# Dictionary of American Conservatism

# Dictionary of American Conservatism

by
Louis Filler

Preface by Russell Kirk

CITADEL PRESS
*Secaucus, New Jersey*

# CONTENTS



Published 1988 by Citadel Press
A division of Lyle Stuart Inc.
120 Enterprise Ave., Secaucus, N.J. 07094
In Canada: Musson Book Company
A division of General Publishing Co. Limited
Don Mills, Ontario

By arrangement with Philosophical Library, Inc.
200 West 57 Street, New York, N.Y. 10019


Manufactured in the United States of America

**Library of Congress Cataloging-in-Publication Data**

Filler, Louis.
Dictionary of American conservatism.

Includes index.
1. Conservatism—United States—Dictionaries.
I. Title.
JA84.U5F55 1986 320.5'2'0321 86-22665
ISBN 0-8065-1087-0

# Introduction to the Paperback Edition

## *A Time for Bridging Gaps*

This new printing of *Dictionary of American Conservatism* offers the author a chance to comment on its particular relevance to present cases. There have, of course, been many crises in our past which have pitted groups and partisans against each other. There have even been what one entry in this work calls Social Wars involving ethnic, religious, political, minority, and other factions. They can be found here treated under various headings and the names of their major figures. But strangely, our present confrontations take place in a time when group antipathies, especially their expression, are all but barred by law. In theory, there should be no difference among attention-seekers and would-be office holders anywhere. All need the consideration and votes of men and women everywhere.

And yet there are interest groups which, before our very eyes, amass majorities favoring several and sometimes single issues, and not necessarily because their elements are agreed on by all of them. All are homogenized into a single voice, a single slogan. It is as though the opposition did not exist, with its own feelings and its own experiences. I sometimes think that these factions are like the Gulf Stream in the Caribbean, which cuts through its waters as though steel walls separated them. And yet all major currents are part of the same society and share its premises and traditions.

More interesting in some ways are the non-voters among us: passively non-endorsing those of passionate conviction. Among those non-voters may be found all the nuances missing in those who are uncompromising, and who will not be moved. All the non-voter needs to show life and make himself or herself directly felt is a deeper sense of self and of the history which created self. But there must be many tomes and dialogues before such enlightenment is wön.

This dictionary tries to contribute to the implicit dialogue. It is not a conservative dictionary. It is a dictionary of conservatism. Inevitably, it involves liberalism: a subject long of concern to the author. Ours is a liberal country. How could it be less, with its long history of opportunity, change, and upward mobility? Fortunately or unfortunately, change always involves discomfort. Old ways are shaken. The new is strange and inconvenient.

But woe to him who dances blithely into a new time without sophistication regarding the old. Instinctive thoughts and feelings are not lightly disregarded. They find subtle means for keeping up with the procession and influencing it. An example in our own time is the work of T.S. Eliot. His interests would have seemed made for consignment to the rubbish heap of history. Religion, ancient languages and literature, manners—and yet in books and on stage he continues to absorb readers and audiences throughout our Western world. To understand why is to help ourselves in our dilemmas.

This is said to be a conservative era, and in one sense it has been true. We have had to cope with conservative viewpoints and personalities more intensely than in previous decades. This is partly because traditional liberal forces have been passed by, or are in disarray. Their followers have made their appeals with catch-phrases rather than hard-won and established experiences. Some of this will be found illustrated in the following pages. A somewhat similar process has been going on in Great Britain, where the winning Conservative Party has actually worried over the decadent state of its labor opposition. There, Conservatives know that a strong country needs strong opposition parties for health and good prospects.

Here, conditions are not markedly better among our factions. There are those among the conservatives who consider other conservatives fuddy-duddies, so far as one can judge because they are bemused by tradition and don't like rock music. Some *with-it* conservatives want to research us on the grounds that they have reasoning powers superior to our own, though their sense of conservative principles—let alone history—often seems no deeper than that of anyone else. Others among us pass as liberals who, on any objective scale, could more properly be termed radicals, yet who denounce avowed conservatives for deviating from the ideals of "true conservatives," all happily dead.

What seems missing in all such partisans is some element of common purpose: an openness toward others, especially as they show themselves as trying to live according to their own best lights. Thomas Jefferson's First Inaugural Address is always helpful; in it he said: "We are all Republicans, we are all Federalists." Both of Lincoln's Inaugural Addresses always repay careful reading, especially since they involve the fate of millions of us, black and white. To understand one another we must know one another, and that will take reading—as well as thought.

Louis Filler

# PREFACE

by Russell Kirk

As a term of politics, "conservatism" is about one hundred and eighty years old; it has been employed in American public discourse ever since the days of John C. Calhoun and Orestes Brownson. Curiously enough, all that while there has been published no dictionary or other work of reference concerned with conservative ideas, movements, and persons—perhaps because conservative views have not been approved by the publishing trade, whatever the sentiments of the American public.

This Dictionary, a welcome addition to serious studies in American civilization, is a companion volume to *A Dictionary of American Social Change* (1982), also the work of Professor Louis Filler. Readers may be interested in a glimpse of the scholar who has produced these two lively and useful studies, and many other books.

At the heart of the Michigan village of Ovid, far from the madding crowd, stands a tall handsome old church-building, now a house. Within this strange and grand residence, now styled The Belfry, Louis Filler drew up this Dictionary.

Surrounded by thousands of books on everything under the sun, shelved or piled on the old church's various levels, the cheerful and loquacious Dr. Filler turns out historical studies, literary criticism, anthologies, and a diversity of articles, his spirits and his productivity undiminished by more than four decades of writing and teaching. One would never guess that Filler was born in Odessa, for nobody is more heartily American than this bushy-haired scholar in the discipline of American civilization, who is more energetic than professors half his age. His young wife (an accomplished editor herself) and their two winsome little children complete this picture of the union of love and learning, there in the dim religious labyrinths of The Belfry.

It was at conferences in the Newberry Library that, in the early Fifties, I first met Louis Filler; I was much taken with his humor, his sound sense, and his freedom from ideological snares. When I began to edit the quarterly *Modern Age*, he wrote to me that the conservative movement in America had become the only body of thought worth serious consideration. I was somewhat surprised at this encouragement from a professor at institutions not renowned for their attachment to immemorial ways; besides, Mr. Filler was then, or soon would become, the author or editor of books about Edwin Markham, Wendell Phillips, Horace Mann, John Bach McMaster, David Graham Phillips, Randolph Bourne, and other worthies who are not looked upon as pillars of orthodoxy. He was the historian of the Progressive Movement (although, as once he remarked to me, Progressivism was conservative essentially) and the author of *A Dictionary of Social Reform* and of *The Crusade against Slavery*. But Professor Filler, like Lincoln, nourished a preference for the old and tried in America over the new and untried; and like Falkland, he knew that when it is not necessary to change, it is necessary not to change. In the three decades of our friendship, I have discovered him to be one of our more generous and perceptive defenders of America's permanent things.

What Dr. Filler has given us in this Dictionary is a well-organized body of clues to the character and the significance of conservative thought and action in the American Republic. Probably no words have been more abused, both in the popular press and within the Academy, than "conservatism" and "conservative." (Some people who ought to know better write the word with an extra syllable, "conservativism," and confound it with nineteenth-century liberalism.) The *New York Times*, surely not with malice prepense, now and again refers to Stalinists within the Soviet Union as "conservatives." The master of an Oxford college, on learning at high table that I had written a book entitled *The Conservative Mind*, exclaimed to me indignantly, "You must be in favor of Malan in South Africa!"

Professor Filler aspires to diminish such widespread ignorance by endowing us with some accurate definitions and descriptions. Conservative convictions and policies being in the ascent in America nowadays, it is of some importance to know whereof one speaks, and not to mistake the American conservative impulse (always a strong influence in the United States) for some neat and impractical ideology.

Permit me, then, to offer you some paragraphs about the nature of the conservative mentality, as supplement or perhaps as guide to Professor Filler's admirable definitions of terms and names that are related to conservatism past and present.

* * *

The attitude we call "conservatism" is sustained by a body of sentiments, rather than by a system of ideological dogmata. It is almost true that a conservative may be defined as a person who thinks himself such. Permanence counts for more than change, in conservatives' affections—although a conservative knows, with Burke, that healthy "change is the means of our preservation." A people's historic continuity of experience, says the conservative, offers a guide to policy far better than the abstract designs of coffee-house philosophers.

Although there exists no conservative Test Act of Thirty-Nine Articles of conservative belief, still one may suggest the political and social mentality of the typical thinking conservative in America near the end of the twentieth century. He believes, to begin with, that there endures a moral order natural for mankind. He has found human nature to be a mixture of good and evil, and that it may not be perfected. He defends custom, habit, common sense. He says that the chief virtue in politics is prudence—judging any measure by its long-run complex consequences. He is attached to a society of diversity and opportunity; he is suspicious of any ideology that would govern the great mysterious incorporation of the human race by a single abstract principle, whether that principle should be "equality" or "liberty."

He supports the institutions of private property and a competitive economy. He knows that sound government, repressing violence and fraud, providing for the common good, is necessary for the survival of civilization. He assumes that politics is the art of the possible, not the path to Zion.

Now to judge by election returns and by polls of public opinion, the substantial majority of Americans today subscribe to such conservative views of the civil social order—although of course most of them could not express their political persuasion so succinctly or abstractly, any more than most liberals or radicals could set down their first principles in coherent form.

Such is the core of conservative sentiments, opinions, or prejudices. In practical politics, however, a body of general convictions ordinarily is linked with a body of interests. Thus the old Tory party of seventeenth-century England, for instance, with its affection for king and Church, obtained electoral and military support chiefly from the agricultural interest, led by its bluff squirearchy. What interest or group of interests backs the conservative element in American politics?

That question is not readily answered. Many rich Americans back liberal or radical causes; affluent suburbs frequently vote for liberal men and measures; attachment to conservative sentiments does not follow the line that Marxist analysts of politics expect to find. The owners of small properties, as a class, tend to be more conservative than do the owners of much property (this latter often in the abstract form of stocks and bonds). One may remark that most conservatives hold religious convictions; yet there are numerous exceptions to this rule, and the national officers of "mainline" Protestant churches, together with church bureaucracies, frequently ally themselves with radical organizations. Half a century ago, it could be said that most college professors were conservative; that could not be said seriously today; yet physicians, dentists, lawyers (or the majority of them), and other professional people subscribe to conservative journals and generally vote for persons they take to be conservative candidates.

In short, the conservative interest appears to transcend the usual classification of American voting-blocs according to wealth, age-group, sex, ethnic origin, region, and the like. If we may speak of a conservative "interest," this appears to be the interest-bloc of people concerned for stability: those citizens who find the pace of change too swift, the loss of continuity and permanence too painful, the break with the American past too brutal, the loss of community dismaying, the designs of innovators inhumane. Certain material interests are bound up with this resistance to insensate change, of course: nobody relishes having his savings reduced to insignificance by inflation of the currency. But the moving power behind the renewed conservatism of the American public is not some scheme of personal or corporate aggrandizement; rather, it is the impulse for survival of a culture that wakes to its peril at the end of the twentieth century.

* * *

Dr. Filler casts his net wide, all the way from *In His Steps* to *Atlas Shrugged*. He is well aware of the diversity of conservative factions, and of their frequent failure to consist one with another; he is their recorder, not their apologist.

In this Dictionary's pages the browser will encounter terms and persons he may never have heard of before, among them the Goo Goos and Albert Mordell's book *Dante and Other Waning Classics*. Louis Filler is a latter-day Isaac Disraeli for curiosities of literature. But also this volume is a work of much reflection. Some of the entries are polished little essays: Gentility and Culture, for instance, or the pieces on William James and Henry James.

Practically everybody of significance in America, connected with conservative concerns, is included in this Dictionary—and a good many British subjects, too. Gerald Heard, for one, obtains a hearing. So does George Washington Cable. One encounters John Henry Cardinal Newman cheek by jowl with the *New York Times* and Newspeak. Some eminent liberals or radicals find their places in these pages, as involved in controversy with conservatives. What a range of subjects: Victimless Crimes, Over-Achievers, Prayer in School, Featherbedding, Calamity Howlers, Consumerism, Invisible Hand, Siege Psychology!

Always civil, Dr. Filler is temperate throughout, despite temptation to be ironic about much in today's politics. Conservative eccentrics, silly books of a conservative cast, and the wilder shores of "conservative" movements are not omitted. One is surprised to note how many books have been published, since early in the Fifties, in attempted refutation or derision of conservative thought and action. Most of those publications have been thoroughly forgotten now, by liberals as well as conservatives: an instance of the vanity of human wishes. Incidentally, Dr. Filler appends to many entries useful brief bibliographies.

For anybody much interested in politics, either practical or theoretical, this is an admirable bedside book, what with its sketches of personality, its succinct examination of burning issues, its references to a wide range of literature, and the brief acute comments of its author. This Dictionary reveals much about what Raymond English has called "the forbidden faith."

More, it is of serious value to liberals and radicals, that they may understand their conservative adversaries and not contend against phantoms. Most of all, this Dictionary ought to be in the possession of every man and woman who thinks of taking some part in the present conservative movement, intellectual or electoral. As F.J.C. Hearnshaw wrote half a century ago, "Ordinarily it is sufficient for conservatives to sit and think, or perhaps merely to sit." Sedentary conservatism, however, will not suffice in a time when conservatives in office must make decisions that cannot be undone.

A great many Americans of conservative inclination know very little about past or present complexities of conservative discourse or policy; nor do they know where to turn for information. Thus they stand in danger of justifying John Stuart Mill's supercilious remark that conservatives form "the stupid party." Dr. Filler's Dictionary can direct them to sources of knowledge, extending from the middle years of the eighteenth century to the closing years of the twentieth. Honest in conception and marvellously accurate in detail, this *Dictionary of American Conservatism* will help to instruct the rising generation of serious students in the arts of political prudence.

"To make dictionaries is dull work," Samuel Johnson informs us. But this Dictionary is not dull reading—not at all. Dr.Johnson employed a crew of Scots to assist him in his lexicographical labors in his Gough Square house; Dr. Filler might cry, with Coriolanus, "Alone I did it!" Clearly he took pleasure in his labors, there in The Belfry; and pleasure as well as instruction he bestows upon us.

# FOREWORD

There is no way in which a dictionary of American conservatism can expect to be definitive. Issues and personalities gain and lose nuances as time goes by. This being a first such dictionary, it is likely to require emendations and additions as events indicate need.

Still, it is significant that modern developments have called for such an assemblage of data. The fluid nature of American life continues to create new alliances and definitions, but also new polarizations which must be recognized in order to make proper judgments. A basic point which helps understanding is that conservatism and liberalism, and even radicalism, have intermingled as well as separated. The American Revolution, for example, was not like other revolutions. It is helpful to keep Thomas Jefferson and John Adams (*qq.v.*) in mind as a measure of social differences and common interest: at one in rebellion, separated for many years in political conflict, friends in older age.

This is not a *Who's Who* of conservatism, past or present. *Representative* figures, *visible* personalities, and *symbolic* slogans and ideas have been sought. Important has been the concept of transitional (*q.v.*) figures, whose careers help define magnetic fields in society. Edmund Burke (*q.v.*) defending American colonial rebels and Edmund Burke denouncing French revolutionaries are one and the same Burke. Recognizing that fact can diminish much blind argument and declamation.

A vital factor often too lightly and even irresponsibly handled is culture. It measures feelings and understandings better than does dogma—which seems strong in social war—but is weak in crises, and especially weak in the long run, when dogma loses its force. The weakness of literature and history in contemporary debates, their subservience to political stances, is one indicator of inevitable change in coming crises.

The *issues* affecting major trends have been fairly constant, and are reflected throughout this work. War and peace, elections, the working world, communication, minorities—in a nation of minorities, men and women, youth, cities and suburbs: these are factors affecting life at any time.

Included items are intended to be evocative as well as informative. They are implemented by cross reference "Quod Vide" (*q.v.*), meaning "Which see," allowing the reader to follow such threads of conservatism as particularly interest him or her. Many issues and figures are treated in the texts, and often ramify through cross references.

My *Dictionary of American Social Change* has included many items also treated in this work, but from different perspectives and involving variant materials. There has seemed no gain in including here information not directly relevant to the issues at hand. For readers wishing to contrast treatments given here and in the other Dictionary, I indicate their presence there as: Filler, DASC.

The *Bibliography* has been selective to avoid losing the forest for the trees. Books have been noticed for their distinction, coverage, or contrast. They often contain further bibliographies for those wishing to pursue a topic in depth.

References have been to topics, rather than to a key or specific word, priority being given to that having the greatest currency or connotation. Thus, "Reforms and Conservatism" is also the reference to reform, reformer, reformist, etc. In cross references it has not been thought necessary to align precise variants for uniformity.

My best appreciation is due the Marguerite Eyer Wilbur Foundation, a grant from which helped ease the expenses which attended the preparation of this dictionary.

L.F.

# INTRODUCTION

It may appear paradoxical that this should be the first dictionary of conservatism in a land which has had such leaders as George Washington, John Quincy Adams, Abraham Lincoln, Grover Cleveland (*qq.v.*), and others in a direct line of conservatives, sponsoring conservative ideals. Moreover, all of them in their time were under severe pressure from forces ranging from liberal to radical (*qq.v.*). It would appear that those who approved of their lives and work, and those who did not, would have wanted aid in building their defenses or opposition.

It helps to look at one or two large-scale works in America's past, and to discuss their general tendencies.

*The New American Cyclopaedia* (1859 ff.), in sixteen volumes, was a formidable work, much of it to be sure now obsolete, but illuminating in and of its time. It was edited by important people. George Ripley was a founder of Brook Farm, which had intended to transform society; and his co-editor, Charles A. Dana, had been secretary of Brook Farm. Both had come far from their utopian (*q.v.*) days, and Dana was to go farther as the brilliant and cynical editor of the *New York Sun*: a clearly transitional (*q.v.*) figure.

Their encyclopedia was indeed "a Popular Dictionary of General Knowledge," much of it far from ideology. It was even-handed toward abolitionists (*q.v.*), for example, but also toward Czar Alexander II, whom it saw as "religious, and sincerely attached to the national church, but without fanaticism." Considering the sweep of the work, and its contributors, who included Ralph Waldo Emerson (*q.v.*), one ought not lightly to generalize about *The New American Cyclopaedia*. It seems accurate, however, to judge it conservative. It did not seek "solutions" to matters grounded in nature. It did not emphasize the critical approach to society, looking forward to change, so evident in W. D. P. Bliss's later formidable *Encyclopedia of Social Reform* (1897 ff.).

Again, John J. Lalor's *Cyclopaedia of Political Science* (1881) is clearly conservative. Its bulky three volumes recognized and sanctioned the status quo in banking, trade, political affiliations, and other aspects of individual and social life. The volumes were informative and often fascinating in reflecting contemporary states of mind among the learned and authoritative. Many of their ideas would be blown to the wind in time by economic crises, wars, inventions, and an ever-increasing democracy. But the sense of working from eternal principles dominates their work.

For example, speaking of the *Entrepreneur* (*q.v.*), the French writer Joseph Garnier declared that his workmen were partners "who, being bound only by temporary engagements and not being willing to participate in the bad chances, renounce the good ones and content themselves with a compensation regulated by the law of supply and demand." The world changed, so that later conservatives would find it necessary to modify that "law" in order to make it better comport with other conditions of the century following.

Nevertheless, an encyclopedia is not a dictionary. An encyclopedia may be conservatively inclined, but its primary mission is information or alleged information, rather than definition. The Ripley-Dana and Lalor volumes spoke for a basically conservative society—a society with no need to identify itself further, except as sociologists would care to study its aspects and describe them for those interested in the poor, the rich, the military, the farmers, the entertainers, and so on through occupations, age groups, and sex.

Since then, whole regimes in the world have declared themselves committed to anti-conservative principles—communist, "Marxist," socialist, and radical (*qq.v.*)—and challenged language as well as economics in behalf of their own official attitudes and interpretations. The vocabulary of liberalism has seemed to many to become all but predictable. All persons who refer to "Keynesian principles" (*q.v.*) have not read Keynes, but they know enough of his economic theories to communicate their partialities. "Liberalism" (*q.v.*) in 1986 does not infer what it did in 1912. Its new attributes, however, have been well explicated; indeed, the old ones have been largely forgotten. "Compassion," "Victimless Crime," "Pro-Choice," "Racist," "Anti-Nuke," "Environmentalist," and "Alternative Life-Style" could not be mistakenly identified with conservatism. "Pro-Life," on the other hand, does not mean "Anti-Capital Punishment" (*qq.v.*).

Because conservatives identified themselves with what T. S. Eliot (*q.v.*) called the permanent things, they had fewer slogans of agitation and unrest. Family, faith, and nation would not appear to require defense in a society which valued its security and continuity. Yet it is evident that all of these have been called in question. On the one hand, the nation has appeared to accept its astonishing statistics of mayhem and corruption almost fatalistically. On the other hand, it has produced a new agitation which, from Barry Goldwater even through Watergate, has made famous spokesmen as varied as

Rev. Jerry Falwell, Strom Thurmond, Henry Kissinger, William F. Buckley, Jr., and Ronald Reagan (*qq.v.*).

In 1980, Ronald Reagan achieved the Presidency, and with him to Washington came scores and hundreds of individuals once known, if at all, to local conservative chieftains and conservative interest groups. Now they occupied offices, new seats in Congress, and positions in conservative institutes. They helped make programs for the entire country. Their intention was to roll back developments which had taken half a century to create and to formalize.

Who were they? Whom did they represent? What were their positions in the world as well as in the nation? There are no certain answers to many such questions. Significant names come and go, and are sometimes surprisingly lost even to persons committed to tradition. Evidently, tradition has meant different things in America and elsewhere. This was more manifestly the case in earlier eras of conservatism than in the present, now that factions and programs have been formalized to meet particular challenges created by bureaucracies, Presidential initiatives, and the Supreme Court (*qq.v.*).

One of the conclusions which has emerged from a consideration of the conservative heritage is how little it has affected the present. The Founding Fathers (*q.v.*) are apposite in this connection, to the extent that their Constitution (*q.v.*) is a chief binding force in our lives. Liberals and Conservatives appeal to the Constitution for endorsement of their current sentiments. It cannot be said that either camp has been strong in bringing out for modern constituents the reality of the lives of those who made the Constitution. Thomas Jefferson (*q.v.*) is peculiarly apposite in this respect.

The result has been to shift attention from the Founding Fathers to recent Justices who have sworn to defend and abide by the Constitution. Although this has been inevitable to a degree—with enigmatic results and prospects—it would no doubt add a dimension to public debate to assess the times and temperaments of those who made and interpreted the original document.

Such subjects of law and direction link with others like education (*q.v.*) and the public will. It helps to recall the great Lincoln-Douglas debates (*q.v.*) of 1858, delivered before undiscriminated audiences in the marketplaces of Illinois, and probing the most delicate questions of law and tradition regarding slavery. It is fair to say that these extraordinary speeches would challenge the logic and attention of a good part of the educated public today, accustomed as it is to headlines, television (*q.v.*) summaries, and the views of commentators. If one of our present-day tasks is to raise the level of public discourse about issues, it would seem the duty of conscientious citizens to revive interest in such high points of our conservative heritage, of which there are many. The Federalist Papers, the Gag Rule, Crédit

Mobilier, and the Granger Cases (*qq.v.*)—such landmarks in American life can throw light on the character of our present-day debates, and those who engage in them.

This Dictionary defines past and present conservative concepts, and illustrates their workings with examples and references according to the best knowledge of the author. The reader gives life to those concepts by choosing among them for his current purposes. A. J. Nock (*q.v.*) emphasized that history was experience. This Dictionary does not distinguish between past and present in displaying its understanding of American conservative experience.

LOUIS FILLER
The Belfry
Ovid, Michigan

# Dictionary of American Conservatism

# A

**Abolitionism,** a 19th-century movement vital to the long dissatisfaction with the slavery system of labor. Slavery was held to transgress religious tenets, in the American North, and free enterprise (*q.v.*) principles central to those which inspired the Revolution. Although conservatism entered into abolitionist developments, it did so irregularly. Thus, antislavery advocates in the Quaker, Methodist, and Congregationalist denominations tended to disrupt the even tenor of their churches, and finally to become "Come-outers," asking friends of the anti-slavery movement to leave congregations which were held to be in complicity with slaveholders. The followers of William Lloyd Garrison were clearly extremists (*q.v.*), certainly not conservative. They embraced women's rights and held anti-government views which kept them in opposition to the major forces of the society of the day. Distinguished conservatives like Judge William Jay, son of Chief Justice of the Supreme Court (*qq.v.*) gave strength to abolitionism and such related causes as peace (*q.v.*), but did not carry the burden of abolitionism as agitators and crusaders. Such businessmen as Lewis Tappan (*q.v.*) were both evangelical in religion and persistent in their abolitionism, but were a minority among businessmen. Not until abolition became Free Soil (*q.v.*), and demanded that slavery not be spread beyond where it was already legal, did conservatism become a major force in abolition, and then only as it could be separated from libertarianism (*q.v.*), which asked for women's rights, free churches, separation from the "tainted" South, and other reforms. Conservatives who sought peace with the South at any price can be better seen as reactionary. Abraham Lincoln's (*q.v.*) growth during the Civil War showed a turn from a cautious conservatism to one verging on liberalism. (See also Filler, DASC.) After World War II, and especially as a result of the radical movements of the 1960s, Southern (*q.v.*) sympathizers in the history profession and many radical historians began to look at the abolitionists with a critical eye. The radicals seemed especially interested in emphasizing the accomplishments of black 19th-century anti-slavery figures over those of the abolitionists. Courses in the condemnation of slavery flourished in universities, while courses in pre-Civil War reform and abolition dwindled. Abolitionists were often portrayed as neurotic, patronizing of blacks and slaves, rhetorical rather than real, and either responsible for the Civil War or irrelevant to forces making for emancipation. They were finally seen as objects for sociological examination, rather than as the courageous partisans of freedom they traditionally seemed to be; see L.J. Friedman, *Gregarious Saints* (1982). See also Louis Filler, *Crusade Against Slavery* (1986 ed.).

**Abortion,** one of the momentous issues of the late twentieth century. In 1973 the Supreme Court (*q.v.*) ruled, seven to two, in *Roe v. Wade* that no state could pass a law interfering with the patient-physician decision for abortion during the first three months of pregnancy. The decision, based on a gang-rape of housepainter Norma McCorvey, overthrew a Texas law and comparable laws in some thirty states. In the meantime, the baby had been born and taken away at birth. Additional cases and rulings seemed to make abortion possible at almost any time during pregnancy. The bitter battle between "Pro-Choice" partisans and

"Pro-Life" opponents brought the issue to the forefront of public debate. Meanwhile, it was estimated that a million and a half legal abortions were performed each year following the historic decision. There were efforts to return abortion to its earlier status as state regulated, and contrasting efforts to expand its public endorsement, mainly through increased Federal and state funding, presumably in the interests of the poor. The issue was seen by many as a moral issue, involving female and fetus rights and the legitimate powers of government. Had a few judges in Washington the right, constitutionally and otherwise, to take from the states and their constituents the power to regulate abortions? Were fetuses human beings? Ought Congress to subsidize abortions? What were the responsibilities of individuals and families? It seemed that many individuals had no sense of responsibility; a popular writer had explored this irresponsible attitude toward sex (Ralph Keyes, *We, the Lonely People* [1973]) in the year of the *Roe* decision. Did these individuals merit Federal or any funding? The argument ranged beyond abortion to society's incitements to sex, the general moral climate, and the state of the family and society, but it paused at particular junctions. Did fetuses suffer in abortion? Were fathers to be taken into consideration? If babies were "unwanted," could they not be given to those who wanted them? What of the "Squeal Law" (*q.v.*)? What of eleven-year-old pregnant girls? Ought a pediatric surgeon, C. Everett Koop, who opposed abortion, be made U.S. Surgeon-General? Battles waged in behalf of abortion by such agencies as the American Civil Liberties Union and Planned Parenthood held the line generally for the basic 1973 decision, but they aroused opposition in Congress, the Health and Human Services Department, and in the states. Eventually, public funds were drastically diminished for abortions, leaving much of the battle to the private sector. The ACLU Reproductive Freedom Project not only protested government support to the states in regulating abortions and efforts to separate abortion and family-planning clinics, it also denounced the 1981 Adolescent Family Act, sponsored by conservative Senators Jeremiah Denton and Orrin Hatch, as being a "chastity Act" using "the power of the purse" to establish official religious beliefs in America. The Act would make grants to religious organizations and specifically refuse them to pro-abortion groups. In 1983, abortions were said to be "down," though how significantly could not be spelled out. A striking fact was that the easy acquisition of contraceptives and sophisticated medical treatment seemed to do nothing at all for either pregnancy control or the spread of sexual diseases through much of the society. "Birth Control," once fought for by Margaret Sanger and others who had advocated family-planning clinics, seemed to do little to halt the alarming rise of teenage pregnancies and abortions. Many advocated a return to traditional social and moral restraints. However, democratic decisions were hard to reach. Euphemisms (*q.v.*) about the termination of pregnancy could be matched with pitiful cases of lonely, impregnated children who did not know where to turn. With so much "sex education" seen by many as irresponsibly partisan, a social consensus was not at hand. See also *Single Issues*, and James Di Giacomo, ed., *Abortion: A Question of Values* (1975); Thomas Hilgers and D.J. Horan, *Abortion and Social Justice* (1973); L.R. Sass, *Abortion: Freedom of Choice and the Right to Life* (1978); L.B. Francke, *The Ambivalence of Abortion* (1978).

**"Abscam,"** a program sponsored by the F.B.I. (*q.v.*) in 1980 and 1981 to trace corruption in public operations. It used allegations and informants to test the probity of individuals. The most sensational were those who responded positively to tempting bribes, allegedly by Arabs (Arab-"scam," scam being a colloquialism for a fraudulent conspiracy). Legal proceedings brought the conviction on charges of corruption of seven members of Congress and one Senator. Some liberals criticized the enterprise as having created crimes which might otherwise not have taken place. The F.B.I. defended itself as having to "get beyond the street and the bagman [bribe-carrier] and the insulation." F.B.I. Director William H. Webster saw "Abscam" as part of an undercover activity which, costing some

$7.5 million, led to recoveries of property worth more than $109 million, and resulted in 2,723 arrests with 1,064 convictions. It was hoped that the catastrophes which harmed the careers of a few congressmen would alert others to the dangers of bribe-taking.

**Absurdity,** a philosophical attitude derived from the despair and confusion coming out of World War II (*q.v.*), with its mass slaughters, its "absurd" loyalties, and the interminable insecurities created by the emerging nuclear (*q.v.*) threat. In such a context, a sense of the irrational in human nature was developed which made living a well-founded life a chimera. Many conservatives responded by reaffirming faith in God's purposes and the validity of the family and a law-based society. Albert Camus of French Algeria, with such others as Jean-Paul Sartre in France, rejected the possibility of a God (*q.v.*), or at least a just God, and held themselves to be strangers in the universe. Samuel Beckett also perceived Man as a pawn of incalculable forces, but in his famous *Waiting for Godot* (1956) seemed to hope that signs of salvation might make their appearance. Some conservatives countered the absurdist version of the irrational with a respect for or belief in the mystic experience. See Patrick McCarthy, *Camus: A Critical Study* (1982). Compare Lewis, C.S.; Huxley, Aldous.

**Abuse,** of children and of wives, was prominent in the news in the early 1980s, decades after the welfare and civil rights (*qq.v.*) movements had tried to abolish economic and social causes for individual and group dissatisfaction. Causes for family abuse were found by some liberals in poverty, ignorance, revenge for past or present social treatment, and the need for therapy and understanding. It was noted that abuse had often been unheeded in the past, that there was always more abuse than was now surfacing. Many people wondered why it had previously gone unreported. The agreed-upon breakdown of the family and neighborhood no doubt contributed to the rise of such abuse. The government, taking over responsibilities on the local and federal levels, was seen by many as interfering with the traditional obligations of family life. Cases of wives killing husbands and alleging abuse as a defense brought out social attitudes, some of which seemed to be political rather than humanistic. Some women's-rights activists (*q.v.*) charged male-dominated society with encouraging the abuse, thus directing attention away away from the individual (*q.v.*) involved. Some liberals emphasized the needs of the abuser for counseling and understanding, but in the meantime many apparently unfit parents were allowed to raise their children. Some educators (*q.v.*) defended children's rights as equal to those of adults. A few activists saw children themselves as equal if not superior to adults. Children's rights were invoked as an argument against the "Squeal Rule" (*q.v.*). The Atlanta murders of black children in 1981 made nationwide headlines. Some radicals used these murders as an example of white racism, but with the arrest and conviction of a black man for the crimes they quickly lost interest. School teachers were severely restricted in their ability to discipline children in classrooms, partly as a result of the increasing emphasis on children's rights, and many teachers felt powerless to control unruly and delinquent behavior by their pupils. Vandals, bullies, and exploiters of other children were dangers to teachers as well in "the blackboard jungle." Many conservatives emphasized the traditional values of family, religion, and discipline and the need for learning, social and academic, to encourage normal and secure growth. Liberals accused some conservatives, however, of being more interested in restricting people's freedom and promoting traditional bigotry and sexism. Many liberals called for greater social expenditures for counseling, day-care centers, schools, and rehabilitation institutions. They urged changes in social attitudes which they believed would further emancipation while curbing abuse. To many conservatives, Supreme Court (*q.v.*) decisions undermined traditional family values without ensuring child guidance or child security. See J.E. De Burger, ed., *Marriage Today: Problems, Issues and Alternatives* (1978); Peter D. Chimbos, *Marital Violence: A Study of Interspouse Homicide* (1978); Donald F. Cline, ed., *Child Abuse and Neglect: A Primer for School*

*Personnel* (1977); R.E. Heffer and C. Henry Kempe, eds., *Child Abuse and Neglect: The Family and the Community* (1976); Marilyn C. Collins, Harold Rugg (*q.v.*) and Ann Shumaker, *Child-Center School: An Appraisal of the New Education* (1928); E.J. Anthony and C. Kouperniks, eds., *The Child in His Family: Children at Psychiatric Risk* (1974); Naomi F. Chase, *A Child Is Being Beaten: Violence against Children, an American Tragedy* (1976); Norman A. Polansky et al., *Child Neglect* (1972); John Steinbacher, *Child Seducers* (1970); Norman K. Denzin, *Childhood Socialization* (1978); Robert Coles, *Children of Crisis* (1967-1973); Ray Homings, *Children's Freedom: The Summerhill Idea* (1972); B. and R. Gross, *Children's Rights Movement: Overcoming the Oppression of Young People* (1977); Roger Langley and Richard Levy, *Wife Beating: The Silent Crisis* (1977); Jane Scott, *Wives Who Love Women* (1978); R.D. Chotiner, *Marriage and the Supreme Court* (1974); Sidney Ditzion, *Marriage, Morals, and Sex in America* (1978 ed.).

**Academe,** a general term for education and the educational community. In the 19th century higher education, the source of many leaders in business, the liberal arts, government, and education (*qq.v.*), was basically conservative in regular practice and philosophy, so much so that William Graham Sumner (*q.v.*), though committed to Social Darwinism (*q.v.*), principles which took little account of compassion or equalitarianism (*qq.v.*), was considered suspect at Yale University for advocating Free Trade (*q.v.*) policies in government. Legal and academic freedom cases from 1880 to 1920, centering around campus advocates of free inquiry, underscored the conservative character of education at all levels. Disillusion following World War I introduced elements of experimentation in teaching and textbook writing, but traditional standards of conduct and adherence to conventional methods continued to guide teachers, educators, and curricula, except where they could gain followers in conspicuously experimental and radical schools, or win respect and influence through writing or personality, as at the Dalton School in New York or the Parker School in Chicago (see Filler, "The Progressivist Tradition in America," *History of Education Journal*, vol. VIII). Many radical and experimental teachers became enamored of the Soviet "experiment" in the 1920s and 1930s, but Russia's first atomic bomb in 1949, combined with the victory of the Communists on the Chinese mainland that same year, caused a reaction in the United States which undermined radical and experimental teaching methods as exemplified by such organizations as the Progressive Education Association. The 1950s saw a rise in apathy among students (*q.v.*), which upset many educators. Students looked off-campus for their diversions. In the 1960s campus storms of protest—against discrimination and the war in Vietnam—coupled with uprisings within the education (*q.v.*) field by discontented teachers, researchers, and even administrators shook the foundations of conservative principles in education. These principles were undermined by liberal influence in government agencies, notably the Department of Health, Education and Welfare (later divided into Health and Human Services and the New Department of Education). Liberals often used government funds to advance their interpretations of American history and politics, American policy toward minorities, and foreign affairs. In the 1970s the decline of campus radicalism and hard economic times turned new waves of students into seekers after economic security, and lessened the liberal (*q.v.*) principles. It also gave birth to new, aggressively conservative teachers and student leaders, who asserted patriotic, religious (*qq.v.*), and other ideals on campaigns and in schools. Liberalism had reached its peak and began to decline. A crucial question involved those parents who sought to evade busing, the lack of open prayer in schools, and "affirmative action" (*q.v.*) by moving their children out of urban public schools. The escapees (*q.v.*), usually to the suburbs or to private schools, were criticized by many liberals as forsaking the ideals of equality and contributing to de-facto "re-segregation." Many liberals were further outraged by conservative attempts to legalize the "tuition tax credit," which in effect helped parents with the costs of moving their children into private schools. Proponents of the tax credit, however, argued that public education had already been hurt by the busing and desegregation battles which followed *Brown v. Topeka* (*q.v.*).

**Academic Freedom: An Essay In Definition** (1955), by Russell Kirk (*q.v.*), an effort to determine the meaning of "freedom" (*q.v.*) in an institution requiring goals and results. Kirk attacked both indoctrination and individualism (*q.v.*), neither of which he found satisfactory. Indoctrination was wrong and ineffective, while individualism focussed on the person rather than on the heritage of life and tradition. Kirk believed there was such a reality as Truth, and that teachers must be its bearers. This truth was drawn from past disciplines, past experience. It contradicted the goals of educational "levellers" and the "dogmas" of pragmatism and progress. There were, however, blatant contemporary examples of mindless and frightened transgressions of academic freedom, not all involving conservative interests, which were spelled out in detail. Kirk stated that he did not know of any administrator who would "knowingly engage a Communist." He made no such assertion about Marxists, however. See also Education.

**Achievers,** see Over-Achievers

**ACLU,** see American Civil Liberties Union

**Acquisitive Society, The** (1920), by R. H. Tawney, a criticism of the capitalist (*q.v.*) system in its later stages as no longer able to produce with adequate efficiency, because of the breakdown in the community organization which would allocate duties and rights according to an agreed system of values. Capitalism, Tawney argued, had "worked" in earlier stages because of the use of force; but as labor gained strength, earlier scales of values no longer applied. The argument was somewhat along lines developed by Thorstein Veblen, but without his indirection and special terminology.

**Actions Speak Loud** (1968) by J. Daniel Mahoney, described a movement intended to diminish what was perceived as Nelson Rockefeller's (*q.v.*) dilution of Republican conservative principles. Resentful that Rockefeller had deprived the Nixon (*q.v.*) campaign of its anticipated New York electoral vote, losing him the Presidential election in 1960, young conservatives organized their new political party, challenged the influential Liberal Party for votes, and in four years first won legal status. The Conservative Party eventually outpolled the Liberal Party, giving conservatism in New York a strength it had previously lost.

**"Activist,"** a term associated with radical protests of the 1960s and later broadened to include those in the forefront of many causes, including minority rights, ethnic rights, gay rights, and the ERA (*qq.v.*). Though the term was originally applied to proponents of liberal and radical-left causes, it later came also to be applied to those in the forefront of conservative and radical-right causes, including the successful fight against the ERA and the growing protests against abortion (*q.v.*). The activists of the 1960s were famous for impeding everyday activities in the interest of their causes; indeed, it was one of their contentions that the world's work must be stopped to emphasize the urgency of their message. They often seemed to have little or no understanding of the causes they espoused. Their techniques included the shouting of slogans, often endlessly and into the night, as well as so-called symbolic acts: going limp in the hands of peace officers, being chained to gates before the White House, and the like. A cartoon in a London newspaper depicted a motion-picture director complaining that he had called for "Action!" and seen all the people in his studio walk off the set.

**Acton, Lord** (1834-1902), of a notable Catholic family, he early absorbed himself in historical studies, seeing them as requiring moral perception as well as proper training and implementation. His liberalism, not unrelated to the minority position of Catholics in England, expressed itself in parliamentary service and close friendship with William E. Gladstone. Although he was known as one of the most scholarly of British historians, it was through his lectures at Cambridge, rather than in books. He planned the great *Cambridge Mod-*

*ern History* series but lived to see only one volume of the work. His conservatism expressed itself in his acceptance of authority and tradition as first principles, and in studies of such conservative figures as de Maistre (*q.v.*). It led him to see the breakdown of the United States during the Civil War as inevitable, due to its being based on false democratic (*q.v.*) principles. Known generally for his epigram regarding power and corruption, he was in fact profuse in evocative observations; see "Extracts," in his posthumous *Essays on Church and State* (1952). Other posthumous works, drawn from his contributions, mainly to Catholic periodicals, and his own papers and lectures include *Lectures on Modern History* (1906) and *Historical Essays and Studies* (1907).

**Adams, Brooks** (1848-1927), less famous than his brother Henry, he worked more strenuously to interpret the progress—or decay—of American civilization. His overview of societies as advancing or declining according to the human energy of their constituents influenced his brother's views (see *Law of Civilization and Decay* [1895]). His defense of silver (*q.v.*) as resisting the reign of gold-holders showed his partisanship toward whatever would help his class of bond and property-holders, though he opposed currency manipulation in the abstract. See also his *Theory of Social Revolution* (1913), which again revealed his fear of the commercial (*q.v.*) classes and his lengthy preface to Henry Adams' *The Degradation of the Democratic Dogma* (1920).

**Adams, Charles Francis** (1807-1886), son of John Quincy Adams (*q.v.*), and a "Conscience Whig," who founded as an organ of Free Soil (*q.v.*) the Boston *Whig*. Although he had occasion to denounce Martin Van Buren (*q.v.*) when he was President for pro-slavery actions, Adams ran as his Vice-Presidential partner on the Free Soil Party ticket in 1848. Adams served with distinction as Minister to Great Britain during the Civil War, and, in 1872, was a possible candidate for President on the *Liberal Republican (q.v.)* ticket. See *M.B. Charles Francis Adams* (1961).

**Adams, Charles Francis, Jr.** (1835-1915), like his brother Henry a critic of the new society unfolding from a higher technology, but in addition willing to work to modify its excesses. His *Chapters of Erie* (1871) was an example of early muckraking (*q.v.*), though in impeccable prose calculated to reach the cultural elite (*q.v.*) of the time rather than the general public. As chairman (1869) of the pioneer Board of Railroad Commissioners in Massachusetts, he sought to bring the massive industry under law, and as president (1884) of the Union Pacific Railroad to help control its policies. The industrial marauder Jay Gould ousted him from his position with the railroad several years later. Adams contributed valuable historical essays as well as memorable civic service. See his autobiography (1916).

**Adams, Henry** (1838-1918). The scion of two Presidents and son of Charles Francis Adams, who might have been President, Adams felt increasingly alienated from a nation which could elect a Ulysses S. Grant to its highest office and engage in the sordid commercial (*q.v.*) enterprises which characterized the post-Civil War era; his novel *Democracy* (1880) constituted an early example of muckraking (*q.v.*), as well as a regal exercise in language and conservative disdain. Although Adams professed himself a "failure," he served Harvard College as a pioneering scholar in historical research and seminar direction, and a larger genteel (*q.v.*) public as editor of the *North American Review*. His *History of the Administrations of Jefferson and Madison* (1885-1891), in nine volumes, though partisan, illustrated the argument of some conservatives that a secure income in proper hands could result in distinguished public service. His novel *Esther* (1884) obviously depicted his wife. Later women's rights activists argued that his wife, who committed suicide, had been depleted in spirit by male dominance: a doubtful assertion at best. Adams, like others of his family, was a paragon of conservatism who transcended class attitudes thanks to his national outlook. Later liberal historians sometimes tried to ignore his achievements. His patently elitist outlook, however, was seen by many conservatives as preferable to what they regarded as liberal elitism in attitudes and behavior toward the so-called lower classes.

**Adams, John** (1735-1826), second President of the United States, and key figure in American conservative thought. His defense of the British soldiers charged in the "Boston Massacre" (1770) displayed his faith in law, as well as his personal courage. In 1774-1775, his "Novanglus" letters made him one of the American lawyers who formulated reasons for colonial resistance to British law. He was a pillar of strength in the difficult work of reconciling order and rebellion during the Revolution, as well as after, in his *A Defence of the Constitutions of Government of the United States* (1786-1787). Adams never saw himself as anything but a conservative; his clearest exposition of principles is in his *Discourses on Davila* (1791). As President he led an aroused Federalist Party, fearful of democracy (*q.v.*) and ready for war. Though he signed the Alien and Sedition Acts, which later generations of liberals have tended to denigrate, he was judicious in enforcing them. Faced with a war situation with revolutionary France, he moved toward negotiations, flying in the face of Federalist demagoguery and ending his own career. The power of Revolutionary conservatism is best approached by reviewing his friendship with Thomas Jefferson (*q.v.*), renewed in old age despite his principled opposition in political philosophy; see their correspondence, Paul Wilstach, ed. (1925). His son, Charles Francis Adams, edited his works (1850-1856).

**Adams, John Quincy** (1769-1848), sixth President of the United States, a study in conservatism made liberal by opposing forces. He was raised to be a statesman, accompanying his father on political missions abroad and himself serving as Minister to the Netherlands and to Prussia. He served with continuing principle and distinction as a nationalist, literary man, and statesman. No man was better trained for the Presidency. Yet his victory over Andrew Jackson (*q.v.*) in the elections of 1824 incited Democratic opposition in Congress which prevented him from accomplishing any of his major goals: the binding of the states by roads, a Pan-American Union, and a lessening of the tensions of slavery. Defeated in the elections of 1828, he returned to Congress as a Massachusetts Representative, and became the leader of Northern resistance to the extension of slavery. His long battle against the "Gag Rule" which the South used to block freedom measures in Congress, and his general defense of the Bill of Rights are unexampled in history, and resulted from his conservative heritage, backed by his life-long religious faith. His lengthy "memoirs" are a national treasure. See S.F. Bemis, *John Quincy Adams and the Foundations of American Foreign Policy* (1949), and [*JQA*] *and the Union* (1956).

**Adams, Samuel** (1722-1803), noted firebrand of the American Revolution, whose resolution and intransigence led later historians to search for the unique source of his bitterness and his unwillingness to consider compromise with the British Crown. As interesting was his post-Revolutionary turn to conservatism which, as governor of Massachusetts (1794-1797), made him unheeding of populist discontent. Adams compares with Patrick Henry in Virginia: also unswervingly for revolution, also turning conspicuously to conservative measures and outlook as governor of his state. They were both examples of action-seekers and ideologues for a particular cause—in this case, severance from the authority of an overseas power—which, when achieved, permitted them to return to more integral concerns. See also Transition, Figures in; Turncoats.

**Addams, Jane** (1860-1935), of a gracious Illinois family, noted founder of Hull House in Chicago, which helped generations of immigrants accommodate themselves to strange and difficult American conditions. Addams would have seemed immune to criticism from later generations because of her forty years of service to the poor and her fight for peace during World War I, which made her an upright and distinguished symbol of legitimate pacifism (*q.v.*). Nevertheless, she was ill-remembered by conservatives, and was viewed skeptically or with scorn by some elements of liberal academe (*q.v.*), as having patronized the poor and as having sought to inculcate American values in them rather than accepting their mainly European heritage; see Settlement Houses, and D. Levine, *Jane Addams* (1971).

**"Adversary Politics,"** see Stockman, David A.

**Adversary Role**, opposition to a dominant political party or belief. In modern times many conservatives saw themselves in such a role, with the implication that liberals were controlling public opinion on popular issues and needed to be resisted through criticism and satire. Oddly, this continued even when the Reagan Administration came to power in 1981. The *National Review* spent substantial energy ferreting out liberal implications in *New York Times* reports; *Chronicles of Culture* did the same for cultural reviews in the *Times* and in the *New York Review of Books*. "Creationists," pro-life advocates, and other crusaders also labored to resist the power of liberals in the school, the press, and government bodies. Many of them believed that they were coming from below to protest dominant power and propaganda. Phyllis Schlafly and other conservative activists used their adversary role to defeat the ERA. But in 1986 many conservatives continued to believe that liberals controlled the organs of power and communication. (*Qq.v.* for above.) See also Advocacy and Siege Psychology.

**Advertising** has traditionally been important in commercial activities and should be distinguished from Propaganda (*q.v.*). As an adjunct of business, advertising's main need has been to advance sales, rather than promote improvements, as shown in James Rorty's *Our Master's Voice* (1934) and underscored in Frederic Wakeman's fictional *The Hucksters* (1946). The Advertising Council of America claimed a public-service function in "educating" the public to values in new products, warning against disease, and other campaigns. Advertising attracted some unconventional types, including the poets Hart Crane and T. S. Eliot, the latter writing blurbs for his publishing firm. Commercialism (*q.v.*) in advertising did not hesitate to exploit anti-social movements, as in urging young people to "do their thing" in the 1960s. Later a cigarette advertiser exploited women's rights by the way they promoted products with the slogan "You've come a long way, baby." Advertisers kept a sharp eye on public trends. Mobil Oil became well-known for its skillful advertisements defending company policies, which some liberals called Propaganda. "Subliminal" advertising attempted to influence public attitudes through words and phrases flashed momentarily in the middle of television (*q.v.*) programs and motion pictures. The extent of its use and its effectiveness were widely debated. In the 1980s advertising techniques became more and more important in political campaigns, and in many elections were more influential than ideas or issues.

**Advisors**, a term applied to American aides and troops, then in small number, in South Vietnam (*q.v.*) during the Kennedy Administration. The term was finally abandoned when the number of troops there increased precipitously. It surfaced again in the 1980s in El Salvador (*q.v.*), alarming some observers who foresaw "another Vietnam." Many American officials tried to downplay the connotations of the term, however, hoping to allay any public fear of Vietnam-type operations in Central America.

**Advocacy,** journalism and organizations. The term advocacy came to be associated with liberal causes in their post-Watergate (*q.v.*) phases. Advocacy grew from earlier social impulses which had created Progressivism (*q.v.*) into one centered on a network of minority, poor, legal, and urban concerns. It engaged committed social elements, and enjoyed the support of influential journalists in the media. Many advocacy organizations were created by Federal legislation or supported by grants from private foundations. Their emphases could be readily discerned in an association of causes. Thus, they favored "compassion" (*q.v.*) for the poor, emphasized society's failings as a cause of crime, and favored an array of social programs—welfare, entitlements, health care, school and student aid, women's rights, and environmental legislation (*qq.v.*). They enlisted lawyers, research groups, and propaganda (*q.v.*) to carry their messages to the larger public. Ralph Nader (see Filler, DASC) was prominent in advocacy operations, though emphasizing consumerism and alleged government wrongdoing. Although conservatives also sought public impact, they were at first less rooted in advocacy approaches, due to their opposition to Big Government (*q.v.*). However, in the 1980s many conservatively oriented advocacy groups came to the fore.

**Affirmative Action**, in the 1970s the name given to efforts to improve education, income levels, and social opportunities available to blacks. It soon became associated in the minds of many with preferential treatment for blacks and other minorities in education and employment. Many proponents, including *The New York Times*, sought to justify this preferential treatment as "reparations" for centuries of oppression. Many conservatives, however, wondered which social grouping in America had not at one point or another suffered similar oppression. Conservatives and indeed some liberals tended to see affirmative action as "reverse discrimination." To them, the spread of such preferential treatment would weaken the quality of education and job performance. The Bakke Case (*q.v.*) limited such preferential treatment, though the Supreme Court decision indicated that affirmative action merited pursuit when it did not transgress legitimate rights. Thus, the ultimate decision regarding affirmative action lay with the larger public. See also Lionel Lokos, *The New Racism: Reverse Discrimination in America* (1971).

**Affluence**, the result of some of the best and worst tendencies in American history. Overall, conservatives defended the push to affluence. Other lands also had abundant resources but were less able to use them to create opportunity for their people. American exploitation of national resources was indeed done with little foresight and according to debatable principles. But this has to be balanced against many compensatory factors. Thus, the taking of Texas from Mexico in the 19th century, declared wrong by such as Robert F. Kennedy, was stormily defended by Texans who pointed to conditions in Mexico at that time. All but unknown in America is that the entrance of Texas into the Union was under the auspices of land-speculators. Many new states were admitted into the Union with retroactive approval of land-grabs before admission. This was justified by appealing to natural rights rather than to law (*q.v.*). It is unclear whether liberals or conservatives bore more responsibility for such policy. Affluence born of war and war production, including that of the Civil War (*q.v.*), was always a perplexing problem in morality and patriotism unless treated in individual terms. Henry Adams, taking a conservative position, criticized the government for having financed the war with unbacked paper dollars, debasing the value of debts. Yet later, seeing his friends who lived on inheritances ruined by depression and closed banks, he saw value in the Silverites (*q.v.*), who sought to diminish the value of gold: a Populist (*q.v.*) position. Affluence in the 1920s was based on America's superior position in a world exhausted by World War I and on expanded industry and credit, and created vast new industries and modernized facilities. Although identified with commercial conservatism, it also involved liberal dreams of expanded democracy. The 1929 economic collapse asked unnatural fortitude of a people accustomed to affluence. The New Deal was a liberal victory, responding to human need; but the "prosperity of the 1920s," due to war work and production, and the adoption of "deficit spending," instead of valid expansion credit, began a cycle of affluence emphasizing services *as* production, rather than as an adjunct to necessities, and what seemed to many to be frivolous pursuits which degraded the values of affluence. This persisted in Truman's "Fair Deal," and even the subsequent Eisenhower Administration. Democratic and Republican efforts to stem the rising cost of government failed to halt the mounting deficit. Under Lyndon Johnson it went totally out of control. America's loss of prestige, thanks to the Vietnam fiasco and the year-long humiliation of the Iran "hostages" crisis, threatened as well America's role as an industrial leader. The paradox of inflation and rising unemployment, at home and abroad, forced the realization that a program for curbing both would have to be found. Reagan's call for sacrifices, though controversial, at least raised issues and forced debate. Looming ahead was the possibility that if the economic cycle of upturns and downturns could be overcome—through quality production and healthy reciprocity with friendly and even unfriendly nations—conditions might be right for an easy drift to unearned increment and aimless living. (*Qq.v.* for above.) For a conservative view of affluence, Larry R. Williams, *How to Prosper in the Coming Good Years* (1981), a Regnery (*q.v.*) publication. See also Stanley Marcus, *His and Hers: the Fantasy World of the Nieman-Marcus Catalogue*, and *Quest for the Best* (1979).

**Afghanistan**, a glaring example of Soviet aggression. In 1979 the U.S.S.R. installed a pro-Soviet puppet government in Afghanistan, which it bordered, and began relentless military efforts to quell popular opposition and a widespread desire for independence. By 1986 the Soviets still had not defeated defiant Afghan tribes. To conservatives, Afghanistan was another instance of the worldwide Soviet expansionism which many liberals had tended to overlook or excuse. The Soviets' proximity in Afghanistan to oil-rich areas seemed to signal trouble for the West when and if new international crises should arise in those areas. Anthony Arnold, *Afghanistan: The Soviet Invasion in Perspective* (1981); J. C. Griffiths, *Afghanistan: Key to a Continent* (1981); Anthony Hyman, *Afghanistan under Soviet Domination, 1964-81* (1982).

**Africa**, largely colonized by European nations in the 19th century. By the mid-1980s the European colonies had become independent native states of varying degrees of viability. Clearly, the native Africans had by and large been ill prepared for independence. Many African nations were beset by widespread famine, poverty, and disease. Neither natural wealth, as in Nigeria's oil deposits, nor dry and unfruitful soil, as in Ethiopia and Somalia, appeared to make any difference in prospects for attaining growth in the fundamentals of agriculture, peace between tribes, and working governments run by responsible chiefs of state. *Zimbabwe*, formerly Rhodesia, made independent by the British Tory government in 1979, inherited a sound economy and establishment, but faced the loss of skilled whites, who found themselves a scorned and jeopardized minority, and civil war resulting from the discontent of tribes and demobilized revolutionary soldiers. *Nigeria*, despite its oil, suffered a downturn in its economy which threatened the lives and fortunes of much of its population. In 1983, it forcibly removed half a million Ghanians from within its borders, expelling them to live or die as they could. *Uganda*, having rid herself of the murderous Idi Amin, nevertheless struggled with a depleted treasury and internecine war. *Angola* was controlled with the help of Cuban soldiers, who worked with guerrillas to invade South African territories. *Ethiopia* and *Somalia* shed blood over border areas which all observers agreed had no economic or strategic value. Other African areas suffered under spendthrift dictators. Meanwhile, the minority white population of the *Republic of South Africa* (*q.v.*) maintained its hold on political power in its nation by denying political rights to all non-whites. Clearly, South African whites were appalled by the excesses which had occurred in black-ruled countries elsewhere on the continent. Many conservatives, while deploring the racism of South African internal policies, pointed to its general stability on a continent marked by internal turmoil and noted that the standard of living of South African blacks was far above that of blacks in other nations of Africa. The conservative columnist Alice Widener (*q.v.*) in the *Indianapolis Star*, in May of 1982, denounced the head of the World Bank for wanting more American aid given to African countries: "President Mobutu Sese Seko of Zaire, a client of yours who owes not only our country but also many European countries billions of dollars he can't pay is occupying the entire 35th floor of an exclusive [New York] Park Avenue Hotel. There are 80 persons in his entourage, including 21 children.... He brought along three native chefs from Zaire to learn how to make the kind of American griddle cakes he likes so much." The major concern of American conservatives was that the continent might fall, not only into irresponsible hands, but into Marxist and ultimately Soviet hands, giving the latter strategic positions from which they could strangle Western economics and the will of democracies to act as an influence abroad or maintain their way of life at home. The dilemma faced not only by conservatives but all supporters of Western democracy was the fact that South Africa seemed to be not only the most internally stable nation in Africa, but Africa's staunchest foe of Communism. K. Borgin and K. Corbett, *The Destruction of a Continent: Africa and International Aid* (1982); David Larub, *The Africans* (1982); Frank S. Meyer (*q.v.*), ed., *The African Nettle* (1965).

**Agar, Herbert** (1897-1980), born in New Rochelle, New York, but identified with the Southern Agrarians. He attended Princeton University, and in 1933 gained the Pulitzer Prize for his *The People's Choice*. He made his American career on the *Louisville Courier Journal*, but soon found himself more comfortable in London. He was literary editor of the *English Review* (1930-1934), though he continued to write of America in skillful prose which was well received, but made less impact than the symposium he edited with Allen Tate on *Who Owns America?* (1936). *A Time for Greatness* (1942) was his contribution to the war effort, *The Perils of Democracy* (1965) an effort to relate to the evident social crisis, from which, however, he was too remote for effect.

**Aged**, see Old Age

**Agnew, Spiro** (1918- ) rose precipitously from county executive of Baltimore, Maryland (1961) to governor of Maryland (1967), and to Vice President on the 1968 Nixon ticket. Agnew's firm stand on law and order deeply satisfied conservative gatherings from coast to coast. His developing career seemed to set him up for the highest office, after the Nixon Presidency had run its course. As Watergate (*q.v.*) closed in upon his chief, allegations and evidence surfaced which exposed him as the recipient of illegal payoffs. Agnew's claim that he could have proved his innocence, but at the expense of his family's peace of mind, is untenable. His resignation from office helped undermine President Nixon; it is unlikely that Congress would have threatened impeachment with Agnew next in line for the White House. Eventually the entertainer Frank Sinatra had to rescue the ruined former Vice President with funds from his own bank account. Agnew's best-selling novel, *The Canfield Decision* (1976), was an illuminating account of Washington politics. His *Go Quietly...or Else* (1980), non-fiction, was much less interesting.

**Agony of G.O.P. 1964, The** (1965), by Robert D. Novak. It attempted to analyze the results of the 1964 Presidential election, seeing it, as did many observers at the time, as a catastrophe for conservatism. But, from the conservative point-of-view, the Goldwater (*q.v.*) defeat had many positive results. For one thing, it introduced the general public to the fact that there were too many conservatives who could not be dismissed as merely "kooks." It also highlighted the role of the media as forums for creating and disseminating opinions, a role which became increasingly prominent in later years for Republicans as well as Democrats. See Nixon, Richard M. See also Republicans, Conservative.

**Agrarianism**, harking back to Thomas Jefferson's (*q.v.*) concern for farmers as the basis of a good society, it maintained its radical base with such city workers as Thomas Skidmore in the 1830s, persons who feared the poverty and inequality in the major cities, dreamed of owning their own land, and, at the extreme, demanded an equal division of land. The word survived among post-Civil War farmers seeking, not drastic solutions to their problems, but relief from oppressive freight rates and banking difficulties.

**Agrarians**, a phenomenon of Southern culture, involving a number of Vanderbilt University intellectuals with relations elsewhere. In 1930, they published a volume of essays, *I'll Take My Stand*, in which they looked back to pre-industrial days and reaffirmed their principles of tradition, elite culture, and, indirectly, the values of slavery. All this, in the midst of a deepening depression, should have made their essays quaint and bizarre. However, their contributors included Stark Young, an esteemed *New Republic* theater critic; Robert Penn Warren, with a career of best-sellers ahead; John Crowe Ransom, whose *Kenyon Review* was to capture academe with principles of the New Criticism; and others distinguished in scholarship and culture. *I'll Take My Stand* survived even while civil rights agitation reached into the Southern universities, implemented by Federal law, and was one rallying point for a second South not ready or willing to accept the perspectives of the civil libertarians. In 1980 it celebrated half a century of influence. See also *Southern Partisan, The*, and Louis Filler, "Prophets in the Promised Land," *Book Forum*, vol. 6, no. 2.; and Twelve Southerners, *I'll Take My Stand* (1980 ed.); Thomas D. Young, *Waking Their Neighbors Up* (1982); William C. Havard and Walter Sullivan, eds., *A Band of Prophets* (1982); Clyde Wilson, ed., *Why the South Will Survive* (1981).

**Airlines**, see Deregulation

**Alcoholism**, see Temperance, Prohibition

**Alien and Sedition Acts** (1798), a bone of contention between the Federalist Administration of President John Adams and the out-of-office Democratic-Republicans headed by Thomas Jefferson. The 1790s were an era of fierce antagonism between the parties, heightened by scurrilous journalism and opposed attitudes toward the French Revolution. Too, the conservative Federalists deemed it necessary to strengthen the Federal government against unruly or seditious elements, such as had led the Whisky Rebellion of 1794, flouting federal tax collectors, or contemplated separating parts of the West from the Federal Union. How much harm aliens who approved of the French Revolution could have done to the United States cannot be known; certainly there was an element of hysteria (*q.v.*) in some Federalists' reactions. Their resentments of the Jeffersonian (*q.v.*) journalistic abuse of the President did not wholly distinguish between antipathy and sedition. The resulting Alien and Sedition Acts of 1798 at a time of possible war between the United States and France set dire penalties for subversives. The provisions restricting aliens were not enforced, though they frightened or subdued visitors from England and France. Federalist courts did, however, penalize some twenty-five Jeffersonian editors with fines and jail sentences. Meanwhile Jeffersonians attempted to repudiate the Acts on the basis of states rights (*q.v.*). Jefferson in the Virginia Assembly and Madison in Kentucky obtained official resolutions declaring that they were "not united on the principle of unlimited submission to their general government." Their attempt to win other states over to this principle, however, was a failure. They did set a precedent for the Hartford (Connecticut) Resolutions of 1814, which denounced "Madison's War" and appeared ready to leave the Union, and an even more somber precedent for the Secession movement which brought on the Civil War. (*Qq.v.* for above.)

**Aliens**, see Immigration

**"Aligned,"** and non-aligned nations, those that claimed independence from Communist and anti-Communist influence, notably that of the Soviet Union on one side and the United States on the other. In pre-nuclear eras, such lands had been subject to war and controversies, and been ruled by governments acceptable to reigning imperialists (*q.v.*). In periods which saw East and West in general confrontation, the tiniest nation or quasi-nation could command respect and a measure of influence merely by playing off the Soviet Union against the United States, or by designating itself as "non-aligned." The power of such nations as Libya, Saudi Arabia, and Nigeria, for example, lay solely in the oil which they had "nationalized" without Western reprisals and which gave them a base for international prestige. An organization of "non-aligned" nations, some 120 in 1984, sometimes met and came up with seemingly impractical programs calling for massive financial assistance and world peace. There was continuing danger, however, that one or more of them, from internal or external disruption, might come under the control of the United States or the Soviet Union thus disrupting the precarious balance of world peace.

**Allende, Salvador**, see Latin America

**"Alphabet Agencies,"** see New Deal, The; Thirties

**"Alternative,"** a term common in the 1960s and 1970s, intended to suggest a widening of democratic choices, as well as an indirect or direct criticism of those already available or known to American traditions. The phrase "alternative life-style," though somewhat amorphous in concept, was generally attached to non-traditional patterns of living and behavior. Liberals tended to be more tolerant of such life-styles than conservatives, whose perspectives in social, sexual, and other areas were generally traditional. Many academics rushed to join what they perceived to be the non-traditional wave of the future, which produced curious results. Thus, John L. Thomas produced *Alternative America: Henry George, Edward Bellamy, Henry Demarest Lloyd, and the Adversary Tradition* (1983). In some liberal circles the term "alternative" became a replacement for "adversary," being less confrontational and less likely to arouse opposition.

**Alternative, The**, see Tyrrell, Emmett, Jr.

**Amendments to the Constitution**, see Fifth, Tenth, Bill of Rights

**America First**, an emergency effort between September 1940 and December 7, 1941 to halt America's drift toward intervention in the European War by rousing and organizing the forces against war through publicity and the encouragement of political action. Although there were pro-war groups and pacifist groups, America First sought to create a center for larger, non-doctrinaire non-interventionist forces. Thus, the American Peace Mobilization was Communist controlled and sought only the defense of the Soviet Union, by peace or war. Pacifists represented various purposes which did not necessarily place "America first." The new America First organization attracted many well-known or distinguished persons, such as Burton K. Wheeler, once a famed reformer; Philip LaFollette, carrying on the non-intervention tradition of his father; Senator Gerald P. Nye, who had probed munitions scandals; and, best known of all, Charles A. Lindbergh, Jr. (*q.v.*). Head of the New York chapter was John T. Flynn (*q.v.*), already a vigorous crusader against war profits. Although the Committee attracted a few liberals of distinction, such as Oswald Garrison Villard, it drew mainly conservatives and Republicans. Leader of the pro-British side was the Democratic President himself, Franklin D. Roosevelt, and his followers, most of them liberal on one or more points in politics or social outlook, and not a few of them tolerant of or even sympathetic to apparent Soviet aims. America First partisans saw little fruitful in the Soviet program. A negotiated peace between the embattled nations seemed wise. Lindbergh feared that Germany was too strong to risk war. Despite such sincere opinions, America First was shadowed by charges of anti-Semitism (*q.v.*) and by association with fascist and demagogic groups. In addition, it was evident that pro-Nazis were eager to cooperate with and use non-interventionists, in order to aid the cause of Hitler. Although America First did not grow substantially, its publicity reached curious or anxious people, and helped slow down the drive toward intervention as the Nazis advanced over Europe. The Japanese assault in Pearl Harbor, December 7, 1941, put an instant end to America First. Wayne S. Cole, *America First: The Battle against Intervention* (1953), James J. Martin, *American Liberalism and World Politics, 1939-1941* (1964).

**America We Lost: The Concerns of a Conservative, The** (1968), by Mario Pei, a mournful protest by a distinguished scholar of language, recalling the America to which he emigrated as one of opportunity and freedom, now restricted in outlook, material processes, and hope. Indicative of his spirit was his belief that the *New York Times* (*q.v.*), in refusing to print his letter of protest against an article by the liberal Henry S. Commager defending an all-powerful Federal government, was as a private property justified in its policy. William F. Buckley, Jr. (*q.v.*) provided an introduction.

**American Association of Retired Persons**, see Pepper, Claude; Old Age

**American Civil Liberties Union**, born in the struggle of 1917 to defend radicals, aliens, and opponents against intervention in the European War, under the leadership of Roger N. Baldwin (1884-1981) and such socialists and pacifists as Norman Thomas (see Filler, DASC). It attracted the dislike and deprecation of conservatives as being vulnerable to Communist infiltration and causes, and thus harmful to American security as well as to a proper understanding of civil liberties; see

*The Truth about the American Civil Liberties Union*, published c. 1958 by Organization Research Associates, one of the then-scattered conservative groups resisting dominant liberal opinion. The profound decline of domestic Communist organizations focused conservative antagonism to the ACLU more sharply on its role in promoting such causes as abortion, separation of church and state as in the school-prayer issue, and "affirmative action" (*qq.v.*).

**American Commonwealth**, see Bryce, Viscount James

**American Conservatism in the Age of Enterprise, 1865-1910** (1951), by Robert Green McCloskey, a liberal consideration of William Graham Sumner, Stephen J. Field, and Andrew Carnegie (*qq.v.*) which saw them extending the gospel of wealth; Sumner in material rationalizations of behavior, Field in moral justifications for private property, Carnegie in linking capitalist ethics with philanthropy. The author saw these approaches as carrying inner contradictions which, being so perceived by the American people, enabled them to move away to new viewpoints which made theirs obsolete.

**American Conservative Union**, founded in the middle 1960s, became a leading conservative action organization, setting up centers throughout the country, for raising funds and issuing publications and lobbying in Congress. Unhappy with Nixon's (*q.v.*) policies—his budget deficits, his wage and price controls, his welfare-state Family Assistance Plan—it took no part in his overwhelmingly successful 1972 re-election campaign.

**American Democrat, The** (1838), by James Fenimore Cooper (*q.v.*), illustrated Cooper's particular ideas of democracy. He believed in the rule of the best, and defended the American social system as superior to that which he perceived as dominating Europe. But he was made sensitive to what he saw as the evils of excessive equalitarianism by the uprising against perpetual tenancy (the patroon system) which had been practiced by the aristocratic Dutch landlords in upstate New York. Cooper favored aristocracy, as opposed to monarchy, and encouraged everyone to do his best whatever his station in life. He pleaded against universal suffrage on grounds that it would result in inadequate leadership.

**American Dissent, The** (1966), by Jeffrey Hart, a faithful report on the positions taken by the *National Review*, as displayed in writings by James Burnham, Willmoore Kendall, John Chamberlain, Russell Kirk, and the editor, William F. Buckley, Jr. (*qq.v.*). They variously stressed tradition, free enterprise, the heritage of the Constitution-makers, social morality, and anti-Communism, among other tenets. Although the *National Review* had risen in circulation from 8,000 readers in 1955 to 100,000 in 1966, it was notable that its interpreter still saw his as the party of dissent, rather than parity, and not merely because it was a minority in politics. Central authority and welfare had so deeply infiltrated the public consciousness and operations, according to Hart, as to raise questions of whether the trend since New Deal (*q.v.*) years could be reversed.

**"American Dream,"** a concept engaging writers and political aspirants in many forms, involving a belief that the nation was destined for great and democratic achievements. Hence it was improper, almost unnatural, for Americans to accept meager goals and shoddy products. Conservatives approved the prospect, though, in better eras, with less rhetoric than faith. Almost all Presidential aspirants made the implicit "calls to greatness"; it was the sign of a new uncertainty that Jimmy Carter (*q.v.*), in his 1980 campaign, beset by troubles, made a low-keyed appeal for "realism": times were hard, and there would be no miracles. His opponent, Reagan, made the traditional appeal. Norman Mailer's novel *American Dream* (1964) exploited the concept negatively. See also F. I. Carpenter, *American Literature and the Dream* (1955).

**American Enterprise Institute**, a frankly conservative "think tank," founded in 1943 to promote free-enterprise ideas. In subsequent years it attracted business and economic analysts in and out of government, including such well-known figures as Herbert Stein and William E. Simon (*q.v.*). It considered itself in opposition to the liberal Brookings Institute, which admitted that it was not entirely impartial but protested that its concern was primarily with analyses of economic conditions. Nevertheless, the determination of the new Reagan Administration to reverse the liberal direction of government found a friend in the American Enterprise Institute such as it did not have at Brookings.

**"American Fear of Literature, The,"** Sinclair Lewis's (*q.v.*) acceptance speech, December 12, 1930, on receiving the Nobel Prize for Literature. Making a major effort at ecumenical statement, Lewis took off from the public statement of the conservative author, pastor, and diplomat Henry Van Dyke, who had declared it an insult to America that such an author as Lewis should be awarded the Nobel Prize. Van Dyke was also a member of the American Academy of Arts and Letters, and this gave Lewis an opportunity to review persons honored with membership in it and the greater number of distinguished authors not so honored. Lewis balanced his salutes, to Theodore Dreiser and Willa Cather (*q.v.*), to Upton Sinclair and H. L. Mencken (*q.v.*), to Eugene O'Neill and James Branch Cabell (*q.v.*). His contrasting references ran from François Villon to John Galsworthy (*q.v.*). He saw the paucity of writers then formally in academe (*q.v.*) as evidence of America's fear of new literature, and noted that America had not produced a Brandes, Taine, Goethe, or Croce in criticism. American writers had to work alone, and in resistance to such outlooks as that of the new Humanists (*q.v.*), who could not honor distinction unless it expressed itself in Greek. Lewis opposed Emerson (*q.v.*) and deplored Hamlin Garland's fall from realism: as a Midwesterner himself, this touched him personally. He concluded by honoring such younger talents as Hemingway, Wolfe, Faulkner, and the Communist Mike Gold. Some of Lewis's speech reflected Twenties (*q.v.*) attitudes, some his own judgment; but the effort at breadth was generous and perceptive. It was ironic that the Academy would in time honor authors whose quality, often radical, was approximately on a par with those of the Van Dyke era.

**American Federation of Labor**, see Gompers, Samuel.

**American Legion, The.** Organized in 1919 following World War I, it proved a powerful lobby acting in behalf of veterans' interest. It was also noted for anti-communist and patriotic (*q.v.*) activities, many of which were denounced as "extremist" by liberals. In a time of wide public interest in the Soviet Union as a great "experiment," and with American commercial (*q.v.*) firms anxious to sell their products to the Soviets, the American Legion held firm in its opposition to "godless communism" and commercial relations with Soviets. For that, and for seeking to influence education so as to develop a more patriotic outlook among students, it drew accusations of being "reactionary." The *American Legion Magazine* reflected its several interests. Raymond Moley (*q.v.*), *The American Legion Story* (1966). See also Patriotism.

**American Mercury**, best known as the organ of H. L. Mencken (*q.v.*) and George Jean Nathan from 1924 to 1933. It was then taken over by others who generally shared Mencken's outlook, particularly his anti-New Deal sentiments, but the magazine had less of the high spirits and variety which it had been known for at its peak. From 1936 to 1939 the magazine featured Mencken himself, Charles Beard, the forthright fascist Lawrence Dennis (known for his contributions on "The State of the Union"), George Santayana, G. K. Chesterton, and A. J. Nock (*qq.v.*).

**American Opinion**, magazine publication of the John Birch Society (*q.v.*).

**American Party**, the name for minor political parties in addition to the more famous or notorious Know-Nothings. They included the National Christian Association (1872) and the American Party (1887), eccentrically nativist (*q.v.*) in their suspicion of or rejection of immigrant strains newer than themselves, and generally reactionary rather than conservative in their unrealistic unwillingness to recognize change and the rights of others whose basic goals were little different from their own. Their self-righteousness seemed to serve prejudice more than it did patriotism (*qq.v.*).

**American Protective Association**, see New Immigration

**American Revolution**. Although accorded a mountain of studies and special monographs, it furnished an example of how history invited continual reinterpretation as time goes on. In the twentieth century conservatives tended to accord the American Revolution more regard than did their opponents, who in many instances abandoned earlier liberal and radical efforts to align their causes with those of the Revolutionary fathers. The rise of pacifism in connection with the Vietnam War tended to color liberals' attitudes toward the Revolution. Emphasis on the "economic causes" of the War for Independence hinted at calculation and exploitation. "Debunking" such figures as George Washington (*q.v.*) became fashionable in some liberal circles. One profitable approach was to compare the American Revolution with the later French Revolution, for development and results. Edmund Burke (*q.v.*), as friend of the colonists and as foe of the French Revolution, made for profitable reflection. C. D. Hazen's *Contemporary American Opinion of the French Revolution* (1897) was also helpful. B. Quarles's *The Negro in the American Revolution* (1967) approached its subject with scholarship. Some others contributed to a balanced and more objective view of the Revolutionary Era. See also Adams, Samuel; Henry, Patrick; Dickinson, John; Paine, Thomas; and related topics.

**American Spectator, The**, see Tyrrell, Emmett, Jr.

**American Telephone and Telegraph**, see Deregulation.

**Americans for Democratic Action (ADA)** see *Unravelling of America, The*

**Ames, Fisher** (1758-1808), famous for his Federalist (*q.v.*) eloquence, which he brought to bear against equalitarians. A Massachusetts aristocrat and lawyer, he was unequivocal in speaking up for the "wise and good and opulent" as the natural guardians of liberty. After helping to win Massachusetts support for the new Federal Constitution in 1787, he came to Congress in 1789, where he emerged as its outstanding orator, dazzling even the Jeffersonian opposition with the force of his eloquence, many of his speeches being regarded as masterpieces. A high point in his Congressional career was his defense of Jay's Treaty with Great Britain, April 28, 1796, in the face of popular denunciation of the Treaty as a betrayal of the Revolution. Ames's impassioned speech turned the tide and won ratification of the Treaty for the Federalists. A sick man, he left Congress for home, where his anxiety for the government increased with the victory of the Jeffersonians in 1800. From an ardent defender of central power, he began to look to the states to preserve liberty as he defined it. See his *The Dangers of American Liberty* (1805). See also his *Speeches in Congress* (1871), and W. E. A. Bernhard, *Fisher Ames* (1965).

**Ames, Oakes**, see Crédit Mobilier

**Amway Corporation**, a successful world-wide private business, begun in 1959 by two friends in the Grand Rapids, Michigan area, Jay VanAndel and Richard Devos. It was essentially a mail-order, door-to-door retailer of household and personal items, some of which Amway manufactured, some of which it had manufactured for it, and some of which it handled for Sears, Montgomery Ward, and other large firms. Amway prospered swiftly, expanded world-wide, and soon became a billion-dollar-a-year operation. It differed from other commercial (*q.v.*) ventures in several respects; operating on a cash-only basis, so that it was uniquely debt-free, and employing an estimated one million salespeople who paid for their initial "kit" and received aid in developing their techniques. Successful salespeople were accorded notable status in the company. Amway did much for Michigan business and helped maintain the city of Grand Rapids as a desirable living area. Amway's own headquarters in nearby Ada included a manufacturing showplace and a convention center, and attracted many people, both businessmen and sightseers sympathetic to its philosophy. Amway claimed to be much more than a commercial operation. It held itself to exemplify free enterprise (*q.v.*), and encouraged its personnel to exemplify this. It was therefore startling in 1982 when Canadian Customs accused Amway of having sought to defraud Canada of some $28 million in customs charges through false declarations. The alleged export scheme enabled Amway to lower the cost of its goods before submitting them to customs. The Amway officers denied these charges completely, and claimed that the conditions of entry had been candidly presented to and approved by Canadian authorities. In November 1983, Amway Corporation and its Canadian subsidiary admitted to the Canadian operation as fraudulent, and were fined a total of $20 million for depriving the Canadian government of $23 million of unpaid duties on imported products: the highest criminal sentence ever imposed in Canada. In exchange, the government agreed to withdraw all criminal charges against four top executives. Still open was a $119 million civil suit for penalties and back taxes. Amway advertised immediately in major newspapers, neither admitting nor denying guilt, and asserting only that Amway's chiefs had "misplaced their confidence and wound up paying a high price for the unfortunate advice they were given." C. P. Conn, *An Uncommon Freedom: The Amway Experience and Why it Grows* (1982). See also Commercialism.

**Analysis**, a 4-page monthly broadsheet begun by Frank Chodorov (*q.v.*) in 1944 in which to express his libertarian views. In 1951, he merged *Analysis* with *Human Events* (*q.v.*).

**Animal Farm** (1945), see Orwell, George

**Anthem** (1937), by Ayn Rand (*q.v.*), a novel depicting her anti-utopia (*q.v.*), intended to show into what degradation mankind had fallen through the evils of community. The individual in the world of *Anthem* had disappeared; persons referred to "We" and "They." They lived grubbily in places lit with candles. Sex took place on schedule in the Palace of Mating. Older times were "Unmentionable Times." Places which had gone to grass were uncharted and forbidden to the helots. Love came to the dissidents in such phrases as: "We are one. . .alone. . .and only. . .and we love you who are one. . .alone. . .and only." Their fulfillment in an "uncharted" forest—we learn nothing of the charted areas—involved no more than living together and liking it. How humankind descended to this state is not indicated.

**"Anti-Anti-Communist,"** a term sometimes applied to those liberals who opposed what they regarded as the conservative fixation on the menace of Communism.

**Anti-Conservative**, see *Ominous Politics*

**Anti-Democratic Thought, Patterns of** (1949), by David Spitz, a learned and keen analysis, especially concerned with the American "political mind" of the time. It closely considered James Burnham's (*q.v.*) "economic-political oligarchy," Ralph A. Cram's "the nemesis of mediocrity," George Santayana's "natural aristocracy," and Irving Babbitt's "restrictive authoritarianism" (*qq.v.*), among others. Spitz concluded that "democracy, alone of the forms of state, provides the necessary mechanism for its own correction." Profound and refreshing as were Spitz's examinations, he failed to account for the success of totalitarianism, and the need of lovers of democracy to adjust their actions and judgments to this reality. Nor did he cope with the patent failures of democracy, for example its inability to impede the rise of totalitarians.

**Anti-Imperialism**, in American politics of the 19th century a tendency among conservatives, many of whom carried the burden of resistance to popular imperialistic demands. A legitimate argument, covering the history of America and much more, opposed the concept of "expansion" to that of "imperialism," (*q.v.*) noting vast territories ill-used or not used at all which might be open to an expansion which would not be imperialism. Nevertheless, missionaries, adventurers, explorers, friends of Indians, anti-militarists, and others protested such expansion and demanded justice, reparations (*q.v.*), education for freedom, citizenship, and still other measures to modify the evils of imperialism, from colonial times onward. Theodore Frelinghuysen pleaded for the Cherokee Indians (*qq.v.*), numerous distinguished Americans protested the Mexican War (*q.v.*), and the rise of admitted imperialists in the 1890s inspired such patent anti-imperialist conservatives as E. L. Godkin (*q.v.*), the businessman Edward Atkinson, and the lawyer Moorfield Storey of the Anti-Imperialist League. Although no one could deny their anti-imperialism, some liberal critics felt free to impugn their motives. Little attention has been paid to the pro-imperialism of the American public at large. E. B. Tompkins, *Anti-Imperialism in the United States* (1970).

**Anti-Nuke**, see Nuclear War

**Anti-Semitism**, a small factor in pre-Civil War conservative America because of the small number of Jews in the country and Puritan regard for the Old Testament. After the Civil War the growth of the cities directed some rural resentment against the idea of an alien people, now coming in large numbers to work in sweatshops, though there was still more fear of the Irish Catholics, who were identified with the "bosses" (*q.v.*) in city political machines. Jews were sometimes identified with "international" finance, of which the Rothschilds were one symbol and perceived by frustrated individuals as cunning at money manipulation at the expense of producers. Rumors of European anti-Semitism, from France to Russia, as explicated by the theoreticians Gobineau and Chamberlain (Richard Wagner's son-in-law) contributed to American conservative feeling on the subject. Richard Hofstadter's later attempt to identify anti-semitism with Populism (*q.v.*) was rejected by many scholars. Jews were well-regarded by Progressives, who dominated the 1900-1914 era. However, their general hatred of Czarist Russia and of capitalist war lost them some empathy in conservative centers. Anti-Semitism touched an unfortunate nerve in so central a figure as Henry Ford (*q.v.*); see Albert Lee, *Henry Ford and the Jews* (1980). The rise of Nazism in Germany and the Great Depression of the 1930s stirred anti-Semitism among domestic fascists seeking scapegoats. However, World War II slogans and goals made blatant anti-Semitism unfashionable. Laura Z. Hobson's *Gentleman's Agreement* (1947), which depicted an undercover anti-Semitism in social and business relations, sold some two million copies and became a highly successful motion-picture. After the war, stereotypes and "gentlemanly agreements" sustained a measure of anti-Semitism, as in the Princeton dignitary who quietly confided to another WASP (*q.v.*) that they were getting undesirable elements on campus, referring to Albert Einstein, and the more or less open understanding of quotas (*q.v.*) for students in schools generally and graduate schools in particular, notably in law and medicine. Deans argued that they sought "representative" students, or that Jews, being "too smart," might create imbalances in student percentages. The rise of the New Conservatism, coinciding with the counterculture eruptions of the 1960s, undermined such attitudes and personalities. New Conservatives, being a minority, and emphasizing law and principle, could find no justification for anti-Semitism, and repudiated its manifestations at the grassroots. The youth counterculture, urging equality and scorning education as such, became a threat to institutions which could only be met by patent non-discrimination and even "affirmative action" (*q.v.*). Although Jewish elements were not the center of such pressures they gained from it. Though anti-Semitism still continued, the easier rationalizations and code words lost much of their usefulness. In the late 1970s and 1980s, however, anti-Semitism became fashionable among many radical leftists, who identified with the radical Arab regimes opposed to the state of Israel. Such anti-Semitism was also seen by many as a continuing problem in the American black community, which similarly tended to be sympathetic to radical Arab and Third World regimes.

**Anti-Trust Laws**, see Trust

**Anti-Utopia**, see Utopia

**Apartheid**, see Africa; South Africa

**Apathy**, a reaction to perceived injustices in society, typical of such groups as the "Beats" of the 1950s, who felt distaste for what they saw as a killing social conformity and elected not to participate in traditional social roles. The "Beats" encouraged unconventional sexual activities, drug experimentation, and a general "bohemian" lifestyle. Conservatives have appeared less inclined to apathy, even when resentful of government actions. Henry Adams (*q.v.*) refused to listen to "treason" in his own house, when discontented conservative guests sneered at Woodrow Wilson's (*q.v.*) policies. Conservatives who detested Franklin D. Roosevelt and his New Deal (*q.v.*) sought the action of Republican politics, rather than lapsing into apathy.

**Apprenticeship**, see Vocational Education

**Aquinas, St. Thomas**, see Thomism

**Arendt, Hannah** (1906-1975), social and political thinker, German born and educated, a refugee from fascism (*q.v.*) who gained academic and general distinction for such books as *Origins of Totalitarianism* (1951), *The Human Condition* (1958), *On Revolution* (1963), and *On Violence* (1969). Although her works were applauded by many thoughtful and intelligent liberals and conservatives, they leaned toward the values of conservatism in weighing good and evil and avoiding vain anticipations. Her researches had found imperialism and anti-Semitism (*qq.v.*) at the root of totalitarianism. Her report on *Eichmann in Jerusalem* (1963), concerning the notorious Nazi executioner's trial and condemnation, raised questions of responsibility and justice which troubled commentators in the West.

**Aristocracy**, a lost cause in America from the beginning, since few nobles cared to settle in the country. Southern plantations offered better opportunities than Northern for aristocratic ways, as reflected in such lives as that of William Byrd (1674-1744), whose uncommercial prose in *A History of the Dividing Line* and other writings reflected a lord-of-the-manor viewpoint. Washington Irving (*q.v.*), of a commercial family, enjoyed fashionable and moneyed company. James Fenimore Cooper (*q.v.*), a Northern landowner, fought in print and the courts for the rights of his class, though many quasi-aristocratic scions disdained to do so. Theodore Roosevelt (*q.v.*) saw aristocrats as clearly failing their duty to the nation, and worked to change this. Many of aristocratic bearing were but one generation removed from farmers and clerks. Henry Adams (*q.v.*) was three generations removed, and labored to prove himself free of the madding crowd. Aristocrats could be found in reform movements, practicing forms of *noblesse oblige* (*q.v.*). Civil service reform (*q.v.*) was created by aristocrats. Aristocratic airs were possible in persons of modest background, such as A. J. Nock (*q.v.*). Franklin D. Roosevelt (*q.v.*), on the other hand, practiced warmth and confidentiality with his public, as did Nelson A. Rockefeller (*q.v.*). New conservatives varied in their attitudes toward aristocratic goals or aspirations.

**Aristocracy in America** (1839), by Francis Joseph Grund, an Austrian, graduate of the University of Vienna, who emigrated to the United States in 1827. He interested himself in journalism and politics, and was, to a degree, influenced in his own work by de Tocqueville's (*q.v.*) *Democracy in America*, taking, however, an entirely different tack. Where de Tocqueville was speculative and analytical, Grund responded to individuals and social groups, offering lengthy versions of their conversation and attitudes. Much of what he reported was personal and stereotyped, but left an impression of accuracy. Sharply perceived were class discriminations, with the newly wealthy seen to be as pushy and aspiring as members of the lower classes. Also instructive were Grund's comparisons with the language, gestures, and expectations of comparable classes abroad.

**Aristotle** (384-322 B.C.), a major figure in ancient Greek philosophy, honored by many conservatives as well as reactionaries. His emphasis on deductive reasoning and materialism made him less important for conservative thought than Plato (*q.v.*). Much of Aristotle's overview of science has become outdated. His emphasis on reason and contemplation passed through Thomism (*q.v.*), has been highly regarded by traditionalists. His ethics and politics—seen by him as related—continue to offer points of reference for new solutions to problems of social goals and justice. Aristotle saw the purpose of science as knowledge, but the goal of ethics and politics as good conduct. Using happiness as a measure of virtue, he could be seen as closer to the utilitarians (*q.v.*) of much later date than to Plato (*q.v.*), but his pronouncements on virtue, honor, and related qualities reveal that he saw true happiness as the result of contemplated choices and moderate actions. Aristotle's view of man as a political animal placed emphasis on community, family, and the state as demanding measures of virtue such as seem to comport better with traditional conservative standards than with relativistic views of human nature. His teachings, too, regard order (*q.v.*) with high respect. Aristotle viewed the various forms of statehood—from monarchy to democracy—for what they could give family and the individual, in terms of happiness and stability. H. B. Veatch, *Rational Man: A Modern Interpretation of Aristotelian Ethics* (1962); H. F. Cherniss, *Aristotle's Criticism of Plato and the Academy* (1944), Stephen R.L. Clark, *Aristotle's Man* (1975).

**Arlington House**, conservative publishing firm which furnished an outlet for a number of distinguished conservatives including Russell Kirk, Eric von Kuehnelt-Leddihn, and Isaac Don Levine (*qq.v.*). The latter edited *Plain Talk* (*q.v.*), an anthology that drew together anti-communist writers who had resisted left-wing defenses of and apologetics for Stalinism (*q.v.*). Internal confusion appears to have diminished the firm's ability to survive, and it became an "imprint" for Crown Publishers.

**Arnold, Matthew** (1822-1888), poet and literary critic, like John Stuart Mill (*q.v.*) apparently more liberal than conservative, but, like him, more bound to ideals of order and tradition identified with conservatism. Like Mill, he had a famous father more intensively bound to conservative tenets than the distraught industrialism and, later, Darwinism (*q.v.*) of their time permitted. Arnold made his first reputation as a poet, in such verses as "The Strayed Reveller" (1849) expressing a sense of the insecurity of life which would find its austere yet passionate fulfillment in the immortal "Dover Beach" (1867). It was his sense of society's need which drove him to become a poet-prophet, whose basic ideas are patently as urgent at the end of the twentieth century as in the nineteenth. *Culture and Anarchy* (1869), *Friendship's Garland* (1871), and his *Essays in Criticism* (1865, 1888) linked literature with life, exalted the worth of creative spirits, and treated intellectual products as equally tangible with material things. His famous categories of Barbarian, Philistine, and Populace, referring in order to the upper classes, the middle classes, and the working classes, though requiring some adjustment for changing times and circumstances, provided a measure for assessing the relationship of life to mind. Arnold's *Literature and Dogma* (1873) and *God and the Bible* (1875) reconciled his spiritual perplexities by finding the poetry in revelation sufficient. Beauty was truth, truth beauty. Although John Stuart Mill lived a different life, like Arnold he worked to create patterns which could satisfy human needs. See Lionel Trilling (*q.v.*), *Matthew Arnold* (1939), E. Alexander, *Matthew Arnold and John Stuart Mill* (1965), P. J. MacCarthy, *Arnold and the Three Classes* (1964).

**Aron, Raymond** (1905-1983), French political thinker and anti-Marxist, whose studies and views were influential in the West and among French politicians. A fellow-student of Jean-Paul Sartre at the Ecole Normale Superieure, he took an opposite road in his view of political developments. Impressed by de Tocqueville (*q.v.*), he also pondered the workings of society, in numerous books and as a perennial writer for newspapers. During World War II he joined the Free French in London, edited a newspaper, and spoke on the BBC to occupied France. A follower of General de Gaulle, he returned with him to engage in editing and writing. Typical of his writings, branded by his opponents as "reactionary" but scornful of all forms of totalitarianism, was his *Progress and Disillusion* (1968). See his *Memoirs: 50 Years of Political Reflections* (1983).

**Articles of Confederation**, first instrument of the emancipated British American colonies, intended to assure that the new government could not claim power over the states as had Parliament and the British King. The new government which succeeded it, under a Federalist Constitution, did what it could to demean the Articles, by holding them impotent and their Presidents figureheads. Yet George Washington (*q.v.*) himself honored its first President, his neighbor John Hanson, and delivered up his sword to him. Hanson's government, under the Articles, achieved peace with Great Britain, recognition and trade relations with several countries, arrangements with Indians (*q.v.*), and an administrative apparatus. Most important, it passed the Northwest Ordinance (*q.v.*), which assured that there would be no slavery (*q.v.*) in the Old Northwest, from Ohio to the Mississippi River. A Southwest Ordinance failed in Congress by one vote; had it passed slavery could not have expanded westward. Thus, the Articles were by no means impotent; the powers of the central government were deliberately kept limited to prevent the abuses which had brought about the Revolution. The Articles provided for a transition period during which the new nation could determine the directions it preferred. They were radical in many respects. The genius displayed by the Federalists, and their powers of persuasion, indicate that the citizenry agreed with them in essentials. M. Jensen, *The Articles of Confederation* (1940).

**Assembly Lines**, efficient methods of factory operation as formulated by Frederick W. Taylor (*q.v.*) and carried out for the production of steel, automobiles (*q.v.*), and other manufactured goods. It came to refer to social projects which carried out prior arranged plans, usually sub rosa, for electing someone, instigating strikes, gaining grants from foundations under allegedly "open competition" conditions, and the like. Infiltrating organizations with useful personnel, or "stooges," to create assembly lines was an important preliminary to gaining a desired appointment, decision, or other end. The National Endowment for the Arts was widely suspected of employing assembly lines for the allocation of grants for applicants.

**AT&T**, see American Telephone and Telegraph

**Atheism**, apparently more tolerated in liberal circles than in conservative circles, where it is often viewed as a deviation from traditional patterns of thought. Militant atheism seems an inconsequential factor in the American dialogue; some philosophical conservatives deemed it less of a threat than religious apathy. Although such groups as the American Humanist Association include some religious "seekers," their "humanism" appears closer to atheism than to anything else. Atheism was perceived by some as being itself a species of religion, in its ardor and concern. Gonzalez-Ruiz, *Atheistic Humanism and the Biblical God* (1969); P. Masterson, *Atheism and Alienation* (1971); Bertrand Russell, *Atheism: Collected Essays: 1943-1949* (1972); M. M. O'Hair, *Atheist Epic: Bill Murray, the Bible, and the Baltimore Board of Education* (1970).

**Atlantic Monthly**, begun 1857, one of the most distinguished of "genteel" (*q.v.*) publications. It began under the editorship of James Russell Lowell (*q.v.*), attracted writings from among the most notable writers of his time, and with *Harpers, Scribner's, Century*, and other publications in the same rank provided standards of education and social stability which encouraged civility in the period after the Civil War. It printed Walt Whitman and Henry Thoreau; Mark Twain (*q.v.*) and his collaborator on *The Gilded Age*, Charles Dudley Warner; Julia Ward Howe's "Battle Hymn of the Republic"; and Edward Everett Hale's *The Man Without a Country* (*q.v.*). Changing times pointed up some of its evasions of poignant social issues and its overemphasis on secondary issues, but it continued to give limited outlet to newer writers as the decades went on. It published many essays by William James, Hawthorne, Francis Parkman, Edith Wharton (*qq.v.*). In recent decades it has featured Steinbeck, Thurber, Hemingway, and others, though rarely in their most challenging form. Ellery Sedgwick, comp., *Atlantic Harvest* (1947), with a valuable memoir; L. Desaulniers, *119 Years of the Atlantic* (1977). See also M. DeWolfe Howe, *The Atlantic Monthly and Its Makers* (1919).

**Atlas Shrugged** (1957), by Ayn Rand (*q.v.*), see *Fountainhead, The*

**Atomic Bomb**, see Nuclear War

**Atrocities**, see also Genocide. Atrocities have occurred in all ages. Those of the 1950s and, increasingly, the 1960s and 1970s were different in that rationalizations were provided for those who committed them. The perpetrators were seen as victims protesting against a false civilization or as opponents of civic and national leaders who were leading the nation to catastrophe. Conservatives persisted in distinguishing between direct atrocities committed by individuals and groups, and such actions as were carried out by United States bombers over Libya, in retaliation for official Libyan murders perpetrated abroad. But sympathetic interpretations were offered for both individual atrocities and comparable actions endorsed by governments, ranging from the actions in the 1960s of Charles Manson to terrorist (*q.v.*) exploits of the 1970s and after. When all else failed in court and in the media, and as sympathy and empathetic vibrations diminished for those such as Manson, the insanity plea (*q.v.*) interposed to inhibit possibly more effective solutions to the social conditions involved. They remained unresolved in the 1980s.

**Attack on Corporate America, The** (1978), edited by M. Bruce Johnson. It was an extensive rebuttal of charges directed against corporations and involving social responsibility, employee relations, management, information control, state and federal chartering, prices, innovation, profits, and antitrust and regulation issues. The contributors were drawn from economics, law, business, and related fields. Backed by formidable documentation, and contradicting such critics as Ralph Nader and John Kenneth Galbraith, they saw corporate incentives (*q.v.*) as promoting quality in production, equitable treatment of employees, and overall propriety in production and consumption. Thus, Galbraith's belief that advertising (*q.v.*) forced unwanted goods on customers was seen as unjustified by the facts. Arthur Laffer (*q.v.*) found no need for additional information for investors other than what the market itself produced. Profits found their legitimate level, it was maintained. Although the work was intended to provide a "quick fix" against allegations and accusations of the critics and the media (*q.v.*), it raised questions. Could a "quick fix" counter lurid and memorable news reports of corporate misconduct? In the mid-1980s it was revealed that defense contractors had outrageously inflated the cost of items sold to the Pentagon. The "invisible hand" of competition had not, apparently, driven the profiteers from the field. Moreover, the book's failure to anticipate such future developments as the growth of corporate involvement in political action committees (PACs [*q.v.*]) limited its subsequent usefulness. Compare the work of Roger Blough (then chairman of the United States Steel Corporation), *Free Man and the Corporation* (1959), a volume in a series sponsored by the Graduate School of Business, Columbia University. This series also included volumes by Ralph J. Cordiner (chairman, General Electric), *New Frontiers for Professional Managers*; Crawford H. Greenewalt (President, E. I. du Pont Nemours), *The Uncommon Man*; and Theodore V. Houser (formerly chairman, Sears, Roebuck), *Big Business and Human Values*. Cordiner won Reagan with the freedom granted him on his media show; see Reagan, *Where's the Rest of Me?* (1965). See also Commercialism.

**Augustine, Saint** (354-430), from a Roman family in Africa. He lived a worldly life as a school master until converted from Manichaeism to Christianity, being baptized on Easter in 387. He became a priest and, as Bishop of Hippo, in present-day Algeria, a Church Father of paramount influence, in his own time and after. He was known for his life as a teacher and a writer who gathered his lore from Plato (*q.v.*) and Cicero as well as the early Christian authorities. He influenced such masters as St. Thomas Aquinas (see Thomism), but is now perhaps best known for his *Confessions* (c. 400), which detailed his life before and after conversion in human terms readily recognized. *The City of God* (c. 412) is his durable defense of Christians from the fury and assaults of Romans made desperate by barbarian onslaughts, who blamed the Christians for the decay of Roman power. Augustine's numerous critiques of other religious sects, including those with which he had consorted, summed up views of life and divinity which became foundational for Christian thought and dogma. Augustine saw the Church as Christianity's authority, with its apostolic succession as the basis of salvation. He died during an assault on the city of Hippo by Vandals. Robert J. O'Connell, *Saint Augustine's Confessions: The Odyssey of a Soul* (1969); Karl Jaspers, *Plato and Augustine* (1966); Etienne Gilson, *The Christian Philosophy of Saint Augustine*

(1960); J.J. O'Meara, *Augustine Reader* (1973).

**Austrian School of Economics**, see Mises, Ludwig von; Hayek, Friedrich A.

**"Authoritarian States,"** a term made popular by Jeane J. Kirkpatrick (*q.v.*) to distinguish certain modern states, marked by strong authority or dictatorship, from "totalitarian states," which attempted to control every aspect of life within their borders. "Authoritarian" states limited or prescribed political opposition, but within them it was possible for varying degrees of free expression to exist or even flourish. Thus, the Germany of Kaiser Wilhelm II was controlled by the military and police, educators and officials, yet in it flourished numerous geniuses in the arts and sciences. Hitler's Germany, which succeeded the rickety Weimar Republic, was a totalitarian state which eliminated any freedom of expression. Soviet Russia, under its "dictatorship of the Proletariat," was expected by its partisans to mandate freedom, but lost its prestige with the totalitarian excesses of its Stalinized party apparatus. The subsequent "Cold War" between East and West had observers examining states in Africa, South America, and Asia for signs of authoritarianism or totalitarianism. Pro-socialist sympathizers saw in the Chilean Salvador Allende (*q.v.*) a "freely elected" Marxist, not so much as an "authoritarian," though his drive to nationalize Chilean industry moved swifter than his narrow margin of victory warranted. Similarly, liberals, while critical of American actions in Vietnam, found nothing to criticize the workings of the North Vietnam organization. El Salvador-Nicaraguan (*q.v.*) differences were predictably distinguished by liberals and conservatives in 1986. Their assessments were often colored by their basic political views.

**Automobiles**, initially reluctantly received by many conservatives as creating an unhealthy tempo in society, used as status symbols by the wealthy and ambitious. Henry Ford was more highly regarded for his homely virtues than his assembly lines (*qq.v.*), and in the 1930s was the target of labor unions (*q.v.*) seeking recognition. As a result of mass production, automobiles influenced and were affected by public response, which firmly rejected such models as Ford's "Edsel." Whether commerce or the public was responsible for such bizarre features as the "fishtail" effect in the 1950s is undetermined. General Motors' mean attempt to disgrace Ralph Nader in the 1960s alienated the public and ruined production of its "Corvair," but many of its owners cherished that model. With automobile production becoming the key industry in American life, its tendencies helped shape American attitudes. Henry Ford II's support of "controlled depreciation" (*q.v.*)—the making of parts which would deteriorate according to plan—was a plan for full employment, but also a temptation for the production of shoddy goods. Autoworkers' salaries far outstripped those of workers in other American industries. Economic recession and the rising popularity of foreign cars forced management and workers to think—the former about cutting unprofitable plants and wages, the latter about salary and other concessions. Many urged protectionist trade policies to aid the American auto industry. Although automobiles continued to be a power in the economy in the 1980s, they had lost much of their centrality and cultural impact. Eaton Manufacturing Company, *A Chronicle of the Automobile Industry in America 1893-1949* (1950); Frank Ernest Hill, *The Automobile* (1967).

**Avery, Sewall**, see Higher Law

# B

**Babbitt, Irving** (1865-1933), though often thought of as remote and library-trained, was a product of Middle America. He was born in Dayton, Ohio, a town which produced the Wright Brothers and the inventor Charles F. Kettering. Babbitt himself took time developing, at one point in his youth living as a cowboy in the West. He was taken with the power of literature and by 1894 had become Professor of Romance Languages at Harvard. Early in the next century he became alarmed for the future of classical literature as a controllnig force over man's reckless nature, and opposed the democratic tendencies of Progressivism (*qq.v.*). *Literature and the American College* (1908) and *The New Laokoön* (1910) went against the spirit of the time. His masterpiece, *Rousseau and Romanticism* (1919), was a major indictment of romanticism as leading men and morals astray. Identified with the New Humanism (*q.v.*), he was almost certainly the inspiration for the name given by Sinclair Lewis (*q.v.*) to the central character of his novel *Babbitt* (1922), though Babbitt himself had none of the qualities which marked that character. Peter Viereck (*q.v.*) later invented "Gaylord Babbitt": a modern Philistine (see Arnold, Matthew) who, far from rejecting modern artistic experimentation, sought status as an intellectual with wide sympathies—"I go for culture in a big way." That the real Babbitt was indeed formidable was seen in the anger and derogation he received from Twenties (*q.v.*) intellectuals. His later works included *Democracy and Leadership* (1924) and *On Being Creative* (1932). How effective Babbitt could be in a new time of revaluation is problematic. Another New Humanist, Stuart Sherman (1881-1926), abandoned the faith to be more receptive to such experimenting talents as Sherwood Anderson, and to express his new vision in the popular press, yet he also suffered neglect after his death. A revived conservative criticism would almost certainly be heavily influenced by the cultural vision of Babbitt. See also More, Paul Elmer; and pros and cons expressed in Norman Foerster, ed., *Humanism in America* and C. Hartley Grattan, ed., *The Critique of Humanism: A Symposium*, both published in 1930. See also F. E. McMahon, *The Humanism of Irving Babbitt* (1931), and F. A. Manchester and Odell Shepard, eds., *Irving Babbitt: Man and Teacher* (1941).

**"Back to Basics,"** a slogan raised to oppose that of "progressive" education (*q.v.*), urging a renewed emphasis on school instruction in the basics of reading, writing, and mathematics. (See The Graves of Academe.) Observed that such "basics" would no more than enable otherwise illiterates to read the want ads, and did not define education. A second concept of "basics" may be found in *Back to Basics* (1982), by Burton Yale Pines of the Heritage Foundation (*q.v.*), his "basics" including authority, discipline, and a moral order with a hierarchy of values. *Back to Basics: The Traditionalist Movement That Is Sweeping Grass-Roots America* (1983), by Burton Yale Pines, a conservative report, the result of across-country interviews, a study of polls, and discussions with "repentant" liberals and others, as well as socially conscious conservatives.

**Bagehot, Walter** (1826-1877), British social and political commentator who achieved fame because of his grounding in economics and politics, and his literary skill and sense of personality. The son of a banker, and a banker himself, he became editor of the influential *Economist*. His essays mixed literary allusions and allusions to various eras and civilizations. His application of his classical training to practical topics made him evocative to a range of readers. His essay on *Parliamentary Reform* (1859) made an impression, as did his *English Constitution* (1865), which, with its sense of growth and decay, seemed of permanent value. *Lombard Street* (1873) covered financial modes and transactions with authority. Bagehot's aim was, in effect, to take the processes of living out of the realm of conjecture and treat them with certitude. His *Physics and Politics* (1872) was a pioneer effort to find science in experience. Bagehot's unusual eye for connecting links—Sir Robert Peel and Lord Byron both at Harrow at the same time, for example—made his writing interesting without impugning the value of his judgments. Woodrow Wilson (*q.v.*) admired him without qualification, and sought to attain his directness and variety. William Irvine, *Walter Bagehot* (1939); Norman St. John-Stevas, *Walter Bagehot* (1959).

**Bakke Case** (1978), a Supreme Court decision which offered hope to conservatives fearing the effects of "affirmative action" (*q.v.*) and seeking ways to maintain standards of competence in social and civic affairs. The *New York Times* held as did Liberal extremists that the United States owed "reparations" (*q.v.*) to blacks for the time they had been enslaved, and that the way to pay them was through "affirmative action" (*q.v.*), in education making way for them in graduate schools even when their grades were lower than non-black candidates. That a less competent class of professionals might be released to treat sick people for example appeared, evidently, a small price to pay for the earlier years of limited opportunity. The Bakke decision, finding in favor of a white applicant to medical school who had been passed over in favor of apparently less competent blacks, seemed to many conservatives a step in the right direction; it chagrined many liberals. T. Eastland and W.J. Bennett, *Counting by Race* (1980), J. C. Livingston, *Fair Game?...Affirmative Action* (1930).

**"Banana Republics,"** see United Fruit Company

**Banfield, Edward C.** (1916- ), an urban government specialist who examined a number of city conditions offering recommendations or publishing analyses. *The Moral Basis of a Backward Society* (1958) concerned itself with Italy, but developed several of his premises, such as the difference between an upper and lower class; the one working in anticipation of a future, the other present-minded. *Political Influence* (1961) and (with James Q. Wilson) *City Politics* (1963), among other books, continued his investigations. However, his great coup was *The Unheavenly City: The Nature and Future of Our Urban Crisis* (1970), which stirred up a storm and established him as a leading conservative in his field. He had, to be sure, done work under the auspices of the American Enterprise Institute (*q.v.*). The reasons for his approach seemed to be many. Banfield recognized that an urban crisis existed which required more than money for control. His documented and scholarly techniques did not project a foreseeable future, and did little to enhance the image of the urban underclass. He observed that "poverty" was a function of statistical methods, and that "redistributed income" would not eliminate it. "Social guilt" did not necessarily inspire improvement, he observed, and was no justification for anti-social behavior. Not all the unemployed wanted to work. Schooling was not the same as education (*q.v.*). It might be necessary to abridge freedoms to control crime (*q.v.*). The use of contraceptives and the withholding of children from delinquent parents could help lift the quality of life of the lower classes. Most infuriating to liberals was Banfield's chapter on "Rioting Mainly for Fun and Profit." Despite the use of certain statistics in his work, Banfield emphasized that his examinations did not disparage blacks as such, but concerned the urban underclass in general. He made many suggestions to overcome the urban crisis, but concluded that they would probably not be followed.

**Banking**, a long-standing political concern in America. In the early 19th century the Second Bank of the United States became a major political issue for its alleged control of credit, which the Jacksonians (*q.v.*) claimed was anti-democratic. President Jackson's removal of government deposits from "Nicholas Biddle's Bank" began its ruin; the action was hailed by partisans who little noticed that Jackson then deposited the funds with bankers favorable to the Administration. Private bankers in post-Civil War decades varied from the cruel and oppressive skinflints lurid in Populist lore to shrewd but kindly David-Harum types exemplifying humanity in monetary dealings. Nevertheless banks expanded, as typified by the financial dealings of J. P. Morgan and other monopolies (*qq.v.*). Many were powerful enough to be able to begin or end panics by ordering credit and money manipulations, as in the Panic of 1907, induced by the fall of the Knickerbocker Bank in New York. This, and the Pujo Committee hearings of 1912 (see Filler, DASC), resulted in the creation of the Federal Reserve System, intended to support valid banks squeezed for credit and otherwise to control the money supply. The Fed's inadequacy for emergencies was revealed in 1929, when its too-easy credit policies contributed to the stock market crash and set off a decade-long depression. By the end of World War II, banking was becoming highly internationalized, and even politicalized. The International Monetary Fund was set up (1945) to help stabilize the postwar situation and aid "developing" nations to secure their economic bases. Many immature and dictatorial governments were given loans not granted to more responsible governments. These countries amassed enormous debts which in many cases could not be repaid in the foreseeable future. The euphemism (*q.v.*) of "rescheduling" debts was devised. Some of these countries threatened to turn to America's and the West's foes for aid. Since many of them were professedly "Marxist," it was not clear how long they could be kept tolerant of their capitalist creditors, or whether it was worthwhile attempting to keep them to their commitments. Some conservatives were tempted to steer loose of the less-promising nations. Others feared a collapse of the entire international "system" of banking if debtor nations were called to account. G. C. Fischer, *The American Banking Structure* (1968); R. C. H. Catterall, *The Second Bank of the United States* (1902); H. G. Grubel, *The International Monetary System* (1969); Martin Mayer, *The Bankers* (1974).

**Banned Books** (1955), by Anne Lyon Haight, second edition, a valuable overview of censorship (*q.v.*) of books: "some 330 of them from 850 B.C. to the present, from Homer to Hemingway." It noted largely sexual and religious works which were driven from circulation, and in its description of circumstances emphasized prudishness and intolerance which many liberals often identified with conservatives. The sweeping intolerance of many leftists was less emphasized. Note was taken of 1926 Soviet instructions to libraries to bar religious writings, but not of that government's wholesale interdict of social and political works from at home and abroad. Mentioned was the Soviet ban (1929) of Conan Doyle's *Adventures of Sherlock Holmes*, this because of Doyle's interest in the occult and spiritualism. Nazi censorship practices were carefully detailed.

**Barlow, Joel** (1754-1812), an early example of a transitional (*q.v.*) figure in American political outlook. As associated with the "Connecticut Wits," a varied group of talents notable in various fields other than the verse which brought them together, he extolled the American destiny and was a conservative. In France as a businessman at the time of the French Revolution, he was caught up in its raptures and hopes, and turned radical. His *Advice to the Privileged Orders in the Several States of Europe, Resulting from the Necessity and Propriety of a General Revolution in the Principle of Government* (1792, 1795) was a total repudiation of his past. He later became a friend of Thomas Jefferson and James Madison (*qq.v.*), the latter making him ambassador to France in 1811. See J. Woodress, *A Yankee's Odyssey* (1958).

**Bastiat, Frédéric** (1801-1850), French Free Trader (*q.v.*) and foe of extended government power. He chose as foes the socialists of his time who sought to expand government privileges to the poor through designated government bureaucracy (*q.v.*): his views anticipated those used later by American critics of the New Deal (*q.v.*) and its successors. See Bastiat's *Harmonies of Political Economy* (1860 translation), and George C. Roche III (*q.v.*), *Frederic Bastiat: A Man Alone* (1971).

**Bauer, P. T.**, see *Equality, the Third World and Economic Delusion*

**Bay of Pigs**, see CIA

**Beard, Charles A.**, see *Progressive Historians, The*

**Beaumarchais, Pierre A. C. De**, see French Revolution

**Behavioral Persuasion in Politics, The** (1963), by H. Eulau, an example of the effort to apply behavioral principles in the area of social decisions. Eulau believed that Thoreau's political principles were "wrong" and impractical in actual life, and employed the basic concept of with the intention of revealing the inner meaning of group and class operations in politics. Although the book claimed to "invite inquiry," it seemed to many to direct the student into particular lines of thinking and action, first by loosening his or her loyalties by giving unnatural "roles" to play, suggesting the interchangeability of all roles, and then by emphasizing new roles in terms of social approval and results. To many, such behavioral "persuasion" had its intrinsic defects, lacking insight (as in Thoreau) in the real dynamics of the "role" played, and in the results obtained from social rewards. Thus in theory the prosperity of the middle classes (*q.v.*) in the 1950s should have produced a happy, docile generation, as predicted by Clark Kerr, Chancellor of the Berkeley Campus, University of California. Instead, the 1960s saw large-scale student protests which all but destroyed the liberal arts on many campuses. Social rewards, it seemed, could produce unpredictable behavior.

**Behaviorism**, an evident product of post-World War I disillusionment (*q.v.*), the unseemly death rate contrasting tragically with the earlier optimism of the Progressive (*q.v.*) era and suggesting the expendable nature of humanity. J. B. Watson of the University of Chicago, experimenting with animal behavior, concluded that it could be controlled by administrations of pleasure and pain, as could human behavior: a modern and dehumanized version of Jeremy Bentham's philosophy (see Rationalism). His *Behaviorism* (1925) fitted too with the Twenties' fear of robots assuming human characteristics. It was significant that Watson largely abandoned science to enter into advertising (*q.v.*). His natural successor was B. F. Skinner of Harvard University, whose recipe for rational living was the fullest degree of behavioral modification possible. His reductive principles anticipated rigorous formulas for modifying individual behavior to comport with that of the masses. For such work, Skinner received kudos and honorary degrees. His *Walden Two* (1948) is a disturbing novel about a behavioral "utopia" (*q.v.*) which has little relationship to the utopia of Henry David Thoreau. Skinner's *Beyond Freedom and Dignity* (1971) was respectfully received.

**"Behemoth University,"** see Education

**Bell, Daniel**, see Radical; Kristol, Irving

**Bellamy, Edward** (1850-1898), see Filler, DASC, famed author of *Looking Backward* and its subsequent *Equality* (*q.v.*). Many conservatives maintained that they fed the illusions of liberalism, though being religiously intended. The crux of the matter was whether all cooperative efforts of any kind were anathema to a determined conservatism. Bellamy in many ways was a precursor of the New Deal as it was originally conceived. See Arthur E. Morgan, *Edward Bellamy* (1944).

**Belloc, Hilaire** (1870-1953), British novelist, versifier, historian, controversialist. He was mainly directed in his thought and actions by a constant and unswerving Roman Catholicism. His tireless writing, traveling, and intervention in public issues produced a body of work which, whatever its uses subsequently, established the Catholic point of view in the English literature of his time. Allied with G. K. Chesterton (*q.v.*), he attacked both the capitalist and socialist viewpoints. He served as a Liberal Member of Parliament (1906-1910)—leaving the field in a cloud of scorn for parliamentary democracy—and wrote fiction, essays, histories, and biographies almost too numerous to mention. He attacked "Protestant" history, but his own view of history, though vivid and entertaining, was not taken seriously beyond its time. Belloc was at his best as an essayist, ironicist, and poet. Especially enjoyable are his *Bad Child's Book of Beasts* (1896) and his various collections of essays on anything, everything, and, as he entitled it, nothing "and kindred subjects." His *The Path to Rome* (1902) involved travel as well as affirmation. *The Servile State* (1912) contributed to an anti-state philosophy. *The Jews* (1922) embarrassed many of his friends but his *Essays of a Catholic Layman in England* (1933) redeemed his reputation. ·Robert Speaight, *The Life of Hilaire Belloc* (1957).

**Benét, Stephen Vincent** (1898-1943), American author with a strong love of country and the goal of reconciling its parts and unfolding its essential greatness. The son of a military man, with Northern and Southern ancestors, he studied at Yale and the Sorbonne; but while many of his contemporaries made the rounds of Paris Bohemia, he visited the Forty-second Street Library in New York in furtherance of his poem *John Brown's Body* (1928). The work was a landmark in Twenties (*q.v.*) literature, though resisted by many academics and experimentalists. It was all but unique in its particular grasp of American cultural continuity. As the Poetry Society of America had furthered Edwin Markham's career so the *Saturday Review of Literature* and related publications served Benét through the Depression (*q.v.*). His strong vein was fantasy, which complemented the realism and poetic insight of *John Brown's Body,* and which included *The Devil and Daniel Webster*, a classic story subsequently made into a film and even an opera. Benét's major project was a large, panoramic vision of America, of which only a section, *Western Star* (1943), was left at his death. It included his "invocation," like the one in *John Brown's Body* among the best of its kind in American literature. Fragments of his work were still to be collected for an adequate portrait of a great aspiration and achievement. Q. A. Fenton, *Stephen Vincent Benét* (1958), ed., *Selected Works* (1942) and *Selected Letters* (1960).

**Berger, Raoul** (1901-1985), maverick law authority. He followed a career in music by becoming a Doctor of Jurisprudence and a professor of law at Harvard University. Berger proceeded to issue works which, in their close reading of law, raised questions respecting the functioning of the Supreme Court (*q.v.*) in the modern period. In *Congress v. The Supreme Court* (1969), he studied "judicial review." His other works include *Impeachment: The Constitutional Problems* (1973) and *Executive Privilege: A Constitutional Myth* (1974). Berger's *Government by Judiciary* (1977) came close to what many conservatives were maintaining, and his study of the Supreme Court's treatment of *Death Penalties* (1982) further questioned the court's constitutional readings. Although his findings did not always comport with a conservative consensus, his tenacious concern for constitutionality won him many conservative advisers.

**Bergh, Henry** (1823-1888), conservative reformer of the post-Civil War era, who made his cause the humane treatment of animals; see Filler, DASC. This was especially needed because of the rise of the city, which was hard on such animals as horses that were more adapted to rural conditions. In 1866 he led the movement which created the American Society for the Prevention of Cruelty to Animals, and he himself became a picturesque figure in his high hat and tails stopping draymen and forcing law cases to prevent the brutal whipping and abuse of horses on the cobbled streets. Bergh was subject to ridicule, but also to appreciation and respect. City circumstances by 1875 also called into action the Society for the Prevention of Cruelty to Children. Z. Steele, *Angel in Top Hat* (1942).

**Berkeley, George** (1685-1753), British theologian and logician who, utilizing the instruments of scholasticism (*q.v.*), undertook to refute materialist conceptions inherent in Deism (*q.v.*) and the explorations of Descartes. His *Theory of Vision* (1709), *Treatise Concerning the Principles of Human Knowledge* (1710), and, most popular, *Three Dialogues between Hylas and Philonous* (1713) undertook to prove that all knowledge originated in the mind and was given by God (*q.v.*): matter had no existence outside the mind. Berkeley's lucid prose was impressive to believers, a challenge to such skeptics as David Hume (*q.v.*). Bishop

Berkeley's long and effective career included plans for a college in Bermuda for the training of Anglican clergymen in the New World.

**Berlin Wall**, see Escapees

**Berns, Walter F.** (1919- ), seminal conservative scholar in the law. His *Freedom, Virtue, and the First Amendment* (1957) was an indictment of the liberal interpretation of freedom as having the effect of sanctioning depravity. The Court's function was to discern virtue in freedom of expression and contrast virtue with its opposite. Berns also wrote *For Capital Punishment: Crime and the Morality of the Death Penalty* (1979). Following academic service, he was a resident fellow at the American Enterprise Institute (*q.v.*) in Washington, where he also offered courses at Georgetown University.

**"Better Red Than Dead,"** see Nuclear War

**Bible, The**, unarguably the most important influence on Western civilization, to many believers in the Judaeo-Christian tradition the inspired word of God. Its accounts and personalities so involve human experiences and analogies as to be a force in most Western aims and enterprises, in the mortal struggles of the West and in its processes of contact with other areas of the world. The Bible also provides historical perspective, in that the conditions under which it was given to mankind obviously differ from those of later times. Thus the Bible requires interpretation in terms of facts and metaphors to be persuasive among varied peoples. Standard in English has been the King James Version of the Bible (1611). The sacredness of the text of both Old and New Testaments, with some exception, has been common to both Protestants and Catholics. The Old Testament is central to the Jewish faith. The Bible seen as literature, with the extraordinary lilt and vibrancy of numerous, famous passages in the King James version, has moved and impressed even unbelievers. For believers, the Bible is a basic element in their faith. Fundamentalists (*q.v.*) believe it is the literal word of God. Modern social unrest as it has affected many churches and sects also affected attitudes toward the Bible. One key point of contention was the subordinate role assigned women in church services and responsibilities, with controversy attention centered on the Bible itself as embodying male domination. Although Peter Simple (*q.v.*) had long had his "far out" clergyman suggesting that it was time He retired in favor of a younger man, such attitudes had seemed in the area of satire, rather than program. The multiplication of women in churches and synagogues as pastors, rabbis, vestrypersons and others preceded the National Council of Churches organizing a committee to withdraw male-biased passages from their lectionaries (compendiums of scripture selections that direct affiliated congregations through the church year). Two years after, in 1983, the committee unveiled the result of its work, which they were determined would begin a new era in church programs. *An Inclusive Language Lectionary* directed congregations to substitute "sovereign" for "Lord," "monarch" for "king," "sisters and brothers" or "friends" for "brethren." Other changes substituted "Father and Mother" for "Father," "Human One" or "Child" for "Son," and otherwise evaded what one of the committee saw as a book "all wrapped up in men." Since the Bible was understood by numerous religious persons to be the word of God, it appeared that the National Council of Churches had the choice of rejecting it or acceding to its language. Reaction to many of its alterations in traditional translations has so far been mixed.

**Bierce, Ambrose** (1842-1913?), journalist and author of classic tales of the Civil War (*q.v.*), in which he served, including *Tales of Soldiers and Civilians*. As a columnist he was caustic and cynical. He is known to conservatives for his scorn and hatred of socialism. His lack of a positive view of life, however, undermined his use to any social tendency. *The Devil's Dictionary* (1911) contains many items relevant to the liberal-conservative debate, such as: "Conservative: A statesman who is enamored of existing evils, as distinguished from the Liberal, who wishes to replace them with others," and "Radicalism: the conservatism of tomorrow injected into the affairs of today." Most touching was his definition of *Mugwump*, the name given, notably in 1884, to Republicans who could not in good conscience accept their party candidate, James G. Blaine, who was tainted with corruption: "In politics one afflicted with self-respect and addicted to the vice of independence. A term of contempt."

**Big Business**, often identified with conservatism, as more concerned for profit than the public weal, and as identical with free enterprise (*q.v.*). It was identified with the Robber Barons (*q.v.*) of post-Civil War industry. New conservatives found a moral component in Big Business, as in works by Ayn Rand and George Gilder (*qq.v.*). Interestingly, Lenin (*q.v.*) had predicted that he and his party would overthrow capitalist regimes with means provided by the capitalists. His own crucial 1907 meeting in London, which gave him control of the Bolshevik faction, was made possible by money provided by Joseph Fels, of Fels-Naphtha soap. See also Commercialism. Richard D. Steade, *Business and Society in Transition* (1975); Bert F. Hoselitz and Wilber E. Moore, eds., *Industrialization and Society* (1963).

**Big Government**, a *bête noire* of conservatism, which held that government should do as little and be as small as possible, in keeping with the national needs of the people, who should otherwise care for themselves and associate with such groups as they fancied. This goal, once the frank ideal of conservative ideologues as late as the Grover Cleveland (*q.v.*) administration, became increasingly hard to contain, as "private" business and cities became formidable, requiring controls if the well-being of citizens was to be preserved. Liberals of the Progressive era saw government as an honest broker between interests, large or small. Left-wing liberals in time came to argue that government had actually become an adjunct of big industry; see for example J. Weinstein, *The Corporate Ideal in the Liberal State* (1968). The patent growth of Big Labor, however, and its influence in Welfare State (*q.v.*) policies, gave conservatives reason to turn the argument around, and to demand a modification of government in the interests of greater individual and corporate freedom.

**Big Labor**, see Unions; Immigration; Majority

**Bill of Rights** to the Constitution (*q.v.*), subject to conflicting interpretations by conservatives and liberals. Thus many liberals see the First Amendment as providing a "wall of separation" between religion and the state which is absolute. Many conservatives say that the Government has traditionally encouraged the practice of religion and should continue to do so, despite such Supreme Court rulings as that in *Engel v. Vitale* (1962). On the other hand, many conservatives regard the right to bear arms as absolute. Many liberals say that this right has been traditionally subject to abridgement and should be abridged even more. The First Amendment was invoked by persons called before the House Un-American Activities Committee who often refused to testify on alleged Communist affiliations. When this was struck down by Supreme Court decision, witnesses at committee hearings and in court proceedings invoked the Fifth Amendment ban against "self-incrimination" in their refusals to testify. It was evident that the language of the Bill of Rights was subject to changing interpretations of "rights," and also to particular uses seen in them. Thus, the "Gag Rule" (see Adams, John Quincy) was sustained by legislators who saw its peculiar necessity to the health of the Union. The Tenth Amendment (*q.v.*), giving to the states and citizens all rights not specifically alloted to the government, opened wide vistas for states-rights partisans, but was less effective than many of them hoped.

**"Biopsychology,"** see Weyl, Nathaniel

**Birth Control**, see Abortion

**Bitch-Goddess Success, The** (1968), a compilation of views taking off from the famous phrase by William James, including such conservatives as de Tocqueville, Washington Allston, and Maxwell Perkins, and such liberals as Walt Whitman, John F. Kennedy, and George F. Kennan, among others. It provided evidence that success was not a partisan goal, but an American concern. Curiously, all depreciated success, and several claimed not to need it. Yet all knew it affected their lives, and were inspired to bitter or defensive statements. De Tocqueville saw that it drained Americans of contentment. The architect Louis H. Sullivan, deprived of usefulness, warned of dreadful costs. See, however, Franklin, Benjamin, for evidence of less negative qualities. Edwin P. Whipple, *Success, and Its Conditions* (1871) still makes profitable reading.

**"Black Anger,"** see Violence

**Black Market**, see Wage and Price Controls

**Blacks**, originally a term invidiously employed by racists (*q.v.*) who saw no reason to distinguish between various elements in the numerous and distinctive Negro communities. The notorious evasion employed by white individuals in the South who wished to pretend courtesy without giving it was to pronounce the word Negro as "Nigra." Negroes concerned for intra-race civility for many years often preferred the phrase "Colored ladies and gentlemen"; their major organization for many years used "National Association for the Advancement of Colored People," shortened to NAACP. As the civil rights drive of the 1960s developed, young Negroes, often dark skinned, insisted on being called blacks, and were critical of older members of the Negro community who were unused to the designation (A. Meier and E. Rudwick, *CORE* [1973]). It became one of the insignia of the on-going and continuing drive for Negro civil rights, and as such was accepted by conservatives as well as others. City and state elections brought forth black candidates of varied power and credentials, many favoring the concerns of their black constituents just as, they held, Irish and Italian and other groups did. The Jimmy Carter (*q.v.*) Administration saw blacks addressed nationally, and receiving, not "token" offices, but national and even international responsibilities. The Reagan (*q.v.*) Administration sought to broaden the concept of minority representation by appealing to Hispanic (*q.v.*) and other groups. Although black communities had had an irregular voting record, such 1980s figures as Jesse Jackson of Chicago labored to make of them a voting bloc. This contributed to the election of a black, Harold Washington, as mayor of that city. Jackson's spontaneous slogan of "We Want It All," apparently aiming at the Presidency, struck concerns among conservative politicians who feared that a black bloc added to a female-activist bloc, plus others, might undermine Republican advances in the polls. Though many of the most stable elements of black communities were socially conservative, they and other blacks voted in overwhelming numbers for Democratic and liberal candidates in most elections. Such politically conservative blacks as Walter Williams and Thomas Sowell (*qq.v.*) knew themselves to be minority voices among blacks as a whole. See also Negroes.

**Bloc Voting**, see Voting Rights Act (1965)

**"Block Busting,"** see "White Flight"

**Bohemian Life**, mainly a product of nineteenth century social and industrial developments. They created the bourgeois society closely examined by Émile Zola, and also its opposite, the youth (*q.v.*) who scorned conformity, practiced art and the art of living, and were democratic in their associations, particularly sexual. Henri Murger's *Scenes from Bohemian Life* (1845-1849) told their story, from the ateliers to respectability, in Paris, which became the model for bohemian life in other cities. William Makepeace Thackeray wistfully recalled "the brave days [in Paris] when I was twenty-one." Many bohemians mixed conventional life with the exotic—as with Paul Gaugin, who moved from business to a painter's life in the South Seas, and Arthur Rimbaud, whose brief career as an experimental poet was followed by years of business and intrigue. Most bohemians had little to show for their lives. G. K. Chesterton (*q.v.*), thinking of his London, saw bohemians as a tribe of persons who lived the life they could not write. He himself, writing and moving freely about, scribbling articles on street corners and exulting in beer and fantasies, was the model of a conservative who saw himself as free within Christian tenets. Many found conservatism an emancipation from mere liberal routine; see for example Russell Kirk (*q.v.*), *Confessions of a Bohemian Tory* (1963). A. J. Nock (*q.v.*), in his love of Rabelais, reflected aspects of conservative emancipation, though without regard for Rabelais's earthy aspects. Classic bohemianism mixed with wealth and patronage to produce an elitism (*q.v.*) which was typified by James Joyce and Pablo Picasso. The conservative T. S.

Eliot (*q.v.*), however, whose work indirectly indicted much of what they stood for, ranked with them as a modern innovator. Bohemians who fell into a rut in and out of the Soviet Union were the theme of Max Eastman's (*q.v.*) *Artists in Uniform* (1934). The youth (*q.v.*) rebellion of the Beats of the 1950s gave way to a youth offensive against civilization which was almost devoid of art, and scarcely rated the name of "bohemian." Louis Filler, *Vanguard & Followers* (1978).

**Bolingbroke, Viscount**, see Idea of a Patriot King

**Bonus Marchers**, see Thirties

**Bookmailer, The**, predecessor to the Conservative Book Club (*q.v.*), begun in 1952 as a combination book service and outlet for conservative publications and views. Its president, Lyle Munson, a former worker for the Office of Strategic Services (OSS), was concerned that Communism was advancing around the world and that its goals were being furthered by Americans in government employment. Along with his regular services, therefore, he undertook to supply readers with books which were "right wing" in purpose—he protested that there was free talk of "right-wing conspiracy," (*q.v.*) but not of "left-wing conspiracy"—and himself published numerous books by conservative authors, including the *National Review Reader* (*q.v.*). He himself edited *For the Skeptic*, 188 pages of testimony from official hearings, and *Who Will Volunteer*, as well as works about Communist conspiracies and UN (*q.v.*) operations.

**Boorstin, Daniel J.** (1914- ), early transitional (*q.v.*) figure from radicalism (*q.v.*) to conservatism. He was an outstanding student at Harvard and Oxford, where he was taken into private political avant-garde circles. During the conservative 1950s, he became a notable public witness against his past associates. His *The Lost World of Thomas Jefferson* (*q.v.*) (1948) indirectly reflected his varied experiences. Freed of Marxism, Boorstin sought and found a new direction in *The Genius of American Politics* (1953), that "genius" being non-philosophy and consensus (*q.v.*). Americans had been "given" a vast empire which needed no romantic illusions for compensation, as in constricted Europe. No fundamental theoretic differences separated American political parties. Our national well-being reduced the impulse toward bitter feuds. Boorstin went on to survey "The National Experience" in volumes marked by novel expressions for popular concepts. He appears to have first thought of the Founding Fathers (*q.v.*) as having "invented America," a phrase picked up by Garry Wills (*q.v.*). Boorstin saw Western ranchers as "go-getters," and the emphases on localities and localisms as uniquely American. The aim was to indicate American affluence and indigenous qualities. Many of his concepts were debatable, such as his views that Charles A. Lindbergh (*q.v.*) was turned from a hero (*q.v.*) into a "celebrity" and that America was a "disproving" ground for utopias (*q.v.*). Boorstin warned readers of the dangers of illusions in advertising (*q.v.*) slogans, decried the "pseudo-events" of journalism, and turned on a later brand of radicals as "barbarians." Overall, however, he found a sum of positive achievement in American records. Identified as a conservative, he distinguished "discoverers" (Christopher Columbus) from "explorers" like the Pilgrims, who could explore as a community, or who could, like the great inventors, make great "leaps" across the "dark continents of technology." All such presentations were calculated to redound to the good repute of capitalism; see *The Exploring Spirit* (1976) and his lengthy survey of impulses and principles in *The Discoverers* (1983). His textbook for eleventh-grade readers (1981) continued his long habit of finding curious details—clipper ships were so called because in their swift course they "clipped" time in transit. Nevertheless his account of America's rise was strikingly traditional, with clash and jeopardy dampened to inconsequence. His American Revolution (*q.v.*) was not a revolution, but a struggle for independence. His Civil War was no war at all, but a sectional struggle. Radicals were troubled enclaves of workers, rather than challengers and antagonists, and provided no dynamics for change or growth, or decline. Much of Boorstin's placid view of America seemed inappropriate to many involved in the contentious and divisive political struggles of the 1980s.

**Boredom**, an endemic feature of modern life, often associated with increased prosperity and the inability to find satisfaction in one's work or leisure. Earlier generations of laborers, in their search for bread and comfort, had no opportunity for ordinary boredom. Eric Hoffer (*q.v.*) believed that boredom was a major cause for revolution. It is likely that the ceaseless round of sniping and atrocities in Northern Ireland (*q.v.*) has much of its source in the traditionally drab life existing in the Six Counties. "Boredom" on the job, complained of by workers in the 1970s and the topic of numerous sociologists, clearly diminished in the 1980s when jobs were less plentiful. Russell Kirk (*q.v.*), "The Architecture of Servitude and Boredom," *Modern Age*, Spring, v. 26, 114 ff. See also his "The Problem of Social Boredom," in *A Program for Conservatives* (1954).

**"Boring from Within,"** a notorious tactic of Communists who professed democratic principles in order to gain entry into unions (*q.v.*) and other organizations, where they went on in concert to subvert susceptible elements to their point of view. Their aim was to gain a working effectiveness and dominate policy. Conservatives labored to expose this strategy before others, and cited it as evidence that Communism was not a legitimate viewpoint in society but a conspiracy (*q.v.*) against it. However, it usually took a variety of factors to undermine Communists; when they revealed themselves, such a tactic as "boring from within" could then be seized upon by former sympathizers as an occasion for deserting the cause.

**Bosses**, originally identified with "boss rule" in cities of the post-Civil War era, where the needs of impecunious minority groups were cared for to a degree by ward and city politicians. The bosses became a special target of Progressive (*q.v.*) reformers such as Lincoln Steffens and also Joseph Folk of St. Louis, who took on bribers and other corrupt officials; see Filler, *The Muckrakers*. The key fact was that the rapid growth of cities, housing unprecedented numbers of new citizens from abroad, made it impossible for "bosses" to dominate their city-demesnes with any degree of efficiency (*q.v.*). New bosses who suceeded the disgraced and deposed bosses abjured old-fashioned truculence and blatant corruption. The new rulers worked more carefully with educated officials and union and industrial leaders. Although corruption (*q.v.*) was far from obliterated, the new city and special interest leaders were able to deliver more tolerable services. Chicago (*q.v.*) became noted among its apologists as "the city that works," that is, which better ministered to the wants of its different ethnic (*q.v.*) and other elements. Conservatives found the formula less satisfying than did liberals who saw corruption as an informal means for "the people" to express their wants and preferences; see for example J. G. Sproat, "*The Best Men*" (1965), a scornful examination of the work of reformers. From that perspective, the bosses were the best men.

**Bowery**, a street in New York, symbolic of Skid Row degradation in American cities. Welfare state (*q.v.*) policies, plus employment opportunities during World War II and affluent years afterward, reduced its prevalence somewhat though alcoholism and unemployment (*qq.v.*) kept the population of Skid Rows constant. In Communist propaganda the Bowery was seen as a byproduct of capitalist heartlessness and greedy economics.

**Bozell, L. Brent** (1926- ), a founder of and contributor to the *National Review*, (*q.v.*). With his brother-in-law William F. Buckley, Jr. (*q.v.*), he wrote *McCarthy* (*q.v.*) *and His Enemies* (1954). Bozell's *The Warren* (*q.v.*) *Revolution* (1966) expressed conservative antipathy to its liberal direction. He edited the Catholic *Future*, and then *Triumph* (1966-1975). Later interests included Catholics United for the Faith. In 1986, Bozell published a collection of his essays under the title of *Mustard Seeds*.

**Brace, Charles Loring** (1826-1890), pioneer in rehabilitation work among the poor, especially poor children. He made studies abroad of prisons and institutions, and undertook missionary work in New York City. He helped found the Children's Aid Society, established a newspaperboys' lodging house, and industrial schools for Germans and Italians. His works included *The Dangerous Classes of New York* (1872). Loring was among those stigmatized by subsequent reformers as meliorative, rather than "basic," in his approach to society's ills. He was also forgotten by conservatives who were too involved in controversy to find time for education in their own traditions.

**Bradbury, Ray** (1920- ), writer of science fiction and fantasy (*qq.v.*) both of which contributed to conservative psychic expression. Bradbury was less conservative than, for example, C. S. Lewis (*q.v.*), being closer to popular impulses, some of which were of liberal derivation. His recollections of youth, as expressed in *Dandelion Wine* (1957), gave him some doubts respecting the values of technology, but did not make him as skeptical of technology as it did many conservatives. In one tale, Bradbury had Jesus taking a rocket ship into space, where, "since Darwin," life had deteriorated. Bradbury's greatest success was *The Illustrated Man* (1951), made up of tales of varied quality. "The Other Foot" commented on old oppression of blacks on earth, now succeeded on Mars by black oppression of whites, the moral being that both ought to start over again. "The Veldt" and "Kaleidescope" both saw futuristic technology as having produced evil results. "The Fire Balloons" was reminiscent of Gerald Heard's (*q.v.*) fantasies. In this instance priests came to Mars to build a church, and discovered they were not needed: "The way I see it there's a Truth on every planet. All parts of the Big Truth." Some tales, like "The Long Run," placed on Venus, offered no evident moral or lesson, but captured attention by sheer imaginativeness.

**Brain Trust**, identified with the New Deal (*q.v.*); conservatives had no equivalent for it for themselves, possibly because of their proliferation of theoreticians and institutes. The term was coined as "brains trust" by Dr. James M. Kieran, then president of Hunter College, and included academic and other professionals, some of whom later disassociated themselves from the New Deal. See also Kitchen Cabinet.

**Brainard, Maurice W.**, see Socialism

**Brandeis, Louis Dembitz** (1856-1941), won fame in the 1900s as the "people's attorney," and in 1916 elicited anti-semitic prejudice from former President William Howard Taft (*q.v.*) as he attempted to prevent Woodrow Wilson's appointment of Brandeis to the United States Supreme Court. Brandeis's greatest liberal achievement was the development of the "Brandeis Brief," supporting a law by cumulative data more than by precedence. His connection with Justice Holmes (*q.v.*) in drawing up notable legal dissents during a strongly conservative era in law created the famous "Brandeis and Holmes" combination which resulted in memorable phrases relating to civil rights, social philosophy, and other key issues. Evidence recently arose that Brandeis had secretly been in contact with his follower Felix Frankfurter, providing him with funds for influencing political events (B. A. Murphy, *The Brandeis/Frankfurter Connection* [1982]). This raised interesting questions about Brandeis's career. One of Brandeis's early coups had occurred during the "Ballinger Case," involving questions of legitimacy in Alaskan land distribution, in which he had discovered that President Taft had been involved in unpublicized activities in the matter. It is possible that, had the Brandeis-Frankfurter "connection" been known while they were active in public life, they might have been forced into private life over this issue. See A. T. Mason, *Bureaucracy Convicts Itself* (1941).

**Bricker Amendment**, introduced June 15, 1953 by Senator John W. Bricker, Republican Senator from Ohio, in order to give Congress the power to regulate all Executive agreements. This was in response to conservative resentment over the Yalta (*q.v.*) agreement, which they saw as a sell-out to Soviet imperialism and pregnant with future ill for the United States. The Bricker Amendment stipulated that any provisons in conflict with the Constitution were to be null and without effect. Controversial was Section Two of the Amendment, which seemed—Bricker to the contrary—to give the states the ability to ignore Executive treaties when they deemed that necessary. Eisenhower opposed the

Amendment, but such was the restlessness over possible Soviet expansionism that it won formidable endorsements. But Bricker's intransigence over its wording lost him support, and it was defeated February 25, 1954, having failed to win a two-thirds majority vote. Had it passed, even in modified form, it would have called sharp attention to a Congressional role in Executive international negotiations, and perhaps forced more responsible commitments abroad from future Presidents, as during the Vietnam (*qq.v.*) involvement.

**"Brief Me,"** see Propaganda

**British Conservatism**, see *Conservative Tradition, The*

**Brodie, Fawn N.** (1915-1981), American historian. In *No Man Knows My History* (1945) she sought to trace down and interpret the facts of Joseph Smith's life. Though judged to be in error by the Mormon Church, which she had left, her book seemed well-spoken and courageous to readers outside. Brodie's somewhat more impertinent biography of Sir Richard Burton, *The Devil Drives* (1967), was nevertheless stimulating and subject to reasonable checks and qualifications. She then published *Thomas Jefferson* (1974) (*q.v.*), intended to reveal a secret liaison between the statesman and one of his slaves, a Sally Hemings. In fact, there did not seem to be a shred of evidence for this, as was spelled out in Virginius Dabney's *The Jefferson Scandals: Rebuttal* (1981). Yet Brodie's book was a Book of the Month Club selection, and a later novel based on the tale by Barbara Chase-Ribout (1979) a Literary Guild item. To many the episode glaringly illustrated how history as a serious pursuit had fallen. Brodie's posthumous book on Nixon was a publishing success, despite what many saw as questionable methods of scholarship.

**Brook Farm**, see Brownson, Orestes A.; Dana, Charles A.

**Brookings Institution**, see American Enterprise Institute

**Brown vs. Board of Education of Topeka** (1954), landmark decision in the field of education and race relations which wiped out the "separate but equal" doctrine enunciated in *Plessy vs. Ferguson* (1896) and set off a train of decisions affecting every aspect of social life. See Segregation. *Brown* was based on liberal doctrine, but its implementation certainly involved, if not formal conservative opinion, a substantial portion of conservative agreement and assent, persuaded by legal opinion, media presentation, religious teaching, and other forces. "White flight" to the suburbs from inner cities, private school proliferation, and resistance to future busing mandates derived not so much from conservative teachings as from deteriorating conditions in urban schools. By the mid-1980s the future of the *Brown* decision was still indeterminate, in terms of actual practice.

**Brownson, Orestes A.** (1803-1876), a religious and social seeker, an early transitional (*q.v.*) figure who rose in public estimation in the yeasty atmosphere of Transcendentalism, and whose general influence declined following his entrance into the Catholic Church. Because of his high cerebrations about the nature of democracy (*q.v.*) and the urgency of religious premises, and his experience with the nature of communism, he has fascinated some current conservatives as one who foresaw many modern conditions. As a clergyman, he entered into many sects, savoring them and leaving them: Congregational, Methodist, Presbyterian, Unitarian, and Universal. He created his own Society for Christian Union and Progress. Entering into the processes of society as manifesting God's will, he helped found Brook Farm and joined the Democratic Party. As editor of the *Reformer*, and then of the Boston *Quarterly Review* (1838-1842) and the *Democratic Review* (1842-1844), he promoted a spiritual purpose behind mundane matters, but was himself disillusioned with politics by the Democratic defeat in 1840. His essays on "The Laboring Classes" in the *Quarterly Review* of 1840 interested later "radicals" for their insight into American conditions. His turn to Catholicism (*q.v.*) in 1844 created a sensation, but because of the Church's separation from the mainstream of American religion and tradition of the time, it disengaged Brownson from his earlier career. His *The American Republic* (1865) provides a type of synthesis for those interested in continuity. L. Roemer, *Brownson on Democracy and the Trend toward Socialism* (1953).

**Bryant, Anita**, beauty queen, singer, television personality. She became a commercial spokesman for Florida citrus products. Upset by the effort of homosexuals (*q.v.*) in Dade County to advocate laws curbing prejudice against them, she undertook what she called a Save the Children crusade and became nationally known for her anti-homosexual advocacy. Although Bryant won her particular campaign, despite television humorists and commentators, Dade County homosexuals claimed that it advanced their cause substantially. Bryant's involvement in such controversy eventually cost her her role as a commercial spokesman. She later underwent a conversion to "born-again" Christianity and repudiated some of her previous anti-homosexual statements.

**Bryant, William Cullen** (1794-1878), the first American poet to be acclaimed on both sides of the Atlantic, and a transitional (*q.v.*) figure from Federalism to the Democratic Party (*qq.v.*). Raised in an intensely anti-Jefferson (*q.v.*) household, at the age of fourteen he published a bitter satire, *The Embargo* (1808), of which he was later ashamed. At the same early age he was pondering nature and death, writing in 1811 his first draft of "Thanatopsis." When it was published in 1817 it made his reputation. *Poems* (1821) contained several other of his most famous verses. Unable to make a living as a poet, he turned to journalism (*q.v.*) and, as editor of the New York *Evening Post*, became famous. He was considered by many to be New York's (*q.v.*) leading citizen. His later sympathy toward labor's aspirations, religious tolerance, and other liberal concerns was mixed with a conservative reluctance to press the slavery (*q.v.*) issue until war became a fact. He consistently advocated manners and refinement in social affairs. Bryant raised standards in journalism with his insistence on well-written and accurate prose. See H. H. Peckham, *Gotham Yankee* (1950), and Allan Nevins, *The Evening Post* (1922).

**Bryce, Viscount James** (1838-1922), British historian and social analyst and, like de Tocqueville (*q.v.*), author of a classic study of American democratic behavior. Although Bryce was a liberal in the European sense, his call for social order and responsibility in *The American Commonwealth* (1888) can be seen as conservative. He did not rationalize the systems of corruption which he found dominating municipal administrations, but showed them as inevitable where demagogues and appeals to special interests could dominate. Bryce was Ambassador to the United States during much of the Progressive era (*q.v.*), which was reflected in his *Modern Democracies* (1921).

**Buckley, James L.** (1923- ). He was persuaded by his brother, William F. Buckley, Jr., and the Conservative Party of New York (*qq.v.*) to run for the U.S. Senate against the popular Jacob Javits in 1968, and made an impressive showing. In 1970, he ran again and won. As a Senator he made difficult decisions, one of the most painful being to urge President Nixon to resign because of the shadow cast by Watergate (*q.v.*) revelations. He also resisted Nixon's wage and price controls policy. His consistent conservative policies were spelled out in his *If Men Were Angels* (1975), and included opposition to Federal bureaucracy, judicial activism, and policies which he believed encouraged crime. In his speech at the 1976 National Republican Convention, he held that the sanctity of the American family was at stake in the election. That same year he was defeated for re-election. In 1980 he was named an Undersecretary in the Department of State by President Reagan.

**Buckley, William F.** (1925- ), one of the key conservative figures of his time as editor of the *National Review*, commentator on public events, television personality, essayist, and novelist. Conscious that he was fighting a powerful liberal tradition, Buckley developed a style of argument and wit which won him admirers as well as foes. His *God and Man at Yale* (1951) created a furor with its attack on the power of liberalism in academic humanities, but twenty-five years later it was still being read. His *McCarthy and His Enemies* (1954) dealt with the dangers inherent in communism and in the liberal support of its premises, and gave the benefit of the doubt to the often dubious anti-Communist crusade of Senator McCarthy (*q.v.*). Decisions of the Warren Court (*q.v.*) and later Supreme Court decisions involving busing, abortion, prayer in schools, and defendants' rights in criminal trials increased Buckley's audiences and their receptivity to his arguments. Buckley's mixture of good humor toward persons hostile to his frame of reference with the sharpest criticism of policies he deemed harmful to civilized living created a running controversy reflected in such books as *Up from Liberalism* (1959), *The Jeweler's Eye* (1969), and *A Hymnal* (1978). His penchant for eye-catching phrases was illustrated by the title of his anthology of writings by conservatives, *Did You Ever See A Dream Walking?* In reality the book detailed "American Conservative Thought in the Twentieth Century," as its subtitle indicated, with copious notes and explanations. Buckley awed many with his extensive information on an array of subjects. His grasp of the cultural factor in liberal-conservative controversies was perhaps less sure.

**Bugging**, the use of recording devices secretly installed. Bugging figured prominently in the problems of the Nixon Administration. Many liberals and others conjured up visions of a police state, prepared at any time to use illegal surveillance in offices and private homes. Especially damaging to Nixon were the revelations of the tapes. They weakened and then undermined his Administration, and brought on the Freedom of Information Act (*q.v.*). Later revelations that bugging had been practiced in earlier Administrations by CIA specialists, and that tapes had been regularly employed by preceding Presidents, including Johnson, Kennedy, and even Franklin Roosevelt (*qq.v.*), were downplayed and contributed to a general public skepticism about the operations of Government.

**Bunker Hill**, a key battle of the American Revolution, symbol of the American Revolutionary spirit, and site of a noted monument, near Charleston, Mass. It is close to Breed's Hill, where (June 17, 1775) the battle between Patriot and British forces actually took place.

**Bureaucracy**, a relatively modern topic in America, its importance underscored by an increasing sense of the costs of government and the problem of getting it to respond to public needs. Bureaucracy developed with expanded social services during the Depression and the needs of World War II. After the war Republicans tried to curb federal bureaucracy, but under President Eisenhower (*q.v.*) the Government continued to expand. Lyndon B. Johnson's Great Society programs created a further proliferation of bureaucratic offices and agencies. Richard M. Nixon (*q.v.*) was unable to curb the bureaucratic establishment. Although Ronald Reagan seemed more than willing to reduce the bureaucracy, he also found it difficult. Conservatives continued to give lip-service to the streamlining of government agencies, and especially service agencies, and to denounce liberals for corruption and waste, but little was done during the 1980s. It was uncertain whether automation and computer technology would create more or less bureaucracy. See Robert Ewegen and Byron Johnson, *B.S.: Bureaucratic Syndrome* (1982).

**Bureaucracy** (1944), by Ludwig von Mises (*q.v.*). It was issued the same year as Friedrich Hayek's (*q.v.*) *The Road to Serfdom*, and like it defended the free enterprise system. Mises contrasted it with that evolved from the welfare state or socialism (*qq.v.*). Although he agreed that there was bureaucracy in many free political states, he held bureaucracy to be central to socialism, the bureaucrat having no function but to carry out codes and regulations from the central authority. Under the "market system," the goal of production was to serve the consumer, according to Mises. Under socialism, the goal was to serve the state.

**Burger, Warren**, see Supreme Court

**Burke, Edmund** (1729-1797), British Parliamentarian and early progenitor of modern conservatism. He was born in Dublin of a Protestant father and Catholic mother, which gave him a breadth later reflected in his public actions and addresses. Not a directed student in youth, he enriched his learning with wide reading. Though he disappointed his father, who wanted a finished lawyer, he developed a grasp of legal principles which affected Parliamentary history. His 1756 volumes, *A Vindication of Natural Society* and *A Philosophical Inquiry into...the Sublime and Beautiful*, won attention. He joined a famous circle which included Dr. Johnson (*q.v.*) and Oliver Goldsmith. His thirty-year association with the *Annual Register* gave him a grasp of the world's turnings. As a conservative Whig in Parliament he spoke against the Stamp Act foisted on the American colonies, even though it was legally imposed. He thus underscored one of his major principles, that tradition and fraternity were more important than formal law. And though he was unsympathetic toward the radical John Wilkes, he protested Crown efforts to keep him from his seat in Parliament, voters having the right to prefer whom they would. Burke's *Thoughts on the Causes of the Present Discontents* (1770) pointed again, not to legal majorities, but to the furtive Royal policies which were fomenting governmental disorder. That year began the ascendency of Lord North, which was to conclude with the loss of the American colonies. Burke opposed the hated Tea Tax. His *Speech on Conciliation with the Colonies* (1775) was to become for more than a century a favorite with American schoolteachers. In 1780 Burke opposed his Bristol constituency's desire for the restriction of Irish trade, declaring that a representative was not bound by his constituents' instructions. He subsequently endured stormy political years, which reached a height with his protracted effort to gain the conviction of Warren Hastings, English Nabob of India, on the grounds of extreme corruption and cruel administration. His speeches demanding the impeachment of Hastings represented a high point in conservative principle, in opposition to the greedy and cynical operations of British commerce. Although Hastings won acquittal, Burke's seven-year effort brought Indian reform. However, it was the French Revolution (*q.v.*) which drove a wedge between Burke and many of his associates, who bore with its excesses. Burke's *Reflections on the Revolution in France* (1790) affirmed him as a Tory, and drew from Thomas Paine (*q.v.*), then in England, a full response in the first part of *The Rights of Man*, a work which eventually required Paine to leave England. Burke's *Thoughts on French Affairs* (1791) followed events in France with increasing, and prophetic, horror. Burke's became the major voice opposing the course of revolution in France—as the royal family was beheaded, the march of the tumbrels to the guillotine increased its pace, and the Jacobins enshrined the Goddess of Reason. His opponents made a distinction between the Burke who defended colonial rights and the Burke who cried out that the glory of Europe had departed forever. Others, who appreciated Burke's faith in constitutional principles, had less difficulty in perceiving what held them together. Peter J. Stanlis, ed., *The Relevance of Edmund Burke* (1964); Russell Kirk, *Edmund Burke* (1967); Charles R. Richeson, *Edmund Burke and the American Revolution* (1976).

**Burnham, James** (1905-1987), transition (*q.v.*) figure and anti-Communist analyst. He had an early career as a follower of the anti-Stalin Communist Leon Trotsky (*q.v.*), during which he saw capitalism as without a future and a correct Communist program as a viable alternative. As a professor of philosophy at New York University, along with Sidney Hook (*q.v.*), he held on to his convictions until 1940. When, convinced that Communism in any form was a false road for humanity, he broke with old associations. *The Managerial Revolution* (1941) (*q.v.*), made him famous to a large reading world, impressed with his view of a world run, not by capitalists, but by managers: essentially people able to organize and administer rather than merely having the trappings of power. In his later works, Burnham sought to penetrate into the maze of power politics, especially as controlled by Communists, and to expose them to democratic eyes. A dedicated conservative, he published *The Web of Subversion* (1954), which recognized Communist infiltration in American government agencies with the intent of aiding Communist foreign policy abroad. Burnham's essential point, spelled out in great detail in terms of foreign developments, was that of his former affiliations, seen, however, from an American-interest viewpoint. Communists used their raw power whenever they could, he maintained. Where they could not, they entered "popular fronts," but only to gain status with naive associates or states, in order to take full power. Thereupon democracy was outlawed and dictatorship instituted. This was the message which helped to give weight to his pages in the *National Review* and to inform his *The Struggle for the World* (1947), *The Coming Defeat of Communism* (1950)—which saw "the democratic side" as superior to its foes except for strategic position and political leadership—and *Containment or Liberation?* (1950). Burnham saw a Third World War in progress and labored to help the American side. In 1983 he was awarded the Medal of Freedom by President Reagan.

**"Burnout,"** a phenomenon noticed in the late 1970s and early 1980s which aided the conservative argument that Americans needed less random "freedom," and more routine and responsibility for work and family: that irritability, fatigue, forgetfulness, as designated by psychologists, were a product of aimless living and false attitudes toward work. This diagnosis was the reverse of liberal response which had earlier asked for fewer work-demands, more recreation and diversion, and a burden of proof for poor production on the employer. "Burnout," the opposite of "boredom" (*q.v.*) seemed likely to have a brief career, as the need for work diverted attention from both.

**Bushnell, Horace** (1802-1876), a clergyman of conservative social and religious principles who was honored in general society for his views in *Christian Nurture* (1847). It flouted doctrines of original sin by conceiving of the child as a Christian, to be taught and directed as a person: an early step in raising the child's status in society.

**Business**, see Big Business; Commercialism; Industrial Revolution; Monopoly

**Business Unionism**, see Unions

**Busing**, see Civil Rights

**Butz, Earl**, see Censorship

# C

**Cabell, James Branch** (1879-1958), writer, especially well known in the Twenties (*q.v.*). He had already written works which, without the derring-do of the "romantic" fiction of the 1890s and 1900s, could qualify as romantic because of their aversion to contemporary realism. Implicit in Cabell's measured prose could be found a disillusioned chivalry, a southern equivalent of what Edwin Arlington Robinson's "Miniver Cheevy" found in the North. Cabell's quiet career was interrupted in 1919 by publication of his novel *Jurgen*, which seemed to include erotic concepts serious enough to stir controversy and cause the book to circulate under counters at twenty dollars a copy. His novels were read in the Twenties and were widely regarded as the works of an established master. The 1930s were catastrophic for Cabell. The call for "socially significant" fiction plummeted him from established author to nonentity: a lost cause in conservative melancholy and gentility (*q.v.*). Although Cabell never resumed his place as a national author, he was respected by cultural elements in the South, especially the Agrarians (*qq.v.*). Desmond Tarrant, *James Branch Cabell: The Dream and the Reality* (1967); J. R. Himelick et al., *James Branch Cabell* (1974); R. Canary, *The Cabell Scene* (1975).

**Cable, George Washington** (1844-1925), a prototypical transitional (*q.v.*) figure, conservative in his social outlook and manners, whom occasion forced to serve a liberal cause. A soldier in the Confederate Army during the Civil War, he was persuaded that only equal civil rights for Negroes would serve his beloved South. An artist, rather than a propagandist, he issued famous novels with a fine ear for Creole talk and ways, *Old Creole Days* (1879) and *The Grandissimes* (1884), which indirectly pleaded his cause. His forthright *The Silent South* (1885), however, ruined his reputation in the South and drove him North. His art, however, apparently needed the tension of direct conflict to flourish, for his later works lacked the qualities of nuance and spontaneity which had made his earlier works distinguished; see A. Turner, *George Washington Cable* (1956).

**Calamity Howlers,** a derogatory phrase with which Republicans (*q.v.*) in particular, during the Presidential campaign of 1888, attacked members of the Farmer's Alliance, the Grange, the American Federation of Labor, (*q.v.*) and other groups which deplored the state of the country, it seemed to demand of its defenders an optimistic outlook independent of conditions.

**Calhoun, John C.** (1782-1850), American politician. Though conservative in his passionate defense of slavery, his later political course was much more revolutionary. A nationalist and a "War Hawk" during the War of 1812, he asked for protection (*q.v.*) of home industries, hoping to build Southern factories to compete against those of New England. Disappointed in his hopes, he turned to free trade (*q.v.*) as a defense against the North. He published his "South Carolina Exposition" (1828) anonymously, still hoping to achieve the Presidency and unwilling to commit himself to his pamphlet's principles of states rights and nullification (*qq.v.*). Andrew Jackson's (*q.v.*) break with him in 1832 turned him into an outspoken sectionalist. Although he hoped for many years that self-interest would give Northern industrialists and Southern slaveholders a common platform, he lived long enough to foresee that moral reformers and Northern entrepreneurs would find a basis in fellowship between abolitionism and "Free Soil" (*qq.v.*). His final hope for saving the Union without war, published posthumously in his "Discourse on the Constitution," lay in a dual Executive, in the North and South, each acting for his own section. His *Disquisition on Government* (1850) had offered a rationale for secession. Although *The Wisdom of Conservatism* (*q.v.*) agreed that Calhoun was a reactionary, he was seen as part of the conservative heritage.

**Cambodia,** part of the tragedy of American intervention in Vietnam (*q.v.*). Much was made in anti-war circles of America's "illegal" entrance into Cambodian territory to bomb Vietnam bases. The subsequent genocide (*q.v.*) practiced by the communist Pol Pot Khmer Government, and additional atrocities (*q.v.*) by invading Vietnamese Communists, showed the brutal nature of Southeast Asia's Communist regimes, and seemed to many to give some justification in retrospect to America's controversial Vietnam role.

**Canada,** an increasing presence in North America, and one United States citizens found it more and more necessary to notice. Toronto boasted, that it was a city of graciousness and civilization, such as American cities once claimed. Montreal, for all its problems with British Canada, still had an Old World flavor. French separation threatened Canadian unity in the 1970s, but lost much of its political force under the Governments of Prime Minister Pierre Trudeau and his successors. Canadian assertiveness on issues as far apart as China and nuclear cooperation demanded American respect. The *National Review* (*q.v.*) feared Trudeau's alleged "Marxist" predilections, but others preferred the path of friendliness and trust. American culture, especially popular culture, pervaded many aspects of Canadian life—much to the chagrin of many Canadian nationalists. The close association of the American and Canadian nations can be seen in the career of William Lyon Mackenzie. He is vivid in Canadian annals as the firebrand of 1837 separatism from the British Empire. Mackenzie fled Canada following the collapse of his abortive revolution. In the United States he became a pioneer muckraker (*q.v.*) with massive exposures of fraud and chicanery in Jacksonian (*q.v.*) America. A subsequent amnesty brought him back to Canada to acclaim. See Filler, *Appointment at Armageddon.* Although Canada's fear of "acid rain" caused by American industry, various fishing controversies, and Canada's nationalistic economic policies continued to raise issues between the two countries, their long friendship and unmilitarized borders ensured continued cooperation.

**Cannibals All! or Slaves Without Masters** (1857), by George Fitzhugh, a famous reactionary (*q.v.*) view of society. Its author argued that it was hypocrisy to pretend that all could be equal; there had to be slaves and masters, and the slaves of the South were better treated than the allegedly free men of the North, who could be used up by their masters and flung into the streets. Slavery, on the other hand, was kind and the society it maintained was stable, as compared with the hectic and cruel results of a competitive society. Fitzhugh was especially bitter about the British, whom he accused, not only of interfering in American affairs, but of maintaining an industrial system of barbaric ruthlessness. Harvey Wish, *George Fitzhugh, Propagandist of the Old South* (1943).

**Capital Punishment,** traditionally one of the major targets for reform. Organized opposition was based on its irregular application in the various states, the troubling possibility that innocent persons could be executed, and doubts that capital punishment was a deterrent to other potential murderers. Reform movements brought forth distinguished advocates of abolition; see Filler, DASC. However, the modern crisis in the field was a product of the Supreme Court and the civil rights drive of the 1960s. It was noted that blacks suffered a disproportionate number of executions. It was also held that execution was a social-control factor, especially in the South. Meanwhile, those arguing in behalf of particular clients marshalled a more traditional array of issues. In 1972, the Supreme Court wiped out all the laws of the several states, finding capital punishment "cruel and unusual," in transgression of the Eighth Amendment. Although the ruling left loopholes for new state laws, the abolitionists had gained a major victory. Subsequent developments, with mass murderers given jail sentences and many perpetrators of cruel and unusual killings being let out into the streets to kill again, stirred debate on every level. Arguments raged over gun control, the issue of deterrence, vivid cases of innocent persons found guilty, the operation of parole and pardoning boards, the state of prisons, and alternative prisoner housing. Conservatives leaned toward supporting the death penalty as a just outpouring of society's outrage against the criminal. Liberal opposition often seemed contradictory. Joseph Sobran noted that liberals were horrified by the death of a convicted murderer, but dull to the enormous toll of abortions (*q.v.*). Russell Kirk (*q.v.*) called the death penalty merciful to a tormented life. That the public was partly instructed and partly entertained by such a case as that of Gary Gilmore, who in the late 1970s asked to be executed and resisted abolitionists' pleas to fight the penalty, cannot be doubted; Norman Mailer's *The Executioner's Song* (1979) exploited this case. On a higher level, Pope John Paul II denounced the death penalty, especially for political culprits. Raoul Berger (*q.v.*), opposing "government by judiciary," thought the question of capital punishment should be back in the hands of the people: that is, the states. It was hoped by proponents of capital punishment that new Supreme Court appointments would bring about more favorable rulings. After all, "cruel and unusual punishment" had not, until 1972, meant capital punishment. Although it gave pause to think that lives could be lost or saved by the addition or subtraction of several Supreme Court justices, the larger problem involved measures which might promise hope for a public haunted by crime. T. Sellin, ed., *Capital Punishment* (1967); Michael Melsner, *Cruel and Unusual* (1973); H. A. Bedau and C. M. Pierce, eds., *Capital Punishment in the United States* (1976).

**Capitalism,** the major economic basis of modern conservative thought. It suffered attack but also received ample defense during the more than one hundred years it dominated Western industry. It claimed to represent venturesome capital, industrial growth, economic leadership, incentive, and philanthropy. Its foes emphasized the word "capitalism," being more than reluctant to admit that they opposed "free enterprise" (*q.v.*). The new conservatives, following World War II, faced with a tenacious welfare state (*q.v.*), found it urgent and necessary to accept capitalism as historically valid and working as well as possible under adverse conditions. They qualified their endorsement, however, when they perceived its leaders or spokesmen as displaying myopia or following harmful policies. Conservative intellectuals did not always find it easy to obtain commercial (*q.v.*) support for cultural projects. They were frustrated when businessmen proved eager to deal commercially with Communist countries, even when it harmed American policies or competition. They noted with disapproval great foundations subsidizing radical ventures. Nevertheless, they found much to approve in entrepreneurs who acted the part of statesmen in business and politics, and who worked to turn back welfare statism. William Ebenstein, *Today's Isms* (1970); Milton Friedman, *Capitalism and Freedom* (1962); Daniel Bell and Irving Kristol, eds., *Capitalism Today* (1971); J. D. Forman, *Capitalism, Economic Individualism to Today's Welfare State* (1973).

**Capitalism and the Historians** (1954), edited by F. A. Hayek (*q.v.*), a publication reflecting the proceedings of the Mont Pèlerin (*q.v.*) Society in 1951, which was addressed by the British economic historian T. S. Ashton, the American economic historian Louis M. Hacker, and the French conservative economic historian Bertrand De Jouvenel (*q.v.*). Hayek's introduction emphasized that myths about early capitalist conditions, as propagated in Marx (*q.v.*), the Webbs, and others, had persisted and grown despite their patent falseness. Ashton showed that writings of the early 19th century portrayed capitalism as destroying the standards of living of workers who were drawn from supposedly idyllic farmlands. Hacker, a convert from 1930s

Marxism to 1940s Manchester Liberalism, condemned apologists for the slavery system, and denounced Charles A. Beard for finding the money-motive rampant in American leaders. Jouvenel found a similar suspicion of capitalist motives on the continent. A paper by Professor W. H. Hutt of the University of Capetown examined reports on the workings of the factory system in the early nineteenth century and their effects on morals, health, and children, and found these reports prejudiced by Tory distaste and lack of information. Nevertheless, according to Hutt, their conclusions persisted in later socialist (*q.v.*) and quasi-socialist tracts.

**Capitalism and Welfare,** although well-known in western Europe, where doles, pensions, housing regulations, and other meliorative social actions aided the lower classes, the Welfare State transgressed American habits of thought and expectations. Only bitter struggles and controversies put an end to debtors prisons, took charity operations from the hands of dilettantes, and forced railroads to curb their arrogant treatment of towns and farmers dependent on their patronage and rates. The Progressive era (*q.v.*) labored to stabilize social services, mainly through voluntary (*q.v.*) organizations interested in helping immigrants adjust to new conditions, setting up food and lodging facilities, and helping distraught families to live through crises. "Welfare Capitalism" (*q.v.*) sought to create dialogue on labor's and capital's needs and duties, on a voluntary basis. E. Berkowitz and K. McQuaid, in *Creating the Welfare State* (1980), saw Welfare Capitalism as a prelude to the New Deal (*q.v.*), but underplayed its voluntary nature, as well as the apparently temporary basis of the New Deal, created out of an economic catastrophe and intended to dwindle as the crisis dissipated. The creation of a bureaucracy (*q.v.*) to sustain the New Deal's workings brought on permanent agencies of welfare and permanent farmer's subsidies. This created a social and voting constituency especially devoted to the Democratic (*q.v.*) Party, and was augmented during President Truman's Administration. It continued under the Republican Administration of President Eisenhower, because of irresistible affluence (*q.v.*) and a careless attention to the poor and subsidized. The system fitted well also with local political machines based on patronage (*q.v.*). The Welfare State reached its apogee under President Lyndon B. Johnson. But, in seeking to satisfy and even encourage numerous interests while at the same time carrying on war in Vietnam (*q.v.*), he lost his following and augmented by inflation raised the national deficit (*q.v.*) to dangerous heights. President Reagan's determination to turn back the welfare state roused public attention to its elements: the relation of the government to its constituents, and the role of economics in their goals. Liberal economists denounced capitalists as "greedy," in effect asking for a distribution of assets and resources. Their answer to the patent demoralization noticeable in society—ruined cities, helpless welfare clients—was more money. Free-market economists asked for a diminution of government planning and a new emphasis on individual initiatives. Harold L. Wilensky, in *The Welfare State and Equality: Structural and Ideological Roots of Public Expenditures* (1975), argued that welfare was the majority tendency of modern society; conservatives challenged that assumption.

**Capone, Al,** a 1920s gangster, symbolic of the irresponsible commercialism (*q.v.*) and social conditions produced by the advent of Prohibition (*q.v.*), as distinguished from temperance, to which it had been made equivalent. Basically criminals like Capone fought competing criminals for control of the bootleg liquor market, in the process influencing and even dominating local political administrations. Those who denounced him as a symbol of crime insufficiently faced the fact that he was a folk hero of sorts because of the power he wielded—as Jesse James had been before him—partly because Big Business was not in high repute, partly because his example offered hope to the poor, insufficiently imbued with pride and certain that only money gave dignity and possibilities for happiness. Motion pictures based on his life as well as those of other Prohibition-era criminals mixed violence with images intended to "humanize" the criminal, and in the process imparted the indirect message that his was the road to fame. A later generation of criminals "went respectable" by buying into legitimate businesses. Subsequent revelations of "white-collar crime" further complicated the task of setting up a social ethic. The mass distribution of drugs after World War II implicated large sections of the population, conservative as well as liberal, as illegal liquor had in the 1920s. However, drugs seemed to many more demoralizing and deleterious to society. The cost to society, in terms of health and morals, suggested the need for a new approach to crime (*q.v.*) and criminals. See also *Godfather, The.*

**Capp, Al** (1909-1979), a cartoonist and conservative social commentator. His cartoons, centered about the character and associates of "L'il Abner," a backwoods hillbilly, attained international celebrity and the admiration of such intellectuals as John Steinbeck (*q.v.*). The cartoon strip lightheartedly noticed and commented satirically upon politics, social fads, the family, economic depression, and other themes. Capp was deeply offended by the youth (*q.v.*) movements of the 1960s and their evident corruption and hypocrisy and directed his satire effectively at their manifestations in crime, education, drugs, and general degradation. He added to his career by campus appearances in which he sought to appeal to conservative impulses among students and administrators. Evidence that he had compulsively sought to use female students libidinously cast shadows on his campaign, and though the scandal was treated lightly in the news it harmed the conservative cause.

**Captive Nations**, a term applied to the Communist-controlled nations of Eastern Europe. An Assembly of Captive European Nations was organized in 1951 in Independence Hall, Philadelphia. It included representatives of Albania, Bulgaria, Czechoslovakia, Estonia, Hungary, Latvia, Lithuania, Poland, and Romania. They held that their native peoples were prisoners of the Soviet Union (*q.v.*), kept in bondage through puppet governments. Anti-Communist outbreaks in Czechoslovakia, Hungary, and Poland, though crushed or suppressed, gave validity to these claims, which were kept alive in conservative circles and journals. The Assembly's watch upon developments and social changes in Eastern Europe also furnished conduits of information respecting conditions inside the various totalitarian states. See also Dissidents.

**Caring,** see Compassion

**Carlyle, Thomas** (1795-1881), British historian and social philosopher of individual work and achievement. In vivid and dramatic prose he saw *The French Revolution* (1837) as a morality play featuring careless living and responsibility, and admired great men as necessary to the world's work, as in his *Frederick the Great*, to which he dedicated many years of labor. He upbraided his native country for laxness in life and administration. His satiric *Sartor Resartus* (1833-1834) made a metaphor of his principles. The courage which enabled him to rewrite the first volume of his *French Revolution*, accidentally destroyed, became part of the legend of his greatness. Nevertheless, his scorn of abolitionism (*q.v.*), as displayed in his "The Nigger Question" (1850), reduced his usefulness to conservatives, especially in a world which had to cope with emerging African peoples and nations. Sensitivity to outbreaks of fascism in 1930s enabled anti-fascists to see Carlyle as a precursor of fascism. Carlyle's character and prose, nevertheless, were sustained by biographers and historians throughout the twentieth century, in the multivolume biography of D. A. Wilson (1923-1934) and in studies by Eric Bentley (1944) and Julian Symons (1952), among others.

**Carnegie, Andrew** (1835-1919), Scottish immigrant boy whose life exemplified the American dream (*q.v.*) of a rise from poverty to riches and the conservative view of wealth as constituting a stewardship. (See, however, Rand, Ayn.) Carnegie's role in building and developing the steel industry was challenged in his time; see James H. Bridge, *The Inside History of the Carnegie Steel Company* (1902). His vast selling of his assets in order to retire and practice philanthropy (*q.v.*) raised other questions. Was society best served by private giving or by public social expenditures? Philanthropists like Carnegie avoided charity, for the most part. They sought instruments which served society as a whole. Finley Peter Dunne (*q.v.*) waxed ironical about Carnegie libraries, though they proved durable throughout the century. Still unanswered is the comparative value of government work as opposed to that of such Carnegie endowments as his Foundation for the Advancement of Teaching (1906), his Endowment for International Peace (1910), and his United Kingdom Trust (1913). See also Carnegie's *The Gospel of Wealth* (1900).

**Cartel,** an international concept covering firms which extended their holdings abroad, enabling them to have an impact on the economy of other nations and on the production and distribution of raw materials such as chrome and rubber. A scandal of the pre-World War II era involved cartels which linked American firms to Nazi-owned and dominated German firms, in effect involving them in war production opposed to American interests: an important episode in the history of commercialism (*q.v.*). The criticism which such activities drew appeared to discredit "cartels." In the 1980s so-called multinational corporations came to the fore. A resurgent Japan and suddenly affluent Middle East oil interests were able to buy into American industries. So intricate had international business relations become by then that it became difficult to determine which nation might be influencing the others economically or in social attitudes. Most visible in 1980s was liberal activism (*q.v.*) intended to cut American business ties with the Republic of South Africa (*q.v.*).

**Carter, Jimmy** (1924- ), President of the United States (1977-1981). He served briefly as governor of Georgia and, with little political experience, went to the country in 1975 as a candidate for the presidency. Carter was sincere, and basically conservative; but his vulnerability to liberal slogans and his faith in Detente (*q.v.*) abroad seemed to conflict with the personal shrewdness which had advanced him so far so rapidly. He was master of neither Congress nor, despite formal power, of his own party. His Panama Canal treaty was opposed by many conservatives. The Camp David accords between Israel and Egypt were recognized as a devout hope rather than a firmly-established base for future developments. His year-long hostage crisis, (1979-1981), during which American diplomats and embassy workers were held captive by Iran, appalled friend and foe alike as revealing apparent American weakness. American opinion turned conservative and Carter lost his 1980 bid for reelection. See Betty Glad, *Jimmy Carter* (1980); Filler, "A Nation Stumbles: The Carter Mind and the Presidency," *University Bookman*, Autumn 1981; also Filler DASC.

**Cartoons,** in America originally a vehicle for political commentary, often invidious. They began a new career in the 1890s as entertainment, exploiting sidelights on human behavior, jokes, sentimental notions, eccentric characters, and the like. They matured into middle-class family situations and continuity with conservative limits to the imagination they tolerated. During the 1930s, radicals attracted some cartooning talent, like that of Syd Hoff, and the anti-capitalist William Gropper. Conservatism was served, to a degree, by the sophisticated pictorial comments of the *New Yorker*. Most promising as cartoonist-commentator was Crockett Johnson, who was more delicately anti-establishment, but his vogue, expressed in *Barnaby*, petered out. Herblock, as a consistently liberal editorial cartoonist, and Al Capp (*q.v.*), as an irreverent social observer turned mordant conservative, probed different aspects of the post-World War II scene. The youth movements of the 1960s brought female and minority cartoons into the entertainment and social picture. Gary Trudeau gained a national following in the late 1970s with his "Doonesbury" comic strips. They satirized politics and social and cultural trends and pretensions. At first even-handed in its approach, Trudeau's work later seemed to many to become more and more anti-conservative. When he returned to work from a "sabbatical" in 1984, his approach was criticized by some as increasingly heavy-handed. The clearly conservative Jeff McNelly was a popular cartoonist of the mid-1980s. Allan Nevins and Frank Weitkampf, *A Century of Political Cartoons* (1944); *Cartoons and Illustrations of Thomas Nast* (1974); Charles Press, *The Political Cartoon* (1981).

**Carver, George Washington** (1864?-1943), distinguished Negro scientist, the son of slave parents, and famous for the original investigations in agricultural problems he carried on at Tuskegee Institute. His work with soybeans, sweet potatoes, and peanuts won him wide acclaim. His birthplace became a national landmark. Carver's modesty and religious outlook was notable. However, in the 1960s and 1970s some black militants accused him of being an "Uncle Tom." They contrasted him, for instance, with Dr. Charles Richard Drew (1904-1950), who developed the modern blood bank and who was outspoken in his denunciation of racial discrimination. The 1980s have returned to a more balanced view of Carver's character and achievements.

**Cather, Willa** (1876-1947), one of the great American writers. Her intrinsic conservatism was never on the surface, but could be traced even in her most austere fictions. Like her contemporary Edith Wharton (*q.v.*), she was a dedicated artist, and "feminist" only in her will to self-expression. An editor for S.S. McClure's *McClure's Magazine*, she was responsible for the art which went into making his *Autobiography* (1914) a folk classic. Her female protagonists in *O Pioneers!* (1913), *The Song of the Lark* (1915), and, best of all, *My Antonia* (1918) are all marked by their spirit of independence. *The Professor's House* (1925) implied Cather's sense of a decline in American moral certainties. *A Lost Lady* (1923), her masterpiece, had already dealt with that decline in a poignant tale of disintegration. Cather's attraction to Catholicism appeared in the care she gave her *Death Comes to the Archbishop* (1927) and *Shadows on the Rock* (1931), though, formally, her art was all that engrossed her. She stipulated that no biography was to appear about her, but there was no way in which critics and students of her life could be kept from drawing upon these and other writings, which included memorable short stories and a volume of essays, *Not Under Forty* (1936).

**Catholics,** a traditional bastion of conservatism in American life. The Church professed traditional morality but, with such practices as Confession, appeared able to embrace those fallen from grace. The unrest of the 1960s, however, shattered monolithic attitudes among American Catholics. Such extremists as the Berrigans assaulted government offices in protest against the Vietnam War (*q.v.*). Many priests and nuns revolted against traditional Church strictures. Although many non-Catholics had long looked down at their education as dogmatic and restrictive, the deterioration of the public schools put Catholic schools in a new light as unsegregated, well ordered, and capable of teaching information and proper deportment. The sheer numbers of Catholics—some 25% of the population—made them a strong force in all sectors of society. Beside their panoply of publications, they gave America such contemporary national figures as Rev. Andrew Greeley and William F. Buckley, Jr. of the *National Review* (*qq.v.*). Moreover, official Catholic positions on national issues often drew the sympathy of liberals ordinarily antagonistic to the Church. The election of John F. Kennedy (*q.v.*) to the Presidency in 1960 had helped mute such anti-Catholicism as that expressed in books by Paul Blanchard. In the 1980s there was increasing opposition by American Catholics to the Church's official teachings on various aspects of sexual morality. The statements of American Catholic bishops on nuclear warfare and on the economy aroused considerable support but also considerable controversy. See James Hennesey, *American Catholics: A History of the Roman Catholic Community in the United States* (1981). In the mid-1980s, under the leadership of Cardinal O'Connor of New York, the American Church mounted a drive to make abortion illegal. Whether ecumenical movements contributed significantly to Catholic power, or diminished it, is difficult to judge. Efforts of Protestant and Catholic prelates to heal the over four-hundred-year split between British Anglicans and Catholics roused as much anger and protest as they did approval. Pope John Paul II, as a Polish leader in the enormous struggle for freedom under Communist and Soviet domination, seemed to be sympathetic to the West, but he criticized capitalism with some vehemence. Educational tax benefits for Catholic and other private school students aroused the opposition of many liberals, who saw it as a church-state issue. See K. W. Underwood, *Protestant and Catholic* (1956); James Adams, *The Growing Church Lobby in Washington*; Garry Wills, *Roman Culture* (1963) and *Bare, Ruined Choirs* (1974); *Politics and Catholic Freedom*, intro. Will Herberg (*q.v.*) (1962); *Andrew M. Greeley, Catholic High Schools and Minority Students* (1982), and other works by Greeley. See also John Courtney Murray, *We Hold These Truths: Catholic Reflections on the American Proposition* (1960), concerned for a "post-modern world" which offered a choice between the "democratic monism" of Jacobins and the "democratic pluralism" of the Founding Fathers (*q.v.*). See also Vatican II.

**Cato Institute, The,** a conservative think-tank with headquarters in Washington, D.C., named for Marcus Porcius Cato (95-46 B.C.), known as Cato the Younger. Of a distinguished conservative Roman family, he was remembered for his resistance to Caesarism and his defense of Rome against conspirators. As an example of the Institute's publications, see *Freedom, Feminism, and the State: An Overview of Individualist Feminism* (1982), edited by Wendy McElroy. The Institute published *The Cato Journal.*

**Cattle Kingdom, The,** referred to the Great Plains area of the West, extending north from Texas, over which in the 19th century cattle grazed on the way to market. Walter Webb's *The Great Plains* (1931) held that life there had been different from that in the East; a life of individualism, simplicity, and the elemental virtues of courage, loyalty, and direct relationship to nature. It was treated fictionally by Eugene Manlove Rhodes and A. H. Lewis; see also *Old Wolfville*, edited by Filler. The Negro and "racist" element is emphasized in W. L. Katz's *The Black West*. Webb's outlook, underscored by his subsequent *Divided We Stand*, held that the freer West was "oppressed" by Eastern capitalists.

**Censorship,** see Filler, DASC. Often traditionally identified with conservative restrictions of free expression, especially on sexual subjects, much of it done by social consensus in the 19th century. In the 1920s, such organizations as the Watch and Ward Society in Boston aroused opposition for their efforts at censorship. H. L. Mencken (*q.v.*) identified the "Bible Belt" and "booboisie" with censorship. Communists in the 1930s were often identified with sexual freedom, though in fact Communist regimes have been extremely puritanical and very prone to censorship in practice. The "free speech" movement at Berkeley during the 1960s, centered around the public use of four-letter words, helped spark the youth movements of the decade which emphasized sexual and verbal license as part of their approach to society. The civil rights movements of the 1960s and 1970s led to social and public strictures against terms deemed invidious to racial and other minorities—though such strictures were enforced more by custom and peer pressure than by law. Many liberals seemed overly concerned with the proper use of "approved" or politically and socially "correct" terminology when referring to women, minorities, and other social groups. Such conservative political figures as Spiro Agnew (*q.v.*), Earl Butz, and James Watt were castigated by their opponents for offhand jests about various minority groups. On the other hand, Jesse Jackson's offhand remarks about American Jews during his 1984 bid for the Democratic nomination for President also aroused a storm of controversy, alienating many liberals who were sympathetic to his radical-left ideas. The historian Philip Foner adopted the form of "n____" in quoting documents dealing invidiously with blacks. But, while racial and ethnic terminology seemed severely restricted by custom in the mid-1980s, public use of "vulgar" and "obscene" speech and the open discussion of intimate aspects of sexuality were tolerated if not accepted by large segments of society. To many this seemed an ironic reversal of the situation prevalent in America in the 19th century. Dr. Earl Butz, President Ford's Secretary of Agriculture, lost his position because of a distorted version of a statement of his respecting blacks played up by the liberal media. Since all public people used their own ethnicity or other minority (*q.v.*) qualities, and those of others, to seek to gain political points, it was evident that levels of language and connotation were in the making which would finally determine the parameters of inter-ethnic discourse.

**Censorship, Literary**, traditionally identified with conservatism and with evasion of the facts of human nature as well as of social and working-class concerns. The famous "disillusionment" of Twenties (*q.v.*) created numerous censorship cases which called attention to books and issues which might otherwise have passed unnoticed. James Branch Cabell's (*q.v.*) *Jurgen* was sold under the counter, though today it sits on library shelves mostly unread. James Joyce's *Ulysses* helped break down American censorship laws in the 1930s. The excessive concern of Boston's Watch and Ward Society for the purity of books caused many authors such as Samuel Putnam to long to be denounced as an incentive to sales. Mark Twain's (*q.v.*) *Huckleberry Finn* has been continually dogged by censorship. Originally denounced by schoolboards as vulgar and unfit for youthful eyes, it nevertheless gained a vast scholarly following for its subtle, liberal nuances of character, respect for Negroes, and understanding of Americans of the North and South. It is now commonly regarded as an American classic. Yet in recent years some blacks have protested its use of such words as "nigger" and its portrayal of the Negro slave Jim, and have called for its removal from libraries and school classrooms. In one case, in Prince George's County, Virginia, it was made available to students only under close analytical supervision. In the mid-1980s American writers clearly had considerable legal freedom from censorship in their descriptions of sexual and other behavior and their use of "vulgar" and "obscene" expressions. See Anne Lyon Haight, *Banned Books* (1935, 1955), an excellent though somewhat outdated study.

**Center for Strategic and International Studies,** at Georgetown University in Washington, D.C., one of the conservative-directed bodies which report on government policies: seen by liberals as part of the "new conservative labyrinth," as in *Ominous Politics* (*q.v.*). The Center cooperates with such other Washington-based centers as the Heritage Foundation (*q.v.*), exchanges visitors with them, enjoys the association of such luminaries as Jeane Kirkpatrick (*q.v.*), and issues reports on foreign policy and related topics.

**Central America,** see Latin America

**CETA,** see Comprehensive Employment and Training Act

**Chamberlain, John** (1903- ), early transitional (*q.v.*) figure who turned from neo-Marxism to conservatism. He was impressed when a Yale College student by A. G. Keller, a friend and colleague of William Graham Sumner (*q.v.*), but turned while reviewing books for the *New York Times* to derogation of the Progressive (*q.v.*) tradition. His *Farewell to Reform* (1932) did serious harm to that tradition. As early as 1936 he was also associated with *Fortune*, and later served with *Barron's*. By then, he could re-issue *Farewell to Reform*, viewing reform negatively from the right. Among his books approving capitalism were *The American Stakes* (1940) and *The Enterprising Americans* (1963). Chamberlain wrote an account of the Hillsdale College (*q.v.*) programs, *Freedom and Independence* (1979). He was an early and long-time associate at *National Review*. One of his disillusioned conservative ventures was as an editor of the 1950-1952 *Freeman* (*q.v.*), which he helped with his wide acquaintanceship among authors and social activists. He later conducted a conservative daily syndicated column, *These Days*. See his memoir, *Life with the Printed Word* (1982).

**Chamberlin, William Henry** (1897-1969), one of the early foreign correspondents disillusioned with the Soviet regime, along with Malcolm Muggeridge and Eugene Lyons (*qq.v.*). A *Christian Science Monitor* journalist sent to the Soviet Union to report news in 1922, he stayed till 1934. Since he had been a quiet sympathizer of the Bolshevik Revolution while in New York, and written of it in the radical press under a pseudonym, he was ready, along with other American correspondents, to believe its reports of progress and freedom, and to pass lightly over such blemishes as he saw. His first accounts of Soviet planning and operations, written while in the Soviet Union, did not challenge common opinion, which was positive respecting the "Great Experiment." *Russia's Iron Age* (1934) and *The Russian Revolution* (1935) expended more care and objectivity, but could not compete for public interest with Leon Trotsky's (*q.v.*) *History*, as translated by Max Eastman (*q.v.*). By then, Chamberlin's disillusionment was complete. His *Collectivism: A False Utopia* (1937) was an early anti-Soviet book repudiating socialism in any form, and was followed by his *Confessions of an Individualist* (1940), the word "individualist" being favored by the anti-Communists of the time. Chamberlin went on to become a columnist for the *Wall Street Journal*, an associate of *Human Events* (*q.v.*) editors, and of the Revisionist (*q.v.*) historians. As such, he published with Henry Regnery (*q.v.*) an account of *America's Second Crusade* (1950), the unfavorable reviews of which startled him with their fury and influence. A precursor of the coming New Conservatism, he published his *Evolution of a Conservative* (1959).

**Chambers, Whittaker** (1901-1961), a phenomenon of modern conservatism. His personal testimony did much to give modern conservatism its character and influence. Earlier conservatism had been weak in its grasp of the world scene. Chambers, having lived in the two worlds of American dreams and communist vision, and having survived to relate his experiences with both, provided material for newer conservatives to explore. His youth had been agitated, his Columbia University experiences unfulfilling. The Communist world seemed to give him a goal which he translated into tales which pleased them with the image it projected of their purposes. The Communists wanted agents more than poets, however, and he was taken into their espionage system in 1932. As an agent he worked with Alger Hiss (*q.v.*) to procure state papers which could then be passed on to the Soviet Union. The harsh Stalin purges were intolerable to Chambers. In 1938 he broke with the Party, though fearing assassination. (See Trilling, Lionel.) The next year he joined the staff of *Time* and rose swiftly to a senior position. Chambers made efforts to apprise government officials of the presence of what would later be called "moles" in responsible posts, but was not able to stir interest in his story, even for investigation. In 1948 he put his career on the line by testifying before the House Committee on Un-American Activities about his former espionage activities, implicating Hiss. The spirit of the time was indicated in the distaste which was felt for his awkward figure and poor teeth, as compared with the trim, handsome appearance of the then-head of the Carnegie Endowment for International Peace. The subsequent trials and torments involved an awesome clash of opposed social spirits, which was not wholly resolved by Hiss's sentence to prison. Chambers's *Witness* (1952) was recognized as an extraordinary memoir, though whether it was too much for the public to bear is difficult to say. It did not seem to move the intellectual establishment, and offended part of it. See his *Cold Friday* (1964), and *Odyssey of a Friend: Whittaker Chambers's Letters to William F. Buckley, Jr., 1954-1961*, Buckley, ed. (1970).

**Champions of Freedom** (1974), see Socialism

**Champions of Freedom,** a series of lectures on free-enterprise themes maintained at Hillsdale College (*q.v.*) in honor of Ludwig von Mises (*q.v.*) drawing on well-known figures in the world of conservatism, and being issued in volumes, the number reaching nine in 1983. Speakers included economists, politicians, journalists, and figures in such institutions as the American Enterprise Institute (*q.v.*).

**Channing, William Ellery** (1780-1842), a founder of Unitarianism, and seen as a religious liberal and an apostle of peace, which patriots and imperialists identified with dissidence. Nevertheless, Channing was moderate in his response to such liberal to radical causes as antislavery, women's rights, and related causes. Like some other conservatives of his time, he was reluctant to plunge too far ahead to views which threatened the Union and traditional family ties and expectations. His *Slavery* (1835) put him clearly on the antislavery side and swayed northern public opinion in its behalf, though the book was unsatisfactory to radicals. He refused, also, to align himself with peace advocates who sweepingly disavowed "carnal" weapons, and with pacifists who preached "no-government" when it transgressed conscience. Channing was thus a transitional (*q.v.*) figure from earlier conservatism who helped other conservatives to adjust their minds to newer concepts of civic responsibility. R. L. Patterson, *The Philosophy of William Ellery Channing*(1952); A. W. Brown, *William Ellery Channing* (1961).

**Chapman, John Jay** (1862-1933). Of distinguished Revolutionary and dissident background, he took an individualist position which recommended him to later libertarians (*q.v.*). His most famous act was, in 1911, hiring a hall in order to commemorate a Negro who had suffered lynching. The meeting was attended by two persons: one a Boston Negro, the other an informer; see Chapman's *Memoirs and Milestones* (1915). Admirable in his *Cause and Consequences* (1898) and *Practical Agitation* (1900) as calling attention to social problems which required cure, his opinions were marred by anti-Semitism and anti-Catholicism; see R. B. Hovery, *John Jay Chapman* (1959).

**Chappaquiddick,** as symbolic in many ways for the public assessment of the Democratic Party and its Kennedy legacy as was Watergate (*q.v.*) for that of the Republican Party. In 1969 Edward M. Kennedy, Senator of Massachusetts, was involved in a mysterious automobile accident on Chappaquiddick Island, Massachusetts. He was driving a car which went off a bridge, trapping a young woman companion inside who subsequently drowned. Kennedy himself escaped, and the accident was not reported until many hours later. James McGregor Burns, whose early endorsement of John F. Kennedy for the Presidency had made him famous (*John Kennedy: A Political Profile* [1959]), attempted to do the same for his brother Edward M. Kennedy, in his *Edward M. Kennedy and the Camelot Legacy* (1976). He defended and rationalized Kennedy's actions and evasions following the automobile accident. The *New York Times* (*q.v.*) spoke of "unanswered questions." *Reader's Digest* (*q.v.*), following exhaustive examination of the evidence, concluded that Kennedy's "sworn account...is false." Despite the efforts of such allies as James McGregor Burns, Kennedy's political career was clearly hurt. Nevertheless, he fought for the Democratic nomination for President in 1980. Although his bid was frustrated by President Carter's firm use of Democratic Party regulations governing the choice of delegates, he received startling ovations from them, and his speech to the Democratic Convention topped in sensational response that of the renominated Carter. Although he did not run for nomination in the 1984 primaries, it was held not impossible that if the major contenders cancelled each other out, Kennedy would be the nominee of the Democratic Party.

**Charities,** see Filler, DASC. Liberals of the pre-World War I generation fought for adequate wages and human rights. They scorned "charity," though it had classic meanings of compassion (*q.v.*) and human duty. Radicals went further in denouncing philanthropy (*q.v.*) as assuaging the guilt feelings of the undeserving wealthy and creating apologetics of social service and vanity for the self-made affluent. Social Service, however, was devised and made professional through endowments of often immaturely drawn-up programs. The Great Depression demanded emergency measures of both state and government aid, as well as direct charity. Wartime and subsequent peacetime prosperity diminished the need for both. However, the continued existence of the poor and of elements of society which could not care for themselves gave "case work" to Catholic, Jewish (*qq.v.*), and other charities, as well as to organizations created during the Depression. Negroes adrift from the South to Northern cities, Puerto Ricans new to the American mainland, unregistered Mexican aliens (*qq.v.*), migrant laborers, alcoholics, drug addicts, and homeless children needed care. Almost invisible, but useful to large numbers of their fellows, were fraternal organizations which built hospitals and centers. With the welfare state (*q.v.*) now in full swing, many liberals gave little thought to means for avoiding dependency on government. Traditional virtues of temperance, self-control, and austerity were often ridiculed and demeaned. The sweeping assault on conservative social standards in the 1960s (*q.v.*) seemed to multiply the evils of dependency. The collapse of radical-left along with "Great Society" programs (*q.v.*) forced a confrontation between those who preached "compassion" and those who urged "voluntarism" (*q.v.*) as a first step toward reconstituting a viable society.

**Chatterton, Thomas,** see Suicide

**Chesterton, Gilbert K.** (1874-1936), journalist, poet, storyteller, Catholic apologist. He was famous in his day, his paradoxes adding a signature to his varied writings. His basic, original plea was for the romance and joy of life, which he expressed in books on Robert Browning (1903) and Charles Dickens (1906). He produced sound literary studies on each to which he added a study of George Bernard Shaw (1909). Chesterton was in controversy with Shaw on the meaning of life, Shaw's socialism (*q.v.*) offending his sense of personality and religion. Chesterton's quest led him officially to the Catholic Church (*q.v.*) in 1922. Earlier, in tales and essays he had attacked self-centered, calculating, and joyless men. His verse, which ranged from doggerel to much more than that, was spirited and convincing. His fiction, of which *The Man Who Was Thursday* (1908) was typical, stressed fantasy and swift judgment on those who questioned life. *The Innocence of Father Brown* (1911) gave him an even larger and more popular audience, attracting those who enjoyed crime and detection fiction, weighted with moral purpose, but with intriguing pardoxes; the best of the Father Brown detective stories are read even today. Chesterton's turn to Catholicism diminished his influence to a degree but provided a base of conservative thought which carried his personality, and some of his writing, into the future, where he became a fixture of the New Conservative establishment; the New Conservatives relished his stinging prose and verse and approved his social politics. Maisie Ward, *Return to Chesterton* (1952); F. A. Lea, *The Wild Knight of Battersea* (1945); Garry Wills (*q.v.*), *Chesterton: Man and Mask* (1961); A. S. Dale, *The Outline of Sanity: A Life of G. K. Chesterton* (1983).

**Chicago.** In the 1900s Chicago was involved in the era reform movements, but by the 1920s it was more readily identified with the presence of Al Capone (*q.v.*) in neighboring Cicero. From there he ruled a cheerful if degrading empire. Under Mayor Daley in the 1960s and 1970s Chicago was known as "the city that works." A system of political patronage kept city breakdowns at a minimum, with favored neighborhoods not only maintaining their character, but actually reviving under local enterprise. The death of Mayor Daley led to schisms in the machine and among ethnic elements, and the election of Mayor Harold Washington put substantial power in the hands of the black community. Although still a Democratic and liberal stronghold, the evidence of loose, unintegrated power elements gave conservatives hope that coming elections would give them free play for greater effect.

**Chicago School of Economics,** highly effective in stimulating conservative thought and feeding it ideas in the economic and social sectors, it was instituted by Henry C. Simons (*Economic Policy for a Free Society* [1948]) and Frank Knight (*Freedom and Reform: Essays in Economic and Social Philosophy* [1947]) and attracted others who saw a relationship between economic policies and the fortunes of society in general. The school succeeded in making the study of conservative economics exciting and influential. Its most notable additions were Friedrich A. Hayek and Milton Friedman (*qq.v.*).

**Chicago Tribune,** one of the major newspapers in the nation. It contributed greatly to the election of Abraham Lincoln (*q.v.*) and later maintained a tradition of Republicanism and regard for the principles it espoused, including a paternalistic view of blacks (*q.v.*). Under Robert R. McCormick, it was dedicated to patriotism, free enterprise, and anti-union sentiments, and gained a tight hold on Chicago and Midwestern readers. Isolationist (*q.v.*) and suspicious of British diplomacy, it provided news and viewpoints in opposition to the New Deal of the 1930s. The city's deterioration after World War II due to urban (*q.v.*) conditions affecting most American cities, focused attention on the Democratic city machine, made conspicuous by political deals which were believed to keep Chicago together. The ability of the *Tribune* to maintain its power over readers, despite the resentment of City Hall and the political machine, baffled its critics. However, the death of McCormick in 1955 saw the *Tribune* shift gradually from a rigid pro-capitalist stance and conservative outlook. *Tribune* columnists were often cynical about the city's politicians and followed closely their financial deals. Although sentimental conservatives thought the *Tribune* had declined from what it had been under McCormick, many saw it preferable to such papers as the *New York Times* (*q.v.*).

**Children,** see Abuse

**Chile,** see Latin America

**China,** second only to the Soviet Union (*q.v.*) as a long-term challenge to American prospects and ideals. All historical precedents—from the Chinese Exclusion Act of 1880, through John Hay's (*q.v.*) Open Door Policy, later American interest in Chinese railroads, concern over Japanese aggressions on the Mainland and expansion there during World War II—were overthrown in 1949, when the Red Chinese Army forced the Chiang Kai-shek regime to flee and thereupon set up a People's Republic on the Mainland. Many conservatives blamed Communist sympathizers in the State Department and in the Institute for Pacific Relations for confusing public opinion on the imminence of this event, and for preparing it to accept the Communists as legitimate and humane rulers of China. Conservatives feared a Communist invasion of the Chiang Kai-shek stronghold on the island of Taiwan. Conservatives were dismayed by the dismissal of General MacArthur (*q.v.*) for wishing to carry the Korean War to the Chinese Communist Army which had entered it on the side of North Korea. Meanwhile, there were reports of ruthless Chinese violence against "enemies of China," the herding of millions of Chinese into communes, the regimenting of slave labor to force rapid modernization. In contrasts, such figures in the IPR as Owen Lattimore (see Filler, DASC) talked of a free and happy people acclimated to communism. Conservatives denied that there was a subversive "China Lobby" maneuvered by capitalists who feared peace and freedom (see *Plain Talk*). In the 1960s they denounced American student infatuation with "Chairman Mao," whom they saw as a ruthless totalitarian and ideologue, a danger to civilization as the Russians were. Conservatives took some satisfaction and hope from the upheavals of the Chinese Cultural Revolution led by Maoist extremists, and from the rift which developed between Mainland China and the Soviets. Taiwan was seen by many, conservatives and others, as a capitalist success which merited every American consideration. The Nixon-Kissinger initiative which took the President to the Mainland in 1972 alarmed conservatives as an extension of Detente (*q.v.*) which would cost Americans in the end. Later, President Carter seemed to hint at an end for American support to Taiwan, and Congress itself felt it necessary to reassure Taiwan that its autonomy was not to be sacrificed. In the late 1970s and 1980s, the successors of chairman Mao turned away from his extremist policies to allow a greater freedom and the beginning of free enterprise in Chinese society, though still within the context of a totalitarian police state. China's abandonment of many traditional principles of Marxism seemed to many a dramatic indication of the bankruptcy of communism and a portent of things to come in the Soviet Union and elsewhere. Meanwhile, China remained an important factor in America's balancing of forces in the world. President Reagan seemed able to deal with the Chinese without yielding principle. Frank N. Trager, William Henderson, eds., *Communist China, 1949-1969* (1970); Richard C. Thornton, *China, the Struggle for*

*Power, 1917-1972* (1974); Edwin J. Feulner, ed., *China, The Turning Point* (1976); H. C. Hinton, *China's Turbulent Quest... Foreign Relations since 1949* (1972 ed.); Fox Butterfield, *China: Alive in the Bitter Sea* (1982); John K. Fairbank, *Chinabound: A Fifty-Year Memoir* (1982).

**Chodorov, Frank** (1887-1966), a transitional (*q.v.*) figure, the son of immigrants who, infused with the liberal spirit, left business to follow the Single-Tax doctrines of Henry George. He became head of the Henry George School, which issued the master's work and associated materials. His concern was individualism (*q.v.*), rather than the later wide-sweeping "conservatism." For the publisher Regnery he produced several pamphlets, including *Taxation Is Robbery*, *From Solomon's Yoke to the Income Tax*, and *The Myth of the Post Office*. He also wrote *One Is a Crowd*. A sponsor of young William F. Buckley, Jr., he called Regnery's attention to Buckley's manuscript of *God and Man at Yale* (*q.v.*). Chodorov helped edit *The Freeman* (*q.v.*) and *Human Events*, and was one of the early group which helped Buckley launch the *National Review* (*q.v.*).

**Choice, Not An Echo, A** (1964), by Phyllis Schlafly (*q.v.*). It sold over a million copies in several months, and was credited with having helped push Barry Goldwater (*q.v.*) to the Republican nomination for President. The book held that "a few secret kingmakers based in New York" had selected the Republican nominees for President from 1936 to 1960. A coldly documented account of Communist victories and American defeats all around the world was followed by the declaration that Republicans could not lose the coming election if they emphasized the disgraceful record of both Democratic and Republican Chief Executives. The book depended on such concepts as "the hoaxters" and "the big steal" and emphasized a conspiracy (*q.v.*) theory: Americans were being sold candidates whom they did not want.

**Chronicles of Culture**, its name altered to Chronicles: A Magazine of American Culture, a publication of the Rockford Institute in Rockford, Illinois, a conservative center. Edited by the late Leopold Tyrmond, it undertook to expose what it saw as the shallowness, false values, and bullying by approval or disapproval of a wide variety of fiction and social commentary—especially in the *New York Times* and *New York Review of Books*, but touching such other publications as the *Nation, New York*, and the *New Republic*. Its reviewers, strongly conservative, though often with modest credentials sought in their advertising to deflate "Vidal, Mailer, Vonnegut, Doctorow, et al...." Although some of their articles were trenchant and observant and by such notables as Russell Kirk and Robert Nisbet (*qq.v.*), others amounted to no more than alternative readings of the works and authors in question. What the critiques did not do was probe the reasons for the influence of several of the publications it attacked, or show awareness of the diminished power of such organs as the *Nation*. The approach of the *Chronicles*, of being against liberal writings and reviewers, rather than building a positive intellectual world, seemed insufficient to some conservatives. Under a new editor, the classics scholar Thomas Fleming, it expanded its program. It utilized a wider range of critics, set up new departments, and sought a less parochial approach to readers within its basis premises.

**Church and State.** The First Amendment to the Constitution (*q.v.*), said: "Congress shall make no law respecting an establishment of religion, or prohibiting the free exercise thereof...." In the 19th century the existence of a dominant Christian ethic—with tradition, ritual, and ceremonies—was recognized as implicit in society; in the twentieth century this was broadened to include the Judeo-Christian tradition. The assault on this concept, by militant atheists, the American Civil Liberties Union (*qq.v.*), and other dissidents, interpreted the constitutional stipulation, as projected into the twentieth century prohibiting any recognition of religious concepts or ceremonies in civil activity. This viewpoint won a victory in 1962 with the Supreme Court decision outlawing public prayer in schools (*q.v.*). Thereafter the conflict grew between those who thought the state should encourage religion and those who thought it should not.

Earlier national practices, such as religious services to Indians (*q.v.*) who were wards of the state, complicated the argument. Especially controversial were educational grants to parochial schools, even though Catholics and others paid taxes part of which went for public education. With "mainline" churches and synagogues fighting to clarify their roles internally and in the larger community, with fundamentalism (*q.v.*) alive and growing with persons who had been cast adrift by social eruptions, and with courts under pressure from skilled legal technicians from both sides, the full status of church-state relations remained undetermined. P. B. Kurland, *Church and State: The Supreme Court and the First Amendment* (1975); E. J. Hughes, *The Church and the Liberal Society* (1961); P. Schaff, *Church and State in the United States; or, the American Idea of Religious Liberty* (1888); H. Stroup, *Church and State in Confrontation* (1967); A. W. Johnson and F. H. Yost, *Separation of Church and State in the United States* (1948).

**Churchill, Winston** (1874-1965), see Filler, DASC, a major figure of pride for Western conservatism, his brief period as a Liberal (1905-1908) helping to describe the difference between liberalism in Great Britain and in the United States. His career, aside from his "finest hour" as Prime Minister resisting the Nazi onslaught against Great Britain (1940-1945), helped to diminish the cliches which separated the Liberal, Labor, and Conservative Parties. He fought in South Africa as an imperialist (*q.v.*) in opposition to the Boers, and later helped build the welfare state with "conservative socialist" measures, but held out against the principles of nationalization. His war against Hitler required collaboration with Stalin, but he himself declared the need for the Cold War (*q.v.*) once the Soviets had lowered the Iron Curtain across Europe. He declared his unwillingness to release India from under the British Raj, but later did so. In his years British journalists were critical of his "rhetoric" during World War II. But to many his wit and wisdom were more memorable than his critics, and his reputation seemed safe for posterity—as statesman, orator, author, and even soldier.

**CIA,** Central Intelligence Agency. It was involved in controversial undercover activities which alarmed many liberals. Most conservatives believed that American security required such undercover operations for the defense of the nation. Established in 1947, under the directorship of Allen W. Dulles, the CIA organized a coup which overthrew the Government of Iran in 1953. It was also involved with the Bay of Pigs fiasco in 1961. The CIA has come under attack for illegal wiretapping and mail surveillance activities, and was a favorite target of radical leftists in the 1960s and 1970s. In 1973 it helped overthrow the Marxist President of Chile, an action denounced by many liberals but applauded by many conservatives. Americans generally agreed that the CIA was vital to American interests. In the late 1970s a former CIA operative began to expose the names of agents and details of their activities and this led to at least one death. An Intelligence Act passed Congress in 1980 in an effort to rebuild internal CIA control. Y. H. Kim, *Central Intelligence Agency: Problems of Secrecy in a Democracy* (1968).

**Civil Rights.** The concept of civil rights arose with the Fourteenth Amendment and was implemented, modified, and expanded in later Supreme Court decisions dealing with the rights of Negroes. (See Voting Rights Act.) The World War I suppression of dissidents resulted in the creation of the American Civil Liberties Union with its concern for civil rights. During the 1960s efforts were made to extend the concept to include women, ethnic minorities and homosexuals. The concept of "affirmative action" (*q.v.*) was put forth by many liberals, but to conservatives it seemed to be a form of reverse discrimination. Efforts to desegragate school systems were thwarted by "white flight" and resegregation. The question of applying civil rights to such groups as illegal aliens caused many problems for the courts. While the status of blacks had improved considerably since the beginning of the 1960s, a large black "underclass" remained which seemed resistant to government efforts to improve its lot. Conservatives believed, in fact, that such efforts exacerbated the problem. What were the "rights" of illegal aliens? Or of employers charged with job discrimination? Although the Supreme Court (*q.v.*) could affirm various views, and influence thousands of actions in towns and states, there were public opinion and a Congress (*q.v.*) to initiate changes. Such watchdog agencies as the Equal Employment Opportunity Commission and the Washington Council of Lawyers could chide the Department of Justice for inadequate action, without necessarily losing its prestige. Moreover, civil rights partisans could be found wanting in other respects. A university economist found that while they were pursuing their particular causes, while a small portion of black professionals were accruing economic gains, the larger black community had actually lost ground in comparison to the whites since the eras before the civil rights drives. Friends of the black people and of urban development might well wonder what the civil rights drive had accomplished for the country, or how the downward chart of black conditions could be halted. In 1986, this question was not faced. The road continued to be marked by civil rights suits. One black spokesman even wished to go "beyond" the civil rights movement to what he thought of as a "U.S. Mainstream Commission" which, while protecting civil rights "gains" would also "make sure that our national goals and timetable accurately measure black American progress." J. Anderson, *Eisenhower, Brownell, and the Congress: The Tangled Origins of the Civil Rights Bill of 1956-7* (1964); A. J. M. Milme, *Freedom and Rights* (1968); H. J. Abraham, *Freedom and the Courts* (1972).

**Civil Service, United States,** established in 1883 with a classified list of Postmasters and others. It began a process which expanded into all areas of federal, state, and local government. Leaders in the original drive to institutionalize standards for government employment were Dorman B. Eaton, George William Curtis (*q.v.*), and Carl Schurz. The Hatch Act (1940) forbade political contributions by office holders. The growing bureaucratization (*q.v.*) of government employees led many conservatives to call for cutbacks in staffing and reorganization at the federal, state and local level. Carl R. Fish, *Civil Service and the Patronage* (1904), P. Van Riper, *History of the United States Civil Service* (1958); F. C. Mosher, *Democracy and the Public Service* (1968).

**Civil War.** The American Civil War was at one time a source of inspiration and patriotism for Northerners and Southerners alike. Its major figure was Abraham Lincoln (*q.v.*), his life and work summing up what the Union stood for. Woodrow Wilson (*q.v.*) represented North-South reconciliation when he was elected President in 1912. He believed that a single nation which admired both Lincoln and Robert E. Lee symbolized the spirit of a great people. In the 1960's and 1970's radical left historians and others tended to cast doubt on the motives, conduct, and results of the war. Allan Nevins's (*q.v.*) six-volume *The Ordeal of the Union* was a typical approach to the subject. Daniel Aaron's *The Unwritten War: American Writers and the Civil War* (1973), which sees the Civil War as sentimentalized by such writers as Ralph Waldo Emerson (*q.v.*), is typical of the "revisionist" historical approach. See Filler, "The Civil War as Myth and Reality," in *Reviews in American History* (vol. 2, no. 3).

**Civilian Conservation Corps,** see Public Works

**"Class Action" Suits,** see Legal Services Corporation

**Classics,** to many conservatives involving the best traditions of the past, but the subject has been complicated by changing trends and concerns, notably those involving democratic tastes and preferences. Matthew Arnold (*q.v.*) held that, for those responsible for upholding civilized standards, Homer was a more crucial poet to know and understand than Lord Byron. Albert Mordell (*q.v.*), in *Dante and Other Waning Classics* (1915), held that only the human aspects of alleged "classics" truly survived; modern readers, he maintained, would give little more than lip-service to archaic fancies and superstitions. Such conservatives as

Irving Babbitt and Paul Elmer More (*qq.v.*) made conscious intellectual war in behalf of mainly foreign classics, and were in open combat with those who admired the democratic writings and language of such newer 20th century authors as David Graham Phillips, Sinclair Lewis, John Dos Passos (*qq.v.*), and others who deviated from "classical" standards. Conservative critics particularly disparaged writings which exploited looser sexual patterns and vulgar prose, and were antipathetic to writings which showed sympathy with socialist (*q.v.*) ideals at home or abroad. The concept of "classics" was debased to a degree by American readiness to apply it in the fields of commerce and popular culture. One branch of conservatives who asserted their presence on the post-World War II American scene held to older fashions and saw time as an important factor in estimating the quality of literary work. Others, more closely embroiled in contemporary debates, used admiration and scorn to effect the quality of contemporary literatures, and fought the gradual abandonment of "classical" standards.

**Clay, Henry** (1777-1852), conservative statesman. His long career in Washington provided numerous examples of his love of country and tolerance of human nature. A poor boy who left his native Virginia and went to Kentucky, he came to the Capital as a young hothead who wanted war with Great Britain. Affable and shrewd, as a peace commissioner at Ghent he was able to save Detroit from transfer to British hands as a result of the War of 1812. His two great compromises, those of 1820 and 1850, dealt with North-South conflicts over the expansion of slavery; it is likely that they gave forces of freedom in the North the time necessary to forge an alliance among diverse elements, from abolitionists to Unionists (*qq.v.*), to help them to resist Southern secessionists and expansionists. Clay's "American System" was basically an economic system of protection, intended to advance American industry, bring the sections of the country closer through roads and canals, and defend the country. His battle with Andrew Jackson (*q.v.*) over the recharter of the Second Bank of the United States showed his conservative belief. His early efforts to create a Pan-American Union, while Secretary of State under John Quincy Adams (*q.v.*), foundered on Democratic reluctance to deal courteously with dark-skinned officials south of the American border. Clay's approach to slavery was moderate, expressing a willingness to curb and diminish it, a stand which roused impatience in the North and South but which served the dream of Union. He opposed war with Mexico. Overall, in a nation producing numerous partisans of stature who were ready to sink the Union in pursuit of their goals, Clay was a figure of goodwill and grace who spoke for what the nation had been and could be.

**Clayton Act** (1914), see Unions

**Clemens, Samuel L.,** see Twain, Mark

**Cleveland, Grover** (1837-1908), a conservative whose phenomenal rise to the Presidency somewhat paralleled that of the liberal Jimmy Carter (*q.v.*) almost a century later. In 1882 he was Democratic mayor of Buffalo, N.Y. That same year he became governor of New York, and two years later President. His solidity of character satisfied the Democratic need for a candidate who could challenge the powerful Republican Party, and his firmness in resisting pension frauds and lax postmaster appointments augmented his reputation for honesty. His courageous turn to Free Trade (*q.v.*) contributed to his re-election defeat. It gave him a reputation for liberalism which was, however, ideological rather than compassionate. (See Godkin, E. L.) In 1892 he obtained the Presidency once more. His second term featured a run on the U. S. Treasury, which he settled on hard terms with J. P. Morgan (*q.v.*) Company, and a mixed imperialist, anti-imperialist record. He held off on a forced treaty giving Hawaii to the United States, claiming the duties of great nations to small ones (Hawaii was later simply annexed, during the Spanish-American War), but then threatened war with Great Britain, when it attempted to settle unilaterally a dispute over land with Venezuela. Although Cleveland undoubtedly acted from principle, his actions seemed to many to reflect the nation's confusion in a narrowing world. Allan Nevins, *Grover Cleveland: A Study in Courage* (1932); and *Letters* (1933).

**Clichés of Socialism** (1962), a publication of the Foundation for Economic Education (*q.v.*). It provided free-market and conservative answers to such statements and questions as, "If we had no social security, many people would go hungry"; "The size of the national debt doesn't matter because we owe it to ourselves"; and "If free enterprise really works; why the Great Depression?" The answers engaged such authors as the libertarian Murray N. Rothbard (*q.v.*), author of *Man, Economy, and State* (1962); Robert LeFevre, president of the Freedom School and editor of the Colorado Springs *Gazette Telegraph*; and R. C. Hoiles, president of a chain of *Freedom Newspapers* with headquarters in Santa Ana, California.

**"Clients,"** see Surrogates

**Clio from the Right: Essays of a Conservative Historian** (1983), by Edward S. Shapiro (1938- ), a collection of essays, articles, and reviews which touch upon methods and opinions in the history profession and the place of conservatism in it. Shapiro emphasized the Agrarians, the New Deal, aspects of World War II, centralization tendencies opposed to decentralization, and Jewish roles in society. Strong on bibliography and liberal-conservative differences, his work threw light on history in the schools, as in his review of Irwin Unger's textbook, *These United States*.

**Cobbett, William** (1762-1835), a British transitional figure who rose above his early Toryism and later Radicalism (*qq.v.*) to win honor as one of the greatest of journalists, master of a lucid and riveting style, author of the classic *Rural Rides*, and a persuasive foe of cruelty and lover of justice. Of humble country stock, he became a self-taught student of life and letters. He served with honor in the army, but, having charged officers with fraud, was forced in 1792 to flee to the United States. There, as "Peter Porcupine," he wrote in the spirit of Federalism, denouncing his fellow expatriates Dr. Joseph Priestley and Thomas Paine (*q.v.*)—loosely condemned as atheists (*q.v.*), though they were in fact Deists (*q.v.*)—and carrying his party's war against the Jeffersonians (*q.v.*). In 1800 he returned to England, where he was welcomed by the Tories. In 1802 he began his famous *Weekly Political Register*, which he maintained until his death. It is considered by many to be remarkable for its commentary on British life and politics. Cobbett's hatred of the harsh military system and awareness of the ravages caused by the new industry turned him into a Radical (*q.v.*) in 1804, and once more he was subject to official surveillance. He was imprisoned (1810-1812) for his denunciations of flogging in the service, and in 1817 fled once more to America in fear of seizure and confinement. He returned in 1819, carrying with him the bones of Thomas Paine. He was not allowed to bury them, however, and they were scattered and lost. Before his death, and despite continuing harassment, he gained a seat in Parliament. A farmer for much of his life, despite his almost incredible literary production, he maintained earthy values even when confronted by repressive measures which required protest.

**Code Words,** distinguished from euphemisms (*q.v.*), an effort to disguise coldness or antagonism toward members of ethnic or racial groups. They are often found in public discourse, and mainly by run of the mill conservatives, in which the coldness or antagonism must be maintained beneath a polite veneer. Demeaned people had no need for code words, and expressed themselves freely respecting "honkies," "pigs," and "Mr. Moneybags," "WASPS," (*q.v.*) and "Anglos." "Aggressive" could characterize Jew, Catholic, or, later, Negro. With insults put outside the law and non-WASPS made leading figures in business, education, and public service, code words lost much of their function. Racists could vent their feelings freely in private meetings. In public, old code words lost some of their precision, with "New Yorker" not certainly a Jew, and "law and order" not certainly a call for white policemen, with so many of them in black cities.

**"Coercion,"** see *Invisible Hand, The*

**Coexistence,** a liberal slogan supplementing the concept of Cold War (*q.v.*) which liberals claimed had been maintained against the

Soviet Union since 1917, its year of revolutionary triumph. Before World War II there had been many years of capitalist-Soviet commercial relations, and during World War II massive aid had been given by the United States to the Soviets. Coexistence was initially a liberal response to Soviet arms parity. Its aggressive movements in Berlin, Cuba, and elsewhere indicated a program for unending expansion of influence and power. This, coupled with an American military "build-up," threatened a nuclear showdown dangerous to civilization. The efforts at Detente (*q.v.*) pushed by Presidents Nixon and Ford (*qq.v.*) and Democratic leaders resulted from the principles of coexistence and roused much conservative criticism. Conservatives held that Communists understood nothing but power, and that only evidence of the will to win could curb Soviet aggression. President Reagan's evident determination to bolster American military power alarmed liberal proponents of "coexistence" as well as some conservative European leaders whose countries were on the front line of Soviet might. Coexistence presumed a competition toward peace, with West and East proving the ability of their respective systems to create prosperity among their peoples. Its actual practice involved a constant alert against aggression everywhere, directly or through surrogate (*q.v.*) forces. Conservatives worried about the relative strength of American and Soviet forces, and emphasized the need to move swiftly and without equivocation whenever Soviet military logistics required checkmate. In the mid-1980s many liberals began to see the propriety of the conservatives' call for vigilance. George F. Kennan, *On Dealing with the Communist World* (1964); Henry G. Aubrey, *Coexistence: Economic Challenge and Response* (1961); Richard M. Nixon, *The Real War* (1980) and *The Real Peace* (1983).

**Cold War, The,** a somber product of World War II which massed the Soviet Union and its satellites against the United States and the other NATO (*q.v.*) nations. Many conservatives expressed increased bitterness over government decisions during and after World War II which they blamed for allowing an all-but-prostrate Soviet Union to become one of the greatest military powers on earth. Whether decisions at the great conferences at Teheran and Yalta constituted a betrayal of national interest can never be proven; many liberals argue that the Soviets could not have been prevented from dominating eastern Europe and the East generally. Conservatives, however, have tended to hold that subsequent aid plans to halt Soviet expansionism—the Truman Plan, the Marshall Plan, the Alliance for Progress—were grossly mismanaged, putting arms and power in the hands of those notably Marxists who conflicted with American needs. Government spokesmen in response argued that America could not impose its form of government and economy on others, and that the generally agreed aim of "coexistence" (*q.v.*) with the Soviet Union required a flexible approach which recognized differences while distinguishing basic foes from nations accepting principles of freedom. The *National Review*, as a spokesman for modern conservatism, denied this premise. Socialism (*q.v.*), it asserted, is a failure everywhere: a fact which must be faced. To sustain it anywhere with aid and recognition is to drain the West of its resources and to organize its defeats. Walter Lippmann, *The Cold War* (1947); N. A. Graebner, ed., *The Cold War* (1976).

**Coleridge, Samuel Taylor** (1772-1834), British poet and philosopher whose eccentric career represented a romantic, individualistic reaction to the Utilitarian (*q.v.*) outlook. His early career was that of a poet and friend of nature. He was an associate of William Wordsworth, and a transcendentalist (*q.v.*) who first hailed the French Revolution (*q.v.*) as an emancipating force. Hope for humanity turned to hatred of Napoleon and all he symbolized in opposition to social order and religion. How much Coleridge's idealism and sense of virtue in government and piety owed to his disorganized life and long addiction to opium is difficult to judge. His best conservative writings built on principles enunciated in social and political terms by Edmund Burke (*q.v.*). Coleridge's notable conservatism went hand in hand with an unconventional lifestyle, a union unimaginable to many liberals. His works are varied, brilliant, and memorable in all his fields; see his *Biographia Literaria* (1817) and *Essay on Church and State* (1830), among *Collected Works*, ed. K. Coburn (1969-1972); also the famous scholarly adventure into the sources of his poem remembered from a dream, "Kubla Khan," J. L. Lowes's *The Road to Xanadu* (1930). Coleridge was an inspiring and persuasive conversationalist, and influential on such later conservatives as Russell Kirk (*q.v.*).

**Collectivism,** basically abhorrent to conservative philosophy. The term is used somewhat more precisely among Europeans, referring to socialist states which force the building and habitation of collectives at the expense of free choice and free enterprise, and also to the general power wielded by a Stalin or Hitler (*q.v.*). There being no such condition in America, extreme American conservatives viewed with suspicion those who studied cooperation or sponsored cooperatives, thus appearing to take a first step toward the more horrendous programs abroad. This made Edward Bellamy (*q.v.*) a collectivist to these conservatives as well as a utopian (*q.v.*). E. Merrill Root, in the 1953 *Freeman* (*q.v.*), called the famous poet Archibald MacLeish a collectivist.

**Colonization,** like "imperialism" (*q.v.*) made infamous by Third World (*q.v.*) agitation. Agents of colonization in the 18th and 19th centuries were seen as ground-breakers and bearers of light, progress, and Christianity. In contrast are Third-World descriptions of colonized lands as paradises of peace and fruitfulness overcome by brutal exploiters. India offered the complex situation of an older civilization with British modes and features superimposed. Chinese patriots found bitter memories in the Open Door Policy (see Hay, John). "Native Americans" was used to describe American Indians (*q.v.*), suggesting to some their original title to the American mainland. Although colonies and colonization movements went back to antiquity, they appeared to have no future in the contemporary etiquette of international relations. The term "colonization" has persisted in the language of space probes; see Erik Bergaust, *Colonizing the Planets* (1975). See also Expansionism.

**Coming Defeat of Communism, The,** (1950), by James Burnham (*q.v.*), an analysis valued by many intellectual conservatives as presenting a plan for resisting and overcoming Communist machinations and asserting the principles of freedom and free enterprise. Such principles came sharply from one who had been himself pro-Communist somewhat more than a decade earlier.

**Comintern,** agency of the Third International, set up under Lenin (*q.v.*) as a combination of Communist parties everywhere to carry on the work for world revolution. It was early seen as a sinister force by conservatives, who made efforts to persuade the general population of the threat it posed to American freedoms. In fact, it posed a threat to the national Communist parties as well, organized under expectations of contributing to the creation of a "new world." It soon became evident that the U.S.S.R. was not just another Communist-led land, but the actual ruler of the Comintern. Stalin's rise to power, his expulsion or execution of "old Bolsheviks," and his dictatorial powers were applied also to the Comintern, the annual meetings of which he curtailed. National parties became subject to his direct rule, dissident factions being expelled and denounced as agents of capitalism. The Comintern perished of lack of use. Some of its functions were assumed by the Warsaw Pact (1955), uniting countries behind the Iron Curtain (*q.v.*) and subject to Soviet domination. Other Communist parties in the world received direct aid or instructions from the Soviets or their agents and sympathizers. Conservatives worked to expose Soviet domination in Cuba, Nicaragua, Angola, and numerous other lands, and to urge a foreign policy which helped friends and harmed foes. Jeane J. Kirkpatrick (*q.v.*), ed., *The Strategy of Deception: A Study in Communist Tactics* (1963).

**Commentary,** a magazine originally intended to give an outlet to Jewish intellectuals. It attracted substantial talents, mainly of a liberal persuasion; see *The Commentary Reader*, edited by Norman Podhoretz (1966). For a sense of their accomplishments see M. J. Friedman's "The Enigma of Unpopularity...

Wallace Markfield," an exposition of Markfield's *To an Early Grave* (1964) (Filler, ed., *Seasoned Authors for a New Season* [1980]). Non-Jewish authors also contributed to *Commentary*. The turn of Podhoretz (*q.v.*) away from liberalism was part of the emergence of neo-conservative publication, arousing the abuse of many of his liberal colleagues.

**Commercialism,** a key factor in the perceptions of conservatives, especially as identified with the rise of industry and its attendant characteristics. The British economic historian Richard H. Tawney, in his *Religion and the Rise of Capitalism* (1926), saw conservatism and commercialism as related, commercialism being accompanied with "pious ejaculations"—though expressions of devoutness could be found among all classes. Although persons of conservative outlook were indeed dominant in commerce, and furthered business above other values, many strove to rationalize their major concerns. Some became notorious when social values failed them as when Cornelius Vanderbilt proclaimed that he was above the law ("I've got the money, haint' I?"), or when the financial buccaneer Jim Fisk delivered himself of the view that nothing was lost in his activities except honor. Carnegie and Rockefeller (*qq.v.*) were notable among those industrialists who held themselves to be "stewards" of the funds they amassed, to be expended for the social good. Ivy Lee (*q.v.*) was notable for creating a public-relations operation to justify the actions of free-wheeling entrepreneurs. Advertising (*q.v.*) and public relations became major avenues through which commercialism was best furthered, both receiving vigorous defense as well as criticism and worse. A constant flow of news and revelation showed industrialists contriving monopolies, using "controlled depreciation" (*q.v.*) to produce shoddy products, trading with the nation's enemies, and otherwise substituting commerce for stewardship. However, the rise of labor and the welfare state introduced such new commercial concepts as workers' benefits, wealth redistribution, democratic opportunity, and compassion (*q.v.*). Although principled conservatives deplored the excesses of capitalism and repudiated its crasser manifestations in commercialism, their fear of planning and their will toward social order placed limits on many of their strictures, as did their sensitivity to labor and welfare malfeasance. Many liberals were pleased when they could discover deviations from high principles in conservatives; *New York* magazine was gratified to learn that William F. Buckley, Jr. (*q.v.*) owned a radio station which played rock music, a form of music Buckley professed to despise. Russell Kirk (*q.v.*), reminiscing about the founding of *Modern Age* (*q.v.*), noted his difficulty in acquiring well-to-do conservative support for intellectual enterprises such as his own. Norman S. Gras, *Business & Capitalism* (1939); Thomas M. Garrett, *Business Ethics* (1966); C. C. Walton, ed., *Business and Social Progress* (1970); Richard D. Steade, *Business and Society in Transition* (1975); Neil H. Jacoby, *Business-Government Relationship: A Reassessment* (1975); Alan Heslop, *Business-Government Relations* (1976); Bert F. Hoselitz and Wilbert E. Moore, eds., *Industrialization and Society* (1963). See also Free Enterprise; Rand, Ayn; Gilder, George.

**Communism,** with its variants of socialism and collectivism (*qq.v.*), the major enemy of conservative thought. Although it emerged from socialism, with the advent of the Soviet Union (*q.v.*), it differed from socialism in its sharper sense of class war and its totalitarian control of society. Socialism was all but liberal in its expectations of electoral victories, and attracted liberal sympathy, and even some conservative sympathy, especially when seen as a transitional concept toward greater government social and economic regulation. "We are all socialists today" was a popular statement before World War I. After the war "socialist" and quasi-"socialist" governments emerged which non-socialist governments had to recognize for expedient reasons. Although anti-communism harked back to the fear and horror evoked by the Paris Commune of 1871, and although Communism was often used to explain away corruption and incompetence (Warren G. Harding's [*q.v.*] corrupt Attorney-General Harry M. Daugherty blamed his troubles on the machinations of Communists), its major role in conservative thinking derived from the 1930s. The persisting Depression seemed to indicate to people of all classes intimations that free enterprise was obsolete and the Soviet Union the wave of the future. Stalin's (*q.v.*) failure to stem Fascism alone, plus revelations of his treacheries and mass murders, further hardened conservative opposition to Communists. The extensions of Soviet power and Russian development of the atomic bomb, thanks in part to the treason of some Western intellectuals, along with the rise of Chinese Communism, aroused conservative anti-Communism often buttressed by philosophical and religious principles, which often extended to socialist and collectivist programs of any kind. Liberal viewpoints were seen by some conservatives as leading to Communism. A basic conservative contention was that despite diplomatic and cultural exchanges, the fundamental enmity of Communists for the Free World remained unchanged. The struggle between Western and Communist nations for influence among aligned (*q.v.*) and "unaligned" nations, involving momentous considerations of raw materials and strategic defense, ensured that the arguments for and against cooperation with Communist or "socialist" nations would continue indefinitely. Alarming to conservatives were the elements at home who, fearing atomic war, were ready for all compromises which might seem to protect "peace."

**Communist Imperialism**, a phenomenon of the post-World War II era, see Imperialism and Reform, Filler, DASC. Earlier, Soviet inroads into adjacent territory could be justified or defended by many as the spreading of a workers' revolution, as a "defense of the Workers Fatherland," or as uprisings by nations oppressed by feudal or capitalist regimes. Even the Soviet takeover of Latvia, Lithuania, and Estonia was accepted abroad as reflecting Soviet sensitivity to its place in a world of powerful capitalist nations eager to undermine the "great socialist experiment." Stalin's (*q.v.*) destruction of the Third International—symbol of a community of Communist parties around the world—his creation of an Iron Curtain (*q.v.*) behind which he plundered nations freely and, most important, his development of the atomic bomb achieved partly through the efforts of traitors in Western countries, all built a perception of the Soviets, and later to a lesser degree of the Mainland Chinese, as aggressive forces seeking to dominate the world with armed might established at the expense of their own people. Revelations of the "Gulag" (*q.v.*) helped mold images of Communist oppression. As Soviet and Chinese adventures in Poland, Hungary, Afghanistan, Tibet, Indochina, Korea, and elsewhere multiplied it became more difficult to identify imperialism solely with Western activities. The image of a greedy West opposed to peace-loving Communist nations became harder to maintain, especially as Soviet arms were used to implement surrogate (*q.v.*) nations in confrontation with others supported or advised by Western powers. Matters came to a head on September 1, 1983, when a Soviet plane, after firing "warning shots with tracer shells," brought down a South Korean commercial airline carrying 269 passengers, 50 of them American. The Soviets later claimed that the plane had been on a "spying" mission and transgressing Soviet air space. To most observers this claim was outlandish, to say the least. The incident was a lurid reminder of the May 7, 1915 sinking of the British transatlantic steamer *Lusitania* by a German submarine, an incident which led to American entry into World War I. Colin Simpson, *The Lusitania* (1973); J. J. Stephen, *Sakhalin* (1971); G. Lichtheim, *Imperialism* (1970); K. E. Boulding and T. Mukerjee, ed., *Economic Imperialism* (1972); A. B. Ulam, *Expansion and Coexistence: Soviet Foreign Policy 1917-1967* (1968) and *The Rivals: America and Russia since World War II* (1971).

**Compassion,** a classical word denoting graciousness, social conscience, and human understanding. Since the 1960s it has been increasingly used by liberal advocates of government social programs for the poor and needy. The implication has been that only those who advocate such programs can be said to have compassion. Conservatives reply that reducing such government activities and relying more on free enterprise would stimulate the economy and provide the jobs that the poor and needy require to better their lives. To many conservatives the word "compassion" has become a liberal euphemism (*q.v.*). Republicans tended to feel for the little man, much in the same manner of William Graham Sumner (*q.v.*), the Free Trade advocate.

**Competition,** basic to the philosophy of conservatism, which sees the competitive factor as necessary to maintaining a nation's vigor and optimum use of resources. The modern conservative understanding of competition differs from earlier Darwinism, as expounded by Thomas Henry Huxley, in rejecting its biological basis. It is also in opposition to cooperation as an element in socialism, and shows no interest in such investigations as those of Prince Kropotkin, whose *Mutual Aid* (1902) maintained that nature was not warlike and aggressive, but gave evidence of a division of labor. Although capitalists praised competition as bringing out the best in workers and researchers, their critics pointed to the movement within industry toward monopoly (*q.v.*) and the control of researchers in the interest of profits. Defenders of big business, however, found zest and competition even within large consolidations. They were also gratified when the Soviet Union and other Communist nations felt compelled to institute more and more elements of competition and free enterprise in their economies in order to overcome economic and industrial failures. See also Commercialism.

**Comprehensive Employment and Training Act,** see Unemployment

**Computers,** see Social Sciences

**Comstock, Anthony** (1844-1915), often used as symbol of a repressive censorship. His *Fraud Exposed* (1880) made many legitimate points about the society of its day. That Comstock endangered free speech and communication in his crusade, however, was beyond doubt. Fortunately, there were rational people at the time who knew that his zeal threatened freedom and the finer impulses in society, to say nothing of its threat to classical literature. Comstock stirred numerous anti-Comstocks to action. In sum he was a man with a cause, rather than a symbol of society. Heywood Broun and Margaret Leech, *Anthony Comstock: Roundsman of the Lord* (1927), Robert W. Haney, *Comstockery in America: Patterns of Censorship and Control* (1960).

**Comte, Auguste** (1798-1857), French philosopher known for his "Positivism," on the face of it liberal, in essence a conservative view of life and social operations. His *System of Positive Politics* (1852-4) saw the history of mankind as having passed through theological and metaphysical stages, and having entered into a "positive" stage, to be final and stable. Though apparently open to all necessary changes, Comte saw reigning traditions as good and required. This should have endeared him to Establishment figures; but they were, instead, offended by the details of his social system, which he seemed to arrange arbitrarily according to his religious, sexual, and even class and national preferences. Comte's credibility with the Establishment of his day was ruined. He lost disciples and his academic post. Although his ideas have continued to intrigue many, his role as a conservative force has diminished.

**"Conceptualizations,"** see Social Sciences

**Concessions,** denoting a curious change in labor-management relations. Labor traditionally fought for concessions with respect to wages, hours, union organization, rest periods, and rights in the hiring and firing process. As a result of great gains during the New Deal era, World War II, and after—through mediation, law, and the fruits of an expanding economy—labor was able to wield great power in its negotiations with management. Management was generally content to give in to labor's demands so long as the costs could be passed along to consumers. The late 1970s, however, revealed a dismal picture of inflation, municipal coffers, depressed industries, low productivity, and strong foreign competition. Despite labor protests, industries began to rid themselves of burdensome plants and redundant employees, and fought demands for increases in labor perquisites of various kinds. Labor unions were constrained to make "concessions" to management to prevent catastrophe. The irony was not lost on many students of American industry.

**Congress.** It has fluctuated in popular and partisan regard, depending on its membership and personalities. The House of Representatives, as the most popular branch, has attracted a variety of picturesque characters, sometimes of the distinction of John Quincy Adams (*q.v.*), but as often with the demagogic (*q.v.*) qualities of a David Crockett. He was put up as the Whig answer to his fellow-Tennessean Andrew Jackson. Jackson's follower refused to run against Crockett on the grounds that he did not care to represent people who would listen to such absurd rant as Crockett provided. Congress was a fertile breeding ground of "bunk" which often amused those who followed its operations, as when Felix Walker of the 16th Congress suggested that fellow-members need not listen to his peroration since it was only intended for his constituents in Buncombe County, North Carolina. As famous was Webster Flanagan's, of Texas, question at the 1880 Republican Convention which mooted the possibility of Civil service planks for curbing the growth of patronage jobs: "What are we up here for?" House of Representatives "czars" who kept tight hold of its Rules Committee later met bipartisan efforts at reform among its members. The Senate, created as an American equivalent to the British House of Lords, also had its distinguished and less distinguished eras. Willmoore Kendall (*q.v.*) complained, as did many others, that Congress had the power to resist infringements on the Constitution, but had not adequately used it. Dismay over Supreme Court (*q.v.*) decisions caused many conservatives to look to the Congress for legislative relief. James Burnham, *Congress and the American Tradition* (1959); R. and L. T. Rienow, *Of Snuff, Sin and the Senate* (1965); Paul Van Riper, *History of the United States Civil Service* (1958).

**Conjecture,** a more serious and less popularized version of efforts to prepare for contingencies than Futurism (*q.v.*), it entered into philosophical efforts to establish possibilities of arriving at truth, and also of projecting forecasts which could aid practical efforts at preparing for new conditions or emergencies. Bernard de Jouvenel (*q.v.*) was a principal in the development of the *Futuribles*, a group which issued publications seeking to define problems in conjecture which needed conscious attention in order to avoid false premises and assumptions. His *The Art of Conjecture* (1967) brought together many of their findings. See also Karl R. Popper, *Conjectures and Refutations: The Growth of Scientific Knowledge* (1963), dedicated to Friedrich A. von Hayek and constituting an approach to his philosophy of rational trial and error.

**Conscience of a Conservative, The** (1960), by Barry Goldwater (*q.v.*). It circulated in numerous editions throughout the country. The book is generally credited with giving his bid for the Republican Presidential nomination in 1964 its original and increasing impetus. (See also *Choice, Not an Echo, A.*) In his book Goldwater covered all vital areas: states rights, civil rights, the farmer, labor, taxes, welfare, education, and the problems of the Soviet Union (*qq.v.*). His examinations were forthright, constitutional, and well-presented. Though Goldwater lost the election, many conservatives declared that his campaign had been a success. It had given them a program, provided them with leadership, and prepared the way for further campaigns.

**Consensus,** a deceptive concept which may from time to time seem valid, but may also disappear unexpectedly. Daniel Boorstin (*q.v.*), among others, held that there was a long-tried liberal consensus in America: this was essentially, and because of its history (*q.v.*), a liberal country. The hypothesis required passing over much of America's past. Nevertheless, it was true that commercialism (*q.v.*) had transcended nativist, activist, even anti-Soviet (*qq.v.*) sentiments. Americans did not seem to harbor major grudges against one another, though the country has often been split by large-scale sectional (*q.v.*) and political differences. Thomas Jefferson (*q.v.*), in his First Inaugural Address, said, "We are all Federalists. We are all Republicans." This, however, was an aspiration, rather than a fact. Nevertheless, it did work, to a degree. Conservatives have never had a full consensus among themselves. Members of the John Birch Society felt far removed from "Moderate Republicans."

Intellectuals often had limited appreciation of the vagaries of business. Many conservatives tired of Ayn Rand, and were unsure of what to make of libertarians (*qq.v.* for above). They did at times achieve consensus of a sort. Transitional (*q.v.*) figures were often welcomed. New Rightists (*q.v.*) were not happy with all of Reagan's (*q.v.*) policies, but they agreed that they had "nowhere else to go." Reagan was seen as seeking to "appease" them from time to time. Regard and respect for religion (*q.v.*) provided a basic premise for almost all conservatives. James P. Young, ed., *Consensus and Conflict: Readings in American Politics* (1972); D. Cummins and W. G. White, *Consensus and Turmoil: The 1950s and 1960s* (1973); B. Sternsher, *Consensus, Conflict, and American Historians* (1975).

**Conservatism,** always a factor in social and human affairs, sometimes more visible in one era than another. It should be distinguished from reactionism (*q.v.*), though its foes labor to associate the two concepts. It involves differences with commercialism (*q.v.*), which can ramify through all classes. Although the well-to-do are often equated with conservatism, it can show surprising strength among the less affluent. Lenin (*q.v.*) predicted that, when the revolution came, it would be funded by the rich. Indeed, they have often subsidized movements intended to overthrow the reigning establishment. The American Revolution (*q.v.*) is unimaginable without the adherence and leadership of conservatives. The constant problem of keeping order in the settled parts of America and of controlling the populations which were attracted by the opportunities on the frontier (*q.v.*) was largely dealt with by conservatives. They took as ideological mentors such spokesmen as Edmund Burke, James Madison, John Adams, John Randolph, Fisher Ames, William Graham Sumner, and Abraham Lincoln, (*qq.v.*) They created a political line which extended from Federalism into the Whig movement, and then into the long history of Republicanism. Although there were indeed large numbers of conservatives among the Democrats of the mid-19th century who from their standpoint saw "radicalism" in an anti-slavery Republican Party, other issues separated conservatives from liberals and radicals at that time. The Democrats adhered to the Free Trade (*q.v.*) doctrine, hoping it would provide better exchange goods for cotton; the largely conservative Grover Cleveland (*q.v.*) was won over to Free Trade, though not for the cheaper bread and wool for the poor which motivated some reformers. Conservatives generally abjured such panaceas (*q.v.*) for hard times. They were suspicious of the newly arrived immigrants (*q.v.*), sharing such sentiments with Populists (*q.v.*), whom they nevertheless had reasons to hold at arm's length for business reasons. They viewed the more militant trade unionists (*q.v.*) as upsetting the social order. Still, conservatives could be found supporting a wide range of reforms. William Ellery Channing and Andrew Carnegie (*qq.v.*) favored peace, rather than war, with Mexico and later Spain. Josepine Shaw Lowell (*q.v.*) demanded a more humane outlook toward the poor, the imprisoned, and women generally. Jane Addams (*q.v.*) welcomed immigrants and helped them adjust to strange conditions. Conservatives could be found in many parts of the Progressive (*q.v.*) movement, concerned for a better railroad policy, a better conservation policy, municipal rectitude, better and more democratic schooling, and the like. Even many social democrats of the era were clearly conservative in their approach, though they could be distinguished from those who feared change on principle. World War I intervention separated liberals from conservatives, and gave the former a receptivity to change, even radical change, such as more firmly set conservatives did not respect. It produced Herbert Hoover's (*q.v.*) intransigent attitude toward Depression conditions, and put conservative doctrine in the shadows through the era of Franklin D. Roosevelt (*q.v.*). A new conservatism, signaled by the appearance of Russell Kirk (*q.v.*), resulted from the rising power of the Soviet Union and Communist China, the disintegration of erstwhile imperialism, the ominous message of the atomic bomb, the need for domestic security from subversive elements, eroding bureaucratic and welfare (*q.v.*) systems, and a general sense that possessions and opportunities were no longer in individual hands and potential. The decline of the cities, the decay of patriotism, and the evidence that decisions abroad directly affected possibilities at home suggested the need for a regrouping of Americans according to interests and power. With labor equal and sometimes more than equal in influence in local and national administrations, old liberal tenets based on the powerless lost persuasiveness and required refreshment. In the mid-1980s conservatives touting free enterprise and individual initiatives found themselves in a better position to win voters and attention. D. H. Fischer, *The Revolution of American Conservatism* (1965); Glenn D. Wilson, *The Psychology of Conservatism* (1973); N. M. Wilensky, *Conservatism in the Progressive Era: The Taft Republicans of 1912* (1965); Edwin L. Dale, *Conservatives in Power: A Study in Frustration* (1960); James Reichley, *Conservatism in an Age of Change: The Nixon and Ford Administrations* (1981); The Conservative Society of America, *A Declaration of Conservative Principles* (New Orleans) (1960); G. Kolko, *The Triumph of Conservatism* (1963).

**Conservatism and Reform.** In British politics the two were identified after the Reform Bill of 1832, resulting in a long history of "Tory socialism." The identification of reform with liberalism was an American development. Many radical leftists in America held that famous reforms were "really" conservative or even "reactionary," standing in the way of "true" reform, which would point toward socialism. Compare Filler, *Appointment at Armageddon*. For the British experience, see Sir Arthur Bryant, *The Spirit of Conservatism* (1929); Harold Macmillan, *The Middle Way* (1938); and Paul Smith, *Disraelian Conservatism and Social Reform* (1967). See also Reform and Conservatism.

**Conservative Book Club,** founded 1964 by Neil McCaffrey. It made a profit for fourteen years, with a high mark of 36,000 members late in the 1960s. It suffered bad management (1978-1982), but then came back to McCaffrey. Helped too by the rise of modern conservatism, it regained financial health and lively, efficient marketing, and had promising prospects.

**Conservative Caucus, The,** an activist conservative organization with headquarters in Washington which kept watch over government operations, gave testimony before committees, issued publications, and helped organize campaigns. Its *Conservative Manifesto* was a general statement of principles. Other publications for stimulating support nationwide included *Senate Issues Yearbook*, *Senate Report*, *Grass Roots*, *Members Report*, and *Annual Report*. Its causes in 1983 included "defunding of the Left"; the Caucus argued the government funds were made available by stratagem to thousands of liberal organizations. It also demanded a single tax rate of 10 percent to end the bureaucratic (*q.v.*) operations of Internal Revenue, and a "restoration" of the Monroe Doctrine. See Constitution of the United States.

**Conservative Decade, The,** (1980), by James C. Roberts, an overview of the conservative movement, its structure and personalities, programs and issues, with a prophetic introduction by Ronald Reagan (*q.v.*) contributed before his own nomination for the Presidency. Its most significant feature is its tracing of individual careers in conservative circles, suggesting the impressive scope of the conservative movement. It describes the mailing empire of Richard Viguerie (*q.v.*) and touches on the fields of journalism, research, Christian advocacy, political organization, and student, legal, and other enterprises. Their targets include such liberal centers as unions, major papers, Ralph Nader activist groups, and the Democratic Party. The major conservative organizations, with their budgets and staff, are also included. Staffs were not always commensurate with budget. The American Conservative Union, with a budget of $2.8 million had 19 staff members; the Pacific Legal Foundation, with a budget of $3 million had 55. The American Tax Reduction Movement, highly prized in conservative labors, declared 15 staff members, and a budget of some $5.75 million. The powerful American Enterprise Institute (*q.v.*) employed no fewer than 150 persons, with a $7 million budget. The same budget carried out the work of the

National Right to Work Foundation, with its 45-member staff. See Right to Work.

**Conservative Illusion, The** (1959), by M. Morton Auerbach, a Ph.D. thesis which predicted the imminent demise of conservatism. The book moved through historical forms of conservatism, from Plato to Edmund Burke (*qq.v.*) and beyond, finding, them all moving against the tide of expanding freedoms, and, in the United States, against tradition itself—which was wholly liberal. "Reactionaries" like Paul Elmer More and Irving Babbitt (*qq.v.*) were succeeded by a variety of "confused" would-be conservatives like Weaver, Kirk, and "McCarthyite liberals" like Buckley (*q.v.*). All operated against a tide which would eventually pull them down.

**Conservative Intellectual Movement in America, Since 1945**, by George H. Nash (1976), a hard-worked Harvard thesis, which broke ground in following through tendencies and major individuals who came together or flew apart while creating a new conservatism able to create programs for a complex time. Asking "What Is Conservatism in America?" Nash described the different approaches of such protagonists as Kirk, Buckley, Kendall, Burnham, and Chodorov (*qq.v.*), among numerous others, described philosophies near to or far from them, from Burke to Leo Strauss (*qq.v.*), and weighed their potential for the new time.

**Conservative Mind, The** (1953), Russell Kirk's (*q.v.*) epochal book which caught attention at home and abroad and gave conservatives a history and a program. It discussed divine intent in contemporary issues, individualism and its sense of life as varied and mysterious—though controlled by social order and classes, and the sanctity of personal property. Although all these ideas were known to a spectrum of conservatives, none earlier had brought together so clear and cohesive a roster of cultural figures and accompanying personalities in one work: beginning with Edmund Burke and highlighting Macaulay, de Tocqueville, Disraeli, Cardinal Newman, and Walter Scott abroad, and John Adams, Alexander Hamilton, John Randolph, Calhoun, and James Fenimore Cooper at home, as well as such critics and commentators as More, Babbitt, and Santayana (*qq.v.*). As featured in *Life* and numerous other publications, *The Conservative Mind* sounded a tocsin not only to conservatives, but to liberals and radicals who helped make a symbolic figure of Kirk and who were not infrequently moved to change in their own outlook and philosophy. The book also gave boost to its publisher Henry Regnery (*q.v.*), whose work and future it affected.

**Conservative Papers, The** (1964), with an introduction by Melvin R. Laird, provided a range of opinions which contributed to the gathering conservative movement. Articles included one by Edward Teller on the uses of nuclear energy; warnings on Soviet satellite countries and conditions in Asia; Henry A. Kissinger (*q.v.*) on "The Essentials of Solidarity in the Weak Alliance"; E. C. Banfield (*q.v.*) on foreign aid doctrines; Milton Friedman (*q.v.*) discussing "Can a Controlled Economy Work?"; and articles on the underdeveloped nations, deficits, labor power, federalism, and civil and religious liberty.

**Conservative Party, NY,** see *Actions Speak Loud*

**Conservative Reformers** in England included "transitional" (*q.v.*) figures in the university who sought to modernize their educational offerings without destroying the heritage of the past. Thus, they worked to maintain religious devoutness and traditions while showing greater receptivity to the truths of natural law (*q.v.*), and to emphasize the values of pre-Christian lore as not in conflict with later revelations. See Aristotelian Ethics and Politics; Platonism. They followed the teachings of Bishop Whately (*q.v.*) while accepting the evidence of material change in life. While Anglicanism held on to its social dominance, it was forced to make way for greater tolerance toward dissenters. D. Newsome, *Godliness and Good Learning* (1961); S. Rothblatt, *Tradition and Change in English Liberal Education* (1976); B. Heeney, *A Different Kind of Gentleman* (1976); M. M. Garland, *Cambridge* [University] before Darwin (1980). See also Shaftesbury, Disraeli.

**Conservative Tradition, The** (1950), edited

by R. J. White, an anthology which traces the roots and growth of conservatism in British political and social life. Selections from Edmund Burke, Benjamin Disraeli, Samuel Taylor Coleridge (*q.v.*), and others down through Randolph Churchill and T. S. Eliot (*q.v.*) show a line of thinking which separates conservatives from the more commercial-minded (*q.v.*) Whigs on one side and the Liberals (*q.v.*) on the other. The tone of the selections makes clear—and *tone* is essential to the program—that Tories placed a special emphasis on order and tradition as instruments of freedom and on monarchy as a binding force in society, a force limited in commercial-minded America. Although conservatism produced a Prime Minister Wellington, with his readiness to ride down striking workers, it also won power for a Disraeli, who distinguished between the poor, meriting all consideration, and the working class, meriting some, but within the confines of freedom rather than socialism. State measures furthering housing and other humane legislation could be positively viewed by many conservatives; what they despised was statism, in which the state took on the bureaucratic and authoritarian character of socialism. See also Shaftesbury, Earl of; Hugh Cecil, *Conservatism* (1912).

**Conspiracy.** Many political groups have professed to see conspiracy against them. There is indeed paranoia, but how to distinguish it clearly from legitimate fears? How to distinguish conspiracy from agreement among friends? A liberal collection, *The Fear of Conspiracy* (1971), edited by D. P. Davis, defined paranoia in politics as a weak, incompetent group being seen as "powerful, monolithic, and virtually infallible organization." Yet a group might be small and able to inflict harm. Certainly, the Communists in America were all but monolithic. The journalist Murray Kempton, himself a former Communist, in his *Part of Our Time*, noted that Communists had been a minority, but that they had comprised a majority of the dedicated—and had been capable of harm. Americans were, indeed, liable to look for scapegoats, rather than more basic causes, and to evade looking into their own hearts. Thus the Birchites (*q.v.*), reviving John Robinson's *Proofs of a Conspiracy against All the Religious and Government of Europe...* (1797), and creating a secret order of their own. *Fear of Conspiracy*, an anthology, brought together allegations about Masonry, Mormonism, Popery, Monopoly, Foreign Powers, the Slave Power, Jews, Reds, Blacks, Labor, the "conspiracy" against silver, and others. Although a liberal bias is apparent, it is regarded by many as more temperate than Richard Hofstadter's *The Paranoid Style in American Politics*. The historian D. H. Fischer observed in his *Historians' Fallacies* that Hofstadter's work itself was paranoid. See Sidney Hook (*q.v.*) *Heresy Yes, Conspiracy No* (1953).

**Constitution of the United States.** It is believed by many conservatives to be the keystone of their faith. One of its most intense interpreters was one of the founders of modern conservatism, Willmoore Kendall (*q.v.*) for whom reading the Founding Fathers (*q.v.*), "accurately" was a first consideration. He saw the Constitution as part of a great, ultimately indomitable tradition: a conservative tradition based in natural law—not Hobbes's (*q.v.*), but reflecting a divine will. Although Locke's (*q.v.*) Social Contract theories had affected the founders' rhetoric, Kendall denied that they had anticipated an equalitarian society. Most of them had been opposed to the Bill of Rights (*q.v.*), he maintained, and the Constitution had to be understood in the context of their larger thoughts and experiences. Conservatives held that in the 1960s the Warren Court (*q.v.*) had led a revolution against the Constitution as given, and that only action by Congress, by the Executive (when called upon to appoint Supreme Court justices), and when necessary, by Constitutional Amendment would bring the law back in line with American traditions and understanding. Liberals satisfied with the trend of Court findings saw in conservative opposition an attempt at building a reactionary law structure, and overthrowing all the liberal gains from the inauguration of the New Deal (*q.v.*). It was evident that social war (*q.v.*) had entered seriously into legal debates extending from municipal courts to the Supreme Court, affecting policies on abortion, civil rights, the death penalty (*qq.v.*) and other vital areas—extending even to foreign affairs and the status of the military. In 1984, eleven liberal members of Congress filed suit claiming the American invasion of Grenada (*q.v.*) had been unconstitutional, and asking the U. S. District Court in Washington to order all American troops out immediately. Another lawsuit, this one by the Conservative Caucus, held that the Administration's intention to abide by the terms of the SALT II (*q.v.*) agreement in the interests of Detente (*q.v.*) transgressed the Constitution and should be halted by court order. Were such suits to be successful, it was obvious that the operations of the Executive and the Defense Department would be seriously, perhaps fatally, curtailed. The Federal Government might even decide to ignore the courts in the interests of national security. This Lincoln had done, in suspending the writ of habeas corpus during the Civil War; see J. G. Randall, *Constitutional Problems under Lincoln* (1926). Although the Supreme Court was often judicious in not pressing law beyond the tolerable, and resisted following the more daring decisions of lower courts, many of its interpretations were highly controversial especially in conservative circles. Whether the Court would follow the new conservative mood of the nation was still undetermined in the mid-1980s. E. S. Corwin, *The Constitution and What It Means Today* (1973 ed.); Rexford G. Tugwell, *The Emerging Constitution* (1974); Paul L. Murphy, *The Constitution in Crisis Times, 1918-1969* (1972); Forrest McDonald, *Novus Ordo Seclorum* (1985).

**Consumerism,** a cause identified in the minds of many with liberalism. Consumerists work to curb negative practices in industry (*q.v.*) and promote increased standards of safety and quality in consumer products. In 1890 Josephine Shaw Lowell founded the Consumers League of New York, putting pressure on merchants and industrialists who mistreated women employees. The League utilized the boycott as well as other means for advancing its cause. It grew into the National Consumers League, which fought against "sweated" labor in the home, and exploitation by cruel and underpaying employers. In the 1930s Consumers Research advised members on the quality and value of consumer products, but also included a radical criticism of capitalist economics in its research. A radical contingent split from the organization to form the Consumers Union. J. B. Matthews (*q.v.*), disillusioned with his associates in the parent organization, left them to become an early resister to Communist programs and techniques. Ralph Nader (see Filler, DASC) rose to the leadership of a new consumerist movement when he published *Unsafe at Any Speed* (1965), an attack on safety standards in the automobile (*q.v.*) industry. Exposure of efforts by General Motors agents to spy on his private activities in order to disgrace him turned public feeling in his favor. With money from the settlement of a subsequent lawsuit he was able to set up agencies to monitor business and government activities which might be wasteful, deceitful, or against the public interest. He attracted young lawyers and others who wished to join him in this work and soon became a national figure. He was applauded for trying to bring to light government and private malfeasance, but his efforts to foist his standards on others by law roused conservative opposition and disturbed many consumers. Nader's calls for increasing government regulation ran counter to the conservative mood of the 1980s, which favored deregulation and less government interference in the marketplace. Interestingly, Nader called for the finances of private business, even though the finances of his own organizations were not made public; see D. M. Burt, *Abuse of Trust: A Report on Ralph Nader's Network* (1982). Meanwhile the Consumer Product Safety Act of 1972 had set up a Consumer Product Safety Commission, partially in response to public interest. The result was the establishment of the Consumer Federation of America. Clearly the ultimate fate of consumerism was in the hands of the public itself. By the mid-1980s the movement seemed to many to have lost much of its strength of earlier decades.

**Continuity,** a basic concept in conservative thought, though not always honored by conservatives themselves. Conservative thought was held to have developed with different nomenclature and emphasis, in a recognizable line from before Plato through the Roman Empire and the Middle Ages—in tradition, culture, and experience. Its economic, industrial, and religious permutations were occasioned by national and international stances and the needs of various peoples and nations. Conservatives, however, held no monopoly on civilization and progress. The use of the term conservative itself was subject to debate. The liberal I. F. Stone, for example, saw Socrates as a conservative; many others saw Christ as a radical. A famous speech by the rebellious Roman slave Spartacus, known to generations of schoolchildren, was in fact written by the 19th century writer Lydia Maria Child, who saw in Spartacus a revolutionary American love of freedom. Ecumenical movements in the 20th century narrowed the distance between followers of Martin Luther and the Catholic (*q.v.*) Church, even while coming to terms with Luther's inordinate hatred of Jews. Deep divisions existed between admirers and critics of Rousseau (see Babbitt, Irving) and the Romantic Movement which had drawn inspiration from him, even among conservatives. Clearly many non-conservatives had added color and vibrancy to life throughout history. Orestes Brownson (*q.v.*), for example, had feet in all camps. So too with a host of other figures and movements involving transitional (*q.v.*) experiences. Continuity, then, could be a shibboleth or a reality. In 1982 a number of professed conservative academic historians began a publication named *Continuity*, issued by the Intercollegiate Studies Institute, a conservative body (*q.v.*).

**Contras,** see Sandinistas

**Contraception,** see Abortion

**Contract Labor,** endorsed by the Office of Commissioner of Immigration in 1865 and permitted to continue until 1885, when agitation forced its abolition. It authorized commercial (*q.v.*) firms to admit laborers from abroad under agreements which made them liable for a year of work to pay off the cost of their passage to the United States. In effect, it created a species of indentured servitude (*q.v.*) and a body of labor which would keep wages low. In practice, it exploited the unready workers and their families, who needed years of travail before they could gain some control of their lives.

**"Controlled Depreciation,"** see Quality Control

**Cooke, Janet,** see Journalism, Investigative

**Coolidge, Calvin** (1872-1933). He was made President of the United States by the death of President Harding (*q.v.*), and re-elected in 1924. In an age of "Disillusionment" (*q.v.*) he could be seen as, ironically, a symbol of business growth, the proliferations of gangsters, and labor unrest. His inactivity became legendary. Many liberal historians saw him as a typical example of Republicanism; see Thomas B. Silver, *Coolidge and the Historians* (1983). His relevance to the modern conservative experience, however, is unclear. His policies have been defended by some conservatives, but without much illumination. His defense of the Republican protective tariffs of 1921 (Emergency Tariff) and 1922 (Fordney-McCumber) on grounds of defending home industry begged the question of the effect of protection in an increasingly interdependent world. Certainly, to conceive of Coolidge as a penetrating intellect can hardly be justified by a reading of his *Autobiography* (1929) and press conferences (H. H. Quint and R. H. Ferrell, eds., *The Talkative President* [1964]). The old problem still remains: Coolidge's attitude toward the Harding scandals, as they overlapped into his Administration's operations; his view of government's responsibility toward industry and toward farmers' interests; his sense of foreign policy, especially as it followed up on the American intervention in World War I. Donald McCoy, *Calvin Coolidge: the Quiet President* (1967); Jules Abels, *In the Time of Silent Cal* (1969); Filler, ed., *The Ascendant President* (1983 ed.).

**Cooper, James Fenimore** (1789-1851). In his time he was judged to be, with Washington Irving (*q.v.*), in the forefront of American literature. Later critical opinion found profundities in Nathaniel Hawthorne which Irving and Cooper both lacked. Both Irving and Cooper were united in conservative sympathies, Cooper being the far more active and concerned of the two. Inspired by Sir Walter Scott—who, like Cooper, took pride in being well-born—and with an equally sharp eye for caste and class, tradition, and the role of women, Cooper produced numerous novels. His *Leather Stocking Tales* were far and away the most popular. They eventually came to be seen as fare for young readers in search of adventure, and were mordantly examined by Mark Twain (see his "Fenimore Cooper's Literary Offenses," *North American Review*, July 1895). Still, they have the validity of myth and give a vivid sense of the changing frontier. In themes, characters, and treatment they have been enormously influential in the subsequent development of American creative writing. Cooper also wrote extensively in defense of conservative values. Abroad, he defended American democracy against the denigration it earned from English and Continental aristocrats. At home, he found an aggressive Jacksonian (*q.v.*) democracy and farm tenants in upper New York anxious to break the bonds of the feudal system established by Dutch patroons. With New York dominated by Whigs, Cooper declared for Jackson though his aim was really Jeffersonian (*q.v.*), positing the rule of the best rather than of mere majorities. With the upstate farmers in revolt, demanding the right to buy the land they had worked, sometimes for generations, Cooper took his stand with his fellow-landowners. He recorded his principles in the too-little-read *Littlepage Chronicles*, comprised of *Satanstoe* (1845), *The Chainbearer* (1845), and *The Redskins* (1846). An interesting work of fiction—which, like all his later works, shows a conscious effort to display his understanding of democracy—is *Ways of the Hour* (1850), a tale of crime and detection. Cooper's essays are clear and unequivocal; of most interest to conservatives are *Notions of the Americans* (1828) and *The American Democrat* (1838). See R. E. Spiller, *Fenimore Cooper, Critic of His Times* (1931); and J. F. Ross, *Social Criticism of Fenimore Cooper* (1933).

**Cooperation,** see Competition

**Cooperatives,** originally identified with idealistic dreams of expanded democracy and socialism. In the 19th century they attracted Robert Owen in Great Britain and the brilliant radicals and intellectuals who developed Brook Farm in Massachusetts, among many others; see Filler, DASC. Farmer's troubles after the Civil War brought forth cooperative efforts intended to ease their problems, with little thought for theories of price and distribution. Although cooperative ideas and social experiments inspired such idealists and socialists as Edward Bellamy (*q.v.*) and Upton Sinclair, the emphasis of many cooperatives on commodities and techniques for saving began to interest conservative supporters of capitalism. The Cooperative League of the United States of America, founded 1916, was more centrist than radical. Government offices eventually began providing information regarding the setting up of cooperatives for the use of farmers and others interested in consumer's stores and credit unions. To most people cooperatives are a form of private enterprise. Some conservatives, however, see them as a first step toward socialism.

**Corn Laws,** see Shaftesbury, Earl of

**Corporations** (1904), by John P. Davis, a classic work. Published posthumously—the actual manuscript having been completed in 1897—it traced the rise of the corporation through ecclesiastical, feudal, municipal, and guild bodies, and such later developments as regulated companies, joint-stock companies, and colonial companies. Regretfully, this mature scholar did not live long enough to write his projected history of modern corporations. He could only note the great tendency toward organizations of every kind, whether "corporations" in name or in essence. According to Davis, the citizen "discovers, in fine, that citizenship in his country has been largely metamorphosed into membership in corporations and patriotism into fidelity to them."

**"Corrupt Bargain,"** see Elections

**Corruption,** a perennial in political human affairs, but often seen differently by conservatives and liberals. Big-city corruption in the late 19th century was considered a priority by "Goo Goos" (*q.v.*), less so by Progressives, who were more concerned with massive theft of public resources by oil, timber, and other "barons" of industry. Progressives identified "reform" groups with conservative hatred and fear of New Immigrants (*q.v.*). However, the Progressive movement itself engendered more vigorous reform movements, which modernized city administrations without necessarily ending the corruption attending favoritism, the manipulations of political machines, and connections with vice and crime. Corruption raged and waned throughout the 20th century, and no level of government seemed immune to its deleterious effect. See also PACs.

**"Counter-Revolution,"** a term common in radical (*q.v.*) history and thought. Radicalism assumed progress (*q.v.*) in social development, with a progression of changes from obsolete forms of society to "higher" or more "modern" relations. Since it was assumed that "reactionary" (*q.v.*) elements would not willingly give up their privileges, revolution (*q.v.*) by popular consensus or by bloody travail was thus justified. A few social forces, such as those seeking to sustain the Czarist cause in Russia gladly assumed the title of "counter-revolutionary," but most opponents of Communism scorned the phrase as revolutionary jargon and preferred other nationalistic or conservative descriptions of their cause. The entrenchment of Communist regimes, with repressive institutions of their own, impugned their revolutionary origins, and even made them appear to be "counter-revolutionary" to their radical critics. Trotskyites, for example, advocated "permanent revolution." But the professed revolutionary origins of Communist nations continued to give meaning to the idea of "counter-revolution," especially for the foes of revolution (*q.v.*).

**Cozzens, James Gould** (1903-1978), outstanding conservative novelist of the 20th century. He developed his art slowly in a period not suited to his talents, and held persistently to the values of conservatism. His characters probed the moral dilemmas of faith, justice, patriotism, and law. Increasingly, his fiction included newer elements in society—persons of foreign extraction, for example—while maintaining conservative values. His three most challenging works—disturbing to many liberal critics but with wide circulation—were *The Just and the Unjust* (1942), *Guard of Honor* (1948)—which won the Pulitzer Prize, and *By Love Possessed* (1957)—which stirred the greatest controversy of all. All the books gave evidence of close attention to telling detail and knowledge of law and of social mores, and, in the case of *Guard of Honor*, of the military establishment. *Guard of Honor* has been called one of the very best of World War II novels. Liberal critics such as Dwight MacDonald attacked *By Love Possessed*; see "By Cozzens Possessed" in *Against the American Grain* (1962). However, even William F. Buckley, Jr. found it unsatisfying, although without citing evidence of its alleged failures. Yet to many the novel contained subtleties of great distinction. See Filler, ed. *A Question of Quality: Popularity and Value in Modern Creative Writing* (1976).

**Cram, Ralph Adams** (1863-1942), architect and author. He was famous for his neo-Gothic architectural designs, most notably the Cathedral of St. John the Divine in New York. Although he wrote influential books in architecture, his works in defense of the conservative viewpoint were less influential, among conservatives as well as others; see *The Nemesis of Mediocrity* (1918) and *The End of Democracy* (1937), among other writings. Robert Muccigrosso, *American Gothic: The Mind and Art of Ralph Adams Cram* (1980).

**Crane, Philip M.** see *Democrats' Dilemma, The*

**"Creationism,"** a term employed by religious partisans who see the theory of evolution as inconsistent with a literal interpretation of the Book of Genesis. Some creationists, who call themselves scientific creationists, see the theory of evolution as scientifically unsound or inadequate to explain the origins of life and the universe. Although there are some scientific theories which are tantalizingly close to the Biblical account of creation—the "Big Bang" theory of the origin of the Universe, for example—most scientists accept evolution as valid and uncontroversial. The question as it has entered the political and social arena involves what is to be taught in science classes in the public schools. Shall children of devout fundamentalists, for example, be taught, in effect, that the Book of Genesis is not to be taken literally? Some conservatives, supporting the right of creationists, link the issue with school prayer (*q.v.*) and the Constitution. Interesting is the fact that most mainline churches see no contradiction between the theory of evolution and the religious accounts of creation. Also interesting is the fact that the theory of evolution is generating increasing scrutiny and some skepticism in the scientific community. (See Darwinism.) Ronald L. Numbers, "Creationism in 20th-Century America," *Science*, November 5, 1982.

**Crédit Mobilier,** a construction company set up under Congressional authority to carry out the purposes of the bill, signed by President Lincoln in 1864, to create the Union Pacific Railroad. A Congressman, Oakes Ames of Massachusetts, was placed in charge of contracts and construction. In 1872 it was revealed that Administration figures, including Vice-President Schuyler Colfax and Senator James A. Garfield, later to be President, had received stock in Crédit Mobilier. It was charged that these transactions had been in return for political influence. Congressman Ames was made the central figure in the alleged plot. It was also claimed that some $40 million in costs was unaccounted for. Crédit Mobilier became a symbol of political corruption (*q.v.*) in the Grant Administration. Shortly following his censure in Congress, Ames died. He was later posthumously exonerated in his home state. Despite the allegations of scandal the Union Pacific Railroad found itself in notable financial condition. The original charges fitted well with the "Robber Barons" (*q.v.*) concept, but to most disinterested observers they remained unproven. Still, Daniel J. Boorstin's (*q.v.*) *A History of the United States* (1981), written with Brooks Mather Kelley and Ruth Frankel Boorstin, speaks of bribed politicians and railroad officers making "enormous sums" from the "swindle." See, however, Robert William Fogel, *The Union Pacific Railroad, a Case of Premature Enterprise* (1960); J. B. Crawford, *The Credit Mobilier of America* (1880); Charles Edgar Ames, *Pioneering the Union Pacific* (1969). Allan Nevins (*q.v.*), in his article on Ames in the *Dictionary of American Biography* (1928), vindicates Ames.

**Crime**, one measure of the state of society, its causes and cures often differently perceived by conservatives tended to concentrate on measures against the criminals themselves, liberals on alleviating the conditions which they saw as creating criminals. In the 1970s the crime rate jumped enormously throughout the United States. In many areas the criminal justice system was unable to handle the increasing number of cases. A growing concern for the rights of defendants, sparked by Supreme Court (*q.v.*) decisions and a liberal social climate, further hampered the efforts of the courts to mete out justice. Overcrowded prisons also added to the problem. The result was that crime became more "profitable" for the average criminal. There was little chance of being arrested by an overworked police force, and less chance of ever going to trial, being convicted, and spending substantial time in prison. The growing percentage of young people in the population exacerbated the problem, a result of the postwar Baby Boom. Young people tended to commit a disproportionate share of crimes—especially violent crimes. In addition, the era was marked by lack of respect for authority, which many conservatives saw as the result of liberal social attitudes. Clearly, the liberal tendency to "explain away" criminal behavior did little to prevent or deal with such behavior. More conservative social attitudes in the country in the 1980s, coupled with a gradual aging of the population, helped national crime rates to stabilize and even diminish. There was growing protest over what many perceived as excessive concern for defendants' rights in criminal cases, and this began to lead to a hardening of judicial attitudes. Concern for the rights in crime victims found legislative support at all levels of government. Still, there was much to be done before the crime rate would even return to pre-1970 levels. See Gun Control.

**Crime and Detection**, a literary genre generally seen as a time-passer, read by responsible people as a diversion from serious topics, but a factor in social attitudes, and intended by numerous authors to advance their liberal or conservative attitudes. Edgar Allan Poe, acclaimed as the "father of the detective story," was in fact a displaced Virginia gentleman, driven by his needs to feign the inordinate calm and "ratiocination" of his macabre tales. Dostoevsky's *The Brothers Karamazov*, though embodying a "mystery," was scarcely a tale for the idle hour. G. K. Chesterton's "Father Brown" stories patently served his conservative interests. Dashiell Hammett's fictions were curious, being whodunits while gaining unexpected consequences from his anti-McCarthy posture. *The Big Clock*, by Kenneth Fearing, noted as a left-wing poet, gained from the understanding that it derogated Henry Luce of *Time*. Among distinguished proponents of conservative crime and detection fiction were Josephine Tey, whose *Daughter of Time* was influential in complicating opinion respecting the alleged crimes of Richard III and whose other fiction in the genre derogated democracy, and John Steinbeck, whose *The Winter of Our Discontent*, traced American social corruption in the subtle misuse of mental science. Gerald Heard's religious seeking and scientific grasp found expression in his celebrated *A Taste for Honey*. Chester Himes's crime novels of Harlem were distinctive as using the genre for developing attitudes toward the black community. Jacques Barzun and W. H. Taylor's *A Catalogue of Crime* (1971) emphasized the "entertainment" aspects of the genre, thus missing significant works. E. L. Gilbert's *The World of Mystery Fiction* (1983) opens views on the subject, though from a limited perspective. See also Jurgen Thorwald, *The Century of the Detective* (1964); and C. Steinbrunner and O. Penzler, *Encyclopedia of Mystery and Detection* (1976).

**"Cruel and Unusual Punishment,"** see Capital Punishment

**Cuba,** see Latin America

**Curtis, George William** (1824-1892), a once-esteemed intellectual leader identified with post-Civil War gentility (*q.v.*). He was impressed as a youth with Emersonian (*q.v.*) idealism and social responsibility. Receiving early opportunities on the *New York Tribune*, he was able to write travel books and graceful essays. His oration, "The Duty of the American Scholar to Politics and the Times" (1856), was read with appreciation in his own time. Curtis himself wrote in opposition to slavery, and, as editor of *Harper's Magazine* and a public personality, contributed to the fight for a Civil Service (*q.v.*), for women suffrage, and industrial harmony. Curtis and *Harper's* were mediating forces between embattled radicals and reactionaries, and helped modify the anti-social elements in both. Gordon Milne, *George William Curtis & the Genteel Tradition* (1956).

**Cyclopaedia of Political Science, Political Economy, and of the Political History of the United States,** edited by John J. Lalor (1881-1884), 3 volumes. It presents a substantially conservative view of American affairs, as set down by historians, economists and others. Some, like Ernest Renan, wrote from abroad, for the *Cyclopaedia* meant to present an account of the world as well. As to its premises, Léon Faucher warned against social interventions: "Progress is born of difficulties. By taking poverty out of the world we would be taking labor out of it, and the law of labor is the very law of existence." A. Joseph Garnier praised liberty and competition, but, citing the Physiocrat Quesnay, did not probe the ways of commerce and industry deeply. The *Cyclopaedia* can be compared with another massive work of the same era, edited by the Christian Socialist W. D. P. Bliss, *Encyclopedia of Social Reform* (1897, revised 1908, 1910). It treated similar subjects with greater detail and a positive attitude toward workers and reformers.

# D

**Dahlberg, Edward,** see *Freeman, The*

**Dana, Charles A.** (1819-1897), journalist who helped mold the conservative outlook on post-Civil War developments through his influential *New York Sun.* A transitional (*q.v.*) figure in that he was an influential force in the utopian (*q.v.*) colony of Brook Farm (1841-1847), he was sufficiently disillusioned by its labored and unsuccessful effort to control human nature to turn his talents in other directions. He joined Horace Greeley's *New York Tribune*, and later served as a correspondent in the Civil War and at the War Department. In 1868 he began his long service with the *New York Sun*, which he made a model of clarity and accuracy. He was famous for his cynicism, hatred of labor unions, and scorn for reformers, notably E. L. Godkin (*q.v.*) of the *New York Nation* and *New York Post* and Joseph Pulitzer of the *New York World.* Pulitzer was a brilliant immigrant from Hungary, and the *Sun* once printed one of his speeches in dialect spelling. David Graham Phillips's (*q.v.*) apprentice novel *The Great God Success* (1901), describing the intellectual downfall of a newspaper editor, was long rumored to have been influenced by his years with Pulitzer; actually, Phillips had also been employed on the *Sun*, and the picture of an editor fallen from idealism better reflected Dana's career than Pulitzer's. C. J. Rosebault, *When Dana Was the Sun* (1931); Candace Stone, *Dana and the Sun* (1938).

**Dante and Other Waning Classics** (1915), by Albert Mordell, a Philadelphia lawyer and litterateur who received praise and regard from such scholars and critics as George Brandes. Mordell was a pioneer in materialistic criticism reflecting Darwinian assumption. He was a quiet, methodical person who intended no more than a naturalistic view of existence, but his writings and wide correspondence helped fuel the ideological conflicts of late decades; see his *The Erotic Motive in Literature* (1919), *The Literature of Ecstasy* (1921), and *T. S. Eliot's Deficiencies as a Social Critic* (1951)—all, including the Dante book, in later editions. His original challenge was sweeping. He argued that Dante, Milton, Bunyan, Thomas A. Kempis, St. Augustine (*q.v.*), and Pascal only appealed to us as we recognized in them experiences we could share. When they appealed to "absurd" cosmology, "irrational" historical sequences, and "unnatural" human feelings and relationships, we could not be moved as were readers of the authors' own period. There is no reason, for example, in Dante's punishments. Lucifer's war with the angels inspires us with contempt, yawns, and disrespectful amusement. *Pilgrim's Progress* causes us to regret that Bunyan did not describe "Vanity Fair," which would have been interesting. And so with Thomas A. Kempis, St. Augustine, and Pascal. Mordell did not find Pascal's famous "wager" persuasive. An interesting appendix brings together notable persons who offered adverse views of classic books and authors. A.B. Feldman, *Albert Mordell: A Prophet Not Without Honor* (n.d.).

**Darkness At Noon,** see Stalin, Josef

**Dartmouth College,** see Taney, Roger B.; Youth

**Darwinism,** a term used to apply to the philosophical implications of the work of the English naturalist Charles Darwin (1809-1882). In the 19th century Darwin's theory of evolution was both applauded and condemned as being inimical to the teaching of Christianity. Not only did it contradict a literal reading of the Book of Genesis, it also seemed to suggest that human beings were no more than animals, different in complexity but not in kind from the lower forms of animals. Extremist disciples of Darwin and those opposed to religion tended to encourage these interpretations of Darwin's ideas. In the 20th century the general tendency has been to see Darwin's ideas as religiously neutral. Religion has consistently taught that man is more than an animal, and about this science can say little. Most mainline churches no longer read the Book of Genesis literally, and thus have made their peace with evolution. Fundamentalists, however, who regard Genesis as literal fact still see evolution as contradictory to the Bible. Robert Nisbet (*q.v.*), in his *Prejudices*, put it in a class with Marxism and Freudianism—as debased by popularization and false leaders, as pretending to be scientific while saturated with presumptions and special goals. "Events, jumps, macromutations" Nisbet thought, could "be ignored by the mandarinate no longer." They were, however, ignored by such as Stephen Gould, fondled by liberals, in such books as *Since Darwin* (1979). See also Creationism; Social Darwinism.

**Daugherty, Harry M.,** see Communism

**Dawes Act** (1887), see Indians

**Death Penalty,** see Capital Punishment

**"Debunking,"** see Washington, George

**Decadence,** originally an artistic term referring to a period of deterioration or decline. The term has come to be applied to social mores which appear to represent a deterioration or decline from past standards or present ideals. Totalitarian states tend to identify decadence with opposition to or freedom from their total control of society. Nazi Germany campaigned against "decadent art" as an enemy of the state. The Soviet Union has consistently identified decadence with capitalist or "bourgeois"—anti-Communist—attitudes or customs. Conservatives, with their basic respect for tradition and history, are often ready to view any manifestation of contemporary culture as representing a decline from the past. Liberals, on the other hand, with their basic commitment to change, are often ready to embrace contemporary cultural manifestations simply because they are new, different, and contemporary. Thus many conservatives saw the counterculture of the 1960s as decadent. See also Robert M. Adams, *Decadent Societies* (1983). Many liberals embraced it uncritically, partly perhaps because it was new and different. Ironically, in the 1980s many liberals have denounced the new conservative mood of the nation as itself decadent, a decline from the "idealism" of the 1960s. The youth claimed that it was American society which was decadent, rather than themselves and, indeed, it could be noted that hedonism without purpose could be detected among social components which had once been seen as the "pillars" of society. Obviously, the youth could have accomplished little without their cooperation or tolerance. C. E. M. Joad, in his *Decadence* (1949) observed that non-decadent eras were often disagreeable in many respects, and only supported out of necessity or through social sanction. To conservatives, however, even imperfect standards are better than none at all, and a reluctance to change far better than change for change's sake.

**Decadence and Renewal in the Higher Learning** (Kirk), see Education

**Declaration of Independence.** Some people confuse it with the Constitution of the United States (*q.v.*); the academic Leslie Fiedler, with insight into such thinking, noted that the Rosenbergs (*q.v.*) died in the electric chair because they could not distinguish one from the other. It contains elements disturbing to both conservatives and liberals. Conservatives for example, protested that "all men [being] created equal" does not mean that they continue to be equal. Still, since they are also said to possess "inalienable Rights" which include "Liberty," the slavery then in force seems to be gravely impugned. Only the sense of the Declaration as constituting an aspiration, with the new freedoms implied, can give validity to the passage in its historical context. The heaping upon the King's head of all the infamous acts, rather than upon Parliament, a changeable body, indicated a separation from monarchy and a fixed head of government: a sweeping renunciation. No war could be fought without acknowledgment of the popular will, and that will, in the North, resented the Proclamation of 1763, which had given to "a neighboring Province" (Canada) control of the terrain west of the colonies—especially since that province was Catholic. Most troubling for liberals is the paragraph which charges: "He has excited domestic insurrections amongst us"—that is, among blacks—"and has endeavored to bring on the inhabitants of our frontiers, the merciless Indian Savages, whose known rule of warfare, is an undistinguished destruction of all ages." To be a firm staff in a long journey, it had to be seen as both a constant battle cry, and as one voiced in a particular time. C. L. Becker, *The Declaration of Independence* (1922); David Hawke, *A Transaction of Free Men* (1964).

**"Decriminalization,"** see "Victimless Crime"

**Deficit Spending.** Always necessary during wartime, the practice was introdudced by the New Deal (*q.v.*) Administration in the peacetime 1930s to finance programs for combatting economic depression. It gave new powers of taxation (*q.v.*) to government, adding what many saw as a socialist (*q.v.*) component to the American economy. It was defended by reformers and revolutionists, denounced by conservatives and Manchester Liberals (*q.v.*). Maintained following World War II for "Cold War" (*q.v.*) purposes, and to meet the increasing demands of weapons and space development, it was fought by many conservatives who wished to reduce the bureaucracy (*q.v.*) and unwarranted Federal services. In the 1970s growing evidence indicated that many federal social programs had done little to help the poor for whom they were intended. President Ford's (*q.v.*) effort to address the problem, however, was rebuffed, as was President Carter's (*q.v.*) later attempt. President Reagan (*q.v.*) was able to push through many proposals for tax cuts and spending reductions. The Federal deficit continued to grow during his Administration, however, partly as a result of increased military spending. After his overwhelming re-election in 1984, however, Reagan began to mount an all-out attack on deficit spending. He lent his prestige to efforts to pass a Constitutional Amendment mandating balanced Federal budgets in peacetime. More immediately, he advocated drastic Federal spending cuts, mostly in social programs, in an effort to reduce and eventually eliminate the yearly Federal deficits. At the very least, the Reagan Presidency had placed economics high on the list of political priorities.

**Deism,** see Filler, DASC. Though holding to generalized tenets of religious faith, it rejected Revelation, as in Thomas Paine's (*q.v.*) critique of the Bible. Yet many conservatives of the Revolutionary era, notably John Adams (*q.v.*), held Deist sentiments. Adams's Deism caused him great distress when his beloved wife died and he could not persuade himself that he would see her again in afterlife. Jefferson (*q.v.*), also a Deist, though of a liberal persuasion, and friendly to Adams in their old age, was distressed that he could not offer Adams consolation and hope.

**Demagogues,** a natural product of democracy (see Filler, DASC) and apt to flourish under difficult or frustrating conditions, as well as when crises of economics or war provide dominant elements with occasions to give vent to their fantasies. Curiously, many extreme conservatives have been identified as demagogues, but few extreme liberals. Populism (*q.v.*) did become identified to some extent with demagoguery, however, as some of its more impassioned spokesmen were derogated as either insane or criminal. Franklin D. Roosevelt (*q.v.*) was viewed as a calculated demagogue by many irate conservatives. For the most part, though, attention has been traditionally focused on conservative demagogues. Reinhard H. Luthin, though a superb student of demagogues, was aware that there were ranters on the liberal side as well as the conservative. However, the era of his *American Demagogues* (1954), and the spirit of the time, called for information about conservatives rather than liberals. Accordingly, his book discussed Huey Long, Theodore G. Bilbo of Mississippi, Bill Murray of Oklahoma, "Pa and Ma" Ferguson of Texas, and Gene Talmadge of Georgia as Southern demagogues. His Northern examples included Joseph McCarthy (*q.v.*), Boss Curley of Boston, and Big Bill Thompson of Chicago. Boss Hague of Jersey City was also included as a demagogue preying on minorities. Vito Marcantonio was elected to Congress, but ran afoul of his Communist sympathies during the early Cold War (*q.v.*) period. The youth rebellion of the 1960s (see Youth Uprising) went hand in hand with the rise of many radical-left demagogues. Many black and minority demagogues, in the 1960s and afterwards, attempted to exploit real and imagined grievances for personal and political power. Jesse Jackson, a black minister based in Chicago, first came to national prominence with his calls for self-reliance and hard work on the part of blacks and other minorities. His abortive try at the Democratic Presidential nomination in 1984, however, with his increasingly virulent attacks on American society and foreign policy, caused many to wonder whether he too had entered the ranks of demagogues. Modern demagogues employing the new Rhetoric distorted certain words' meanings to connote metaphors for murder, arson, stealing ("liberating" money, goods, guns, and whatever came to hand). The concept of rhetoric was important to youth leaders who would deny all wrong-doing when brought to trial on criminal charges. The decline of the youth uprising showed them as having been demagogues to a world of their own; their rhetoric of violence proved of little use to new leaders emphasizing social and political power, rather than alienating threats, though threats of various sorts were occassionally used.

**De-Managing America: The Final Revolution** (1975), by Richard Cornuelle (1927- ), an influential book among conservatives. It preached a species of free enterprise in management, and was anti-bureaucratic (*q.v.*) and scornful of the "front-office mentality" as being separated from reality. Cornuelle praised "the invisible hand" (*q.v.*) of a worker's individual energy and creativity and denounced such government operations as Housing and Urban Development (HUD)—the "$100-billion mistake"—as catastrophic whenever they intervened in human productivity. We are trying to solve our problems, Cornuelle declared, by managing others, rather than permitting them to function freely. As a former bureaucrat, he held that he had "seen the future and it doesn't work," echoing Lincoln Steffens's once-famous phrase respecting Soviet Russia which maintained the opposite: that it *was* working. Cornuelle set down much evidence of bureaucratic incompetence. One curious reference, in the light of later revelations, was to John De Lorean, who claimed he had "quit" General Motors in 1973 because it was "insulated" from the country. During the glaring publicity which attended De Lorean's later fall, it was suggested that he had been seen as irresponsible by G. M. and had been let out. See also Cornuelle's *Reclaiming the American Dream* (1965) and *Healing America* (1975).

**Democracy.** Some conservatives see unrestrained democracy as unwieldy or wrong for a nation like the United States, but others see it as a positive challenge. Similar distinctions could be found among liberals. Some liberals longed for measures which would increase the "cooperative" aspects of democracy, while others feared any restraint on the democratic process. Conservatives generally agreed that the Founding Fathers (*q.v.*) had not intended a "democracy" as generally understood, but rather had set up a Republic, seen as the rule by the best. De Tocqueville's *Democracy in America* (1835) and Bryce's *American Commonwealth* (1888) (*qq.v.*) are generally regarded as the best examinations of America's working. Remarkably both authors were foreigners. Embattled conservatives like William F. Buckley, Jr. questioned unexamined democracy. Buckley observed that lynchings, which most people find undesirable, are nevertheless "democratically" arranged, and with a sense of virtue. Democracy, moreover, is not "democratic;" depriving as it does children, criminals, and the insane, among others, of the right to vote. See also *Anti-Democratic Thought, Patterns of.*

**Democracy in America,** see Tocqueville, Alexis de

**Democrats, Conservative.** Though the modern Democratic Party is generally identified with liberal causes and programs, a strong conservative strain runs through its history. Jefferson limited slavery in his Northwest Ordinance. On the other hand, Jackson's rise to the Presidency was seen as a victory for the slavery interests. Franklin Pierce was a Northern "doughface," cooperating with slavery forces. Grover Cleveland became a famous convert to Free Trade, but as an economic measure, not as an aid to the poor. He also cooperated with a J. P. Morgan consortium to stop a run on the U. S. Treasury. The result gave the consortium unwarranted profits. In the 20th century Woodrow Wilson saw himself as a conservative Democrat bent on Free Trade; it was the Progressive push in his party which carried him beyond "conservative"—or reactionary—Democrats of the big city machines. Franklin D. Roosevelt ran his 1932 campaign on a conservative economic platform; the key to his subsequent actions was his readiness to experiment. The New Deal momentum committed future Democrats to liberal programs, but the party still found room for such men as Charles Sawyer, Truman's Secretary of Commerce. Sawyer fought for the status of industry in national affairs, opposed "giveaways" in foreign aid, feared Communism and inflation, and disagreed with Truman's removal of MacArthur in the Korean War; see his *Concerns of a Conservative Democrat* (1968). Lyndon Johnson began as a conservative but became more and more liberal. Jimmy Carter was in many ways conservative, but unable or unwilling to fight the radical-left elements in his party. The decisive election victories of Ronald Reagan in 1980 and 1984 caused many Democrats to question their liberal assumptions. Political observers forecast a revival of conservative Democratic attitudes and actions. (*Q.q.v.* for above.)

**Democrats' Dilemma, The** (1964), by Philip M. Crane, then a professor of history, later a favorite among conservatives. His book held that the party had been captured by zealots determined to foist on the country programs inimical to its well-being. It named such organizations as the League for Industrial Democracy (LID), Americans for Democratic Action (ADA), and the Center for the Study of Democratic Institutions as guiding the Democratic Party's policies.

**Depression, The,** often called the Great Depression (*q.v.*). It lasted from 1929 to 1940, and was ended not by New Deal (*q.v.*) measures, but by the coming of war and the consequent revival of industry. The Depression was as much psychological as real, kept alive in the minds of the people by many vivid experiences and images in the streets, suicides ("Do you want a room for sleeping or leaping?"), the hopeless search for jobs, strikes, and unemployment parades. Panaceas (*q.v.*), like the Townsend Plan for giving away government money to the aged, were proposed. The era saw the rise of radical, notably Communist, opinion in culture and politics. Conservative views sounded feeble and elitist (*q.v.*) in such times, and were identified with important patriotic and free-enterprise (*q.v.*) attitudes, support of Ku Klux Klan and Fascism (*qq.v.*), and isolationist opposition to aid to anti-Fascists abroad. Wartime affluence did little to improve the image of conservatism. Much attention was given to the anti-Fascist aspects of the war and the U. S. alliance with Stalin (*q.v.*), despite his known brutalities. The Depression has never been a favorite conservative topic, since it originated in a Republican era and from Republican policies. Conservative attention has centered mainly on Franklin D. Roosevelt's (*q.v.*) deficit-spending policies and his Administration's tolerance of radicals. See Inflation; Economics; Great Depression.

**Depressions,** in the course of history, had been stimuli for demagogues, reformers, revolutionists, economists, and conservatives, all of whom contributed to their lore. Murray Rothbard's (*q.v.*) university thesis was an examination of the 1819 Depression. Marxists (*q.v.*) saw in depressions evidence of the "contradictions" in capitalism, reformers the need for compassion—until depressions in welfare (*q.v.*) states revealed their own contradictions. Conservative economists worked with cyclical theories; see Filler, DASC. Free-enterprise and monetarist theoreticians blamed bad fiscal measures, though not always taking into account the effect of unprincipled manipulators and of human nature. The Great Depression (*q.v.*) was a crisis in capitalism which conservatives seemed inept at handling, and from which radicals of the left profited, in and out of government. Efforts to insure against such a depression ever occurring again linked with welfare measures and wartime expenditures to produce an affluence (*q.v.*) which made it difficult for political conservatives to advocate free-enterprise ideals. Mounting deficits, inflation, and unemployment (*qq.v.*) in the 1970s forced attention to conservative economic views. However, many conservatives insisted that the worst that could happen under free enterprise was better than the best that could happen under socialism or socialistic tendencies. This tended to play into the hands of radicals and their associates, who accused conservatives of a lack of compassion. Thus, even Herbert Hoover's effort to stimulate industry by setting up the Reconstruction Finance Corporation to loan money to businesses was interpreted by some conservatives as "socialistic." They blamed the Federal Reserve System for expanding credit without warrant in the 1920s, and saw the Smoot-Hawley Tariff—the high protective tariff sponsored by the Republicans—as the chief barrier to economic recovery during the Great Depression.

**Deregulation,** the name given to the attempt in the 1970s and 1980s to lessen or eliminate government efforts to supervise and regulate (*q.v.*) private businesses. These efforts had been originally intended to promote greater efficiency and fulfill the public interest. However by the 1970s it was evident that something had gone wrong. Huge government bureaucracies had grown up and regulations had multiplied to the extent that whole industries were strangled in red tape. Innovation, competition, and efficiency were discouraged in the process, and the public interest was hurt rather than helped. Or so it seemed to many observers. President Carter attempted to break through bureaucracy by deregulating airlines and the trucking industry. His successor, President Reagan, came to office prepared to continue the process. Nevertheless, there were developments which gave pause. The airlines' losses immediately after deregulation were catastrophic: $280 million in 1980. The next year, the twelve largest carriers lost $641 million. Losses continued the year after, as bankruptcies multiplied. Deregulation had been expected to unleash free enterprise. Instead, the largest airline companies were absorbing the smaller. In 1984, it appeared that seven airlines would eventually dominate the industry. Much the same was happening to motor carriers, with hundreds of truck lines going into receivership as they lost control of their price structure and books. When American Telephone and Telegraph was stripped of its monopoly, and broken up into regional companies, investors and consumers awaited the results anxiously. Would service deteriorate, produce unfair rate schedules, cause chaos to individuals and businesses? No one knew. As carefully as the new companies planned their operations, the immediate result was still a good deal of confusion among subscribers. It occurred to numerous observers to ask whether the breakup of AT&T had been necessary. Had service been that bad? Had it been inordinately expensive? In its beginnings the telephone had been subject to free enterprise, which had proved inefficient. It had been efficiency, not monopoly, which had brought on unification. Could deregulation become a shibboleth, as regulation had?

**Desegregation,** see Civil Rights

**Destabilization,** term in vogue in foreign affairs in the 1970s and 1980s. It referred to efforts short of outright war to upset the status quo in nations which seemed peaceful, secure, or tightly controlled. The Soviet Union attempted to destabilize many nations allied to or friendly with the United States and the Free World. Its tools included misinformation, propaganda, subversion, assassinations, and terrorism. The intent was to create conditions which could be exploited on behalf of "Marxist revolution." The Reagan Administration undertook its own efforts at destabilization, most notably in the case of Marxist-ruled Nicaragua. These were exposed by many liberals and others who feared "another Vietnam" (*q.v.*). While some called U.S. destabilization efforts "descending to the level of the enemy," many conservatives spoke of "fighting fire with fire." In 1985 South Africa (*q.v.*) became a major target for destabilization.

**Detente,** see Filler DASC. A concept complementary to Coexistence (*q.v.*), it involved a supposedly mutual effort to relax the strained relations between the United States and the Soviet Union. Many people were alarmed by the growing military might of both sides. It was argued that neither had anything to gain by large military expenditures. Both had everything to lose if nuclear weapons got out of control and monstrous warfare was unleashed. Detente includes efforts to limit the development and production of such weapons. Richard Nixon admitted that 1972 being an election year had something to do with his summit meeting in both the Soviet Union and Red China; see his *The Real War* (1980). Yet he also noted a general state of "euphoria" which encouraged hope that weapons limitation would be achieved. The key question was whether neutral observers would be allowed to check stockpiles of nuclear warheads. Many conservatives doubted whether the Soviet Union would honor the terms of the Nixon-Brezhnev Strategic Arms Limitation Treaty (SALT I). They were dismayed by President Ford's initiative in connection with a new treaty (SALT II). Many liberals discounted such fears; the American military, they declared, had enough arms to destroy the Soviet Union "many times over." But key questions remained concerning first-strike capabilities and the Soviet Union's massive military build-up, nuclear and non-nuclear, during the 1970s. In his later writings Nixon argued that Detente had become confused with Entente. Entente was "an alliance between nations with a common interest." With interests as different as they were between the United States and the Soviet Union, no agreement of significance could be achieved unless participants were forced to accept genuine nuclear controls. And that would come about only if American armed forces had superior capability and were used with will and resourcefulness. In effect, according to Nixon, Detente no longer had any practical meaning. M. Wilrich and J. B. Rhinelander, eds., *SALT* (1974); D. K. Simes, *Detente and Conflict: Soviet Foreign Policy 1972-1977* (1977); Charles E. Timberlake, *Detente: A Documentary Record* (1978); Alexander Solzhenitsyn (*q.v.*) et al., *Detente: Prospects for Democracy and Dictatorship* (1976).

**Determinism,** of lesser interest to an era rendered insecure by the presence of nuclear (*q.v.*) weapons than to an earlier era which saw progress (*q.v.*) as "inevitable," or saw Darwinism (*q.v.*) as implying a master plan of evolution or a process which resulted in higher species independent of divine will. Marxism (*q.v.*), maintained that human behavior was determined by historical and economic conditions. If the conditions were changed, the human behavior would also be changed. Most conservatives found determinism repulsive because of its denial of freedom (*q.v.*) and its simplistic views of humans and human nature (*q.v.*). See also Behaviorism, and Sidney Hook (*q.v.*), ed., *Determinism and Freedom in the Age of Modern Science* (1958).

**Deterrent,** see Capital Punishment

**Dewey, John** (1859-1952), philosopher of Pragmatism (*q.v.*) and experimentalism. His original experiments in "progressive" education were cordially received by teachers interested in the basic elements of learning but overburdened by the rise of cities, larger classes, and bodies of students of varied backgrounds. To them, Dewey's efforts in his Experimental School connected with the University of Chicago made much sense. He sought to elicit the interests of students, to help students find the best means for developing those interests, and to probe the variety of methods which built students' competence. His students were better than average, however, and this limited the general applicability of his method. Many teachers began to apply them without much thought in less favorable conditions. The result was a gradual decline in the standards and achievements of public education, though other factors also contributed to the decline. Dewey himself, under pressure from his followers, tried to create a liberal philosophy critical of American society and with little concern for the traditions in which he himself had been raised. *Individual-*

*ism Old and New* (1930) saw America as a money culture with a religion of prosperity. Himself removed from religion, Dewey saw a need for a new materialism which would improve on that created by mass culture. Although he was reluctant to term himself a socialist, he believed that Americans lived in a "collective" age with a "redistribution of wealth" inevitable. In his later years it seemed that Dewey had come a long way from the premises which had earlier guided him.

**Dewey, Thomas E.** (1902-1971), Republican leader with substantial roots in the party. His grandfather had been one of its organizers in Michigan in 1854, where Dewey himself was raised. Transplanted to New York City, he precociously emerged on the national scene in 1935. He was so effective against entrenched rackets and criminal operators as to make him a Republican hope. As governor of New York, 1942-1955, he displayed administrative ability of a high order, resisting corruption while leading a liberal Republican coalition which approved of many features of the New Deal (*q.v.*). Yet he is mainly remembered as having lost the Presidential election of 1948 to Harry S. Truman, an election he had been expected to win easily. He continued to wield enormous power in his party, and helped make Eisenhower its Presidential candidate in 1952 over Taft. His power extended to 1968, when he endorsed Nixon (*q.v.*) for the nomination. Dewey's loss of public appeal contrasts sharply with that of Henry Clay (*q.v.*), also precocious, also apparently destined for the Presidency. Clay failed to obtain it, but his influence was such that Abraham Lincoln thought him the "beau ideal" of an American statesman. Involved in Dewey's loss of public appeal seems to have been a failure in personality rather than in competence. Although he could be friendly and relaxed, his competitiveness and perceived aloofness hurt him with the larger public. In 1944, when he ran against Franklin D. Roosevelt with a neo-Rooseveltian program promising greater efficiency, he came off as carping and without understanding. Against Truman, despite widespread unease with public spending and lax administration, he failed to persuade voters that he would handle their problems with good temper and executive finesse. Modern conservatism's search for new directions, different in kind from the New Deal, involved repudiation of those Dewey had followed. See his *The Case Against the New Deal* (1940); see also Richard Norton Smith, *Thomas E. Dewey and His Times* (1982).

**Dialect**, see Dunne, Finley Peter

**Dialogues in Americanism,** (1964), a series of three debates held in Pasadena, California on November 17, 1963, and on January 22 and February 23, 1964. They pitted William F. Buckley, Jr. (*q.v.*) against Steve Allen, an entertainer and partisan of the National Committee for a Sane Nuclear Policy (Buckley arguing for a strong response to Soviet activities everywhere, including Cuba and Berlin); the educator Robert M. Hutchins controverting Brent Bozell, an editor of the *National Review*, on the validity of Supreme Court decisions concerning civil rights; and James MacGregor Burns opposing Willmoore Kendall (*q.v.*) on the rights and wrongs of majority rules.

**Dickinson, Emily** (1830-1886), one of the greatest American poets. She was unknown in her day, though of gracious family and with many prominent friends, among them Helen Hunt Jackson (*q.v.*). By the 1920s, many of her poems had been made public, and some of her lines and verses popularized, George F. Whicher's *This Was a Poet* (1938) soundly dealt with Dickinson's religious thought and womanly frustrations. Some later critics found it difficult to accept that these were the source of her genius. See T. H. Johnson's three-volume edition of her poems (1955) and an equally expansive collection of her letters (1958).

**Dickinson, G. Lowes** (1862-1932), humanist and social thinker. His works survive, like those of many of his generation, almost independently of his life. Those interested in ancient Greece keep in print *The Greek View of Life* (1896) and *Plato and His Dialogues* (1931). Those concerned about the World War I era consult *The European Anarchy* (1916) and perhaps *The International Anarchy* (1926). His writing as an essayist receives less attention. Nevertheless, *A Modern Symposium*, published before World War I and reflecting his sense of Greek dialogue, brings back a world in which opposites addressed one another in civilized terms. It directly counterposes a Tory, a Liberal, a Conservative, a Socialist, an anarchist, and others, including a poet and a "man of science," to express their outlooks on human affairs. Their precision and even eloquence helps describe the world which died on the battlefields short years later. Although Dickinson was famous, and continued to be published to the end of his life, it is probable that his reputation suffered because of his advocacy of a "League of Nations," his main recipe for peace. This tied in with Great Britain's efforts to maneuver the United States into entering the war on the side of the Allies, although there is no evidence that Dickinson consciously intended that goal. A valid review of the humanist streams which were submerged in the military operations of World War I, on both sides of the battle, might do more for a realistic peace today than any study of diplomatic history. See Filler, Introduction to *A Modern Symposium* (1962); and E. M. Forster, *Goldsworthy Lowes Dickinson* (1934).

**Dickinson, John,** (1732-1808), famed for his *Letters from a Farmer in Pennsylvania to the Inhabitants of the British Colonies*. His political development helps explain why so unlikely an event as the American Revolution (*q.v.*) took place at all. Rich and conservative, Dickinson had no need to profit from disruption. He hoped for reconciliation, and would not sign the Declaration of Independence (*q.v.*). Yet he was "the Penman of the Revolution," asking for justice and respect for property. He stirred patriots, but could not move the mercantilists (*q.v.*) of London. Once the Revolution was underway, he contributed state papers for the Continental Congress and sharpened his views of freedom. His major cause was states rights (*q.v.*), which found expression in his draft of the Articles of Confederation (*q.v.*).

**Dies, Martin** (1900-1972). A predecessor in Congress of Joseph McCarthy (*q.v.*). His chairmanship of the Special House Committee for the Investigation of Un-American Activities roused storms of protest from Communists and leftists, who made "Dies Lies!" a famous phrase of the 1930s. Dies was indeed prone to emphasize Communists in his hearings and investigations, though his mandate was supposed to include Fascists as well. The erection of a Grand Alliance against Hitler, which included the Soviet Union, put a damper on his crusade, which he was unable to re-ignite after World War II with the onset of the Cold War (*q.v.*). See also House Un-American Activities Committee; A.R. Ogden, *The Dies Committee* (1945).

**Dignity**, "bourgeois" word which reappeared following the excesses of the Youth (*q.v.*) uprising. Norman Mailer in *The Deer Park* (1955), while still seriously considered as a writer, satirized it as employed by Hollywood persons who scrounged and twisted in ways described in Budd Schulberg's *What Makes Sammy Run?* Partisans proclaimed the value of euthanasia (*q.v.*) and "dying with dignity" for children afflicted with handicaps, old people who had suffered mental and physical hardships, and victims of accidents which deprived them of limbs or consciousness.

**Dilling, Elizabeth,** see *Red Network, The*

**Directions In Contemporary Literature** (1942), by Philo M. Buck, Jr., a professor in Comparative Literature at the University of Wisconsin. He faced the threat to humanism in World War II with appeals to authors who favored tradition, individualism, and the criteria of beauty. To these he opposed what he saw as the "tribal aggressions of Hitler's *Mein Kampf* and Marxian outlook in Mikhail Sholokhov's fiction." America, according to Buck, contributed "The Search for Beauty" of George Santayana, the return to religion of T. S. Eliot (*qq.v.*), and the troubled odyssey of Eugene O'Neill. Buck rejected cynicism, materialism, and dogma. He found hope in "The Waters under the Earth," in Marcel Proust, in the Indian idealist Tagore, in Aldous Huxley's (*q.v.*) rejection of 1920s skepticism, in Jules Romain's positive world of *Men of Good Will*, and in Thomas Mann's humanism—deepened by an acceptance of divinity.

**Disabled Persons.** Physical and mental disabilities had been long held a misfortune, and the concern of religious and other voluntary groups. The civil rights drives of the 1950s and 1960s focused attention on many groups which claimed discrimination by society at large. The physically and mentally disabled became regarded as such a group. Lyndon Johnson's (*q.v.*) Great Society (*q.v.*) programs increased Federal aid and support for the disabled and their families. The Department of Health, Education, and Welfare was especially important. Equal opportunity laws curbed discrimination to a degree. Although there was resistance against equitable treatment of handicapped persons, there were some evident gains. For example, sidewalks and public places were planned with inclines to permit persons in wheelchairs to move about more readily. Newspapers gave more space to legal, business, and other news affecting the disabled. Hospitals were directed to make special provision for persons requiring special treatment. Degrees of mental competence were studied and productivity assessed, often with surprisingly positive results. However, the abortion (*q.v.*) issue and the related issue of handicapped newborns soon created controversy. Tests which could determine future physical and mental disabilities of fetuses in the womb led many parents to choose to abort those fetuses rather than carry the pregnancies to term. Some parents were selfish and resented the inconvenience of a disabled child. Others were truly concerned with the suffering a disabled child, if born, would have to endure. Abortion's opponents, however, denounced the practice. It was soon revealed that doctors and hospitals had long been allowing severely handicapped newborn infants to die rather than face what they regarded as a lifetime of suffering. Abortion opponents maintained that abortion of handicapped fetuses was euthanasia (*q.v.*). How, they argued, are such practices any different from the policies of Nazi Germany, which eliminated those thought to be inferior biologically or racially. George Will (*q.v.*), the conservative television and newspaper commentator, revealed that a child of his who was said to be suffering from Down's Syndrome was not only dear to his family but without definable limitations. Woven into the debate were basic attitudes toward religion, society, biological needs, and life itself. John D. Kershaw, *Handicapped Children* (1973 ed.); Frank Bowe, *Handicapping America: Barriers to Disabled People* (1978); V. Carver and Michael Rodda, *Disability and the Environment* (1978).

**Discrimination,** a major charge during the post-World War II years of agitation for equal rights, especially for blacks. Although discrimination had been memorably denounced by Justice John Marshall Harlan in 1896 in *Plessy vs. Ferguson*, his was a minority opinion favoring constitutional "color blindness"; the Court majority voted for "equal but separate" public accommodations. When this was overthrown by the Brown (*q.v.*) decision of 1954, agitators' concerns went beyond discrimination to "restitution" for blacks because of alleged past group wrongs and "affirmative action" (*qq.v.*) in furtherance of black social and economic ambitions. Conservatives argued that such goals were a form of "reverse discrimination": an interpretation which accompanied the more than thirty years of argument over experience in black-white relations. At bottom of the debate lay the question of how far an individual might be enabled in law and practice to discriminate among social and individual offerings in his own behalf, without transgressing law and custom. See also N. Glazer, *Affirmative Discrimination* (1976); Equality.

**"Disillusionment,"** a famous mood of the post-World War I period which contrasted with the high expectations of the war era and its preceding Progressivism (*q.v.*). These had anticipated a broadened democracy and a world made safe for democracy. It became evident that the latter had not materialized, the Communist slogans were challenging the democratic, and being sharply repressed by censors and the police. A spirit of cynicism and irony expanded among intellectuals and expressed itself popularly in frivolous activities seriously pursued. "Debunking" in history and an almost universal disrespect for the law of the land as embodied in Prohibition were two of the signs of disillusionment with gangsters such as Al Capone becoming heroes to many. The Great Depression (*q.v.*) brought about a renewed belief in leftist causes among many intellectuals including a sympathy for the Communism of the Soviet Union and a hatred of Fascism. Revelations of Stalin's purge trials in the late 1930s and the Nazi-Soviet Pact of 1939 created some disillusionment with Communism, but this diminished during the Great Alliance with Stalin and World War II. The Cold War, more revelations of Stalinist horrors and of domestic treason, and the postwar economic failures of Communism—coupled with the "empty" material prosperity brought about by capitalism—stimulated new disillusionment among intellectuals in the 1940s and 1950s. This left many of them susceptible to the causes and programs which proliferated in the 1960s as an antidote to cynicism and despair. Post-war "disillusionment" still meant disillusionment with the "crusade for democracy." See W. E. Woodward, *Bunk* (1923).

**"Disinformation,"** a neologism referring to material presented as factual truth which is actually distorted or false. It is contrasted with propaganda in that the appearance of objectivity and balance is maintained, and often the source of the disinformation itself is unknown. Disinformation has traditionally been practiced by governments during war, with the intent of confusing or deceiving the enemy. The development of world communications after World War II and the proliferation of political and ideological conflicts has led to an increased use of the techniques of disinformation by governments and groups. See KGB, CIA.

**Disloyalty,** see Patriotism

**Disraeli, Benjamin** (1804-1881), British statesman and novelist. His personality and outlook created a conservatism which met the demands of a rising democracy, and became part of the conservative heritage. His own background, including distinguished Jewish grandparents and a father famous for his *Curiosities of Literature* (1791-1834) and *Calamities of Authors* (1812), contributed to a career which added depth and culture to the conservative impulse, in England and abroad. Vain, fickle, and intemperate, Disraeli nevertheless struggled with talents of insight and eloquence, winning honors for himself and Great Britain. His first fictional success, *Vivian Gray* (1826), later embarrassed him with its persistent popularity, but it gave him his start in public life. He continued to write and seek election to Parliament, finally being returned for Maidstone in 1837. Meanwhile he was refining his approach to the Tory (*q.v.*) party and to his own "Young England" of Tories. He set it forth in three of his novels which he saw as a trilogy, and which advanced him among readers as well as party rulers. *Coningsby* (1844) took as its theme the origin of English political parties. *Sybil* (1845) gave the country a phrase; it was subtitled "The Two Nations," and described England as divided between the rich and the poor. *Tancred* (1847), he himself explained, was intended to provide a picture of the moral and physical condition of the people, and how they were to be elevated. Earlier, in his *Vindication of the English Constitution* (1835), he had provided a first draft of his vision: a union between Crown, people, and Church. (Disraeli had himself been baptized in the Anglican Church at the age of thirteen.) A generous aristocracy, a revived church, "restoration of the past" by a reconstituted Tory Party: such was Disraeli's program. In 1842 he married for money, and stayed for love. He moved from protection of landowners' interests to anti-protection, from anti-reform to his own Reform Bill of 1867, as effective in debate when he was out of power as when he was in. His duels with the Liberal leader William Ewart Gladstone helped set up an essentially two-party system. Disraeli was Prime Minister briefly in 1868. In 1874 he came back to add a brilliant coda to his career. He passed laws promoting health, housing, and other workers' needs. He won an interest, later to be a controlling interest, in the Suez Canal Company. His complex relations with Queen Victoria culminated in 1877, when he had her designated "Empress of India"; the next year, by order of the Queen,

Disraeli became the First Earl of Beaconsfield. His cautious movements through European intrigues won him the admiration of statesmen. Although the peace he promoted would be treated later with disdain by some writers looking at the shambles of World War I, it looked better to others who were less impatient of compromise. W. F. Monypenny and G. E. Buckle, *Life of Benjamin Disraeli* (1929); Stephen R. Graubard, *Burke, Disraeli, and Churchill* (1961); *Novels and Tales by the Earl of Beaconsfield* (1881).

**Dissent,** see American Dissent, The

**Dissidents.** Since the 1960s the term has come to be identified with elements mainly among the intellectual classes of the Soviet Union. They were inspired by the post-Stalin "thaw" to seek an expansion of respect and a tolerance of human rights (*q.v.*) in their country. Although they were a minute fraction of the Soviet intelligentsia, and had no effect on the Soviet working class, the dissidents included many persons of distinction. The Soviet government had long had problems with nationalists, the religious-minded, and minorities, but it also had long experience in dealing with these groups through mass executions, imprisonment, pressure, rewards and flattery. Dissidents, however, were different. Their historic concepts transgressed the premises of Soviet rule, forged during its 1917-1921 civil war, which divided friends peremptorily from enemies. Enemies had come to include anyone who deviated from the Soviet premise of a dictatorship in the name of the proletariat. The dissidents, who tested the limits of that dictatorship of the proletariat, were thus accused of directly or indirectly aiding the enemy. They included a variety of serious and distinguished persons: Vladimir Bukovsky, who was arrested for public demonstrations which were in theory legal; Valery Chalidze, who labored to extract justice from Soviet law; Roy Medvedev, who feared that the "thaw" would disappear and Soviet practices return to that of the tyrant Stalin; and Tatyana Velikanova, a mathematician who was repelled by the processes which brought KGB (*q.v.*) operatives into suspects' homes and secreted political prisoners in labor camps. Dissidents made their presence felt, if not to the general Soviet public, at least to the KGB. Their samizdat (*q.v.*) underground papers reached the outside world. Alexander Solzhenitsyn (*q.v.*) became a world celebrity. The Gulag (*q.v.*) was made infamous as a symbol of Soviet repression. A particular gain was the dissidents' exposures of "psychiatric hospitals," created by the KGB to punish Soviet dissidents and portray them as imbalanced people who distorted the reality of Soviet life and justice. The "hospitals" were a nightmare of the 1984 (*q.v.*) variety: a twisting of medical arts in the service of insulated power. (Compare Hinckley, John; and Pound, Ezra.) A notable dissident was Andrei Sakharov, Nobel Prize winner, whose fight for human rights led to exile from Moscow, the loss of all honors and privileges, and the denial of needed medical treatment for himself and his wife. Although dissidents were extremely limited in their capacity to reach other Soviet citizens and the outer world, the development of world communications forced Soviet authorities to deal less peremptorily with their activities than they otherwise might have. The Sakharov case was relatively well publicized and brought Soviet "leaks" to the Western media intending to show that Sakharov was still alive and in good health. Soviet Jews, either as dissidents or as individuals and families disheartened in a militantly atheistic state, were also well publicized in the West, which followed avidly their efforts to gain official permission to emigrate. All in all, the dissidents provided the West with needed insights into the workings of the Soviet Government and society and with a reaffirmation of Western ideals which too many in the West seemed to take for granted. Joshua Rubenstein, *Soviet Dissidents: Their Struggle for Human Rights* (1980).

**Dodsworth** (1929), by Sinclair Lewis (*q.v.*), a distinguished novel about an American businessman, accepted by critics and readers as a durable work of art. Lewis's main idea, updated in accordance with his genius, was taken directly from David Graham Phillips's *The Husband's Story* (1910), which contrasted a forthright businessman and his shallow wife in their response to Europeans who weigh them in mercenary terms. With Lewis's commercial elite now as diminished as Phillips's and Europe's nobility all but pulverized by democratic and radical triumphs (see *Leopard, The*), it would take a new historic vision to make such novels effective in the contemporary cultural world.

**Domino Theory,** used during the 1960s to justify American involvement in Vietnam. Proponents of the "domino theory" argued that the fall of South Vietnam to Communist forces would inevitably lead to a Communist takeover of all of Southeast Asia. Indeed the 1970s saw the installation of Communist regimes in Laos and Cambodia as a direct result of the defeat of the pro-Western government in South Vietnam. The brutal Communist regime of Pol Pot in Cambodia was later driven out by Communist troops from North Vietnam. In the 1980s the North Vietnamese worked to consolidate their control in Cambodia against Communist and non-Communist guerilla forces. Liberals denied that the overthrow of a government friendly to the United States would have a "domino" effect on adjacent lands. When it happened, they turned off the argument, accused the American government of having offended the radical, "Marxist," or whatever government, and suggested foreign aid to them, as reparations, compensations, or simple goodwill, alleged to redound to our benefit in terms of international opinion. Although the fall of the South Vietnam government to the northern communists resulted in the new government's military offensive in Cambodia little honor accrued to those who held to the "domino" theory. No new phrase, such as "another domino situation" developed; rather, comparable situations were bruited as "another Vietnam," suggesting that American aid to communist-targeted countries must fail as it had failed in Vietnam. See also Grenada.

**Dos Passos, John** (1896-1970), among the most significant transitional (*q.v.*) figures in the culture of his time. He moved from radical to conscious conservative, expressing his later vision of America in *The Theme Is Freedom* (1956). His earlier, poetic phase the 1920s, can be found in the novels *Three Soldiers* (1921) and *Manhattan Transfer* (1925). His famous trilogy, *U.S.A.* (1930-1936), began with *The Forty-Second Parallel.* Its characters and interwoven plot showed his distaste for conservatives and his hope for unlettered persons of "working-class" background. The novel introduced his "Camera Eye" techniques and other innovations intended to explore the inner workings of society. It showed the author's sensitive ear for varied speech and clichés. Dos Passos wrote here as an outsider. Succeeding novels in the trilogy, *1919* and *The Big Money*, showed him alienated not only from the mainstreams of American life, but also increasingly from the radical movement which was to have infused America with new vitality. By the close of the trilogy, his Communist protagonists had revealed themselves as robots moved by dogma. Though Dos Passos had voted Communist in 1932, by 1936 he had lost all radical conviction. His excellent essays inspired by his travels reflected his most natural feelings. The Moscow Trials (*q.v.*) and the brutal operations of the Communists in Spain brought Dos Passos to a new, individual approach. His second trilogy, *District of Columbia*, began with a subdued account of Communist treachery in Spain, continued hectically with an account of the career of the demagogue (*q.v.*) Huey Long, and found focus in its contempt for those involved with Roosevelt's New Deal (*q.v.*), seen as careerists and hypocrites. Dos Passos's ear for contemporary speech was still in evidence, but the portrait of America was as partial as that of *U. S. A.* More successful was his *Mid-Century* (1961), in which he revived his literary artifices and presented a coherent picture of the world he had earlier rejected: the world of his affluent lawyer-father and his own youth. Nevertheless, the literary establishment continues to treat his *U. S. A.*, with its negative vision of America, as his "masterpiece," and to write off his later work as a decline. Townsend Ludington, ed., *The Fourteenth Chronicle: Letters and Diaries of John Dos Passos* (1973).

**"Doughface,"** see Democrats, Conservative

**Douglass, Frederick,** see Washington, Booker T.

**Dred Scott Case,** 1857, Chief Justice Roger Taney's (*q.v.*) effort to assert the authority of the Supreme Court on the institution and national effect of slavery (*qq.v.*). Arguing with justification (Dred Scott *v.* Sanford, 19 How. 393) that the rights of Negroes had never been recognized in United States courts, and that efforts to make slavery unacceptable in free states were not law, Taney forced on the North a choice of accepting his dictum or defying it. Overwhelmingly, the North chose to defy it; the decision was reprinted by Republicans as a campaign document.

**Dreele, W.H. Von,** see *If Liberals Had Feathers*

**"Drop-Outs,"** see Radicals

**Drugs,** once seen as a medical and health concern, later became concern to society at large. The radical youth (*q.v.*) movement, in the 1950s and after, declared that drugs were not harmful—"less" harmful than liquor—and that many drugs were not harmful at all, marijuana being cited as a notable example. The subject was subsumed by liberal ideologues under "victimless crime" (*q.v.*). Nevertheless, marijuana took innumerable victims: it easily led to heroin use and dulled sensibilities, ruining school and family careers. It also brought on the rise of a massive international drug empire. The subject was thus taken out of party conversation and intellectual pyrotechnics and became a matter for the police, health authorities, and governmental debate. See also Apathy, Life-styles. L.H. Bowker, *Drug Use at a Small Liberal Arts College* (1976); B. Hogins and G. Bryant, *Drugs and Dissent* (1970); K.L. Jones, *Drugs and Alcohol* (1973); A.S. Trebach, ed., *Drugs, Crime, and Politics* (1978).

**"Dual Loyalty,"** see Patriotism

**Due Process,** a system in law which reflected the relations between individuals and the state, the state and the superior courts. In post-Civil War eras, burgeoning industries raised questions of the power of the states to limit the free exercise of corporations in matters which vitally affected the large body of citizens. Thus railroads and grain elevators could ruin farmers by arbitrarily charging whatever rates they pleased for carrying and storing products. Chief Justice Waite's (*q.v.*) famous decision that business involved in the "public interest" was subject to restraints by state commissions was a victory for the average citizen. However, the growth of "due process" encouraged corporation lawyers to keep cases in the courts, taking state findings to circuit courts, and on up to the Supreme Court, in the meantime earning the businesses enormous profits at the expense of often hapless farmers and others. Although the Supreme Court was free to reject appeals, leaving lower court decisions as they were, in its conservative phase it regularly received the corporate appeals and regularly found for the corporations even following the passage of the Sherman Anti-Trust Act in 1890. Decades were required before urban, farm, and social conditions provided some equity in the operations of "due process." Post-New Deal conservatism, however, increasingly found itself opposing "judicial activism," which reached its apogee in the Warren Court (*q.v.*) and beyond, when state laws were often subjected to "due process" and rejected on appeal. Conservative viewpoints were rejected by the courts on issues ranging from abortion to school prayer (*q.v.*). With Congress slow to determine the will of its constituents, and elections delivering sometimes enigmatic results, a period of uncertainty for conservatives was the result. Conservatives looked to changes in Congress and in the personnel of the various courts as a hope for the future.

**Dulles, Allen W.,** see CIA

**Dulles, John Foster** (1888-1959), U. S. Secretary of State in the Eisenhower Administration. He was born in a family which had served in the Department of State, and was well grounded in its affairs. He was at the Paris Peace Conference in 1919, and, following World War II, at the San Francisco Conference which drafted the United Nations Charter. Dulles was appointed U. S. Delegate to the United Nations General Assembly. In 1949 he was appointed to serve out a term as

U. S. Senator from New York, but, not a charismatic person, was defeated in the election the following year. In 1953, he became President Eisenhower's Secretary of State, and the major target of liberal criticism in foreign affairs. Dulles was clear on the need to oppose the Soviet Union's program of expansionism by arming and joining friends and preparing for the worst with massive arms accumulations. All this appeared provocative to many liberals, who accused Dulles of dangerous tactics which might cause world catastrophe. A Dulles article in 1956 noted that the Administration had moved to the "brink" of war as necessary, and that doing so involved the art of diplomacy, and this gave rise to the word "brinkmanship," with which Dulles was harassed. Dulles's policies included U. S. support of Taiwan, threatened by Communist China, and close attention to Middle Eastern tensions. Though ill, Dulles traveled widely to promote readiness for what he plainly called "massive retaliation" against the Soviet Union should the need arise. His resolute anti-Communism earned him a notable place in conservative annals. Richard Goold-Adams, *John Foster Dulles: A Reappraisal* (1962); M. A. Guhin, *John Foster Dulles: A Statesman and His Times* (1972); Blythe F. Finke, *John Foster Dulles: Master of Brinkmanship and Diplomacy* (1972); Leonard Mosley, *Dulles... and Their Family Network* (1978).

**Dunne, Finley Peter** (1867-1936), once nationally and even internationally famous as the creator of "Mr. Dooley," a philosophical barkeep whose wise and ironical remarks made him an honest broker between heated reformers and skeptics, and conservatives who found reformers too intense in their crusades. Dunne's essays, written in Irish dialect, were published in newspapers, and read in the street by passersby as well as intellectuals. Many of his remarks entered into the language and were reproduced in standard English as well as in the original dialect, as in "No matter whether th' constitution follows th' flag or not, th' supreme coort follows th' iliction returns," and "Thrust ivrybody—but cut th' cards." Although Dunne was often brought up in print on matters of domestic policy or international crises, the once-universal familiarity with "Mr. Dooley" definitely declined, in part, no doubt, because of the very dialect which had once been easily made out and admired by such intellectuals as A.J. Nock and Theodore Roosevelt (*q.q.v.*), dialect having become disturbing to persons over-sensitive to ethnic (*q.v.*) identification; see Filler, ed., *The World of Mr. Dooley* (1962).

**Dynamics,** see Social Dynamics

# E

**East Germany,** see Escapees

**Eastman, Max,** see Filler, DASC, and *National Review*

**Eaton, Dorman B.,** see Reforms and Conservatism

**Economic Interpretation of the Constitution** (1913), by Charles A. Beard. It was an interpretation which saw the Constitution as conservative, though not in the complimentary sense intended by later conservatives. Beard's was a daring qualification of earlier versions of history. He saw conservatives as molding the Constitution to curb a government which, under the Articles of Confederation (*q.v.*), had maintained a populist spirit and states' rights (*qq.v.*). These had been necessary for a successful Revolution. But after the Revolution conservatives needed a "strong, central government" capable of paying off those who had debts against it. This thoroughly denied any idealism associated with the Constitution. But Beard tried to evade the implications inherent in his work. "An economic interpretation," he called it, as though he intended no more than an historical exercise. He hastened to say that he was not saying—while saying it—that the patriots wanted a new government mainly to collect their debts. He avoided eloquence and used short paragraphs to give the appearance of simply jotting down facts. But many professional historians did not agree with his facts. Several wrote in hot contradiction. Beard, a product of Jeffersonian thinking and writing in the Progressive (*q.v.*) era, nevertheless attracted a following. See also *Progressive Historians, The.*

**Economics,** see Commercialism; Inflation; Deficit; Supply Side; Keynes, Lord; Chicago School of Economics; Federal Reserve System

**Economist, The,** see Bagehot, Walter

**Economy of Happiness, The (1906),** by James Mackaye, a late attempt to modernize late-18th-century Utilitarianism (*q.v.*) and early-19th-century English Radicalism (*q.v.*) by emphasizing the "common sense" elements of Bentham's pleasure-pain and materialistic principles. Although it scorned commercialism (*q.v.*) and held opposition to its formulas for satisfying human needs to be "conservative," it interested neither conservatives nor liberals. Its main value was in unconsciously calling attention to the difference between mid-19th century conditions and those of 1906, and reminding readers of the influence John Stuart Mill (*q.v.*) had had earlier and was to have again.

**Ecumenical Movement,** a term referring to efforts among Christian churches to draw closer together. It involved attempts to repair the historic divisions in Christianity caused by the split of the Eastern Orthodox Churches from Rome and by the later Protestant Reformation. Differences in doctrine and organization, however, made ecumenical efforts difficult. A key event in the ecumenical movement was the Second Vatican Council, known as Vatican II (*q.v.*). One result of the ecumenical movement was a new spirit of tolerance and acceptance among the mainline Christian churches. Interfaith services and cooperation became more and more frequent. Christian relations with Jews became more cordial as well, partly as a result of the ecumenical movement. There were also centripetal movements intended to make Jewish, Christian, and other communities more satisfying to their inhabitants through more emotive or flavorsome joining and ritual. Differences over the peace (*q.v.*) issue also separated co-religionist groups.

**Edison, Thomas Alva** (1847-1931), the master of American invention. He rose from humble beginnings to achievement and wealth. Self-educated in electricity and chemistry, in 1876 he established himself in Menlo Park, N. J., where he organized research projects related to electricity. His major achievements included the phonograph, the incandescent lamp, and motion-pictures. He also developed the storage battery, the signal box, and the dictaphone. Criticism of him emphasized his building on the labors of others, as well as his commercialism (*q.v.*). He had little philosophy beyond the ethics of work. Nevertheless, his inventions revolutionized modern society.

**Education,** see Filler, DASC. Education in America has endured numerous crises of goals and results, all of them traceable to changes in society. Many of these changes were functions of growth and demand for opportunity (*q.v.*), and justified themselves by their product. In the 19th century mechanics institutes were organized by workers themselves, recognizing that knowledge was power—and not only material knowledge but ideas and culture as well. Higher education for women grew against tradition, as individual women worked to prove that they could master fields traditionally reserved for men. Nothing came easily to men or women. Horace Mann (*q.v.*), despite prestige and achievement, had to fight meager salaries and grants to establish his pioneer normal schools in Massachusetts, and to overcome skepticism respecting his high goals for educators. High schools and vocational schools grew to meet the needs of a complex and growing civilization, with cities which could drown their populations in anonymity and injustice, if they were not ordered and directed through literacy and skills. Also required was the development of leaders with character. Progressive education was welcomed during the late 19th century because of the evident need for experiment to determine the most suitable means for servicing the various classes of child and student. But basic at the time was the family (*q.v.*), responsible for imparting a sense of humanity, love, loyalty, folk wisdom, and tradition to the child, who was then given over to others to become socialized and to unfold individual traits and abilities outside family and neighborhood. As the family went, so went education. In the main, it proved a cohesive agency which carried on American and group traditions and intellectual resources through public, private and parochial schools, all of varied qualities and distinctions. The 20th century crisis in education manifested itself slowly. Many schools called themselves "progressive" merely because they permitted teachers with too many pupils to relax discipline and standards. A lack of sufficient programs or personnel for individual or group attention added to the problem. (See Filler, "Main Currents in American Progressivist Education," *History of Education Journal*, 1957.) John Dewey (*q.v.*) became the symbol of progressivism to teachers who were unfamiliar with his writings. Many of the products of such schools returned to other schools as teachers or instructors. Schools of education became notorious for providing "easy" curricula. Truly "progressive" schools consciously sought to get away from disciplines interfering with "progressivism." For example, Arthur E. Morgan, a self-taught and original-minded engineer interested in "social engineering" (*q.v.*), while reinvigorating Antioch, Horace Mann's old college, deliberately sought history teachers who were untainted by the formal study of history. The resulting lack of depth and knowledge was more evident as time went on. The rise of Communism and Fascism in the 1930s created what seemed a greater crisis in education: a crisis in "knowhow" as opposed to the liberal arts. A. J. Nock's (*q.v.*) distinction between education and vocational education (*q.v.*) had no impact on a society determined on technology at the expense of knowledge, and on propaganda (*q.v.*) rather than understanding. The prosperity of World War II and later years multiplied school facilities and made the National Education Association (NEA) a powerful guardian of teachers' interests. The Soviets' acquisition of the atomic bomb created waves of alarm and inept demands for "patriotic" stances in the schools, as well as vendettas against "progressive" educators (see Rugg, Harold). In 1951 William F. Buckley, Jr. (*q.v.*) jolted the educational establishment with his *God and Man at Yale.* It stirred many conservatives to declare their distaste for modern America as it was reflected in education. Russell Kirk (*q.v.*) burst into the national limelight with *The Conservative Mind* (1953), which gave conservatives a background and direction. Kirk went on to follow the course of education through the 1950s and after, visiting campuses and engaging in debates with other educators—and even with the campus disrupters of the 1960s. He made regular assessments of "Behemoth" University, mostly in the *National Review*, reporting on worthless curricula and incompetent educators, and on occasion on colleges and administrators fighting the downward trends. His reports were finally brought together in *Decadence and Renewal in the Higher Learning* (1978). Although there were continual efforts to search for "improved" education, "successful" educational experiments, and the like, any achievements were relative to the general decline. Meanwhile higher education increasingly encouraged "fragmentation" and specialized "research" in the humanities and sciences. The president of Johns Hopkins University said that the schools were producing "educated barbarians," meaning specialists who could not see beyond their specialty. Whether among them there would be liberals or conservatives dissatisfied with their own results and able to join others in broader goals and comprehension was the question of the future. Martin Mayer, *The Schools* (1961); W. L. Griffen and J. D. Marciano, eds., *Education for a Culture in Crisis* (1972); Sidney Hook, *Education for Modern Man* (1973 ed.); J. E. Coons and S.D. Sugarman, *Education by Choice: The Case for Family Control* (1978). In 1986 Reagan's Secretary of Education William J. Bennett appeared to offer guidelines more positive to conservatives.

**Education of American Indians** involved perplexing questions. How should Indian youth be directed? Toward reverence for Indian tradition, and if so, as tribes or as a whole people? Or should they study adjustment to the larger framework of American ways and conditions? A hundred years of experience, in a general atmosphere of indifference, showed discouraging results. The social turmoil of the 1960s added to the confusion of goals and interests, while bringing forth Indian leaders and would-be leaders. See William E. Coffer, *Sleeping Giants* (1979).

**Eighth Amendment,** see Capital Punishment

**Eisenhower, Dwight D.** (1890-1969), commanding general in the European Theater in World War II, later President of the United States (1952-1960). There were many differences between Eisenhower the soldier, and Eisenhower the public man. As a soldier he was precise, unequivocal, and alert to errors of subordinates. As a public man he harked back to his youth in small-town Kansas, where one assessed people and situations quietly and spoke in generalities until precision was required. As a young soldier he studied regulations and his role within them. To satisfy his curiosity, he quietly learned to fly a plane, though doing so was outside his duties. He drily noted, but without disrespect, that he had "studied dramatics under [MacArthur] for five years in Washington and four in the Philippines." When he received his magnificent chance in Europe he assumed desperate responsibilities, but at the same time showed ease with ordinary soldiers and newspaper people, and courtesy and his famous smile with personages of high rank. His postwar choice as president of Columbia University was viewed askance by liberals and conservatives. He then undertook to organize the military forces of NATO (*q.v.*). As Republican candidate for the Presidency in 1952 he promised to visit Korea to settle the war there. Eisenhower repeatedly displayed a sense of popular feeling in the campaign which Adlai Stevenson, his opponent, lacked. Eisenhower's two Presidential terms saw him generally well protected from criticism. The most pointed complaints came from conservatives. They could not understand that he looked to goals, not finances, as a result of his military background. He promoted many Federal programs, such as the building of superhighways, which conservatives saw as fiscally irresponsible. He supported Supreme Court decisions outlawing racial segregation which many conservatives of the day regarded as judicially unwarranted. His foreign policy toward the Soviet Union was less confrontational than many conservatives desired. Some called Eisenhower "soft on communism." Birchites (*q.v.*) went so far as to call him a Communist. More responsible conservatives were appalled and embarrassed by the Birchites, but they still questioned many of Eisenhower's policies. Eisenhower himself had determined, however, that the state of society in the free nations, including the United States, did not permit any military confrontation with the Soviet Union. On January 5, 1957, he enunciated the Eisenhower Doctrine, which in effect placed new responsibility on the government to aid other nations which were resisting Soviet or Soviet-controlled domination. In a remarkable discussion, June 22, 1959, Eisenhower and Herbert Hoover (*q.v.*) agreed that, the state of the nation being what it was, only a middle of the road position was feasible, liberal and conservative positions being what they were (R. H. Ferrell, ed., *The Eisenhower Diaries* [1981]). His Administration is remembered fondly by many as a time of prosperity and tranquility before the turbulent 1960s. See also R. L. Treuenfels, ed., *Eisenhower Speaks* (1948); Robert L. Branyan, comp., *The Eisenhower Administration, 1953-1961* (1971); Fred I. Greenstein, *The Hidden-Hand Presidency* (1982); and R. F. Burk, *The Eisenhower Administration and Black Civil Rights* (1984).

**El Salvador,** see Latin America

**Elections.** They often reflected a conservative response to fatigue or frustration of various kinds, as well as division among the populace. For example, John Quincy Adams's (*q.v.*) election to the Presidency in 1824, when Henry Clay (*q.v.*) threw his votes to Adams, represented an effort to control the burgeoning democratic tide of the time which threatened to give power to elements not used to public office and capable of misusing it. Falsely denounced as a "corrupt bargain," it nevertheless incapacitated what should have been the best of Administrations in view of Adams's long experience and love of country. Other Presidential elections similarly demonstrated the ebb and flow of popular feeling. Following the Federalist (*q.v.*) era of small government and small budgets, corruption (*q.v.*) became a problem in city and state administrations. "Throw the rascals out" became a relevant slogan, descending to a cliché as alternatives to "patronage" (*q.v.*) were controverted. Glaring corruption rose and fell in city halls and state houses with varied conditions. Grover Cleveland's (*q.v.*) rise was partly due to the integrity he displayed as mayor of Buffalo and governor of New York, but partly resulted from divisions in the Republican Party and the growing public acceptance of Democrats, previously split by the Civil War. Tammany Hall became a symbol of big-city Democratic corruption in the late 19th century, but Democrats in the 1920s were quick to see Teapot Dome (*q.v.*) as representative of Republican and big-business (*q.v.*) corruption. Both Tammany Hall and Teapot Dome have faded into history, but liberals and conservatives of distinction and achievement continue to effect and be affected by new conditions.

**Eliot, John,** see Indians; Puritanism

**Eliot, Thomas Stearns (T.S.)** (1888-1965), arguably the most influential poet of the 20th century. He was distinctly a man of the right, whose influence, however, was so widespread as to reflect tendencies rather than further conservative causes. He was indeed as much made by the spirit of the times as making it or even shaping it. His main impulses appear to have been a sense of lost faith in the positive tendencies in society and a need for inner strength against the disintegration he discerned in the midst of what others saw as a forward, progressive movement of humanity. From Paul Elmer More and Babbitt (*qq.v.*) he learned of the defense provided by culture. The Symbolism of French poets and the metaphysical poems of John Donne suggested means for expressing his feelings. Dante and Milton provided visions of heaven, earth, and hell against which he could judge the passing scene. Most of all, the idea of culture, not as an adjunct to life but as life itself, informed his work. This could have kept his few poems and sometimes esoteric essays in obscurity had they not filled a hunger in more flamboyant contemporaries. Eliot moved among a substantial but still limited literary crowd in London, having abandoned Harvard University and America, but his work carried a message with universal overtones. Its burden was World War I, which blasted the lives and hopes of a generation, and all but destroyed chivalry and the ideals of patriotism (*q.v.*). Eliot's "Love Song of J. Alfred Prufrock" shocked readers and critics on both sides of the Atlantic, and signaled poetry's movement away from such popular styles as those of Vachel Lindsay and its concentration in fewer and fewer hands. Eliot was the effective spokesman for an elite (*q.v.*) which endeavored to define among itself proper attitudes toward life and the spirit. His own work—sharp, chiseled, responsive to the intonations and symbols of classical experience—was a point of reference, however small in quantity. *The Waste Land* (1922) was a sensation as James Joyce's *Ulysses* was a sensation offering guides to method, private language, and symbols which in inferior hands could give a feeling of superiority to those "in the know." It opened vistas for many individuals seeking solutions in a time of social crisis. This was true not only for those impatient with the vagaries of the masses, but also for those who hoped to lead them to socialism—despite reservations about his evident distaste for vulgarity ("Sweeney") and for undue optimism. His measured stanzas, evocative references, and obscurities, as well as his anticapitalist and religious ironies and his pessimism, appealed to a broad range of intellectuals. In "Ash Wednesday" (1930) he revealed his turn to Anglicanism. Eliot was also famous to millions of non-readers, and this fame would accompany his name up to and beyond the grave. (See Russell Kirk, "Pilgrims in the Waste Land," in Filler, ed., *Seasoned Authors for a New Season* [1980].) Eliot's plays were a phenomenon in their own right, from *Murder in the Cathedral* (1935), dealing with the last hours of Thomas à Becket, to *The Elder Statesman*, mixing light talk with ominous and resonant lines—poetry and prose which roused recollections from the Elizabethans to Oscar Wilde, and not accidentally. Eliot was famous for his gift of borrowing lines and rhythms from great authors and common speech. To some this was plagiarism and buffoonery; others saw an original mind at work which brought the past and present to life. A thousand books are said to be in the British Museum which deal with Eliot's life and works; there can be no doubt of the impress he has made on letters and attitudes. How much he has served the conservative cause it is difficult to judge. He was not happy with what he saw of the *National Review* (*q.v.*), which, he thought, gave the impression that all issues are decided in advance. There was, he thought, a need for "a dispassionate discussion of a number of current *idées reçues*" (Kirk, *Eliot and His Age* [1971]). His own *Criterion* (1922-1939) had had a quiet but powerful influence on academic criticism, like the *Kenyon Review*, which drew principles of "explication" from it. Eliot was capable of startling his professed admirers. When he introduced an edition of Rudyard Kipling's (*q.v.*) verse, expressing his regard for it, the fact astonished many. Kipling had been made a symbol of the old, discredited doggerel written in support of an infamous colonialism. Although much of the periphery of Eliot's fame is bound to fall apart, the heart of his achievement—fine lines and individual associations, a life of integrity, a profound commitment—will have the regard of discerning readers. T. S. Matthews, *Great Tom: Notes Toward The Definition of T. S. Eliot* (1974); Hugh Henner, ed., *The Pound* (*q.v.*) *Era* (1971); and Kenner, ed., *T. S. Eliot: A Collection of Critical Essays* (1968); F. O. Matthiessen, *The Achievement of T. S. Eliot* (1935).

**"Elitist,"** once applied as a perjorative term by liberals to conservative intellectuals, seen as defending a society in which they could be accorded respect for being the best educated and informed, the most intelligent, to whose opinions lesser mortals should bow. Rising conservative opinion, striking back at democratizing pressures, developed the view that the liberals were themselves "elitists," seeking to be the mouth of a scruffy democracy; in appealing for the "rights" of their half-educated fellows—often more emotional than thoughtful and, as products of the welfare state, often unproductive—they were speaking for constituents who they hoped would make liberals dominant voices of the new democracy. Thus, it seemed, anyone, liberal or conservative, could aspire to being an "elitist." See also Envy.

**Eloquence,** to be distinguished from demagoguery (*q.v.*). Conservatism could claim such giants of debate as Fisher Ames, Theodore Frelinghuysen, Daniel Webster, and the low-keyed but penetrating Abraham Lincoln (*qq.v.*). A factor more identifiable with conservatism than other social impulses was patriotism (*q.v.*), which often led to rant, but also to memorable sentiments. Southern partisans in and out of the Union, and after slavery (*q.v.*) as well as before, were often famous for their eloquence. Woodrow Wilson (*q.v.*), as a transitional (*q.v.*) figure between liberalism and conservatism, won plaudits for eloquence. Ronald Reagan (*q.v.*) was credited with having an effective "delivery," and with being a "great communicator," thanks to his earlier film career. The great Nixon-Kennedy debates (*q.v.*) were less notable for eloquence than for television emphasis on "image," which many observers felt swung the balance. Television (*q.v.*) was a significant and growing factor in politics from the 1960s on, in the opinion of many reducing the need for eloquence in public life. See DASC, and Filler, *The President Speaks* (1983 ed.).

**Emancipation Proclamation,** see Lincoln, Abraham

**Embargo,** see Jefferson, Thomas; Webster, Daniel

**Emerson, Ralph Waldo** (1803-1882), one of the great figures of American life and letters. He is viewed with some distaste and suspicion by conservatives who seek stability in the American tradition, and who feel that his apostrophes to Nature at the expense of orthodoxy, his faith in spontaneous expression, his willingness to be ruled by whim, and his call to Youth (*q.v.*) to lead the nation left a legacy of irresponsibility. Moreover, though not an abolitionist (*q.v.*), he was with the abolitionists in spirit: an attitude not calculated to appeal to Southern conservatives (see Agrarians) and those sympathetic to their tenets. This view of Emerson was matched by liberal revisionist views of the Civil War as a futile blood bath sustained by the idealism of Emerson and others. (See Daniel Aaron, *The Unwritten War: American Writers and the Civil War* [1973], a decidedly unfavorable portrait.) Emerson's true cause was individualism (*q.v.*), a theme conservatives theoretically approve. It gave him the ability to accept Walt Whitman, whose life and ways otherwise conflicted with those Emerson preferred.

**Employment,** see Unemployment

**Endless Crisis: America in the Seventies, The,** ed., François Duchêne (1970), a symposium under auspices of the International Association for Cultural Freedom. It was theoretically a cross-section of social scientific opinion, in fact a gathering of liberals. It gathered such black "activists" as Harold Cruse, the white activist Sam Brown (who complained that others like himself had not been invited), Lillian Hellman, Allard K. Lowenstein, Daniel Bell, Edward Shils, and others. Among the national figures involved were John Kenneth Galbraith, A. M. Schlesinger, Jr., George F. Kennan, Zbigniew Brzezinski, and Henry Kissinger. Foreign visitation included J. J. Servan-Schreiber, Alastair Buchan, and others from around the world. Topics discussed included Europe, "The Rape of Czechoslovakia," Latin America, Asia and "Dilemmas of Development." The president of the organization had formerly been with the Ford Foundation, which subsidized the sessions. Major domestic concerns included black dissatisfaction with opinion ranging from separatism to accomodation and the youthful uprisings of the 1960s (which were generally approved). In foreign affairs, the United States was seen as having to accomodate itself to future developments.

**Entente,** see Detente

**"Enterprise Zones,"** see New Federalism

**Entertainment,** more a factor in liberal-conservative differences in post-World War II decades than earlier, when entertainers were seen as a relief from oppressive problems rather than as contributive to their solution. Thus Frank Sinatra emerged from a position of teenage idol to fund-raiser for and friend of Presidents, and personally raised from penury the discredited Spiro Agnew (*q.v.*). Jane Fonda's work as film star was recognized as a factor in public perception of American participation in the Vietnam war. The actor Ed Asner, acting a television role of conscientious newspaper editor attained popular credence for his views of public affairs. Conservative writers recognized the power of entertainers to influence public-interest issues, and followed their careers as entertainers and opinion-makers with care. William F. Buckley, Jr., as talk-show commentator and host, recognized that participants had to entertain as well as inform, in order to attract audiences. Generally, liberal-minded entertainers were more effective than conservatives in reaching the public with their messages. Norman Lear, widely recognized for his liberal principles, in his long-running "All in the Family," was ingenious in utilizing a conservative setting within which to express his viewpoint.

**Entitlements,** a government term indicating obligations under law. Entitlements were limited under the original New Deal, which was presented as a relief measure for an abnormal time. Aid to the needy was termed "Relief," indicating that it was to be suspended as changing times permitted. Changing times, however, expanded rather than diminished disbursements to several classes which were not always needy. Although President Truman was not able to attain his "full employment" goals, which would have created a full measure of entitlements, he was willing and able to maintain Federal programs which helped create a permanent class of recipients. This trend was given an air of permanence under President Johnson, whose drive to end all traces of poverty created scores of agencies which increased the bureaucracy (*q.v.*) to monumental proportions. To end entitlements under such circumstances, with the poor (*q.v.*) a fact of life, and with the addition of the "new poor" (*q.v.*) created by economic and industrial vagaries, seemed hardly possible; at best, entitlements could be curbed or diverted into more fruitful channels, depending on society's direction.

**Environmentalism,** seen by Robert Nisbet (*q.v.*) as a new religion. Modern concern for the environment, the so-called environmental movement, can be traced to the publication of Rachel Carson's *Silent Spring* in 1962. In many ways similar to conservatism (Filler, DASC), environmentalism emphasized not only land taken out of private ownership or exploitation, but also the uses of the land and the results of particular land policies. The movement for preserving the environment was accelerated by the back-to-the-land impulses of the 1960s counterculture, by fears of nuclear power and its potential for catastrophe, and by the inadequate disposal of chemical and industrial waste by some manufacturers. Key to the environmental movement are the Resource Conservation and Recovery Act and the Safe Drinking Water Act passed by Congress in the mid-1970s. The Sierra Club, long a watchdog of environmental policy, cooperated with the League of Conservation Voters in its watch over the Federal Environmental Protection Agency, and with the Environmental Defense Fund, subsidized by Congress, in court actions. Environmentalists eventually became identified in the minds of many with liberal and radical-left activism. Many environmentalists seemed more interested in opposing capitalism and industrialism than in protecting the land and its resources. Their opposition to President Reagan's Secretary of the Interior James Watt (*q.v.*) helped lead to his resignation. But by the mid-1980s the environmental movement appeared to have lost much of its momentum. Concern for jobs and development in a changing economy outdistanced environmental concerns in the popular mind. Conservatives generally agreed that the land and its resources should be protected from exploitation and destruction, but they deplored the radicalism and fanaticism they saw in many environmentalists. Roy Arnold, *At the Eye of the Storm: James Watt and the Environmental-*

*ists* (1983). See also Censorship.

**Envy,** often employed to characterize the motives of malcontents. "Peter Simple" (*q.v.*) was scornful of liberal journalists and activists who encouraged such feelings, and in doing so brought down social standards of outlook and behavior still further. Liberals in turn held that conservatives, as "elitists (*q.v.*)," spoke for the well-to-do, without concern for the just ambitions of those lower in the social scale.

**Epithets.** They were often intended to depreciate others, and reflected group and national prejudices. Ethnic and class humor, once considered good-natured, and a check on pomposity and over-serious self-esteem, were highly diminished by laws opposing discrimination (*q.v.*) and subsisted, to the extent that they did, behind closed doors; for a variety of concepts, See Filler, DASC. The same conditions affecting international discourse, it is likely that some epithets, like "Hun," were incomprehensible to newer generations. "Rat" continued to be a universal epithet among foes everywhere. Some elements in society, given status by wider democracy or law, evaded definition, even when accurate, as in the case of "dope fiend." Homosexuals were given the word "Gay." Many conservatives made "liberal" an epithet, refusing to distinguish between its usages in various eras. They also sometimes carried the words "Red" and "Communist" far beyond their legitimate usage. Many liberals, on the other hand, often used "Fascist" and "reactionary" indiscriminately to refer to their opponents. "Bourgeois" and "middle class" were often epithets of American liberal intellectuals. "Intellectuals" itself was an epithet to those who disparaged them. The time level of political discourse in the 1980s tended to discourage the public use of disparaging epithets.

**Equal Rights Amendment (ERA),** see Schlafly, Phyllis

**Equality,** a favorable *bête noire* of many conservatives, made more troublesome and complex by recent government efforts over several decades to create "equal opportunities" at great expense, human and material, and with controversial results. Conservatives found it extremely difficult to persuade the general public that it should examine the validity of such "opportunities" (*q.v.*) and the accompanying "affirmative action" (*q.v.*). The famous words in the Declaration of Independence (*q.v.*), that "all men are created equal" were often quoted by equal rights partisans. Many conservatives argued them to mean that men were so *created*, but not necessarily so endowed. They were equal before God, but not before other human beings. Yet such conservatives had to face the reality of the "one man, one vote" (*q.v.*) principle: men and women *were* equal—at the polls. The conservative who wished to be effective, to move society, had to find some means to victory in elections. Some conservatives found difficulty in reconciling themselves to many of the inherent problems. They questioned some of the positions of Eisenhower, Nixon, and Reagan (*qq.v.*). They traced the confusion over the role and limitations of "equality" to the French Revolution (*q.v.*) and the philosophy of Jean-Jacques Rousseau (*q.v.*), which had exalted material equality at the expense of the spiritual, and had seen it as a goal to be maintained at all costs. This being impossible to attain, such a philosophy could only institutionalize unrest, envy and mean-mindedness as its gift to the future. Along with this philosophical base went more: bitter memories of mistreatment by aristocrats, their petty retainers, and servile supporters, succeeded by greedy merchants and hypocritical church and cultural establishment. And further, the dream of equality had raised heroic champions of freedom, romantic poets and composers, and cold-eyed and accurate chroniclers of an unjust society. Conservatives opposed a different picture of results, beginning with Edmund Burke's (*q.v.*) apocalyptical view of the chaos brought on by the Revolution. Burke's successors saw a democratic course of events which led to communism and fascism abroad, and, with the welfare state (*q.v.*) at home, to the degradation of family, education, selfhood and society. Also, as sheer result, the ruin of the very earth on which such human needs were nurtured. Rule there must be, but it must be the rule of the best. Equality could not be denied, but it must be interpreted in terms of an individual's resources, productivity, status in law, and merit. How far such an interpretation of "Equality" could be achieved, individual conservative spokesmen spelled out, noting the vagaries of law, the attainment of a community opinion, and the role of media (*q.v.*) in fostering particular standards and attitudes. See also Bellamy, Edward.

**Equality, the Third World and Economic Delusion** (1931), by P. T. Bauer, an influential conservative critique of the principles guiding Western democracy in its attempts to mitigate poverty and abysmal living standards in Africa. The book was in part a refutation of the arguments developed by the socialist R. H. Tawney in his well-regarded *Equality* (1929). Tawney had satirized "The Religion of Inequality," claiming that capitalism had operated without distinction, and that "the people" could be depended upon to administer society more rationally and competently than self-proclaimed masters. All they needed was "opportunity" (*q.v.*). Bauer pointed out that Tawney had expected opportunity to result in an equality of income. He had not taken into account what bureaucracy (*q.v.*) could do to social classes. Black Africans, he pointed out, persecuted black Africans. Moneys drawn into black economies were not distributed among the people, but collected in the hands of a few elite (*q.v.*) elements, the remainder of the population being left to feed on demagoguery or to starve. Bauer noted how natural economies had been uprooted in the interests of a "modernization" which did not modernize, but which had harmed a natural and necessary agriculture. See also Foreign Aid.

**Equity,** see Fairness

**Escapees,** the most dramatic and irrefutable evidence of the failure of the communist systems in the "Iron Curtain" countries patrolled by the Soviet Union and its nationalistic agents. Although East German authorities made feeble efforts to explain the desperate attempts of its citizens to flee their land under fire as involving traitors, criminals, American agents, and insane persons, the Berlin Wall and the graves of those who had been shot down by the wall in West Berlin stood as living evidence of the will of East Germans to leave their country. Similar events took place elsewhere by plane, boat, and automobile. In Soviet Russia itself, and in Red China to a lesser degree—due to fewer democratic lands adjacent as goals for flight—pleas for permission to emigrate, escapes from consulates, vacation spots, sports and artistic events gave testament to social unrest. See also Dissident.

**Essays on Hayek,** (1976), a Hillside College publication of the Mont Pèlerin Society (*qq.v.*), comprising essays on aspects of Hayek's work. Contributors include George C. Roche III, William F. Buckley, Jr. (*qq.v.*), U.S. Senator Roger W. Jepsen, and several other free-enterprise advocates, as well as Professor Shirley R. Letwin, a student of Hayek, and the University of Vienna-trained Professor Fritz Machlup.

**Establishment,** a term borrowed from the British tradition of relating church and state, modified in America to indicate influential connections between elements of government and other pursuits. It was used by both conservatives and liberals, often to indicate entrenched, influential, and even conspiratorial opposition to their policies and beliefs. Thus, liberals in the 1960s spoke of "the Establishment" as a conservative bastion opposed to change and progress. In the same period conservatives spoke of the "Eastern Establishment" as a cohesive force influential in promoting liberal policies. That such an "Eastern Establishment" did exist could not be denied; see Leonard and Mark Silk, *The American Establishment* (1980). Its centers included Harvard University, the *New York Times*, the Ford and Rockefeller Foundations, and the Washington-based Brookings Institute. This "Establishment" was qualified by strong elements in other educational institutions and journals, however, and moved between liberal and conservative tendencies. Since public opinion often ran against that of notable "Establishment" figures, it was sometimes difficult to estimate its power. The "Establishment" all but made Thomas E. Dewey (*q.v.*) President. It could not elect Nelson Rockefeller (*q.v.*) to that position. Conservatives saw the "Establishment" as helping to bring down the Nixon Administration and opposing the Vietnam War (*q.q.v.*). The Reagan Administration came to Washington flanked by a wide array of conservative institutions, such as the American Enterprise Institute, the Heritage Foundation, and the Conservative Caucus (*qq.v.*), and with journals and newspapers to interpret its program to the public. Whether these would add up to an Establishment was yet to be seen. A. M. Ducovny, *The Establishment Dictionary* (1971); Art Buchwald, *The Establishment Is Alive and Well in Washington* (1969). See also Ominous Politics.

**Ethic, Social,** a state of society in which a number of classes feel they have a stake. The conservative ethic tended to maintain roots in the past: to honor country, family, and duty to associates, and to maintain a regard for religion; to recognize the needs of young and old, the handicapped and the stranger; and to perceive the necessity for an education which transmitted a sense of these basics. The liberal view was more open, tolerating insults to the nation in recognition of a large loyalty, honoring "alternative lifestyles" even when they infringed on or insulted larger community ways, fearful of state activism in recognizing religious feelings, but welcoming state activities in separating itself from them; seeing the welfare state as a moral duty which could not be overdone. It sought an open education which, aside from technical skills, cut down differences between pupil and teacher, and met expectations, rather than inculcated them. Thanks to the youth (*q.v.*) uprising of the post-World War II era, and the entrance of many of the formerly embattled youth into the various institutions of society, the social ethic became a mixture of old and new, with many areas such as sex, deportment, the use of drugs, educational tenets, and attitudes toward crime, loyalty, and traditions in controversy.

**Ethnicity,** a term showing a consciousness of difference in customs, characteristics, language, and common history, whether involving a minority status or not. Thus WASPS (*q.v.*) could manifest a conscious sense of difference from others even where they were not singled out by laws or expectations, or held to be bigoted or insensitive by aggressive non-WASPS. Nathaniel Weyl (*q.v.*) revealed a sense of ethnic differences which many found challenging. American Indians and elements from India residing in urban American areas were likely to show such a sense of consciousness of group difference, as separating them from other minority (*q.v.*) communities. A.H. Greeley, *Ethnicity in the United States* (1974); G.B. Tindall, *Ethnic Southerners* (1976); M. Schneider, *Ethnicity and Politics: A Comparative State Analysis* (1978); C.H. Mindel and R.W. Habenstein, eds., *Ethnic Families in America* (1976).

**Euphemisms,** a greater problem in modern times than formerly when gentle or evasive words communicated to a class, and could be relatively ignored by other classes. "He passed on" could read sourly to an atheist, but read or sound appropriate to friends of the deceased. The long triumph of liberalism (*q.v.*), augmented by minority, youth, and other eruptions which carried with them visibility and material means demanded euphemisms for coating over otherwise questionable actions. "Alternative lifestyles" suggested free choice and equal legitimacy, though it often masked bullying and unhealthy activities. "Peccadillos" as a euphemism for fornication was pompous as well as inaccurate. "Liberating" for stealing, "drug culture" for taking drugs, and "pro-choice" for abortion seemed as unwarranted as calling housewives "slaves." As the party of dissent, conservatives tended to be critical rather than euphemistic, preferring to remain silent rather than absurd when one of their number was apprehended in less than adequate actions. They relished verbal triumph when President Carter (*q.v.*) having no policy concluded to "stay in the Rose Garden." Liberals envisioned a thoughtful and patient President pondering civilized choices for the seized "hostages" in Iran. Conservatives, in their turn, viewed him as empty-handed and impotent. Nevertheless, conservatives won significant power in 1980, and became themselves subject to a combination of bureaucratese (*q.v.*) and euphemism, with Department of the Interior Secretary James Watt being sometimes "misspoken," at other times dealing with "national species of special emphasis," that is, endangered species which could be killed. It was bureaucratese rather than insincerity which allowed "zero funding" for lopped-off programs, but euphemism for reluctantly approved "revenue enhancement," since the Administration was not happy to institute the resultant taxes. With George Orwell's (*q.v.*) *1984* (*q.v.*) looming over society, it remained to be seen how far apart double-talk would be estimated to be from his totalitarian "Newspeak." See Mario Pei, *Double Speak in America* (1973). See also Censorship.

**Euthanasia,** the act or practice of painlessly putting to death persons suffering from incurable or distressing disease. Euthanasia has undoubtedly been secretly practiced throughout human history. With the development of modern medical technology, however, questions have arisen as to how far medical treatment should be prolonged in cases involving incurable conditions. It is often possible, for instance, to maintain individuals who are brain dead on life-support systems for indefinite periods. Should the life-support system be disconnected? Similarly, many individuals with incurable diseases can be kept alive, conscious, and in great pain although there is no hope for their recovery. Should they be kept alive? If the answer in both cases is no, does this involve euthanasia or "mercy-killing"? By the mid-1980s these problems just began to be dealt with. Many conservatives, concerned with the value of human life, watched the situation closely. See also Abortion. William Munk, *Euthanasia*, ed. Robert Kastebaum (1977 reprint of 1887 ed.); A. B. Downey, ed., *Euthanasia and the Right to Death* (1970).

**Evangelicals,** see Falwell, Rev. Jerry; Moral Majority

**Evans, M. Stanton** (1934- ), hard-hitting conservative journalist and editor. He began his work, briefly, with the *Freeman*, then moved to the *National Review* and *Human Events*, for which he wrote and edited. In 1959 he moved to the conservative *Indianapolis News*. His books included *Revolt on the Campus* (1961), *The Liberal Establishment* (1965), and *The Assassination of Joe McCarthy* (1970).

**"Executive Privilege,"** see Filler DASC, a critical factor in the modern Presidency and its relations with Congress. How far can the White House go in protecting its internal workings from Congressional scrutiny? In the Watergate (*q.v.*) controversy, President Nixon claimed Executive Privilege in refusing to turn over to Congressional investigators tape-recordings of his meetings with key White House aides. His claim was denied by the Supreme Court, voting 8-0 against him. Subsequent administrations have claimed Executive Privilege when key aides, Cabinet officers, agency officials, and even records have been subpoenaed by Congress. A certain amount of confidentiality is necessary for any Administration to deliberate and arrive at policies. The extent of that confidentiality, however, is a source of controversy. See Raoul Berger (*q.v.*), *Executive Privilege: A Constitutional Myth* (1974).

**Expansionism,** often equated with Imperialism (*q.v.*), and indeed a term employed by those who approved of the seizure of the Philippine Islands in 1899 by President McKinley. Historically, however, the two concepts differed. Imperialism referred to the seizure or domination of lands by threat of force of arms against the will or traditions of a particular indigenous people. Expansionism described a situation in which large terrains, little used or sparsely populated or without the domination of an indigenous people, were settled from without. The historical growth of the United States involved both imperialism and expansionism. American courts, adjudicating claims and complaints from early times onward, were often forced to distinguish between the two.

**Expatriates**. They were a few in number in colonial times and the decades afterward, being limited to such persons as the traitor Benedict Arnold, Tories who settled elsewhere after the Revolution, and such later fugitives as the Jacksonian (*q.v.*) Samuel Swartwout. Such writers as James Fenimore Cooper and Washington Irving (*qq.v.*) visited abroad for longer or shorter periods. Centers of art in Rome, Paris, and London attracted groups of Americans in the 19th century, some artists and writers, others well-to-do or supported by money from America. These "colonies" of Americans in England and on the Continent grew in post-Civil War years as American fortunes increased and marriageable women sought titles abroad. In their turn, titled Europeans visited America in search of wealth; David Graham Phillips (*q.v.*) wrote one of his early novels, *Golden Fleece* (1903), about them. Most famous of all American expatriates was Henry James (*q.v.*), whose novels dealt mainly with Americans abroad. Before the 1920s expatriates were largely conservative and had relatively little impact on American thought. American intervention in World War I exposed large numbers of soldiers to European life. A popular song of the day, "How You Gonna Keep Them Down on the Farm after They've Seen Paree?" dealt humorously with the impact of this exposure. In the 1920s many American intellectuals and would-be intellectuals settled in Paris and elsewhere on the Continent, in self-imposed exile from the "stultifying" cultural scene at home. Their impact on American arts and letters was substantial. Their work often encouraged experiment in culture and living and skepticism toward traditional values. The Left Bank in Paris became synonymous with American expatriates who dedicated themselves to art, scorned material success, and lived a hedonistic, bohemian (*q.v.*) life. T. S. Eliot (*q.v.*), however, wrote with a strong sense of cultural tradition. The works of Stephen Vincent Benét (*q.v.*) were marked by an atypical patriotism and love of country. The Depression (*q.v.*) and the subsequent outbreak of World War II drove many expatriates home. Ezra Pound, however, remained in Italy, radio broadcasting treasonous commentaries to the American armed forces. After the war many Americans again settled abroad, but their influence on American culture and thought was small. In the 1960s the expatriate Henry Miller, whose writings many considered to be little more than pornography, enjoyed a vogue among some sympathizers with the youth (*q.v.*) counterculture. Isabel Ross, *The Expatriates* (1970).

**Expedience**, a pressure bearing on both liberals and conservatives. When a group is out of power or in the minority it can hold more firmly to its principles. When the group is actively seeking power, however, or face-to-face with the need to wield that power effectively, it must appeal to and deal with persons and groups with differing points of view. The line between compromise and expedience is often elusive. Many conservatives were disappointed with the policies and programs of the Eisenhower and Nixon (*qq.v.*) Administrations and commercial (*q.v.*) Republicanism. President Reagan (*q.v.*) found it difficult to satisfy his many and varied conservative supporters, though the overall tone of his Administration was more satisfying to most conservatives than that of previous Republican Administrations from Eisenhower's on. The rise of "single-issue" (*q.v.*) politics in the 1980s posed difficulties for both conservatives and liberals, with the idea of compromise itself becoming more and more suspect. The Democratic Party foundered in the 1980s by attempting to appeal to a myriad of single-issue groups. Thoughtful conservatives were concerned lest the same fate befall the Republican Party in the post-Reagan years.

**Experimentalism** see Dewey, John

**Explication,** see New Criticism

**Extremists,** a term traditionally applied in America to those farthest from the political "center" or urging radical departures from current practices and attitudes. Barry Goldwater's defense of "extremism" in the cause of freedom, in his 1964 campaign for the Presidency, was highly controversial. Some conservatives and liberals tend to identify each other with the most extreme examples of conservative or liberal thought. To such conservatives all liberals are "Communist revolutionaries." To such liberals all conservatives are "Fascist reactionaries."

# F

**Fairness**, a long-sought ideal among liberals responsive to social issues. "A fair wage" was long a labor objective. World War II (*q.v.*) permitted generous, rather than merely fair, wages. Postwar affluence led to demand by blacks for fairness in hiring, housing, and education. Despite President Kennedy's statement that "life is unfair," liberal sentiment in the 1960s and 1970s increasingly urged government efforts to ensure "fairness" in all aspects of life, especially where blacks and other minorities were concerned. Affirmative action (*q.v.*) was intended to promote such fairness. Many conservatives and others pointed out, however, that this often entailed unfairness to other groups and individuals. They wondered how government activities and social engineering could ensure that each human being's life would be happy and "fair." The growing conservative mood of the 1980s put stress on individual opportunity and initiative and downplayed government efforts at ensuring fairness. Twentieth Century Fund, *Fair and Certain Punishment: Report on Criminal Sentencing* (1976); National Committee against Discrimination in Housing, *Fair Housing and Exclusionary Land Use* (1974); Piers Beirne, *Fair Rent and Legal Fiction: Housing Rent Legislation in a Capitalist Society* (1978); David Listoken, *Fair Share Housing Allocation* (1975); Brian Percusson, *Fair Wages Resolutions* (1977); Steven J. Simmons, *Fairness Doctrine and the Media* (1978).

**Falkland Islands**, an important issue in international relations in 1982. Argentina took control of the islands by force from Great Britain, claiming that the islands had originally belonged to Argentina and had been lost to Great Britain illegally. The Thatcher (*q.v.*) government determined to retake the islands at whatever cost necessary (the final cost of the war being in excess of 1 billion pounds). Since Great Britain had given up control of an empire stretching from India to Africa, this raised questions about the meaning of sovereignty in modern times. The Falklands were in fact retaken, which toppled the Argentine government and raised Thatcher's prestige. The whole episode underscored the close ties between Great Britain and the United States, which was supportive of Great Britain. Although it seemed likely that Great Britain might ultimately give up "possession" of the Falklands, which contained only a handful of British subjects and cost London an estimated 400 million pounds a year, the incident emphasized the need for international diplomacy in the shadow of the great nuclear threat—diplomacy which could diminish the special interests which had diminished the authority of the United Nations (*q.v.*) *Sunday Times* of London, *War in the Falklands* (1982); Joe Laffin, *Fight for the Falklands* (1982).

**Falwell, Reverend Jerry**, evangelical minister and founder of the Moral Majority (*q.v.*). His "Old Time Gospel Hour" broadcasts reached an estimated 15 million people. Although one of numerous evangelicals, Reverend Falwell was successful in linking his message with the conservative social and political trends which led to the election of Ronald Reagan (*q.v.*). See Jerry Falwell and Elmer Towns, *Capturing a Town for Christ.* Dinesh D'Souza, *Falwell Before The Millenium: A Critical Biography* (1986).

**Family**. Conservatives place great emphasis on family values, and this affects their views on such subjects as abortion, human life, feminism, the ERA (*qq.v.*), and related topics. Conservatives perceived Supreme Court (*q.v.*) decisions curbing prayer in school and legalizing abortions as contributing to the disintegration of the family. Many believe that welfare (*q.v.*) as it has developed has also hurt the family. Other factors demoralizing to family cohesiveness, in the eyes of many conservatives, include the easy prosperity of World War II and the postwar years, the increased mobility of American life, the development of a homogenized culture neglectful of goals and traditions, and the counterculture of the 1960s with its direct assault on family values and promotion of "alternative life-styles" (*q.v.*). The new conservatism that crystallized in the 1950s has supported the traditional family whenever possible. Disquieting was the growth of two-job and single-parent families. The decline of the counterculture and the reassertion of many traditional values in the 1970s and 1980s were reassuring but the divorce rate continued high throughout the country. Many of the least wounded elements sought refuge in more conventional routines. The "futurist" (*q.v.*) Alvin Toffler's prediction that society was moving toward a "menu of family styles" could be seen as injudicious. The family was still very much in trouble, and much of the trouble came from a shaken society in an insecure world. Ira L. Reiss, *The Family System in America* (1971); L. and J. Scanzoni, *Men, Women, and Change* (1975); Selma Fraiberg, *Every Child's Birthright. A Defense of Mothering* (1977); Theodore Caplow, *Middletown Families: Fifty Years of Change and Continuity* (1981); Philip Slater, *Footholds...Shifting Sexual and Family Tensions in Our Culture* (1977); A. S. and J. H. Skolnik, *Family in Transition: Rethinking Marriage, Sexuality, Child Rearing, and Family Organization* (1981); C. McDannell, *The Christian Home in Victorian America, 1840-1900* (1986).

**Fantasy**, see *Myth, Allegory, and Gospel*

**Farmers**, see Filler DASC, traditionally seen as conservatives in social, religious, and economic principles, yet also as mainstays of such political "revolutions" as characterized the Jackson and Populist (*qq.v.*) uprisings. Their problems were largely economic and even self-inflicted, as when they took advantage of war needs and prosperity to expand their holdings and machinery unrealistically, using borrowed funds which had to be repaid, whatever their troubles with drought, flood, over-production, or competition abroad. In addition, the rise of the cities drew away their youth and voting power. They raised aspirations among erstwhile farm stay-at-homes which produced bitterness, envy, and confused objectives. Thus farmers, a dwindling social element, were both conservative and liberal in outlook. They became increasingly part of the mainstream of American opinion, and, as "agribusiness," of American business and industry. D. C. McCurry and R. E. Rubenstein, *Farmer-Labor Party History* (1975 reprint ed.); E. T. Benson, *Farmers at the Crossroads* (1956); E. C. Higbee, *Farms and Farmers in an Urban Age* (1963); M. Perelman, *Farming for Profit in a Hungry World* (1978).

**Fascism**. It is often associated with conservatism, though commercialism (*q.v.*) was more important to the rise of Hitler in Germany. In the late 1930s liberals accused America First (*q.v.*) partisans of fascist sympathies. Visible fascist elements in the United States have had little in common with any conservative philosophy and program. Liberals were confounded by the 1939 Nazi-Soviet Pact; many gave up "fellow traveler" (*q.v.*) status, but it was difficult to term fascist our subsequent ally opposing Hitler; some defended the Soviet assault on Finland as being a defense of communist borders against a "fascist" neighbor. Despite the fall of Hitler and Mussolini, the epithet "fascist" has persisted in use among many liberals. Nevertheless, there has been increasing public awareness that little if anything Communist actually distinguished the career of fascist Hitler and Mussolini from that of Stalin. Hannah Arendt, *Origins of Totalitarianism* (1966); N. Greene, ed., *Fascism: An Anthology* (1968); Walter Lequeur, ed., *Fascism: A Reader's Guide* (1977); Daniel Guerin, *Fascism and Big Business* (1977); William

Eberstein, *Today's Isms* (1973 ed.); Anthony J. Joos, *Fascism in the Contemporary World* (1978).

**"Fat-Bellied Capitalists,"** a cliché (*q.v.*) of 1930s radicalism, which saw "bosses" and "exploiters" as dining excessively at the expense of their underpaid employees and the unemployed (*q.v.*).

**FBI**, Federal Bureau of Investigation, see Hoover, J. Edgar

**Featherbedding**, the practice of unions (*q.v.*) requiring employers to hire unneeded workmen, to pay for unnecessary or duplicated work, or to limit the amount of work done by a given employee. Featherbedding is generally written into union contracts with employers. Thus, the Supreme Court felt constrained to approve a union rule of 1944 which enabled it to punish workers who went over production quotas set by themselves. The decision affected workers in the Wisconsin Motor Corporation in Milwaukee, members of the United Automobile Workers (UAW), four of whom were fined $50 to $100 and suspended from the union for a year for exceeding the production ceiling for piece workers.

**Federal Highway Administration**, part of the U. S. Department of Transportation, established 1966 in the Johnson Administration. Road-building, however, made significant steps under Eisenhower (*q.v.*), who set under way the great drive to build interstate and intercity highways. By cutting into and around cities and creating new, artificially nurtured commercial complexes, engineers and politicians made debatable impress on neighborhoods and society across the country. H. S. Firestone, *Man on the Move* (1967); Wilfred Owen, *Wheels* (1967). See also Automobile.

**Federal Reserve System**, originally intended to curb such unnecessary economic dislocations as resulted from the failure of the Knickerbocker Bank in New York in 1907, despite ample but not fluid assets. This brought on the "Money Panic" and lost savings for depositors across the land. Establishment of the Federal Reserve System was fought by bankers (*q.v.*), who saw it as an infringement on their prerogatives. However, they soon adjusted themselves to its use. In theory, its ability to control the money supply should have made significant economic depressions obsolete. The crash of 1929 gave evidence that this was not the case. The economy was tied to many factors, not the least psychology, and the coming of the New Deal (*q.v.*) added a mighty component of government intervention which required an adjustment of the role the "Fed" played in the economy. The swift expansion of goverment debts, taxes, and international commitments finally confronted the country in the 1970s with dilemmas of inflation, high interest rates, and high unemployment. The "Fed's" various efforts at tightening the money supply to pull down inflation, to "ease" the money flow to bring down interest rates, and otherwise to act as a mediating factor in banking and business brought it an unprecedented attention, and made the name of its chairman, Paul A. Volcker, as well-known as any in the land. One economist called him the most important man in the world. His policies affected world trade. However, continuous attention to those policies made clear that they were only one factor in the economic chain of government, business, unions, and ultimately saving, public spending, and earning—which could only to a degree be cajoled into lifting the economy to a secure plateau. Daniel S. Ahearn, *Federal Reserve Policy Reappraised* (1963); Martin A. Larson, *The Federal Reserve and Our Manipulated Dollar* (1975); R. D. Erb, ed., *Federal Reserve Policies and Public Disclosure* (1978).

**Federalists**, originators of conservatism in American politics. They made their mark in opposition to the new government under the Articles of Confederation (1783-1787), which they condemned as unable to enforce the laws it passed. In their sweeping censure of life under the Articles, they forgot that the Revolution had taken place against centralized power and that power in the states was its goal. Moreover, they ignored the confederation's achievements: the negotiations of a treaty of peace with Great Britain, treaties with France and Spain which gave form to the new government's status among nations, and above all passage of the Northwest Ordinance. It stripped Virginia of her claims to the West, which would have stopped the new nation's growth and made Virginia an empire. It also provided for education in the Old Northwest and for the admission of new states into the Union. And it ensured that there was to be no slavery in the territory which extended from the Ohio River to Canada. Federalism was, in fact, a revolutionary movement tied to the acceptance of the new Constitution by the States. This acceptance was urged successfully by the *Federalist Papers*. Federalists controlled the country's politics and life under two presidents, George Washington and John Adams (*qq.v.*). They forced acceptance of the Constitution by quelling anti-tax insurrections, notably in western Pennsylvania, where a tax on whisky was resisted. With Alexander Hamilton (*q.v.*) as Secretary of the Treasury, they imposed a conservative fiscal policy, which included funding of the public debt and encouraging industry through subsidies and high tariffs. Involved in an undeclared war with France, they prepared for hostilities, only to have the bubble of nationalism pricked by President John Adams's realistic negotiations. Federalists were swept out of office in the 1800 elections, with only the Supreme Court still in their hands and with a strong Federalist sentiment still in New England. They all but opposed "Mr. Madison's War" of 1812. The growing numbers of white voters served the Democrats more than it did the Whigs, successors to the Federalists. Not until 1840, with the opportunistic candidacy of General William Henry Harrison and John Tyler of Virginia—"Tippicanoe and Tyler too"—did the Whigs learn the demagogic stratagems which had been employed by the Democrats. The Democrats continued substantially to dominate the scene in an alliance of slaveholders and mechanics until the rise of the Republican Party in the 1850s, which changed perspectives for conservatives in both the North and South. (*Qq.v.* for above.) D. H. Fischer, *The Revolution of American Conservatism: The Federalist Party in the Era of Jeffersonian Democracy* (1965); J. C. Miller, *The Federalist Era* (1960); Paul Goodman, *Federalists versus the Jeffersonian Republicans* (1977).

**Federalist Papers, The**, a series of 85 political articles appearing in the press, 1787-1788, as written by "Publius." The chief author was Alexander Hamilton, with contributions by James Madison and John Jay (*qq.v.*). The articles were intended to persuade New Yorkers to approve the new Federal Constitution (*q.v.*), which Federalists intended to succeed the Articles of Confederation. It was indicative of the time that there was suspicion of steps which would increase centralized government, especially among rural elements which remembered that power had once been centralized in London. It was the supreme achievement of Hamilton and his associates that they spelled out in classic terms the balance of powers intended by the new Constitution which would curb overweening authority. Hamilton was especially keen in perceiving that the wealthy would be a significant "minority" as the population expanded, and that they would need a more independent and strong Senate to control the majority rule of the House of Representatives. Gottfried Dietze, *The Federalist* (1960); Clinton Rossiter (*q.v.*), *The Federalist Papers* (1961).

**"Fellow Travelers,"** a Leninesque (*q.v.*) concept. Communism would be advanced not only by dedicated communists—"professional revolutionaries"—but also by others less dedicated but "traveling in the same direction." In fact, not a few "fellow travelers" were able to be more effective than Communists because of strategic positions in society and their ability to move among social elements and concerns, gathering information, studying alignments, and putting weight or pressure where they could do the most good for the cause. The decline of Communism as such in America led to the disappearance of "fellow travelers." Those sympathetic to Communism tended to involve themselves with liberal and radical-left circles. See *Odyssey of a Fellow Traveler*.

**Fels, Joseph**, see Social Dynamics

**Femininity**. It was brought into question by women's rights militants in the 1960s and 1970s. Femininity was held to be an indication of subservience, a means of limiting women's abilities on jobs and in homes, and a transgression of their needs. Extremists repudiated child-bearing, encouraged hatred and disgust for men, and promoted lesbianism as an alternative. As women competed more and more for jobs with men, femininity was seen by many as a hindrance to that effort. See New Chastity, The. George Gilder (*q.v.*) met the issue head-on in *Sexual Suicide* (*q.v.*). Many conservatives ignored it, preferring to deal with women's issues on legal or realistic grounds. In 1984 a best-selling author, Susan Brownmiller, whose *Against Our Will* (1975) had denounced rape, issued *Femininity*. In it she noted a "resurgence of feminine wiles." This, she believed, was due to a diminution of the number of available men—she counted half a million more women than men in New York, and a male homosexual population there of from three to four hundred thousand—and the greater difficulty of women in attaining jobs.

**Feulner, Edwin J., Jr.** (1941- ), a Richard Weaver (*q.v.*) Fellow at the Intercollegiate Studies Institute (*q.v.*), he attended the London School of Economics. He later went to Washington as assistant in the Department of Defense, and then worked for Congressman Philip M. Crane (*q.v.*). He became president of the Heritage Foundation and publisher of *Policy Review* (*qq.v.*). His publications included *Congress and the New International Economic Order* (1976) and *Looking Back* (1981). He edited *China, the Turning Point* (1976) and *U.S.-Japan Mutual Security* (1981).

**Field, Stephen J.** (1816-1899), Associate Justice of the U.S. Supreme Court from 1863 to 1897. It was one of the longest terms of service in court history. Admired for his defense of private property by conservatives, he was also noted for his conscientious concern for moral principles, notably in his opposition to anti-Chinese laws passed in his adopted California. He denounced them as racist and discriminatory, as in his opinions concerning *In re Ah Fong* (1874) and the "Queue Ordinance" case (*Ho Ah Kow v. Nunan*, 1879). His dissent in *Munn v. Ill.* (1876; see Waite, Morrison R.) was clearly in defense of large capital over small, though couched in Constitutional terms. Since he saw every man as a capitalist his opposition to the income tax as "an assault upon capital" (*Pollock v. Farmer's Loan*, 1894) was less a defense of capitalism than of opportunity (*q.v.*). Carl B. Swisher, *Stephen J. Field: Craftsman of the Law* (1930); A. M. Paul, *Conservative Crisis and the Rule of Law* (1930).

**Fifth Amendment.** During the 1950s the Fifth Amendment to the Constitution gained public attention in connection with Congressional hearings on Communist influence in government and elsewhere. With general anxiety heightened by Soviet development of the atomic bomb, aided by Americans with access to military secrets, and China overrun by Communist armies, it seemed urgent for the nation to investigate Communist activities at home. The House Un-American Activities Committee held hearings and called witnesses. Many of them refused to testify. They invoked the key phrase of the Fifth Amendment, that no one "shall be compelled in any criminal case to be a witness against himself" and maintained that any answer of theirs "might tend to incriminate" them. Implied in the transaction was the possibility of criminal charges, though not necessarily criminality. Many conservatives took the position that the issue was defense of American interests, and that loyalty should be proved by cooperation. Since the intent of the Fifth Amendment was to place an emphasis on evidence rather than self-incrimination, the hearings should have concentrated on elucidating social positions and their effect on society. Instead, abuse and counterabuse turned the spotlight on irrelevant features of the proceedings and pulled liberals and conservatives apart even further. See Sidney Hook (*q.v.*), *Common Sense and the Fifth Amendment* (1957).

**First Amendment,** see Bill of Rights; see also Fifth Amendment

**Fish, Hamilton** (1808-1893), New York aristocrat and public servant. He reached the height of his conservative career as Secretary of State in the Administration of Ulysses S. Grant (1869-1877). Using firmness and negotiating power, in the Treaty of Washington (1871) he peacefully settled Civil War claims which could have brought on war with Great

Britain; calmed a crisis with Spain over the seizure of the ship *Virginius* and the shooting of Americans aboard (1873); and achieved a commercial treaty with Hawaii (1875), a step toward final annexation by the United States. Allan Nevins (*q.v.*) *Hamilton Fish* (1936).

**Fluoridation**. The fluoridation of drinking water to prevent tooth decay among children aroused great controversy in many communities in the 1950s and afterwards. Some extremists saw it as a radical plot to stupify Americans and make them easier prey to Communist machinations. William F. Buckley, Jr. (*q.v.*) saw the campaign to put fluoride in drinking water as a "liberal mania." The *National Review*, however, saw the issue as one of choice rather than compulsion. The usefulness of fluoride seemed medically supported, the issue in many communities indeed being choice: whether they cared to spend their funds on "forced medication." Many communities thought not. By the 1980s, however, the general public seemed persuaded of fluoride's value and it was used extensively in toothpastes and mouthwashes.

**Flynn, John T.** (1882-1964), a fiery advocate of both liberalism and conservatism. He first made his reputation as a critic of capitalism, or rather of how capitalism was functioning. It was this which brought him to the attention of the radical *New Republic*. A long-time journalist and editor, in 1933 Flynn began a column for the magazine entitled "Other People's Money." He took his title from Louis D. Brandeis's (*q.v.*) book on the Congressional investigation of "money trusts" of 1912. Flynn had already published *Graft in Business* (1931) and *God's Gold* (1932), the latter a critical review of John D. Rockefeller's (*q.v.*) career. His earlier *Investment Trusts Gone Wrong*, (1930) had blamed the economic crash on wrong policies and faithless people. Flynn favored the New Deal (*q.v.*) as an opportunity to put proper policies into effect. He was quickly disillusioned, seeing it as authoritarian and politically dangerous. He saw "fascist" potentials in the National Recovery Administration program, and he perceived connections between businessmen and munitions manufacturers. In 1936 for President he favored socialist Norman Thomas. When, however, he concluded that Franklin D. Roosevelt was an unconscionable Machiavellian, likely to bring America into a war on the side of imperialist Great Britain, he was repudiated by his colleagues and his *New Republic* column ended. His *Country Squire in the White House* (1940) lost him old associates and gained him new ones. He was a founding father of America First (*q.v.*) favoring non-intervention in the European War. With such supporters as Henry Ford (*q.v.*), who was accused of anti-Semitism, and Charles A. Lindbergh, Jr. (*q.v.*), who was suspected, perhaps unfairly, of pro-Nazi sympathies, Flynn had to fight anti-Jewish tendencies in his organization. In *As We Go Marching* (1944) and *The Roosevelt Myth* (1948) Flynn joined the revisionists (*q.v.*) in claiming that war had come as a result of a government conspiracy that had continued in the Yalta (*q.v.*) agreement. Flynn was a defender of McCarthy (*q.v.*) and his cause, but was disappointed with the postwar conservative turn away from non-intervention to a program for fighting communism, not only at home, but on the world arena. Michele Flynn Stenehjem, *An American First* (1976); R. Radosh, *Prophets on the Right* (1975).

**Food Stamps**, a welfare state (*q.v.*) program designed to enable the poor and needy to receive adequate nutrition. Qualified applicants were given allotments of stamps which they could use to purchase food. Many conservatives in the 1970s and 1980s alleged excessive waste and fraud in the federal food-stamp program. Procedures were tightened somewhat, but the question of who was eligible for food stamps—that is, the income level at which one would be defined as poor and needy—was a bone of contention between the Reagan Administration and Congress. In 1983, some 22 million people were receiving food stamps at an estimated cost of 11.3 billion dollars. The year before Congress had approved a $2.3 billion cut at President Reagan's request, reducing recipients by about a million persons. Future projections, however, promised little diminishing of the number of recipients.

**Ford Foundation**, see Foundations; Social Dynamics

**Ford, Gerald** (1913- ), a long-time conservative Republican leader in Congress, successor to Spiro Agnew as Vice President and to Nixon (*qq.v.*) as President. He compiled a record in two and a quarter years which conservatives, despite caveats, generally approved of but which they found disappointing in some respects. His pardon of Nixon for any crimes committed during his term of office was denounced by many liberals. Faced with a Democratic Congress, Ford could do nothing to lessen Federal expenditures and fight inflation (*q.v.*). Nor did he have much freedom in dealing with Vietnam (*q.v.*) because of congressional weariness with the war. He did, however, resist the Cambodian seizure of the American Merchantman Mayaguez (see 1975) as well as North Korean probes against South Korea (see MacArthur, Douglas). A string of trivial accidents during his public appearances hurt his Presidential image and made him appear clumsy and inept. His televised statement that Poland was not dominated by the Soviet Union and his refusal to support Federal aid to prevent New York City's bankruptcy (which cost him the electoral votes of New York State) undoubtedly hurt him in the close 1976 Presidential election. Unfortunate to many conservatives was his support of SALT II (The Second Strategic Arms Limitation Treaty), signed in 1979 under Jimmy Carter (*q.v.*), which conservatives felt gave the Soviets respectability and the opportunity to build armaments detrimental to American security. Ford felt, however, that such agreements were inevitable and necessary. While not the ideal Chief Executive to many conservatives—he approved of ERA and would later endorse the Panama Canal (*q.v.*) treaties—he was a respectable transition President in a time of acute national crisis. See John Hersey, *The President* (1975); Clark R. Mollenhoff, *The Man Who Pardoned Nixon* (1976); Ford's own *A Time to Heal* (1979); Malcolm D. MacDougall, *We Almost Made It* (1977).

**Ford, Henry** (1863-1947), pioneer in assembly-line manufacturing. He helped to transform the country by making automobiles available to the masses. David Graham Phillips's (*q.v.*) fear had been that the automobile would create a new elite which looked down on the man in the street. Instead it became an inevitability which transformed environments, distances, and homes. Ford exemplified an American tradition of energy and initiative, of humble beginnings and a rise to wealth and authority: a mixture of commercialism (*q.v.*) and social virtues. He also mixed welfare capitalism (*q.v.*) and old industrial tenets with his innovative five-dollar minimum wage and his distrust of unions. He disturbed fellow industrialists with his unilateral attempts to mediate peace during World War I, and in the early 1920s he subsidized inquiries involving anti-Semitic suppositions. Nevertheless he impressed some analysts of the American scene as worthy of a political role in an industrial society. The economic crisis of the 1930s harmed his reputation, when he tried, through agents, to resist union (*q.v.*) activities by force. His Ford Foundation evolved from conservative premises into an agency interested in encouraging social change in liberal directions. Ford's value for modern conservatism is still unclear. Allan Nevins and F. E. Hill, *Ford (1954-1962)*; R.M. Wik, *Henry Ford and Grassroots America* (1970).

**Foreign Affairs**, see Detente; Isolationism; Korea; Vietnam; Dulles, John Foster; Kissinger, Henry; Poland; South Africa, Republic of.

**Foreign Aid**, see Filler, DASC. Since World War II it has been a key problem for conservatives looking abroad. In 1960 Barry Goldwater (*q.v.*) noted that foreign aid had strengthened friendly nations to resist the Soviet juggernaut at a time when it had threatened to move over Greece, Turkey, and other areas, thus diminishing the terrain available for the Cold War (*q.v.*). But, Goldwater added, foreign aid had been handled without care and discrimination. Some money outlays had not been necessary; the nations involved would have fought for their freedom without them, and been more firmly attached to their freedom as a result. Some policies had been questionable—for example, shipping farm products abroad in ways which gave anti-

Americans a chance to claim America was interested in profits, not freedom. And some outlays had been to foes of America: Marxists, Communists, and Soviet surrogates who had used the aid to turn against their American benefactors. Although foreign aid survived many domestic protests—thanks in part to ignorance, indifference, and the power of American agriculture and other domestic interests—attention to it increased because of growing conservative opposition and because a tightening American economy brought more scrutiny of budget expenditures. Victor Ferkiss, *Foreign Aid: Moral and Political Aspects* (1965); K. W. Thompson, *Foreign Assistance: A View from the Private Sector* (1972); Melvyn B. Krauss, *Development without Aid* (1982). See also *Equality, the Third World and Economic Delusion*.

**Foundation For Economic Education**, organized in 1946 by Leonard E. Read (1898-1982) and dedicated to promoting the least government activity possible in the economic sphere. Encouraging "voluntarism," it attracted the interest and support of business people and educators inspired by its vision. It spread its message through speakers and its publication, *The Freeman*. It also sponsored seminars and debates and a Freedom Library, with works ranging from Frederic Bastiat's (*q.v.*) *The Law* to William Graham Sumner's (*q.v.*) *What Social Classes Owe to Each Other*. Henry Hazlitt (*q.v.*) was much admired by the Foundation. George C. Roche III (*q.v.*) of Hillsdale College worked with the organization. Leonard Read himself contributed numerous publications to its library, with such titles as *Elements of Libertarian Leadership, Thoughts Rule the World*, and *Talking to Myself*. He admired Herbert Spencer and Murray N. Rothbard, and also Grover Cleveland and Calvin Coolidge (*qq.v.*).

**Foundations**, see Filler, DASC. At one time foundations, like charity (*q.v.*), were viewed skeptically by many liberals and radicals as being attempts by capitalists to quell social unrest and justify the status quo. In recent years foundations have come under more critical attack as tax-dodges, and for building power structures in education, medicine, administration, and other areas. Social turbulence following World War II posed fundamental problems for the nation, with such foundations as the Ford Foundation distributing multi-million-dollar grants for experiments in such areas as housing and education. Many conservatives wondered whether such foundations, like many liberal organizations, were ignoring tradition and common sense in favor of an amorphous "social engineering" and change for the sake of change. In the 1980s conservatively oriented foundations began to come to the fore, such as the Ingersall Foundation; (see Ingersall Prizes, The).

**Founding Fathers**. Since the Founding Fathers were of varied minds, they could be claimed by both liberals and conservatives. Democrats celebrated Thomas Jefferson's birthday, Republicans that of Abraham Lincoln. Complexities created by the rise of the Soviet Empire, the dissolution of the British Empire, and the emergence of interest groups in the United States which found little relevance in the American past—many of whom despised its historical treatment of blacks, Indians, and others—appeared to make the Founding Fathers less urgent to a reorganization of the nation's social and political systems. Whether their essential doctrines and personalities might seem more necessary in the future could not be guessed. Although a certain amount of scholarly industry continued in the collection of papers and the production of monographs, they had little effect on journalism, conservative or liberal, and were balanced between ritualistic appreciation and studied efforts to demean; see, notably, Jefferson, Thomas.

**Fourteenth Amendment**, see Due Process

**Fourth Amendment**, see Violence

**Fourth International**, see Comintern

**Fountainhead, The** (1943), by Ayn Rand. The novel aroused critical interest more on the basis of its principles than its art. Its hero was Howard Roark, an architect and an undefiled realist-idealist. He was a man who could pronounce the Parthenon a failure, and certainly irrelevant to the present. He also could turn away multi-millionaire clients who presumed to tell him what they wanted in a building he would design. He helped lesser men to fame and wealth, and worked at manual labor while waiting for lucrative offers to do what he wished to do. Roark came from nowhere and wanted nothing. Yet the novel itself was a great success and treated seriously by Rand's followers, and conservatives were repelled by her message of unbridled individualism and atheism. *Atlas Shrugged* was an equally massive and successful work and equally incredible. See also Rand, Ayn.

**Franklin, Benjamin** (1706-1790). Many liberals have seen him as a wise radical sponsor of revolution some conservatives, on the other hand assess him as conservative in spirit and actions. Though a Deist (*q.v.*), he thought it judicious to attend church, to set an example to the people, and suggested prayer to open revolutionary conferences for the same reason. Franklin approached revolution as a last resort. D. H. Lawrence despised him for his calculating nature; see Lawrence's *Studies in Classic American Literature* (1923). Evidence concerning his somewhat unruly personal life has served to humanize one of America's greatest figures. See W. Randall, *A Little Revenge: Benjamin Franklin and his Son* (1984).

**Fraternal Organizations,** see Charities; Rotary

**Free Enterprise**, a paradoxical tenet of conservatism, emphasizing as it does liberty from restraints and faith in the "free market," while approving many of the workings of large corporations which dominated smaller concerns in their fields and sought and received government cooperation, financial and otherwise, and which, thanks to the intricacies of production and distribution, were dominant factors in other fields and industries. Conservative spokesmen were often willing to disavow fraud and suppression of rights in connection with free enterprise, from the scandals which defaced the Warren G. Harding (*q.v.*) Administration to those which emerged in succeeding years. However, it was the contention of farsighted conservative advocates of free enterprise such as Milton Friedman (*q.v.*) that, despite tragedies and frustrations which marred its workings, the record and potential of free enterprise were vastly better than those of socialists or "planners," who created self-serving bureaucracies operating on presumptions rather than facts, and whose policies encouraged non-productivity and fraud in their economics at the expense of suffering populations. Although planned-economy advocates pointed to the Great Depression (*q.v.*) as evidence of the obsolescence of "free enterprise," conservatives pointed to nations committed to socialism (*q.v.*). They noted Soviet Russia's long-term failure in agriculture, a failure which it exported to its satellite nations. They observed how nationalized industries in Great Britain had drained its work force of incentives and competence, and how its welfare policies had destroyed self-respect and the will to work in large sections of the population. The dynamics of the New Deal and government actions following World War II (*q.v.*) involving subsidies to farmers, defense contracts in connection with the Cold War (*q.v.*), and an affluence which enabled politicians to avoid coming to terms with monetary, social, and welfare-state problems brought on a build-up of dissatisfaction which war and partisan scandals could not quell. The conservatively oriented administrations of Eisenhower, Nixon, and Ford (*qq.v.*) failed to turn the nation's direction toward "free enterprise" principles. The Reagan Administration took office on the heels of Margaret Thatcher's (*qq.v.*) triumph in Great Britain. Thereafter, both Reagan and Thatcher attempted to turn back their respective states to principles and practice more in keeping with "free enterprise" principles. France's turn toward "socialism" provided one point of comparison with the U. S. and Great Britain. Taiwan was hailed by conservatives as a modern industrial miracle, in contrast to Communist China's use of its population and resources. Although individuals everywhere were obviously more subject to outside forces than in eras and locales which more openly welcomed "free enterprise"—such an era as had, for example, produced a Benjamin Franklin (*q.v.*)—and nations more firmly related than ever before, it seemed likely that "free enterprise" would continue to be of importance to conservatives, and to others in need of evoking social enterprise and energy from associates and themselves. See also Gilder, George; Laffer, Arthur; Smith, Adam; Industrial Revolution, The; Free Trade.

**Free Soilers**, often confused with abolitionists, but emphasizing at their inception and in the 1848 elections not so much slavery's sinfulness and its offensiveness to God (*q.v.*) as its trangression of American goals in the settlement of Western land. Indeed, the Free Soil candidate in 1848 was former President Martin Van Buren, more than tolerant of slavery, and willing to see it perpetuated to the extent that it did not curb Western opportunities for Northerners or prospects for capitalist developers. True abolitionists (*q.v.*) divided between those seeking to politicize anti-slavery by supporting the Free Soilers and others who refused to vote for Van Buren in view of his record. Many Free Soilers developed a rhetoric which gave them the outward appearance of abolitionists, but they were willing to negotiate and compromise with pro-slavery partisans to limit the spread of slavery or preserve the Union, as in the case of Abraham Lincoln (*q.v.*). Free Soilers were most extreme in their speech and actions in Massachusetts but were present throughout the North. J. G. Rayback, *Free Soil: The Election of 1848* (1970).

**Free to Choose** (1980), by Milton Friedman (*q.v.*) and Rose Friedman, a "personal statement" explaining and illustrating their views of the money flow as the central medium of exchange. This readable work helped put money in its current conservative context. It referred to historical matters and discussed economic mechanisms which were seen as subject to adjustment. Thus, the rise of great businesses in the post-Civil War decades was seen as products of "19th-century liberalism" (*q.v.*) and the businessmen themselves as "choosing" ventures which succeeded and enriched the nation. The problem was with the role of government, which the Freidmans recognized could not avoid a certain amount of interference. But of what kind and when? The Panic of 1907 was shown to be responsible for the creation of the Federal Reserve System. (The fall of the great Knickerbocker Bank in New York had triggered the Panic, which emphasized the need of a mechanism for providing funds to solvent banks requiring immediate cash to cope with customer "runs.") The Friedmans failed to note evidence, however, that the Panic had been deliberately caused to force a change in the administration of the Knickerbocker Bank. This would have required a recognition of the difference between conservative theory and commercialism (*q.v.*), which often limited freedom in the free market. The Friedmans were aware of the role of leaders in capitalist enterprise, and they perceived the nature of "mismanagement." Their monetary emphasis caused them to underplay the role of misleaders.

**Free Trade**, a potent avenue for the expression of social, class, and sectional feelings. In the 19th century it was resisted by Protectionists (*q.v.*), who claimed to be defending home industry from foreign competition. The South's (*q.v.*) cotton economy gave it an interest in the availability of low-priced goods. This led to secession (*q.v.*) and war when the slavery issue became unsolvable, and the Republicans, a Protectionist and Northern party, triumphed in 1860. After the Civil War, Democrats North and South argued for Free Trade, and thus claimed to be the party of the people, who needed low prices for food, clothing, and shelter. The Free Trade argument was eventually modified by the Reciprocity idea, which asked a *quid pro quo* of foreign producers. With the rise of powerful Japanese, German, and other economies in the 1970s and after, and the failure of American industrial productivity, a clamor began among American labor unions (*q.v.*) for protection from foreign products, notably automobiles, but affecting many other products, producing dilemmas for a nation intertwined politically as well as economically with other nations.

**Free World**, a self-designating phrase adopted by Western democracies to call attention to their own free societies as well as to the lack of freedoms in the Soviet-dominated areas of the world.

**Freedom**. The term has been utilized by all factions to advance their programs, but with different shades of meaning. Freedom was a watchword of the Revolution, and carried over into the battle against slavery (*q.v.*) and, later, against "wage slavery." Various pro-labor (*q.v.*) crusades appealed to freedom for the working man. Franklin D. Roosevelt (*q.v.*) enunciated "Four Freedoms" in 1941: freedom of speech, freedom of worship, freedom from want, and the enigmatic freedom from fear. The civil rights (*q.v.*) movement of the 1950s and after employed the slogan of freedom, though with less regard for the past and its heroic figures. The youth movement (*q.v.*) of the 1960s called for freedom for unconventional, "alternative" lifestyles. Conservatives have traditionally emphasized individual rights and duties as going hand in hand with freedom. They have followed up on Herbert Spencer's *The Man versus the State* (1884) by demanding limits to state control and intervention, curbs on bureaucracy (*q.v.*), and above all the dismantling of the welfare state (*q.v.*). Liberals have protested that conservatives only want state intervention when their economic interests are involved. Conservatives, on the other hand, have pointed to the relatively large amount of freedom permitted under capitalism, and how freedom is routinely repressed by authoritarian regimes elsewhere, many of which have received liberal sympathy and aid. A. T. Mason and Richard H. Leach, *In Quest of Freedom: American Political Thought and Practice* (1959); Eric Voegelin, ed., *Freedom and Serfdom: An Anthology of Western Thought* (1961).

**"Freedom of Choice,"** a euphemism (*q.v.*) of those favoring the legalization of abortion (*q.v.*). They held that women had a natural right to control their own bodies and to decide whether or not to bring their pregnancies to term. Many of those favoring the legalization of abortion argued that the freedom of choice required government aid to enable poor and needy women to obtain abortions. See also Squeal Rule.

**Freedom of Information Act** (1975), in part a response to the Watergate (*q.v.*) episode involving the Nixon (*q.v.*) White House. With limited qualifications, it made available large portions of Federal Government files to the general public. The intent was to protect against Federal abuse of power. Such agencies as the FBI (*q.v.*) protested that the Act interfered with normal activities of government while threatening security and even lives of others. Gangsters, for example, could and did probe into protected files to learn of persons who had provided information about them, and whom they could then murder. Efforts were made under the Act to prove that the government had lied in the Hiss and Rosenberg (*q.v.*) cases, but investigations of government files confirmed the general validity of the charges made in each case. The FBI and CIA insisted on modifications of the Act to enable them to function with better efficiency, and some changes were made. By the mid-1980s the effect the Act would ultimately have on government operations was still unclear.

**Freedoms Foundation at Valley Forge**, a conservative organization concerned for patriotism and the free-enterprise ideal. It appealed to educators, created school programs, made various awards, and sponsored seminars which explored aspects of justice, communication, and economics with the aid of government, college, and foreign-service speakers, many of international repute.

**Freeman, The**, magazine publication of the Foundation for Economic Education (*q.v.*).

**Freeman, The** (1920-1924), one of the distinguished publications of its time. It represented a high point in the public life of its editor, A. J. Nock (*q.v.*). Although it termed itself "radical" on the grounds that, unlike other organs such as the *Nation*, it did not believe politics made a difference—that only the return of the land to the people would make a difference—its editorial policy did not press the point. Nock asked only for clearness and coherence in language and point of view. His associates shared his conviction that American intervention in World War I had been a catastrophe, which the peace continued. They viewed American industry and affluence with skepticism, opposed imperialism as practiced in the Caribbean and through fiscal penetration elsewhere, and scorned the super-patriots of the war era and afterwards. At the same time, they honored classical wisdom, expressed themselves in Latin when they so chose, and treated culture as a paramount concern. Undoubtedly, they contributed to the disillusionment, individuality (*qq.v.*), and freedom from cant which counteracted the hazy patriotism (*q.v.*) and commercialism (*q.v.*) of the time. They also offered a range of experience and interests which enriched all experience. They welcomed essays as expressing personality. Francis Neilson's (*q.v.*) long experience as actor, entrepreneur, and political figure inspired marvelous reminiscences. Geroid T. Robinson was a vivid expositor of Russia and the Continent. Other contributors included Charles A. Beard, the distinguished Irishman George W. Russell (A.E.), the expatriate Harold Stearns, Lincoln Steffens writing on the just-deceased John Reed, William Henry Chamberlin (*q.v.*), Van Wyck Brooks,—there were others, like Lewis Mumford, Susanne La-Follette (*q.v.*), and the publisher B.W. Huebsch, who wrote on the *Odyssey*, changes on the Supreme Court, James Joyce, the relevance of rhyme, and even baseball. See *The Freeman Book: Typical Editorials, Essays, Critiques*...(1924: reprint 1978).

**Freeman, The** (1950-1953), an important development in the rise of a New Conservatism. It was begun on October 2, 1950 by editors Henry Hazlitt, John Chamberlain, and Suzanne La Follette (*qq.v.*). Although it looked back with respect to A. J. Nock's old *Freeman* of 1920-1924, it took into account the failure of Suzanne La Follette's *New Freeman* of 1930-1931, recognizing that there had since been a severe economic depression, a major war, and the rise of a totalitarian Soviet Union. It recognized too that vast numbers of intellectuals and other opinion-makers had not been disillusioned by Stalin's bloody regime, its expansion throughout Eastern Europe, or its evident plans for further expansion. *The Freeman* mounted a campaign against domestic welfare programs, current educational policies, the economics of inflation, and Harry Truman's Administration. The editors called upon many of their colleagues and friends for contributions. These included Isaac Don Levine, Frank Chodorov, George Sokolsky, George S. Schuyler, Eugene Lyons, and Ludwig von Mises (*qq.v.*). In addition, they printed many other writers of varied attitudes and interests, such as: Harold Loeb, who wrote about technocracy, the poet and neo-Marxist, James Rorty (who wrote as a critic of advertising), the novelist Louis Bromfield (who wrote about agriculture), and the song lyricist Morrie Ryskind (who had abandoned his former left-wing views). A striking addition was Edward Dahlberg, a one-time radical novelist who had become increasingly interested in the mystique of sex and art. Although Dahlberg was not interested in *The Freeman's* cause (see *Epitaphs of Our Times, the Letters of Edward Dahlberg* [1967]), his presence gave evidence of the breadth of interest allowed in the publication. All the editors had cultural interests and training. Nevertheless, the goal was conservative: to stand up to Communists at home and abroad, to support American interests in Korea (*q.v.*) to resist leftist tendencies in the United Nations (*q.v.*), and to defend free-enterprise ideals. Aside from criticism of "leftist clergy" and an appreciation of William F. Buckley's (*q.v.*) *God and Man at Yale*, there was no strong religious emphasis in *The Freeman*. The editors had hoped for a circulation of 15,000; after two years, they had reached 21,000 and appeared firmly established. Nevertheless, publication was abruptly discontinued in the fall of 1953.

**Freeze**. The term was identified in the 1940s and 1950s with wage and price control. In the early 1980s it became associated with efforts to curb the arms race between the United States and the Soviet Union, especially in the field of nuclear weapons. Although "Anti-Nuke" partisans claimed to be seeking a "freeze" affecting both belligerents, it was evident that they could be heard and effective only in the United States. The question was whether their activities would encourage Western military weakness and Soviet belligerence. See Richard M. Nixon, *The Real Peace* (1983).

**Frelinghuysen, Theodore** (1787-1862), famous as the "Christian statesman." His memorable speech pleading the cause of the Cherokee Indians (*q.v.*) in the U. S. Senate (April 9, 1830) has long been cherished by some conservatives. Although the speech ignored the fact that Northern Indians had already been moved to reservations and to the West, and failed to see the issue from a Southern standpoint, its sincerity was transparent and spoke for enlightened American opinion. Frelinghuysen was Vice-Presidential candidate with Henry Clay (*q.v.*) in 1844, and later president of Rutgers College.

**French Revolution** (1787), one of the momentous events of the past two hundred years. Questions about its causes and effects and whether it could have been avoided have persisted to this day. Edmund Burke's (*q.v.*) horrified reaction has been echoed by mid-twentieth century conservatism. Most conservatives have little sympathy with Voltaire's scorn of the well-endowed Church establishment or Diderot's emphasis on materialism. Rousseau (*q.v.*) became the theme of Irving Babbitt's (*q.v.*) most esteemed study. *The Marriage of Figaro* (1784), "the firecracker which set off the Revolution," deserves renewed attention to see how a mere play by Beaumarchais could excite opinion and crystallize feelings which those affected hardly knew they had. The comedy, which the King attempted to suppress, revealed a bored and amoral nobility. Later conservatives expressed respect for the Physiocrats (*q.v.*), who honored free enterprise. They read with satisfaction such defenders of piety and monarchy as Maistre (*q.v.*). They were less moved by the dreams and tragedies of such as the revolutionary Camille Desmoulins, doubtless because their eloquence and hopes had stirred to life not only constitutionalists, but also fanatics bent on destroying society. Carlyle's (*q.v.*) powerful depiction of the forces engaged in the Revolution and his brooding, moralistic view that its degradation was the doing of all participants is still appreciated. Although liberty, equality (*q.v.*), and fraternity were too great a burden for human nature (*q.v.*), it is difficult now to take sides on the issues of the time—though such repulsive figures as the Marquis de Sade deserved condemnation. Nevertheless, the issues and events of the French Revolution have continued to reverberate in the politics and ideologies of the 20th century.

**Friedan, Betty,** (1921- ), American author and women's-rights activist. Her book *The Feminine Mystique* (1963) gave an important impetus to the women's rights movement. It crystallized a widespread dissatisfaction among middle-class women with their lives as housewives and mothers and helped legitimize women's efforts to seek careers outside the home. The excesses of women's rights extremists, with their total rejection of men and motherhood, led Friedan, herself a women's rights spokesman, to write *The Second Stage* (1981). In it she argued for the value of motherhood and the need of women also to be dependent. Some critics maintained that these were the very things she had abandoned back in 1963. However she appeared to merit a recollection for her comment on Phyllis Schlafly (*q.v.*) in the course of a public debate, in May 1973: "I'd like to burn you at the stake." See Carol Felsenthal, *The Sweetheart of the Silent Majority*.

**Friedman, Milton** (1912- ), one of the most visible and esteemed of conservative economists, a Nobel Prize winner and consultant to foreign governments, as well as influential in the Nixon and Reagan Administrations. Friedman's rise was a measure of the need for governments to find means for resisting democratic demands for endless social expenditures. As many conservatives saw it, these expenditures could only result in merciless inflation, gaps between classes, demagogic slogans, and authoritarian government. A member of the "Chicago School" (*q.v.*) of economics, a U.S. Treasury specialist, and a founder of the Mont Pèlerin Society, he gave slogans to conservatives which idealized 19th-century capitalists as "liberals"—presumably because of their free-enterprise principles. He went on to create concepts of proper monetary policy which constituted a major assault on welfare-state economics. A master of mathematical economics, he also developed a communicative style which made him known beyond economic and government circles. Friedman dealt not only with the flow of money, but also with associated social components, and his ideas were prolific and provocative. Military expenses, welfare programs, and educational expenditures all came under his analysis, often causing debate among conservatives—as with his "negative income" plan which would have guaranteed an annual income for every citizen. Friedman's "voucher" plan for education challenged liberal perspectives. He also advocated an all-volunteer army. It was evident that the success of his recommendations depended not solely on the money made available or withdrawn, but on social response. Conservatives and others have criticized Friedman's economic approach. He fails to realize, they say, that economies are subject not only to "government mismanagement" (for which Friedman blamed the Great Depression [*q.v.*]) but to the minds and traditions of a nation and its connections with other nations. Thus, Friedman would see a Protection (*q.v.*) policy on imports as a fault of government, as though domestic manufacturers did not think they had a stake in such policies, and the capacity to influence them. Nevertheless, Friedman, formulating economic policies in a language laymen could understand, was an important force in the modern conservative movement. See his *Essays in Positive Economics* (1953), *Capitalism and Freedom* (1962), *Inflation: Causes and Consequences* (1963), *Dollars and Deficits* (1968), *There's No Such Thing as a Free Lunch* (1975), and, with his wife Rose Friedman, *Free to Choose* (1980). This last (*q.v.*) was a national best-seller.

**From Wealth, To Welfare: The Evolution of Liberalism**, by Harry K. Girvetz (1950), an authoritative survey showing how classical liberalism, with its emphasis on the pressure for democracy and the rights of the individual, led to modern liberalism, which broadened definitions of democracy and extended the rights of the individual to take in rights not envisioned by eighteenth- and nineteenth-century protagonists: Free Traders, Utilitarians, anti-state individualists, and others. New rights, however, required state activism and intervention; the author found, in planning, controls over private enterprise, and nationalization, among other policies, a freedom for the masses "heretofore reserved for the classes." Conservatives were able to view events since the book's publication as evidence that liberalism had misread the lessons of history—even the history of liberalism—and made assumptions respecting human nature (*q.v.*) not endorsed by experience. Of particular relevance was Girvetz's criticisms of Ludwig von Mises and Friedrich A. Hayek (*qq.v.*), defenders of the free market, whom Girvetz found inadequate in explaining the rise of fascism. He denigrated them for minimizing the role of monopolists in helping the Nazis to power, and for making German working-class organizations party to their own destruction during the Nazi crisis.

**Frontier**, classically a concept which made no distinction between conservatives and liberals. Conservatives invested in frontier lands from early times; poorer elements were eager to make themselves felt on the frontier by clearing it for families and industry. Frederick Jackson Turner's famous 1893 essay which saw the frontier as largely disappeared emphasized the democracy which it had inspired. The frontier should theoretically have signalled an end to the slavery system as obsolete. Instead, southern pioneers gone west took slaves along with them; northerners in their westward movement opposed slavery, but not the segregation or debarment of blacks. The concept of a "new" frontier—of science and technology—tended to be seen differently by liberals and conservatives. The latter preferred to leave settlement and organization of new territories to competition. The liberals professed a concern for the "little man" who might suffer by the impositions of capitalists. By John F. Kennedy's administration, the idea of a "new frontier" had become largely inspirational. John F. McDermott, ed., *The Frontier Re-Examined* (1967).

**Full Employment**, see Unemployment

**Fundamentalism**, an important element in the conservative movement of the post-World War II era. Fundamentalism assumed the Bible to be the literal word of God. In the early 20th century its followers were numerous, but their impact was often dulled by divisive factors. They differed, for example, on the importance they attached to the Old Testament, denying the third "Testament" of the Mormon prophet Joseph Smith and well removed from the ritual of the Catholic Church. (See, however, Ecumenical Movement.) Although there were substantial schools and institutions of higher learning, the emphasis of fundamentalism upon the common people kept its tenets simplified and often without nuance: a fit subject for H. L. Mencken's (*q.v.*) satire. Before the 1970s most fundamentalists had eschewed politics. The counterculture movement of the 1960s, with its attacks on traditional morality and lifestyles, and such events as the Supreme Court's ban on public prayer in schools and its legalization of abortion galvanized many fundamentalists into increasing support of conservative candidates and causes. Such fundamentalist spokesmen as Rev. Jerry Falwell (*q.v.*) became nationally known for their outspoken political views. Jimmy Carter (*q.v.*), though a "born again Christian," seemed unable or unwilling to link his fundamentalist religious principles with the growing fundamentalist political movement. Ronald Reagan (*q.v.*), following after him, seemed more in tune politically with fundamentalist beliefs on the family and society. See Filler, *Vanguards and Followers.*

**Futurism**, a development of the 1970s. It came out of earlier efforts to project future interests and needs, and from "science fiction" (*q.v.*) which suggested radical changes in future human life. Anxieties stirred by scientific progress toward bio-engineering and by the potential for nuclear destruction were widely shared, and aroused or soothed by such popular successes as Alvin Toffler's *Future Shock* (1970). Conservatism had little involvement with futurism, however. See Kahn, Herman.

# G

**Gag Rule**, notorious measure introduced in the House of Representatives in 1838, intended to end the debate on slavery (*q.v.*) there. It stipulated that all petitions bearing on the subject, notably those requesting that slavery be ended in the District of Columbia, be "laid upon the table"—that is, ignored. Since the measure transgressed the Constitution, which specified (in the First Amendment) that the people were free "to petition the government for a redress of grievances," this pro-slavery rule created a strong issue for abolitionist (*q.v.*) agitation. It also roused former President John Quincy Adams (*q.v.*) now a Representative, to a defense of the Constitution which continued session after session, and which gave him an incomparable position in House affairs. The rule was finally overthrown in 1844.

**Galsworthy, John** (1867-1933), British novelist and playwright. Perhaps his best-known work is *The Forsyte Saga* (1922), the story of a wealthy family through succeeding generations. Galsworthy appeals to many cultural conservatives seeking a thoughtful and responsible treatment of social problems along with concern for moral values. His play *Justice* (1910), a story of prison life, helped change laws; it showed Galsworthy's honest search for values, without sentimentalizing or distorting. *Strife* (1909, dealing with labor-capital relations), *The Skin Game* (1920), *Loyalties* (1922), and *Escape* (1926) also gained from Galsworthy's calm and yet probing honesty. His short story "Quality" was once used in schools to teach the value of quality as reflected in modest, unassuming lives. D. Barker, *The Man of Principle* (1963); A. Fréchet, *John Galsworthy: A Reassessment* (1982).

**Gavin, John** (1932-     ), American actor, appointed U. S. Ambassador to Mexico by President Reagan (*q.v.*) in 1981. His appointment aroused considerable opposition by opponents of Reagan, who pointed to Gavin's Hollywood past and accused him of being unqualified for so sensitive a diplomatic post. In fact, Gavin had specialized in Latin American affairs while at Stanford University and had served in Korea as an intelligence officer. From 1961 to 1973 he had been special advisor for Latin American affairs to the Secretary General of the Organization of American States. As a State Department official observed, Gavin had not been a "career" official; he had been a professional in the field. He had also been president of the Screen Actors Guild (as had Reagan) and his union (*q.v.*) experience was relevant to problems involving Mexican and American unions, especially as they concerned Mexican "illegals" in the United States and immigration generally. As head of the American Embassy in Mexico, Gavin was chief of one of the largest U. S. diplomatic missions, with over 1,000 employees, and had a central role in hemisphere development. He resigned his post in 1986 to return to private life.

**Genetic Revolution**. The 1970s and 1980s saw tremendous studies in the scientific understanding of how genes operate. Genetic research was aimed at using this knowledge to treat hitherto untreatable diseases with genetic origins, such as sickle-cell anemia (afflicting blacks) and Tay-Sachs disease (afflicting Ashkenazi Jews). Genetic-engineering techniques gave promise of one day extending human longevity, and even creating or altering human life itself. Scientists became increasingly adept at "tailoring" bacteria genetically to meet specific medical or commercial purposes. By the mid-1980s the Lilly Company had received Federal permisson to market insulin made by such bacteria. Many conservatives were wary about such developments. They pointed to the dangers involved in genetic research conducted without any ethical or moral guidelines. They pointed especially to amniocentesis, a common prenatal test which can detect genetic defects of a fetus in the womb. The presence of genetic defects often lead prospective parents to opt for abortion rather than bringing the pregnancy to term. Not only conservatives have been concerned by the genetic revolution. (See Luddites.) The National Council of Churches, reporting in 1983, warned of the risks in "unfettered" genetic research. It spelled out the need for ethical thinking, taking in the sacredness of human life, the interdependence of life systems, and the rights of the public in deciding the course of research. For a pro and con discussion of the genetic revolution under the conservative auspices of Hillsdale College (*q.v.*) see "Releasing the Genetic Genie: How Risky?" *Imprimis*, June 1983.

**Genocide**, the effort to exterminate an entire group or ethnic (*q.v.*) component repugnant to a government with the power to carry through, or to attempt to carry through such an enterprise. Its existence was affirmed by the Nuremburg Tribunal in 1945, and the onus placed upon the late Hitler (*q.v.*) government in Germany and its leaders. Some critics warned against the charge, saying that it could be used by any power in position to declare any foe guilty of genocide. Nevertheless, the crime was made official by the United Nations in 1949. Later agitation accused various nations of practicing genocide against elements at home or abroad, making it a function of war propaganda, rather than a documented and valid charge. Americans were accused of practicing genocide against Indians, Paraguay against its Indians. Despite reprimands won at sessions of the United Nations, and monitoring of nations by several agencies, the accusation of genocide continued to present problems. Thus, the Soviet Union was part of the United Nations, yet well-documented evidence of essentially genocidal actions, from the Katyn Forest (*q.v.*) murders to enormities commited against Ukrainians and others could not be pursued because of the military might of the Soviet government. Thus, genocide settled into a phenomenon widely recognized and widely employed to describe new or alleged large-scale atrocities (*q.v.*). They involved actions denied or defended by friends of the governments involved, recalled by foes of those regimes. N. Robinson, *The Genocide Convention* (1960).

**Gentility**, once a binding force among the various classes of people in the United States. The ideal of gentility allowed people to pursue their individual ethnic, social, and political activities, but called for standards of deportment on ritual or other occasions. Weddings and funerals, for example, called for certain kinds of dress and behavior. Genteel gestures and communication received severe blows from expanding democracy in the 19th and early 20th centuries, the disorders of the World War I period—which suggested that graciousness and courtesy were grotesque in a world of mass killings, and from the Depression of 1929 and after—which left beleaguered individuals and families exposed to uncertainties. By then, gentility seemed lost forever, especially in the eyes of social historians. It had been forgotten, however, that gentility stemmed from the concept of "gentleman," and that manners of "gentlemen" had varied through the ages. Nor was it noticed that T. S. Eliot's patently genteel writings were studied and emulated with care, in method often coarse beside the work of their mentor. Efforts at social ritual and conformity could still be found everywhere at gatherings of many sorts. Although older gentilities were doubtless in history, it seemed likely that new modes of accepted social behavior would continue to take their place. George Santayana, *The Genteel Tradition at Bay* (1931); John Tomsich, *A Genteel Endeavor* (1971).

**Gentility and Culture**. The association of the two concepts seems to have little future in a world of democratic pressures, with the need for writers and politicians to seek wide audiences among those accustomed to abrasive and simplistic viewpoints. Nineteenth-century gentility had argued that being human was to minimize animal nature, to emphasize the ideal in social attitudes and communication. It had encouraged euphemisms (*q.v.*), some of which became notorious in later generations, as when "limbs" was substituted for "legs." Nevertheless, the genteel way of life produced the writings of Henry Adams, Henry James, and Emily Dickinson, among others. It also produced the journalism of E. L. Godkin (*qq.v.*), and such distinguished publications as the *Atlantic Monthly*, the *Century*, and *Scribner's*. It gave rise to the Civil Service (*q.v.*) as a limiting factor on political patronage and corruption. Progressives (*q.v.*) helped to undermine gentility in their quest for a higher democracy; David Graham Phillips stated that he abjured the words "ladies" and "gentlemen" because of what they had come to mean—he equated them with snobbishness and trivial pursuits. Later works impugned all gentility past as well as present; see for example, J. G. Sproat's *The Best Men* (1965), which preferred the corrupt politicians of the Gilded Age to the reformers. Yet gentility could claim to have contributed standards of deportment and social activity, not only to its direct representatives, but also to others lost in the backwoods or embroiled in the rudely developing cities. *The Ordeal of Mark Twain* (1920) by Van Wyck Brooks accused gentility of having curbed Twain's natural energies; other studies gave evidence that it had helped give them form. Although conservative publications of later vintage did not employ gentility as a concept, such organs as the *National Review* (*q.v.*) practice some of its principles. They took pride in "good English," honored cosmopolitan culture, and were suspicious of uncontrolled democracy. They saw virtue in the rule of the best, and respected the principle of "noblesse oblige" (nobility gives reponsibility). A related concept, "the gentry," was oddly maintained in the term "gentrification." Although this referred to an urban phenomenon, in which poor people were forced out of a once-excellent, decayed neighborhood to make room for the well-to-do—who might not necessarily be genteel, the process involved elements which could well augment gentility. See Walker Percy, *The Last Gentleman* (1982). See also Ellery Sedgwick, comp., *Atlantic Harvest* (1947); and Arthur John, *The Best Years of the Century: Richard Watson Gilder...1870-1909* (1981).

**Geopolitics,** see Mackinder, Halford J.; Heartland

**Georgetown University,** see Center for Strategic and International Studies

**Gilder, George F.** (1939- ), American author and social critic. From a distinguished family (see Gilder, Richard Watson), he attended Harvard, was involved in Ripon (*q.v.*) politics, and associated with the liberal *New Leader*. He became a speechwriter for political figures including Nelson Rockefeller, Richard M. Nixon (*qq.v.*), and Senator Robert Dole. His *Sexual Suicide* (1973) did not sell well, but it established his method, which was to examine the bases of human relations by employing statistical findings to support its view of man-woman relations. Gilder saw those relations as wounded by feminist propaganda and attitudes. His *Naked Nomads* (1974) continued the theme, interpreting feminist agitation in terms of what it did to families and society. *Visible Men* (1978)—a play on Ralph Ellison's famous *Invisible Man*—turned its attention to the difference between what government policy was supposed to do for the poor and what it in fact did. Gilder's *Wealth and Poverty* (*q.v.*) came out in the early days of the conservative Reagan Administration (1981), with its policies based on supply-side economics (*q.v.*). It was a national bestseller, with its efforts to diminish the gap between statistics and human nature and need inherent both in government and in commerce. Gilder's later essays include "Paying for Children," in *Human Life* (*q.v.*), Winter 1984.

**Gilder, Richard Watson** (1844-1909), an exemplar of gentility (*q.v.*). The son of a well-esteemed minister, he served in the Civil War, apprenticed in journalism and magazine work, and at age twenty-six became managing editor of *Scribner's Monthly*—later more famous as *Century Magazine*. In 1881 he became its editor, and published many of the most distinguished authors of the era. Although his poems were overpraised and admired for their "spirituality," his civic services, like those of other "Goo Goos" (*q.v.*), were commendable. He was the first president of Kindergarten Associates, which advocated free kindergartens. He founded the Society of American Artists and the Free Art League, and, among other such enterprises, contributed to the People's Municipal League.

**Gitlow, Benjamin**, a founder of the American Communist Party, its Vice-Presidential candidate in 1924. He was the principal in *Gitlow v. People of New York* (1925), in which Oliver Wendell Holmes, Jr. voiced a memorable dissent favoring free speech. Disillusioned by a Communist International of violence and dictatorship, Gitlow pioneered revelations respecting Communist life and thought in *I Confess* (1940) and *The Whole of Their Lives* (1948). The latter title came from a quotation by Lenin defining the "professional revolutionist" as committing the whole of life to the cause. The vivid, detailed memoirs helped mark the passing of an older radicalism, but offered little direct guidance to the new. See also Philbrick, Herbert A.

**"Giveaways."** In modern times both conservatives and liberals have denounced government "giveaways." Each group, however, tends to define "giveaways" differently. For conservatives, the emphasis has been on government social programs which developed during the New Deal (*q.v.*), grew during the Truman (*q.v.*) Administration, and reached their peak in the administrations of John F. Kennedy (*q.v.*) and Lyndon Johnson (*q.v.*). Conservatives argued that many of these programs were unnecessary, ill-advised, wasteful, and even injurious to their supposed beneficiaries and society as a whole. Payments to welfare families, for example, tended to keep them in a state of apathy and dependency. Public impatience with many of these social programs began to grow in the late 1970s and led to increasing sympathy for conservatism and the New Right (*q.v.*). The election of Ronald Reagan (*q.v.*) was interpreted as a national mandate to curb government "giveaways." Growing concern about Federal deficits in the 1980s led to an increasing emphasis on efficiency in government spending and on curbing unnecessary government programs. Liberals, on the other hand, have traditionally opposed government "giveaways" to the wealthy and to large corporations. Many conservatives have argued, however, that such "giveaways" are beneficial to society since large corporations and the wealthy provide jobs and opportunities for the poor and needy.

**Glazer, Nathan** (1923- ), a transitional (*q.v.*) figure, from liberalism to neo-conservatism (*q.v.*). He served as an editor on *Commentary* (*q.v.*) (1945-1953) and worked in publishing, before joining Harvard University as a sociologist. Having become a critic of Communism and Communist sympathizers in the 1930s and after, he wrote *The Social Basis of American Communism* (1961). Originally a liberal, in his later years he turned neo-conservative (*q.v.*). His *Affirmative Discrimination* (1976) was a criticism of sentimental liberalism. He became a co-editor of *The Public Interest* (*q.v.*).

**"Gnosticism,"** see Voegelin, Eric

**"Gobbledygook,"** a slang phrase referring to obscure or evasive pronouncements in bureaucratic (*q.v.*) language or the language of officialdom in general. It was utilized by conservatives in combat with "New Deal," "Fair Deal," and "New Frontier," "Great Society" programs. Thus, in the community action programs which proliferated under Lyndon B. Johnson (*q.v.*) funds were allocated "to establish decentralized multi-functional information." Liberal commentators joined the attack on "bureaucratese" and "euphemisms" (*qq.v.*) over the years, but their complaints tended to be more in defense of language generally, or in opposition to such supposed conservative phenomena as "Pentagonese," the mangling of language by the military. See also Mario Pei's (*q.v.*) essentially conservative *Double-Speak in America* (1973).

**God**, see Filler, DASC. A belief in God has traditionally been acknowledged as significant in American affairs, a sword and shield to controversialists who faced antagonistic spectators, from Wendell Phillips to Martin

Luther King. Skeptics and atheists (*q.v.*) were rarely notable, Thomas Paine's (*q.v.*) Deism (*q.v.*) serving later skeptics more than it did him. Robert G. Ingersoll's repudiation of the Bible (*q.v.*) earned him substantial scorn among conservatives despite his devotion to Republican Party tenets. Marxism by self-definition is atheistic, and Communist countries have consistently persecuted those who believe in God. In modern times, overturning its tradition, the Supreme Court (*q.v.*) has generally interpreted the First Amendment to the Constitution (*q.v.*), which forbids the establishment of a religion by the Federal Government, as forbidding government encouragement of any religious practice. The government according to the Court should be "neutral," not only among religions, but also between religion and non-religion. Its decision prohibiting public prayer in the public schools was especially controversial. The growth of Fundamentalism (*q.v.*) in the 1970s and 1980s was fueled in part by reaction to Supreme Court decisions, as well as by disillusionment with Marxism and with the counterculture movement of the 1960s. In the 1980s many conservatives continued to emphasize the traditional importance of religion in American life.

**God and Man at Yale**, see Buckley, Jr., William F.

**Godfather, The** (1969), by Mario Puzo, a novelist who turned from writing novels of acknowledged distinction to writing and publishing a novel which *Time* termed the "fastest-selling book in history." As a motion picture, it repeated this triumph, both in its original version and in a sequel. *The Godfather* equated the workings of organized crime with that of regular American business: a judgment which readers and viewers appeared to accept. Its portrayal of Italian-American gangsters was criticized by some for inaccurately glossing over many aspects of criminal life. See also Capone, Al.

**Godkin, Edwin L.** (1831-1902), journalist, editor, advocate of Free Trade (*q.v.*) without being a reformer. Born in Ireland of English parents, he wrote a *History of Hungary and the Magyars* at age twenty-two. He himself later said it contained interesting materials which were irrelevant. The work sufficiently impressed the editor of the *London Daily News*, however, and he sent Godkin to the Crimea (1853-1855) to cover the Russo-Turkish War. Having distinguished himself as a correspondent, he then emigrated to the United States. He studied law, and worked as a journalist reporting on the South, exhibiting a curious realism while missing the passions beneath the surface. His reputation enabled him in 1865 to found the *Nation (q.v.)*, ostensibly as an organ for adjusting former slaves to freedom. This aim soon disappeared, as the *Nation* drew some of the most elite and distinguished writers of the time to comment on cultural and social affairs. Godkin himself, in his editorial pages, developed a clear, penetrating style. His program, however, overlooked the desperate needs of farmers, laborers, and minorities in the cities and countryside. His main cause was Free Trade, which he saw as permitting an interchange among major nations. Free Trade would also prevent war, with its attendant social instability and disorder. Godkin was also a foe of corruption in politics, fearlessly denouncing the city "rings" which plundered coffers and bribed and bullied their way to election victories. Reformers denounced him as being sensitive to the thievery of the Irish in politics, but not to the massive thefts by great corporations. Godkin's was indeed the morality of a genteel (*q.v.*) generation, but his strange public coldness of temperament deprived him of the regard accorded other genteel litterateurs and politicians. William James noted that privately, in his own home, Godkin was warm and friendly, but as an editor he was capable of having a job applicant in for an interview, and never so much as informing him that his application had been rejected. In 1881 he became editor of the *New York Post*, to which he imparted his high editorial standards and his philosophy. In 1883 he became the editor-in-chief of both the *Post* and the *Nation*. The Spanish-American War was a blow from which he did not recover. Rollo Ogden, ed., *Life and Letters of E. L. Godkin* (1907).

**Gold**, once a key factor in international exchange, accepted as a standard of value, and affecting domestic currency and exchange arrangements. The increased capacity of government to influence prices, interest rates, bond holdings, and other components of banking and finance made the gold standard only one more factor in domestic and foreign transactions. Maintaining or "going off" the gold standard, therefore, became not so much a central factor as an indicator of public financial interest and demand. Jack Kemp (*q.v.*), however, believed that the gold standard could be a stabilizing and unifying element in a free-enterprise economy. See also Silver Issue, The.

**Goldman, Eric**, see Lee, Ivy

**Goldwater, Barry** (1909- ), Republican Presidential candidate in 1964 and an influential voice in conservative circles through the mid-1980s. A long-time Senator from Arizona, he has been known to many as "Mr. Conservative." Goldwater's 1964 campaign ran into determined liberal opposition. He was portrayed as a trigger-happy war-monger, liable to use nuclear weapons in Vietnam and elsewhere. He was opposed by Lyndon B. Johnson (*q.v.*), who ran as the "peace candidate." Johnson's later massive escalation of American involvement in Vietnam provided an ironic postscript to the 1964 campaign. The political humorist, Art Buchwald, later wrote a column in which he pretended to describe the horrid things which might have occurred if Goldwater had been elected. Goldwater lost the Presidential election in a landslide, but his efforts galvanized conservatives nationally. Many blamed liberal falsehoods for the election defeat, but it was clear that Republican ineptitude contributed as well. Their candidate was a successful businessman, a pilot in the USAAF during World War II and a Reserve Major-General with responsible views of discipline and constitutional government. He had published the interesting *Arizona Portraits* and *Journey Down the River of Canyons* (both 1940). He was alarmed, as were many, over runaway budgets and the state of Social Security, and as Senator (1953-1964) had offered plans for dealing with them, in speeches and further volumes. But the campaign was poorly run, and public opinion was not yet ready for many of Goldwater's ideas. He later returned to the Senate and gained a reputation as "the conscience of conservatives." Although *With No Apologies* (1979) had a defensive title, it reflected integrity, as well as stirring some controversy. See also John H. Kessel, *The Goldwater Coalition: Republican Strategies in 1964* (1968). See also Robert D. Novak, *The Agony of the G.O.P.*, 1965.

**Gompers, Samuel** (1850-1924), labor leader who dominated the American Federation of Labor from its beginning in 1886 until his death. Because of his insistence that labor unions had to be able to survive, and not only in times of depression or capitalist assaults, he gave priority to established, conservative unions (*q.v.*) capable of dealing with employers and having members who could support the unions' existence. He was thus attacked by more "militant" leaders adept at confrontation but not necessarily able to win concessions (*q.v.*) from employers or survive to fight again. Gompers disdained unions which lacked financial security or which threatened the leadership of the American Federation of Labor. He earned the enmity of radicals by cooperating with the National Civic Federation, which sought mediation between labor and capital, but which radicals claimed was intended to weaken the drive for militant unions. During World War I, Gompers served on President Wilson's Council of National Defense, in effect preventing strikes, though with the full employment of wartime they were not necessary. Although he believed that he had thus institutionalized labor in government, the alliance fell apart after the war, as employers worked to keep labor in line and prevent radical union organization. Following his death, Gompers was identified by radical intellectuals as a conservative, and even as a "labor faker." Bernard Mandel, *Samuel Gompers* (1963); see also Gompers's *Seventy Years of Life and Labor* (1925).

**"Goo Goos,"** a social response to the burgeoning cities of the post-Civil War decades, which urgently needed reform; see Filler, DASC. Although radicals called for fundamental change, usually meaning socialism and eliminating "root causes" (*qq.v.*) of the cities' problems, strong elements of the urban gentility (*q.v.*) centered attention on municipal corruption, civil-service reform, sanitation services, and housing built in dangerous haste for the incoming New Immigration (*qq.v.*). All this was offensive to the political bosses whose power was built on patronage and political deals. The journalist Dana (*q.v.*) jeered at such civic leaders as Richard Watson Gilder (*q.v.*) and others who fought the city bosses in the interests of good government, dubbing them "Goo Goos." Still, they created the laws and techniques by which better government could be achieved, in the 1880s or the 1980s.

**Gothic Romance**, a literary genre which can be traced back to the late eighteenth century. Its most notable titles included Horace Walpole's *The Castle of Otranto* (1765) and Mary Shelley's *Frankenstein* (1818). The genre featured mysterious places, strange rumors, noises and whispers, and tended toward melodramatic plots. Its most talented practitioner in the early twentieth century was Gabrielle Margaret Vere Campbell Long, whose best-known novels appeared under the names of "Marjorie Bowen" and "Joseph Shearing"; see, for example, her *Moss Rose* (1935). The majority of "gothic romances" were far from memorable. Russell Kirk (*q.v.*) was credited with having given the genre a renewed vitality.

**Government**, a major field for careerists, attracting liberals and conservatives in equal number. Although Democrats claimed to speak for the "people" in greater number than the Republicans, they produced wealthy "dollar-a-year" heads of departments and ambassadorships as readily as did their opponents. So crucial a department as that of State attracted bureaucrats (*q.v.*) of every persuasion, from Alger Hiss to John Foster Dulles (*qq.v.*). All learned a diplomatic language which accreted every conceivable nuance of interpretation. Although popular support had a strong influence on government trends, it was limited by the subtleties of communication. Thus, the *New Republic*, with small circulation, had an influence during the Woodrow Wilson Administration out of proportion to its readership. The *National Review* (*q.v.*) was a similar force in the Reagan Administration.

**Grand Alliance**, the anti-Nazi accord which placed Great Britain and the United States on the side of the Soviet Union in the war against Hitler (*q.v.*). Although there was considerable distaste on the part of those who remembered the Nazi-Soviet treaty which had enabled the Germans to unleash war against Europe, there seemed a practical need to muster arms and resources in order to put down so formidable a foe. Conservatives hoped that, with Hitler quelled, it would then be possible to control or put down their repugnant Soviet ally. Many of them had been opposed to intervention, hoping that Nazis and Communists would destroy one another and enable more civilized regimes to take over in their lands. Winston Churchill, as a British Tory (*q.v.*), felt too immediately threatened by the Germans to wait for such a solution; as he said, he was interested in anyone who would kill Germans. Although Franklin D. Roosevelt (*q.v.*) seems sincerely to have been taken in by Stalin, and believed him a legitimate leader of Russians, his successors were left to face an insatiable "ally" who was in fact a foe, with whom it was necessary to enter into the "Cold War" (*q.v.*).

**Granger Cases**, see Waite, Morrison R.

**Grassroots**, a political term referring to the "people" or to movements or sentiments among them. Liberals and radicals in the 20th century have traditionally believed the people at the grassroots level supported their programs and ideas. With the rise of conservative sentiment in the 1970s and 1980s, however, conservatives began to look to the grassroots level for support of their own ideas and programs. This went hand in hand with the rise of Fundamentalism (*q.v.*). Imbued with a traditionally American suspicion of and distaste for cities and those inhabiting them, conservative spokesmen sought to appeal to "heartland" (*q.v.*) populations, those of the rural "grassroots" imbued with what they considered true American instincts and memories. The historian Richard Hofstadter attacked these "pseudo-conservatives," and impugned once-respected Populists (*q.v.*) as narrow-minded, anti-Semitic (*q.v.*), and regressive. However, Jimmy Carter (*q.v.*) presented himself as both liberal and populist. By the mid-1980s conservatives seemed to have garnered much grassroots support particularly outside the major urban areas. See *Grassroots*, a "leadership" publication of the Conservative Caucus (*q.v.*).

**Graves of Academe, The** (1981), by Richard Mitchell. It is a corrosive examination of the harm "educationalists" have done to education through an absence of standards permitting students to advance without regard to achievement. Mitchell, a professor at Glassboro (New Jersey) State College, traces this collapse of education to the findings of the Commission on the Reorganization of Secondary Education (1913-1918). Its report on "Cardinal Principles of Secondary Education" gave priority to health, home, vocation, and other principles at the expense of scholarly disciplines. As administered under the auspices of such groups as the National Education Association, this approach downgraded reading, writing, history, mathematics, and other fundamentals. With teachers educating teachers in the new priorities, Mitchell saw a precipitous decline in simple literacy, not only for students but for teachers themselves. Mitchell's own printed leaflet, *The Underground Grammarian*, exposed unreadable and illogical statements by influential educationalists. To blame the 1918 "Cardinal Principles" for all this, however, is probably unfair. It had not occurred to the Commission that its principles would be permitted to supersede basic elements of education and communication.

**Great Britain**, long a feeder of conservative ideas and an inspiration to Americans, conservative and otherwise. Tories were a strong part of the colonial establishment, and following the American Revolution were able to reorganize and push for the Constitution (*q.v.*). John Jay's (*q.v.*) equitable Treaty with Great Britain settled questions left over from the war. Succeeding Administrations quarreled with the British but made peace with conservative spokesmen, even following the War of 1812. Much appreciated was Britain's readiness to secure the U. S.-Canadian border, its later avoidance of trouble over the Panama Canal, and its non-intervention in U. S.-Cuban relations. A bitter anti-British epigram had it that American intervention in World War I paid off Great Britain for her tolerance of the Monroe Doctrine. As a creditor nation following the war the U. S. received as little regard from Great Britain as from its other debtors, but the ambitions of Hitler in the 1930s, and of the Soviet Union, forged U. S.-British relations which held during subsequent Labour and Conservative administrations. Keynesian (*q.v.*) theories rode high in the Franklin D. Roosevelt (*q.v.*) Administration and succeeding Democratic Presidents, and were not seriously disturbed even during the Eisenhower and Nixon (*qq.v.*) eras. Margaret Thatcher's (*q.v.*) rise to the office of Prime Minister in 1979, however, and the victory of Ronald Reagan (*q.v.*) in the United States a year later put conservatism in command in ways which marked a historical turning-point. With both nations deep in welfare-state (*q.v.*) economics and programs, could the new leaders turn or at least stem the tide, now a way of life to half their populations? Both leaders tried, Thatcher to denationalize industries and cut services, Reagan to "deregulate" (*q.v.*) industries, and limit entitlements. Both saw their countries as needing strength to curb Soviet expansionism and to lead world opinion against it. Both needed to show a will to act, Thatcher in the Falklands, Reagan in Grenada (*qq.v.*). Both compromised principles, to stay in power and to gain time to determine the most expedient approaches to financial and bureaucratic problems. Both avoided deadly confrontations with Soviet leaders while calling other nations to join them in exerting pressures on Soviet activities. A major problem for Americans was to realize that Britishers were not Americans, that there were numerous differences in language and outlook which could create misleading judgments. Stripped of their colonies and harassed at home by ethnic and economic crises, Britishers found themselves fighting for life and dignity, both of which took priority over American friendship. See also Burke, Edmund; Mill, John Stuart; Carlyle, Thomas; Smith, Adam; Ricardo, David; Huxley, Aldous; Churchill, Winston; Orwell, George; Oakeshott, Michael; and related personages and events.

**Great Depression**, once a major argument for the cause of liberalism, and a major embarrassment to conservatives. As the 1930s receded into history, however, its political importance began to recede as well. It was soon almost universally realized that Roosevelt had not conquered the Depression; the coming of World War II had accomplished that end. Wartime prosperity had been followed by postwar prosperity which, shallowly handled, bolstered government spending and inflation (*qq.v.*). The youth revolt of the 1960s, chaotic and false as it often was, nevertheless revealed some of the weak foundations on which this "prosperity" had been based. Massive bureaucracy and a welfare nightmare, along with ruined cities and an increasingly unproductive workplace helped conservatives gain support from what they had been in 1929-1939 so as to make the "Great Depression" academic to current students and their elders. Ronald Reagan was able both to remember the time and to criticize Democratic handling of it in terms of bureaucracy, unnecessary interposition into private industry, and augmented rather than diminished welfare programs (*qq.v.*). In effect, the Great Depression ultimately had no more impact than earlier depressions; all attention turned to specific economic proposals and their impact on segments of the population.

**"Great Society,"** a phrase used by Lyndon B. Johnson (*q.v.*) to refer to his programs for eradicating poverty and inequality in the United States. The collapse of so ambitious and comprehensive a blueprint was only partially the result of the domestic agitation caused by the Vietnam conflict. Social demoralization, symbolized by the counterculture movements of the 1960s, went hand in hand with the individual demoralization promoted by an unproductive affluence (*q.v.*) of the time. Many began to question what the grants and loans and blandly recognized "giveaways" actually accomplished. Family planning, job training, neighborhood improvement, crime prevention, educational programs, and the like did little to halt the visible deterioration of values and facilities in all areas. The funds, however, were spent and renewed with bureaucratic persistence. Politics defeated Johnson's program, but also the false assumption that funds generously dispensed would eradicate social evils. During the 1980s government bureaucracies fought to maintain their funding and existence, despite an economic downturn and Reagan (*q.v.*) Administration policies. Evidently, people's expectations would have to be altered. See Concessions; Welfare State; Corruption.

**Greed**, see Envy

**Greeley, Andrew M.** (1928- ), one of the most popular Catholic social and cultural writers. He captured attention as a sociologist (Ph.D., University of Chicago, 1961) who challenged ethnic assumptions with vigor and data in such books as *The Church and the Suburbs* (1959), *The Education of American Catholics* (1966), and *The Catholic Experience* (1967). Father Greeley made active and influential his National Opinion Research Center in Chicago. His essential conservatism derived from Catholic positions on abortion and the family and reached many readers through a syndicated column. He attained further distinction by writing best-selling novels, such as *The Cardinal Sins* (1981). Critics deemed some of his books simplistic and repetitive, but he was well-regarded by some scholars and general readers. In 1984 he provided $150,000 for an annual lectureship at a Catholic seminary , and $850,000 to endow a chair in Roman Catholic studies at the University of Chicago, to be shared by the university's social science division and its divinity school.

**Grenada**, an important incident in the development of a Reagan foreign policy which showed American determination to resist Soviet power and Soviet surrogates (*q.v.*) while being prepared to seek peace and accommodation with nations great and small. Grenada, a tiny republic with British Commonwealth status in the Caribbean, had been taken over by radical Marxists friendly to Cuba. Reagan feared the island was becoming a base for Cuban military activities. On the island too were American students who might well be held hostage in future confrontation with the U. S. In October 1983, Marines moved to take over the island. They found a nearly completed airstrip suitable for military operations and Soviet arms in profusion. Most of the population of Grenada welcomed American intervention and later U. S. efforts to restore democratic rule. American journalists had been kept from accompanying invading American troops—Vietnam (*q.v.*) being in mind—and many called this a violation of freedom of the press. Many of Reagan's opponents charged him with imperialism. Most striking, though inevitable, was the protest from British Prime Minister Margaret Thatcher (*q.v.*) for not having been consulted with regard to the operation. This did little, however, to sour British-American relations. American public opinion all in all was clearly behind the President.

**Grove City College**, a private coeducational school in Grove City, Pennsylvania, over a hundred years old with an enrollment in the mid-1980s of 2,200. It was conservative in its views and resistant to government intervention in its affairs. Although the college did not practice sex discrimination, it was required as a condition of receiving Federal aid to sign a pledge that it would not do so. The college sued the Federal Government in court. The Government argued that Grove City's acceptance of students receiving Federal aid gave it the right to prevent discrimination in all of the college's operations. Grove City spent $400,000 from 1977 to 1984 denying the contention. The Supreme Court finally concluded, six to three, that only the financial aid program was subject to Government jurisdiction. See also Hillsdale College.

**"Guardian Angels,"** see Self-Help

**Guilt**, see White Guilt

**Gulag**, see Slave Labor

**Gun Control**. A cause generally identified with liberals, who attributed much of the rise in crime during the 1960s and 1970s to the easy availability of guns in much of the United States. Many argued that the Fourth Amendment guarantee of the right to bear arms applied only to state militias and not to individuals. In 1911 the tragic killing of the novelist David Graham Phillips (*q.v.*) by an unbalanced stranger had inspired a young coroner in New York City to push for a gun-control law. Oddly, the resulting Sullivan Law came not from reformers but from a local political boss. Despite efforts to push for the law in states beyond New York, it failed to rouse the necessary support; Americans were either indifferent or, in some parts of the country, openly hostile to such efforts. The new push for gun control was met by lobbyists for the National Rifle Association. A rash of assassinations and attempted assassinations, from John F. Kennedy in 1963 to Ronald Reagan in 1981, gave impetus to gun-control advocates pushing for national legislation. NRA propagandists, in reply, said that "people kill people, not guns." Hunting and fishing enthusiasts, gun hobbyists, defense-minded civilians and soldiers, and conservatives generally agreed.

# H

**Hale, Edward Everett**, see *Man Without a Country, The*

**Hale, Sarah J. B.** (1788-1879), most famous, or notorious, for writing "Mary Had a Little Lamb." She was in fact an influential editor, an encourager of women writers, and an advocate of higher education for women, deeply involved in many civic enterprises. Turning to journalism after the death of her husband, in 1837 she became editor of *Godey's Lady's Book*, and arbiter of fashion and manners. Her most durable work was *Women's Record, or Sketches of All Distinguished Women from the Creation to the Present Day* (1853). A large work, it traced a line of influence and achievement which was individual and conservative, but showed thought and study and efforts to be fair. O. W. Burt, *First Woman Editor* (1960).

**Halifax, George Savile, Viscount**, see "Trimmer, The"

**Hall of Fame**, see Heroes

**Hamilton, Alexander** (1755-1804), first Secretary of the Treasury under President George Washington (*q.v.*) and originator of the "Hamiltonian system," intended to build a capitalistic economy in the United States. As detailed in his "Report on Manufactures," he intended America to institute a Protective Tariff (*q.v.*), encouraging native entrepreneurs at the expense of foreigners. The government was to subsidize agriculture, and to augment its funds by an excise tax. It was to fund its debts, assuming also all the state debts incurred by the Revolutionary War. All this was to insure that the central government was strong, with all other authorities subservient to it. Hamilton had already, as a major figure in the organization of the new Federal Government, given it all the power he could. He would have made Washington a king had the temper of the people permitted; as it was, he doubted whether such a loose collection of states could keep from slipping back into British control. His basic tenets—lack of faith in unbridled democracy and the need for strong conservative reins—made him a guiding light to conservatives and a figure of fear and contempt to ardent Jeffersonians (*q.v.*). Yet, when he lost his life in a dual with Jefferson's Vice-President Aaron Burr, Burr had to flee the country to avoid arrest, such was the popular resentment at Hamilton's death. See G. Stourgh, *Alexander Hamilton and the Idea of Republican Government* (1969).

**Handicapped, The** see Disabled Persons

**Hanighen, Frank C.,** see *Human Events*; Morley, Felix

**Hanna, Marcus A.** (1837-1904), Cleveland, Ohio businessman and politician, credited with having organized the then-modern Republican Party (*q.v.*) during the first candidacy for President of William McKinley. As a streetcar magnate, Hanna fought the reform efforts of Tom L. Johnson to create public transportation. Involved in Ohio politics, Hanna groomed McKinley for the 1896 Presidential race. He became famous for his fund-raising ability and notorious as having "bought" Indiana for his friend and candidate. Himself winning a United States Senate seat, Hanna soon became conspicuous for his concern for big-business opportunities. He was a valued advisor to McKinley and his successor Theodore Roosevelt, and was being talked of as a successor to Roosevelt as President when he died suddenly. He was admired by Herbert Croly, who made reform a nationalistic enterprise to which he later dedicated his magazine, the *New Republic*. His belief that bringing America to a premier place in the world required astute and powerful leadership was expressed in Croly's *Marcus Alonzo Hanna* (1912).

**Hanson, John**, see Articles of Confederation, The

**Harding, Warren G.** (1865-1923), President of the U. S., considered to be a low point in the history of the Republican party and of conservatism generally. He is rarely invoked by either and survives mainly as an academic topic. He is notable as the first businessman in the Presidency. Harding had been owner and editor of the Marion, Ohio *Star*, where he paid higher wages than union rates; Norman Thomas, later leader of the Socialist Party, recalled him as a gracious and generous employer when Thomas was a newspaper boy in Marion. A Republican Party regular, Harding delivered the keynote address at the 1912 Republican convention which nominated William Howard Taft (*q.v.*) for the Presidency. His slogan was a return to "normalcy" when Harding was elected President in a landslide in 1920. His opponent was another Ohio newspaper proprietor, James M. Cox, also a state governor and a man with little more distinction than Harding; see Cox's autobiography, *Journey through My Years* (1946). Of major interest was the public which turned to such candidates, following World War I, presented as a crusade for freedom. See Samuel Hopkins Adams, *The Incredible Era* (1939), and R. K. Murray, *The Harding Era* (1969).

**Harper's**, see Curtis, George William

**Harris, Joel Chandler** (1848-1908), Georgia journalist and storyteller. He created in his "Uncle Remus" tales a complex vision of Negro thought which was helpful in attempts to understand the realities of blacks as Southerners and Americans. Thus, it is evident that "Br'er Rabbit" is a subconscious image of the black: though physically (socially) weak, he lives freely and victoriously thanks to his native wit. Harris also collected Negro folk sayings and stories.

**Hart, Jeffrey**, conservative columnist, *National Review* (*q.v.*) editor, Dartmouth College professor; see *American Dissent, The; Political Writers of Eighteenth-Century England; When the Going Was Good.*

**Harvard Hates America** (1978), by John LeBoutillier, an irreverent work by a Harvard graduate. It created some stir by saying that Harvard, with exceptions, had become a magnet for students and mentors who found American policies and ways decidedly alien. It could be compared in some ways with William F. Buckley, Jr.'s (*q.v.*) *God and Man at Yale* (1951). LeBoutillier tried for a career in politics, but lost his Congressional seat after one term.

**Harvey, Paul** (1918- ), radio and television personality whose crisp, knowing comments on American life have been followed by millions of listeners. He based himself in Chicago, from which he believed he could best reach ordinary people. Generally conservative, he decried welfare cheats, drug abusers, Communists, and bureaucrats. His oppositon to the Vietnam disaster and acceptance of the ERA (*qq.v.*), however, showed his ideological independence. An expose in *Esquire* in 1978 revealed more turmoil in his life than his swift, confident style seemed to indicate. Paul Harvey, *Autumn of Liberty* (1954) and *The Rest of the Story* (1978).

**Haushofer, Karl**, see Mackinder, Halford J.; Geopolitics

**Hawthorne, Nathaniel** (1804-1864), American author. He is often thought to have favored reform because of his sympathetic portrait of Hester Prynne—who bore a child out of wedlock in *The Scarlet Letter* (1850)—his short stay at the reform commune Brook Farm, and his tale "The Maypole of Merry-Mount," referring to an incident in Puritan New England involving merrymaking between English and Indian. Although Hawthorne was indeed disturbed by memories of his ancestors, who included a judge at the Salem witchcraft trials, he was formed by long years of seclusion from society. He quickly found the Brook Farm oppressive, and, once married, retired to his family and art. His work reflected his Calvinist tendencies toward fatalism and predestination. It is too rarely noticed that *The Scarlet Letter* gives no indications of expecting justice or condoning "sin." Hawthorne satirized Brook Farm in *The Blithedale Romance* (1852). His deepest friendship was with his former classmate at Bowdoin College, Franklin Pierce, who had served in the Mexican War (*q.v.*) and who was put up for the Presidency by the Democratic Party in 1852 because of his indifference to the slavery issue. Hawthorne wrote his campaign biography, and was rewarded by a consulship at Liverpool, England, which he held till 1860. He is praised, at the expense of Emerson (*q.v.*) among others, in George M. Frederickson's *The Inner Civil War* (1965) for having viewed the Civil War (*q.v.*) realistically as death and destruction. Actually Hawthorne was indifferent to its moral purposes. Of interest to scholars is Hawthorne's strange apathy in his last years; he died for no apparent reason. It has been conjectured, though with scholarly evidence, that his need for religion to implement his conservative outlook, and his lack of religion, deprived him of a reason to go on; see Henry G. Fairbanks, *The Lasting Loneliness of Nathaniel Hawthorne: A Study of the Sources of Alienation of Modern Man* (1965). See also R. von Abele, *The Death of the Artist: A Study of Hawthorne's Disintegration* (1955).

**Hay, John** (1838-1905), American Secretary of State, best known as formulator of the Open Door Policy permitting equal commercial opportunities in China, and thus diminishing the chances of war among great powers. Henry Adams (*q.v.*) deeply admired his friend's expertise in the transaction. Hay is less known as a transitional (*q.v.*) figure from Indiana and Illinois liberality to a reserved statesmanship. At twenty-one, he joined Abraham Lincoln's (*q.v.*) staff in the White House as assistant and private secretary. Following positions in the Foreign Service he joined the *New York Tribune* as a journalist. During that time he published his *Pike County Ballads* (1871), which saluted his background in open, democratic dialect, the poem "Jim Bludso" attaining particular fame. Hay found himself disturbed by rising labor unrest, and in 1883 he published anonymously the anti-labor novel *The Bread Winners*. It lacked narrative skill, and held malcontents and incompetents responsible for labor riots. By then, his transformation into an Eastern gentleman had been completed. His work with John G. Nicolay on ten volumes of *Abraham Lincoln: A History* (1890) was at the time considered a publishing coup. It was soon superseded in public interest by Ida M. Tarbell's gathering of insightful materials and information from still-living personages who had known Lincoln, which was published as *Early Life of Abraham Lincoln* (1900).

**Hayek, Friedrich A. Von** (1899- ), conservative economic theoretician, much revered. He protested that he was not a conservative but actually a liberal. A product of the University of Vienna, where he taught economics from 1929 to 1931, he left for England, where he was a professor at the University of London from 1931 to 1950. His reputation grew with such works as *Monetary Theory and the Trade Cycle* (1929), *Prices and Production* (1931), and *Monetary Nationalism and International Stability* (1937). He attracted the attention of economists because of the moral component he found in monetary transactions. Originally a friend of government's inevitable role in trade, he was repelled by what he saw as the inevitable results of "planning," on the Continent and, prophetically, in Great Britain's turn to Labour. *The Road to Serfdom* (1944) alerted conservatives and alarmed partisans of the welfare state (*q.v.*); see Herman Finer, *Road to Reaction*. Hayek's humanistic personality helped make him a leader among free-enterprise economists, as did such publications as his *John Stuart Mill and Harriet Taylor* (1950) and *The Constitution of Liberty* (1960). In 1974 he was awarded the Nobel Prize for Economics. See *Essays on Hayek*.

**Hazlitt, Henry** (1894- ), a noted conservative economist. His writings drew on decades of financial experience which, helped by a lucid style, gave force to his free-market opinions. He began with the *Wall Street Journal* in 1912 and continued as financial editor for a number of New York papers. In 1925 he became literary editor for the *Sun* and continued until 1929. He was editor of the *American Mercury* from 1933 to 1934. His literary interests expressed themselves in *The Anatomy of Criticism* (1933). He was co-editor, then editor-in-chief of the *Freeman* (*q.v.*) and in 1936 became literary editor of the *Nation*. A pioneer among new conservatives, he published *Economics in One Lesson* (1946), widely disseminated in conservative circles. A major critic of Lord Keynes (*q.v.*), he trumpeted *The Failure of the New Economics* (1959). A humanist as well as an economist, Hazlitt linked morals and finance in his writings. The evident problems inherent in deficit spending gave new authority to such of his later books as *Man vs. the Welfare State, The Conquest of Poverty* (1973), and *The Inflation Crisis and How to Resolve It* (1978). His fear of government, which had been building the welfare state, put him in substantial opposition to members of the Chicago School (*q.v.*), who saw the State as a possible instrument for advancing free enterprise.

**Heard, Gerald** (1890-1971), born Henry FitzGerald Heard. He is best known as "H. F. Heard," author of remarkable tales mixing scientific materials with moral questions, and as "Gerald Heard," who wrote more directly on religious and mystic themes. In his early years he was a Christian Socialist, but his experiences convinced him that moral values would have to be linked with events for there to be positive change that did not waste human endeavor. He employed the findings of science and speculation to show that the Bible was in truth the word of God. Heard's *These Hurrying Years* (1934) and *Morals Since 1900* (1950) were remarkable in seeking cause-and-effect relationships between government and social impulses, and so unfolding the "moral climate" of the times. Such books as *A Dialogue in the Desert* (1942) and *The Eternal Gospel* (1946) more directly pondered the weight of Christian tenets and revelation in the lives of people. Heard's best known follower was Aldous Huxley (*q.v.*), drawn by Heard's remarkable combination of strict scientific studies and mystic explorations. Heard's name was probably more widely circulated among followers of fantasy and science fiction, and for his subtle fictional forays into criminal psychology. *A Taste for Honey* (1941) and *Reply Paid* (1942) were durable narratives of strange conditions and abnormal gifts, as was *Weird Tales of Terror and Detection* (1944).

**"Heartland,"** a concept of Halford J. Mackinder (*q.v.*), who also pioneered geopolitical analyses intended to define the pivotal nations from which world power would radiate. During Richard M. Nixon's administration, his political "heartland" was seen as the Middle West, composed of people who were seen to show him American ideals and feelings to which he could freely appeal. When they tired of his Presidential misadventures, his support collapsed.

**Helms, Jesse** (1921- ), a Baptist and former newspaperman who became one symbol of conservativism in Congress. A United States Senator from North Carolina since 1973, he protested such Supreme Court decisions as that on school prayers and abortion and Congressional acts implementing them. He won the Conservative Congressional Award in 1976. His forthright opposition to liberal causes made him a standard object of liberal condemnation and conservative approbation. In 1983 he made a symbolic stand against the declaration of Martin Luther King, Jr.'s birthday as a national holiday.

**Helsinki Charter** (1975), see Human Rights

**Henry George School,** see Chodorov, Frank

**Henry, Patrick,** (1736-1799), American patriot. Like Samuel Adams (*q.v.*) in Massachusetts he was an example of the radical turned conservative following the Revolution, which gave both the opportunity to distinguish themselves. Unlike Adams, whose fixed opposition to British rule has been traced to family fortunes in decline because of British colonial policies, Henry's was a tale of democratic opportunity in aristocratic Virginia. He seized on the discontentment of rising classes and the limiting force of the Navigation Acts to declare with unprecedented eloquence that it was the purpose of the British Crown to put chains upon the people. In his speech of March 23, 1775, reported secondhand but rousing patriot excitement, he declared for armed resistance to the authorities. The next year he was made governor, and served the Revolution. His conservatism grew in two stages: first in defense of states rights (*q.v.*), which caused him to oppose ratification of the new Constitution (*q.v.*), submitted in 1788; later as a full-fledged Federalist (*q.v.*) in resistance to Jeffersonian doctrine.

**Herberg, Will** (1909-1977), religious and conservative thinker whose career illustrated the transitions (*q.v.*) from extreme radicalism to extreme conservativism. A precocious youth and Columbia University Ph.D. (1932), he was led by Marxist writings and the force of Communist politics to intellectual leadership in the movement. He joined Jay Lovestone when he was expelled by Stalin from command of the American party. Herberg labored to rationalize Communist policy while being active in the "Lovestoneite" stronghold, the International Ladies Garment Workers Union (ILGWU). Stunned by the Nazi-Soviet Pact, the Lovestone faction disbanded, and Herberg began an intellectual odyssey first inspired by the thoughts of Reinhold Neibuhr. They led him to the Judeo-Christian (*q.v.*) tradition and positions he would follow for the rest of his life—first as a lecturer and writer and then as a professor at Drew University in New Jersey, where he taught Judaic Studies and Social Philosophy. He became one of the ex-radicals who turned to the *National Review*, adding an ecumenical tone to its developing program. Typical of his thought was *Protestant, Catholic, Jew* (1955). Believing that those who hated God were closer to Him than those who indulged in a watered humanism, he pondered such writers as Albert Camus and mused over *Four Existentialist Theologians* (1958): Jacques Maritain, Nicolas Berdyaev, Martin Buber, and Paul Tillich. With others, he prepared *Religious Perspective in American Culture* (1960) for the American Enterprise Institute. See Bernhard W. Anderson, ed., Herberg, *Faith Enacted as History; Essays in Biblical Theology* (1976), and J.P. Diggins, *Up from Communism* (1975), treating Herberg among others in transition.

**Heritage Foundation, The,** a Washington-based public-policy-research institution committed to free enterprise, limited government, and a strong national defense. It published *Policy Review*, and such works as *Agenda '83*, intended to offer suggestions on a variety of matters to the Reagan Republican Administration. It maintained informal relations with such other institutions as the Hoover Institution (*q.v.*) and the Center for Strategic and International Studies at Georgetown University (*q.v.*). One of its many publications was Number 13 of The Heritage Lectures. Russell Kirk's (*q.v.*) *Reclaiming a Patrimony* (1982), a collection of lectures including a retrospect on conservative developments; "Then and Now" on Edmund Burke, Dr, Johnson, and Adam Smith as "pillars of order"; and discussions of such other topics as libertarians, church and state, and the criminal character (*qq.v.*).

**Heroes,** mainly products of nationalistic advance, but more numerous for groups identified with particular causes or pursuits. It is evident that the fame of Nathan Hale and his once-famous "I regret that I have but one life to give for my country" was a product of the desperate gamble of patriots; the American Revolution needed heroes. Zebulon Pike was of the stuff of heroes. The discoverer of Pike's Peak and other Western terrain sought fame and earned it with his death during the War of 1812. The Civil War contributed more heroes than the mind could hold, or cared to hold, as Northerner or Southerner. Allan Nevins subtitled his biography of John D. Rockefeller "The Heroic Age of American Businessmen," but those who mistrusted the purposes or achievements of the entrepeneurs created their own pantheon of heroes (see Heroes, Filler DASC). The "disillusionment" (*q.v.*) of the Twenties created "debunkers" of American history, but did not impede operation of such institutions as New York University's Hall of Fame, situated in the Bronx, New York. The rise of ethnic agitation and dissatisfaction with WASP (*q.v.*) domination of American ideals, mixed with widening international problems and responsibilities, shook the loyalty to traditional heroes, even those who had founded or helped save the nation. Although the need for heroes continued, despite the attention paid to "anti-heroes," it was evident that fresh understandings of American duties were necessary. Superficial enthusiasms produced literally thousands of "halls of fame," while New York University's Hall of Fame of

Great Americans eroded in a decaying Bronx. In the 1960s some radical elements in America revered such figures as Cuba's Che Guevara and China's Chairman Mao. Meanwhile they demeaned such American heroes as George Washington and Abraham Lincoln. The entire subject became politicalized (*q.v.*) in the interests of narrow groups. It was evident that such atomization of feelings could not continue indefinitely. The 1980s saw a new respect for traditional heroes. R. B. Browne et al., eds., *Heroes of Popular Culture* (1972); M. W. Fishwick, *American Heroes: Myth and Reality* (1954); O. E. Klapp, *Heroes, Villains and Fools: Reflections of the American Character* (1962).

**Hewitt, Abram S.** (1822-1903), one of the most distinguished conservatives of the second half of the nineteenth century. A graduate of Columbia College, he worked with the businessman and philanthropist Peter Cooper to advance iron manufacturing in the pre-Civil War period, and himself introduced the Bessemer process in America. He assisted in the work of laying the Atlantic cable in 1858. During the Civil War his works were invaluable in providing gun metal for the Union Army at fair rates. In 1874 he was elected to the U. S. House of Representatives, where he rose to leadership. He managed Samuel J. Tilden's campaign for the Presidency two years later, and guided the Democratic Party through the dangerous disputations following. He also undertook and completed the work involved in establishing Cooper Union, a distinguished New York institution of learning. His papers on gold, free trade, and labor relations were realistic and highly informed. As mayor of New York in 1886, having defeated Henry George and Theodore Roosevelt (*q.v.*) he gave the city a reform administration. His sound money arguments were reminiscent of those which appeared in the early 1980s. Allan Nevins, *Abram S. Hewitt: With Some Account of Peter Cooper* (1935) and ed., *Selected Writings of Abram S. Hewitt* (1937).

**"Higher Law,"** one of the imponderables in the programs of social activists, from radical to conservative. The great governor and senator William Henry Seward, denouncing the Fugitive Slave Law of 1850, declared that there was a "Higher Law" than the Constitution. He was startled to hear himself branded as a radical and, even more, defended and praised from Northern pulpits. How far could one go who believed in law yet felt compelled to defy it? Conservatives unwilling to abandon John Brown for his 1859 assault on Harpers Ferry in effect urged an insanity plea. The post-Civil War era was less receptive to appeals to Deity in matters involving law and business. In 1902 George F. Baer, railroad and coal-mine operator while resisting strike demands drew a line between old appeals and new necessities when he declared that workers were best protected by those to whom "God in his infinite Wisdom has given control of the property interests of the country." So merciless was the response of the public that it required the best services of the pioneer publicity man Ivy Lee (*q.v.*) to restore Baer's reputation. Controversial were such later crises in higher law as Montgomery Ward head Sewell Avery's 1944 defiance of the National Labor Relations Board, and the much later air controllers' attempt to strike against Federal regulations in behalf of still higher wages.

**Higher Patriotism,** see Patriotism

**Hillsdale College,** in Michigan, a small liberal arts institution over a century old which became nationally known for its unwillingness to receive Federal or other funds which would entail having to accept bureaucratic (*q.v.*) regulations. Insisting that it chose students for entrance on the basis of their credentials, it defied U. S. Health, Education and Welfare demands that it adopt a quota (*q.v.*) system of student selection. Taking HEW to court, and finding aid and support in the name of academic freedom, Hillsdale was able to stop Federal interference. Its president, George C. Roche III, presided over lecture series and meetings which brought famous conservative speakers and personalities to the campus, including the Center for Constructive Alternatives and a wide variety of publications explaining the college's philosophy and goals. *Imprimis* reprinted many of these lectures and circulated them to some 90,000 readers. *Alternatives* was sent out to clients which included *Reader's Digest* (*q.v.*), and in monthly issues discussed such subjects as welfare and government regulation (*qq.v.*). The Shavano Institute, located in Colorado, brought together public figures to discuss topics of national import, and instituted *Counterpoint*, which broadcast debates pitting the socialist Michael Harrington against the free-enterprise champion Walter Williams (*q.v.*), the Rev. William Sloane Coffin against Winston S. Churchill II, and Right-to-Work's (*q.v.*) Reed Larson against the head of the Machinists Union, William Winpisinger. With its endowment growing, and its long lists of nationally recognized visitors regularly in the news, Hillsdale became a Midwest center of conservativism.

**Hinckley, John.** He attempted the assassination of President Ronald Reagan in March 1981. Hinckley, then 27, later stated that he was attempting to impress a young movie actress with whom he was in love from afar. Hinckley's subsequent trial was important for his reliance on the insanity plea (*q.v.*). Earlier attempts on Presidents had been dealt with by courts peremptorily. Tried in a Washington, D.C. court, he was judged innocent by reason of insanity at the time of the shooting. He was sent to St. Elizabeth's Hospital. If in the future hospital authorities decided he was no longer insane, they could conceivably set him free. There was great controversy over the trial's outcome and the insanity plea. The judge of the proceedings averred that ending the insanity defense would mean a "retreat to the Middle Ages." George F. Will saw law as evading the issue of responsibility. Strom Thurmond (*q.v.*) and others demanded that the defense be required to prove insanity, rather than the prosecution, as had been the case in Hinckley's trial. St. Elizabeth's kept its own counsel in the case as it had in that of Ezra Pound (*q.v.*): a case comparable in showing lack of reverence for American institutions, or duty toward them. See also Dissidents.

**Hispanics,** an overall term denoting Spanish-speaking people in the United States. They derived from different lands—Mexico, Cuba, and Puerto Rico for example—and variant traditions. Puerto Ricans were American citizens by law. Most Hispanics were Catholic, but their lifestyles differed considerably. They totaled some 14.6 million, and were mainly centered in New York, New Mexico, New Jersey, Illinois, and Texas. In 1980 some 3.5 million registered to vote. Hispanics gained the office of mayor in San Antonio and Miami and in 1983 elected a young, forceful lawyer mayor of Denver: a city in which Hispanics were only 18 percent of the population. Although conservative in many respects, they were generally poorer than other social groups and tended to favor liberal candidates. However, in 1980 they gave Ronald Reagan 30 percent of their votes, 20 percent more than blacks. The Reagan Administration attempted to reach out to Hispanic communities, seeing them as natural supporters of many of its programs.

**Hiss Case,** see Filler, DASC, a landmark in liberal-conservative relations. It was clearly a product of experience and commitments in the Thirties (*q.v.*), of Soviet credibility amassed before and during World War II, and of fear and hatred of fascism (*q.v.*) especially as developed in Germany under Hitler (*q.v.*). None of this should have affected attitudes toward treason and perjury, but they did. Alger Hiss was personable, a New Deal establishment figure, competent and successful. Whittaker Chambers (*q.v.*) was unattractive, with a conflicted personality and a tendency toward abstract thinking. In his early effort to reach New Deal figures with his evidence that Hiss was dangerous to American security, he failed to impress them. Hiss had a commendable record in government, had been a State Department advisor during the Yalta (*q.v.*) conferences, and had become deputy director of the Office of Special Political Affairs and then its director. He had helped draw up the United Nations (*q.v.*) Charter, and had become president of the Carnegie Endowment for International Peace. Chambers, meanwhile, had been a Communist and an agent of the Comintern. His charges that Hiss had been his friend and a Communist, and that Hiss had copied sensitive State Department records for transmission to Soviet agents, appeared incredible. Before the record was fully aired, and two trials completed in 1949 and 1950, the public had seen two major approaches to the issue. Exhaustive efforts by the Department of Justice produced torrents of witnesses and evidence. Richard M. Nixon (*q.v.*) proved vital to the effort to find and pursue a case. Secretary of State Dean Acheson, however, stated that he would not turn his back on Alger Hiss. Strangely Hiss was unable to produce witnesses contradicting Chambers. Meanwhile, conservatives used the Hiss case to indict liberal thinking and capabilities. Liberals saw Hiss as a victim of conservative persecution. Although books were written to prove Hiss victim of a diabolic government plot, they found little interest. Chambers wrote *Witness*, a soul-emptying autobiography; Hiss's *In the Court of Public Opinion*, on the other hand, was oddly abstract and lacking a human dimension: a lawyer's brief picking and choosing among evidence. The *coup de grâce* was delivered in 1978 with publication of *Perjury*, by Allen Weinstein, then an academic. He had studied case papers under the Freedom of Information Act, which Hiss himself had consulted. Weinstein had found proof of Hiss's guilt. See also Trilling, Lionel.

**History,** see *Clio from the Right*, Continuity, *Progressive Historians*, Revisionists. In general, the "new" history attracted liberal investigators, though both "conceptualized" theses and "quantification" also attracted broader based historians to provide useful historical information. "Psychohistory," however, which encouraged writers to psychoanalyze historical figures, was much more controversial, since it could offer seemingly persuasive portraits and judgments, and so feed biases with little controls. H. J. Grass and P. Monaco, *Quantification and Psychology: Toward a "New" History* (1980); Salvatore Prisco III, *An Introduction to Psychohistory: Theories and Case Studies* (1980). See also Brodie, Fawn.

**Hitler, Adolf** (1889-1945), made infamous by his demagoguery, military actions, genocidal (*q.v.*) operations, and twisting of the German heritage into one of blond conquerors, cultural bigotry, and gross international adventures. A few Americans of conservative bent openly saw good in his projected program, and commercial (*q.v.*) elements sanctioned business arrangements with German firms. Ann Morrow Lindbergh's (*q.v.*) book, *The Wave of the Future* (1940) caused controversy when it appeared, by seeming to justify indirectly the Hitler revolution. The larger part of American conservatism, as represented by America First (*q.v.*), proved more isolationist and patriotic than empathetic to Hitler and his cohorts. The new conservatism of the post-World War II era agreed that nothing justified the ruin which Hitler had brought on Germans and others. The new conservatives differed from liberals, however, by insisting that it was improper to heap hatred on Hitler without also consigning to infamy Stalin (*q.v.*) and the policies he had preached and practiced. In a newly matured conservative era, they were able to link the two dictators with some success, though some liberals protested that they could discern differences in the origin and development of the Soviet and Nazi systems, however compatible they might appear in results. See also Levine, Isaac Don; Solzhenitsyn, Alexander (*qq.v.*); and A. Bullock, *Hitler: A Study in Tyranny* (1971); R. V. Daniels, ed., *The Stalin Revolution: Foundations of Soviet Totalitarianism* (1972); James E. McSherry, *Stalin, Hitler and Europe* (1977).

**Hobbes, Thomas** (1588-1679), rationalist philosopher. His view is rejected by most conservatives, who see more in man than Hobbes envisioned. A tutor to the aristocratic Cavendish family, Hobbes interested himself in the science of politics. He was at odds with the Parliamentarians who ultimately overthrew Charles I. Hobbes left England for France where exiles found his cold materialism unpleasant. His dedication to the monarchy lacked the warmth, Christianity, and tradition which they found attractive. Hobbes saw people as mere organisms, the lives of which were "solitary, poor, nasty, brutish, and short." Qualifying natural law (*q.v.*), which conservatives saw as positive and God-given, he saw the need for a social contract to prevent mutual slaughter by concentrating full authority in a monarch. Such peremptory authority led, conservatives felt, to the French Revolution and later revolutionary uprisings which lacked humanistic aspects. See Gateway edition, Hobbes' *Leviathan* (1956), with introduction by Russell Kirk (*q.v.*). See also Strauss, Leo; Oakeshott, Michael Joseph.

**Hoffer, Eric** (1902-1983), a phenomenon of social history. He was a migratory worker in California early in the 1940s, then became a longshoreman with a penchant for philosophical inquiry and varied historical reading. A major concern for him was the frame of mind and experience which drew people to mass movements. Avoiding dogmas, he studied the impulses of desire, the misfits, the bored (*q.v.*), and others. He struck with ardor at factions by noting "the interchangeability of mass movements," found the roots of self-sacrifice in such elements as make-believe and "depreciation of the present," and otherwise deflated what he saw as pretension. Made famous by his *The True Believer* (1951) and possessed of a homely, photogenic personality, Hoffer was encouraged to speak his mind on television and in interviews. *The Passionate State of Mind* (1955), *The Ordeal of Change* (1963), and *The Temper of Our Time* (1967) broadened his ruminations from what had essentially been a consideration of Communist compulsions. During the intense civil-rights and other agitations of the 1960s Hoffer's forthrightness on blacks and others embarrassed many. His opinion that "unlucky countries have revolutions, lucky countries learn from other people's revolutions" was controversial in a time which idolized revolution. Hoffer retired from public view. His later books were *Working and Thinking on the Waterfront* (1969), *First Things Last Things, Reflection on the Human Condition* (1973), *In Our Time* (1976), and *Before the Sabbath*.

**Hoffman, Abbie,** symbol of youthful unrest and anti-American behavior, as manifested in such 1960s behaviors as campus disruption, anti-Vietnam protest, and the encouragement of drug consumption (*qq.v.*). He was the evident protagonist in the film, *The Big Fix,* reviewing it himself in the *Village Voice,* a New York paper, though he was then living disguised to evade police. See Filler, *Vanguards and Followers: Youth in the American Tradition.*

**Hofstadter, Richard,** see *Progressive Historians, The*

**Holmes, Oliver Wendell** (1809-1894), once considered of paramount literary distinction, so much as to outweigh his scientific achievements, notably in the study and control of puerperal fever. Among his poems, the patriotic "Old Ironsides" and the reverent "The Chambered Nautilus" were once highly prized, and his "Wonderful One-Hoss Shay" survives as a masterpiece showing in metaphor the crumbling of the Calvinist establishment. A Boston Brahmin and an exemplar of gentility (*q.v.*), he was the "Autocrat" of the *Atlantic Monthly* (*q.v.*) whose opinions on all subjects were accepted with delight by informed readers of the time. As a pioneer in what became the field of psychiatry, he wrote fiction which attracted less attention from his admirers; see C. P. Oberndorf, *The Psychiatric Novels of Oliver Wendell Holmes* (1944).

**Holmes, Oliver Wendell, Jr.** (1841-1935), as Associate Justice of the Supreme Court, he rose above his father in fame, particularly among liberals, for his apparent openness to change. Much quoted was "the Great Dissenter's" minority opinion, endorsed by his Court collaborator, Justice Brandeis (*q.v.*), that if "in the long run, the beliefs expressed in proletarian dictatorship are destined to be accepted by dominant forces of the community, the only meaning of free speech is that they should be given their chance and have their way" (*Gitlow* [*q.v.*] *v. New York*, 268 U.S. 652, 673 [1925]). This was less quoted by conservatives, when quoted at all, than was his opinion in the same dissent, which would have applied to conservatives as well as liberals, that "[i]t is said that this manifesto [of Gitlow's] is more than a theory, it is an incitement. Every idea is an incitement." Other of Holmes's dissents were also made famous by liberals, but not those which reflected his pride in having served in the Civil War and holding war a legitimate expression of sovereignty. The writer Max Lerner, in his liberal-radical phase, looked doubtfully at Holmes's loyalty to traditional American ideals (Lerner, *The Mind and Faith of Justice Holmes* [1948]). Holmes could have served a vigorous conservatism in the fallow post-World War I years more than he did, with such views as "the great act of faith is when man decides that he is not God" and—following up on Chief Justice John Marshall (*q.v.*)—"the power to tax is not the power to destroy."

**Holocaust,** see Anti-Semitism; *Human Life Review*

**"Home Industries,"** see Protectionism

**Homosexuals**, see Filler, DASC. For many centuries a forbidden subject, though realized by scholars of ancient history as evident even in classic writings. The Oscar Wilde scandal of the 1890s drew together many threads, hinted at or evaded in earlier public opinion. Wilde's talent and fame, the exposure of matters ordinarily hidden behind elite walls, and the presence of respectable and esteemed individuals forced society to come to terms with the obvious, beyond the "depravity" anticipated in outcasts or the dissolute poor. Well-known writers openly praised Wilde's *Ballad of Reading Gaol*, and were moved by his *De Profundis* (Out of the Depths). Publishers issued books about him, and reprinted his tales and plays. Although Radclyffe Hall's *The Well of Loneliness*, detailing a lesbian love affair while avoiding private details, was a 1920s scandal of sorts, it also drew appreciation for fine writing and evident sincerity. A.J.A. Symons's *In Quest of Corvo* (1934) similarly saw beneath a tormented life a genuine talent and compulsive needs. However, the turmoil of the 1950s precipitated to the fore numerous rebels against the established order, including homosexuals, many of whom were determined to "get out of the closet" and into social life. Generally, the new conservatives held to the norm of family and heterosexual relations, and loyalty to country. Liberals, too, when co-workers were revealed in homosexual roles, tended to blame ill-health for the event. During the exposure of President Lyndon B. Johnson's close aide, Walter Jenkins, friendly journalists blamed overwork for Jenkins's humiliation. Homosexuals accumulating in number in various centers, notably San Francisco and New York, became a political factor which challenged public leaders to recognize their strength while not offending their basic constituencies. Conservatives sought to be understanding when a favorite of theirs was revealed in a deviate role, and accepted his plea of illness. However, his turnabout in support of his sexual preference caused them to leave him to his own devices. Homosexuals sought visibility and success in liberal politics. They achieved both gains and losses. In San Francisco, its Retirement Board agreed that the homosexual lover of an assassinated city offficial merited survival benefits; but an effort to have the unmarried partners of all city employees, whatever their sexual preference, given the same benefits was overruled by the mayor. The march of homosexuals to civic parity received a setback by revelations that they were particularly subject to the deadly failure of their immunity systems to withstand certain disease patterns; that, moreover, they were able to pass on their infirmity to heterosexual persons. Particularly distressing to many was the fact that the disease (AIDS) could reach even children. Nevertheless, such was the power of numbers that the New York City Council was persuaded to pass an ordinance making illegal discrimination against homosexuals in civic concerns. Enrique Rueda, *The Homosexual Newwork: Private Lives and Public Policy* (1981).

**Hook, Sidney** (1902- ), long-time head of the philosophy department at New York University. As a young man he was a brilliant expositor of Karl Marx (*q.v.*), as in *The Meaning of Marx* (1934). Since Marx posited action as well as words, Hook made efforts to cooperate with the Communists of the time. Disillusioned by the capacity of Stalinists (*q.v.*) to follow party orders like automatons, and the inability of their Communist opponents to accomplish more—he termed Trotskyites (*q.v.*) "midget totalitarians"—he turned from the movement to concentrate on logic and education. In the 1960s he met apologists for campus disturbances with sharp reasoning. Some conservatives saw him as a companion in arms. See his

*Heresy, Yes, Conspiracy, No* (1953) and *Academic Freedom and Academic Anarchy* (1970). See also Paul Kurtz, ed., *Sidney Hook and the Contemporary World* (1968).

**Hoover, Herbert** (1874-1964), American President who bore the brunt of the blame for the Great Depression (*q.v.*). He was world famous as "the great humanitarian" as a result of his services during World War I, when he headed expanding commissions to feed, clothe, and provide medical supplies to populations in war-devastated zones, beginning with Belgium and reaching into demoralized areas of Russia. As Secretary of Commerce under Harding (*q.v.*) and Coolidge, he brought his administrative talents to bear on industry, persuading leaders to agree on standards of production, especially concerning new materials multiplying under assembly-line conditions. Seemingly the ideal businessman for presiding over an industrial society—educated, a student of history, and with worldwide experience as a mining engineer—Hoover overwhelmingly defeated his opponent, Alfred E. Smith, from the city streets of New York, in the 1928 Presidential election. Hoover was victimized by a Depression (*q.v.*) he had not foreseen and which conflicted with his philosophy of free enterprise and hard work; he had himself been born poor. He saw his task as President to continue his World War duties, encouraging local initiative to aid those in dire need and encouraging industry to rehire workers and resume production. Although he initiated some government projects, and finally set up the Reconstruction Finance Corporation to loan money to industrialists, he could not cut into the business slowdown. In the process his image suffered. His proud, reserved manner worked against him, as did the optimistic forecasts he felt it his duty to offer as leader. With the encouragement of the opposition Democrats the shanty towns used by homeless people for shelter became known as "Hoovervilles." Harmful too was Hoover's response to the "Bonus Marchers," desperate men encouraged by radicals to demand an immediate cashing of compensation certificates held by veterans. Camping out near the Capitol in shacks and unused buildings, they appealed to Congress, which denied their petitions. They were offered transportation home; those who refused it were ordered to disperse. Following a violent confrontation with police they were evicted by Federal troops under General MacArthur and his aide Dwight D. Eisenhower (*qq.v.*). These events contrasted sharply with measures taken by Governor Franklin D. Roosevelt in New York, who instituted a "Little New Deal." Although it did little to improve the economy, and involved "leaf-raking" (*q.v.*) and other cosmetic features as well as modest welfare allotments, it provided a modicum of hope which Hoover could not supply. There were many who approved his courageous defense of principles, but when he ran for re-election he defended his record completely, in effect promising that another four years would bring nothing more. Hoover was overwhelmed at the polls in 1932. He described the ensuing New Deal as *The Challenge to Liberty* (1934), and published numerous other books and memoirs. War prosperity and post-war revaluations threw a better light on Hoover than the Depression era had permitted. Soon scholarly books appeared describing with respect or appreciation of Hoover's numerous deeds and experiences. Notable was Eugene Lyons's (*q.v.*) *Our Unknown Ex-President* (1948), Lyons having been a well-known radical intellectual. In 1949, President Truman (*q.v.*) appointed Hoover head of a commission to study the condition of the Executive Branch and to make recommendations for its reorganization. Truman reminded the public of Hoover's early reputation for administrative expertise. Meanwhile, the Hoover Institution on War, Revolution, and Peace had been established in 1919 to process Hoover's long-gathered papers and to acquire more, and had become, at Stanford University, his alma mater, one of the world's leading research centers. At his death he was acknowledged to have been a leading Republican of his time, and to have forged a philosophy of life and duties relevant to American ways.

**Hoover, J. Edgar** (1895-1972), embattled head

of the Federal Bureau of Investigation, with a record of anti-radicalism which went back to World War I. He began to fight crime in the changing years of the 1920s (*q.v.*) which produced new and more formidable criminals, of whom Al Capone (*q.v.*) became prototypical. In time, Hoover became accused of self-publicity, aggrandizement of power, and the maintenance of secret files against rivals and civilians. In the 1920s and 1930s, however, he developed a formidable body of operators whose courage and resourcefulness became legend. During the 1930s (*q.v.*) he also began his campaign against Communists as enemies of the state. He was vehemently opposed by radicals, and by liberals persuaded that he was a foe of freedom. His *Masters of Deceit: The Story of Communism in America and How to Fight It* (1958) gave a substantial account of the growth of the Communist movement and its workings in America. Yet the fierceness of the sustained attack on him by radicals and liberals helped harm his reputation. By keeping files on hundreds of thousands of citizens—many, as it turned out, cataloging words rather than deeds—Hoover compromised his best intentions when they were most needed to build rapport among loyal citizens. His vendetta against Martin Luther King, Jr. became notorious even among persons whose regard for King was qualified, suggesting as it did that any of an individual's vagaries might become part of an official dossier and subject to distortion by an official with a partisan point to make. Although revelations obtained through the Freedom of Information Act (*q.v.*) with respect to F. B. I. files helped cloud Hoover's reputation, he was still appreciated by many as a dedicated public servant who had created modern standards of service and techniques for meeting them. William W. Turner, *Hoover's F. B. I.* (1971), Ralph De Toledano (*q.v.*), *J. Edgar Hoover: The Man in His Time* (1973).

**Hoover Institution on War, Revolution and Peace**. It was established in Palo Alto, California in 1919 by Herbert Hoover as the War Library, to hold the papers he had collected during his various services as a relief administrator. It expanded its holdings to include vast quantities of associated papers and developed research and publication programs. Seen as a conservative "think tank," it stirred resentment among Stanford University liberals and radicals, some of whom in 1983 tried to disassociate the university from the Hoover Institution.

**"Hoovervilles,"** a term referring to shantytowns during the Hoover (*q.v.*) Administration. It formed a brilliant campaign on the part of the Democratic Party in 1932 and succeeded in fastening upon Herbert Hoover, fighting for re-election, the onus for decayed buildings and rudely erected shelters housing homeless drifters in that depressed year. Although the charge was technically "unfair," the fact remained that the imputation clung to Hoover, and remained even after he had been long rehabilitated. The nation evidently concluded that, considering Hoover's optimistic forecasts before his election and during his Presidency, the existence of such tragic enclaves could be reasonably related to him. However, the same nation rejected attempts during the Reagan (*q.v.*) Administration to ascribe "Reaganvilles" to him, evidently realizing that the setting up of shanties across the street from the White House was mere play-acting, and that the decay of the cities, despite high inflows of Federal funds, had long preceded Reagan (*q.v.*) and was clearly not the result of unemployment but of social decay.

**"Hostages,"** see Carter, Jimmy

**House Un-American Activities Committee, HUAC**; see Filler, DASC. Its high points of activity involved Martin Dies (*q.v.*). At bottom were issues of national security and privacy. During the Dies era, however, liberals argued that Communism did not threaten the United States, whereas fascism, underplayed by the HUAC, did. The war against Nazism, in association with the Soviet Union, undermined the efforts of Dies. Russia's development of the atomic bomb, and evidence of domestic treason contributing to that development, gave fresh impetus to HUAC. However, the discrediting of McCarthy (*q.v.*), and the dwindling of the Communist Party turned attention to traitors who could be presented in court, rather than Communist sympathizers, the traditional targets of the HUAC. See also Hiss Case.

**HUAC**, see House Un-American Activities Committee

**Human Events**, a conservative publication, began in 1944 by the pacifist journalists Frank C. Hanighen and Felix Morley (*q.v.*). It grew into an anti-New Deal, anti-Democratic-Party outlet opposed to augmented Federal power, Executive-mandated wars, and readiness to cooperate with the Soviet Union. It thus appeared an "extremist" publication to foes, but was highly respected within the conservative family of publications. It maintained a Congress watch, gave space to a variety of conservative commentators, and was as sharply critical of conservative leaders including President Reagan (*q.v.*) when it deemed them deviating from conservative goals as of liberals.

**Human Life Review**, published since 1975 by the Human Life Foundation, and dedicated to the "Single Issue" (*q.v.*) of opposition to abortion. As such, it received a striking amount of original matter bearing on the family, children, literature, and psychology from such writers and personalities as William F. Buckley, Jr., Malcolm Muggeridge, Mother Teresa, Michael Novak (*qq.v.*) and others, providing arguments and experience for those engaged in fighting what it referred to as the "Human Holocaust."

**Human Nature**, a staple in conservative thought and action. Many radicals have believed that the vagaries of humanity—cheating, competition, violence, careless living, and other destructive behavior—result from the influence of capitalism. When the socialist state arrives, such impulses and individualistic actions will disappear. "Human nature" will be benign nature. The foes of socialism continually deny such forecasts. Believers in original sin, human weakness, and imperfect nature, they see individualistic living, with whatever faults, superior in kind to any form of collectivism, which they identify with enslavement. They distinguish this from what they consider the negative results of "human nature." They maintain that life under capitalism, with all the tragedy involved, still offers choices which permit higher forms of idealism than could socialism. The savage crushing of dissent in Soviet Russia and China, once defended by sympathizers in capitalist countries as necessary in order to establish the "workers' state," according to their beliefs cannot be defended nor can it be defended in countries dominated by Russia and China, such as Hungary, Poland, and Afghanistan, which long to preserve their own ways and preferences.

**Human Rights**. The concern for human rights was deemed by the Carter (*q.v.*) Administration as constituting one of its major achievements, turning the world's attention to the UN Human Rights Commission and to its principles in the Mideast, in Central and South America, and elsewhere. Conservatives were enraged that the UN ignored the notorious policies of Communist nations with respect to their dissidents and their wholesale slaughter and abuse of those alien to their culture. They were angry with President Gerald Ford (*q.v.*) for having signed the Helsinki Charter of 1975, which pledged its signatories to respect human rights at home. The Soviets ignored the Charter, notoriously mistreating their own nationals and others who stood in their way. Yet human rights were obviously the issue of the hour and era. How could they be furthered? In general, conservatives were suspicious of the responsibility exercised by the media (*q.v.*) at home, which they deemed overly influenced by liberal outlooks. Their capacity to influence media presentation was undetermined.

**Humanism**, a modern permutation of earlier Rationalist (*q.v.*) movements. It appeals largely to the educated middle class, and is largely Deist. Humanism is divided into a firmly atheistic (*q.v.*) branch on one side and a "seeking" element on the other, sometimes involved in modern Unitarian and Ethical Culture activities. Humanists generally reject Biblical and traditional church tenets, holding that they encourage superstition and irrational longings for reassurance concerning the supernatural, that they give unwarranted power to the clergy, and that they retard progress (*q.v.*) and the acceptance and enjoyment of the living world. Although unable to achieve wide influence, Humanists have taken pride in such associates as Harry Elmer Barnes, Corliss Lamont, and Sir Julian Huxley. They find little good in Catholicism, approve abortion (*q.v.*) as reasonable, seek inspiration in the good evolving from science, and scorn a literal interpretation of the Bible. See also Neo-Humanism.

**Hume, David** (1711-1776), Scottish philosopher whose studies of human nature challenged the idealism of those who sought change while they opposed the religious tenets of conservatives. Hume's hard-headed materialism aided the logic of such social thinkers as Adam Smith (*q.v.*), whose free-trade principles emphasized the realities of trade exchange in defiance of Mercantilist (*q.v.*) premises which exalted civic duties in terms of empire. Hume's *Treatise of Human Nature* (1739-1740), *Enquiry Concerning the Principles of Morals* (1751), and *Dialogues Concerning Natural Religion* (1779) add up to an empirical attack on both the rational (*q.v.*) conjunction of truth and the principles of faith. His skepticism thus served the Establishment more than it did those who might wish to alter it. See his posthumous *Autobiography* (1777). See also D.W. Livingston and J.T. King, eds., *Hume, A Re-Evaluation* (1976).

**Hutchinson, Thomas** (1711-1780), a notable American Tory (*q.v.*) of pre-Revolutionary years. He was a descendant of the liberal religious leader Anne Hutchinson and the last royal civilian governor of Massachusetts. Although broad in his outlook and tolerant of diverse political opinion, he became unpopular by reason of his determination to uphold the law, a stance which brought on the Boston Tea Party and closed the ranks of anti-government forces. He is best remembered for his *History of the Colony and Province of Massachusetts*. His career illustrates the intensity of the drive toward independence, which the most generous and indigenous Tory opinion could not appease; see William Pencak, *America's Burke: The Mind of Thomas Hutchinson* (1982).

**Huxley, Aldous** (1894-1963), a figure in transition. He linked his grandfather, Thomas Henry Huxley, whose studies in Darwinism (*q.v.*) made him an atheist, with his own course from skepticism to mysticism. His early novel *Chrome Yellow* (1921) proclaimed him a stylist, and *Point Counter Point* (1928) a mixture of skeptic and seeker. *Brave New World* (1932) showed him turned against materialists. He became a follower of Gerald Heard (*q.v.*), dedicated to a search for evidence of the truth of Christianity. Huxley's Darwinian heritage was now firmly in the past. Among Huxley's works as a seeker, see *The Perennial Philosophy* (1945). His brother, Sir Julian Huxley (1887-1975), a biologist, found no reason to abandon his birthright, which he reconciled with humanism (*q.v.*); see his *Religion without Revelation* (1927) and *Evolutionary Ethics* (1957).

**Hypotheses**, see Social Sciences

**Hysteria**, an alleged feature of times of social crisis. The period of the Alien and Sedition Acts in the John Adams (*q.v.*) Administration has been seen in retrospect as one of hysteria. Although there was unwarranted persecution during the Civil War, recognition that there was a momentous threat to the Union has curbed some criticism of its dimensions. World War I vigilante action against pacifists, radicals, and persons of German background suggested hysteria to many people. In 1941 the unknown dimensions of Japan's threat to the United States led to measures to ensure that Japan was not receiving aid and comfort from Japanese-Americans, which many ascribe to hysteria. McCarthyism (*q.v.*) was linked to hysteria; his partisans argued that the Communist menace was real.

# I

**I Led Three Lives** (1952), by Herbert A. Philbrick, a pioneer memoir of an FBI undercover agent, with an average American background, whose testimony helped convict top-ranking Communist Party functionaries for conspiracy (*q.v.*) to overthrow the American government. Although the Party was becoming of secondary importance to a Soviet Union made powerful by possession of the atomic bomb and its direct hold over adjacent nations and penetration of lands elsewhere, the revelations of Philbrick helped create a demarcation line between older conditions and new. Philbrick exposed dedicated "comrades" and associates, unions (*q.v.*), and Communist "fronts." After Philbrick, Communist sympathizers masqueraded as Americans concerned for peace and peaceful relations abroad, civil rights, and other progressive causes at home. "Marxists" tended to be not members of an insignificant Communist Party, but citizens and professionals who saw capitalist economists and policies as impediments to a freeing of populations everywhere. An interesting detail of Philbrick's book was an appendix which sought to distinguish the Communist from the liberal. Thus he defined a Communist (*q.v.*) as one who "interprets and misinterprets history for his own purposes; a liberal (*q.v.*) studies history honestly and learns from it." Other points contrasted liberals and Communists in connection with the role of the individual, violence, the uses of culture, and other areas. See also Gitlow, Benjamin.

**Idea of a Patriot King, The** (1749). The fruit of Viscount Bolingbroke's complex political life which took him as Henry St. John from heights of political power and admiration under Queen Anne to exile on her death in 1714. This brought the Hanoverians to power, along with Whigs who honored commerce more than tradition. Bolingbroke tied his fortunes to those of James, who aspired to become James III, but whose fortunes ended in 1714 as far as Bolingbroke was concerned. Pardoned, he returned to England, where he furthered Tory causes. A distinguished Tory despite his religious skepticism, he learned from Machiavelli without conceding that victory was virtue. As the major contriver of the Peace of Utrecht (1713), his own high point of power, he valued negotiation above conflict. His Patriot King would rule for all the people, rather than for a faction. Bolingbroke was much approved by Disraeli (*q.v.*). Jeffrey Hart, *Viscount Bolingbroke, Tory Humanist* (1965).

**Idea of a University, The,** see Newman, John Henry Cardinal

**Ideas Have Consequences**, see Weaver, Richard

**Ideas That Became Big Business** (*q.v.*) (1959), by Clinton Woods, with a foreword by Dr. Richard D. Weigle, president of St. John's College. A comprehensive study and description of 200 businesses and their 700 originators and entrepreneurs. The stories told exemplified the conservative argument that there was work and wealth in the nation for those who were willing to look for them, and willing to battle discouraging prospects and conditions. Wants and needs met or created included the "convenience store," the Talon Zipper, Cream of Wheat, Root Beer, flowers by wire, wood pulp, fertilizer, the safety razor, the thermos, and Johnson's Wax.

**Identity Cards.** The issuance of identity cards was suggested by some conservative commentators and others to control illegal immigration in America and such other modern dangers as those created by terrorists. Many liberals, and indeed many conservatives, denounced identity cards as suggesting a police state and as being against American traditions. They pointed to use of identity cards as "internal passports" to control population movements in the Soviet Union and other Communist countries. Yet many Western European democracies routinely issue identity cards to their citizens. And for many Americans drivers licenses, credit cards and Social Security cards among many other identifying documents routinely function as "identity cards." In the mid-1980s the issue was still unresolved.

**Ideologue**, a term often used by political partisans to suggest that opponents are committed to abstract principles, rather than to human and factual realities. A curious, influential book *The End of Ideology* (1960) by Daniel Bell, an ex-radical turned sociologist, mostly concerned with "left" ideology, stated that "[t]he intellectual begins with *his* experience, *his* individual perceptions of the world, *his* privileges and deprivations, and judges the world by these sensibilities." Bell's thesis was that ideology had "ended" in the 1950s, a thesis which failed to anticipate the 1960s and their aftermath in ERA, supply side economics, and other dedicated causes.

**If Liberals Had Feathers...Gee** (1967), by W.H. von Dreele, one of the genuine satiric talents of the New Conservatism. The rest of his title ran: "What a Hunter I Would Be." Von Dreele, who edited a management newsletter for IBM World Trade Corporation, was impressively consistent in the quality of his verse and parody of liberal attitudes, euphemisms, and resistance to facts. With a variety of verse forms, mixing poetic symbols with flat statements, and adapting song, slogans, and phrases to new conditions, he made his pieces for *National Review* a constant delight.

**Imagination**, a vital function in human thought. Liberals were often influenced by romanticism (*q.v.*), so often at odds with order and tradition. Romanticism did indeed produce a Coleridge (*q.v.*), though mainly in his poetic phase; see J. S. Hill, *Imagination in Coleridge* (1978). And it touched all political leanings as shown in E. B. Gose, Jr., *Imagination Indulged: The Irrational in the 19th Century Novel* (1972). Poe (*q.v.*) and others constituted a conservative imaginative heritage, though little used; they were adjuncts of conservatism, more than a working conservatism proper. See Kirk, Russell; Lewis C. S.; Bradbury, Ray; Utopianism.

**Imagination** (1963), a posthumously published effort by Harold Rugg (1886-1960) a progressive educator, he tried to rescue what he could of the collapsed progressive structure he had labored to erect. Soundly raised and educated, Rugg worked to develop student materials which were substantive but also calculated to stimulate the mind and suggest relevance to the student. But his was a time of popularity for the "developing" Soviet Union, with intellectuals from Bernard Shaw in England to Walter Duranty of the *New York Times* finding much to praise in Soviet life. Rugg and his colleagues of the Progressive Educational Association cited with approval the Soviets' apparently enlightened educational techniques. The very popularity of Rugg's works called him to American Legion's (*q.v.*) attention, and made him an early victim of its fear of Soviet influence. The effect upon his textbooks by Legion protests was devastating; they were driven from circulation. Rugg, considering what could be done to preserve the core of his approach—the stimulation of student intelligence—hit upon imagination as the key. He sought evidence and examples in the lives of famous personalities showing that mere grubbing had not been the essence of their achievement. A surprising number of distinguished people had solved baffling problems, not during their rote studies, but with their minds and psyches at rest and working on their own. Rugg's book was indirectly a plea for individuality and creativity. However, the educational machine had by then gotten out of hand, and not even progressives were interested. For Rugg's apologia, see *That Men May Understand* (1941).

**Immigration**, see Filler, DASC. Immigration has often been identified with conservative response and exploitation and often more appropriately seen as a function of sectional, capitalist, or labor interests. The colonial era was receptive to immigrants as representing needed labor, much of it involuntary in the form of enslavement or indentured servitude; see Slavery. The Irish were a controversial center of interest once they grew in numbers of immigrants early in the nineteenth century because of their Catholicism (*q.v.*), but they were still exploited at mean and hard labor. The South, protecting its "peculiar institution," discouraged their immigration below the Mason-Dixon Line. Their bitter times provided justification for the Irish as Democratic urban "bosses" and corrupt officials in the major cities in the East during and following the Civil War. The resultant growth of industry caused states and particular industries actively to seek immigrants, especially from southern Europe, on contract terms which amounted to involuntary servitude. Though struck down by law, variant oppressive arrangements persisted which required humanitarian and reform movements to mitigate. "Goo Goos" and Civil Service reformers like George William Curtis and E. L. Godkin (*qq.v.*) represented conservative interests which gave form and efficiency to civic government. Little was done for the Orientals, brought in to service workers building the transcontinental railroads or smuggled in by Chinese entrepreneurs to do the menial work of the West Coast towns. Despite rude handling and betrayals, Chinese and Japanese, baited by labor demagogues, persisted into better times. The Progressives (*q.v.*) turned such efforts into a national enterprise intended to Americanize newer immigrants through settlement houses, "Americanization" classes, and civic education in the schools. The end of the 19th century saw picturesque communities with new Americans adding to the color and tragedy of life. The golden age of vaudeville featured ethnic dress, songs, irony, sentimentality, stereotypes, and jokes. Early efforts to limit immigration from the 1880s onward often reflected the prejudice and malice of the American Protective Association, but not infrequently asked questions about disease and criminals, and the capacity of groups to become part of the American structure, which warranted answers. The Democratic Party, with its long record of interest in immigrant votes, took the lead against such efforts. World War I intervention had turned invidious attention on Germans, Irish, and Jews, some of which was reflected in the 1924 Johnson National Origins Act, providing quotas. Although it included patently unfair stipulations, it turned attention on a question requiring modern revaluation. Also modern was Franklin D. Roosevelt's salute, in an address to the Daughters of the American Revolution, to "my fellow immigrants." Employers of his era began a shortsighted process by bringing into their mines and orchards illegal Mexicans to labor at meager wages superior to what they could have gained at home. During World War II, some Puerto Ricans were brought to the mainland to do the work war workers were no longer interested in doing, and they started to come in large numbers after the war. Although the liberal establishment had grown large through an expanded bureaucracy it faced a less integrated but substantial conservative alignment in Congress and elsewhere after World War II. The McCarran-Walter Act of 1952 sought to screen out subversives entering the country, and was roundly abused by liberals, defended by conservatives. Although American immigration policies compared favorably with the best in the world, and offered opportunities beyond most, they were to suffer unremitting criticism, at home and abroad, and to face unprecedented problems. President Eisenhower recognized inequities in McCarran-Walter, but moved less rapidly than his critics preferred. The 1953 Emergency Refugee Act was intended to help refugees from Communism, but was denounced as doing nothing. Almost unnoticed was the response of immigration authorities to the defeated 1956 Hungarian uprising, following which tens of thousands of refugees, including highly trained professionals, were admitted to the United States. The need for a strong immigration policy mounted. Refugees from Castro's Cuba multiplied in Florida. The movement of illegally entering Mexicans from across the border reached overwhelming proportions in the

1960s. The departure of America from Vietnam in the 1970s brought catastrophe to the populations of Vietnam, Laos, and Cambodia, and demands that the United States help out with refugees from the slaughter conducted in those countries. "Boat people" from Southeast Asia and from the Caribbean led many liberals to invoke memories of Ellis Island and the "generous" years of welcome to all people seeking a better life. Yet conditions in 1980 were not what they had been a century before, in the United States or abroad. Americans lived with unemployment, uncertain industries, declining cities, dangerous budgets, and a welfare system under heavy review. Immigration could not be unchecked. Employers required controls, and protested official surveillance. Aliens had to be known, yet identity cards (*q.v.*) were denounced "totalitarian." The *New York Times* fought "mean," "cruel," and "racist" policies. A curious editorial (March 10, 1982) was entitled "Holding Haitians Hostage." Haitians illegally in the United States were being held in government camps. "Not even accused criminals are imprisoned without the opportunity for bail. Yet the Haitians are not criminals. They are poor blacks fleeing poverty, or persecution. To put them in camps is discriminatory and cruel....Every day that these detention camps continue is a day our country defames itself." The *Times* did not say, to whom, or to what the Haitians were hostage. It stated there were "a large number of foreign migrants—maybe half a million, maybe two and half million." The figures were strange; some estimates of illegal migrants ranged beyond ten million. Strangest was the fear of foreign opinion, though all evidence was that those who chose to hate America would hate it no matter what it did. It appeared best for the country to do what was best for it.

**Impeachment**, see Berger, Raoul

**Imperialism**, once a sensitive topic for conservatives, thanks to decades of liberal and socialist criticism which identified it negatively with capitalism. The formal emancipation of numerous lands, notably India, gave imperialism a bad name, so that it was difficult to recall that the British, for example, had once proudly designated Queen Victoria as "Empress of India," or that the word carried connotations of power and victory which went back to the Roman Empire and beyond. The word properly contained memories of reform as well as repression, numerous states having been prepared for independence by leaders trained in the government service and schools of once dominant nations. They were, however, too tempting a target for patriotic rhetoric and as explanations for economic and other difficulties experienced by cruel or inept leaders for gratitude to accompany their reigns. "Economic imperialism" could be denounced, when there was no other imperialism to blame. (See also Anti-Imperialism.) Most confusing to proponents of a modern anti-imperialism was the phenomenon of self-proclaimed socialist and Marxist (*qq.v.*) states patently practicing extreme forms of imperialism, as when the Soviet Union following World War II took control of Eastern Europe. Even African states, though often with meager resources, practiced forms of exploitation against neighbors which recalled harsh aspects of older imperialism. The word thus survived as an epithet, to be employed whether relevant or irrelevant. Because of the dissolution of the British Empire and the independence of many former colonies the number of states claiming opposition to "imperialism" mounted, and they tended to dominate the United Nations (*q.v.*). John A. Hobson, *Imperialism* (1902), a work found useful by V. Lenin (*q.v.*); W. Gurian, ed., *Soviet Imperialism* (1941); R. Robinson and J. Gallagher, *Africa and Victorians* (1961); J. A. Schumpeter, *Imperialism and Social Classes* (1919).

**Imprimis**, a series of lectures and speeches published by Hillsdale College (*q.v.*) covering a wide spectrum of conservative interests and drawing on businessmen, politicians, educators, and writers of every kind.

**In His Steps**, see Sheldon, Charles M.

**Incentive**, seen similarly by both conservatives and liberals, but differently in terms of actual strategies for society and survival. Both factions professed adherence to ideals of patriotism as relevant to the nation's workings. Liberals, however, were more understanding of the feelings of disaffected and alienated elements. Although conservatives and liberals both understood the incentive of gain, "wanting more of the pie" was a liberal phrase. Conservatives saw tax (*q.v.*) cuts as an incentive for greater productivity (*q.v.*), bolder investment. Expansion of social "entitlements" (*q.v.*) was a liberal slogan. Law and order (*q.v.*) was underscored by conservatives. Lyndon B. Johnson (*q.v.*) tried to eradicate poverty and improve education by government subsidies. Giveaways to gang chieftains in Chicago became notorious for failing to instill them with "pride" and ideals of leadership; instead, they assaulted one another for possession of the loot. Most critical were approaches to the problem of how to cut welfare (*q.v.*) recipients, with many families in their second or third generation of welfare. Years of "opportunity" (*q.v.*) projects, job "training," and counseling had done little for welfare "clients" or their neighborhoods, which continued to erode. Ronald Reagan (*q.v.*) offered "workfare" (*q.v.*) to able-bodied persons in California, which had the significant result of causing some of them to give up welfare, whatever else it may have done for their pride, incentive, or ambition. As a candidate for the Presidency, Reagan proposed "enterprise zones" for ambitious entrepreneurs: tax benefits and other encouragement for those willing to set up businesses in ruined neighborhoods and help to revive them. Hunger and need had no status as incentives.

**Income Redistribution**, a liberal euphemism (*q.v.*) of the 1970s and after, which essentially meant taking from the rich and giving to the poor (*q.v.*). It compared social inequity created by unsocial business practices abetted by government taxation and other policies variously labeled as "corporate liberalism" and "reactionary Keynesianism" (*qq.v.*), with liberal administration of income. Conservatives argued that such policies harmed incentive (*q.v.*) and distorted actual social conditions, encouraging chaos. For a valid society, income had to be a function of the value of work done, not of claimed need or desire. A third party "redistributing" private income would sooner or later become a tyrant.

**Income Tax**, largely involving a conservative pillar of principle, liberals being more concerned with what they saw as just "distribution" of income aiding social equality (*q.v.*). The stark conditions of the 1930s encouraged the concept of a "progressive" income tax, essentially taking from the rich allegedly in aid of the poor. The long prosperity of the post-World War II era raised questions regarding the workings of the Welfare State (*q.v.*). A new conservatism formulated its demands in terms of social effects and economic results. Tax cuts, the need to repay venture capital, harmful pressures on an expanded middle class, and related concepts added up to "Reaganomics" (*q.v.*), which drew from such ideologues as Arthur Laffer, George Gilder, and Jack Kemp (*qq.v.*). They sought to slow the growth of liberal policies, and to reverse them as political conditions permitted. See also Taxation; Proposition XIII. Frank Chodorov (*q.v.*), *Income Tax: the Root of All Evil* (1959); B.E.V. Sabine, *A History of Income Tax* (1966).

**Incredible Bread Machine, The** (1974), a successful, popular exposition of conservative economic principles prepared by students of the Campus Studies Division of World Research in San Diego, California. Working with metaphors and puns ("The Sun Also Rises," "Kneading Bread," "Better Bread than Dead"), it traced federal intervention in economic matters, and found it uniformly harmful to society. It was government giveaways of land which produced problems for the railroads, free enterprise producing a better record than critics of the "Robber Barons" (*q.v.*) realized. Unsound money issues, the protective tariff, and Federal Reserve Board manipulations were seen as responsible for depressions. (The Civil War [*q.v.*] created the 1873 depression.) Keynesian (*q.v.*) doctrine was contrasted with that of Friedman, Rothbard, and others. Labor unions (*q.v.*) with closed shops and the combination of high wages and low productivity bore the responsibility for demoralized industry. In sum: "[W]hen economic freedom is limited, personal freedoms ultimately diminish."

**Indentured Servitude**, see Slavery

**"Independence Party,"** see *Making of the*

*New Majority Party, The*

**Independent, The.** It was originally founded in 1848 by religious leaders of the Congregational Church to further their tenets in opposition to other Protestant sects, and to oppose the spread of Catholic doctrine in the West. It became a leading conservative force opposing the spread of slavery before and during the Civil War (*q.v.*), under such ministers as Leonard Bacon and Henry Ward Beecher. Later historians tended to overlook the conservative nature of *The Independent*. During the Progressive era (*q.v.*), under Hamilton Holt, it was more distinctly liberal in principles. Filler, "Liberalism, Anti-Slavery, and the Founders of the *Independent*," *New England Q.*, Fall 1954; Warren F. Kuehl, *Hamilton Holt* (1960).

**Indianapolis News**, conservative newspaper which had, among its notable contributors, editor M. Stanton Evans and columnist Alice Widener (*qq.v.*).

**Indians**, see Filler, DASC. Work on behalf of Indian rights and prospects was largely a conservative achievement which went back to colonial days. Colonial efforts on behalf of Indians included the private ministry of John Eliot in Massachusetts and the treaties wrought by William Penn. Aggression against Indians drew mainly from popular ambitions rather than those of the elite (*q.v.*). Moreover, savagery was not confined to white settlers on the frontiers. Theodore Frelinghuysen (*q.v.*) was one among many who tried to modify the war and unrest which characterized Indian-white relations. Logan, Black Hawk, and Chief Joseph were among many Indians whose names and deeds were rescued from oblivion by empathetic whites; the Smithsonian Institution would later do matchless work to rescue the very languages of the numerous tribes and their artifacts. The highpoint of white-Indian debate in the pre-Civil War times involved the Cherokee and their destiny in Georgia and environs; see Filler and A. Guttmann eds., *The Removal of the Cherokee Nation* (1976 ed.). Memorable was Sequoyah, whose Christian training freed his genius and enabled him to create a written language for his people. A name among names in the post-Civil War era is that of Helen Hunt Jackson (*q.v.*), whose labors in behalf of Indians reached the public conscience and helped bring on the Dawes Act of 1887, making Indians wards of the state and helping them in their unequal fight against exploiters. Friends of the Indian fought for their cause in succeeding decades, working with the Bureau of Indian Affairs against public prejudices and ethnic dilemmas. Basic was the problem of whether Indians would choose to live with ancient tribal customs and memories or leave them for newer ways. It was a dilemma which could not be resolved, though reform efforts and changing conditions gave some Indians clearer choice than had been possible earlier. The tragedy of Jim Thorpe, Indian athlete unfairly stripped of Olympic honors in 1912, was invoked by liberals of the 1960s and 1970s as an historic example of prejudice against Indians.

**Individualism**, an earlier version of free-enterprise conservatism which identified capitalism with freedom and socialism with slavery (*qq.v.*). Conservatives of the progressive era pointed to heroes (*q.v.*) of invention, business, and politics to illustrate their views. Advocates of cooperatives (*q.v.*) and socialists argued that they were working to save whatever of individualism could be legitimately saved, and pointed to "wage slaves" in mines and factories who were at the mercy of unscrupulous entrepreneurs. The apogee of the individualistic defense was reached in Herbert Hoover's (*q.v.*) highly publicized concept of "rugged individualism," which was harshly satirized during the Depression decade. A revived conservatism preferred other concepts. "Individualism," focusing on the person rather than the movement, became the equivalent of liberty, and was advocated by libertarians (*q.v.*). Since neither socialists nor free-enterprise partisans admitted to heartlessness or unwillingness to cooperate, it rested with the great classes in the middle to determine which side would most benefit society. The socialists raised visions of forlorn children, hounded minorities, and hungry and homeless masses "in the midst of plenty." Conservatives saw ahead to "collectives": slave-like hordes ruled by masters and regulations immune to criticism or change. David Riesman, *Individualism Reconsidered* (1954); F. A. Hayek, *Individualism and Economic Order* (1958); D. Klingaman and S. Prejovich, *Individual Freedom: Selected Works of William H. Hutt* (1975).

**Individualist, The** see Intercollegiate Studies Institute

**Industrial Revolution.** Seen somewhat too formalistically as identical with capitalist (*q.v.*) economics, it progressed in 19th-century lore on two levels: one emphasizing the biographies of discoverers of steam and electricity and inventors of mechanical means for augmenting production; the other interpreting the "revolution" as one creating increasing misery for the masses. The first was intended to prove inspirational to ambitious young men, the second to inspire humanitarian sentiments and to direct reformers and radicals to the problems of the poor and desperate. In the United States, the transformation of industry extended from Eli Whitney and his cotton gin (1793), with its effect on the slave economy, which had seemed doomed by inefficiency, to the towering career of Thomas A. Edison (*q.v.*), which awed the youth of his time. Diminished interest in the great entrepreneurs and inventive spirits proceeded in part from great industrial consolidations which took attention from individuals and turned it on the policies of corporations. Edison's numerous properties, for example, involving thousands of dramatic experiments under his direction, became in time the General Electric Company, with its problems of unions, pricing, and production. With capitalism itself under attack during the 1930s Depression (*q.v.*), there was little time or interest available for attention to the lives of forceful individuals as enterprisers or inventors. Hundreds of biographies circulated to little purpose. Thus, the biography of Hugh Roy Cullen by two newspapermen, E. Kilman and T. Wright (1954), told a colorful tale of a bold man whose ventures in oil made him both a tycoon and philanthropist, in his latter role giving some $175 million to charity and education. Yet Cullen was known, when at all, for his conservative opinions. More modestly published was Estelle H. Ries's biography of her father Elias E. Ries (1951), whose scores of inventions netted him little in funds from the great companies or in fame. Although the conservative drive of the 1950s and after to give new dignity to the individual involved such persons by implication, it was too embattled in contemporary issues to find space or time for a revaluation of the industrial revolution and its effects. T. S. Ashton, *The Industrial Revolution* (1948); P. N. Stearns, *The Impact of the Industrial Revolution* (1972); C. S. Doty, ed., *The Industrial Revolution* (1976).

**Inflation**, a major conservative interest, since it depreciated the currency, harmed banking by permitting repayment for debts not matching original value, and lost industry the return on production. In times of economic stress, harassed debtors welcomed inflation, and even sought to force it in law. In post-World War II decades, various sectors of society were similarly driven by inflation. Liberals were more ready to chance inflation by means of public expenditure, despite its notorious effect on the economy, in order to curb unemployment. They derogated military expenditures as unnecessary and a threat to peace. Thus, inflation had become a political as well as economic issue. Reagan's success in curbing inflation while maintaining his generosity to the military, his critics said, was at the expense of social entitlements (*q.v.*). However, inflation was perceived as a world-wide phenomenon and carrying dangers beyond the economic forced critics to seek ideas and examples which would impress varied interest groups. Congressional Quarterly, *Inflation and Unemployment* (1974); H. Hazlitt (*q.v.*), *Inflation Crisis, and How to Resolve It* (1978); L.C. Harriss, *Inflation: Long-Term Problems* (1975); B. Griffiths, *Inflation: The Price of Prosperity* (1976).

**Ingersoll Prizes, The**, established in 1983 with funds from the Ingersoll Foundation. The T.S. Eliot Award for literature, and the Richard Weaver Award for scholarly letters recognize "authors who address the themes of order and virtue." Fears that the prizes would be tarnished by ideology were quickly allayed by the distinguished list of winners. Eliot

Award: Jorge Borges, Anthony Powell, Eugene Ionesco, and V.S. Naipaul; Weaver Award: James Burnham, Russell Kirk, Robert Nisbet, and Andrew Lytle.

**Insanity Plea**. It presented a paradox for the legal system in the mid-1980s. Psychiatric "experts" could and did disagree over the sanity of defendants in trial. Often it was up to untrained juries to make the decison. Following the Hinckley (*q.v.*) case, the presiding judge insisted the insanity plea was a vital part of the judicial system. Critics focused on the fact that, when a defendant pleaded innocent of a crime by reason of insanity, the prosecution had to prove his sanity. Far better, they argued, to make the defendant prove his insanity. In 1983, the American Medical Association recommended that the insanity plea be dropped, but retained as a consideration in sentencing. See also Pound, Ezra; Restitution.

**Inside Right: A Study of Conservatism** (1977), by Ian Gilmour, a survey of British Conservative politics, philosophy, and historical background, including a section on its operations in post-World War II years. It treated notable figures including George Savile (see "The Trimmer"), Lord Bolingbroke (see Patriot), David Hume, Edmund Burke, Samuel Taylor Coleridge, Disraeli, Michael Oakeshott (*qq.v.*), and Lord Hugh Cecil—himself the author of *Conservatism* (1912), considered a classic account. The longest section discusses Conservatism as such under a number of headings.

**Installment Plan**, see Twenties

**Institute for Pacific Relations**, see China; *Plain Talk*

**Institute for Policy Studies**, Washington, D.C. a long-time center for radical and liberal formulations, the fellows and directors of which often appeared in columns for the *New York Times* and similar publications. They were consistent in weighing Soviet and American interests equally, and in their positive view of Marxist regimes everywhere. Their work was closely watched by conservative institutes as indicators of current liberal nuances in interpreting government policy. The Institute was in the news in 1976 when it gave sanctuary to Orlando Letelier, formerly an associate of Allende in Chile (see Latin America). Letelier died when his car was blown up with a bomb, at the direction of the Chilean secret police: a fact which was related with horror in the liberal community. Less publicized was the fact that Letelier's papers gave proof publicized in conservative publications that he had been an agent of Cuba's intelligence service, and on its payroll.

**Integration**, see Segregation

**Intercollegiate Studies Institute**, originally founded in 1953 by Frank Chodorov (*q.v.*) as the Intercollegiate Society of Individualists, with William F. Buckley, Jr. as its director. It published *The Individualist*, and gained increasing influence among campus conservatives as its program expanded and attracted notable educators of the quality of Robert A. Nisbet, Richard Weaver, Russell Kirk, and Will Herberg (*qq.v.*). The Institute developed programs of lectures and publications, the latter including *The Intercollegiate Review*, the *Political Science Reviewer*, and the *Academic Reviewer*. Later it took over *Modern Age* (*q.v.*). Its Richard M. Weaver (*q.v.*) Fellowships helped promising students further their careers as conservatives, and an Alumni Association helped additionally to give cohesiveness to its program. In 1980, the ISI claimed some 30,000 members on 350 campuses with a program of seminars, institutes, summer schools, and book and cassette distribution. See *Ominous Politics*.

**International Monetary Fund**, see Banking

**Intervention**, crucial to United States relations in the world. Thomas Jefferson (*q.v.*) hoped to avoid being implicated in the war between Great Britain and France by imposing an Embargo (*q.v.*) on shipping with the belligerents. Nothing came of his effort but bitter protest from conservative New Englanders who cherished their trade with the British—and eventually "Mr. Madison's (*q.v.*) War." American intervention in World War I (*q.v.*) was momentous for the world, and carried through by a union between conservative and liberal forces. Intervention in World War II (*q.v.*) was again debatable, since it saved the Stalinist (*q.v.*) regime and gave it authenticity. By then it was evident that the United States was caught between choices of isolationism (*q.v.*) and intervention, with no simplistic solution at hand. R. Chakrabarti, *Intervention and the Problem of Its Control in the Twentieth Century* (1974); Herbert S. Dinerstein, *Intervention against Communism* (1967); Robin Higham, ed., *Intervention or Abstention: The Dilemma of American Foreign Policy* (1975).

**Investigative Journalism**, see Journalism, Investigative

**Invisible Hand, The** (1963), ed., Adrian Klaasen, a collection of essays taking its title from the famous phrase of Adam Smith's (*q.v.*) and helping to make the case for free enterprise. Authors were in the main academics. They included F. A. Hayek on "The Moral Element in Free Enterprise," Gottfried Dietze on "The Vital Importance of Property Rights," and Ludwig von Mises, who held that it was "impermissible to question the free market's choice of the entrepreneurs." Milton Friedman, concerned as were all free-market economists about "coercion," wrote of the relation between economic and political freedom (*qq.v.*). Guy Alchon, *The Invisible Hand of Planning ...in the 1920s* (1985).

**Iran**, see Carter, Jimmy

**Ireland, Northern**, see Terrorism

**"Iron Curtain,"** Winston Churchill's (*q.v.*) famous phrase used in 1946 to describe the results of the Soviet Union's (*q.v.*) actions following the anti-Hitler Grand Alliance. These actions involved the division of Berlin (*q.v.*) and Germany; the outlawing of republican forces in Poland (*q.v.*), Hungary, and Czechoslovakia; and the completion of a belt of states around the Soviet Union, including Rumania, Bulgaria, Albania and Yugoslavia. The result was an "iron curtain" stretching across Europe. Yugoslavia soon broke free of Soviet control. Although Western powers generally welcomed Yugoslavia's independent stance, conservatives maintained a dislike of its "socialist" measures and recalled the ruthless march to power of Marshall Tito, its dictator. The Iron Curtain nations subscribed to the Warsaw Pact (*q.v.*) (1955), the Soviet answer to NATO (*q.v.*)

**"Iron Law of Wages,"** see Ricardo, David

**Irrational**, see Absurdity

**Irving, Washington** (1783-1859), American author. He was considered in his own time the best of American stylists, but lost fame rapidly to more challenging writers. Socially concerned conservatives saw usefulness in James Fenimore Cooper (*q.v.*), but none in Irving. Overlooked was his *History of New York* by "Dietrich Knickerbocker" (1809). It had generations of students laughing at what was apparently a satire on war and pompous authority, but what was in actuality a subtle and carefully researched attack on the Thomas Jefferson (*q.v.*) Administration. In his youth Irving was a Federalist (*q.v.*), and despised the burgeoning Democratic politics in New York, with its newly founded Tammany Hall and aggressive artisans. Using the Peter Stuyvesant era as an analogue, he caricatured its activities with verve and relevance. It was for decades imagined that he had concocted the humorous-sounding footnotes with Dutch names and book-titles out of his own imagination, the Dutch language and spelling looking absurd to American eyes. A literary researcher, however, established that he used real books which he had browsed among in his father's library. Thereafter, Irving indeed tired of politics and the American scene, and viewed fiction as a gentleman's diversion rather than as a weapon for social commentary. It was ironic that he became stereotyped as the author of several too-well-read tales. Though he professed indifference to his career as a professional writer, he in fact worked carefully over his prose and earned his title as a stylist with honor. Not creative in plot and characterization, he could nevertheless retell tales with a grace and sense of drama which well repaid reading.

**Isolationism**, see Filler, DASC; in modern times mainly referring to conservative efforts to avoid being implicated in foreign troubles. America First (*q.v.*), a distinctly conservative body in the late 1930s, was clearly anti-Communist, but with pro-fascist sympathies. Although it had some natural support from Midwesterners who were suspicious of all foreign entanglements—but not above selling products to the Soviet Union—much of isolationist sentiment represented big business (*q.v.*) suspicions of Washington and of official labor, deemed sympathetic to Soviet goals. Isolationism was linked too with protective (*q.v.*) policies in foreign trade. The Council of Foreign Relations, which published *Foreign Affairs*, was suspect to conservatives for its liberal outlook. Isolationism expressed itself after World War II in doubts about the value of foreign aid (*q.v.*). Foreign aid was seen as financing nations often having anti-American goals. Isolationists were disillusioned later by recognition of Communist China and by detente (*q.v.*) generally, which they saw as aiding Soviet imperialism with nothing gained in return. The isolationist program, however, was inevitably affected by shifting styles of government, Democratic and Republican, and by such crises as Vietnam (*q.v.*). Radicals and many liberals preached a new isolationism in response to American involvement in Vietnam. The growth of conservatism, including shrewd students of foreign affairs, helped break down the distinction between "international-minded" people and "isolationists," making the issue more what was best for America in a nuclear age. See also Taft, Robert A.; Foreign Aid. A strange development was the turn to isolationism of radicals bankrupted by Soviet militarism and Communist Chinese totalitarianism. The ruthless suppression and slaughter resulting from the Communist takeover of Southeast Asia led many radicals who had called for an end to American intervention there to declare that they had merely been non-interventionists. A major work evolving from the turmoil over Vietnam in America was *Prophets on the Right: Profiles of Conservative Critics of American Globalism* by Ronald Radosh (1975). It made heroes of dissent of the historian Charles A. Beard and the journalist Oswald Garrison Villard. The book also found more pluses than minuses for Robert A. Taft and the "turncoat" liberal-conservative John T. Flynn (*qq.v.*). Most remarkable was the credibility it gave to the acknowledged fascist Lawrence Dennis. He was seen as a victim of interventionist government—which charged him with treason—and interpreted as more socialist than fascist in his analyses of domestic capitalism and foreign relations. The book was interesting as showing how earlier and clear-cut divisions among liberals, socialists, and fascists could be adjusted to changing times to accommodate changes in outlook which amounted to reversals. See also Rosenberg Case.

**Israel**, see Middle East

**Issues of the Sixties**, L. Freedman, C. P. Cotter, eds. (1961), a genuine effort at balancing issues and partisans, yet offering few comments from conservative or quasi-conservative sources. Civil rights was seen as referring to integration. Nathan Glazer offered "Is 'Integration' Possible in the New York Schools?" The legacy of the 1950s was said to be optimism, based on affluence and the disappearance of Stalin (*q.v.*). There was an "escape" from politics, with Russell Kirk (*q.v.*) warning of unrestrained power and "creeping socialism." The "affluent society" was basically unquestioned, as was the welfare state. Dr. Philip E. Jacob reported that students were "gloriously contented." Nikita S. Khrushchev led off a discussion of "peaceful coexistence." Herman Kahn (*q.v.*), however, was able to discuss "first-strike capability." While Erich Fromm gave "The Case for Unilateral Disarmament," Barry Goldwater urged "We Must Be Sure That Foreign Aid Goes Only to Our Friends." James Burnham (*q.v.*) scorned the detente (*q.v.*) attitudes of Schlesinger, Rostow, and Galbraith.

**It Can't Happen Here** (1935), by Sinclair Lewis (*q.v.*). The novel was a phenomenon, as careful a work of detail and intuition within its time as any other of Lewis's masterpieces. Since it ingeniously associated fascism with the loopholes in American democracy, judging Communism to be insufficiently American for domestic triumph, it fit well with Depression circumstances and, as a novel and play, was taken by many to be a warning of future danger. It should rightly have earned a place beside Orwell's (*q.v.*) later *1984*, to which indeed it was superior in some respects. As was in time perceived, Orwell had not been opposed to socialism, but to Stalinism, a legitimate equivalent of Hitlerism. But the Orwellian state was too remote from England to have to compete with its reality. Lewis's account of fascist America was so circumstantial as to be unpleasant without being persuasive. Few critics and readers today give the work place among Lewis's remembered writings.

# J

**Jackson, Helen Hunt** (1830-1885), a friend of Emily Dickinson (*q.v.*) who attained fame as a partisan of Indians (*q.v.*). Her documented work, *A Century of Dishonor* (1881), and even more her fictional *Ramona* (1884), stirred popular indignation and compassion and helped bring on the Dawes Act (1887), which sought to make firmer in law the position of Indians. She also worked with other genteel (*q.v.*) activists, notably in the Boston Indian Citizenship Association, to propagandize for their cause. Although Allan Nevins (*q.v.*) protested that she ignored whole areas of controversial facts in Indian-white confrontation (see Nevins, "Helen Hunt Jackson, Sentimentalist vs. Realist," *American Scholar*, 1941) it has been argued that her work was vital to the Indian cause.

**Jacksonian Era**, also identified in history as the era of the "common man." It was marked by persons such as Andrew Jackson (1767-1845) who expressed the gospel of opportunity and power for any man. This offended such public figures as John Quincy Adams (*q.v.*), who had literally been reared for leadership in an older tradition and whose ideal was to be governed by the best. Jackson was a poor boy who gained wealth and entered politics in frontier Tennessee, a duelist, a breeder of slaves, and a masterful army officer who gave expansionist (*q.v.*) Americans reason to cheer. He gained the popular vote in the election of 1824, but thanks to the political system of the time was defeated when Henry Clay (*q.v.*) threw his bloc of votes to John Quincy Adams. Clay preferred Adams as more learned and responsible. Jacksonians in Congress thereafter, and until the next Presidential election, raised the unfair cry of "Corrupt Bargain." This united their party sufficiently to make Jackson President. It also signaled equal rights for slaveholders in competition with the North for Western terrain. Jackson's approval of the "spoils system" marked the passage of Americans to a larger and more popular government, with more spoils for the victors to divide. Such conservatives as Theodore Frelinghuysen (*q.v.*) found themselves competing with leaders representing such minority groups as the Irish for political honors. Although slaveholders hoped to make union with capitalists of the North in defense of slavery, they found readier support in new Northern city rings, such as Tammany Hall, which dominated in New York. These rings, notorious for skulduggery and corruption, were targets for conservative reformers, who in modern times have been attacked academically as elitists unwilling to open opportunities to new Americans; see J. G. Sprout, *"The Best Men"* (1965); William L. Mackeinzie (*sic*; Mackenzie), *The Lives and Opinions of Benj'n Franklin Butler*...[and others] (1845); A. M. Schlesinger, Jr., *The Age of Jackson* (1945); L. Filler, *Appiontment at Armageddon* (1976).

**Jaffa, Harry V.** (1918- ), conservative academic. His *Crisis of the House Divided* (1959) stimulated New Conservatives during their formative years. An earlier study compared *Thomism and Aristotelianism* (1952). Jaffa was co-editor of *In the Name of the People: Speeches and Writings of Lincoln and Douglas in the Ohio Campaign of 1859* (1959). Significant conservative themes were embodied in his *Equality and Liberty: Theory and Practice in American Politics* (1965) and *The Conditions of Freedom* (1975). He was a founder of the Winston S. Churchill Association, and edited *Statesmanship* (1981), essays in Churchill's honor.

**James, Henry, Jr.** (1843-1916), American author. He was the son of a wealthy religious seeker who wanted his children to see and experience only the best. Henry James, Sr. was known and accepted among the Transcendentalists (*q.v.*), but found greater comfort in the writings of Emanuel Swedenborg. Swedenborg offered entree into the world of spirits, with doctrines which undoubtedly influenced the turn of his children's minds. They were brought up not to involve themselves in temporal concerns, but to appreciate the finest in arts and letters. Henry James, Jr. concentrated on literature, and in half a century produced a formidable number of novels and shorter fiction. He wrote also plays which failed to attract audiences; it was an irony that several of his most famous tales eventually found popular acceptance in the hands of other playwrights and screenwriters. James was not concerned with the workaday world, yet he saw himself as a realist whose focus was on the spirit and minds of his characters. His evolution was from an early tracing of doings and events, through a concentration on motives and the interchange of or clash of spirit, to such a concern with symbol and ultimate meaning as scarcely to involve whole personages. An increasing oddity of his literary conversation was its sexless quality; without names or some material detail one can scarcely identify the speakers in his work as male or female. Although this would appear to comport with the stereotype of genteel (*q.v.*) living as evasive of sex, in James's case it rather underscored his concentration on the purity of motives regardless of sex. Antagonistic critics found impotence, suppressed emotions, and subliminal meanings in his work, but his art fascinated popular readers in a number of cases, and drew a majority of more sophisticated readers to a wide spectrum of his works. James's was the world of the leisure class; it scarcely concerned itself with those who did its work. Yet within that close-knit order he probed avarice, jealousy, hypocrisy, and the search for essences in love and meaning. His middle period struck the best balance between the world in which he moved and his probing pen. *Washington Square* (1880) gave the most in compact form. *The Portrait of a Lady* (1881), generally held to be his masterpiece, contrasts American innocence and Old World hypocrisy, but carries the reader on through revelations rather than denouements. *The Bostonians* (1886) reveals James himself as a skeptic regarding reform. It satirizes distinguished reformers and Boston generally as a hotbed of reform. Lionel Trilling (*q.v.*) thought *The Princess Casamassima* (1886) showed James as subtly knowledgeable in the way of anarchists, a subject which concerned the era. In actuality, the anarchist theme is not advanced; it no more than furnishes the occasion for its major protagonist's ambivalent feelings. *The Turn of the Screw* (1898), another of James's most read tales, featured ghosts. "Ghost stories" were a staple in fiction generally, and could be found in genteel literature going back to Washington Irving (*q.v.*). In James's fiction, which is markedly deficient in religious themes, are reflected aspects of his father's major religious concerns in transmuted form. James's later fiction, increasingly symbolic and disembodied as in *The Golden Bowl* (1904), was read and pondered during a post-World War II era of "explication" (*q.v.*). The counterculture movement of 1960s led to a decline in James's reputation, but in recent years his works have been more appreciated. An old saw has it that Henry James wrote fiction like a psychologist, and his brother William (*q.v.*) wrote psychology like a novelist.

**James, William** (1842-1920), American author. Like his brother Henry (*q.v.*) he was required to ponder the meaning of his life early, as he pursued his father's plans for his education. A nervous breakdown while abroad caused him to reconsider goals, and turned him to the study of physiology, then psychology, which he began to teach at his alma mater Harvard University in 1872. In 1880 he transferred to the Department of Philosophy. Although identified with Pragmatism, a field increasingly distasteful to those to whom it suggested John Dewey (*q.v.*), James took it in a different direction in his landmark *Psychology* (1890) and later works. Instead of seeing the material world as controlling the human mind's responses, James saw the human mind as controlling the outside world. In famous examples, a feather in a field suggested a bird, on a desk a pen. We were not afraid, and therefore ran. We ran, and became afraid. The center of meaning was the mind. James's hope was to find what he could not find in his father's Swedenborgian tenets. In *The Varieties of Religious Experience* (1902) he found an ecumenical center for differing experiences. Paradoxically, his experiments in the rational and irrational aided developments outside his basically conservative concerns. His "stream of consciousness" inspired Gertrude Stein, one of his students, in her prose. His consideration of drugs, as with Gerald Heard (*q.v.*), was intended to evoke religious feelings and understandings, rather than the hedonistic interests so common in the 1960s. See his *Letters* (1920); and R. B. Perry, *The Thought and Character of William James* (1935).

**"Japanese-Americans,"** see Patriotism

**Jarvis, Howard**, see Proposition XIII.

**Jay, John** (1745-1829), a founding father of American conservatives. He served New York as lawyer and judge, and the Revolution as a minister abroad. Jay's Treaty with England (1794) was popularly denounced as having granted too many concessions to the erstwhile foe. He was a moderate foe of slavery, though he kept slaves for terms of service. Author of five of the *Federalist Papers* (*q.v.*), he helped sway the states away from the loose Confederation to the more centralized Union. As Chief Justice of the Supreme Court (1789-1795), he helped give it its conservative coloring.

**Jay, William** (1789-1858), son of John Jay (*q.v.*) and himself a person of distinction, mixing conservative piety with firm dedication to abolitionist and peace principles. *Jay's Inquiry* threw his prestige and eloquence against the movement to rid the country of Negroes through colonization; his *Review of the Causes and Consequences of the Mexican War* advanced peace principles which served later peace advocates as well as those of his time. Although he deplored what he saw as the excesses of libertarians who fought the churches as foes, he did not hesitate to endorse their abolitionist and peace actions; see his *Miscellaneous Writings on Slavery* (1853).

**Jefferson, Thomas** (1743-1826), revered as a Founding Father (*q.v.*). Still, he was suspect to Federalists (*q.v.*) of his own time, and to Whigs, Republicans, conservatives (*qq.v.*), and modern conservatives afterwards for his resistance to Federalist measures, approval of French Revolution radicalism, defiance of the Alien and Sedition laws, and other measures more appropriate to a democracy than to a republic (*qq.v.*). Adopted as a hero by the Democratic Party, Jefferson symbolized freedom and opportunity to aspiring classes. Emphasized in the South was his loyalty to state rights (*q.v.*), as well as his services to education, freedom of thought, and culture. Emphasized in the North were his Northwest Ordinance, which closed the Northwest Territory to slavery, and his cordial attitude toward artisans. Radicals in the 1930s quoted with approval Jefferson's dictum that the tree of liberty must from time to time be "watered with the blood of tyrants."Highlighted in the 1960s among radicals opposed to the American past, was a false and malicious charge that Jefferson had carried on a lengthy liaison with a slave and fathered numerous children, some of whom had been sold into slavery; see Fawn M. Brodie, *Thomas Jefferson: An Intimate History* (1974). For its refutation, V. Dabney, *The Jefferson Scandals* (1981). Jefferson and his political rival John Adams (*q.v.*) were intimates in old age. As the last surviving signers of the Declaration of Independence they died the same day—one in Virginia, the other in Massachusetts—July 4, 1826, exactly fifty years after the signing.

**Jews**. Jews in America have been subject to a range of responses of a social or religious nature, most notoriously involving anti-Semitism (*q.v.*). Thus, the Christian Nationalist Crusade reprinted Martin Luther's centuries-old pamphlet *The Jews and Their Lies* in 1948. The Jewish community attracted generosity, as in Madison C. Peters's *The Jews in America* (1905), and the ungenerous sentiments of Wyndham Lewis's *The Jews: Are*

*They Human?* (1939). A. J. Nock (*q.v.*) professed himself an objective student of the Jewish "problem," while accepting support from several Jewish admirers. The German Holocaust quelled anti-Jewish hatred, except among forthright anti-Semites, but the rise of Israel and its status as an American ally led many radicals into an anti-Semitism cloaked as opposition to American and Israeli policies. Efforts to keep the memory of the Holocaust alive created a going literature. "Peter Simple" (*q.v.*) protested against burdening the youth of Germany with the great crime which had run its course before they were born, and wondered whether part of the campaign memorializing the Holocaust was not intended to divert attention from comparable crimes committed by Communists in the Soviet Union and elsewhere. Jews were identified by anti-Semites with wealth. Yet they were also seen widely as liberal or left-wing in sympathies. The New Conservatism of the 1950s adopted a firm stand against prejudiced views as such, especially as it attracted such talents as those of Will Herberg (*q.v.*) and the playwright Morrie Ryskind, who had indeed been left-wing in outlook and associates but had repudiated both. The neo-conservatives (*q.v.*) included Jewish personalities in education and government. The turn of *Commentary* (*q.v.*) from a journal open to left-wing sentiments to one following conservative tenets created a sensation in intellectual circles. W. D. Rubinstein, in *The Left, the Right, and the Jews* (1983), undertook to explain this turn of events historically. Jews were basically conservative, he argued. They had been pressured into radicalism by an aggressive anti-Semitism. Jewish writers were prominent in modern American literature, with Saul Bellow winning a Nobel Prize. Although conservatives worked to judge Henry Kissinger, Philip Roth, Nathan Glazer, and others on their performance rather than ethnic background, there were still those who harbored a sense of what Jews ought to think, as in Earl Shorris's *Jews without Mercy: A Lament* (1982). Marshall Sklare, ed., *The Jews: Social Patterns of an American Group* (1958); A. I. Gordon, *Jews in Suburbia* (1959); Arthur Liebman, *Jews and the Left* (1978); Ben Zion Bokser, *Jews, Judaism and the State of Israel* (1975). See also *Commentary*.

**Jews In Literature**. In the post-Civil War eras, American Jews had increasing visibility, because of their relatively high numbers in the growing cities, their intellectual output, and the notoriety associated with anti-Semitism (*q.v.*). Divided by economics, they produced notable personages among the wealthy and among their laboring classes. Abraham Cahan, in *The Rise of David Levinsky* (1917), wrote ironically of the "rise" of one of them at the expense of the Jewish community. E. A. Filene, the Boston merchant, typified persons of Jewish descent whose loyalties were to the larger American community. Louis D. Brandeis (*q.v.*), of a Kentucky Jewish family, was similarly directed, but was inspired to embrace the Zionist cause. Charles Angoff's career rose in association with H. L. Mencken (*q.v.*), and Angoff's novels of Boston Jewry emphasized his characters' adaptation to American life. Meyer Levin's trilogy—*The Old Bunch* (1935), *Citizens* (1940), and *Compulsion* (1956)—dealt with Jews in the social setting of Chicago. The rise of the Jewish state of Israel and disappointments with the course of events in the Soviet Union affected Jews variously, some holding to liberal formulations, others turning to conservative prospects. The latter found common cause with the New Conservatives who disdained anti-Semitism and saw promise in the Barry Goldwater (*q.v.*) campaign. Conservatism attracted the wit, idealism, or study of such Jewish Americans as playwright and former radical, Morrie Ryskind, philosopher Will Herberg (*q.v.*), religious philosopher and former radical; and the veteran anti-Soviet writer Isaac Don Levine (*q.v.*). From the 1930s on Jewish writers were highly visible in literary circles, with such well-recognized names as Delmore Schwartz, Philip Roth, and Norman Mailer. For the most part, they did not serve conservative ends, though several of Saul Bellow's novels spoke out on American dilemmas. M. B. Lindberg, *The Jew and Modern Israel* (1969); Z. Y. Gitelman, *Jewish Nationality and Soviet Politics* (1972); Leo Rosten, *The Joys of Yiddish* (1970); C. B.

Sherman, *The Jew within American Society* (1965); Irving Malin, *Jews and Americans* (1965).

**John Birch Society**, see Welch, Robert

**Johnson, Lyndon B.**, see Southwest, The

**Johnson, Paul**, see *Modern Times*

**Johnson, Samuel** (1709-1784), one of the great figures in conservative thought and outlook. His fame was spread and made durable by anecdotes and events culled from *The Life of Johnson*, first issued by Johnson's acolyte and friend James Boswell in 1791. Johnson is highly regarded for his *Dictionary of the English Language* (1755), his edition of *The Plays of William Shakespeare* (1765), his *Prefaces . . .to the Works of the English Poets* (1779-1781), and other works, and has provided industry for generations of academic scholars. Yet it is evident that his personality and the outlook which gave his life coherence were mainly the products of Boswell's long gathering of materials respecting Johnson and his personal recording of Johnson's view of life and the times in which he lived. Johnson's clear and high-minded vision of life and society, expressed in rounded and precise prose, added up to a philosophy which brought religion, tradition, and duty to society and the state into sharp focus. It inspired conservatives in succeeding generations, down the present. Johnson's influence can be discerned in such writers as Russell Kirk (*q.v.*), to whom tradition is a prime consideration along with morality. Johnson's personality, as recreated by Boswell, is the outstanding example of how a successful portrait can keep a figure's writings and times vivid to readers, academic and otherwise. See, however, *Patriot, The.* See also E. L. McAdam, Jr. and George Milno, *A Johnson Reader* (1964); and J. H. Sledd and G. J. Kolb, *Dr. Johnson's Dictionary* (1955).

**Jones, Jim**, see Filler, DASC, His atrocities were helpful to the conservative crusade because they fitted in with what conservatives considered the nature of unbridled liberalism and because of their roots in the social order. Jones, with his false Fundamentalism (*q.v.*) and charisma, was able to marshal a segment of San Francisco residents, mainly blacks, and become a power in city politics. They followed him to Guyana, and murder and mass suicide. That such a person should have been made director of San Francisco's department of housing, and should have been photographed with and praised by influential national figures, was disturbing. The fact that Jones won his malignant place by a species of democratic (*q.v.*) action was a warning that democracy did not produce automatic good, but required control if it was not to degenerate.

**Journalism, Investigative**, a phenomenon of the 1970s, highlighted by the activities of *Washington Post* journalists in connection with the Watergate affair. Its inordinate success with Watergate suggested to other reporters articles critical of American government or society. Investigative journalism focused on particular issues and individuals in discriminating fashion, and was resented by conservatives, who perceived a liberal bias. Janet Cooke, a *Washington Post* reporter, won a Pulitzer Prise for a series of articles which was later found to be largely composed of invention. This indicated the dangers inherent in much investigative journalism.

**Jouvenel, Bernard De** (1903-1987), French author. Of a notable journalist and Parliamentary family, he pondered, like such others of broad vision and aristocratic background as Eric von Kuehnelt-Leddihn (*q.v.*), the meaning of Europe's long experience with classes. Widely traveled and a close follower of European developments, he urged military intervention at the time of the remilitarization of the Rhineland (1936), and was anti-Munich and anti-Vichy. Until France's capitulation to Hitler, Jouvenel served in the French army. Thereafter he addressed himself to historical studies. Having offended authorities he went into hiding; in 1943 he was able to cross the Swiss border. His books, in French and English—one was translated into French from English—included *La Crime du capitalisme* (1933), *Napoleon and Directed Economy* (1942), dealing with his concern for power, *Après la défaite* (1940), his edition of Rousseau's *Du Contrat Social* (1947), *The Ethics of Redistribution* (1951), his highly esteemed *On Power: Its Nature and the History of Its Growth* (1949), and *Sovereignty: An Inquiry into the*

*Political Good* (1957). He also interested himself in Conjectures (*q.v.*) and what he called Futuribles.

**Judeo-Christian Traditions**. They were asserted by conservatives as at the base of American history and ways. However, liberals were fearful of transgressions against church-and-state separation as posited by the Constitution. The actual history of the nation, under the Founding Fathers (*q.v.*) and after them, seemed to support the conservative claim, but liberals argued that government promotion of religion would eventually lead to a state religion. Some extremists labor to ban all aspects (*q.v.*) of religion from official public life. Their causes took them as far as seeking to abolish Christmas, insofar as it involved state and Federal contact. There was no doubt that the public schools labored for secularization, and doubtless with some effect on students. Meanwhile, conservative intellectuals contributed great bodies of knowledge and experience to suggest the urgency of religious thought to full and satisfying living.

**"Judicial Activism,"** see Supreme Court, The

# K

**Kahn, Herman** (1922-1982), American futurist (*q.v.*). He made a career of mathematics and technical advice for the Rand Corporation. His *On Thermonuclear War* (1960) was presented in formal terms and caused no general interest. In 1961 he established his Hudson Institute at Croton-on-Hudson, New York, as a consultant firm to corporations. His *Thinking about the Unthinkable* (1962) was a resounding success, outraging liberals who thought it favored nuclear war. *On Escalation: Metaphors and Scenarios* (1965) saw Kahn as a conscious scourge to smugness, conservative in principles. His conjectures (*q.v.*) in *The Next 200 Years* (1976) or *The Coming Boom* (1982), however, were anticlimactic.

**Kaiser, Henry J.** (1882-1967), an impressive figure in industry. His activities seemed to distinguish him from those of common commercial (*q.v.*) perspectives. He began in road-paving, which brought him prestige among businessmen and politicians. He was chairman of the board formed to build Hoover Dam. Later he was involved in such projects as building the Grand Coulee Dam and the San Francisco-Oakland Bridge. He attained public visibility during World War II when his efficient organization and unusual methods of production enabled him to supervise the massive production of ships and military vehicles required by the war. Once production was underway, the Kaiser Company became known as the firm which sent out a ship a day. Kaiser's postwar effort to enter into automobile production was not successful.

**Katyn Forest Murders** (1943), an infamous episode in the Soviet Union's conduct of World War II. It attempted to break the back of Polish democracy by killing over 4,000 captured Polish officers, imputing the deed to German invaders. The Germans, however, were eager to call in foreign observers to examine the buried corpses, and Soviet officials did what they could to repel inquiries. Since they were wartime "allies" of the U.S., the American government did not press the matter, nor did public interest demand it. It remained, however, deep in the memory of the Poles themselves. J.K. Zawodny, *Death in the Forest* (1972).

**Kemp, Jack F.** (1935-    ), Congressman, formerly a football star, later an assistant to then-Governor Reagan of California. His attractive personality, coupled with a refreshing faith in the power of people to respond to a free-enterprise challenge reasonably presented, won him recognition among many Republicans. Kemp was elected to Congress in 1970 from New York, and proceeded to develop economic views in tune with supply-side (*q.v.*) economists. He believed a balanced budget would result from a series of tax cuts putting money back into the hands of spenders and investors—who would then stimulate industry, create affluence, and relieve the nation of deficits. Teaming with Senator William V. Roth, Jr., he presented the Kemp-Roth tax plan. Since it comported with the Reagan Administration's program for settling the nation's finances, it added new luster to Kemp's image. By 1984, the tax program had been complicated, since Federal tax cuts appeared not to affect the economic picture significantly. Moreover, there was an apparent need for tax increases to offset a formidable deficit. Yet Reagan held to his belief in tax cuts, and Kemp continued to receive applause from supply-side Republicans. It appeared possible that Kemp might require some broadening of his program, should new crises occur which economic principles did not cover. See Bruce R. Bartlett, *Reaganomics: Supply-Side Economics in Action* (1982 ed.), with a foreword by Kemp.

**Kendall, Willmoore** (1909-1967), political scientist, a founder of the *National Review* (*q.v.*), he contributed inspiration and ideas by force of personality and unbending conservative opinion. Born in Oklahoma, where his father occupied a pulpit, he was educated at Northwestern University, was a Rhodes Scholar at Oxford University, and later a Guggenheim Fellow. As a professor at Yale University he developed a strong, authoritative approach which impressed his student William F. Buckley, Jr. (*q.v.*), among others, but was less satisfactory to some of his liberal colleagues. His was a combination of basic assumptions and firm premises and preferences. He argued that the United States was deeply Christian and conservative, that this was its great tradition, which would endure whatever the vagaries of the day. Equalitarianism transgressed the spirit of the Founding Fathers (*q.v.*) and the practice of society, he maintained. The majority of the framers of the Constitution had opposed the Bill of Rights (*q.v.*). Kendall's preferences and antipathies went back to the bases of society. He despised Hobbes's version of "natural law" (*q.v.*) and disliked John Locke's (*q.v.*) version of the "contract theory." Kendall's colleagues on the *National Review* found him a close debater, who kept them alert and eager to learn. He argued for a tight program which would win the country as liberals exposed their ignorance of the modes proper to society. He thought John Chamberlain (*q.v.*) glorified late 19th-century conservatives, and Russell Kirk (*q.v.*) the role of religion. His long view saw triumphs where colleagues feared defeat. HUAC had resisted its enemies for thirty years, he noted. The South's "victories" (this was 1967) had made its cause national (in an article, "What Killed the Civil Rights Movement?"). Tired of the spirit at Yale, Kendall bought out his tenure for $25,000 and went on to the University of Dallas as chairman of its Department of Politics and Economics. His sense of leadership showed itself in "how to" articles, which extended to a book on baseball, *How to Play It and How to Watch It*. "How to Read Richard Weaver" assumed the general reader's limited capacity; Weaver (*q.v.*), Kendall explained, was for a "select minority" of virtuous people. ("Virtuous" was here used to denote those profoundly in tune with conservative principles of life.) Kendall was a careful, yet prolific, writer; among his books were *John Locke and the Doctrine of Majority Rule* (1941); *Democracy and the American Party System* (1955, which he co-authored); *The Committee and Its Critics* (1962), with *National Review* editors; *The Conservative Affirmation* (1963). He translated J. J. Rousseau's *The Government of Poland* (1972). At the time of his death, he was planning books on the "doctrine" and strategy of a conservative movement, and another book on the Bill of Rights. Following his death, a collection of his essays was issued: *Willmoore Kendall contra Mundum* (1971), edited by Nellie D. Kendall.

**Kennedy, Edward Moore**, see Chappaquiddick

**Kennedy, John F.**, see Filler, DASC

**Kentucky and Virginia Resolutions** (1798), see Alien and Sedition Acts

**Keynes, John Maynard** (1883-1946), one of the greatest names in 20th-century economics, known to millions who had never read a word of his actual writings. He was made famous by his *Economic Consequences of the Peace* (1919). Using classical concepts, it gave evidence that the onerous burden put on defeated Germany by the Allies would spread ruin in Germany and beyond. His own preference at the time was for the free market. The ensuing record of inflation, unemployment (*qq.v.*) and international economic disturbances turned Keynes to the panacea (*q.v.*) of government intervention as capable of adjusting economic imbalances and increasing national purchasing power through public works. This program won over New Deal (*q.v.*) administrators in the United States, who entered into a deficit spending (*q.v.*) program which was intensified by the costs of World

War II (*q.v.*) and continued in welfare-state and foreign-aid (*qq.v.*) programs. At the crucial Bretton Woods conference in 1944, Lord Keynes was a proponent of a World Bank. His theories were crystallized in his major work, *The General Theory of Employment, Interest and Money* (1936). It was a bible to "Keynesians," but came increasingly under attack by free-market theoreticians. As the welfare states (*q.v.*) ran into greater and greater difficulties, Keynesians were constrained to modify their principles, arguing that Keynes had not given carte blanche to government controls. Conservative tenets gained influence with the prestige accorded such economists as Friedman, Hayek (*qq.v.*), and others. For pro-Keynes expositions see S. E. Harris's *John Maynard Keynes* (1955) and L. R. Klein's *The Keynesian Revolution* (1966 ed.). For a strong conservative attack on Keynes see Henry Hazlitt (*q.v.*), *The Failure of the "New Economics"* (1959).

**KGB** (From the Russian words for Committee for State Security), the current acronym for the Soviet secret police. The Soviet secret police became quickly notorious after the Communists took power and was known and feared under various names during its history. During the years when the Bolshevik regime was establishing its primacy, it treated all shades of socialist, republican, and monarchist opinion as enemies warranting bloody extermination. Under Stalin, it extended its function to put under surveillance and mark for prison, labor camps, and execution all persons who might be judged to be in any way inimical to Stalin's rule. Notable were the Moscow Trials of 1936 (see Filler, DASC), during which Old Bolsheviks openly charged themselves with unspeakable acts of treason to the Soviet regime. Numerous observers and readers perceived these confessions as unnatural, but the American Ambassador of the time accepted them as real. The trials were a measure of what nations were willing to credit in order to maintain their dreams of socialism and peace. Involved too was doubtless an indifference to Soviet internal warfare as remote and comparable to the killing of gangsters by other gangsters. More complex and immediate to American concerns was the difficulty of establishing a national consensus respecting the increasingly sophisticated world-wide network of KGB espionage, infiltration of sensitive agencies, tapping of American technology—including nuclear weapons—and its constant support with arms, advisors, and principles of destabilizing (*q.v.*) forces everywhere in the 1980s. The earlier public fury respecting traitors and pawns during the time of McCarthy (*q.v.*) was unsophisticated, and confused by liberal denials of significant malfeasance. The deviance from duty by those in responsible positions who knew that Alger Hiss was a traitor in America and Anthony Blunt a traitor in England was also disturbing. Conservative efforts to impress upon fellow-Americans that a transitional Soviet leader, Uri Andropov, had been head of the KGB for fifteen years and thus merited the sharpest scrutiny, did not seem especially successful. Brian Freemantle, *KGB* (1982); Claire Sterling, *The Terror Network* (1981); John Barron, *KGB Today* (1983).

**Kilpatrick, James J.** (1920- ), influential conservative columnist whose long concern for states rights and constitutional (*q.v.*) rights and limitations made him a watchdog of the Supreme Court (*q.v.*) and its tendencies. He edited the *Richmond* (Va.) *News Leader* from 1951 to 1967, and was vice-chairman for the Virginia Commission on Constitutional Government from 1962 to 1968. Well-known on panels which desired to hear the conservative viewpoint, and awarded a variety of honors for his journalistic work, he accounted himself a "Whig" (*q.v.*). He was author of *The Sovereign States* (1957), *The Smut Peddlers* (1960), *The Southern Case for School Segregation* (1962), and, with Eugene J. McCarthy, *A Political Bestiary* (1978).

**Kipling, Rudyard** (1865-1936), British poet and chronicler of imperialism (*q.v.*). He was a boy-wonder whose verses and tales of the British foot-soldier and Indian administrator, written when he was barely into his twenties amazed British, then American and other, readers. Although he honored "the White Man's Burden," he did not fail to note laggards, hypocrites, women of no virtue, and others who offended the smug and pompous of imperial England. His bitter childhood away from a loving family, in the hands of cruel guardians, spoke for others who suffered from unfeeling standards. Many of his phrases went into the language: "Tommy Atkins," "Mandalay," "Gunga Din," "Danny Deever," "Rolling Down to Rio," "The Ballad of East and West," "The Female of the Species" ("...is more deadly than the male"), "Fuzzy-Wuzzy"—the list could be extended. Many of his verses inspired songs which passed into the repertoire. "Recessional" was special as applicable to any nation. His novel *Kim* (1901) presented the British *Raj* (rule in India) in its best possible light by showing the Indian as a hero. Kipling's very power drove anti-imperialists to try to demean his stature. His work lived on at a popular level, but suffered silence or knowing scorn among intellectuals. Many were shocked when in 1942 T. S. Eliot (*q.v.*) issued an edition of Kipling's work wth a positive introduction. The logic of Kipling's life had him fully approve the Boer War. In World War I his son died striving to live up to Kipling's ideal of "manliness." Kipling could not see that the war would erase the premises on which he had founded his writing. It seems fair to grant him a place among the great writers of England. Lord Birkenhead, *Rudyard Kipling* (1978).

**Kirk, Russell** (1918- ), conservative spokesman and raconteur whose *The Conservative Mind, from Burke to Santayana* (1953) is credited with having given form and direction to the New Conservatism of the post-World War II decades. A native of Michigan, which his family had helped build, he took degrees at Michigan State College and Duke University, where he studied the career of John Randolph (*q.v.*). During the Second World War he served in the Chemical Warfare Service. He joined the staff of his College, now a University, and in 1948 took leave to study at St. Andrew's University and to absorb the scenes of Europe. *The Conservative Mind*, when published, provided common ground for numerous persons dissatisfied with what they saw and felt in American life, even after Eisenhower (*q.v.*) had been elected President, and it set Kirk on his way as a critic and commentator. He met the challenge of debate with liberals on platforms from coast to coast. His column, "To the Point," was syndicated in over a hundred papers. He gave up his university post, disdainful of higher education's appeal to mediocrity, and with the advent of the *National Review* (q.v.) wrote a regular column entitled "From the Academy." It reflected many of his visits and stays at educational institutions, as well as his other meetings and experiences. His work in education included *Academic Freedom* (1955) at one end, and *Decadence and Renewal in the Higher Learning* (1978), at the other. Kirk contributed directly to the rising conservative establishment in *A Program for Conservatives* (1954), *The American Cause* (1957), *The Intelligent Woman's Guide to Conservatism* (1957), and, again linking past and present, *Edmund Burke* (1967) and, with James McClellan, *The Political Principles of Robert A. Taft* (1967). However, it was basic to his concerns that conservatism was no mere dogma, but an accretion of human experience and tradition. Even *Academic Freedom*, though carefully researched, was sub-titled, "An Essay in Definition." Kirk never moved far from the essay. His numerous "articles" and introductions to other people's books fell easily into essay form, as did his *Confessions of a Bohemian Tory* (1963), *The Intemperate Professor, and Other Cultural Splenetics* (1965), and even portions of his famous *Eliot and His Age* (1972). Those interested in the configurations of his work also had to deal with his "Gothic" (*q.v.*) fiction, which moved between the supernatural and the powers of evil and of love. Kirk believed in ghosts, and thought he had seen them, even in the family home which he had inherited in Mecosta, Michigan. His sense of evil distinguished his fiction from empty horror tales. His *Old House of Fear* (1961), linking Scottish scenes with dark conceptions, received acclaim at home and abroad, and encouraged him the next year to issue a series of sketches and stories as *The Surly Sullen Bell*. It mixed things he knew with things he had heard or been told. A final chapter offered "A Cautionary Note on the Ghostly Tale" which indicated how much time and reading he had given to apparitions. *A Creature of the Twilight* (1966) told a complex tale of war in Africa and devilish doings. *The Lord of the Hollow Dark* (1979) featured someone who might have been the Anti-Christ and who named his strange crew for characters in T. S. Eliot's work. As William F. Buckley, Jr. noted, Kirk's were spiritual thrillers. Their validity came from the reality of moral crises. Kirk's Michigan home drew a constant stream of visitors, many of distinction, many others whose distinction lay in their variety. See also *The Roots of American Order* (1974), and Kirk's Heritage Foundation (*q.v.*) lectures, *Reclaiming a Patrimony* (1982) also, Charles Brown, *Russell Kirk: A Bibliography* (1981); and Filler, "The Wizard of Mecosta," *Michigan History*, September-October 1979. See also Order; *Portable Conservative Reader, The*.

**Kirkpatrick, Jeane J.** (1926- ), an outstanding member of the Reagan Administration, representing not only power, but conservative principles. A political scientist, she was employed in the Department of State and the Fund for the Republic, and was associated with George Washington University and later Georgetown University. She also served as an aide to Hubert Humphrey. In 1977, she joined the American Enterprise Institute (*q.v.*). Her books included *Mass Behavior in Battle and Captivity* (1968), *Leader and Vanguard in Mass Society: The Peronist Movement in Argentina* (1971), *Political Woman* (1973), *The Presidential Elite* (1976), and *Dismantling the Parties: Reflections on Party Reform and Party Decomposition* (1978). Her concern for Communism was seen when she edited *The Strategy of Deception: A Study in World-Wide Communist Tactics* (1963). See also *Dictatorships and Double Standards: Rationalism and Reason in Politics* (1982) and *The Reagan Phenomenon, and Other Speeches on Foreign Policy* (1983). Despite the fact that she was nominally a Democrat, in 1981 she was appointed U.S. Permanent Representative to the United Nations by President Reagan. In the U.N. she proceeded to reverse earlier policy by speaking firmly in behalf of American interests and expressing American distaste for dictators. Her authority in the field and her readiness to respond to attacks served her well. Writing with women in mind, she stated that it was possible to mix "traditional" roles with professional roles, but one had to start early, work hard and persistently, and have luck.

**Kissinger, Henry** (1923- ), foreign-affairs advisor to Presidents Nixon, Ford, and Reagan. He was a follower of Prince Metternich in his goal of aiding the Establishment by seeking a balance of power in international relations; see Kissinger's *A World Restored: Metternich, Castlereagh and the Problems of Peace* (1957). Kissinger was the architect of Detente (*q.v.*). As such, he was suspect to intransigent conservatives who thought it a priority to see Soviet Russia as the enemy of civilization, rather than aiding its plans with treaties it would break as it chose. Nevertheless, he was closer to conservatives than liberals who saw him as Machiavellian (*q.v.*), and whom he in return resisted as insufficiently concerned for American interests. See his *White House Years* (1979), and Filler, DASC.

**"Kneejerk Liberals,"** a perjorative term used by conservatives to refer to many of their opponents. The intent was to indicate that such opponents had not arrived at their positions through reasoned analysis and with honorable motives, but rather had been manipulated by such code words as "coexistence" and "compassion" and peer pressure. Their liberal positions were seen as robot-like response to such manipulations.

**Knickerbocker Bank**, see Federal Reserve System; *Free to Choose*

**Know-Nothing**, nativist (*q.v.*) movement of the 1850s, notorious for bigotry in its anti-Catholic, anti-immigration stands. It attracted the sympathy or active participation of distinguished personalities, notably Samuel F. B. Morse, painter and inventor of the telegraph. On a larger plane, the American Party provided a half-way house for Whigs and Democrats tormented by the slavery issue, but unwilling to throw off old associations or to accept the logic of secession (*q.v.*). The party crumbled, as leading figures made their critical decisions.

**Koestler, Arthur**, see Stalin, Josef

**Korea**, see Filler, DASC, a milestone on America's pursuit of a foreign policy for a "Cold War" (*q.v.*) world. It was divided by treaty into South Korea and North Korea, the latter in Communist hands. South Korea soon became subject to probes from North Korea. In 1950 North Korea invaded. General MacArthur's (*q.v.*) sterling response saved South Korea, but when he pressed to carry the war to Communist China, he was relieved of command by President Truman. Truman's argument was that he was trying to prevent World War III. It appeared, however, that Communist attacks were not met with sufficient response as a matter of policy. This was to trouble conservatives in the years following. Also troublesome was evidence that American-supported regimes such as those in South Korea tended toward corruption, especially where people were excessively poor. Since information on Communist regimes was hard to come by, this put the democracies at a disadvantage when such scandals proliferated. E. Traverso, ed., *Korea and the Limits of Limited War* (1970); David C. Cole et al., *Korean Development: The Interplay of Politics and Economics* (1971); F. H. Heller, *Korean War: A 25-Year Perspective* (1977); Glenn D. Paige, *Korean People's Democratic Republic* (1966); Hyung-Chan Kim, *Koreans in America* (1974).

**Kristol, Irving** (1920- ), major figure in neoconservatism (*q.v.*). He exhibited a sense of society's workings which gained him great respect from the conservative establishment. Attending City College in New York in the 1930s, he was recruited by the left-wing litterateur Irving Howe into the "Trotskyist" faction of college radicals, but expelled for individualism; see Howe's *A Margin of Hope* (1982). In 1947 he became editor of *Commentary* (*q.v.*), highly regarded for its liberalism and intellectuality, and in 1953 moved to London to help found and edit *Encounter*. He returned home in 1958 to edit *The Reporter*. By then he was esteemed in cultural circles and in business, and became an executive vice-president of Basic Books. The company published several of his own books in collaboration with the sociologist Daniel Bell. They included *Capitalism Today* (1971), which Kristol and Bell edited, and *Confrontation: The Student Rebellion and the Universities* (1969). Kristol also acted as consultant and director for a variety of business firms. In 1967 he was appointed a professor of social thought at New York University, and later joined its Graduate School of Business Administration. He had, in the meantime, with Nathan Glazer (*q.v.*) launched *The Public Interest* (*q.v.*), which linked societal tendencies with politics, and became a figure in Washington as well as New York. He ranked as a senior fellow at the American Enterprise Institute (*q.v.*), and his own writings were eagerly awaited and influential. Notable was his lecture, delivered under AEI auspices, "The American Revolution as a Successful Revolution" (1973). A related paper saw America as a "continuing revolution": a concept taken from the theories of Leon Trotsky (*q.v.*), but adapted to American conditions. Also admired were *On the Democratic Idea in America* (1972) and *Two Cheers for Capitalism* (1978). His *Reflections of a Neoconservative: Looking Back, Looking Ahead* (1984) defined his tendency, considerably augmented since its earlier years, toward intellectual conservatism.

**Kuehnelt-Leddihn, Erik von** (1909- ), Austrian litterateur and social commentator. He studied at several universities, specializing in law and theology, and taught in England and then widely in the United States, where he was welcomed by conservative gatherings and publications. A humanist and scholar, a Catholic and a liberal monarchist, he studied the nature and character of nations and political systems and probed the differences between programs and the realities of human nature. A foreign correspondent of the *National Review*, he offered analyses of trends abroad. His publications included *Night over the East* (1936), *Moscow* (1940), *The Menace of the Herd* (1943), under the pseudonym Chester F. O'Leary, *Liberty or Equality? The Challenge of Our Time* (1952), *The Timeless Christian* (1969), and *Leftism: From Sade to Marcuse* (1972). Kuehnelt-Leddihn traveled annually. In the mid-1980s he had in work his own memoirs and a study on "Eros in Theological

Perspective." His masterpiece was *The Intelligent American's Guide to Europe* (1979), issued by Arlington Press (*q.v.*), which mixed history with analysis in sophisticated measures, and enabled him to draw from his deep experience and reading.

**Ku Klux Klan,** Attractive to persons claiming to revere family values but lacking the regard for law and the awareness of American traditions and individual differences which would give them a place within those areas. Nor could the Klan claim a relationship with the western "vigilantes" (see Filler, DASC), who openly spoke for and to their communities, which were harassed by outlaws and needed to establish a measure of security in civic life. Although "Ku Kluxers" emphasized their native roots, they could not unite their cause with earlier nativists and Know-Nothings (*qq.v.*), whose cause was not only xenophobic, but linked with national issues which drew persons of distinction. New conservatives of the post-World War II era would have nothing to do the KKK adventurers, and knowledgeable liberals avoided making glib connections between them and their own conservative opponents for fear of counter-accusations of malice and bigotry. Studies of the Klan harkened back to the post-Civil War era and that of 1915-1930. See Filler, DASC.

# L

**Labor, Big.** see Unions; Immigration; Majority.

**"Labor Faker,"** see Gompers, Samuel

**Labor Racketeers,** long a painful feature on the labor-industrial scene, but especially malignant as labor became Big Labor, able to manipulate vast resources from pensions and other union assets. Some unions (*q.v.*), often led by such former "militants" as Jimmy Hoffa, stained the labor traditions by betraying the poor and the martyred who had given them their original status. Conservatives, with no stake in clarifying old traditions to which they could lay no claim, contributed to the forgetfulness which made labor history uninteresting or irrelevant. See also Rackets; "Right to Work"; Gompers, Samuel.

**Lacy, Ernest** (1863-1916), a conservative voice in poetry and drama. During his time drama was in a romantic era, often reaching back to classical influences. Poetry at the time was also limited in style, but with some inspiration from Emerson (*q.v.*) and others working with native themes. Lacy was repelled by an industrial civilization, made gloomy by Darwinian (*q.v.*) hypotheses, and empathetic with harassed poets. His one-act drama *Chatterton*, as acted by Julia Marlowe in 1894, impressed critics. His blank-verse *Rinaldo*, produced in 1895, also elicited praise, as did his *Plays and Sonnets* (1900). It included such disparate poems as "To an Ape," "Westminster Abbey," "A Midnight Walk," and "My Theater." His masterpiece, *The Bard of Mary Redcliffe*, published in 1910, was to star a well-known actor of the time, but new tendencies created by the Progressive era and a rising youth movement (*qq.v.*) sank this enterprise. Louis Filler, ed., *Chatterton* (1952).

**Laffer, Arthur** (1940- ), precocious economist who gained national stature in a time deeply concerned about financial trends and results. Educated at Yale, Stanford, and elsewhere and a tenured economist at the University of Chicago at age of 29, he was able to follow his mentor, George Shultz of the Graduate School of Business, to Washington in 1970 as an economist in the Office of Management and Budget. His economic predictions proved intriguing and placed him in high company among theorists. He became a major resource for those fighting for Proposition XIII (*q.v.*) in California, and for others seeing tax cuts as the base of a healthy economy: feeding supply-side (*q.v.*) needs rather than demand, production rather than consumption. The "Laffer Curve" became legendary and supposedly was first drawn on a napkin. It posited that with no taxation there would be no revenue, but that with 100% taxation there would be no revenue either, since there would be no incentive for anyone to work. A proper tax, therefore, had to be found somewhere between those extremes. In fact, this was the purest theory, since there would be revenue in any case, whether by the sword or by less drastic means. Laffer's theories contributed to real situations—as in Puerto Rico, where they might actually have raised revenue—or gained credibility by such other factors as inflation. Although Laffer's basic ideas appeared in President Reagan's economic programs, they were so bound by other elements of monetary policy, including defense and entitlements, as to have an uneasy future. In their will to free enterprise of restriction they were in the conservative line of reasoning, and were featured in George Gilder's *Wealth and Poverty* (*q.v.*).

See also Laffer's *Private Short-Term Capital Flows* (1975) and *The Economics of the Tax Revolt: A Reader* (1979, co-authored).

**LaFollette, Suzanne,** art critic and feminist, she was a relative of the Wisconsin LaFollettes, though not evidently concerned for their Progressive (*q.v.*) causes. As an associate of A.J. Nock (*q.v.*) and *The Freeman*, she scorned World War I and the outrages against civil liberties it had inspired, and saw liberalism as discredited. Her *Concerning Women* (1926) perceived women as in a position to improve their education in order to probe the nature of freedom, which she believed was linked to the "labor question." Her *Art in America* (1929) avoided ideology to seek out American characteristics. In 1930, she sought to revive the spirit of *The Freeman* with publication of *The New Freeman* (March 15, 1930-May 13, 1931), but the economic depression proved inhospitable. Surviving from it was *The Book of Journeyman* (1930), made up of Nock's *New Freeman* essays. La Follette then went into a quasi-radical period which, in 1937, placed her on a Commission of Inquiry to look into the charges aired in the Stalinist Moscow Trials. The trials had been contrived to "prove" that Leon Trotsky (*q.v.*) had conspired with fascists to undermine the Soviet regime. The Commission, head by John Dewey (*q.v.*), concluded that he had not. In 1950, La Follette headed yet another *Freeman* (*q.v.*), this one placing her clearly in the conservative traditions. In February 1953, there was an abrupt change in editors, with LaFollette removed from the masthead.

**Laing, R.D.** (1927- ), influential psychiatrist (*q.v.*) in the 1970s. He concluded, to the satisfaction of social dissidents, that there was no such thing as irrational behavior, no such condition as psychosis, and that those accused of such conduct were evading onerous circumstances which family and clinical solutions did not reach. In effect, Laing put in medical terms what his less-informed partisans put in social terms: that everything was society's fault, not the individual's. Such analyses helped to muddle society's self-protective agencies; whether they did anything for any patient is difficult to establish. Laing's theories were fashionable for a time, but gradually fell into disrepute. See E.Z. Friedenberg, *R.D. Laing* (1973).

**Laissez-Faire,** a term, indicating its European roots, opposed in the 18th century to the then-ruling economic theory of mercantilism (*q.v.*). Mercantilism made of international trade an expansionist activity with national goals and boards of trade. The Physiocrats (*q.v.*) of France urged that prosperity and economic health lay in letting trade go where it would; hence *Laissez-Faire* or *Laissez-Aller* (let it alone). The policy was best associated in England with the Manchester Liberals (*q.v.*). It was identified in the United States with Free Enterprise (*q.v.*). See also Capitalism; Smith, Adam.

**Lasky, Victor** (1918- ), veteran conservative journalist whose wide readership and investigative materials were effective in popular debate. Trained on the *Chicago Sun* and the U.S. Army's *Stars and Stripes*, and in screenwriting, he was a newspaper columnist during the 1960s and 1970s. With Ralph de Toledano (*q.v.*) he published *Seeds of Treason* (1950), an early examination of the Alger Hiss (*q.v.*) case. Lasky edited an *American Legion Reader* (1953). His *JFK, the Man and the Myth* (1963) and *Robert F. Kennedy, the Myth and the Man* (1968) broke ground for further revaluations. He cooperated with George Murphy (*q.v.*) on an autobiography which paved the way for Murphy's friend and colleague Ronald Reagan (*q.v.*). *It Didn't Start with Watergate* (1977) opposed many sanctimonious attitudes. *Jimmy Carter, the Man and the Myth* (1979) was one of Lasky's best-sellers. His *Never Complain Never Explain: The Story of Henry Ford II* (1981) upset the industrialist but was informative to readers.

**Last Puritan, The,** see Santayana, George

**Latin America,** always volatile, attracting American government concern and social interests. In the post-World War II world, freedom movements took various forms in revolution-prone Central and South America and the Caribbean, often taking color from Marxist ideology and Soviet expansionist interests. The fall of Cuba to Castro in 1959 did not immediately alarm the American public or officialdom. Its rise as a base for Soviet plans created crises: the grotesque failure of the American-approved Bay of Pigs invasion (1961) and a confrontation with the Soviet Union when it sought to set down ballistic missiles on Cuban soil (1962). Thereafter, Cuba was a surrogate (*q.v.*) force significant in all American efforts to curb the spread of Marxism in the two hemispheres and beyond. Troops moved from Cuba to Angola. Cuban advisors were in close touch with Chilean Marxists, Nicaraguan Marxists, and others excited by the prospect of tearing loose from or harming the North American "imperialists." Che Guevera, a Cuban revolutionary and hero of the American left in the 1960s and 1970s, was symbolic of Cuban ambitions in the hemisphere. Administrations from that of Franklin D. Roosevelt on had sought cooperative relations with Latin Americans, as opposed to military relations. In the 1970s the status of the Panama Canal (*q.v.*) stirred national debate in the U.S. Nevertheless, the possibility of a rash of successful Communist revolutions south of the American border divided Americans. Liberals insisted that the nations small or large should be able to choose their own governments. Conservatives approved C.I.A. (*q.v.*) intrigues, and held that at the very least democratic process must be furthered. Even the subject of human rights became partisan, depending on the political coloration of the country involved. The Americans experience with Chile was traumatic. Some liberals hailed Salvador Allende's election as President as a democratic victory for socialism. Kissinger (*q.v.*) observed that his margin of victory had been one percent. In 1970 Kissinger asserted that Allende was driving toward a socialist-communist program which was bitterly resented at home and was working to export revolution to Bolivia. (For the program of one of his advisors see Régis Debray, *Revolution in the Revolution?* [1967], *The Chilean Revolution: Conversations with Allende* [1971].) The unfavorable response among liberals to Allende's overthrow by the military and the passionate conviction of many liberals that Allende had been "murdered" gave little promise of dialogue on Latin American affairs. (See James Whelan, *Allende: Death of a Marxist Dream* [1981].) Crucial to Latin America was the role of foreign aid (*q.v.*). Thus Nicaragua and El Salvador emerged as danger spots in the West roughly equivalent to the situation in Lebanon and the Middle East (*q.v.*). Quarrels at home involved not only questions of Americans and Soviet interventions but also the amount of financial and military aid involved. Total separation from developments in the area seemed unrealistic. Again, Cuba's attempt to initiate a chain of Marxist outposts, beginning with Grenada (*q.v.*), appeared likely to bemuse liberals and conservatives in coming years. See also Banking; United Fruit Company. R.A. Humphreys and J. Lynch eds., *The Origins of the Latin American Revolutions, 1808-1826* (1965); Federico G. Gil, *Latin-American-United States Relations* (1971); Harold E. Davis et al., *Latin-American Diplomatic History* (1977); Leopold Zia, *The Latin American Mind* (1970); W. Raymond Duncan, *Latin American Politics* (1976).

**Law and Conservatism.** Conservatives traditionally maintained respect for law in life and society, until many courts undertook to define law in terms of what conservatives saw as liberal premises or interpretations. In the 19th-century the law's concern for property had enabled it to be a support for slavery (*q.v.*). Later, the Supreme Court (*q.v.*) had to deal with the Fourteenth Amendment's (*q.v.*) regard for "persons." In the mid-20th century the law turned its emphases toward civil rights (*q.v.*), often in ways which offended conservative thinking and emotions. Issues involving minorities—including blacks, and women (*qq.v.*), the latter anything but a minority—often bemused the courts. Minority-considerations often influenced elected and appointed judicial officials. Conservatives found distinctions between society's needs, instincts, and traditions and legal enactments which found meanings in the Constitution (*q.v.*) which earlier courts and the nation's founders had not foreseen or intended. Although conservatives had the same means of redress from grievances that were available to liberals, there was always a social factor to leave them discontented with law as such. Extralegal factors sometimes controlled legal decisions. Higher court rulings on crime, abortion, education, civil rights (*qq.v.*) raised questions of whether the higher courts were interpreting the law or making it. The alternative, of forcing legislative action or Constitutional amendment, offended conservative beliefs in community and societal habits and traditions, but seemed to many of them necessary to a society in flux.

**Leaf-Raking,** once cited by conservatives as evidence of the futility of New Deal (*q.v.*) measures for meeting 1930s depression conditions. An Albany legislative committee hearing established that temporary New York City jobs parcelled out to unemployed persons included the raking of leaves in parks; it was not always clear what was done with the leaves once they were raked. "Leaf-raking" was made a symbol of Democratic willingness to do anything to put government into the private sector of employment. However, it had its rationale. Thus, in a time of economic stalemate, it provided the shadow of activity and a promise of more. Still more important, it provided work which did not compete with private initiative, as happened in some other fields, where enterprising general work persons were driven from the market, unable to match offers from government to have churches freshened up with paint, to provide signs for municipalities and pictures for town halls, and to clean up trashed areas, all free of charge.

**League of Nations,** see Dickinson, G. Lowes

**Lebanon,** see Middle East

**LeBoutillier, John,** see *Harvard Hates America*

**Lee, Ivy** (1877-1934), founder of modern public relations. He saw that industrialists needed means to avoid the abuse and derogation which beset them and harmed their business ventures, especially with the powerful middle class, during altercations with labor or when accused of scheming against the public interest. When George F. Baer, head of the Philadelphia and Reading Railroad and leader of an anti-union drive against coal miners, remarked that "God in His Infinite Wisdom has given control of the property interests of the country" to such as himself, Lee decided that publicity and advertising methods had to be devised to appease journalists and others, and persuade them that business people were socially responsible. In subsequent years Lee served numerous industrial clients by presenting their case, earning the contempt of humanists as well as involved labor and socialist elements. Upton Sinclair dubbed him "Poison Ivy" Lee. See Lee's *Human Nature and Railroads* (1915) and *Publicity: Some of the Things It Is and Is Not* (1925). He found an unlikely biographer in Eric F. Goldman, who wrote *Two-Way Street: The Emergence of the Public Relations Counsel* (1948). The author was a liberal who nevertheless presented a positive view of Lee.

**Lee, Robert E.** (1807-1870), of Virginia, commander of Confederate forces in the Civil War. He became a symbol of national heroism through the military exploits of his father, "Light Horse Harry" Lee, in the Revolutionary War, and his own exploits in the Mexican War (*q.v.*). He gallantly refused the leadership of Federal troops offered by President Lincoln in order to serve his own state. Although Northern editors sought to brand him as disloyal, the effort failed. Lee's brilliant defense of Southern lines despite limited manpower made him a legend of chivalrous deportment. Following his surrender to Grant at Appomattox Court House, where it was agreed that his soldiers might retain their horses and small arms as aids in renewing civilian life, he took up the cause of education for a return to citizenship, himself serving as president of Washington College in Lexington, Virginia. Lee emerged as a better symbol of Southern patriots as they saw themselves than Jefferson Davis, President of the Confederacy, and inspired poetry and prose honoring his character and deeds. Woodrow Wilson (*q.v.*) was pleased to think that his fellow-Virginian had become a national hero. Lee was a binding force for conservatives North and South who emphasized duty, family, and religious faith above sectional differences. The classic life of Lee is by Douglas Southall Freeman, 1934, who also published *Lee's Lieutenants* (1942-44), in three volumes, and a life of George Washington (*q.v.*) (1948-1954) in six.

**Left, The,** term traditionally applied to radicals (*q.v.*) and others dissatisfied with society and urging various forms of revolutionary change in the social and political structure. The Left was distinguishable from moderates by the degree of revolutionary change it was willing to accept. Moderate critics of society sought a central position between Left and Right (*q.v.*), constituting an opposition, but a loyal one. In the French Parliament Leftists and Rightists sat on opposite sides of the chamber. The rise of fascism (*q.v.*), with its facade of "socialism," began the downward career of old categories. Some observers failed to see essential difference between "leftists" and "rightists" who lacked deference for the "masses." The Soviet Union's (*q.v.*) growth as a monolithic power, with its totalitarian control of society and its readiness to make every kind of alliance, most notoriously the Nazi-Soviet alliance of 1939, undermined its credentials as "Left" and created general confusion respecting the term. In 1970-1983, the "leftward" turn of the Labour Party in Great Britain topped a struggle for power within its ranks in favor of elements frankly open to Communism, and drove away social democrats who could not tolerate their presence. The weakening of Labour, even in its traditional constituencies, raised alarm, not only among its supporters, but among Conservatives who felt that there was need for a keen and effective Labour opposition. In America, leftists, including Communists, formed the "Progressive" (*q.v.*) Party in 1948, offering Henry A. Wallace as their candidate. In 1972 the Democratic Party Presidential nominee, George McGovern, was perceived by many as a leftist. See also Right, The.

**Legal Services Corporation,** established in 1974 by Congress as an independent agency to provide aid to the needy, who might otherwise be in an unfair position before courts, in comparison with the well-to-do, able to secure competent counsel. LSC grew into a formidable agency involved in an array of liberal causes intended to advance not only the interests of allegedly beset individuals, but of classes of persons—consumers, minorities, women—buttressed by "class action" suits. Reagan Administration appointees to the LSC Board were barraged with criticism by Reagan's opponents. In 1983 the LSC received Federal funds amounting to $225 million. Although the basic purpose had been to provide money for mainly local use, the LSC was able to make the central office a dominating force in local policy. Whether the LSC could be contained to observe its mandated function of giving legitimate aid at community level to the truly needy (*q.v.*) became a question of the 1980s.

**Lenin, Vladimir I.** (born Vladimir Ilyich Ulyanov) (1870-1924), with Karl Marx (*q.v.*) the founder of Communist methods and perspectives, and held in equal disrepute by conservatives striving against both. Josef Stalin (*q.v.*), however, fills more of their working thought. Lenin's reign as head of the triumphant Bolshevik uprising in 1917 was for six momentous years, but a brief period beside Stalin's rule of almost thirty, during which the power of the Soviets was consolidated and eras of peace and war traversed, leaving the Soviet Union one of the greatest powers in the world. Lenin was little known in the world before his accession to authority, but he was well-known and highly regarded among the factions which made up the Russian socialist spectrum in and out of Czarist lands. His deep simplicity of goals placed him far ahead of other leaders who, led by Marxist theories, were uncertain of which steps required priority for the achievement of revolutionary ends. In *What Is to Be Done?* (1902) Lenin laid down a simple road to victory. The revolution needed wholly dedicated people—"professional revolutionaries"—who would have no other task but to rouse the workers and peasants to protest and overthrow through a highly centralized party. Reform was anathema to Lenin: no more than a brush of compassion which directed attention from advance toward "stages" (*q.v.*) of revolution. Profoundly influenced by Marx's forevision of events, he anticipated a major upheaval in technologically advanced Germany, but criticized the revolutionary uprising of 1905 in Russia as having workers and peasants insufficiently directed and without a closely knit center. He lived on party stipends, studied his class foes, and sought to read their destiny in their own words. He was much impressed by the English economist John A. Hobson's *Imperialism* (1902), and used it freely in his own *Imperialism, the Highest Stage of Capitalism* (1916), seeing his party's task to stir nationalistic revolts in colonial lands. He saw the Great War not as a tragedy, but as an opportunity. With the "bourgeois" Russian revolution of February 1917, he eagerly accepted a German offer to permit him to leave Zurich, Switzerland and to travel by "sealed train" to Russia. There the Germans hoped he would create ferment and disruption which would hurt the efforts of the Czar's successors to keep Russia in the war against them. Lenin worked his way throgh vague alliances with other socialist factions, marshalling soldiers and speakers to spread his program of "Land, Bread, and Peace." Thereafter he created a model of Communist tactics, using socialist factions to establish his own, then proclaiming the proletarian revolution and driving the opposition into prison or exile, declaring all power to the "soviets" (local governing body) of which his party took control, mixing peace slogans with war against his political and economic foes as necessary in order to establish a rule of peace and sufficiency. Conservatives would later ask when that rule was to begin. They could deduce from the Lenin-Stalin experience that the Communist tactic was to demand democracy and, once it was established, to destroy it. Communists asked "sacrifices" from their populations, but to no discernible end. Their propaganda against "war machines" in the West was intended to weaken the West; they themselves became first and foremost a war machine which grew without end. The genius of Alexander Solzhenitsyn (*q.v.*) caught *Lenin in Zurich* (1975) in all his intensity and purpose, a man operating by dogma rather than humanity. See also Burnham, James.

**Leopard, The** (tr. 1960), by Giuseppe Di Lampedusa, one of the most distinguished conservative novels of the modern era. It tells of a traditional way of life in Sicily being undermined by the Garibaldian revolution and insensitive elements of the growing middle class.

**Leviathan,** see Hobbes, Thomas

**Levine, Isaac Don** (1892-1980), a pioneer journalist-critic of Communism. So great was American intellectual sympathy for the Soviet "experiment" that Levine, a long-time worker in his field, won little fame in over half a century of exposé writing. Born in Russia, he came to the United States in 1911, and entered journalism in Kansas City. In 1917 he became foreign editor of the *New York Herald Tribune.* His early opposition to the Bolshevik institution of a dictatorship divided him from many newspaper colleagues. As an editor of *Plain Talk* (*q.v.*), he wrote of the Stalinist labor camps, which then seemed lurid to American readers, as did his books on Stalin and the workings of Communism at home and abroad. During the unfoldings of the Hiss case (*q.v.*), he was an advisor to Nixon (*q.v.*). See his memoirs, *Eyewitness to History* (1973).

**Lewis, C.S.** (1898-1963), British author, scholar in medieval and Renaissance literature, Christian apologist, friend of J.R.R. Tolkien and Charles Williams (*qq.v.*), he developed a clear, firm style implemented by striking analogies and a sense of the familiar which enabled him to reach readers far removed from his closest concerns. His most popular work was *The Screwtape Letters* (1942) which detailed a devil's advice on how to tempt people to sin. Among his distinguished works in science fiction (*q.v.*) were *Out of the Silent Planet* (1938), *Perelandra* (1943), and *That Hideous Strength* (1945). This last predicted the atomic bomb, and all of the science fiction works dealt with moral problems and antagonism. Lewis did not distinguish between his scholarship and his explications of the Christian viewpoint. His *Preface to Paradise Lost* (1942) underscored that its meaning derived from the Biblical injunctions to obedience; as Lewis said, "How are we to account for the fact that great modern scholars have missed what is so dazzlingly simple? I think we must suppose that the real nature of the Fall and the real moral of the poem involve an idea so uninteresting or so intensely disagreeable to them that they have been under a sort of psychological necessity of passing it over and hushing it up. Milton, they feel, must have meant something more than that!" Although obedience sufficed for Lewis, he was resourceful in finding other means for explicating Christian tenets, as in his defense of *Miracles* (1947), which took on David Hume's (*q.v.*) old refutations of their possibility and made an impressive case. An example of his techniques had him noting that artists had distinguishable styles: a Rembrandt could never be a Van Gogh. But under powerful lights, one would find variations in the artist's applications of paint, undermining the evident consistency. Such observations made Lewis endlessly interesting to readers not necessarily concerned about his particular argument or theme. See his autobiography, *Surprised by Joy: The Shape of My Early Life* (1955), and his *Letters*, ed., W.H. Lewis (1966).

**Lewis, Fulton, Jr.** (1903-1966), commentator and columnist, an early proponent of conservative and anti-Communist ideas in the press and on radio. Though not so widely syndicated as Paul Harvey (*q.v.*), he preceded him in the popular expression of conservative themes, and was more consistent in the news and opinions he disseminated. Washington-based, he worked for the International News Service in the 1930s, becoming a news commentator in 1937. "Fulton Lewis, Jr. Says" won the ire of Soviet admirers and fellow travelers (*q.v.*) generally, but earned him citations for his anti-Communist principles.

**Lewis, Sinclair** (1885-1951), American author. Though he was considered an iconoclast during the Twenties and early Thirties (*qq.v.*), his essential conservatism became apparent thereafter, though it was not adequately examined. Inspired by H.G. Wells's middle-class vision (he named a son for Wells; see also his introduction [1941] to Wells's *Mr. Polly*), his search for American characteristics expressed itself in such early novels as *Our Mr. Wrenn* (1914). *Main Street* (1920) was a criticism, not a condemnation. *Babbitt* (1922) (*q.v.*) was distorted in interpretation by critics disenchanted with America. *Arrowsmith* (1925) and *Dodsworth* (1929) (*q.v.*) were clearly affirmative views of Americans. Even *Elmer Gantry* (1927), noted for its portrait of a religious fraud, was positive in many aspects, more so than his later *The God-Seeker* (1949). By then his powers had been largely dissipated. *It Can't Happen Here* (1935) (*q.v.*) was his last major achievement, though *Work of Art* (1934), the tale of a man whose respect for fine hotel service was superior to the pretensions of pseudo-artists, deserved better than it received. The Communist Granville Hicks, then influential, denounced Lewis as "a double-crossing apologist for the existing order." John Chamberlain (*q.v.*), then moving between Hicks and *Fortune Magazine*, found it "not a boring book."

**Liberals Arts,** with Social Science (*q.v.*) a key area of controversy in education. There were few arguments respecting teaching in the sciences during the conservative periods of domination in the schools and colleges, though Darwinism, states rights, and immigration (*qq.v.*) produced some wider controversy than more local and sectional issues. Literature, hewing closely to the "classical" model, was long an uncontroversial subject, as was American history, with its emphasis on great men and events. Even John Bach McMaster's *History of the People of the United States*, with its extraordinary ephemera dug out of old newspapers and pamphlets, was basically conservative in conclusions, though praising progress and expanded democracy. The Progressive era unleashed fresh sources for study and controversial judgments, which world crises augmented. It was not, however, until the 1950s that off-campus pundits began to acquire a parity with formal study. In the following decade, campus curricula were shaken to their roots, as formal language, historical presentation, and teacher qualifications were challenged by students with strong partisan feelings they were able to impart to other students and to administrators. Thus, "white" American literature was protested against and large areas of earlier literary study excised from textbooks to make room for "native"

American (Indian), black, women, and other types of writings, without questions of quality being raised. "Black English" (street talk) was argued to be a legitimate form of communication by partisans, though this was protested against by many blacks themselves.

**Liberal Imagination, The** (1950), by Lionel Trilling. It is of curious interest as illustrating the confusion of categories occasioned by changing times and loyalties. Trilling, author of the highly researched and sensitive *Matthew Arnold* (1939) (*q.v.*), aspired, like Arnold, to be a critic of letters and society, but was influenced by the Depression (*q.v.*) to feel empathy with Communist attitudes. As he told the later conservative writer Jeffrey Hart, "Oh, everyone was a Communist during the Thirties" (Hart, *When the Going Was Good!* [1982]). Trilling's novel, *The Middle of the Journey* (1947), was remarkable for containing evidence relevant to the connection between Whittaker Chambers and Alger Hiss (*qq.v.*) *before* their underground attitudes and plots had become public. But Trilling did not put the cultural tone of Communism in general perspective, as Arnold had labored to do with respect to the cultural values of his time. Although Trilling stated in general terms that Communism had produced nothing creative, *The Liberal Imagination* specifically attacked liberalism as a failure of heart and mind, pinpointing V.L. Parrington and Theodore Dreiser for disapproval, and avoiding Vachel Lindsay, Jack London, Meyer Levin, Edgar Lee Masters, and others of an undoubted liberal heritage who could have complicated the argument. Despite his prestige among academics, Trilling's indictment made no impact either among liberals or conservatives: a failure of dialogue, as well as of esthetics. For one answer to Trilling, see Charles Shapiro, "On Our Own: Trilling vs. Dreiser," in Filler, *Seasoned Authors for a New Season: The Search for Standards in Popular Writing* (1980).

**Liberal Papers, The** (1962), ed., James Roosevelt. It showed a different level of concern from that of *The Endless Crisis* (*q.v.*), being almost wholly concerned for foreign policy. However, even with different contributors, there was a line of continuity. Walter Millis prescribed a "Liberal Military-Defense Policy" which approved of a "retaliatory nuclear force" which would deter. It passed over Herman Kahn's (*q.v.*) vision of a cowering people digging into the ground for survival. The radical Arthur Waskow's "Theory and Practice of Deterrence" in effect substituted negotiation for deterrence. Frank Tannenbaum's "Considerations" emphasized his well-known sense of Latin America's profound traditions and its curious "democracy" based on uprisings. Southeast Asia, Japan, and Communist China were also seen as requiring understanding and accommodation. Quincy Wright sought "Policies for Strengthening the United Nations" (*q.v.*).

**Liberal Party** (British). With its roots in the 18th century and the Whig Party, it emphasized the search for social justice more than did the Tories, to whom the Crown and the Established Church were first considerations. Dr. Johnson (*q.v.*) despised the Whigs, whom he saw as incendiary. But as Liberals early in the 19th century, they attracted those who felt for the dispossessed worker, the harshly treated soldiers, and dissenting clergymen. William Cobbett (*q.v.*) spoke passionately in their behalf, and Utilitarians (*q.v.*) preaching reason saw an unjust Britain. The fight for cheap bread, for humane factory laws, and for an expanded suffrage engaged Liberals as well as such great Tories as Shaftsbury (*q.v.*); Liberals were already standing between the radicals and those who spoke for tradition and order, while the pioneer socialist Robert Owen was seeking to organize laboring men and Disraeli (*q.v.*) for the Tories was looking to break down the divisions between classes by humane measures. Liberals fought for free trade (*q.v.*), and as much freedom for labor as free enterprise would allow. Increasingly, they held the balance between the socialist-minded and the traditionalists. Lloyd George's famous budget of 1909, with its heavy tax on the landed gentry, seemed to create a new day of justice and equity. But World War I (*q.v.*), with its seemingly futile slaughter, left the field to those who saw a new day in socialism (or Communism) and others who held to nationalism and the old values. (See also Progressivism, the American equivalent of British Liberalism.) Although Liberals held on, hoping to hold the balance between the partisans of free enterprise, and of radicalism, conditions had changed since Disraeli could talk of "Tory socialism." The future of the fragmentary Liberal Party continued dubious, though in the 1980s it made alliance with the newly formed Social democrats, former Labor Party members disaffected with its extreme leftist policies. See R.J. Cruikshank, *The Liberal Party* (1948); L.T. Hobhouse, *Liberalism* (1911), H. Slesser, *A History of the Liberal Party* (1944), and studies of such significant Liberals as Lord Palmerston, Randolph Churchill, Lloyd George, Lord Beveridge. See also Mill, John Stuart; Arnold, Matthew.

**Liberal Republicans,** an abortive third-party (*q.v.*) movement headed by such figures as the journalist Horace Greeley, the German-American leader Carl Schurz, and E.L. Godkin (*q.v.*). They were dissatisfied with the Republican (*q.v.*) course of the post-Civil War years: its financial scandals, its harsh policies toward the South (*q.v.*), its use of Negro (*q.v.*) voters there to try to build up a permanent political machine. They saw the need too for a Civil Service (*q.v.*) to raise standards for government workers. Without a strong political base, and with the vulnerable Greeley as candidate, they gave little choice to concerned Republicans in the 1872 election, propelling President Grant to a second term. E.D. Ross, *The Liberal Republican Movement* (1919).

**Liberalism,** a product of several conditions, over long periods of time, and changing with it. None of the conditions conflicted with conservatism and some were a product of it, until modern times—which have demanded a clarification of goals and interests. Liberalism in a modern sense developed in the 18th century, connoting liberal arts (*q.v.*), a response to nature and to pagan cultures less regarded by Christian leaders and church authorities, and a flowering from Renaissance concerns which found their way into universities and temporal affairs. It intensified in the following century into a heightened respect for the individual, as world explorations and travels multiplied adventures and made potent names symbolic of worldly interests. Free Trade and Free Enterprise (*qq.v.*) were then descriptive of liberalism, as contrasted with ventures authorized by central authorities and supervised by them. Such liberals produced the philosophy of Utilitarianism (*q.v.*) with its emphasis upon the material world and upon rational solutions to human problems. It was opposed by religious and aristocratic (*q.v.*) viewpoints emphasizing fealty to overlords of church and state. Utilitarianism (*q.v.*) was a force in the American Revolution and in subsequent disorder elsewhere. It gathered ideals of democracy as it stirred ambitions, some clearly radical (*q.v.*), in hitherto lowly classes. Important was the Industrial Revolution (*q.v.*), which harmed their humanity and diminished the connections between aristocratic and religious orders and the poor and humble. Liberalism now emerged under its own name as compassionate force, insisting on democracy, demanding increased opportunity for the worthy, distinguishing between charity as a suppressive force and charitable enterprises created by reformers for the advantage of those—the poor, handicapped, disadvantaged—with rights to opportunity. Such pro-populist and progressive (*qq.v.*) elements did not move or intend to move toward the later welfare state (*q.v.*). On the contrary, it was their intention to defend and save whatever could be saved of individuality and free enterprise and adapted to conditions of mechanical complexity and organization. But the extremes of impersonal war—World War I, with all its brave slogans and chivalry—became intolerable to the most oppressed elements and their well-off sympathizers. Slogans of socialism and cooperation received authentication from the emergence of a Soviet Union which fended off feudal and capitalistic efforts to destroy it. Liberal sympathies here separated from conservative, even though commercial conservatives desired to sell their products to the Soviets. The Great Depression (*q.v.*) further polarized liberals and conservatives, tempting the latter to respond positively to the emergence of a fascist (*q.v.*) force apparently bent on an anti-Communist crusade. Liberals, on the other hand, adopted welfare programs created abroad or at home in order to fight the economic stalemate, which had been predicted by the Marxists. Although relief for the needy (the dole, in England), aid to industry (nationalization of industries elsewhere), the strengthening of trade unions via mediation boards, and manipulation of the currency (borrowed from Lord Keynes [*q.v.*]) were originally supposed to be temporary expedients in a bad time—as in the Temporary Emergency Relief Administration and National Recovery Act—they developed vast bureaucracies (*q.v.*) which increasingly worked for permanency. Even the arts, subsidized by the government in the Federal Arts Administration, found its advocates in a bill by Congressmen Coffee and Pepper (*q.v.*) to make art bureaus normal parts of government. All such projects were protested by conservatives, some of whom were co-opted by subsidies—to farmers, to airline pioneers, to railroad management (the railroads had been nationalized during World War I), and in other areas. The conservative appeals failed in election, as Franklin D. Roosevelt extended his sway from 1932 to his death in 1945. He was succeeded by his Vice-President Harry S. Truman, who extended New Deal policies. Even President Eisenhower (*q.v.*), a Republican, was unable to stem the tide of government spending and bureaucracy and even added to them with his program of road-building, which increased mobility but contributed to the draining of old-line, stable elements from the central cities. Liberalism held its own under John F. Kennedy and blazed into the Great Society under his successor, Johnson. By now, however, its goals were clearly transformed from what they had been before World War I, and even during the 1920s. Liberalism tolerated, and even cooperated with the rioting of the 1960s. It was committed to coexistence (*q.v.*) with Communist regimes abroad, in ways which differed fundamentally from the conservative approach. Conservatives advocated policies which would diminish Communist influence at home and resist its spread abroad. They had been alarmed by the fall of China to the Communists, and the revelation that the Soviet Union had attained the secret of the atomic bomb. They were infuriated by treason among Americans who identified themselves as liberals. Liberal denunciations of "witchhunts" (*q.v.*) drew a further line between those who looked at the advances of Communism without alarm and those who had the will or obsession to fight it. With the Communist Party in America thin and decrepit, and even its "fellow traveler" (*q.v.*) organizations few and feeble, the conservative anti-Communist crusade emphasized the role of liberals in the furthering of Henry A. Wallace's Communist-influenced Presidential campaign of 1948, in the promulgation of such slogans as "Better Red than Dead," and in the support of the radical political movements of the 1960s. Spiro Agnew (*q.v.*) was later to describe them as "radi-libs." Liberals showed strength in and outside of Lyndon Johnson's drastic push for an expanded welfare state, and the conservative effort to oppose them with Goldwater's Presidential candidacy in 1964 was catastrophic. In 1972, however, positions were reversed; liberals went down to dire defeat in supporting George S. McGovern. His opponent, Nixon (*q.v.*) garnered the greatest popular vote up to that time. By then the New Liberals had crystallized a program which all but separated them from liberalism as it had been perceived even in the early years of the New Deal. It had almost no connection with earlier versions of liberalism. It was committed to welfare-state principles, took the broadest possible stance concerning civil rights (*q.v.*), had a meager interest in American traditions—which it interpreted as racist, imperialistic, sexist, and in general an evil heritage best condemned and buried—except when they could be used to support libertarian demands. It labored for coexistence (*q.v.*) with Communism abroad, urged aid and recognition for "freedom fighters" everywhere, and attacked dictatorial regimes friendly to the U.S. while ignoring dictatorial regimes which called themselves Marxist or Communist. A. L. Hamby, *Liberalism and Its Challengers* (1985).

**Liberalism,** see Newman, John Henry Cardinal

**Libertarianism,** a modern movement with premises somewhere between intellectual anarchy and conservativism. In their scorn of taxation, infringement of private property, impositions of labor unions, welfare, subsidies, bureaucracy, (*qq.v.*) and state interventions generally, the libertarians were clearly in the conservative camp. In their more drastic opposition to the state in principle, on the grounds of natural law and necessity, logic put them against censorship of any kind, and closer to radicals than conservatives. They found predecessors in the 17th-century English "Levellers" (*q.v.*) and the 19th-century Lysander Spooner, who set up a postal service in opposition to the United States Postal authorities until stopped by law. Their outstanding figure, Murray N. Rothbard, (*q.v.*) was critical of Robert Nozick, libertarian and chairman of the philosophy department at Harvard, whose *Anarchy, State, and Utopia* (1974) appeared to justify the state. Libertarians' sharp concern for the roots of freedom and conjectures respecting "natural law" and their view of statism as opposed to freedom in philosophers from Plato onward made them stimulating to conservative theoreticians, but of little use at the polls. They therefore played little part even in the operations of the Libertarian Party, the small constituency of which was mainly interested in less taxation by the government. John Stuart Mill (*q.v.*), *On Liberty* (1859); J.M. Swomley, *Liberation Ethics* (1972); John Hospers, *Liberationism: A Political Philosophy for Tomorrow* (1971). John T. Sanders, *The Ethical Argument against Government* (1980) followed the free-market model of Robert Nozick.

**Liberty, Equality, Fraternity,** see Stephen, James Fitzjames

**Lifestyle,** a liberal phrase of the 1960s and after, rarely employed by conservatives. It suggested that all modes of social relations and habits had equal validity. These involved "sexual preferences," "relations between consenting parties," routines in "singles bars," or a passion for "rock" music. The emphasis on style rather than substance highlighted behavior rather than meaning, though emphasizing "meaningful relations." Minimized were traditions, ethnic and male and female characteristics, and history. A variant on "life-styles" affected urban elements which fancied fashionable clothing, vacations, and particular food, drink, and party-going.

**Lincoln, Abraham** (1809-1865), American President. During the Civil War (*q.v.*) he suffered abuse from almost all elements of the country except those officially related to the Republican Party (*q.v.*). Following his assassination he was raised to the highest pinnacle of regard, even above George Washington (*q.v.*). His tale of early poverty and growth to status as a lawyer, a conservative statesman, and a man of humor, compassion, and firmness in the right was told and retold. He was regarded as the finest example of an American, a man with patience and fortitude. Reading in his speeches and papers, all social and political tendencies claimed him. Conservatives saw him as a moderate whose foremost task had been to preserve the Union. They did not think it detracted from him that he had, in his First Inaugural Address, offered to carry out the Fugitive Slave Act if doing so would hold back the Southern states from secession. Liberals emphasized his passion for freedom, how he had pointed out during the great debates with Stephen A. Douglas (1858) that in urging "squatter sovereignty"—the right of settlers in territories due to become states to vote slavery "up or down" as they pleased—Douglas saw no difference between slavery or freedom. Radicals underscored Lincoln's emphasis upon labor as the primary ingredient in industry. Black spokesmen and writers honored his memory, expressing gratitude for his promulgation of Emancipation Proclamation. And Southerners who addressed the nation, in Congress and elsewhere, bitter over Radical Republican Reconstruction measures, increasingly approved Lincoln as having done his duty by the Union and avowed that, had he lived, he would have made a moderate peace and asked no more than that states in rebellion pick up their duties as citizens under the Constitution. Even radicals found enough in his growth and concern for "all mankind" to fancy that, had he been able to see ahead into their times, he would have found grounds to understand their cause. Post-World War II changes in outlook affected perceptions of Lincoln. A general decline in interest in American history modified his relevance to contemporary thought and discussion. A species of negativism raised question about the validity of key American events, including the Civil War and its major figure. Professional historians discovered racial factors in all aspects of American operations. They learned what had once been thoroughly known and discussed of Lincoln's partiality for the white race—and learned too that the Emancipation Proclamation had been more a military measure than a document of freedom. The radical politics of the 1960s tended to denigrate Lincoln as well as other major American figures, but by the mid-1980s this view had declined in influence. Benjamin Quarles, *Lincoln and the Negro* (1962); George Sinkler, *The Racial Attitudes of American Presidents* (1972); Lawrence Minear, *Lincoln and Slavery: Ideals and the Politics of Change* (1972).

**Lincoln Institute for Research and Education,** founded in 1978 by J.A. Parker. It was a conservative black organization in Washington, D.C. which studied public policy as it affected black communities and their prospects. It attracted a variety of talents, both black and white, and undertook such publications as *Black Education and the Inner City* (1981), which offered observations by Senator S.I. Hayakawa, the black Chicago educator Marva Collins, Dr. Vincent Reed (a former superintendent of public schools in Washington made an Assistant Secretary in the Department of Education), and Walter E. Williams (*q.v.*). Parker also began the *Lincoln Review*, which drew black and white writers on such subjects as "The Folly of Rent Control," "Enterprise Zones" (*q.v.*) "Returning to the Goal of a 'Color Blind' Society," "Black Labor in South Africa" and "Black Congressmen...How Representative Are They?"

**Lindbergh, Charles A., Jr.** (1902-1974), one of the great personalities of his time. He embodied qualities of patriotism (*q.v.*) and individualism (*q.v.*) which made him an important figure, more controversial for liberals than conservatives. He was undoubtedly affected by the abuse which his father, a respected Progressive (*q.v.*), suffered during World War I for pacifist opinions, interpreted as pro-German. Young Lindbergh turned to airplanes rather than politics. In 1927 he captured world attention with his lone flight over the Atlantic, displaying heroic qualities in a cynical time. He married Ann Morrow, daughter of the American Ambassador to Mexico, in 1929. The publicity surrounding the kidnapping and murder of his child in 1932 gave him a temporary distaste for America. Ann Lindbergh's *The Wave of the Future* (1940), which seemed indirectly to justify Nazi Germany, came after Lindbergh's acceptance of a Nazi medal and suggested fascist sympathies. This troubled liberals, who failed to notice the similiarities between Lindbergh's and his father's views, both being of Swedish, not German, descent. Lindbergh was a star of the American First Committee (*q.v.*) and consistent in his opposition to intervention in the war. But once America was engaged, he served in and flew missions for the Air Force. Despite controversy, he and his wife continued to appeal to majority opinion at home. Their journals as published revealed humanistic interests and concerns. See K.S. Davis, *The Hero: Charles A. Lindbergh and the American Dream* (1959).

**Lindsay, Vachel,** see Eliot, T.S.

**Literature.** Outstanding American writers can be seen as divided between conservatives and liberals or radicals. Conservative could claim such representative artists as Franklin, Bryant, Poe, Cooper, Hawthorne, Emily Dickinson, and in later decades, Willa Cather and James Gould Cozzens (*qq.v.*). Edwin Arlington Robinson's striking achievement was to take merely conventional meters and endow them with an unconventional content which transformed them. A failure as a poet in his youth, he caught the attention of President Theodore Roosevelt, whose public notice of him changed his life, enraging a hostile critical establishment. Liberals could also claim a line of descent, from Jefferson, the pioneer novelist Charles Brockden Brown, and Philip Freneau ("Poet of the Revolution") through Herman Melville, Thoreau, and numerous writers of the 1920s and 1930s. There were various shifting reputations along the way, as with Mark Twain (*q.v.*). Emerson (*q.v.*) appeared a radical in pre-Civil War decades, a mountain of individualism, useful to conservatives after the war. New Conservatives after World War II were less enthusiastic about his apostrophes to spontaneity and his preferences for nature, rather than God. Walt Whitman seemed the sheerest radical in his own time, though he was better regarded by conservatives then for his patent love of country and mysticism. Although the younger poets of the 1910s welcomed his free verse, notably Carl Sandburg, and Thomas Wolfe found inspiration in his breadth of vision, Whitman's close identity with material America was less compelling to those who felt remote from it. Allan Ginsburg's publishers advertised him as the 20th-century Walt Whitman; Jeffrey Hart of the *National Review* (*q.v.*) saw Whitman as the 19th-century Allen Ginsburg. John Dos Passos (*q.v.*) lived two lives, the first encompassing bohemianism and radicalism and observing American life with cold, unfriendly eyes; see his trilogy *U.S.A.* (1930-1936). Following his disillusionment with the Left, as expressed in *The Adventures of a Young Man* (1939), he wrote a second conservative-based trilogy, *District of Columbia* (1952), which, with the 1939 work, abandoned earlier techniques. Later works picked up the depth which had distinguished *U.S.A.*, but from a conservative standpoint. The lack of study they received, from conservative critics as well as hostile liberal critics, suggested that much in American literature was in flux.

**"Litigious Society, The,"** a concept covering the inability of tradition to prevent restless and resentful attitudes of individuals and groups and to prevent these attitudes from being taken to the courts. Often this created "class action" suits of a frivolous nature, hobbling the economics and operations of society. Britishers saw the American Revolution (*q.v.*) as dominated by "a plague of lawyers." During the 1980s the United States had more lawyers per capita than any other Western nation; and court dockets were overcrowded with lawsuits and legal actions of all kinds.

**Locke, John** (1632-1704), British philosopher, credited with having provided premises for the American Revolution (*q.v.*). He lectured at Oxford University, studied science and medicine, and from them developed materialist views which saw the five senses as the basis of reality. His essay published in 1690, *Concerning Human Understanding* and *Two Treaties on Civil Government*, made him the most influential philosopher of his time. They combined conjectures on origins and empirical observation. Where Hobbes (*q.v.*) had seen a state of nature requiring authority to keep men from destroying one another, Locke saw a time of goodness and tolerance in which men made a contract permitting authority for so long as it operated to their benefit. When it failed to preserve life, liberty, and property, there was a duty to rid society of it: the contract had been broken. Although Locke's view of civil government in part justified the "Glorious Revolution" of 1688, which put William and Mary on the British throne, its actual impact on later revolutions in conjectural. Russell Kirk (*q.v.*), in *The Roots of American Order*, believed that Locke little influenced American rebels in the 1770s; they were responding to larger trends in British traditions. Locke clearly impressed Rousseau (*q.v.*), whose vision of human equality inspired French radicals of the 1780s and 1790s. How far their actions could be traced to Locke was matter for debate. Locke opposed atheism and Roman Catholicism (*qq.v.*) but his essays on religious tolerance gave little nourishment to French extremists. It was perhaps Locke's materialist outlook and his Deistic (*q.v.*) leanings which made him less than inspiring to conservative theorists. John W. Gough, ed., *John Locke's Political Philosophy* (1950); J.D. Mabbott, *John Locke* (1973).

**Lodge, Henry Cabot** (1850-1924), American scholar-statesman from Boston. He edited (1873-1876) the *North American Review* (*q.v.*) and wrote historical works. A U.S. Senator (1893-1924) and friend of Theodore Roosevelt (*q.v.*), he was scorned in David Graham Phillips's (*q.v.*) *The Treason of the Senate* as an heir of New England "rum and nigger" fortunes, a strict defender of gold and Protectionism (*q.v.*), and partisan of war with Spain in

1898. He earned liberal opprobrium for his efforts to limit immigration by quotas (*q.v.*). Later, as chairman of the Senate Committee on Foreign Relations, he opposed President Wilson (*q.v.*) over entry into the League of Nations. Ironically, his grandson Henry Cabot Lodge, Jr. became U.S. representative to the United Nations. Social change was indicated in the contrast between the cold and genteel (*q.v.*) elder Lodge—and the Cabots, who, in a famous verse, "talk only to God"—and the friendly younger Lodge, who all but gained the Vice-Presidency on the Nixon ticket of 1960. John A. Garraty, *Henry Cabot Lodge* (1953), including reconsiderations suggested by Lodge, Jr., and the latter's own *The Stream Has Many Eyes* (1973).

**Lofton, John** (1926- ), journalist and author, a transitional (*q.v.*) figure whose work took him from *Insurrection in South Carolina: The Turbulent World of Denmark Vesey* (1964) to editorship of the *Conservative Digest*, from membership on the national council of the American Civil Liberties Union to a sharp journalistic prose which held up for criticism and concern liberal fetishes and evasions. He became staff columnist for the *Washington Times*.

**Lost World of Thomas Jefferson, The** (1948), by Daniel J. Boorstin (*q.v.*). A product of the author's leftist years, it was a subtle examination of the philosophy of Jefferson and his "circle." The book saw them as materialistic, utilitarian, and averse to speculation. Yet Thomas Paine (*q.v.*), one of the "circle," was reminiscent of Lenin and Marx (*qq.v.*), as seeing society as conceived in "sin" and with class antagonisms. Jefferson was closer in his morality to Jesus than to Andrew Carnegie (*q.v.*); utilitarianism had hardened into capitalist pragmatism (*q.v.*) through the passage of time. Carnegie's world no longer followed tenets such as had made the Revolution. There was some implication that, as Jefferson's world had become "lost" so Carnegie's "world" might also.

**Lowell, James Russell** (1819-1891), a transitional figure from reform which verged on radicalism to a cold and disillusioned distaste for the stormy America of the post-Civil War decades. Of wealth and an old family, he turned poetic wit and genius on the slavery crisis, and took a stand for pacifism, abolition, and separation from the South. With a quick ear for Yankee dialect and homely references and examples, he made his first series of *Biglow Papers* (1848) an arsenal of denunciation of the Mexican War, slavery, and government policy. War he called murder, slavery a first step to universal slavery. Lowell was a force for calling out the most reckless thoughts from his literate readers. Society showered him with honors: a professorship at Harvard, first editorship of the *Atlantic Monthly* (*q.v.*), editorship of the *North American Review*, (*q.v.*) and posts as minister to Spain and to England. His verse grew formal and his literary writings, all highly respected, became removed from contemporary concerns; see H.H. Clark and Norman Foerster, *Representative Selections* (1947).

**Lowell, Josephine Shaw** (1843-1905), one of the great reformers of the 19th century, with unimpeachable conservative credentials; see Filler, *Appointment at Armageddon*. Of distinguished Massachusetts family, she married Charles Russell Lowell, a nephew of the poet James Russell Lowell (*q.v.*), and himself an entrepreneur of great promise. She followed him to war, where he met a hero's death at the head of his cavalry; it was said he was vengefully buried by Confederates among his Negro troops. Left a pregnant widow at 22, Mrs. Lowell began to help former slaves adjust to conditions of freedom in New York. She then broadened her work to take in the full program of the New York State Board of Charities. A striking figure of dignity and beauty, always wearing black, she gained attention with official reports on institutions for the insane, for women, for the feeble-minded, and also for those deemed incapable of proper employment. This led finally to her founding of the powerful Charity Organization of America. In the 1890s she broadened her concerns still further by demanding more responsible labor, capitalist, and consumer operations. Her report on *Industrial Arbitration and Conciliation* (1893) was a landmark in mediation. The next year she led in organizing the Women's Municipal League, which grew into an important pressure group affecting urban developments. She had already pioneered with the Consumer's League of New York. At her death she was buried beside her husband at Mount Auburn Cemetery in Cambridge, Massachusetts.

**Loyalty,** see Patriotism

**Luce, Clare Booth** (1903-1987), known first as a successful executive on magazines and as the author of plays, notably *The Women* (1936), she gained further fame in politics. As a Republican Member of Congress (1943-1947) she attracted the attention of the press corps, which publicized her view of American foreign policy as "globaloney" and her conservative criticism of Franklin D. Roosevelt as having "lied" the nation into war. She had supported the candidacy of Wendell Willkie for the Republican nomination in 1940, and she supported that of Dwight D. Eisenhower (*q.v.*) in 1952. As President he named her Ambassador to Italy, and she later served as Ambassador to Brazil. Converted to Catholicism (*q.v.*), and skeptical of "women's lib" as unnecessary to women who knew what they wanted, she became a grand old lady of conservatism, sought out for her vigorous and witty comments. Wilfred Sheed, *Clare Boothe Luce* (1981).

**Luce, Henry R.** (1898-1967), publisher whose views of what would interest the public affected publishing and to an extent popular taste. Luce believed people wanted to know about others with apparent authority, including personal details. *Sports Illustrated*, *Life*, and *Fortune* reflected various aspects of his commercial, popular, and conservative insights. His central publication was *Time*. It was soon seen as interweaving facts with opinions, and was attacked for thus "slanting" the news by liberals and radicals. The radical poet Kenneth Fearing's *The Big Clock* (1946) was thought by some to have depicted Luce as a villain. He was thought too to have subverted talented writers by offering them tempting salaries; Luce himself did not think they were especially talented, and maintained they chose to work for him freely. Although Luce was generally conservative in his outlook, the nuances of *Time* reporting were such as to make its actual impact of particular personalities and events not always certain. Luce himself admired Whittaker Chambers (*q.v.*) and stood by him in his ordeals. W.A. Swanberg, *Luce and His Empire* (1972).

**Luce, Phillip Abbott,** see *New Left Today: America's Trojan Horse, The*

**Luddites,** referring historically to violent English workers (1811-1817) who, fearing for their livelihoods, took to destroying new machinery which they saw as making obsolete the work they did with their hands. The name came from a mentally defective Ned Lud who, about 1789, became notorious for his irresponsible destructiveness. "Luddites" in modern times came to mean those who might wish to stand in the way of progress (*q.v.*) by seeking to curb new "knowledge" which offended their religious or other preconceptions. *Discover*, a popular science magazine, in 1983 derogated "The New Luddites," who would stop "genetic engineering" (*q.v.*) on plants and bacteria on grounds that "gene-splitting" might loose upon mankind unthinkable evils.

**"Lunatic Fringe,"** a phrase employed by Theodore Roosevelt to characterize social elements outside the mainstream, obsessed with a particular idea, and immune to normal controversy and debate. It was one indicator of changing times meriting comparative study that many he would have deemed outside the range of significant attention in the 1960s often absorbed a considerable amount of that attention. See also Entertainment.

**Lyons, Eugene** (1898-1985), transitional (*q.v.*) figure who moved from Soviet sympathizer to anti-Soviet partisan. Born in Russia, he was early brought to America, and as a youth developed radical sympathies. He attended Columbia University and served as a private in the United States Army in 1918. Thrilled by the Russian Revolution (*q.v.*), Lyons wrote for the left-wing New York press, and for the Federated Press visited Italy, where further revolutionary events were anticipated. As a Communist, but not a Party member, he edited *Soviet Russia Pictorial* (1922-1923), and was a correspondent for TASS, the Soviet news agency from 1923 to 1928. Meanwhile, he had become involved in the case of Sacco and Vanzetti (*q.v.*), who he believed had been railroaded to the electric chair. His *The Life and Death of Sacco and Vanzetti* (1927) made him famous and was translated into several languages. He served as a foreign correspondent in Russia from 1928 to 1934 and from there contributed to the positive image of the Soviet Union and its leaders. One of his "scoops," an early interview with Stalin (*q.v.*) of which he was later ashamed, was highly approved by American editors. Like Malcolm Muggeridge and William Henry Chamberlin (*qq.v.*) it took years before he ran out of rationalizations for a brutal dictatorship. He left Russia in 1934, but his *Moscow Carousel* (1935) still sought a "balanced portrait," which he later recognized as unbalanced. As he later said, he could not then bear to disillusion the American people. By 1937 he could face his disillusionment. His *Assignment in Utopia* presented him as anti-Soviet. His *Stalin, Czar of the All the Russians* (1940) was judged intemperate. In 1939 he took up editorship of the *American Mercury* (*q.v.*), which liberals, using the language of the time, saw as close to fascistic. He retorted with *The Red Decade: The Stalinist Penetration of America* (1941). A pioneer of new conservatism, he published *Our Unknown Ex-President: A Portrait of Herbert Hoover* (*q.v.*) (1948). In 1953 he introduced a theme helpful to developing conservative premises in *Our Secret Allies: The Peoples of Russia*. It held that they should be encouraged in their yearnings for freedom from Soviet bondage. Meanwhile he was one of those who repudiated trendy liberalism and had more confidence in the principles of ordinary Americans. As with Max Eastman (*q.v.*), it was a matter of comment, for liberals and usually interpreted as a "sellout," when Lyons became an editor for the *Reader's Digest* (*q.v.*).

# Mc

**MacArthur, Douglas** (1880-1964), military hero and symbol to conservatives of pride in American power and will to resist Communist expansion on the world scene. MacArthur's career took him through World War I, the superintendency of West Point, and early and later service in the Philippines. His role in breaking up the shabby camps of the "Bonus Marchers" in 1932 in Washington, at the command of President Hoover (*q.v.*), was long held against him by liberals, but brought him the admiration of conservatives. He was revered for his long and brilliant campaign in the Pacific to dislodge Japanese strongholds during World War II and to free the Philippine Islands. As Supreme Commander in the East, he accepted the formal surrender of the Japanese and subsequently served as head of the occupational forces in Japan, where he earned the respect of his erstwhile foes. Called to service again when the North Koreans threatened to overrun the South Korean Republic, he stemmed the offensive, then carried his troops in sight of the Chinese border, over which came men and supplies to support the North Koreans. He planned to bomb Chinese supply bases against the orders of President Truman, and was relieved of command on April 10, 1951. MacArthur returned home to a hero's welcome. He had already been considered for the Republican nomination for President in 1948, but had shown insufficient drawing power at the polls. Conservative bids to run him in 1952 also misfired, his charisma proving less potent than that of his former aide in the Philippines and Washington, Dwight Eisenhower (*q.v.*). His Republican philosophy was that of free enterprise, and he ended his career as a business executive.

**MacBird!** (1966) by Barbara Garson, an infamous "parody" of *Macbeth*. A product of the counterculture movement of the 1960s, it seemed to accuse Lyndon Johnson of the murder of John F. Kennedy. Trading on agitation against the American involvement in Vietnam, the play enjoyed critical success and a good deal of popularity. Its reception reflected liberal bemusement with the radical excesses of the time and the general inability of liberals of the day to distinguish between dissent and disruption. An attempt by Garson to revive her scheme using Nixon as a target failed to stir attention.

**McCarthy, Joseph R.** (1908-1957), U.S. Senator from Wisconsin, catalyst of anti-Communist feelings in the early 1950s. He reflected the alarm conservative America felt over the Soviet Union's development of the atomic bomb and the Communist takeover of China. Weak, and only intermittently interested in foreign affairs, the general conservative public found in McCarthy a protagonist who like themselves recalled the high-level U.S.-U.S.S.R. cordially of the anti-Nazi war years, who noticed the rapid left-wing politicalization of the United Nations, and who was ready to believe that this could not have occurred without the connivance of Communist agents in government. What seemed called for was a campaign to rid the government of security risks, something which should have occurred thanks to such Congressional legislation as the McCormick Act (1938), the Hatch Act (1939), and the Smith Act (1940). The problem was to determine citizens' rights and discern the nuances of perjury. Thus, Communists made a practice of disassociating themselves from the Communist Party itself, technically evading anti-Communist law. Other "fellow-travelers" were even further removed from direct "Party" affiliation. Still others associated with "Communist-front" organizations could or could not be security risks. Since all of this added up to anti-Americanism, it was acutely frustrating to conservative intellectuals and alarming to ordinary citizens with a sense of being endangered by propaganda and government acts. McCarthy had been elected U. S. Senator in 1946 in a sensational upset of Robert LaFollette, Jr., heir to a great Progressive (*q.v.*) tradition. Although there was ample anti-Communist sentiment in the country, crystallized in the case of Alger Hiss (*q.v.*), it lacked a central focus. This McCarthy provided in a Wheeling, West Virginia speech on February 9, 1950. He claimed to have the names of a number of Communists operating in the Department of State. The alleged number, as changed or contradicted, later became the basis of evidence of fraud and insincerity among anti-McCarthyites. The national attention given a hitherto little-known Senator was so overwhelming that it obviously persuaded him that he had struck deeply into the matters of public concern. Thereafter, he sought and received numerous charges of Communist adherence and association. During the same period the Rosenbergs (*q.v.*) were accused of supplying Soviet agents with atomic secrets, and the academic Owen Lattimore of helping to sway government and public opinion in behalf of the Communist Chinese. McCarthy's opponents accused him of conducting "witchhunts" and persecuting individuals for their beliefs rather than for political acts, but his supporters charged that this was an attempt to create hysteria (*q.v.*). Emboldened by his reelection to the Senate in 1952, however, McCarthy obviously flung charges irresponsibly, in an atmosphere of politics and special interests which served neither the nation nor democratic dialogue. He often substituted force for evidence. Embarrassing was his publication of *The Story of General George Marshall, by Senator Joe McCarthy* (1952), which he impudently copyrighted, though it had been written by Forrest Davis. The work took McCarthy on a road which led to his undoing. In essence the question was whether mistaken American policy had led to Soviet triumphs, or whether treachery in high places had. McCarthy opted for treachery, and many conservatives felt they could not disown him under the circumstances. *McCarthy and His Enemies: The Record and Its Meaning*, by William F. Buckley, Jr. and L. Brent Bozell (1954), sought to overcome this dilemma by setting aside standards of personality and purpose—which they rarely did otherwise—to emphasize the "record." But they did not face the fact that McCarthy himself was becoming a burden which liberals and radicals could and did exploit. The televised Army-McCarthy hearings, a Congressional investigation into McCarthy's charges of treason against the U.S. Army, led to a turn in public opinion against McCarthy. He went on to be censured in the Senate, and later died of complications from alcoholism. Although the concept of "McCarthyism" as a persecution of individuals for their beliefs is in many ways contrived and inaccurate, its persistence in popular lore suggests elements which conservatives evade at their own cost. Two formidable studies place the McCarthy phenomenon in their social and political context, Thomas C. Reeves's *The Life and Times of Joe McCarthy* (1982) and David M. Oshinsky's *A Conspiracy So Immense* (1982). Michael P. Rogin's, *The Intellectuals and McCarthy: The Radical Specter* (1967) is of interest in showing, with documentation, how supposedly responsible historians link Progressivism with the rise of McCarthy, to Progressivism's discredit. Insufficient attention has been given to the psychology and circumstances of liberals and radicals of the time. William Benton's liberal viewpoint in his anti-McCarthy thoughts and actions as a Senator is detailed in Sidney Hyman's *The Lives of William Benton* (1969). Carl Marzani, highly trained and educated, lied about his Communist background and was dismissed from the Department of State in 1946. The next year he was convicted on eleven counts of what he called "a framed-up charge," though it was affirmed by the Supreme Court, and served three years as what he called a "political prisoner." He then wrote *We Can Be Friends: Origins of the Cold War* (1952), which sweepingly endorsed Soviet policy. In some ways more interesting, his novel, *The Survivor* (1958), depicted his state of mind under government "persecution." With degrees in literature, philosophy, and economics—which he later taught at New York University—he offered a viewpoint that was not unique. In a second edition of Buckley and Bozell (1961), Appendix G offered the case of a shabby adventurer, Paul H. Hughes, who pretended to be a secret member of McCarthy's staff who would give testimony concerning McCarthy's machinations. Hughes hoodwinked a formidable battery of liberal luminaries, notably the civil rights attorney Joseph L. Rauh, Jr. and the editors of the *Washington Post* and *New York Post*. Buckley's point was that, although they denounced informers, they were eager to find and use them themselves.

**McGuffey, William Holmes** (1800-1873), professor and college president in Ohio and Virginia, best known as compiler of the legendary "McGuffey Readers" (more formally *Eclectic Readers*) for elementary classrooms. As published between 1836 and 1857, and reprinted in 122 million copies, they were credited with having provided the basic education for several generations of children. They were composed of selections from English literature and other materials encouraging patriotism, good manners, and moral outlook. Conservatives contrasted them with the "pap" offered by later compilers operating on "progressive" (*q.v.*) principles. The McGuffey Readers were circulated by the Conservative Book Club (*q.v.*).

**McMaster, John Bach** (1852-1932), one of the great American historians. He determined in his youth to write a democratic history of the United States, as distinguished from earlier ones which focused on great men and events. Diverted for some years by a career in engineering, which itself produced two books on tunnel centers and dams, he then devoted his life to producing his massive *History of the People of the United States* (1883-1913). McMaster pored over old newspapers, pamphlets, and ephemera in libraries and museums, looking for details of everyday life: how people corresponded, what public events they attended, what they ate, thought, and sang. All such matters he transcribed in longhand and used to describe social and routine events, as well as to throw new light on politics and war. So interesting was this new, popular history as to make his first volumes bestsellers, despite a staccato prose which nevertheless imparted novel and even amusing information. Though without graduate training or position, McMaster received an appointment as professor at the University of Pennsylvania, and gained fame in the history profession. His accounts seemed superficially to demean the nation, describing demagogues, riots, prejudices, and corrupt episodes. McMaster, however, saw these phenomena as part of a deepening and improving of American life. As he said in an essay entitled "Four Centuries of Progress" detailing the growth in humane law, education, and institutions: "In the face of these facts it is wicked to talk of degeneration and decay." It was such leading ideas which caused the radical Staughton Lynd to term him a "bourgeois philosopher," and to recommend that his books not be read. For a social selection from his *History*, Louis Filler, ed. (1964).

# M

**Machiavelli, Niccolo Di** (1469-1527), the ever-present challenger to conservatives and liberals, authoritarianism, and, by liberals, associated with the excesses of conservativism. The rise of a Soviet Union and of a Communist China, equally ruthless and concerned only for victory at whatever cost and by whatever means, raised questions of means and expediency about others beside conservatives. Although George Orwell's (*q.v.*) *1984* (1949) was seen as directed at a degenerate Soviet Union, its elements could be detected in professedly liberal states. Accordingly, it seemed necessary to keep an open mind respecting the means for survival in a complex world. See Filler, "Consensus," in J. Waldmeir, ed., *Essays in Honor of Russel B. Nye* (1978). See also James Burnham's *The Machiavellians* (1943) for musings about moderns imbued with the master's viewpoint.

**Mackenzie, William Lyon,** see Canada

**Mackinder, Halford J.** (1861-1947), British geopolitician, creator of the "Heartland" (*q.v.*) concept. He revolutionized thinking about the dynamics of power, as affected by geographic distribution. Mackinder recommended a combination of cultural and empirical education to disseminate understanding of the tasks facing democracies. Educator and Member of Parliament, he went on to serve on the Imperial Shipping Committee and the Privy Council. His service to England during World War I made him suspect to liberals, as did his faith in military victory; his influence on Karl Haushofer, Nazi military advisor, augmented their skepticism. They failed to note that Haushofer advised Stalin as well as Hitler. See A. J. Pearce, ed., *Democratic Ideals and Reality*, by Mackinder (1962 ed.); also J. T. Lowe, *Geopolitics and War: Mackinder's Philosophy of Power* (1981).

**Madison, James** (1751-1836), known as the "Father of the Constitution" (*q.v.*) and crucial to many conservative interpretations of what the Founding Fathers (*q.v.*) had intended in drawing up that document. As a Virginian, he shared many of the influential views of his compatriots; during the uncertain years between the operation of the Articles of Confederation and the signing of the New Constitution (*qq.v.*) (1783-1787), being a member of the Virginia House of Delegates was as important to Virginians as being a member of the national Congress. Madison was reporter for the debates on the Constitution, himself submitted the Bill of Rights (*q.v.*)—first enacted in Virginia, as drawn up by George Mason (*q.v.*)—and contributed to the *Federalist Papers* (*q.v.*), urging ratification of the Constitution. Nevertheless, as a leader in Jefferson's anti-Federalist party, he joined him in drawing up the Virginia and Kentucky Resolutions. They protested the Alien and Sedition Acts of 1798 (*qq.v.*), asserting that the states would not carry out laws passed by Congress which they deemed unconstitutional. Madison served as Jefferson's Secretary of State and succeeded him to the Presidency. His mishandling of the War of 1812 caused disaffection in the New England states and earned the event the name of "Mr. Madison's War." His *Journal* of the Convention of 1787 proved a treasure to later scholars concerned for the meaning and intentions of the Constitution-makers. After the rise of a new conservatism defensive of earlier American values it was studied even more intensively for answers to a liberal Supreme Court and liberal commentators' views of the Constitution. Henry Adams's (*q.v.*) *History of...the Administration of Jefferson and Madison* (1889-1891) carried on his Federalist war against the Virginians, "answered" in Irving Brant's six-volume biography of Madison (1941-1961).

**Maistre, Joseph Marie, Comte De** (1753-1821), French author, a favorite of conservtives for his firm belief in social order, his hatred of the French Revolution of 1789, and his belief that the only means for an enduring control in society was the Pope in his exercise of Christian government. *Du Pape*, published in 1819, was one of a number of works which offered reflections on the Spanish Inquisition, on France, on political constitutions and human institutions. It has continued to be read by those dissatisfied with the course of democracy (*q.v.*), receiving modern publication and review. De Maistre's *Works* were translated by Jack Lively in 1965. Also important for his wit and prose is de Maistre's brother Xavier (1763-1852), who served as a soldier in the Russian army. His *Voyage autour de ma chambre* (1794), written while he was imprisoned for fighting a duel, was enjoyed for its wit and personality. His *Le Lépeux de la Cité d'Aosta* (1811), a conversation between a soldier and a leper, is notable for its Christian spirit and patience.

**Majority**, an enigmatic concept in the shifting sands of popular impression and opinion, involving not only ideas but impact. Power often emanated from the top down, rather than from the bottom up. A conservative goal of the 1980s was to disassemble bureaucracies (*q.v.*), which were held to serve themselves rather than the public. "Big Business" (*q.v.*) was once seen as unfairly ruling a majority of workers; following the operations of the New Deal (*q.v.*), it became evident that a "Big Labor" had emerged which could operate formidably in national affairs. Thus, a truckers' strike in the midst of social crisis or war could threaten the foundation of society. The leaders of such massive unions (*q.v.*) as those of autoworkers and teachers attempted to become key factors in elections. But the majority of their memberships did not always vote with their unions. The massive following of New Right (*q.v.*) preachers and lay leaders suggested their formidable political power. It appeared, however, that great percentages of them, as in the Moral Majority (*q.v.*), were not always at one on all issues or leaders. They were not able to sustain, for example, patriotic and family (*qq.v.*) beliefs during the Vietnam (*q.v.*) era. Gustave Le Bon, *The Crowd* (tr. 1897); W. L. Ransom, *Majority Rule and the Judiciary* (1912); N. R. Yetman, *Majority and Minority, the Dynamics of Ethnic and Racial Relations* (1975 ed.)

**Making of the New Majority Party, The** (1975), by William A. Rusher (*q.v.*). It reflected the bitterness which conservatives felt over the collapse, as they saw it, not only of the Nixon (*q.v.*) Administration, but of the Republican Party itself. Rusher, of the *National Review* (*q.v.*), felt that the Republican Party was going the way of the earlier Federalist (*q.v.*) and Whig (*q.v.*) parties. He attributed this to its compromises with welfare-state (*q.v.*) principles and a willingness to seek accomodations with Communist China and the Soviet Union. What was needed, in the view of Rusher, was a new party, untainted with the failures of the old. He proposed that it be called the *Independence Party*, to which true conservatives could rally. He saw Ronald Reagan (*q.v.*) as a likely candidate for its program and discussed a number of other possible candidates, in Congress and out of it, several of whom disappeared into history. Rusher had admired Spiro Agnew's (*q.v.*) campaign, and regretted his fall. See also Rusher's *The Rise of the Right* (1984).

**Mallock, William Hurrell** (1849-1923), British Victorian apologist for the landed aristocracy. He himself noticed the "apathy" of his fellow-squires to the "alarming socialist measures" being promulgated, in part by such Tories (*q.v.*) as Disraeli (*q.v.*). Mallock's work in "social questions" began awkwardly in such generalized writings as *Social Equality* (1882) and *Landlords and the National Income* (1884). They attempted to prove that all was well with rural England. Labor's increasingly formidable rise reconciled him to that of the commercial classes (see his *The Nation as a Business Firm* [1910]), and gave him contemporary status as a leading anti-radical writer. His *Critical Examinations of Socialism* (1907) drew an answer from Bernard Shaw. Nevertheless his polemical writings were too ephemeral for durability. Mallock's fame rests on his first book, *The New Republic, or Culture, Faith and Philosophy in an English Country House* (1877). All his life he was a devoted country-house visitor, and carefully recorded many of his visits in his *Memoirs of Life and Literature* (1920). He was a friend of such Victorian grandees as Swinburne, Browning, and Carlyle, and more closely a friend of Herbert Spencer (*q.v.*), John Ruskin, Matthew Arnold (*q.v.*), Walter Pater, Thomas Henry Huxley, and the famed Master of Balliol College Benjamin Jowitt. Like them, Mallock was stirred by the Darwinian (*q.v.*) Hypothesis and sought answers to it. Under other names he assembled some of them at a country house, there to enjoy its amenities and to discuss the temper of their times. With brilliant parody—even to writing an Arnold-like verse which did not lose in comparison with the master's poetry—with original recreations of Jowitt's tormented critiques and defenses of Christianity, Pater's faith in art, and Ruskin's utopian dreams of a people's culture, Mallock depicted the intellectuals of his time with durable wit and learning. He concluded with his own sense, as later recorded, of *Religion as a Credible Doctrine* (1902). For a definitive study see J. Max Patrick, editor and annotator *The New Republic* (1950).

**Malpractice,** a formidable offshoot of advocacy (*q.v.*) law, it enabled clients who claimed injury or suffering as a result of medical treatment to sue for restitution (*q.v.*). The sums awarded were often impressive. The parents of a two-year-old who might never walk, talk, or feed herself, for example, because of brain damage allegedly caused at birth, won a settlement from a hospital of $119 million. This led to an unprecedented rise in hospital and doctors' insurance premiums, and created a class of lawyers equivalent to old-fashioned "ambulance-chasers." Since medical professionals rarely received the sympathy of juries, some of them found it easier to go into less hazardous forms of service with a resulting shortage of needed doctors. With law (*q.v.*) providing one of the few binding forces in society, it appeared that there would have to be a rationalization of society's needs, and an agreement on what constituted just settlements, if health services were not to be reduced to chaos.

**Malthus, Thomas** (1766-1834), British cleric and political economist whose formidable *Essay on the Principle of Population as It Affects the Future Improvement of Society* (1798) became a guide to pessimists and upholders of the status quo, as a goad to those who dreamed of social progress and improvement. Malthus's major principle was that population increased geometrically while the means for subsistence increased mathematically. He further stated that war, pestilence, and the mortality resulting from vice and crime were nature's means for keeping population in line with the means of subsistence. This principle was intolerable to the theoreticians of progress and cooperation. Malthus later added "moral restraint" as a check on population, which gave little additional consolation to the partisans of progress. Although Malthus suffered a species of discredit among those who were constrained to give good news to their constituents, he experienced a new endorsement in the late 20th century among those who advocated population control by limiting births. Conservatives generally were more optimistic about humanity's chances for multiplying without over-populating the planet.

**Man Versus the State**, see Spencer, Herbert

**Man Without a Country, The** (1863), by Edward Everett Hale. Written during the Civil War, and inspired by the enormity of secession and the breakup of the Union, it mixed known facts with invention. In the story a soldier in a reckless fashion had entered into a vaguely formulated plot to separate Western land from Federal holdings. At the subsequent court-martial he cried out in a passion that he never wanted to hear his country's name again, and was sentenced to sail American ships but never to hear its name from seamen or visitors. The tale won unprecedented attention and entered into the lore of the nation. People claimed to have seen or known Philip Nolan. In modern times, it was made into an opera and performed in the Metropolitan Opera House (1937). The decline in patriotism (*q.v.*) in the mid 20th century finally dimmed the story's fame.

**Managerial Revolution, The** (1941), by James Burnham (*q.v.*). A step away from Communism by a former Communist on the way to becoming an admired conservative, it became famous for its thought that free enterprise had to be reinterpreted in terms of its actual leaders: managers, rather than entrepreneurial individuals who linked ownership to profits and direction. The inevitable bureaucracy (*q.v.*) raised question of freedom, as well as of efficiency and production. See Productivity; Profits; Incentive; *Demanaging America: Wealth and Poverty*.

**Manchester Liberalism,** named for businessmen in that industrial city who also developed political ideas and influential national policy. The best known Manchester Liberals were John Bright and Richard Cobden, to whom free enterprise (*q.v.*) was not only a way of attaining wealth, but a philosophy of life from which all gained. They held that factories brought well-being and improved living standards to everyone. They also led the fight for free trade as lowering prices and making for international peace. For the unemployed they advocated emigration, which would help build undeveloped lands abroad. The Communist Friedrich Engels denounced the entrepreneurs in *The Condition of the Working Class in England in 1844* (1845), which became a textbook for devout radicals. However, it was to be scorned in its turn by conservative economists as distorted and without perspective; see T. S. Ashton in Hayek, ed., *Capitalism and the Historians* (1954). Conservative intellectuals were only moderately attracted to Manchester liberals because of their utilitarian emphasis and limited concern for morals and tradition. *Cf.* Shaftesbury, Earl of; Disraeli, Benjamin. See also W. D. Grampp, *The Manchester School of Economics* (1960).

**Manion, Clarence** (1896-1979), lawyer and professor of Constitutional law at the University of Notre Dame (1925-1952). As director of the "Manion Forum" on radio, he became known for his sharp attacks on such forces as Communism, which he deemed detrimental to American freedoms. His books included *Lessons in Liberty* (1939) and *The Conservative American* (1964).

**Mann, Horace** (1796-1859), see Filler, DASC. His educational career was paradoxical in appearing "progressive" in his own time, but more conservative in later eras. As secretary of the Massachusetts Board of Education, he became a national legend for his dedication and creativity as he fought unthinking rote instruction and the tolerance of untrained teachers. His annual reports were an inspiration to generations of educators. He forged a work-and-study program for the college he founded in Ohio. It admitted women as well as men, and repudiated race discrimination. Yet his standards were such as to separate him and his message from later "progressives" who fancied "value-free" guidance, and evaded moral and religious challenges as well as standards of competence. Mann's career and its aftermath raise questions about conformity and change. Filler, ed., *Horace Mann on the Crisis in Education* (1983 ed.).

**Mano, D. Keith,** see Wolfe, Tom

**Mao, Tse-Tung,** see China

**Marcantonio, Vito,** see Demagogues

**Maritain, Jacques** (1882-1973), influential French philosopher and litterateur. A convert to Catholicism (*q.v.*), he believed that Christians should be concerned for public questions; his views affected the findings of the Second Vatican Council (*q.v.*). His first book, *Primacy of the Spiritual* (1927), set the tone for his varied writings. They explored art, humanism, and the role of the individual. A Thomist (*q.v.*), he also wrote *The Range of Reason* (1952). See J. W. Evans and L. R. Ward, eds., *The Social and Political Philosophy of Jacques Maritain* (1955).

**Marshall, John** (1755-1835), conservative statesman whose tenure on the Supreme Court as Chief Justice (1801-1835) gave it parity with Congress and the Executive, and whose decisions built up the nationalistic component in law. Feared by President Jefferson (*q.v.*)—who noted that Marshall had not been elected by anyone, but simply appointed by John Adams (*q.v.*)—Marshall labored to avoid being flouted in his decisions by an antagonistic Executive; his appeal had to be to the country, rather than merely to abstract law. The case of *Marberry v. Madison* (1803) gave him his occasion. Marberry, appointed by John Adams just before leaving office, was ignored by incoming Secretary of State James Madison (*q.v.*). Taking advantage of the Judiciary Act of 1789, which gave the Supreme Court power to rule on differences between government officials, Marberry asked Marshall for a writ of *mandamus* forcing Madison to give Marberry his commission. Had Marshall done so, Madison would have treated his order with contempt. Instead, appealing to logic rather than to law, Marshall held that Marberry had indeed a right to his commission. However, nothing in the Constitution gave Congress the right to endow the Supreme Court with the power specified. Marberry would have to seek redress elsewhere. Thus, by giving up his right to issue writs of *mandamus*, Marshall assumed the greater right to judge the Constitutionality of acts of Congress. The Jeffersonians could do nothing to deny him. Had the nation not concurred in Marshall's decision, believing that it needed a Court to judge Constitutionality, Marshall could have been fought on later decisions. It was evident, however, that his basic view was that of the nation. Once the power of the Supreme Court was established, Marshall proceeded to find many "implied powers" not specified in the Constitution, and to expand their scope in the interests of a national government which could overrule states, and the protection of industry. So firm was Marshall's work that his Court was able to survive the challenges of the Andrew Jackson Administration, the Civil War (*qq.v.*) and the "Court-packing" attempts of Franklin D. Roosevelt (*q.v.*)—frustrated by Supreme Court decisions which interfered with his development of New Deal (*q.v.*) policies. Although liberals and conservatives endured eras which offended their principles, few doubted that Marshall's work had been for the best.

**Marx, Karl** (1818-1883). Marx is regarded as a major intellectual foe of conservativism, though this is minimized by the fact that he has become more of an icon than a living inspiration requiring combat. Revered in the Soviet Union, and held in awe by acolytes of Marxism who seek careers under its aegis in underdeveloped countries, he is less reverentially recalled in the West. An attempt to make a landmark of his centenary year in London, where he is buried, produced little in the way of inspiration or exegesis. His (and Friedrich Engels's) *Communist Manifesto* (1948) offers hard, bullet-like prose and predictions which waver when compared with actual events. "The Revolution" did not take place in the most advanced country, ready for socialism. Embarrassed Soviet ideologues had to explain their revolution as that of capitalism breaking at its weakest link. The state did not wither away; it grew like an enormous cancer over the population and its works. Economics were indeed the life-blood of a people, but Marx's "dialectical materialism" insufficiently recognized that man does not live by bread alone. His monumental labors took place in the time of Disraeli (*q.v.*). Like Marx, though from a different perspective, he recognized that England was becoming two nations—of the rich and the poor—and turned his Tory (*q.v.*) party around to do something about it. Others were to do more, though not always wisely. Conservatives later taking issue with Marxists and neo-Marxists found relatively few occasions to cope with Marx himself, whose context of poverty differed so drastically from that which had evolved out of industry, reform, and revolution.

**Mason, George** (1725-1792), distinguished Founding Father (*q.v.*). His post-Revolutionary fame did not match that of his friends and fellow-Virginians Washington and Jefferson (*qq.v.*), in part because he worked for revolutionary goals as a Virginian rather than in national councils. Yet he drew up for the Virginia Convention (1776) the Bill of Rights, which informed Jefferson's Declaration of Independence (*q.v.*) and was a major force for adding the Bill of Rights to the Constitution; others would have settled for less than those guarantees. Mason also saw to Virginia's concession of its title to western lands; without this enormous gift, the nation would have been crippled in its expansion plans. K. M. Roland, *Life of George Mason* (1892).

**Mass Production,** see "Quality Control"

**Matthews, J. B.,** see *Odyssey of a Fellow Traveler*

**Media,** connoting for conservatives power over the public mind and liberal views on domestic and foreign issues. The "media" commentators, "talk show" hosts, and reporters were held, particularly by conservatives, to have dominated opinion during the civil rights (*q.v.*) crises of the 1960s, to have discouraged patriotic unity in the Vietnam (*q.v.*) involvement, and to have furthered liberal views in succeeding Presidential campaigns and state and local elections. Although technically supposed to be reporting news without prejudices conservative critics held that the media sought to influence the public by such devices as raising eyebrows, emphasizing key words in reported statements, creating code words, and asking loaded questions rhetorically to interviewees. Reasons given for such alleged prejudiced approaches varied. Media reporters and personalities were believed by conservatives to suffer from arrogance and need to exhibit power, as well as the need to appeal to malcontents and climbers such as they had been during their rise to visibility. This would explain, suggested the conservative columnist Joseph Sobran, their references to "millionaire William F. Buckley, Jr.," but never to "millionaire Tom Brokaw," a popular TV commentator. Media personalities were thus seen as feeling they were looked down on by people of more distinguished status, and striking back by exploiting democratic tenets. Their partisanship seemed evident in their tenderness toward the Kennedys as well as in numerous discriminations for and against other public personalities. The failure of the media in the 1980 Presidential election was noteworthy. Although they held that the election would be close, uncertain, and possibly victorious for President Carter he was overwhelmingly rejected. Though the media were chastened by the results, they did not appear modified in attitude. Overlooked is the natural tendency of the media to gain audiences and readers by presenting news items in the most sensational and agitational ways possible.

**Medicare,** conceived in compassion, under President Lyndon B. Johnson, it raised questions during the Reagan Administration. Reagan insisted that he aimed only to turn back undesirable aspects of the Welfare State (*q.v.*), and not to leave the "truly poor" or aged in desolation and despair, or the national budget in disarray. Yet efforts to curb indiscriminate distributions of government funds to those not in need roused liberal agitation. It brought protests from interest groups which reminded Congress that they held potent political power. Nevertheless, economic necessities continued to put pressure on Congress and public opinion to find solutions which enable govenment to deal with all the problems involved in servicing the sick, while curbing fraud among recipients and doctors, and controlling the hospital and pharmaceutical sectors, which were halfway between industries and public responsibilities. Also involved were the bureaucratic agencies, the standards and disbursements of which required revaluation for modernization purposes. R.J. Myers, *Medicare* (1970); M.J. Skidmore, *Medicare and the American Rhetoric of Reconciliation* (1970); J. Feder, *Medicare: The Politics of Federal Hospital Insurance* (1977); S. Prozer, *Medicated Society* (1968).

**Mellon, Andrew W.** (1855-1937), U. S. Secretary of the Treasury, 1921-1931, a major target of liberal criticism. "The greatest Secretary since Alexander Hamilton" (*q.v.*) was seen by foes as harming the general economy with his drastic tax cuts. They were interpreted as helping those who needed no help. Though he cut the national debt from $25.5 billion in 1919 to $16.2 billion in 1930, his critics were unmoved. His banks and Aluminum Company of America were held to hold his Pittsburgh as a virtual fief. Mellon was in fact more than a banker for the rich. His own *Taxation: The People's Business* (1924) sought to expound the actual workings of money. Though his policies were unable to prevent the coming of the Great Depression, the good intentions of

New Dealers were unable to control the evils of social welfare. It appeared that one side effect of the new Reaganomics (*q.v.*) would be to refresh the image of Mellon as a well-intentioned servant of the people. For the radical view, see Harvey O'Connor's *Mellon's Millions* (1933); *cf.*, F. D. Denton, *The Mellons of Pittsburgh* (1948); Burton Hersh, *The Mellon Family: A Fortune in History* (1978).

**Memoirs of a Dissident Publisher** (1979), by Henry Regnery, a key volume in the history of post-World War II conservativism by one whose publications furthered it. Beginning with his first two conspicuous successes, Russell Kirk's *The Conservative Mind* and William F. Buckley, Jr.'s *God and Man at Yale* (*qq.v.*), Regnery issued writings which defined aspects of conservative interests, including such titles as Dillard Stokes's *Social Security: Fact and Fancy* (1956), Jameson Campaigne's *Check-Off: Labor Bosses and Working Men* (1961), Donald R. Richberg's *Labor Union Monopoly* (1957), Buckley and Bozell's *McCarthy (q.v.) and His Enemies* (1954), James Jackson Kilpatrick's (*q.v.*) *The Sovereign State* (1957), James Burnham's (*q.v.*) *Congress and the American Tradition* (1958), Frank S. Meyer's *In Defense of Freedom* (1962) and *What Is Conservativism?*, (1964) which he edited; Willmoore Kendall's *The Conservative Affirmation* (1963), Richard Weaver's (*q.v.*) *The Ethics of Rhetoric* (1953) and *Life without Prejudice* (1965), and John Dos Passos's *Occasions and Protests* (1964). The firm also published volumes on Revisionism (*q.v.*). Under the name Regnery Gateway, it prospered from the Reagan (*q.v.*) triumph in 1980.

**Men.** Implied in the critique of feminists and women's rights activists is the belief that, since men have traditionally dominated the home and the workplace, they do not have "problems" requiring solutions as do women (*q.v.*). Yet many have also noted that, in the traditional American division of social roles, men have been held to as strict and unrealistic a standard as women. Thus, men have been expected to be emotionally controlled, warmth and emotion being seen as connoting weakness, "womanishness," and even homosexuality. Male friendships have had to be circumspect lest they too imply traces of homosexuality. When women are seen as the "weaker sex" to be protected, men by contrast must be the strong, self-assured protectors. Any failure in competence, strength, or self-assurance in a man thus has traditionally implied that he is somehow less than a man. Any failure in aggressiveness, any refusal to risk physical injury or death—whether on behalf of a cause or for no cause at all—has also been traditionally seen by society as "unmanly." In recent decades many men who have adapted to their traditional social roles have been confronted with women who refuse to see themselves as weak, submissive, or in need of protection. For such men the choice has seemed to be between remaining a "man" as they understand it, and risk jeopardizing their relationships with such women or becoming "less than a man," and risk jeopardizing their own self-esteem. Thus, men as well as women have had to re-examine, often painfully, their own basic assumptions of what they are and what they should be in the light of the upheaval of social roles that began in America in the 1960s. See James Wagenvoord, ed., *Men: A Book for Women* (1978); Joseph H. Hughes, Jr., *Sex... a Male Primer* (1977); Barbara Habenstreit, *Men against War* (1973); E. Friedl, *Women and Men* (1975); John Money and Anke A. Earhardt, *Man and Women... Gender Identification from Conception to Maturity* (1973); George F. Gilder, *Sexual Suicide* (1973); Joseph H. Pieck and Jack Sawyer, *Men and Masculinity* (1974); Derek Bowskill and Anthea Linacre, *Men: The Sensitive Sex* (1977).

**Mencken, Henry Louis** (1880-1956), social critic. He had his training as a journalist in Baltimore, and made his reputation as co-editor with the drama critic George Jean Nathan of *American Spectator* (1914-1923). He soon became a national figure, and was editor of the *American Mercury* from 1923 to 1933. On the *American Spectator* (*q.v.*) his work linked oddly with that of the youth (*q.v.*) movement of the time—though he was, if anything, royalist in sentiment, while the youth movement ranged from "socialist" to anarchist. Both Mencken and the editors of *The*

*Masses* and *Poetry: A Magazine of Verse* were elitist (*q.v.*) in outlook—Mencken had written *The Philosophy of Friedrich Nietzsche* (1908), a pioneering work and scornful of democratic standards and conventions. Mencken's major battle in that era was in behalf of Theodore Dreiser's fiction. Mencken had earlier praised David Graham Phillips (*q.v.*) as the leading American novelist, who told the truth about life and love in America. But as a pessimist for whom nothing justified living but elemental pleasures and laughing at fools, he found Dreiser's painful fancies and accounts true in a deeper sense, which he was able to further in the declining years of Progressivism (*q.v.*) and during the "disillusionment" which followed World War I—which he vigorously opposed. It was rarely noticed that Mencken was, like Dreiser, of German parentage, that Mencken loved the German beer and good-fellowship he found in Munich, and bitterly resented all that had disrupted it. His outlook comported with many of the socialists he openly ridiculed, and made him appear the friend of democracy he was not. His *American Mercury* was, like A. J. Nock's (*q.v.*) *American Freeman*, open to a broad spectrum of verse, prose, and fiction, making it one of the most stimulating of magazines in an era of creativity and experiment. Mencken himself was both notorious—in the "Bible Belt," as he termed it, and among the "booboisie"—and famous among those who found his volumes of *Prejudices* (1919-1927) rousing and educational. His opinions covered a wide range. He hated Woodrow Wilson, treated Warren G. Harding (*qq.v.*) as a figure of fun, and thought Thorstein Veblen a pompous ass. His views of women were both patronizing and without insight. Yet he was patiently endured by intellectuals whom the latter views pierced to the heart; they rationalized that he represented free expression in a crass, Babbitty (*q.v.*) world. Although many imagined the *American Mercury* was a vast enterprise, it was in fact a small operation mainly run by Mencken's helper, Charles Angoff. Angoff was a Harvard graduate whom Mencken delighted to "needle," but for whom this was the greatest era in his life (see *The Tone of the Twenties* [1966]). The *American Mercury* taught a sense of the connection between culture and society which more than complemented the formal studies of the universities. Mencken had been in the news as denouncing the Dayton, Tennessee "monkey" trial, which set the atheist-evolutionist Clarence Darrow against the defender of the literal intepretation of the Bible, William Jennings Bryan. Meanwhile, Mencken was quietly pursuing his study of *The American Language* (1918, and following), which would be a surprisingly solid contribution to the subject. The coming of the Depression put him on the sidelines. He could not compete with the partisans of Communism and "proletarian literature," and did not try. His *American Mercury* welcomed fascist solutions to the crisis. His later memoirs were *Happy Days, 1880-1892* (1939), *Newspaper Days, 1899-1905* (1941), and *Heathen Days, 1890-1936* (1943). They were among his best writings, though without contemporary impact. Angoff's study *H. L. Mencken: A Portrait from Memory* (1956), though chided by a *New York Times* reviewer as being too true, apparently sold well, and comports with the Mencken of collected letters and other studies. Most instructive was the evidence in Mencken's life that, though he was despised by conservatives in academe as destructive of order and faith, he was himself a conservative, though of a different order.

**Mercantilism,** an economic system outmoded by the rise of industry and Free Trade doctrines. It places its emphasis on the accretion of gold, a flexible medium by which to advance nationalism and home industries. Mercantilists sought to sell more than they bought. They saw colonies as means for acquiring raw materials and for selling finished goods. The American Revolution (*q.v.*) was in part a protest against the workings of mercantilism. War was one of its instruments when linked to nationalism. Free traders thought their policies would reduce war among nations. Although Free Trade survived in modern times, being opposed by Protective policies, mercantilism, with its bold appeal to nationalistic pride and dominance, had little use. Except for the importance of bullion, Communist economic policies came closest to approximating mercantilist philosophy. L. Silk, ed., *Mercantilist Views of Trade and Monopoly* (1972).

**"Mercy Killing,"** See Euthanasia

**Mexican-Americans,** see Immigration; Unions

**Meyer, Frank S.** (1909-1972), a well-esteemed *National Review* editor and transitional (*q.v.*) figure. His career took him educationally through Princeton University and Balliol College, with additional studies at the London School of Economics and the University of Chicago. He became one of those who gave his energies to the Communist cause. Later, disillusioned with its workings, and helped by the transcendental writings of such writers as Eric Voeglin and Jacques Maritain—as well as by the New Conservatives—he forged a philosophy of freedom as virtue which he employed as commentator on American and world developments. For his summary views on Communism see *The Moulding of Communists* (1961); for a survey of his *National Review* contributions see *The Conservative Mainstream* (1969). Other books included *In Defense of Freedom* (1962) and *Left, Right, and Center* (1965). Notable was his *African (q.v.) Nettle: Dilemmas of an Emerging Continent* (1965), which he edited and which brought together a number of analysts and participants, all conservative, including Elspeth Huxley, Sir Roy Welensky, and Thomas Molnar. James Burnham (*q.v.*) concluded the symposium with an essay on "The United States, the United Nations, and Africa."

**Middle Class,** an amorphous term traditionally designating those halfway between the "working" elements of society and the entrepreneurs. Karl Marx (*q.v.*) described the "petty bourgoisie," who mixed labor with small ownership, and other members of the middle class who had somewhat larger holdings but no control of price or production structures. They were conventional in behavior, and supporters of traditional social, familial, and religious tenets. During affluent times, it became evident that "middle-class" ideals were pursued by ambitious elements among workers and among the well-to-do who aspired to public support and thought it prudent not to flaunt their wealth. Being middle class earned contempt during the Depression era (*q.v.*), but post-World War II affluence reaffirmed middle-class ambitions, creating a hunger for the material trappings of life. None of this aided conservative opposition to the welfare state, except as taxation (*q.v.*) affected middle-class budgets. In the embattled 1960s (*q.v.*) the middle class tended to imitate counterculture attitudes and lifestyles, but by the 1980s middle-class life had become more conservative and traditional. True middle class displays, like Thomas E. Dewey's (*q.v.*) manifest efficiency and authority, created a public sense of discomfort. A few upper-class personages like William F. Buckley, Jr. were tolerated as permitting a peep into other-world living. As the middle classes went, so went their group, or the nation as a whole. Its record stemmed from Benjamin Franklin (*q.v.*), who, on the way up, as told in his autobiography, carried his work out in the street with sleeves rolled up, a living advertisement of himself as hardworking and dependable. The middle classes, gone "soft" after World War II, and indulging themselves following the harder years of the Thirties (*q.v.*), inadvertently created the shocking reprisals of the youth (*q.v.*) debacle. Lewis Corey, *Crisis of the Middle Class* (1935); M. Helms, *Middle America* (1975); Charles Evans, *Middle Class Attitudes and Public Library Use* (1970); W. A. Muraskin, *Middle-Class Blacks in a White Society* (1975); W. P. Kreml, *The Middle Class Burden* (1979); R. M. Carter, *Middle-Class Delinquency* (1968).

**Middle East,** a key point of contention between conservatives and liberals involving first of all the actions of the Palestine Liberation Organization (PLO), which claimed portions of Israel and engaged in terrorism (*q.v.*) in pursuit of that claim. It also involved in background the expansionist goals of the Soviet Union (*q.v.*), which hoped through surrogates at least to reach the Persian Gulf and deprive the West of access to vital stores of oil. Comparatively tiny Lebanon became the focal point of contending forces, watched anxiously by American conservatives fearful of Communist gains in the region and by liberals who feared American involvement, "another Vietnam," and identification with reactionary rulers. The presence of numerous factions in Lebanon, separated by religious, traditional, and material interests, invited endless war and destruction. The question was whether they could be kept in relative balance to avoid a cataclysmic showdown. The United States was committed through all political changes to maintain the existence of Israel as the one Western-style democracy in the Middle East. Nevertheless, Syrian, Jordanian, Iraqi, and Iranian interests had to be kept in mind. With Israel determined to defend and fortify its borders despite decisions reached elsewhere, problems of American intervention and withdrawal of forces became a matter of constant surveillance. The bottom line was Israel's right to exist, which the embattled PLO was unwilling to concede. Such a concession would undermine much of the PLO's reason for war. The Palestinians in fact had a homeland; Jordanian leaders had repeatedly said that Palestinians and Jordanians were one people. The famous West Bank, which Israel had modernized, contained Israelis and Arabs living together. Whether East-West conflict could be subordinated to the interests of peace, and cynical appeals to prejudice and greed shelved, was literally a question of life and death. J. C. Hurewitz, comp., *The Middle East and North Africa in World Politics* (1975 ed.); J. Waterbury and R. E. Mallakh, *The Middle East in the Coming Decade* (1978); Don Peretz, *The Middle East Today* (1978 ed.); George Lenczowkie, *Middle East Oil in a Revolutionary Age* (1976); W. A. Beling, ed., *The Middle East: Quest for an American Policy* (1973); John D. Anthony, *The Middle East: Oil, Politics, and Development* (1975).

**Middle of the Journey, The** (1947), by Lionel Trilling (*q.v.*), a novel significantly crossing liberal-radical with conservative development in the 1930s and 1940s. It depicting the clash of ideas in the conversion of "Gifford Maxim" from espionage agent for Stalinism (*q.v.*) to an unqualified religious position. The original for "Maxim" was Whittaker Chambers (*q.v.*) portrayed before revelations which brought him and Alger Hiss into court. Although the novel responded to local scenes and personalities, it revealed little sense of American ways and experience. The emotional credit its protagonists gave the Stalinist regime, despite revelations of its horrors, contrasted with their favored position in American society, and their capacity for influencing naive students and followers. See also Liberal Imagination, The.

**Military,** see Pentagon; Advisors

**Mill, John Stuart** (1806-1873), influential British thinker. Mill at first sight seems closer to liberalism than conservativism. He was raised under the tutelage of his father, James Mill, to follow the rationalistic (*q.v.*) principles of Jeremy Bentham. He was made a prodigy of classical learning, and at the age of twenty found himself in a depressed state. Contact with the ideas of Coleridge and Comte (*qq.v.*) introduced him to the world of feeling and social empathy, but his religious sense was never stirred, nor did he gain significantly by his contact with Thomas Carlyle (*q.v.*). In 1830 he met the wife of a London merchant, Harriet Taylor, whose mind and emotions captured his spirit for the rest of his years. It is likely that, though they met abroad and as often as possible in London, and married following the death of Taylor's husband in 1851, they never experienced sexual relations; such is the view of Michael St. John Packe, a major biographer. Yet their spiritual affinity and purposes were intertwined. Mill's *System of Logic, Ratiocinative and Inductive* (1843), answered to his view, and that of other Victorians (*q.v.*) that only the mind gave significance to human beings. Always a busy writer, he studied the philosophy of history, while searching for moral solutions for the problems of the age, such as the Irish question: in effect, rearing a man-made order of justice and satisfaction. Such was the burden of his *Essays on Some Unsettled Questions of Political Economy* (1844). An enduring achievement was his *Principles of Political Economy* (1848), which broke ground by turning away from the assumptions of earlier economists, who saw "laws" ruling the world's work. Laws there were indeed, but they could be changed and improved to satisfy human needs. Such thoughts separated him from the socialists (*q.v.*), whose determinism saw only one direction in which laws could change. Nevertheless, other of Mill's writings, heavily influenced by his spirited wife's views and experiences, persuaded left-leaning readers that Mill was one of them. *On Liberty* (1859), *Considerations on Representative Government* (1860), and *Dissertations and Discussions* (1859-1875) moved freely into libertarian attitudes. Best known among the radical-minded was *The Subjection of Women* (1869), which gave so decorous a thinker a true place as a pioneer. Friedrich Hayek (*q.v.*) was much taken with Mill and, in addition to his own *John Stuart Mill and Harriet Taylor* (1957), wrote the foreword to Michael St. John Packe's *The Life of John Stuart Mill* (1954). See also R. L. Heilbroner, *The Worldly Philosophers* (1953). See also M. Cowling, *Mill and Liberalism* (1963); and Arnold, Matthew.

**Minimum Wage Law,** see Wages, "Workfare"

**Minorities,** the most momentous factor in American life, though not realized as such till the post-Civil War era. It was then that the "New Immigration" (*q.v.*) raised a strong sense of alarm that "Americanism" was being threatened by a strange, alien, and numerous, people, difficult to assimilate into the social structure. Although there had been some such feeling with respect to the Irish in earlier decades, the power of English and Scottish emigrations had been such as to make them more than a match for such other minorities as Indians, Mexicans, Jews, and the humbly based slave and free-born Negro communities. The influx of increased numbers of Italians, Poles, Russian Jews, Germans and the smaller influx of Chinese and Japanese roused a xenophobia which expressed itself in malice, efforts to prevent "native" neighborhoods from being infringed upon by such elements, organization of an American Protective Association, and political motions to limit immigration and make the acquisition of citizenship harder to obtain. Although the Catholicism of many of immigrants was an acute worry to the more fundamentalist (*q.v.*) Protestant denominations, the goal of a majority of Catholic parishioners was not to foist their feelings and ways upon their neighbors, but rather to be assimilated to the ideals of their new homeland. During the Progressive era (*q.v.*) numerous public servants and educators made efforts to aid them in their endeavor. World War I brought the government into this enterprise, trusting, through "Americanization" classes, to instill a sense of the nation's heritage and ideals. Affluence in the 1920s created wealthy classes among the "minority" elements as well as the more traditional ones. Indigence in the 1930s created unity between afflicted "native" elements and those of more recent vintage. Jews had long been discriminated against and, though in relatively small numbers, credited with enormous wealth and power in disproportion. They and other "minority" communities soon became visible, however, as requiring political and even social respect because of their commanding positions in politics, industry, science, and the arts. The concentration camps set up for Japanese-Americans during World War II, though defended as a wartime measure, called forth a widespread appreciation of their record as citizens, and entered into postwar readjustments which acted to diminish old attitudes. Realization that Catholic-related people made up some one-quarter of the population was chastening to nativist pride. The civil rights (*q.v.*) drive of the 1960s and after, buttressed by government, undermined many old barriers, and raised question of individual rights as distinguished from old nativist presumptions. The new conservativism repudiated old, prideful racial judgments. It asked for quality and a respect for laws and traditions, and denounced demagogery, whether by oldline nativists or newer, self-styled minority leaders. Of interest was the fact that traditional goals of "assimilation" has become questionable, for lack of certainty as to what those goals might be. Ought ambitious Indians become "Americans"? (Indian partisans now referred to them as "native Americans".) Or were they happier with ancient Indian rituals and beliefs? What was the culture of an "Hispanic"?—What connected the Spanish-speaking Mexican and the Spanish-speaking Cuban in America? Older requirements of citizenship had assumed a respect for those who had made the American Revolution, and for those who had preserved its goals in the Civil War. But it was evident that the growing influence of minorities was bound to affect the definition of an American.

**Miranda vs. Arizona** (1966), see Warren, Earl

**Mises, Ludwig von** (1881-1973), leader of the so-called Austrian School of economists and, with F. A. Hayek and Milton Friedman (*qq.v.*), a leading conservative theoretician of free-market economics. Mixing humanistic values with economic analyses, he published such works as *Theory of Money and Credit* (1912), *Omnipotent Government* and *Bureaucracy* (both in 1944), and *Human Action* (1949). His *Socialism* (1922) was especially useful to conservatives, publicizing their opposition to trends and techniques furthering the system. The Ludwig von Mises Lectures were a continuing feature at Hillsdale College (*q.v.*).

**Mobil Oil,** see Oil

**Moderation,** see "Progressive Moderation"

**Modern Age**, founded in 1957 by Russell Kirk (*q.v.*) as an intellectual organ concerned for culture as well as for conservative principles generally. Kirk served as its editor until 1960, and kept in touch with its spirit and contributors thereafter. *Modern Age* kept in mind the distinguished careers of the *North American Review* (*q.v.*) in America and T. S. Eliot's *The Criterion* abroad, and received articles on social and cultural questions from both sectors. Contributors included such philosophic and social-minded thinkers as Richard Weaver, Ludwig von Mises, and Milton Friedman at home and, from elsewhere, Bertrand de Jouvenel (*qq.v.*), Karl Jaspers, and Wilhelm Röpke (*q.v.*). In 1982, *Modern Age* celebrated its Silver Jubilee: a solid, conservative voice in a swiftly changing nation. Kirk, reminiscing, recalled the difficulty he and his associates encountered in acquiring financial aid for publication, and the indifference displayed by financial tycoons.

**Modern Times: The World from the Twenties to the Eighties** (1983), by Paul Johnson, a fierce, detailed, and accusatory study of politics, mainly radical. It deplored a "relativistic" world, the rise of "despotic utopias," the decadence of legitimate rule, and the aggression and genocide which came with the spawning of "devils." Johnson ran through such figures as Lord Keynes, Lenin, Stalin, and others of Marxist or welfare-state associations (*qq.v.*). "Waiting for Hitler" was one of his better subheadings. A product of rising, modern Toryism (*q.v.*), the long, vivid work was the product of one who had been deeply involved with television and had also been the long-time editor of the Socialist *New Statesman*. He was a transitional (*q.v.*) figure created by disillusionment with radical hopes. *Modern Times* was written while the author was Resident Scholar at the American Enterprise Institute (*q.v.*).

**Moley, Raymond** (1886-1975), political scientist, early New Deal "brain-truster," conservative journalist. He was one of those who made an intellectual journey from Progressivism to the New Deal (*q.v.*), and then a change to the conservative viewpoint. His experience in work of national importance was long and fruitful. He had observed the Progressives dealing with corruption at the municipal and national level, and had especially observed the work of the reformer Tom Johnson in Cleveland. Moley studied at Columbia University, directed Americanization work in Ohio during World War I, and taught government at Barnard College in New York. His observations of crime and prosecutors resulted in *The Practice of Politics* (1927), *Politics and Criminal Prosecution* (1929), and *Our Criminal Courts* (1930). His resultant fame and associations brought him to Washington with a mandate from new President Franklin D. Roosevelt (*q.v.*) to prepare an agenda bearing on the economic Depression. He drew on Columbia University professors, who prepared memoranda on approaches to aspects of the crisis. An advocate of moderate action in connection with big business, Moley found himself farther and farther away from the more drastic policies involved in anti-trust actions, Supreme Court "packing," and other New Deal policies. He moved from Washington discussions to a long association with *Newsweek* and the founding and editing of the moderate *Today*. *After Seven Years* (1939) and *The First New Deal* (1966) summed up increasingly critical retrospects of the New Deal. *The American Cen-*

*tury of John C. Lincoln* (1962), Lincoln being an industrialist, affirmed Moley's commitment to free enterprise. By 1962 he had long been a Republican. *The Republican Opportunity in 1964* spelled out criticism of matured welfare-state politics. He wrote *The American Legion Story* (1966), with a foreword by J. Edgar Hoover (*q.v.*). See also his *How To Keep Our Liberty: A Program for Political Action* (1952) and his posthumous autobiography, edited by Frank Freidel, *Realities and Illusions* (1980).

**Molnar, Thomas** (1921- ), born in Hungary, a student of French and world literature, contributor to the *National Review* (*q.v.*). A critic of disorder, he studied the career of the Catholic monarchist Georges Bernanos, the state of education, and of religion. Among his writings were *The Decline of the Intellectual* (1962), *Authority and Its Enemies* (1976), and *Sartre: Ideologue of Our Time* (1968). See also his *Utopia: The Perennial Heresy* (1967).

**Monopoly,** a haunting prospect to 19th-century Americans, with its threat to opportunity for anyone poor or even of moderate wealth. The Jacksonian (*q.v.*) war on the Second Bank of the United States gained popularity by government charter. In the post-Civil War era, would-be monopolists sought, not governmental help, but government non-interference in their "private" ventures. Trusts (*q.v.*) became the instrument for business expansion to proportions threatening to independent ventures. In the 20th century, attention shifted from anti-trust measures to regulation (*q.v.*), with government agencies empowered to control massive combines. The growth of such agencies into complex bureaucracies (*q.v.*) raised new questions of control. That the will toward expansion was rooted not only in business but in people was shown by the long-term popularity of a game called "Monopoly," the purpose of which was to gain the winner a monopoly of the board's holdings. In 1983 a court ruled that the manufacturers of the game could not legally control the commercial use of the word "monopoly."

**Mont Pélèrin Society,** an informal international group of economists, historians, and social philosophers who were brought together annually in the 1940s and after to discuss issues bearing on the free society. Friedrich A. Hayek (*q.v.*) was a leading figure. For an example of their work see *Capitalism and the Historians* (*q.v.*).

**"Moral Climate,"** a prime consideration for anyone concerned with the well-being of society. In the 1960s and after conservatives and others were dismayed by what they viewed as a breakdown in the "moral climate." Liberals and others argued that the traditional "moral climate" was inappropriate to modern society and had caused much needless suffering. The counterculture of the 1960s rebelled indiscriminately against traditional moral restraint. The 1980s saw a return to traditional values, with an attempt to adapt them to modern circumstances. The task for conservatives was to articulate these traditional values while realizing that the 1980s were not the 1880s. *Cf.* Alcoholism; Capital Punishment; Capone, Al; Racketeers; Cartels; Homosexuality; Monopoly; Patriotism; Rackets; Youth.

**Moral Majority,** led by Rev. Jerry Falwell (*q.v.*), a Fundamentalist (*q.v.*) and Evangelical enterprise, but looking beyond the inspirational goals of such ministers as Rev. Billy Graham. Falwell's purpose was to mobilize millions of citizens in defense of religious practices and the family and to employ the ballot and political pressure to those ends. By July 1980 he had registered 2.5 million new voters in a single year. His target was 5 million by election day of that year. Although the base of the Moral Majority was Protestant, its leadership welcomed Catholics and Jews concerned for their causes. Richard Viguerie (*q.v.*) believed it was possible to mobilize up to 85 million voters who could demand and gain the kind of laws and society they felt they needed, of which they were being deprived. See, however, Majority. See also R .C. Liebman and Robert Wuthnow, eds., *The New Christian Right* (1983).

**Morality,** see "Moral Climate"

**Mordell, Albert,** see Classics

**More, Paul Elmer** (1864-1937), a proponent of the New Humanism (*q.v.*), whose work is a monument to it. He was a native of St. Louis, a graduate of its Washington University. Too little known is his stormy youth, which had him struggling with his spirit and goals as a romantic and unattached idealist. At Harvard at age twenty-eight he met Irving Babbitt (*q.v.*), with whom he developed an intellectual sympathy. They agreed that they sought standards in literary study and understanding. Although this was essentially the task Matthew Arnold (*q.v.*) had set out to accomplish, More was both more intrinsically remote from his society, and increasingly clearer on the need for linking religious dedication to his quest for a moral society, than was either Arnold or Babbitt. Moreover, he equipped himself for communicating his findings by long services as editor and writer. He began with verse, troubled autobiographical fiction, and *A Century of Indian Epigrams*. He taught Sanskrit and classical literature at Bryn Mawr College. He became literary editor of the distinguished *Independent*, then of the *New York Evening Post*. He had already withdrawn himself to the Shelburne woods in New England for contemplation in the manner of Thoreau. In 1909 he became editor of the *Nation*; by then his own prose had been honed, and he was deeply learned in languages and literary lore. The Shelburne Essays (1904-1921; 1928-1936) were his claim to fame, comprising a long series of essays on England and America, a tracing of principles and ideas from ancient Greece, and his magisterial survey of religions and their major interpreters. These essays are primarily products of pre-World War I America, and were well-regarded at the time for their scholarship and lucid presentation. A key element in his work was his reconciliation of pagan and Christian thought based on the Incarnation: momentous to a believer. More was little touched culturally by the Progressive Era (*q.v.*), but he came into head-on collision with the experiments, outlook, and prose—cynical, popular, Freudian—of the 1920s. The age saw his humanism as an impediment to reality and the free spirit. Mencken (*q.v.*) acknowledged his scholarship, but saw him as "[s]teadily, ploddingly, vaguely...continu[ing] to preach the gloomy gospel of tightness and restraint." More was attacked for his denunciation, in his *Demon of the Absolute* (1928), of John Dos Passos's (*q.v.*) tender *Manhattan Transfer* as "an explosion in a cesspool." The young rebels won the day; their Twenties (*q.v.*) were established as a high water mark of American writing. Although conservatives paid lip-service to More, and Russell Kirk (*q.v.*) more than lip-service, More's actual life and experience did not penetrate public consciousness and criticism significantly. And yet there were uncertain areas in the general forgetfulness. More's follower Robert Shafer, in his *Paul Elmer More and American Criticism* (1935), courageously printed a short selection from the writers who demeaned More: Mencken, Van Wyck Brooks, Ludwig Lewisohn, Francis Hackett, Ernest Boyd, among others. It is interesting to note that Brooks totally reversed his views of the time, Mencken's role as a literary critic faded, Lewisohn's reputation declined precipitously, and Hackett and Boyd could not survive their time. Thus, the field was open for revaluations. See also A. H. Dakin, *Paul Elmer More* (1960); F. X. Duggan, *Paul Elmer More* (1966).

**Morgan, Arthur E.,** see Bellamy, Edward

**Morgan, John Pierpont** (1837-1913), a financier once so famous that his initials of "J. P." were recognizable as belonging only to him. With John D. Rockefeller ("Old J. D.") he became a symbol of monopoly (*q.v.*). His reputation was somewhat more negative than Rockefeller's because of his lesser interest in public-service endowments, and because of a "money trust" Congressional investigation in 1912 which ominously suggested that Morgan had undue powers over the fortunes of ordinary people. In addition, events were bruited about which tended to darken the image of Morgan as a representative financier; one of the most damning involved the so-called Hall-Carbine transaction. It had Morgan, as a young man during the Civil War, purchasing a lot of condemned rifles from the government and selling it back at inflated prices to General John C. Frémont, then operating in Missouri. The tale was repeated and embellished in several decades of liberal writings, including the esteemed Gustavus Myers's *History of the Great American Fortunes* (1909-1910, later in the well-circulated Modern Library edition), and in the then-liberal John T. Flynn's (*q.v.*) *Men of Wealth* (1941). Although the standard account was denounced in a biography of Morgan by his son-in-law Herbert Satterlee in 1939, this had made no impression. In 1941, however, a Morgan partner, R. Gordon Wasson, set himself to examine the tale in detail. In a private printing of *The Hall-Carbine Affair: A Study in Contemporary Folklore*, he produced endless detail from official sources to indicate that, not only was it a legend far removed from the facts, but its sponsors had done no more than copy each other's allegations. Morgan became known in later decades, not for his business dealing, but for his munificence, which stirred memories of the nobles of Renaissance Italy.

**Morley, Felix** (1894- ), conservative editor and author. Of a Quaker family, he followed his concern for peace and distaste for Communism to become a co-founder of *Human Events* (*q.v.*). A Rhodes Scholar and foreign correspondent during World War I, Morley became a widely informed newspaperman and Pulitzer-Prize-winning editor whose friendships included Herbert Hoover, Robert A. Taft, William Henry Chamberlin, and John Dos Passos (*qq.v.*)—among others who contributed to the new conservatism of post-World War II years. As editor of the *Washington Post* (1933-1940) before its leftward turn, and president of Haverford College (1940-1945), he thought of himself not as an isolationist, but as a non-interventionist (*qq.v.*). He held with Hoover that peace should be maintained by regional powers, protecting the United States from overseas involvement. Morley was an associate with the Brookings Institution before its turn to partisan liberalism, and then with the American Enterprise Institute (*q.v.*). He was slow to abandon hope for the League of Nations, and sought peace beyond the Munich Pact. With the journalist Frank C. Hanighan—co-author of the well-read *Merchants of Death* (1934), an expose of the munitions industry—Morley began *Human Events* (1944) as a weekly newsletter which followed social trends and Congress, notably in connection with Communism's plottings and advance. They were joined by Henry Regnery (*q.v.*) as business manager, and drew together such peace advocates as Hoover, the socialist Norman Thomas, and Oswald Garrison Villard of the *Nation*. The American Enterprise Institute sponsored a series of *Human Events* pamphlets which helped define it as a Washington-based conservative force. Morley's *The Power of the People* (1949) and *Freedom and Federalism* (1959), averse to an over-centralized state, were solid studies. Morley also edited *The Necessary Conditions for a Free Society* (1963), with aid from the William Volker Fund. It sponsored many conservative projects, including the Mont Pélèrin Society (*q.v.*). Morley's autobiography, *For the Record* (1979), was an intimate account of a conservative career.

**Moscow Trials** (1936), a turning point in Western attitudes toward Soviet Russia as a "Great Experiment" which might show the world the way to a better future for "workers" and others. Although well-known spokesmen for an older liberalism and radicalism refused to be swayed, the nightmare of false confessions, the impact of Arthur Koestler's *Darkness at Noon* (1940), and revelations of Stalin's (*q.v.*) barbaric rule turned such consciences of the West as John Dos Passos (*q.v.*) from the older faith and prepared them for an acceptance of conservative ideas. See *Up from Communism* and Transition, Figures in.

**"Muckraking,"** a vital part of the Progressive era (*q.v.*), and like it subject to revaluation in terms of its social impact and direction; see Filler, DASC. Muckraking seemed "radical" in its time, circa 1902-1914, being concerned about municipal problems, state and Federal policies and their manipulators, and the hard-to-control corporations which, appealing to free-enterprise principles, asked government and law to keep out of their private enterprises. Muckrakers made famous by their exposés included Upton Sinclair, whose novel *The Jungle* described harmful and oppressive conditions in the Chicago stockyards of the time; Lincoln Steffens, whose *The Shame of the Cities* told of fraudulent "rings" operating in various locales; Ida M. Tarbell, whose *The Standard Oil Company* culled vast quantities of information to find the Rockefeller (*q.v.*) organization in need of social controls; and David Graham Phillips whose *The Treason of the Senate* occasioned Theodore Roosevelt's (*q.v.*) denunciation of "muckrakers." Such works, written in terms which entitled them to a place in literature (*q.v.*), resulted in the implementation of laws intended to serve society, and agencies intended to further those laws. Although they contributed to American traditions of reform (*q.v.*), and were recalled by early New Dealers (*q.v.*), it would be inaccurate to put muckrakers and Progressives in the category of welfare-state (*q.v.*) advocates. Most surviving figures in Progressivism were too individualistic to support New Deal measures, even when they were presented as stopgap measures. Later welfare-state partisans who saw Progressive reforms as too little termed them essentially conservative. Yet oddly the muckrakers received no more regard from the newer conservatives themselves. A contemporary offshoot of classic muckraking focuses on sensationalistic accounts of celebrities and their alleged doings. "Investigative" reporting, another offshoot, has produced various books, but most of them seem partisan or ephemeral. Whether the combination of insight and authority of the muckrakers would inspire a more responsible train of authors is unclear. Filler, *Appointment at Armageddon* (1976).

**Muggeridge, Malcolm** (1903- ), British journalist, celebrity and Christian apologist. The son of a socialist, he attended Cambridge University, and received modest teaching assignments—which, however, enabled him to visit India and Egypt. The *Manchester Guardian* soon sent him as correspondent to the Soviet Union, where he was disillusioned with Communism. His writing had been well received, but his distaste for "utopias" (*q.v.*) made him an outsider among radicals and liberals, his difficulties creating a caustic, exaggerated style which would make him famous, and which appeared in *In a Valley of This Restless Mind* (1938). *The Thirties* (1940) reflected his long view, which mixed peremptory judgments with vivid portraiture. Service with the Secret Service during the 1939-1945 war increased his circle of knowledge and acquaintances. Appointed editor of *Punch* in 1952, he revitalized it while rousing storms of controversy and himself becoming a celebrity. His appointment with *Punch* was not renewed in 1957, but Muggeridge by then sought time for his writing and opinions. He became a BBC favorite—somewhat analogous to Eric Hoffer (*q.v.*) in America, but to greater effect—as he interviewed celebrities and offered mordant views on social and international matters. He continued to incite hatred and disagreement, but now he had supporters. His developed Christianity made him one of the most visible laymen in media. Beginning with *Jesus Rediscovered* (1969), Muggeridge issued books which served the conservative cause. His *Chronicles of Wasted Time* (1972- ) were well received for their candor in personal relations and their views of famous authors, politicians, and others he had known or whose careers he had followed. His entrance into the Catholic Church in 1983 was followed closely by journalists and readers; critics claimed that he was more an entertainer than an opinion-maker. Ian Hunter, *Malcolm Muggeridge: A Life* (1980); John Bright-Holmes, ed., *Like It Was: In the Diaries of Malcolm Muggeridge* (1981).

**Mugwump,** see Bierce, Ambrose

**Munson, Lyle H.,** see Bookmailer, The

**Murphy, George** (1902- ), entertainer and politician. His successful run for the U. S. Senate from California in 1964 broke the ground for his friend Ronald Reagan's run for governor of the state two years later. Murphy's foes labored hard to portray him as the song-and-dance man he had indeed been for many years. But he had come from substantial family and a famous father, had attended Yale (where he had studied engineering), and, while famous himself as a motion-picture star, had been Reagan's predecessor as president of the Screen Actors Guild. With Reagan he had battled Communist influence in the union. He had, moreover, been deeply involved in Republican politics as an organizer of events, and had known its principals and their relations as well as the issues of California politics. As Senator he was involved in a range of issues and consistently conservative, which he explicated in his autobiography, written with Victor Lasky (*q.v.*), "*Say...Didn't You Used to Be George Murphy?*" (1970).

**Myth, Allegory, and Gospel** (1974), edited by John Warwick Montgomery, a major effort by Christian scholars to explicate the Gospel content in the work of writers of myth and science fiction. The editor was a professor of history, theology, and literature. In his introduction he related the writers covered in the book to other writers such as the Conrad of *Lord Jim* and the Beckett of *Waiting for Godot*. Russell Kirk's (*q.v.*) "Chesterton, Madmen, and Madhouses" surveyed Chesterton's (*q.v.*) fantasies as striving "to defend the hedges of that one spot which is Eden." Edmund Fuller, a journalist and teacher, author of *Affirmations of God and Man* (1967), saw C. S. Lewis (*q.v.*) as a prophet of the moon landings and undaunted by them as a challenge to Christian faith; Montgomery himself explicated Lewis's Narnian series as children's books and as Christian allegory. Clyde S. Kilby, author of *The Christian World of C. S. Lewis* (1965), examined "Mythics and Christian Elements in [J. R. R.] Tolkien" (*q.v.*) and found connections between his fantasy of Middle Earth—with its elves, dwarves, hobbits, and men—and Lewis's Narnia. Chad Walsh, who wrote also on Lewis, assessed one of the lesser-known of the Lewis circle, Charles Williams. Lewis himself had honored his colleague and friend with *Essays Presented to Charles Williams* [1947]. Williams's fantasies differed from those of his better-known friends in not being set in imagined lands or on Mars and Venus, but on earth. *Shadows of Ecstasy* (1933) dealt with an imaginary uprising in Africa, in which Walsh found spiritual and predictive values. *All Hallow's Eve* (1945) mingled the living with the dead. Despite the relatively minor acclaim he received, Williams's work persisted in print, along with his scholarly essays on English poets, Dante, and even travelers in Africa.

**Myth of a Guilty Nation, The** (1922), by A. J. Nock (*q.v.*), an astringent summary of the intrigue and propaganda which foisted the burden of responsibility for the outbreak and continuation of World War I upon a prostrated Germany. Nock's articles, published originally in his *The Freeman*, noted the war budgets of Great Britain, France, Russia, Germany and the Austro-Hungarian Empire before the declarations of war. Thus, the anti-German forces had been anything but "unprepared" for hostilities. Germany itself had been far from belligerent in preparations or diplomacy. Nock's book complemented J. M. Keynes's (*q.v.*) *The Economic Consequences of the Peace* (1919). Keynes spelled out how judging Germany the sole guilty nation and saddling it with intolerable financial "reparations" would result in momentous instabilities. The book made Keynes world-famous. Although Nock's book furnished ammunition for American intellectuals' "disillusionment" (*q.v.*) it did little for softening American attitudes towards Germans, or increasing sophistication respecting them. Financial "plans" for saving the German economy were intended to save the country from falling to the Communists. Such developments only confirmed Nock in his contempt for Americans and their politicians.

# N

**Nation, The**, see Godkin, E. L.; More, Paul Elmer

**National Association for the Advancement of Colored People (NAACP)**, see Blacks; Negroes

**National Civic Federation**, a non-governmental attempt to create a mediation instrument in the 1900s for adjudicating labor-industry disputes, which too often resulted in savage strikes with violence from both sides. A basic problem was unionization itself, which a large percentage of employers opposed. The NCF drew support from both organized labor and industry, but never enough to prevent the most strategic confrontations. Marcus A. Hanna (*q.v.*), though a large employer himself, believed in the necessity for unions as a brake on radical (*q.v.*) actions, and was a strong supporter of NCF. Samuel Gompers (*q.v.*), exploring all means for advancing the cause of organized labor, also played a role in the NCF. The creation of a Labor Department in government weakened the NCF, as did the Clayton Act (1914), which ruled out actions against labor organizations under the anti-trust (*q.v.*) laws. The NCF turned to seeking support from employers as an anti-radical agency, by which time it had lost any national significance.

**National Origins Act,** see Immigration, New Immigration

**National Review,** from its founding in 1955 the central journal of American conservatism. It established its direction early, once it had been able to break out of its internal debate respecting the meaning of conservatism, liberty, the intent of the Constitution, and other matters vital to its editors. Its contributors, and readers, often sought means of extending their influence over the best of the general public without loss of principles. William F. Buckley, Jr. was his magazine's dominating figure from the beginning, and sought associates and controversies which would catch eyes and command attention. His personal growth as a public figure went hand-in-hand with the growth of the *Review's* position among publications. Although its early sense of being beleaguered among powerful liberal forces in government, in the press, and in the midst of a bemused liberal public softened somewhat, increasing wit at the expense of bitterness and irony, it never entirely disappeared, even when conservatives were in the seats of power. A significant percentage of its editors and contributors was Catholic, but it was clear from its sense of issues that the *Review* would not allow itself to be dictated to by the Church. One internal crisis concerned Buckley's brother-in-law, L. Brent Bozell. With Buckley, Bozell had defended McCarthy (*q.v.*), debated the Brown (*q.v.*) decision, and execrated *The Warren* (*q.v.*) *Revolution* (1966). By then, he had become impatient with the *Review* as insufficiently Catholic and in a letter of May 3, 1966 held that statements by Buckley in the *Review* would "legalize euthanasia or genocide." Buckley responded that he was trying to read Vatican II's (*q.v.*) Declaration on Religious Liberty in terms of a pluralistic society. Bozell's fading from the *Review* furnished one sign of its movement toward dimensionality on the American scene. The *Review* followed national affairs intensively, suffering setbacks, as with Spiro Agnew and Richard Nixon (*qq.v.*). It was an early partisan of Ronald Reagan (*q.v.*). Its foreign policy was firmly based on anti-Communism. It held

Detente (*q.v.*) to be a trap. It enraged liberals with its consistent and often ingenious support for regimes the liberals deemed reactionary or worse. Buckley developed a national syndicated column, which he shared with *Review* readers. He also drew personal mail to which he responded independently of the "Letters" section. The high journalistic standards were supplemented with generally witty cartoons, and the highly talented verse of W. H. von Dreele (*q.v.*). The range of contributors extended from those who had been there in the beginning to new writers on a variety of themes, giving less of a sense of parochialism than of coherence. Cultural comment was sometimes political, often individual, and as often as not dependable. It was curious that editors who emphasized tradition had so little occasion to employ it in their columns, or to recognize pros and cons. Critics tended to follow Buckley in liking or disliking works. A notable example was Buckley's dislike of James Gould Cozzens' (*q.v.*) *By Love Possessed* (1957). Though it was by a well-regarded conservative writer, and had been well received, Buckley could not understand why people liked it. His complaint echoed that of the veteran dilettante Dwight Macdonald. Another *Review* scribe used the occasion of Archibald MacLeish's death to deride his poetry, inappositely in the regular section headed "R. I. P." There were rarely criticisms of such opinions, perhaps because readers were sufficiently divided on cultural matters not to feel the need of a flow of comment. Where politics and art joined easily, the *Review* reflected consensus, as in admiration of Solzhenitsyn (*q.v.*) and contempt for Henry Steele Commager, the *New York Times*'s liberal historical apologist. Russell Kirk (*q.v.*) provided a binding thread with his quarter-century of alerts on the state of education. James Burnham continued as a doyen in anti-Communist theory. Jeffrey Hart (*q.v.*) summed up the *Review's* outlook and programs in mid-course, and continued to grow with it. John Chamberlain, Henry Hazlitt, and Ralph de Toledano (*qq.v.*), among others, gave the *Review* a spirit of continuity.

**National Review Reader** (1957), ed., John Chamberlain (*q.v.*), an early collection of articles and comments which emphasized principles and overall views centered on the evil of Soviet policies abroad and Federal policies at home. Nelson Rockefeller and Eisenhower (*qq.v.*) were seen as examples of "Progressive Moderation," which maintained New Deal principles while promising conservative action. Leading contributors included William F. Buckley, Jr., Russell Kirk, Wilhelm Röpke, L. Brent Bozell, James Burnham, Frank S. Meyer, Willmoore Kendall, Ralph De Toledano, Ludwig von Mises, William S. Schlamm, Erik von Kuehnelt-Leddihn, and Richard M. Weaver (*qq.v.*). The *National Review* was an early haven for disillusioned Communists and fellow-travelers (*q.v.*). An amusing title contributed by Max Eastman and reminiscent of the confessions which highlighted the Stalin purge trials was "I Acknowledge My Mistakes"—mistakes which had gone on from Eastman's bohemian days for over thirty-five years. John Dos Passos (*q.v.*), contributing, had become disillusioned with Communism more quickly. There were numerous landmarks in the *Reader*, such as Kendall's reproach of the then-liberal John Roche, whose analysis of "The State of Our Civil Liberties" approved of loyalty but not "Kafkaesque McCarthyism" (*q.v.*). Priscilla L. Buckley repudiated opponents of fluoridation (*q.v.*); it was not a Communist conspiracy, though there was a case against involuntary fluoridation of public water. The *Review* saw itself as resisting towering liberal forces which Burnham saw as including "conservative Communists" throughout the world who were winning their way through "popular fronts." One veteran conservative from the old *Saturday Evening Post*, surveying the Supreme Court (*q.v.*) acting as reformer, as in desegregation cases, declared "The Right to Nullify," calling paradoxically on Andrew Jackson's (*q.v.*) defiance of the Supreme Court for support.

**National Rifle Association**, see Gun Control

**National Security League**, see Preparedness

**Nationalities**. To a great extent the immigration of nationalities to America determined the development of the nation. This immigration divided naturally into colonial, national, and "New Immigration" (*q.v.*) periods, the first two drawing Western and Northern European people, the latter Mediterranean and eastern European nationalities. Although St. Augustine and Santa Fe could quarrel over which was the "first" American city, Spaniards were not the most determined early settlers, nor did they infuse many later Hispanic (*q.v.*) peoples in America with their traditions. Nor did French influence survive strongly on the American mainland. The German immigration created special problems during World War I. Indians became a species of immigrants in their own country. Mexican-Americans proliferated in the Southwest. Conservatives advocated law and immigration controls; liberals veered between generous welcome and labor's fear of low-paid competitors. Most potent in the major timespan of colonial settlement and expansion were the English and Scotch-Irish, with the Irish attaining significance as well as persecution during the national era. Traditions of xenophobia and acceptance developed as blacks and indentured servants (*qq.v.*) were imported for labor, as the Irish were feared for Catholicism. See Filler, *The Rise and Fall of Slavery in America* (1980). See also Immigration.

**Nationalization**, see "Privatization"

**Native Americans**, a curious neologism, prominent among radicals of the 1960s and liberals sympathetic to them. It was intended to substitute for "Indians," which was regarded as somehow demeaning. Certainly Indians had settled on what became American soil long before European settlers arrived. But at that time it was not known as America. Moreover, the Indians themselves were not ultimately "native" to the land, their ancestors most likely having come to the continent across the Bering Strait from Asia. Clearly "Native Americans" was as inaccurate and confusing as "Indians," though the latter term at least had the virtue of accepted and long-standing use.

**Nativism**, an American Protestant reaction to the influx of Catholic (*q.v.*) Irish immigrants beginning in the 1830s and 1840s. Alarmed at the rising social and political influence of the immigrants (*q.v.*), in 1844 concerned Protestants formed an American Republican Association, heightening "nativist" consciousness and helping to bring on bloody clashes with Catholics. The next year a national convention adopted the name of Native American Party, advocating restriction of immigration. The program, which was to manifest itself throughout the century, had its next landmark in the establishment of the American Party, more widely known as the Know-Nothings (*q.v.*).

**NATO**, acronym for the North Atlantic Treaty Organization founded in 1949. Though conservatives were made impatient by its relatively moderate support of causes they deemed worthy of strong support, NATO was a rallying point for defense of Western nations from the Soviet Union, and as such implemented their defense plans and actions.

**Natural Law**, significant in social philosophy as underscoring the human base for "Positive Law," which, if ill-conceived, would transgress human needs and natural rights (*q.v.*). Developed in Roman law and philosophy, the concept of natural law was seen variously by social philosophers and religious thinkers. A. P. d'Enrèves, *Natural Law* (1951). Formative influences were Aristotle, Aquinas (*qq.v.*) and Cicero.

**Natural Rights**, a product of rising civilizations and particular views of human nature. The concept affected both liberal and conservative attitudes toward human nature, the liberal seeing dazzling possibilities for expansion of human potentials, the conservative warning against the excesses which they might unleash. The Declaration of Independence (1776) (*q.v.*) seems expansive in its faith; in retrospect, at least, the French Declaration of the Rights of Man (1789) seems utopian (*q.v.*). Natural *law* seems a more realistic point of departure for discussing human destiny, since "rights" could prove illusory in fact. The later Universal Declaration of Human Rights issued from the United Nations (*q.v.*) was marked by its impotence to influence events. For a pioneer work, see David Ritchie, *Natural Rights* (1894). See also Jacques Maritain, The *Rights of Man and Natural Law* (1943); Julius Stone, *Human Law and Human Justice* (1965).

**Nazi-Soviet Pact of 1939.** It literally stunned the world. Stalin had continuously abused socialists for having paved the way for fascists and for being fascists themselves; in his memorable phrase, they were "social fascists," the other side of the coin. As memorable was the comment by V. M. Molotov, who negotiated the Pact, that fascism was "a matter of taste." It soon became evident that it was also a matter of land; shortly after the signing of the Pact, Nazi and Soviet troops divided Poland between themselves. Interesting were the defenses offered by American Communists once they were assured that the Pact was indeed in operation. The American Communist press held that it was all a brilliant ploy for deceiving the Nazis while gathering forces for a counterattack. It also claimed that the laxity of western powers forced "the Workers' Fatherland" to defend itself. In addition, it was the German people as longing for peace, just as did the Soviet people. Finally, it revealed that the Soviet action had emancipated its portion of Poland by taking it away from tyrants. Interesting also was the American Communist encouragement of pacifism in the period after the Pact. Some of these pacifist writings resurfaced during the Vietnam (*q.v.*) protests of the 1960s. When Germany invaded the Soviet Union, however, pacifism was quickly forgotten.

**Negative Income Plan**, see Friedman, Milton

**Negroes,** see also Blacks. The place of Negroes in American society has been a massive challenge to its traditions and aspirations. Negroes were long aided in their quests by conservative forces in education, philanthropy, and law, but they became of less direct concern to post-World War II conservatives, who emphasized order and tradition. Conservatives in pre-Civil War eras belonged to two major groups. Some, both in the North and the South, held Negroes to be a different and lesser breed of humanity calling all of them "blacks," even when Negroes who were all but white. Other conservatives felt that religion and freedom were in jeopardy so long as Negroes were deprived of religion and the freedom to grow and improve. Southern conservatives included patriarchs of varied quality, mavericks—who made little difference in basic attitudes toward slaves or free Negroes, and the slaveless white poor—who were often more antagonistic toward slaves than the well-to-do. Northerners who had observed the process of emancipation in their states from Revolutionary times through the 1820s employed free Negroes, contributed to education and religious activities, and observed law as it contributed to public order and their own well-being. Uniting them with Southern compatriots was the dream of sending Negroes to colonize Africa. In effect, this would rid the nation of the problem and lessen the pressure on American tenets of justice and liberty. The more conscientious or radical among Northerners helped rescue fugitive slaves, like Benjamin Lundy who dreamed of colonization within the United States or adjacent areas where Negroes could enjoy autonomy, and helped further emancipation and civil attitudes toward Negroes. The abolitionist movement abandoned conservative approaches, ignoring the fears of Negro competition by white laborers, and attracted reformers of every kind. Women seeking civil expression became a powerful force favoring emancipation, producing hundreds of famous crusaders for both emancipation and female suffrage. Negroes themselves engaged in abolitionist and related activities with mainly conservative goals of civility, freedom, and increased opportunity. During the Civil War, they fought for the right to participate in battle; in the South, arch-conservatives felt that employing Negroes as soldiers degraded their war aims. The post-Civil War era brought out Northern philanthropists, who sent school teachers South to open classes for the Negro freedmen. Negro leaders like Daniel Payne (*q.v.*) insisted on education as the open door to new freedoms. The Republican Party became the bastion for Negro political opportunity; in the South, the educated and well-to-do classes fought to maintain their control by patronizing Negroes. The Negroes there were demagogically berated by such ambitious racists as Thomas Watson, who grew wealthy by flattering the poor whites. A major achievement was the battle against hookworm subsidized by John D. Rockefeller (*q.v.*). Hookworm was a debilitating disease which attacked Southern whites and Negroes. Southern battles against Negro equality culminated in the "separate but equal" (*q.v.*) doctrine. Negro partisans argued that it meant separate, but hardly equal. Self-help (*q.v.*) became a major Negro community goal which its ministers, editors, publishers, educators, writers, business people, politicians, and others used to stir up energies and ambitions. Booker T. Washington (*q.v.*) and W. E. B. Du Bois represented the conservative and liberal extremes among Negroes. The National Association for the Advancement of Colored People and the Urban League became important organizations, employing both liberal and conservative talents and created by the Progressive (*q.v.*) impulse of the first part of the 20th century. Woodrow Wilson (*q.v.*), the first Southern President since Andrew Johnson, favored segregation, and maintained it during World War I. Negro talent flourished amid Twenties "disillusionment" (*q.v.*), but conservatism contributed little but traditional philanthropy. Negroes suffered with most of America during the Great Depression (*q.v.*). The perceived horrors of fascism (*q.v.*) encouraged desegregation during World War II, and the years after World War II saw positive treatment of Negroes as individuals and as a community in books, films, and stage plays. President Truman desegregated the Armed Forces, and the 1954 Supreme Court decision in *Brown vs. Board of Education* struck down the "separate but equal" doctrine. The South resisted desegregation and Negro equality. But the civil-rights drives of the 1960s and resulting federal and state legislation helped contribute to bringing Negroes into the mainstream of American life. By the 1970s "blacks" had become the preferred term to denote American Negroes, both inside and outside the Negro community. Carter G. Woodson, *Negro Orators and Their Orations* (1925); Rayford W. Logan and Michael R. Winston, eds., *Dictionary of American Negro Biography* (1982).

**Neibuhr, Reinhold**, see Herberg, Will; Matthews, J. B.

**Neilson, Francis** (1867-1961), social and cultural figure. Though more technically liberal in his social politics, he was a friend and associate of A. J. Nock (*q.v.*). Born in England, he became a musical and theatrical figure, a leader in the British Liberal Party, and an advocate of Henry George's "Single Tax" doctrine. A pacifist, he wrote *How Diplomats Make War* (1915). He served with Nock on *The Freeman*, himself contributing rich and flamboyant memories of New York and Bayreuth of the Gaslight era. His remembrances also gave color to the Georgeite *American Journal of Economics and Sociology*.

**Neo-Conservatives**, a small but significant element in the New Conservative alliances formed in the 1970s, made influential in cultural and political affairs. They were a product of disillusionment with both radical-socialist programs and Democratic Party developments deriving from the New Deal (*q.v.*). Neo-conservatives did not form a cohesive group. Nevertheless they came to be represented in the public eye by Irving Kristol of *The Public Interest* and Norman Podhoretz of *Commentary* (*qq.v.*). Neo-conservatives provided ideas that challenged older liberal and radical assumptions and expectations. Their critics held that they had suffered a failure of nerve due to U.S.-U.S.S.R. confrontations. Neo-conservatives responded that the facts of life had proved the bankruptcy of liberal tenets. Nathan Glazer, E. C. Banfield, James Q. Wilson, and Sidney Hook (*qq.v.*) were several neo-conservatives who wrote influential books raising questions about the working of the welfare state, crime, "affirmative action," equality, Detente (*qq.v.*), and other crucial questions separating liberals and conservatives. Jeane Kirkpatrick (*q.v.*), a neo-conservative, was in Reagan's Administration, as were others less visible for their writings and presence. The American Enterprise Institute (*q.v.*) invited many neo-conservatives to be fellows and to prepare reports on society. Precisely who would rank as a neo-conservative was subject to debate. The sociologist Daniel Bell, a former socialist, was thought by some to be a neo-conservative. But though he had proclaimed *The End of Ideology* (1960), he had also helped formulate the idea of *The Radical Right* (1955) as composed of "pseudo-conservatives," and had himself contributed to *The Radical Papers* (*q.v.*). Though many neo-conservatives had known each other for years, many having been associated at the City College of New York, differences could be perceived. Still they believed programs spawned out of the New Deal mentality to have failed. They made their peace with the free market. They saw the Soviet Union as the enemy to world security; in addition, they were unequivocal in denouncing treason, and saw virtues in patriotism. *The Neoconservatives* (1979), by *Commonweal* editor Peter Steinfels was profoundly critical of neo-conservatism, and included as neo-conservatives many figures who did not belong there—such as Daniel P. Moynihan, Lionel Trilling (*q.v.*), and Richard Hofstadter.

**Neo-Humanism**, an academic impulse, crystallized in the Twenties (*q.v.*), in protest against the reigning movement of social and cultural experimentation which produced such figures as H. L. Mencken (*q.v.*) in criticism and J. B. Watson in Behaviorism (*q.v.*) and a flood of fiction and drama which dealt with undecorous human actions and desires. Neo-humanism defined "human" as that which separated people from animals. It was hampered by the era's "disillusionment" (*q.v.*) resulting from World War I (*q.v.*) and the democratic (*q.v.*) impulses against authority and tradition it had spawned. Irving Babbitt (*q.v.*), in his Harvard lectures, contrasted the dignity of the classics with what he perceived to be the main trends of current literature. When a student reminded him of the gougings, infanticides, bloody slaughters, and other horrors to be found in Greek drama, he confessed to having not read Greek drama in some time. Such episodes and attitudes helped reduce the influence of Neo-Humanism in classrooms, and subsequent economic distress, war, and the challenge of Communist theory and practice did not help. A species of Neo-Humanism appeared in the ensuing New Criticism, which fixed on "explicating" (*q.v.*) the interior meaning of literary works. Despite such conservative New Critics as the Agrarians (*q.v.*), however, it tended to focus on such modern writers as F. S. Fitzgerald and Ernest Hemingway, and did little to revive the reverence for the classics advocated by the Neo-Humanists proper. See, however, *Chronicles of Culture; American Spectator*. L. J. A. Mercier, *American Humanism and the New Age* (1948); J. C. Jansom, ed., *The Kenyon Critics* (1967).

**Neo-Liberals**, a concept which surfaced in 1983, perhaps inspired in part by the success attained by neo-conservatives (*q.v.*). Neo-liberals believed that liberalism had fallen into decline, and that conservatism was more highly regarded by the general public. Liberal "compassion" (*q.v.*) had been emptied of meaning. Keynesian (*q.v.*) theory had become much like Marxism (*q.v.*), more approved of than examined. "Civil rights" seemed less a liberal cause than it had been in earlier decades. As a result, some 300 politicians, educators, and others gathered in 1983 under *Washington Monthly* sponsorship to reconsider their premises. They agreed that the welfare (*q.v.*) system was not operating well, that people not requiring Social Security (*q.v.*) ought not to receive it, that unions and bureaucracies (*qq.v.*) could serve their constituencies better, but that liberty and justice for the needy were still viable concepts. Clearly they felt that liberalism needed revitalization, possibly in the light of what it had sometime been. R. Rothenberg, *Neo-Liberals: Creating the New American Politics* (1984).

**Nevins, Allan** (1890-1971), one of the greatest of 20th-century historians, known for his work for half a century. Although his passion for history and his ability to organize aides took him in many directions, the core of his writing reflected love of country and faith in its progress. Following some years of journalism, he began his formal career with a masterpiece, wholly unsubsidized though it required him to travel extensively studying archives, *The American States during and after the Revolution* (1924). In 1928 he joined the faculty of Columbia University, and from there he carried on his massive projects. Among his major works, which displayed his basic conservative outlook, were *Grover Cleveland* (1932), *Hamilton Fish* (1936), *Abram S. Hewitt*, (1935), and *John D. Rockefeller: The Heroic Age of American Business* (1940) (*qq.v.*). He edited many diaries. Among the most relevant, showing the conservative viewpoint in the 19th century, was that of George Templeton Strong (1952). What became his six-volume *The Ordeal of the Union* absorbed him till his death.

**"New Barbarians, The,"** see Radicals

**New Chastity and Other Arguments Against Women's Liberation, The** (1972), by Midge Decter, a leader in anti-feminist polemics. She traced the development of the women's rights movement back to Betty Friedan's middle-class dissatisfaction, as expressed in her *The Feminine Mystique*, spawned in a time of social unrest featuring black and youth discontent. Friedan's charges of unfulfillment in housework and opportunities outside the home were taken up and expanded to include a variety of discontents with the "male-dominated society." In effect, according to Decter, Friedan really sought to create a female society. Decter saw much of feminist rhetoric (*q.v.*) as a subtle means for seeking to recapture girlhood, and, in fundamental antagonism to males as males, to recapture a form of "maidenhood" which had been lost forever in sexual deviance and excess. "Chastity" could be seen in the odd regard for medieval nunneries, the promotion of lesbianism, and the hatred of conventional sex. Many other paradoxes entered into Decter's analysis, such as protest against being a "sex object" leading to a "liberation" in which the activist was nothing but a sex object. Decter concluded with the blunt claim that the need for protection in womanhood and the child-bearing destiny required marriage, and all that went with it. See also Women, *Single Issues*, Men.

**New Conservatism, The** (1974), edited by Lewis A. Coser and Irving Howe, subtitled "A Critique from the Left." It included essays by the socialist Michael Harrington, David Spitz, the economics teacher Robert Lekachman, (who was to characterize the Reagan Administration as pressing "the politics of greed"), and others. Coser saw "neo-conservatives" (*q.v.*) as liberals who had gotten "cold feet" in the late 1960s. Irving Kristol, who had written in *Commentary* (*qq.v.*) that liberals were fighting for nothing more than status, was denounced for chamber-of-commerce "reductionism." Edward C. Banfield (*q.v.*) drew criticism for concluding, in *The Unheavenly City*, that Negro riots had been undertaken for "fun and profit." Joseph Epstein defended himself as a "democratic radical." Several of the contributors attacked inequality; equality had to be maintained as a goal despite its faults. An educator, D. K. Cohen, thought schooling was more important than I.Q.s. One of the more thoughtful essays, balancing research and analysis, was by H. F. Pitkin, "The Roots of Conservatism." It was a study of Michael Oakeshott's (*q.v.*) outlook.

**New Criticism**, a development of the post-World War II period. It claimed to avoid mere emotional responses to literature and to substitute scientific judgments of the value of work. Along with it went an emphasis on "metaphysical" poetry with its indirection, obscure allusions, and impenetrable phrases as better challenging the mind and emotions. A key figure in New Criticism was John Crowe Ransom, a Vanderbilt Agrarian (*q.v.*), though little concerned for social issues. He founded the *Kenyon Review*, at Kenyon College in Ohio, where his select contributors published their influential essays. Their technique was "explication," based on the much older "explication des textes," which had originally sought insight into such works as those of Shakespeare by studying word-usages and unconscious concerns. The new explication removed emotional response as a component of quality, and substituted images and references to determine how well the poet's verse held together. The movement was, in part, a reaction to "social significance" writing of the Depression era. In Ransom's case, it enabled him and his followers to rise above North-South history and to focus on an individual poet or even poem. The *Kenyon Review*, as well as other publications which practiced the technique, was selective in the poets it explicated. Walt Whitman was not preferred. Vachel Lindsay seemed too uncomplicated to merit analysis. T. S. Eliot (*q.v.*) merited endless analysis, however. The work of Ransom and other Agrarians narrowed the field of poetry, though other factors contributed. Allen Tate, a Ransom associate had insights and observations which would have done little harm as contributions to method, given a broader terrain; see his *Reactionary Essays on Poetry and Ideas* (1936), *Reason in Madness* (1941), and *The Forlorn Demon* (1953). New criticism captured higher education, and even affected secondary schools. In lesser hands the method became grotesque, as when high school teachers offered to show students the "secret" in a poem after they had read it. Horace Gregory's *A History of American Poetry: 1900-1940* (1946), written with his wife Marya Zaturenska, was a product of the New Criticism, and as such subject to its limitations. See also Literature, Neo-Humanism.

**New Deal, The**, recalled by conservatives as the beginning of the welfare state, rather than as an attempt to unfreeze a largely stalled economy and give heart and sustenance to its most vulnerable elements. Although efforts have been made to indicate that there was actual industrial growth during the earlier years of the Depression—indicating that the situation might have worked itself out without the commitments to welfare and government intervention which changed American directions—the argument does not take into account the long frustration which had developed during the years of President Hoover (*q.v.*), and the psychology of people who saw farm foreclosures and closed businesses and factories and demanded action. Ronald Reagan (*q.v.*) was like many young New Dealers who required years of experience to conclude that the many agencies created in the Thirties (*q.v.*) had become rapidly bureaucratized (*q.v.*) and subject to ideological constraints. The New Deal was initially introduced as a series of experiments to get sectors of the economy to distribute opportunities equitably. Thus, the original National Recovery Act (NRA) laid its stress on business (*q.v.*) rather than labor. Its evident failure to provide leadership left a vacuum which had to be filled. Many radicals (*q.v.*) perceived the stopgap nature of early New Deal endeavors and demanded sweeping measures promoting employment controlled by central authority. That the "alphabet agencies"—A.A.A., T.V.A., F.H.A., and others—hardened and became bureaucratized (*q.v.*) was unfortunate, and partially the fault of New Deal opponents who could not persuade voters that they had strong alternative programs. In the end, a public tired of the rigors of Depression, and released by the "full employment" of World War II, was unable to resist the mirage of deficit (*q.v.*) spending ("we only owe it to ourselves") and the further growth of government agencies and activities. The heritage of the old New Deal was thus lost to changing values and conditions. Basil Rauch, *History of the New Deal* (1944); M. Keller, ed., *The New Deal* (1963); K. Louchheim, ed., *The Making of the New Deal: The Insiders Speak* (1983).

**New Federalism**, a Reagan program for the 1980s, part of his drive against overbearing central government, intended to disperse power and decisions among the states. It dovetailed with his plan for "enterprise zones," (*q.v.*). This would withdraw Federal involvement in decayed city neighborhoods, releasing, it was hoped, individual intitiative among business people able and willing to establish themselves in those areas. State officials were suspicious of the "New Federalism" as shifting responsibility from Washington to themselves; the Reagan intention was indeed to do so, giving strength to the most vigorous talents among state and city officials and turning light on the most corrupt. Liberals were reluctant to see power slip away from the largely liberal bureaucracies in Washington. In the mid-1980s New Federalism seemed to have been discarded by the Reagan Administration, preoccupied with new problems and new programs.

**New Freeman, The**, see La Follette, Suzanne

**New History**. James Harvey Robinson of Columbia University touted a "new" history in 1911, and others picked up the concept for their historical essays in later decades. The basic premise was that new conditions required fresh approaches and materials for grasping and explaining new circumstances. "New" history in the 1970s and after, however, involved more radical approaches, suggesting that there was a discontinuity between past and present preventing investigation of the past. New approaches involved "conceptualization" which in effect let the investigator set up his own premises and find materials which substantiated them. This permitted him to hypothesize as suited his preconceptions. If he embraced "quantification," he could support his views with apparently mathematical precision.

**"New Immigration,"** a phenomenon of the post-Civil War (*q.v.*) decades, partially induced by the demands of new industry. It brought strains of people not previously present in significant numbers in America. Mediterranean peoples and others from Eastern Europe came in increasing waves which reached a million a year. Though mainly of peasant and rural backgrounds, they often found themselves huddled in the burgeoning cities, many in firetrap buildings especially erected for them, later to be known as "Old Law Tenements." Some were brought to the mining and lumbering camps, where their unfamiliarity with English and the law placed them first at the mercy of brutal foremen, then susceptible to the arguments of labor agitators. They themselves produced both, their troubles and psychology being too rarely told by sensitive authors. (See Literature.) Conservatives in retrospect tended to emphasize the free enterprise (*q.v.*) argument, refusing to commit themselves retrospectively to the right and wrong of particular conditions.

**New Left Today: America's Trojan Horse, The** (1971), by Phillip Abbott Luce. He was an early New Left leader, whose career from 1961 to 1965 placed him at the center of youthful (*q.v.*) Communist, Progressive Labor, pro-Cuba, and Maoist intrigues. Tired of their strong-arm methods and deceits, he repudiated them in articles and books beginning with *The New Left* (1966), and in activities involving Young Americans for Freedom (*q.v.*), the House Internal Security Committee, and lectures at the U. S. Air Force School for Counter-Insurgency. Although Luce's inside knowledge was of obvious aid to government agents and others, his revelations in terms of a larger public were more historical record than useful.

**New Liberalism**, see Liberalism

**New Meaning of Treason, The** (1949), by British litterateur Rebecca West, an early consideration of the outlook and motivations of those who held they were serving humanity by transmitting secrets of their own nations, stolen under expectations of loyalty, for transmission to the agents of the Soviet Union. Revised and brought up to date in 1965 it ranked as a classic study of the psychology of intellectuals as traitors.

**"New Poor,"** see Poor

**"New Right,"** a term used by liberals to denote conservatism and taking in conservatives, Fundamentalists, and "Moral Majority" (*qq.v.*) elements. It emphasized that, beginning with the 1970s, such groups enjoyed a higher degree of visibility and public impact than they had before. The New Right was marked by a criticism of contemporary American politics and morality and its views enjoyed wide dissemination through newspapers, radio, and television. Liberals warned that liberties were endangered by "New Right" intolerance. In fact, the "rightist" elements did not act in unison. Supply-siders emphasized other issues than the religion-centered rightists. Libertarians were sometimes as close to liberals as to conservatives. Conservatives veered between those who found Ronald Reagan dispensable, and others who did not. S. S. Hill and D. E. Owen, *The New Religious Political Right in America* (1982).

**New Right, 1960-1968: With Epilogue, 1969-1980, The** (1983), by Jonathan Martin Kolkey, an academic survey.

**New Right: We're Ready to Lead** (1980), by Richard A. Viguerie, with an introduction by Jerry Falwell, both a description of the New Right and a record of their plans and interests. It included as well autobiographical chapters about Viguerie himself, the growth of his direct mail business—a key to success in swaying voters and pressure groups—and the issues which required New Right energy and work. The New Right, Viguerie pointed out, had not created such issues as opposition to abortion and religion in the schools. Liberals, by striking at American traditions and emphasizing such single issues (*q.v.*) as civil rights, had. Viguerie wanted more, not fewer, single issues, and he wanted mass energy put into direct mailings which would draw together such constituents as the Moral Majority (*q.v.*). Although he watched Republican maneuvers intensely, he did not feel bound by the Party, which he found too unprincipled to merit confidence. A major disappointment had been the New Right's fight to save the Panama Canal (*q.v.*) for America, said Viguerie. The New Right had made massive efforts to rouse the nation to the danger of it being given away, and it had attained fine results, according to Viguerie, through direct mail. Yet the Republican Party had cooperated with the Democrats in signing giveaway treaties. Viguerie's plan was to do what the liberals had heretofore successfully done: to pursue single issues, win over groups on the basis of mutual interests, infiltrate the Democratic Party, and form coalitions. He believed in principle, holding that the Goldwater (*q.v.*) campaign of 1964 had not been the failure many claimed. It had roused conservative feelings and ambition, called their case to national attention, and stimulated the creation of durable alliances in conservative interest campaigns. Viguerie had no secrets. His book was a manual for strategy.

**"New South,"** a term identified with the Georgia journalist Henry W. Grady (1850-1889). He called for an end to old acrimonies, and looked forward to a South of industry and peace, with its freed blacks working in harmony, though in a subordinate position. The term was revived in the 1980s, describing a South reconciled to black equality and working in harmony for the betterment of all. A nuance saw a portion of the academic community vigorously researching black history and pouring scorn on the Old South (*q.v.*), apparently in tandem with another portion of the community which continued traditional research in Southern themes and treated with good humor the legend that the Old South was no more. What was common to the two elements was the awareness that the traditional South was in question, and could be approached from various standpoints. See also *Southern Partisan, The*; Agrarians, The.

**New York**, enigmatically representative of the progress of the nation. The city was significant from early Dutch times, though for decades it faced stiff competition from such other urban centers as Philadelphia to the South and Boston to the north. It was *A Hazard of New Fortunes*, according to the title of William Dean Howell's novel (1890), to leave decorous Boston's literary establishment for the turbulence of New York. The latter early in the 19th century became a center of popular literary and journalistic development. In the 1890s it responded to the currents of the New Immigration (*q.v.*), which made New York picturesque and a symbol of American opportunity and opportunism—at the head of which stood the canyons of Wall Street, which J. P. Morgan (*q.v.*) dominated. New York at this stage had its social-minded business heroes, from Lewis Tappan (*q.v.*) of pre-Civil War times to the "millionaire socialists" of the Progressive era (*q.v.*). But the larger number of wealthy and conservative New Yorkers were identified with commercialism (*q.v.*). Their influence was shaken by the Great Depression (*q.v.*), which called forth Franklin D. Roosevelt and his New Deal associates: a mixture of wealthy social-minded leaders such as Herbert H. Lehman and others such as Harry Hopkins and Frances Perkins. Nelson Rockefeller (*q.v.*) inherited their combination of faith in government intervention and administrative abilities to head an "Eastern Establishment" of liberal Republicans. In the 1960s it became one of the powerful forces in New York politics. The growth of the suburbs after World War II and the "white flight" (*q.v.*) of the 1960s and 1970s, led to widespread devastation in New York as elsewhere, but the city remained known for its influential citadels of commerce and enclaves of entertainment and conspicuous consumption (*q.v.*). *New York Magazine* became symbolic of the city's hopes and fears, with its reports on New York's joys and interests as well as crime and other urban ills. With the *New York Times* (*q.v.*) as unofficial spokesman the city's politics became identified with liberalism. New York's nationwide influence in fashion, the arts, and social politics was heavily criticized by conservatives, who aimed their scorn at such figures as Andy Warhol, Norman Mailer, Gloria Steinem, Anthony Lewis of the *New York Times*, Rev. William Sloane Coffin, and New York's media pundits. Gerald Ford's (*q.v.*) reluctance to "bail out" an all but bankrupt New York is widely regarded as costing him the 1976 Presidential election. Ronald Reagan's stunning victory in 1980 signaled a decline in New York's political influence on the nation. Its cultural influence remained strong, though observers pointed to the increasing role of California—Los Angeles in particular—in developing national fashions and trends. For a New York Times critic's reflection of the city's emphases, John Leonard, *Private Lives in the Imperial City* (1979).

**New York Times**, see Filler, DASC. The *Times* is widely regarded as a major organ of American liberalism, along with the *Washington Post*, and the *Los Angeles Times*. Though published in and for New York, it enjoyed a nationwide reputation as "the paper of record," indispensable to reference libraries and students of current events. Conservatives criticized its editorial policies and asserted that its news coverage was often slanted to favor liberal politics. Its cultural judgments were widely influential among American intellectuals, but once again conservatives asserted that even its cultural judgments were influenced by liberal politics. Conservatives critical of liberal trends in the arts blamed the *Times* for encouraging these trends.

**Newman, John Henry Cardinal** (1801-1890), British clergyman and author. His 45 years as an Anglican and 45 years as a Roman Catholic (*q.v.*) created a form of ecumenical understanding beyond church dogma. His personal odyssey was illuminated by his literary craftsmanship. His long association with Oxford University created a church-education relationship which went far beyond the Oxford Movement with its church-shaking Tracts, and finally, in 1845, brought Newman into the Roman Catholic fold. Newman's profound studies in the development of Christian doctrine, his personal qualities of eloquence and integrity, and his evident growth within English life and experience attracted the attention of the nation. He lived modestly in the Oratory he founded, and was only slowly accepted by the Catholic hierarchy. His effort to create a Catholic university in Ireland failed. His integrity was challenged in a controversy with Charles Kingsley and this inspired the production of his masterpiece, *Apologia pro Vita Sua* (1864). Though it is centered on his mental development, many consider its artless art and details in a class with St. Augustine's (*q.v.*) *Confessions*. Indeed, he found occasion to cite the famous turning-point in the *Confessions*, when Augustine responded to the words "tolle et lege—tolle et lege" (take it and, read it). Important too was Newman's appendix on "Liberalism," which he wholly repudiated as repugnant to his dogmatic principles. Among Newman's influential books was his series of papers which became *The Idea of a University* (1873). Here he honored literature and other disciplines, but also insisted on the university's mission as involving moral training. Long removed from Oxford, Newman was in 1878 granted an honorary fellowship at Trinity College. When he was finally made a Cardinal by Leo XIII (1879), many Englishmen not of the Catholic faith felt that the recognition belonged to England as well. G. Tillotson, ed., *Newman's Prose and Poetry* (1957); Henry Tristram, ed., *Newman's Autobiographical Writings* (1957); F. McGrath, *Newman's University: Idea and Reality* (1951).

**"Newspeak,"** see Communication

**Nicaragua**, see Latin America

**Nichomachien Ethics**, see Aristotle

**Niemeyer, Gerhart** (1907- ), political scientist and anti-Communist educator. Of German birth and training, he was naturalized an American in 1943. He was a planner for the Department of State and research analyst for the Council on Foreign Relations. In 1955 he joined the faculty of Notre Dame University. Niemeyer was influential in formulating the conservative attitude toward Communism as requiring understanding and defeat. *An Inquiry into Soviet Mentality* (1956) gave little encouragement to the future policies of Detente (*q.v.*). *The Communist Ideology* (1959) and *Handbook on Communism* (1962) built the case for a hard-headed realism. Barry Goldwater's (*q.v.*) *Why Not Victory?* (1961) credited Niemeyer's work with helping him to formulate his anti-Communist approach. See also Niemeyer's *Deceitful Peace* (1971).

**Nihilist**, see Turgenev, Ivan; Radical

**1914**, a milestone year which was the beginning of World War I. It was marked by conservative and royalist forces mixing nationalist loyalties in a conflict which seemed more interesting than ominous. The war on the Western front took hundreds of thousand of lives; but the fact that the bodies could not be gathered up as readily as in the past, and the havoc smoothed over, was not clearly perceived at the time. That socialist and radical ideologues would gain inordinately from the military actions and political maneuverings despite their small numbers, changing the character of society and affecting the future, was not apparent; nor were the coming Bolshevik and Fascist revolutions, in Russia and Italy, anticipated. James Cameron, *1914* (1959). See also *Year That Changed The World, The.*

**1933**, perhaps no more a milestone than many another year, but ushering in a new Democratic Roosevelt Administration, which was required to cope with intense economic crises, and which signaled a change in direction affecting all Americans. The year saw the closing of harassed banks, the abandoning of the gold standard, and the doom of the Monetary and Economic Conference—signifying that international cooperation would not be a major element in the future. Japan moved away from the League of Nations and toward nationalistic adventure. The Nazis rose to full power in Germany. The conservative solutions of the Hoover (*q.v.*) Administration were in complete retreat. Liberalism under Franklin D. Roosevelt was about to reveal its latter-day principles and potential. See Herbert Feis, *1933: Characters in Crisis* (1966).

**1949**, a significant year in the development of modern conservatism. It saw the U.S.S.R. achieve its first atomic bomb, undermining the American monopoly in the field, with the aid of American and British traitors. It also saw the Red Chinese Army drive the anti-Communist Chiang Kai-Shek forces to the island of Taiwan. Public apprehension over these threats to American military superiority, and bitterness toward American nationals who had contributed to them, cooled the attitude toward America's war-time partners and made America receptive to attacks on domestic Communists, fellow-travellers (*q.v.*), and Communist sympathizers. Communist victories abroad opened the way at home for the McCarthy (*q.v.*) phenomenon, and encouraged numerous conservative-minded intellectuals and political activists to reach out to the larger public through cultural appeals and political alignments. They revived Congressional concern for anti-Communism, revitalized HUAC (*q.v.*) to the level of the earlier Dies (*q.v.*) Committee, and gained momentum from the Hiss (*q.v.*) case.

**1960s** see *Unraveling of America, The*

**1975**, important to liberals as signaling the end of a war in Vietnam which was "inevitably" lost, which conservatives viewed as betrayed by liberals and given up by weary loyalists. Conservatives had warned of the "Domino" effect: that if the United States showed weakness in one area, they would be probed and tested in others. This was shown almost immediately when Cambodians seized United States merchantmen on the *S.S. Mayaquez* in the Gulf of Siam. President Ford (*q.v.*) acted quicky and the captured Americans were freed. Liberals criticized Ford as having "over-reacted." Overlooked in the entire controversy over Southeast Asia was the fact that American intervention in Vietnam had been initiated and escalated by liberals.

**1984** (1949), George Orwell's (*q.v.*) prophetic novel. It depicted a grey world dominated by Big Brother and his vast network of agents, suffocating freedom in a totalitarian world in which news was manufactured as his authorities willed, and in which tepid people lived tepid lives according to rote. Dissidents were ferreted out and subjected to such discipline as turned them into willing tools of their masters. Although Orwell's model was evidently Stalin's (*q.v.*) Soviet Union, some Western commentators maintained that Orwell's 1984 had already arrived in 1949, that democratic life was in essence not far different from totalitarianism. Other critics who saw *1984* as a plea for individualism and freedom failed to take into account Orwell's lifelong socialist sympathies, that what he was criticizing was not Communism as such, but Communism as it had been evolving under Stalin's tyrannical hand. Like the Arthur Koestler of *Darkness at Noon* (1940), Orwell had no faith in the free actions of society. He longed for a cooperative society, classless and individual: essentially the Marxist (*q.v.*) dream without Marxist results. His pessimism derived in part from his view of Stalinism as seamless and triumphant. *1984* did not take into account the choices available to Winston, his protagonist: creating a dream world, a second level of discourse, a metaphysics of existence. On being unmasked he could have prepared for death by suicide. Above all, he could have sought others like himself whose existence weakened or leavened the all-powerful state. Orwell lived before the "thaw" which followed Stalin's death, and which produced Solzhenitsyn, Sakharov, and other Soviet dissidents (*q.v.*) whose thoughts and personalities were made available to the West. See Filler, "Machiavelli for the Millions," in D. Madden, ed. *American Dreams, American Nightmares* (1970).

**Nineteenth-Century Liberalism**, often interpreted by conservatives as referring to the free-enterprise proponents of post-Civil War eras named "Robber Barons" (*q.v.*) by their historical foes. However, not only were major commercial (*q.v.*) personalities distinguished from recognized liberal leaders in religion and liberal advocates of civil service, fair elections, labor-industry mediation, and other issues, but also notable conservatives joined these liberals in many of their causes. A. J. Nock (*q.v.*) endorsed the radical Henry George Single Tax proposal. Moorfield Storey, a conservative lawyer, was only one among others of his background and outlook who detested imperialism and worked ceaselessly against it. Henry Adams (*q.v.*), upset by the Depression of 1893, which cost many of his friends their fortunes, endorsed Free Silver. Jane Addams and Helen Hunt Jackson (*qq.v.*) were but two names among many concerned for Indians and immigrants (*qq.v.*) in the cities. See Filler, ed., *Populism to Progressivism* (1978 ed.).

**Nisbet, Robert A.** (1913- ), social philosopher and a transitional figure from liberalism to conservatism. His *Quest for Community* (1962) posited a social impulse toward cooperation, as did his *Social Bond: An Introduction to the Study of Society* (1970). His observations of society, however, made him skeptical of its good will and more sympathetic to the idea of controls. Although his *Twilight of Authority* (1975) saw developments in dark hue, he could never give up looking for positive signs. He developed a slashing style sometimes reminiscent of Eric Hoffer, as often of Malcolm Muggeridge (*qq.v.*). Like them, his work proved irresistible to some liberal readers, as well as to conservatives. His *Prejudices: A Philosophical Dictionary* (1982) covered freely topics of his own choice, from "Abortion" to "Wit," and set down corrosive thoughts on bureaucracy, corruption, death, Darwinism (which he saw in disarray), Futurology, ("extrapolation charlatans"), and other topics. He feared that liberalism was inevitable in a land deeply committed to government power and distribution. See also his *Social Change and History* (1969), *The Social Impact of the Revolution* (1974), and *Tradition and Revolt* (1968).

**Nixon, Richard M.** (1913- ), controversial President of the United States; see Filler, DASC. In 1960, the year of his defeat for the Presidency by John F. Kennedy, he was favored by conservatives for his firm anti-Communism and his role in the Hiss case (*q.v.*). In general he was detested by liberals. Nixon had strong grassroots support, along with a need to represent all the people. Elected President in 1968, he put his public image in the hands of advertising experts and aides whom Henry Kissinger was later to characterize as "people without a past." They would separate Nixon from the complex currents of American life, and act in arbitrary ways which disaffected those who depended on him. Nixon would have been wise to study thoughtfully Joe McGuinness's *The Selling of the President* (1969), an exposé of the behind-the-scene manipulations practiced by his political managers. However, he believed he required their cynical expertise. As President, he sought moderate ways to diminish the welfare state and end the American presence in Vietnam. His domestic efforts displeased conservatives who longed for a head-on assault on welfare policies and Federal expenditures. Although Nixon took large steps in bringing American soldiers home from Vietnam and winding down war, he received no credit from his foes. He was overwhelmingly returned to the White House in 1972, but his "mandate" apparently persuaded him that he could face his adversaries with force and Executive Privilege. Both deserted him as the "Watergate" (*q.v.*), crisis came to a head and his own political supporters concluded enough was enough. Nixon retired once more from the political scene, leaving it to Gerald Ford (*q.v.*). Some principled conservatives, in despair, thought of abandoning the Republican Party as no longer a fit vehicle for their goals; see Rusher, William. Others worked to reweave the fabric of practical conservatism; see Lasky, Victor. It slowly dawned on foes that the former President was far from deceased. His memoirs, *RN* (1978) became an international bestseller, and there was a grassroots demand for his speeches. Rumor had it that he might re-enter the political arena (as one commentator put it, "He wouldn't—would he?"). *The Real War* (1980) was another bestseller. The new President, Reagan, was in regular touch with Nixon, though he made his own agenda. In 1984, Nixon's move back to Manhattan roused speculation that he was somehow to be evident in unfolding political events. See also Nixon, *Leaders* (1982), and "Siege Psychology."

**Noblesse Oblige** (nobility obliges), a concept responsible for many of the bravest and most generous acts of history, but scorned by democratic partisans as patronizing and inadequate in terms of social justice. In turning their backs on tradition, however, they often lost not only General Washington and General Lee, but Nathan Hale, Colonel Charles Russell Lowell, and Sergeant York. Although nobility as a title was impractical in the United States, nobility as a deed could never be.

**Nock, Albert Jay** (1870-1945), eccentric conservative whose work broke ground for modern conservatism in some respects. His life was affected by changing circumstances which he rationalized by emphasizing privacy and principles. Raised in a religious household, he carved out for himself a classical education. From 1897-1909 he served as a minister in several states. He then turned to work on the "muckraking" (*q.v.*) *American Magazine*, having left not only the ministry but family life. Thereafter, his work reflected no part of his experience, including his experiences with the *American*—which continued till 1914 and included interest in such topics as the cost of living, earning power, and efficiency. Nock's principles, as they materialized in print the next several years, included belief in Henry George's Single Tax solution to social ills, fear of the state as repressive of the individual, a selective belief in Thomas Jefferson's (*q.v.*) vision of the good life, and a skepticism respecting the workings of democracy (*q.v.*). Along with these fundamentals he believed that the classics (*q.v.*) constituted the best approach to understanding, since they represented the experience of mankind. His acquired belief that diplomats made war only to serve economic imperialism all but made him a Marxist (*q.v.*), except that his scorn of "lesser people" gave him no approach to them. As he said, in his later memoirs, boorishness had once angered him; but he had then noted that one was not angry at dogs for their offensive traits. Since then he had never again been ruffled by annoying encounters. He was not so much a pacifist in World War I as an icy observer; it was the occasion for one of his best-known books, *Myth of a Guilty Nation* (1922). He became best-known as editor of *The Freeman* (*q.v.*) (1920-1924), which gave space to a wide variety of older and newer talents of the time. Nock himself was only concerned for clarity of expression and significant point: in effect, Nock had reconstituted the standards of expression of the older *Atlantic* (*q.v.*) and *North American Review* (*q.v.*), but for a new time. Nock found patrons, so that he was not forced to earn a living, but his independence was genuine. He lived remotely from his best friends, offering civility and, to a few editors, essays which impressed them with style. Nock believed that only "objective" writing filtered through personality was durable. His book-essays on Jefferson and Henry George, however, though cold and clear, explained neither his subjects' impact nor their residue. Nock's *Journal of These Days* (1934) was a calm voice of dissent in demagogic times. He was aware that he did not have a program to offer as alternative to those programs he despised. He believed his was the role of a Matthew Arnold (*q.v.*), stipulating true culture as basic to good times or bad. Speaking best for him, therefore, was *The Theory of Education in the United States* (1932), which saw non-education where John Dewey (*q.v.*) saw education. The key, of course, was the classics. Nock averred that he had nothing against institutions which taught utilitarian skills; they were performing worthy work. Only let them not be called colleges, he said. Nock knew that his ideas were unlikely to inspire emulation. There was thus a note of pessimism in his most good-humored pages. Henry Regnery (*q.v.*) reprinted several of his works, and it seemed likely that others would be culled from time to time. See his *Memoirs of a Superfluous Man* (1943).

**None Dare Call It Conspiracy** (1971), by Gary Allen, with Larry Abraham, published by the John Birch Society (*q.v.*). It is typical of a class of publications, liberal as well as conservative, "extremist" (*q.v.*) in essence, which string together facts and conjectures to create patterns which indeed few would be willing to call conspiracy. Such works involve a range of conjecture in history, biography, world affairs, and ideology which leave most people lost in a haze of allegations. This publication, which claimed five million copies in print, connected Karl Marx with the older Order of the Illuminati, international bankers with the Bolshevik Revolution, and Presidents with the goal of world order and domination. Although such books feed dim resentment and prejudice, they can never rise above the level of visibility, except when sponsored by totalitarian regimes.

**North American Review, The**, notable as a quarterly founded on conservative principles in Boston in 1815. It published the early distinguished poems of William Cullen Bryant (*q.v.*). It went on to become a monthly which, under such proud editors as James Russell Lowell and Henry Adams (*qq.v.*), maintained impeccable standards of literacy and intelligence in emotional and democratic decades, publishing such luminaries as Ralph Waldo Emerson and Francis Parkman (*qq.v.*), and serving a small number of influential subscribers. See also *Modern Age*.

**North Atlantic Treaty Organization**, see NATO

**Northwest Ordinance**, see Federalists

**Novak, Michael** (1933- ), journalist, religious educator, and conservative theoretician. He made his mark outside religious and academic circles with *The Rise of the Unmeltable Ethnics* (1972). In essence, it sought to focus upon the varieties of American groups as distinct, with different traditions and contributions to make to American life. Novak worked intensively to discern spiritual forces in conservative activities, and to find both in those of a more general nature. *The Joy of Sports* (1976), as an example, talked of exercise and fun in terms of spirituality. Working for the American Enterprise Institute (*q.v.*), he prepared several papers which emphasized spirituality in the operations of capitalism; one was *The American Vision* (1978), another *Toward a Theology of the Corporation* (1981). His project was culminated with *The Spirit of Democratic Capitalism* (1982). In 1981 he was appointed U.S. representative to the UN Human Rights Commission.

**Nozick, Robert** (1938- ), "libertarian conservative." His *Anarchy, State and Utopia* (1974) won the National Book Award and provided sectors of conservatism with ideas for debate. The book attempted to rebut the anarchist position while maintaining libertarian (*q.v.*) premises. Academic to a degree, it made such connections as between the "Invisible Hand" concept and Lockean formulations (*qq.v.*). See also his *Philosophical Explanations* (1981).

**Nuclear War**, the key issue in the world in the mid-1980s. The almost unimaginable horrors of nuclear war, almost certain to destroy a large percentage of established civilization and perhaps make uninhabitable the remainder of the world, raze Africa, South America, and the Far East, at relatively little expense. Alexander Solzhenitsyn (*q.v.*) believed that the West showed few signs of realizing the extent of Soviet determination, or of having the will to meet it and conquer. Western European nations were ambivalent in their readiness to fight, fearful of American leadership, realizing they were on the "front line" before Soviet power. President Reagan's explicit desire to attain military superiority over the Soviets raised as much alarm as it did approval. Aside from the political issue—viewing guns against butter, concern for military cost "over-runs,"—there was liberal fear of "setting off" a nuclear holocaust. "Anti-Nuke" forces, in Europe and America, sought to dramatize their hatred of nuclear installations. Although they claimed to find them repellent on both sides of the Iron Curtain (*q.v.*), they were only able to make their demonstrations more or less freely in democratic countries. The Labor Party in Great Britain committed itself to the goal of unilateral disarmament, a program obviously encouraging to Soviet hopes of peaceful takeover of authority. It was the hope of unilateralists that the expansion of their cause elsewhere would raise a world opinion which would permeate into Soviet territories. But there was a clear relationship between this program and that of those whose slogan had been "Better Red than Dead." Some radical elements even welcomed such Soviet takeover, believing that an initial period of barbarism and totalitarianism would eventually give way to better times. Conservatives saw in such prospects self-deception and irreversible loss, and followed the debate closely. Harry Foreman, ed., *Nuclear power and the Public* (1970); R. C. Lewis, *Nuclear Power Rebellion* (1972); B. Bosky and Mason Willrich, *Nuclear Proliferation: Prospects for Control* (1970); W. R. Kintner and H. F. Scott, eds., *Nuclear Revolution in Soviet Military Affairs* (1968); Jack G. Shaheen, *Nuclear War Films* (1978); P. Quigg, ed., *Henry Kissinger, Nuclear Weapons and Foreign Policy* (1969). See also Robert Jastrow, *How to Make Nuclear Weapons Obsolete* (1985), a positive view of President reagan's Strategic Defense Initiative program, popularly known as "Star Wars."

**Nullification**, a principle of government which emphasized states rights even to permit rejection of a national law when it offended state prerogatives, Although identified with John C. Calhoun (*q.v.*), nullification found precedents in the Kentucky and Virginia Resolutions of 1798, sponsored by Jefferson and Madison (*q.v.*), and in the Hartford Resolutions of 1814, which expressed dissatisfaction with Madison's war with England. See Alien and Sedition Acts. Still later, Wisconsin antislavery fighters expressed defiance against national fugitive slave laws, which implicated the state in police actions against runaway blacks, by accepting a state supreme court judgment which ran counter to national law, making Wisconsin "the South Carolina of the North."

**Nuns**, traditionally a conservative element in the Catholic (*q.v.*) community, often concerned for the contemplative life, though even more often active in charity work, health care, and teaching. Some of them, notably in the United States, were stirred by contemporary currents and the effects of the Second Vatican Council to modernize their clothing and ways of life, and even to become involved in contemporary issues. Sr. Rosemarie Hudson, *Nuns, Community Prayer and Change* (1967); Kathryn Hulme, *Nun's Story* (1977).

# O

**Oakeshott, Michael** (1901-    ), professor of political science at the University of London and one of the most highly regarded theorists of conservatism, which he saw as giving a firm grasp of the bases of human living. He was educated at Cambridge University and studied and wrote of Hobbes (*q.v.*), and was co-author of *A Guide to the Classics* (1936), and author of *Experience and Its Modes* (1933) and *Social and Political Doctrines of Contemporary Europe* (1939). Oakeshott was one of the few political scientists of whom it was said that he wrote too little. His most famous work was a series of essays which made up *Rationalism in Politics* (1962). Other works were *On Human Conduct* (1975) and *On History* (1982).

**Oberholtzer, Ellis Paxson** (1868-1936), American historian and Manchester liberal (*q.v.*) who was extremely conservative in his views of labor and related issues. He contributed to the furthering of honest voting and democratic procedure; see his *The Referendum in America* (1893). Oberholtzer edited *The Manufacturer* (1896-1900) and wrote a two-volume biography of Jay Cooke, the financier. His masterwork was a *History of the United States since the Civil War* (1917-1931), in four volumes.

**Objectivism**, a philosophical project of Ayn Rand's (*q.v.*), intended to overcome what she saw as the evils of altruism and free individuals from the mental chains it forged. As developed by herself and her enterprising follower Nathaniel Branden, it purported to show troubled individuals who suffered a sense of failure and confusion due to self-defeating premises with which they had been confined. Brandon's "institutes" were, in effect, inspirational and intended to lead students on the road to success, Dale Carnegie but with emphasis on "philosophical" underpinnings as pre-conditions to success. "Objectivism" promised to unveil the falsities hidden in such concepts as altruism, cooperation, humanity, benevolence, and all variations thereof. The key to victory was selfishness, ego, self-esteem. The goal was to understand one's own nature and to satisfy it.

**Obscenity**, a youth (*q.v.*) cause of the 1960s, at first identified with events on the Berkeley campus of the University of California, but soon spread across the nation as a criticism of allegedly hypocritical society. It infected academic classes and books. One text, *American Values in Transition* (1972), ed., R. C. Bannister, dedicated nine pages to the thoughts of a "Yippie" leader Jerry Rubin, from his book *Do It!* (1970), one page of which contained only the word f___ endlessly repeated. Obscenity, in addition, moved freely into society at large. The courts encountered difficulties in determining how much freedom should be granted to peddlers of obscenity, or even to determine what writing or speech constituted obscenity.

**O'Connor, Flannery** (1925-1964), distinguished novelist and short story writer and Catholic writer. A Southerner, she mixed harsh crises with commonplace lives and concepts, as in the tale entitled "A Good Man Is Hard to Find," in fashions which faced the reader with facades and mysterious underlays. "Parker's Back" made symbols of beauty, the process of tattooing, and the "seeing" achieved by eyes and by inner light. Hazel Motes, who burns out Parker's eyes so he can "see," has a symbolic name. O'Connor won readers and prizes by her evident appeal to the disturbed feelings of persons who might be otherwise conformist in their social or political preferences or hatreds. Her own infirmities and sharp judgments contributed to her personal legend. See M. J. Friedman and L. A. Lawson, eds., *The Added Dimension: The Art and Mind of Flannery O'Connor* (1966); R. Drake, *Flannery O'Connor* (1966); S. and R. Fitzgerald, eds., *Mystery and Manners* (1969).

**Odyssey of a Fellow Traveler**, (1938), by J. B. Matthews, a pioneer work which described the operations of Communists and quasi-Communists to sway American public opinion in behalf of their causes at home and abroad. Matthews's background in religious studies, his teaching in needy schools and countries, and his approval of socialist tenets, combined with the 1929 Depression, opened him to the blandishments of Communists. They in turn utilized him as speaker, endorser, and head of numerous peace and labor organizations. Matthews exposed the Communist connections of many persons who presented themselves as liberals, such as Arthur Kallet of Consumers Research (see Consumerism) and David L. Saposs, chief economist of the National Labor Relations Bureau. All this incurred the wrath of Communists and their sympathizers. They were further angered when he testified before the Dies (*q.v.*) Committee. Such was their power that they were able to discredit him with the public. Yet his work's documentation was impressive as he surveyed a wide range of organizations and groups.

**Oil**. World production of oil was important to America's national security and to the future of free enterprise (*q.v.*). The crisis of 1973, during which Arab nations supported Egyptian and Syrian invasion of Israel, saw them stopping the shipment of their oil to the United States. They eventually raised the price of a barrel of crude oil from $3.65 to $34. Americans, unused to the resulting escalations in retail price, tended to blame the oil companies, with their "enormous profits." Attention turned to alternative sources of energy for automobilies, and to the development of solar energy. Employees were urged to use vans to transport workers, and they explored the small-car market. All were urged to conserve gasoline. Great Britain's development of her North Sea oil deposits and America's development of Alaskan oil fields were part of adjustments to new conditons. Classical liberal-conservative differences on the status of oil matured, to puzzle the citizen as much as to enlighten him. Liberals demanded government control of national resources, especially in offshore areas. Conservatives argued for local development specifically, and deregulation generally. Mobil Oil was outstanding in presenting the case for the oil companies, arguing that their profits were in fact minimal, especially when placed against the taxes they paid. The companies spent billions in exploration, Mobil argued, often with no return. Taxed less, they could explore more. So effective was Mobil Oil's campaign that liberal commentators protested it unfairly influenced public opinion. Paradoxes abounded. Although oil was supposed to increase American independence and security, it appeared that Alaskan oil went, not to continental United States, but to foreign purchasers. It was claimed that American companies approved of their Arab connections, because of well-organized and predictable carrying systems. Though gasoline prices continued to fluctuate for no apparent reason, in general they declined. Oil reserves mounted, and the United States and other Western nations gained more energy independence. Americans turned away from small cars in great numbers. They were disturbed by oil spills in the Caribbean and Pacific, and not overly impressed by the arguments of oil tycoons, but saw no answer in government regulation. In the 1980s OPEC experienced financial troubles and lost much of its power but similar financial troubles in oil-rich Mexico and Venezuela were not encouraging. Despite problems in understanding the currents of the oil and political wars, and the justice and injustice involved, it appeared that Americans were learning to realize their stake in oil, at home and abroad.

**Old Age**, see Filler DASC. The problems of old age have been a concern for much of the twentieth century, since first given attention by progressives (*q.v.*) seeking to mend the social wound created by the decline in rural values and the rise of the impersonal city. Family, pension plans, and New Deal (*q.v.*) measures helped modify for many the tragedy of age; but the swift decline of the city, the cult of youth (*q.v.*), and the loosening of family ties, plus medical advances which lengthened life for the aging, created difficulties. Social security, intended to implement savings and pensions, often proved too little for decent survival. Although social security (*q.v.*) benefits improved somewhat under Lyndon Johnson's "Great Society," family did not. Conservatives, seeking limited government and responsible budgets, sought cutbacks on social services, which necessarily included those aiding the elderly. Liberals preached "compassion" (*q.v.*), which conservatives attacked as too costly. The American Association of Retired Persons attempted to act on behalf of the elderly. Conservatives, including the President himself, would have had them joining him in restructuring the society into a more stable enterprise, with family love and social generosity substituting for escapist interests.

**Olympics**, see Sport

**Ominous Politics: The New Conservative Labyrinth** (1984), by John S. Saloma, a cofounder of the Ripon Society (*q.v.*). An academic and political science teacher, Saloma surveyed the results of the electoral victory of Ronald Reagan. His liberal book found cause for alarm in the efficient manner in which conservatives were building their centers and programs. The Intercollegiate Studies Institute sought promising students, for example, and found Edwin Feulner—who came to head the Heritage Foundation. It had relations with the Hoover Institution (*q.v.*), which had shifted from the Cold War to "American Studies," though Saloma saw little difference between the two concepts. The Center for Strategic and International Studies was part of the conservative configuration, according to the author, as were other groups and organizations. It appeared to Saloma that conservatives were accreting a power which endangered democracy (*q.v.*). Yet they did nothing which liberals had not also been doing for as many years as they had engaged in public affairs. (*Qq.v.* for above.) See also PACs.

**On the Constitution of the Church and State**, by Samuel Taylor Coleridge (*q.v.*). It is of interest to those concerned for his reputation in the early 19th century as an outstanding defender of conservative views. He was treated almost with awe by visitors who were overwhelmed by his cascades of conversation and references to people and books. Nevertheless, Coleridge has had less direct impact in the late 20th century as a conservative ideologue and is still best remembered for the poetry of his youth. The best approach to the later Coleridge is through his *Tabletalk* (q.v.), collected during his last twelve years by his nephew and son-in-law Henry Nelson Coleridge. See also *Coleridge the Talker*, contemporary descriptions collected and introduced by Richard W. Armour and Raymond F. Howes (1940).

**"One Man, One Vote,"** see Voting Rights Act; Equality

**Open Door, The**, see Hay, John

**"Open Shop,"** see Right to Work

**Opportunity**, see Filler, DASC. Opportunity is a basic American impulse, perceived as Progressivism (*q.v.*) in the pre-World War I era, but with principles which can be traced earlier. It discerned inequities between the rich and the poor in the midst of plenty, and sought not equalization of wealth so much as equalization of opportunity. The Northwest Ordinance (1787), identified with Thomas Jefferson (*q.v.*), and legislating statehood, rights, and education for United States territory, was an example of opportunity written into law—as were the several Homestead Acts which opened western lands to settlement. The Jacksonian (*q.v.*) era with its expediencies (*q.v.*), patriotism (*q.v.*), and opposition to debtors' prisons included Progressive tenets, as did anti-monopoly (*q.v.*) groupings and protests in the post-Civil War era. A feature of all such movements was the effort to modernize rules and relations while seeking to maintain all of individual effort which could be kept. Although the New Deal (*q.v.*) sought to preserve this feature, terming its more drastic and centralizing actions "temporary," the crisis with which it dealt was too deep and too much influenced by world movements and war for the short-term promise to be honored.

New Deal measures were not only maintained, but augmented in President Truman's Fair Deal, so much so that they could not be shaken under Eisenhower (*q.v.*). New Conservatives misread Progressivism as heralding the welfare state, though actual Progressives who survived into the 1950s were wholly opposed to measures infringing on individual prerogatives. Although left-wingers adopted the name of Progressives for the elections of 1948, they scorned the old Progressives for adhering to capitalist ideals. With the crumbling of welfare-socialist expectations in the 1980s, it appeared that Democrats would attempt to reorganize their principles along old Progressive lines. Although conservatives spoke of recapturing their heritage, they appeared more interested in rehabilitating the much-criticized masters of capital and industry, and their political sponsors, than in claiming their share of the Progressive heritage. See Filler, *Appointment at Armageddon* and *Progressivism and Muckraking (q.v.): A Bibliographical Essay*; Equality.

**Optimism**, often associated with conservatism, shallowness, and Babbittry (*q.v.*). Americans seemed willing to accept the academic view of the novelist William Dean Howells, who was seen as fatuous in his preference for the "smiling side" of life. They preferred the pessimistic view of Theodore Dreiser to that of David Graham Phillips (*q.v.*), a fellow writer from Indiana. Phillips, however, preached less optimism than the availability of a fighting chance to create a better world. The symbol of optimism for many years was the *Saturday Evening Post* (*q.v.*), which clearly favored optimistic views of American life and letters. However, the identification of optimism with conservatism was less evident in the New Conservatives of the post-World War II era, many of them perceiving the presence of original sin, faithlessness, and failure in human affairs and threats to the world itself, not only in the nuclear bomb but in the possible triumph of Godless Communism. Pessimism was distinctly a component in the conservative view.

**Order**, a significant word in the conservative lexicon, but clearly distinguishable from the meaning of order in authoritarian countries. Conservatives sought order in human affairs, and linked it with cosmic order, deriving from faith in the purposes of Deity. "Order," according to Alexander Pope, "is Heaven's first law." Within such order, they sought individual preferences and destiny. Both liberals and conservatives were repelled by order as interpreted in the fascist vocabulary, where it meant the suppression of individuals to the demands of the state. Some liberals, however, were less offended by ordered activities and parades in Communist countries. Nor were they overly disturbed by disorder at home, which they saw as legitimate expression of discontent by alienated or dissatisfied elements. Russell Kirk's (*q.v.*) *The Roots of American Order* (1974) was a massive attempt to trace world factors which had contributed to the American struggle for definition. Using history, sacred texts, philosophy, and leading figures from the Old Testament, Greek and Roman times, and the Middle Ages ("The Light of the Middle Ages"), along with the labors of church reformers and the American saga from colonial times through figures and events which led to the Declaration of Independence through constitution making, Kirk found a religious and civil heritage which could be transgressed only at the cost of liberty and freedom. The United States, he said, had not been brought into being "to accomplish the work of socialism." And he quoted with approval Orestes Brownson's (*q.v.*) summary, in his *The American Republic*, of the true meaning of human history "The Jews were chosen to preserve traditions, and so that the Messiah might arise; the Greeks were chosen for the realizing of art, science, and philosophy; the Romans were chosen for the developing of the state, law, and jurisprudence. And the Americans, too, have been appointed to a providential mission, continuing the work of Greece and Rome, but accomplishing yet more. The American Republic is to reconcile liberty with law...." Although this 19th-century version of "American destiny" was not couched to satisfy late 20th-century conditions, it embodied concepts satisfying to many conservatives. See also Voegelin, Eric.

**Organization Man, The** (1956), by William H. Whyte, Jr. Whyte was a basically conservative business person whose critique of the ways of commerce (*q.v.*) was intended to be positive and helpful. He was shocked by tendencies which drained the individual of personality and made him the mere cog in a machine which gained nothing from his services. Whyte's portrait of the faceless man who watered his lawn on Sunday and readily followed his firm wherever it went was refreshing and recognized as true by its many readers. He himself was emancipated by his success and turned to propagandizing for agreements between towns and farmers which would protect tracts of land notable for beauty or breathing space from uncivil exploitation, by preserving town options through compensation.

**Ortega y Gassett, Jose** (1883-1955), Spanish essayist and scholar in metaphysics. He made a distinguished and influential career in Madrid, writing in opposition to the monarchy, and seeking to help in the reconstruction following the 1931 revolution. However, he was equally offended by the results of fascist and Communist revolutions and their production of "mass men," which he expressed in his most famous work, *Revolt of the Masses*, translated into English in 1932. The concept and book were sustained by conservatives abroad, and entered into the lexicon of the New Conservatism.

**Orwell, George** (1903-1950), British author famous for his *Animal Farm* (1945)—an allegory of life under Communism, with its witty observation that under Communism some were "more equal" than others—and *1984* (*q.v.*). At home, he was read as essayist and his associations noted and discussed. Abroad, he was best known to liberal and left-wing litterateurs. His first book, *Down and Out in Paris and London* (1933), was seen as a determined effort to explore the nether world ignored by higher levels of society. His *Homage to Catalonia* (1938) was controversial to friends and friendly critics of Soviet policy in the Spanish Civil War (*q.v.*). Lionel Trilling (*q.v.*) in an introduction to the American edition of this work, evaded its strictures against the Spanish Republicans by saying that Orwell was no "genius" when compared to Henry James (*q.v.*). Although Orwell's determined effort to tell the "truth" was seen by conservatives as limited by his socialist (*q.v.*) prejudices, the effort itself gave interesting and creative results, aided by his genuine sense of humor. *Such, Such Were the Joys* (1953) was an account of his school days, and *Burmese Days* (1935) a novel reflecting his experience as an Imperial policeman in Burma.

**Oursler, Fulton** (1893-1964), successful author, a master of popular trends. Oursler turned a retentive memory and fluency of thought and writing into a success which brought him the widest of acquaintanceships and contacts around the world, a conservative counterpart of the liberal Norman Cousins, though on a less intellectual level. Oursler's association with the physical-culture entrepreneur Bernard Macfadden, and with such properties as *True Story* and especially *Liberty Magazine*—with its striving for significance, brought him contact with celebrities ranging from the actress Norma Shearer to Albert Einstein. In 1924, he reflected an unhappy first marriage and an aspiration toward art in *Behold This Dreamer!* It brought him praise from Sinclair Lewis (*q.v.*) and Upton Sinclair. His convertion to Catholicism (*q.v.*) led to the publication in 1949 of *The Greatest Story Ever Told*, his greatest success. Oursler wrote other "greatest" works, and much successful fiction. As a senior editor of *Reader's Digest* (*q.v.*) he helped guide as well as reflect changing patterns of American thought. See his autobiography, published and edited by his son Fulton Jr., *Behold This Dreamer!* (1964).

**Outdoor Work**, a supplement to voluntary (*q.v.*) aid provided for the unemployed in decades prior to the Depression of 1929, particularly during trying winters. Municipal executives sought when they could to synchronize practical needs involving roads or streets with the needs of unemployed laborers. Such programs were contrived by reformers like "Golden Rule" Samuel M. Jones of Toledo, Ohio, and also by non-reformers such as the kindly William McKinley, then governor of that state. Although outdoor work was too slight a staff to support serious unemployment such as occurred after 1929, it did provide precedence for the "Little New Deal" which Franklin D. Roosevelt (*q.v.*) managed as governor of New York. On meager funds it gave modest employment to laborers and others for freshening parks, refurbishing church interiors, and otherwise serving communities, often with free materials contributed by merchants and others.

**Over-Achievers**. Although technically connoting success, an education (*q.v.*) concept of the 1970s, created by liberal ideologues to explain high unemployment among presumably well prepared graduates. The obverse of "under-achievers," which prayerfully anticipated more from some classes of students, the concept sought to explain the failure in society of individuals to whom academic degrees should have opened economic doors. It mixed bureaucratic (*q.v.*) anticipations with hidden criticism of individualism and intelligence; the person had not prepared in accordance with specifications and available "slots." The concept clashed with earlier aims in education: to inspire students to greater achievement, in part by displaying before them such examples as Thomas A. Edison (*q.v.*), Francis Parkman (*q.v.*), great in historical writing despite the impediment of blindness, and others in other fields.

**Oxford Movement**, see Newman, Cardinal

# P

**Pacifism,** a vital topic in a world fearful of atomic warfare, with both a liberal and conservative background in American history. It differed from peace movements, which sought to interpose solutions to international belligerency. Pacifism had political overtones during the War of 1812, when leading New Englanders were critical of their government as being Southern, rather than national, and as seeking war with England, a bastion of civilization against revolutionary France. Quakers developed a tradition of pacifism, and suffered financial losses and humiliation in that time and during the Civil War (*q.v.*), for being unwilling to bear arms or support warfare. A more radical pacifism was linked with universal reform movements of the time. Politics entered once more into American attitudes toward what was the European War, from 1914 to 1917, before American intervention. German-Americans advocating pacifism were influenced by their inability to gain wide sympathy for the German cause, and hoped to keep the United States from entering into the war on the Allied side. The youth movement (*q.v.*) of the 1960s, in protesting the Vietnam war, mixed terrorist actions with passive-resistance techniques in confrontation with police and the military—going limp in the hands of those seeking to break up their demonstrations, seeking to obstruct activities with their bodies, and the like. "Anti-Nuke" demonstrators a decade later renewed or adopted such stratagems, in order to protest nuclear arms in America and elsewhere. Although some conservative elements—religious, civic—could be found among such demonstrators, they were in the main liberal and radical, many having participated in other liberal and radical campaigns; C. Benedetti, *Peace Heroes in Twentieth Century America* (1986).

**"Packing, Court,"** see Supreme Court

**PACs (Political Action Committees)**, the result of a lengthy effort to reduce political corruption. In 1907, Congress prohibited corporate contributions to federal political campaign. By 1943, labor unions had grown strong enough to be put under the same ban. The unions then created the first organizations working in behalf of favored political contenders with voluntary contributions. In 1971 corporate leaders agreed to support reforms in the system if they were allowed to set up PACs too. Although financial limits were placed on "voluntary" contributions, the PACs soon multiplied into hundreds of special-interest groups, then mounted into thousands. Early in 1983 there were some 3,000 PACs operating in the country, well organized to serve political parties and such special-interest groups as the American Medical Association and the American Dental Association. The "loopholes" in the laws enabled skilled operators to shift contributors about from state to state to help individual political candidates. In 1982 it was estimated that the PACs spent roughly $240 million to influence the November elections. Did these expenditures threaten democracy? Were candidates reached by interests which had not directly approached them? With persons more or less voluntarily giving support to persons or tendencies they already supported, it became a question whether the issue was the power of the tendency, or the corruptibility. Thus, 1984 saw a PAC race between the North Carolina Campaign Fund, which opposed re-election of Republican Senator Jesse Helms (*q.v.*) and his own friendly National Congressional Club. What led to the victory of Helms was far from clear. Elizabeth Drew's *Politics and Money* (1983) saw the PAC as "The New Road to Corruption," but she seemed concerned that Republican PACs might be more skillfully and successfully handled than were Democratic PACs. For a retrospective view of the problem, see Perry Belmont, *Return to Secret Party Funds* (1927). See also J. R. Eccles, *The Hatch Act and the American Bureaucracy* (1981), which complains that a 1939 act intending to divest civil servants of the capacity for political corruption by preventing their participation in partisan politics has done more harm than good.

**Paine, Thomas** (1737-1809). No transitional figure (*q.v.*), he gave evidence of the need for alliances in such crises as the American Revolution (*q.v.*). Paine also exemplified a long-term trend among numerous emigrants to the United States who, having experienced life in various European countries, became more passionate about American freedoms than did the natives. In America little more than a year, he anonymously published *Common Sense*, which emotionally spelled out American grievances against England, the land of his birth and raising. It caught fire and sold an estimated half-million copies. His *Crisis* papers (1776-1783) were a major force in persuading Americans to fight. Paine also served the Committee on Foreign Affairs of the Continental Congress. In 1787 he returned to England and, impressed by the French Revolution issued a rebuttal to Edmund Burke's (*q.v.*) *Reflections on the French Revolution* entitled *The Rights of Man* (1791-1792). It earned him English condemnation on charges of sedition and treason. Paine was given French citizenship but, siding against the dominant radical Jacobins, lost that citizenship and was confined in prison. There he began *The Age of Reason* (1794-1796). Though Deistic (*q.v.*) it sought to demolish the Bible, and lost him much credit in America. On his return he found America in the hands of Federalists (*q.v.*). Nor were the Jeffersonians (*q.v.*) more welcoming. Paine was not disillusioned by his French experiences, and in 1797 issued his *Agrarian Justice*, which advocated wholesale expropriation and distribution of property. Poor and all but forgotten, he settled in New Rochelle, New York, where he died. William Cobbett (*q.v.*), who as a Federalist had despised Paine, as a Whig honored him. Returning from American exile, he brought Paine's bones back to England for reburial. For lack of interest the project failed, and the relics disappeared.

**Palestine Liberation Organization**, see Terrorism, Middle East.

**"Palimony,"** see Family

**Panaceas**, social "cure-alls," usually associated with radical solutions to social problems which were usually economic. Their essence was that they were single solutions, though their supporters claimed that they affected all avenues of life. The Silver idea, the Greenback idea, the Single Tax, and the Townsend Plan were all intended to start stalled economies, and ranged from radical to liberal in social appeal. How far conservatives delved into panaceas is controversial, and depended on the status of other social conditions. Thus, the Independent Treasury of Van Buren's Administration might or might not have rated as a panacea, but it scarcely affected directly American social relations. The same might have been said of Grover Cleveland's (*q.v.*) version of Free Trade and Milton Friedman's (*q.v.*) concept of a Guaranteed Annual Income. Jack Kemp's dedication to the Gold Standard was perhaps a panacea for American economic imbalances, but supply-side economics (*q.v.*) was too involved in larger American economic policies to rate as a single solution. The increased interrelationship of issues and social effects made panaceas harder to find than in more individualistic eras. See also Utopia.

**Panama Canal**, a problem in national attitudes and changing American perspectives. (see Filler, DASC.) American interest in a Panama route for ocean travel precipitated the actions of Panamanian politicians which resulted in the establishment of the tiny republic and the sale of the canal route to the United States. The heroic labors of American engineers and others to control disease and subdue the landscape to operations made up one of the epics of the 20th century. Woodrow Wilson's (*q.v.*) decision to pay Columbia for the loss of its province outraged Theodore Roosevelt (*q.v.*), who took it as a personal insult, but the action did release America from responsibility for the Panamanian Revolution against Columbia. National assertiveness throughout the region in later decades changed the picture, as lands great and small declared against colonialism and imperialism, past and present, and took advantage of major international rivalries to assert their rights. In effect, it seemed better for Americans to make friends than to provide fuel for anti-American propaganda and isolation. Arguments for the amiable road impressed Lyndon Johnson, seemed reasonable to Gerald Ford, and persuaded Jimmy Carter (*qq.v.*). They also impressed William F. Buckley, Jr. Ronald Reagan was vigorous in his opposition to the treaties signed in 1979 which turned over the Canal to Panama by the end of the century, along with substantial sums for upkeep and other considerations. The event left many questions unanswered, and indeed the entire event left the matter open to serious, important debate in time. Had America abased itself before its Latin American neighbors and the world, or no more than asserted its maturity in an interrelated set of nations? Was the Canal inadequate for growing American purposes, and would another canal, perhaps in Nicaragua, better meet modern and future needs? Were we alert to possible misuse of the Canal, and ready to master the situation if necessary? In several years in office, Reagan had added nothing to his opinions voiced before taking office. *Panama: Canal Issues Treaty Talks* (Special Report Series, Center for Strategic Studies [*q.v.*], Georgetown University, March, 1967).

**Papacy**, a powerful factor in all conservative dialogue and projects, with increasing prestige beyond Catholic (*q.v.*) confines. Its career, always hectic, as it veered between secular power and spiritual affirmation, confounded radical expectations that it would dwindle and disappear as revolutionary governments geared their masses to worldly goals. Instead, the very loss of temporal authority, reducing the Popes to spiritual activity, created a contrast between their words and the atrocious deeds of the Nazis in Germany and the Stalinists in the Soviet Union. Pius XII (1939-1958) emerged from the carnage of World War II (*qq.v.*) as a major proponent of peace. Those who had scorned the Church as impotent now sought to criticize him for not having done enough to rescue Jews from the Nazi Holocaust, and for intransigent anti-Communism. Pope John XXIII (1958-1963) directed an *aggiornamento* (updating) of the growing Church establishment the affects of which were felt around the world. His convening of Vatican II (*q.v.*) (1962) and its reconvening (1963-1965) under his successor Paul VI (1963-1978) resulted in findings with incalculable consequences, feared by many, seized upon by others. Liturgical reforms made many conservatives cringe. Lay participation was augmented, encouraging the bishops to assert an independence which often amounted to a flouting of Papal authority. The phenomenal growth of Catholicism in Third World (*q.v.*) countries, often in defiance of revolutionary authorities, drew bishops into politics, with the Church required to determine the limits of this activity. Paul VI's Encyclical, *Populorum Progresio* ("Development of Peoples") appealed to wealthy nations to right the balance with needy nations. But Paul also reaffirmed celibacy for priests in *Sacerdotalis Caelibatus* and decried birth control in *Humanae Vitae*, though birth control was all but universally accepted in the lay Catholic community. The 1978 election of Karol Wojtyla, Cardinal-Archbishop of Cracow, to be Pope John Paul II was sensational, for John Paul was a Pole, and Poland (*q.v.*), intensely Catholic, confronted its Soviet masters and their surrogates (*q.v.*) with nothing but its religious shield: a constant challenge to their atheistic program and prospects, for which their nuclear capability could do little. John Paul, both traditional and approving of popular action and sentiment, was extraordinary in his visibility. His travels in Africa, South America, North America, Southeast Asia, the Far East, and the Middle East drew millions to see and hear him: an estimated 100 million. His visit to

Czechoslovakia, Poland, was awesome. Some three and a half million Poles convened before him. Allegations that the Kremlin was involved in the attempt to assassinate him in 1981, if true, would show how threatening he seemed to the Soviet overlords of Poland. John Paul's own confidential talk with and the pardon of his would-be murderer enhanced his presence among world leaders. Although restlessness among nuns (*q.v.*) and radical gestures among bishops seemed to point to weakness in the hierarchy, Catholic prestige and numbers pointed to a community resolve of power in a world which had otherwise narrowed to one of weaponry and ultimate weaponry. J. J. Delaney and J. E. Tobin, *Dictionary of Catholic Biography* (1961); John A. Hardon, *Modern Catholic Dictionary* (1980); Oscar Halecki and James F. Murray, Jr., *Pius XII* (1954 ed.); Paul Johnson, *Pope John XXIII* (1974); James A. Corbett, *The Papacy* (1956); Francis A. Ridley, *The Papacy and Fascism* (1937); M. Bertrams, *Papacy, Episcopacy, and Collegiality* (1964); Edmund D. O'Connor, *Pope Paul and the Spirit* (1978); Msgr. George A. Kelly, *The Crisis of Authority: John Paul II and the American Bishops* (1981).

**Paris Commune**, see Communism

**Parker, J. A.**, see Lincoln Institute

**Parkman, Francis** (1823-1893), one of the towering figures in American historiography. He was once admired for the fortitude with which he pursued his historical studies and writing, and the literary power with which he recounted the history of the French and Indian wars. His battles with blindness, his rigid standards of accuracy, his triumphs over affliction to produce vivid and arresting narratives of the rise of British rule made him a model of writing even to those who criticized his antipathy to Catholics (*q.v.*). *The Oregon Trail* (1849) and the culminating work of his series on the wars, *Montcalm and Wolfe* (1884), continue to give the best entree to his work. Mason Wade, *Francis Parkman: Heroic Historian* (1942).

**Pascal, Blaise** (1623-1662), French mathematician and philosopher. His precocious intellectual discoveries and investigations gained him early fame. In the quarrel between Jansenists and Jesuits, Pascal contributed the masterly *Lettres Provinciales* (1656-1657), which exposed Jesuits to censure and made their name synonymous with casuistry. His *Pensées*, published after his death, are a masterpiece of Christian thought and feeling: a landmark in their opposition to rationalism (*q.v.*).

**PATCO (Professional Air Traffic Controllers Organization)**. Its fate as a union marked a turning point in how the public and labor unions viewed each other. In 1981 PATCO defied its contract with the Federal Government by going on strike for better working conditions. It appealed to the public's concern for air-passenger safety in its bid for support. President Reagan ordered PATCO back to work, and upon its refusal, fired the striking controllers. Non-striking and military controllers were used to fill the vacant positions until new personnel could be trained. The liberal press and media held that Reagan had been too "legalistic" in a matter meriting negotiation rather than dismissal. The continuation of air service, however and public dissatisfaction with labor unions in general undermined traditional sympathy. The episode heartened those who in business and government sought curbs on union power. In England Prime Minister Margaret Thatcher (*q.v.*) resisted ASLEF, the union of railroad workers, which was denied the support of TUC, the Trade Union Council, for its plans for a major strike. Ironically, in 1985 many of the non-striking controllers who had resisted earlier PATCO pressure and remained on the job also began to call for better working conditions and to raise doubts about the safety of air travel under current conditions. See also Unions.

**Patriot, The** (1774), a pamphlet by Samuel Johnson (*q.v.*). It is of interest as helping to clarify the meaning of his much-quoted "patriotism is the last refuge of a scoundrel," voiced the next year to James Boswell. In that same year he issued an anti-American tract, *Taxation No Tyranny*. Johnson would clearly have despised mere malcontents; as he said: "He is no lover of his country that unnecessarily disturbs its peace." "Patriotism," moreover, was a word which took on the color of the times. In Johnson's, it suggested sedition, factional malice. Its proper use, therefore, required a sensitive and informed mind. See also *Idea of a Patriot King, The.*

**Patriotism**, often subject to confusion, the patriot or the patriot's duty being difficult to discern. Conservative New Englanders resented "Mr. Madison's (*q.v.*) War" of 1812, and not a few of them resented the war with Mexico, which they saw as reflecting the slaveholder's ambitions for expansion. Robert E. Lee (*q.v.*), like many others, was torn between loyalty to the Union and to his native Virginia. Abolitionists (*q.v.*) sought a "Higher Law" than that of the slavery-scarred Constitution (*q.v.*). The constant coming of new immigrants roused suspicions of "dual loyalty"—of Irish Catholics to the Pope, and later of Germans to Germany and Jews to Israel. At the same time, there were counter-repudiations of pompous "patriots," with no record of service to the nation except of "waving the bloody shirt" of others. World War I was a crisis in patriotism, with many fearing involvement in a European War which was none of their own. "Black regiments" separated from white soldiers created a second order of bitterness. Aggressive patriotism on the part of such organizations as the American Legion (*q.v.*) disturbed some loyal Americans and was a target of radical hatred and alarm. The world growing smaller and deadly weapons larger stirred need for new understandings of patriotism. Conservatives saw a love of country as a first requisite to an ordered program. Although few were proud of the internment of Japanese-Americans, an event which outraged many, some saw justification in the imponderables of a two-ocean war. The brilliant revival of the Japanese-American community after the war reminded many that the nation still offered much which less-favored people wanted and could get. The youth uprising of the 1960s stirred a conspicuous amount of anti-patriotic feeling, including obscene misuses of the American flag, and of the *Star-Spangled Banner*; see also *Man Without a Country, The.* Daniel Lang's *Patriotism without Flags* (1974) attempted to encourage and justify anti-patriotic feelings. The 1980s saw a revival of patriotism especially among the young which both helped and benefitted from President Reagan's Administration and policies. See also Heroes; and P. Karsten, *Patriot-Heroes in England and America: Political Symbolism and Changing Values over Three Centuries* (1978); E. C. Murdock, *Patriotism Limited 1862-1865* (1967); J. Eagleson and P. Scharper, eds., *The Patriot's Bible* (1975).

**Patron in the Arts**, identified with traditions of conservative largesse, derogated by Marxists as anti-democratic and no more than a byproduct of unearned profits, though it produced famous patrons, including popes and kings. Best known was Samuel Johnson's (*q.v.*) rejoinder to Lord Chesterfield's offer of patronage, after his *Dictionary* was finished and help unnecessary. Poverty-stricken artists and writers such as Thomas Chatterton and Franz Schubert were often cited as having suffered for lack of perceptive patrons. Patrons were more readily found for established works than unproved individuals, including the upkeep of museums and opera houses, though democratic responses in the form of cliques might determine this or that artist's fate. The Federal Arts Projects of the New Deal (*q.v.*) was a democratic effort to keep arts alive in a time of economic stress, but its legitimacy was scorned or debated. The *New York Times* commented: "They need not starve, but must they act?" Though the projects employed many of the artists later to become well known in art, writing, theater, and even music—they were permitted to slide into oblivion. The later National Endowment for the Arts, initiated in a time of prosperity, was also controversial. Meanwhile, systems of patronage under centralized states such as the Soviet Union resulted in reprehensible systems of suppression and control of the arts. For National Endowment, see Filler, DASC. See also Alan Osborne, comp. and ed., *Patron: Industry Supports the Arts* (1966). See also Congress.

**Patroons**, see *American Democrat, The*

**Payne, Daniel A.** (1811-1893), one of the greatest Negro figures of his time, though less recalled by his people because of his great emphasis on education as the ultimate strength. Nevertheless his career involved crises and even drama. Born in Charleston, S.C. of free parents, he displayed aptitudes which enabled him to study not only English and mathematics, but also French, Latin, and Greek. As a teacher of adult slaves, he was so successful that on December 17, 1834 the legislature passed a law making such studies illegal, and threatened him with a whipping and fine. Payne left the state, prepared for the ministry from 1835 to 1837, and served various churches and opened schools. In 1842, he opened a church in Washington, for which he helped build the pews, and organized the first colored pastors association. Resisting prejudice against an educated ministry, he continued pastoral work, in Baltimore being rejected as too genteel as a pastor who wouldn't "let them sing the cornfield ditties." In 1848 he undertook to prepare a history of his African Methodist Episcopal Church: a task which took him from New Orleans to Canada, searching out and preserving documents despite indifference. In 1852 he was elected a bishop and for the next years opened churches and schools, organized mothers' home-training and education classes, and preached the need for literary societies and the study of history, his own special delight. In 1863 he purchased Wilberforce University in Ohio for $10,000. Struggling with debts and practical problems which had always kept him poor, he set it firmly on its way, with a rigid course of study which was a model for study anywhere. With the Civil War won, he returned in triumph to Charleston, where he founded the South Carolina Conference, a center for A.M.E. church expansion throughout the South. Honored internationally by his church and by the World Parliament of Religions at the Chicago 1893 Exposition, he died a renowned figure, leaving as his masterpieces *Semi-Centenary and the Retrospection of the AME Church in the United States of America* (1866) and *Recollections of Seventy Years* (1888). W. E. B. Du Bois, whom he met, and whom he sought to attract to Wilberforce, saw him as a saintly figure. Louis Filler, in Winston, Logan, eds., *Dictionary of American Negro Biography* (1983).

**Peace**, see Filler, DASC, and Pacifism

**"Peace With Honor,"** phrase associated with Prime Minister Benjamin Disraeli (*q.v.*) as used at the Congress of Berlin in 1878.

**Peaceful Coexistence**, see Coexistence

**Peccadilloes,** a liberal euphemism (*q.v.*) for facts which embarrassed the public image of admired liberals. It was much employed during the high point of open discussion of John F. Kennedy's extra-marital exploits, notably in Judith Exner, *My Story* (1977). Since liberals tended to approve more candid speech including obscenities (*q.v.*) as an adjunct to more readily expressive behavior, they required more defensive words when exposed to criticism. Conservatives tended to lay less stress on such issues, and when embarrassed by the deviance of colleagues to attribute the eccentric turn to illness, sometimes happily overcome. An odd response of liberals to the exposure of a top aide to Lyndon Johnson as interested in homosexual behavior was to attribute his actions to overwork. America's credibility in the world, shaken by such major misadventures as Vietnam and the Iranian fiasco (*qq.v.*) suggested that there might be an increased call for stronger executives with fewer peccadilloes. A curious contrast with the treatment accorded Kennedy was provided by an obscure effort, through forgery, to prove that Richard Nixon (*q.v.*) had conducted an extra-marital affair with an ambassador's wife, thus impugning the sincerity of his apparent love of his family: a fraud which did not inspire "investigative journalism" (*q.v.*) to ferret out the culprit.

**"Peculiar Institution,"** phrase used ironically by Northern ideologues with reference to the slavery (*q.v.*) system as it existed in the South before the Civil War (*q.v.*); used without apology by Southerners of that era and after as involving premises of fact and tradition which those remote from both would not well understand.

**Pegler, Westbrook** (1894-1969), a rough-edged individualist in journalism, whose pioneer skepticism of the New Deal (*q.v.*) uncovered blemishes among administrators and rackets (*q.v.*) in unions, earning him both liberal and conservative readers. His exposés of union terrorists and frauds put several union leaders in prison, and won him the Pulitzer Prize in 1941. Pegler soon became convinced that unions were intrinsically foes of free enterprise. His journalism, always harsh, became increasingly abusive and ill-founded, and lost him a representative readership.

**Pei, Mario,** see *America We Lost*

**Pendleton Act**, see Reform and Conservatism; Civil Service Reform

**Pentagon**, a symbol of the role of the military in American domestic and foreign affairs. Its image wavered between old fears of a Man on the White Horse, symbol of an emergent dictator, and the need of a strong military arm to defend the nation. The *Pentagon Papers* at home raised old suspicions of military intrigue when the *New York Times* printed them, despite being classified material. Evidence that some Pentagon expenditures were either foolish or corrupt did no good to its public image, but Congress tended to meet most of its demands for funds. In effect, the military had become everybody's business, which would be handled by the most persuasive faction, made influential by events. See Filler, DASC, Pentagon; Ellsberg, Daniel; and related items. See also Advisors.

**People, The,** more heavily exploited by liberals than conservatives, the latter anxious that responsible and competent persons address or be addressed. Liberals were more prone to generalize alleged social wants, and feel free to speak to and even for "the people." The word was also liable to demagogic uses, a few individuals appointing themselves "people's" representatives, and creating "people's courts" consisting of themselves, with the power of life and death, at least until confronted with actual representatives in the form of police or judges. In a different class were Abraham Lincoln's (*q.v.*) invocations of the people.

**Pepper, Claude** (1900— ), Florida politician. His long service as a Democrat took him from the 1930s, when he co-sponsored the memorable Coffee-Pepper Bill calling for permanent government sponsorship of the arts, to the 1980s when, as an octogenarian Congressman, he became the hero of the elderly. He called for legislation and government programs to alleviate the problems of the elderly. His major achievement was to call attention to the formidable number of aged for whom he functioned as spokesman, most especially the American Association of Retired Persons (AARP) with its fourteen million members. See also Old Age.

**Perjury**, see Hiss Case, The; Chambers, Whittaker

**"Permanent Revolution,"** see Stalin, Josef

**Permissive Society,** a phrase used to describe American society as it emerged, in laws and "lifestyles," out of the 1960s. Liberals tended to be more sympathetic than conservatives in acknowledging its impact, using the phrase ironically or in accusation.

**"Peter Porcupine,"** see Cobbett, William

**"Peter Simple"** (Michael Wharton), British journalist whose column in the London *Telegraph* (*q.v.*) attacked liberal and leftist politicians and celebrities and many aspects of contemporary society in general. Many of his columns dealt with the mythical locale of Stretchford, Nerdley, "lovely, sex-maniac-Sadcake Park," among other locales, schools, businesses and personalities, but also keeping up with such imaginary figures elsewhere as Alderman Foodbottom 25-stone, iron-watch chained, crag-visaged, grim-booted chairman of the Bradford City Tramways and Fine Arts Committee whose views of proper citizen and artist deportment contrasted sharply with that of liberal or experimental persons in the news. Simple's cast of Stretchford personalities over the years included upper-class Communists, libertarian psychologists, a bizarre clergyman who thought God ought to give way to a younger man, an official chaplain for freeways, and international boring experts. Michael Wharton, *The Missing Will* (1984), was his revealing autobiography. He also imaginatively wrote of a reactionary newspaper which had not conceded freedom to the "perverse colonials" in the United States. In addition, Peter Simple commented on news and individuals in his own voice. When a radical *Observer* scribe noted, "The lowering of the grievance threshold is a feature of our society," Simple noted the evasive phraseology and replied that "ours is a society in which envy, spite, discontent, and petty-mindedness are growing daily, and are being encouraged." Since the daily news provided from strange to weird instances of bizarre opinion and action, it was not always possible to be certain that Simple had or had not concocted a particular incident as an example of what the way of the world had become. His forthright judgments upon pacifists, radicals, rock singers, avant-garde artists, liberal ministers, politicians, and others gained him acclaim on both sides of the Atlantic. Kingsley Amis wrote an introduction to one of Peter Simple's books, *The Stretchford Chronicles* (1980). See also *The World of Peter Simple* (1973).

**Philanthropy.** Traditionally conservative, depending as it did on grants from living or deceased persons of wealth, philanthropy developed under increasingly impersonal conditions as the cities grew. It mixed simple charity with better-directed projects, and produced notable pioneers, Josephine Shaw Lowell (*q.v.*) being among the most distinguished. But even when it took on scientific aspects, as in the famous war on hookworm, sponsored by John D. Rockefeller, philanthropy received the scorn of liberals who considered it conscience money, a tithe returned from what had been "stolen" from workers and their families. The coming of the welfare state (*q.v.*) produced a new species of philanthropists, liberals who administered public funds to alleviate need. Such funds were dispersed in an effort to promote physical and mental health. Conservatives, however, tended to be suspicious of the concept of mental health, preferring to rely on traditional families and communities rather than on medical treatment and psychological counseling. Many conservatives were less than sympathetic to those who did not fit in with traditional families and communities. Conservatives defended voluntarism (*q.v.*) and maintained that much of the state and federal funds allotted went not to clients but to administrators. See also Foundations.

**Philbrick, Herbert A.,** see *I Led 3 Lives*; Gitlow, Benjamin

**Philistines,** Matthew Arnold's (*q.v.*) memorable designation for those who eroded cultural values through ignorance, social power, and coarse cultural standards. Arnold discerned three classes in the society of his time: the aristocracry (Barbarians), the bourgeoisie (Philistines), and the working class (Populace), and held the Philistines particularly culpable in diminishing cultural potential, because of their capacity for eliciting works in "culture," and for bringing it down to their level.

**Phillips, David Graham** (1867-1911), journalist, novelist. During his meteoric career beginning in 1901 he was perceived as "radical" in his criticism of the evil effects of capitalism and crushing urban conditions. In 1911 Phillips was assassinated. After his death his reputation fell victim to the "disillusioned" criticism of the 1920s which seized on a false essay by Granville Hicks, the religious academic turned Communist critic, to consider Phillips a non-subject in literature. See Filler, *Voice of the Democracy* (1978). Although the muckraking and Progressive movements of which he was part were indicted as having been intrinsically conservative, this gave Phillips and his co-workers no status with emergent conservative intellectuals of the time, whose literary equipment was eclectic and whose outlook followed that of Irving Babbitt (*q.v.*) and associated figures. Phillips's indictment, *The Treason of the Senate* (1906) emerged as a classic under obscure auspices, and his novel *Susan Lenox: Her Fall and Rise*, published posthumously, was given status as a "pioneer" pro-feminist work. Nevertheless, he continued to serve neither liberal nor conservative causes: one of a number of cultural figures whose vision and influence gyrated wildly among esthetic impulses as far apart as those of John Steinbeck and James Gould Cozzens (*qq.v.*). See also Gun Control.

**Phillips, Kevin P.** (1940- ), conservative columnist and political researcher. President of the American Political Research Corporation, and publisher of its reports, he was credited for having invented the concepts of the "Sun Belt" and the "New Right," and for having shown capacities for accurate prediction. Whether his *The Emerging Republican Majority* (1969) actually foresaw a majority, or merely gained by cyclical developments, his analyses were mind-stirring, as he weighed historical trends and compared them with apparent developments among classes and sections. Such questions as the Reagan "mandate" and the capacity of the population to arrive at a common purpose made for various conjectures which alerted the reader to possibilities, without informing him of what might eventuate from some powerful movement in one part of the world or another. Nevertheless, the very idea of a *Post-Conservative America* (1982)—at a time when it was not quite certain that there was a conservative America—provided challenges which in Phillips's varied sources—interviews, polls, events—stimulated thought.

**Phillips, Ulrich B.** (1877-1934), formidable defender of the old South, who won Northern honors for publications and instituted a line of Southern historians at Yale University. A native of Georgia, he steeped himself in its lore, studied history in the Columbia University graduate school under William H. Dunning, and published *Georgia and States Rights* (1902), which won him his first prize. It treated slavery as an incident in an overall progressive career. *Life and Labor in the Old South* (1929) won him his greatest distinction, for its prose and for its sense of a rich and fruitful civilization. A major figure in the American Historical Association, he had already published in its *Review* (1928) his most challenging essay, "The Central Theme of Southern History." It held that the theme was not slavery, but preservation of the nation as dominated by its white inhabitants. Phillips touched many graduate students, but made his greatest impact on Gilbert H. Barnes, whose *The Antislavery Impulse, 1830-1844* (1933) was dedicated to Phillips. Barnes offered a thesis which, effective in graduate schools, turned the current of historical writing by denouncing the major abolitionist figures as futile and dishonest, and finding a North-South consensus in an apparent antislavery consensus. This was later explicated when Phillips's successor at Yale, C. Van Woodward, in a 1963 reprint of *Life and Labor in the Old South*, admitting various charges against Phillips's historical presentation, but arguing for giving it the same regard that might be accorded classical historians of the Old Regimes of France and Russia. New editions of other of Phillips's books, with introductions by others, including avant-garde historians, gave evidence that the soundness of his basic materials and presentation insured its durability in changing times. See Louis Filler, introduction to Phillips, ed., *Plantation and Frontier*, two volumes, in J. R. Commons et al., eds., *A Documentary History of American Industrial Society* (1958 ed.); and Filler, "Consensus," in *Essays in Honor of Russel B. Nye*, ed., J. Waldmeir (1978).

**Philosophers,** an adjunct of the conservative-liberal struggle. For liberals, see Deism; Dewey, John; Humanism; Pragmatism. Conservatives employed philosophers for intellectual nourishment, ideas, references, phrasings, and major premises. In addition, they produced such religious-historical interpreters as Eric Voegelin and Leo Strauss (*qq.v.*) in opposition to such as Reinhold Niebuhr's *Reflections on the End of an Era*, as preferring, between capitalist hypocrisy and communist vengeance, vengeance. Russell Kirk (*q.v.*) gained much from philosopher-statesmen, and in Regnery's (*q.v.*) "Gateway Editions" provided introductions to works by Orestes Brownson, Edmund Burke, Thomas Hobbes, John Locke, and John Stuart Mill (*qq.v.*). Conservatives debated the validity of tenets held by these expositors and such others as David Hume (*q.v.*). St. Thomas Aquinas (*q.v.*) ranked high among many conservatives because of his Christian faith and his logic.

**Physiocrats,** see Quesnay, Francois; Smith, Adam

**Plain Talk.** Edited without pay by Isaac Don Levine (*q.v.*), it was an invaluable source of revelations of Communist operations in the United States and abroad, notably in Stalinist Russia and Communist China before and during Communism's triumph on the Mainland. *Plain Talk* was issued between 1946 and 1950. It was begun with a modest grant from Alfred Kohlberg, who was accused of being an "agent" of Chiang Kai-Shek's China because of his having business relations with it. Levine regularly provided articles on the weakness of American diplomatic connections with Stalin (*q.v.*), the role of the Institute of Pacific Relations in neutralizing American opinion toward the Communists in China, the network of supporters of Alger Hiss (*q.v.*) in government and out, and other evidence of malfeasance and treason. Although Levine's cohorts and their enemies treated one another with bitterness and recrimination, the general public itself received news of subversion and subversives (*q.v.*) calmly until the Soviets detonated the atomic bomb. Afterwards, the public supported McCarthy (*q.v.*). Told of the Gulags (*q.v.*) in *Plain Talk*, with a remarkable map of the U.S.S.R. pinpointing locations the public offered no response until Solzhenitsyn (*q.v.*) with his enormous fame, placed the facts before it. *Plain Talk* circulated better in the Soviet underground than in America. It attacked famous people, including Bertrand Russell, William C. Bullitt, Margaret Mitchell (of *Gone with the Wind*), Alexander Kerensky, Eugene Lyons (*q.v.*) and the British Labor Party's Harold J. Laski. A major effort of *Plain Talk* was to have the State Department and other government agencies expose secret information about U.S.-U.S.S.R. dealings for the public's information. Some of it came out by force of often inadvertent revelations, but much of it did not. *Plain Talk* died of financial attrition. Commercial (*q.v.*) conservativism had no money to spare for expanding it or furthering its distribution, though it curiously had funds for many other enterprises, some fairly conservative in nature. The non-success of *Plain Talk* makes an interesting comparison with the success of *National Review*, with respect to format, financing, features, range of articles, and cultural content. See also Isaac Don Levine, ed., *Plain Talk: An Anthology from the Leading Anti-Communist Magazine of the 40s* (Arlington House, [*q.v.*], 1976).

**"Planned Economy,"** seen positively by liberals; as deceptive and leading to the evils of bureaucracy, socialism, and collectivism by anti-statists and conservatives. Although there were obvious uses for experts able to contribute to large national and international projects, and a need for sophisticated plans in a vast array of operations, private and public, such operations were distinguished from a planned *economy*, which placed the individual at the mercy of impersonal boards, politicians with private interests to further, and theoreticians removed from the realities of human nature, traditions (*qq.v.*), and the predilections of persons and communities. In the Thirties (*q.v.*), the exigencies of a stalled economy made planning seem attractive to socialists and others, and suggested such books as the liberal George Soule's *The Planned Society* (1935). In that era too those sympathetic to or open to the expectations of the Soviet Union (*q.v.*) saw it as overcoming the "chaos" of a capitalist economic structure, especially with foreign correspondents reporting the Soviet Union's economic experiences in partisan and distorted fashion. (See Lyons, Eugene.) The expansion of government authority and the welfare state (*q.v.*) caused an unprecedented expansion of planning boards, bureaucrats, consultants, and others who institutionalized planning—and who became targets of the growing conservative revolt. Libraries of books discussed urban planning and reorganization, technological master plans, and housing, educational and other guidelines: projects involving enormous investments. The rise of Third World (*q.v.*) governments brought to the fore endless successions of advisors and administrators to plan and further enterprises, often dangerous to the populations affected. Thus, central water supplies, intended to be more sanitary and efficient than supplanted water-holes, transgressed century-old traditions and religious sanctions, without necessarily placing the new equipment in competent hands. (See Bauer, P.T.) Added to such problems were those of sheer corruption (*q.v.*), incompetence at the highest levels, political cross-purposes, and other dilemmas which less planning might have at the least modified. Conservatives resisted such planning at the various point of production, aided in their cause by the manifest failures apparent in cities and in exposed bureaucratic failures. For an overview, Ludwig von Mises (*q.v.*), *Planning for Freedom* (1974). A sample of studies in the area, of varied quality, include A. H.

Hanson, *Planning and the Politicians* (1969); L. R. Beres and H. R. Targ, eds., *Planning Alternative World Futures* (1975); E. M. Byrne, *Planning and Educational Inequity* (1974); W. I. Jones, *Planning and Economic Policy: Socialist Mali and Her Neighbors* (1976); Jack Rothman, *Planning and Organizing for Social Change* (1974); Michael Shanks, *Planning and Politics: The British Experience 1960-76* (1977).

**Planned Obsolescence,** an idea of conservative-commercial thought. It posited that if goods were produced to wear out, there would always be a demand for more, thus ending once and for all the fear of unemployment (*q.v.*). It is also interesting as having been thought of as "*planned* obsolescence"—high level planning, especially on the government level, being suspect in much conservative thinking. The capacity of private enterprise entrepreneurs to plan was rudely exposed during the first level of National Recovery Administration (NRA) operation. The theory did not take into account the predicament of consumers who should purchase goods marked for obsolescence, who might even then lack funds to purchase more. Many saw planned obsolescence as leading to shoddy goods and shoddy workmanship and destroying "productivity" (*q.v.*). For an early statement of the theory, see Bernard London, *The New Prosperity* (1933).

**Planned Parenthood,** an organization originally devoted to continuing the work of Margaret Sanger, intended to ease the torments particularly of poor and ignorant women made helpless by the constant carriage of children in poverty, or driven to misery or worse by rape or passion. It taught them about contraception and provided means for limiting births. The Supreme Court decision of 1973, legalizing abortion (*q.v.*) created new conditions surrounding the work of Planned Parenthood. Feminists emphasizing women's rights as they saw them interpreted "planning" to mean women's right to dispose of their bodies as they chose. Federal funds, made available to the states for medical purposes which included abortion, were challenged by anti-abortionists. In 1979 the Hyde Amendment cut off this source of funds to the states. Thereafter states became the battleground for persons seeking funds for abortions. Planned Parenthood associations, adjusting to this program, held abortion not a solution of last resort, but, as a New York official stated, a normal part of their information, counseling, and related services.

**Plato** (427?-347 B.C.), a giant figure in the history of philosophy, along with his student Aristotle (*q.v.*), yet more disturbing to modern readers unsympathetic to his goals or conditions because of his attractive flights of fancy and idealism. Karl Popper, who favored *The Open Society*, classed Plato among its enemies. John Jay Chapman (*q.v.*), in his *Lucian, Plato and Greek Morals*, would not take Plato seriously. Warner Fite's *The Platonic Legend* (1934) was obviously influenced by the totalitarian threat of his time, which he thought Plato endorsed with honeyed words. Conservatives reacted in different ways. The world certainly needed the method and order of this disciple of Socrates, this founder of an Academy where students would face a lucid dialectic and learn. Plato's "Socratic dialogues" were masterpieces of inquiry into ethics, knowledge, education, and laws governing human nature, society, and the universe. Plato's search for harmony in life and nature, though it might offend attempts at self-expression and those who feared authoritarianism, seemed capable to many for doing less harm than liberal idealizations of "working-class leaders" and their firing-squads and Gulags (*q.v.*). Although Plato's ideal *Republic* was to be led by an elite, itself dominated by a philosopher-king, he circumscribed his leaders with such necessary virtues as to make them incapable of dishonor. Certainly, their virtues were often ascribed to monsters of totalitarianism, assisted by their controlled media. But Plato was working from his primary concepts of "Forms"—ideas which were eternal, despite the flux and confusion of people and society—and this helped preserve his ideal in the face of discouraging failures. Some of Plato's assumptions were offensive to segments of society—his acceptance of slavery, of homosexual relations, of female subservience, and his stable society which included no democratic fluidity. Such, of course, were the presumptions of his time. But it helped to underscore that Plato's mind was a compound of living experience and the most intensive search for an ultimate reality of ancient times. The very anger his work roused in unempathetic readers was proof of the eternal challenge in his dialogues. Plato's attraction for some conservatives consists of his refutation of moral relativism, his transcendental realism, and his rejection of mass democracy. See also Dickinson, G. Lowes; and Eric Voegelin (*q.v.*), *Plato* (1966); R. S. Crossman, *Plato Today* (1963); Paul Elmer More (*q.v.*), *Platonism* (1931); Glenn R. Morrow, *Plato's Law of Slavery in Its Relations to Greek Law* (1939); John Wild, *Plato's Modern Enemies and the Theory of Natural Law* (1953). See also Utopia.

**"Plenty,"** a liberal cliché intended to expose a society which harbored poor "in the midst of plenty." The concept linked, too, with the liberal demand for income "distribution": essentially a levelling goal, asking increased disbursements from central government to augment the income of the poor. (See Welfare.) A somewhat reverse concept appeared in a reputable historian's book which sought to determine why the nation was so plentiful in material goods, ignoring the contemporary squalor and misery in the midst of entitlements (*q.v.*); see David M. Potter, *People of Plenty* (1954).

**PLO,** see Middle East

**Podhoretz, Norman** (1930- ), editor of *Commentary* (*q.v.*), and transitional (*q.v.*) figure from liberalism to neo-conservativism (*q.v.*). Educated at Columbia University, the Jewish Theological Seminary, and Cambridge University, he joined *Commentary*, where he emphasized socio-literary concerns of a contemporary character; see his *Doings and Undoings: The Fifties and After in American Writing* (1964). His *Making It* (1968) was a combination of autobiography and confession, describing the line of inquiry and direction it required to "make it" in New York among such figures as Lionel Trilling (*q.v.*). See also his *Breaking Ranks* (1979). Increasingly disillusioned with his liberal milieu, after becoming editor of *Commentary* in 1960, he turned its columns into an area for reconsidering liberal premises and history with respect to new issues of the day. Since *Commentary* had grown up with a language and sense of issues closer to that of the *New York Times* (*q.v.*) than of any conservative journal, its change of direction added a dimension to conservative discourse not present before. By the time Podhoretz issued *Why We Were in Vietnam* (1982), his position was firmly conservative; his prose, however, was more capable of reaching liberals somewhat more directly than could the *National Review* (*q.v.*). See also Decter, Midge Rosenthal; Mrs. Norman Podhoretz; and *Neo-Conservatives*, by Peter Steinfels.

**Poe, Edgar Allan** (1809-1849), American author, an example of an essential conservative, driven by guilt and fantasy to a "bohemian" way of life though not as a flouter of social convention. Though Baudelaire thought he recognized a kindred spirit in Poe's writings, Poe's recourse to liquor and drugs, then easily obtained, was misunderstood and maliciously exploited. Poe's adoration of women—masking his tragic impotence, his love of formality when his finances permitted, and his dependence on a child-wife and mother-in-law defined a distraught genius. For a sense of Poe's compulsions, which prevented him from organizing his life, Joseph Wood Krutch's study (1926). See also Marie Bonaparte, *The Life and Works of Edgar Allan Poe* (1949), by a disciple of Freud. For an attempt to define a "normal" Poe who pretended deep feelings, N. B. Fagin, *The Histrionic Mr. Poe* (1949).

**Poetry,** see Literature

**Poland,** see Filler, DASC. In the years after World War II Poland became a satellite of the Soviet Union, but its people maintained their resistance to Soviet control. This was because of Poland's long tradition of antagonism to Russia, its Catholicism (*q.v.*) which resisted official Communist atheism, and its memories of World War II and the Katyn Forest massacre (*q.v.*). In addition its trade unions manifested a power and persistence which challenged Communist authority while avoiding such provocations as had brought upon East Berliners and Hungarian freedom-fighters bloody reprisals. Through strikes, organizations, and demonstrations, Polish workers forced recognition of their major independent union, Solidarity, and its leader, Lech Walesa; both became symbolic of freedom throughout the world, and could not be ignored by Soviet surrogates (*q.v.*). Efforts to discredit both Solidarity and Walesa included arrests, threats, and orders to disband. Especially important to Poland's future in the mid-1980s was the presence in the Vatican of a Polish Pope, John Paul II.

**Policy Review,** a publication of the Heritage Foundation (*q.v.*) which attracted the substantial cultural and educational talents of George Gilder, William E. Simon, Robert Strausz-Hupé, and others who helped refine and update conservative opinion. A Washington quarterly, it focused more on government issues and foreign policy concerns than did *The Public Interest* (*q.v.*), and was less burdened with earlier liberal attitudes than *Commentary* (*q.v.*).

**Political Writers of Eighteenth-Century England** (1964), edited by Jeffrey Hart, an anthology with introduction which provides contrast between such conservatives as Jonathan Swift, Viscount Bolingbroke, Samuel Johnson, and Edmund Burke and more liberal to radical expositors such as John Locke, John Wilkes, and Thomas Paine.

**Politicalization,** valid questions made into causes, and so distorted to make "political" points. Thus fluoride (*q.v.*), advocated by evidently legitimate scientists and researchers, and adopted in numerous cities as a means of resisting tooth decay, was claimed by a conservative element to be part of a Communist plot to poison the American population. Some conservatives were unwilling to argue the matter because of their general antipathy to "big government." On the other hand, they were less upset by evidence that large corporations harmed the water supply by carelessly pouring toxic by-products into streams and rivers. On the liberal side, free speech and self-expression were often encouraged regardless of the consequences. Yet liberals often fought to keep public prayer out of schools, citing Constitutional principles and the views of the Founding Fathers—though evidence of the Founding Fathers' approval of prayer, for reasons of reverence or expedience, was ready to hand. Other subjects vulnerable to politicalization included attitudes toward Communism in theory and practice and toward women, "minorities," gays, abortion, the rights of defendants in court, sexual preferences, cheating on welfare, and the prerogatives of police, the FBI, and the CIA (*qq.v.*).

**Polls.** They have been shown over and over again to give rise to serious difficulties resulting from the intent or the integrity of the polltakers, and yet have often proved to be correct with respect to trends and elections. "Public opinion" has been difficult to assess, because of the enigmas of subjects and persons: did those polled really mean to say what they said? Changing opinion was even more difficult to chart by polls. What was the public meaning to say in 1981 in its extraordinary welcome to the hostages freed by Iran? What changed in the final weeks of the 1948 election which gave an unexpected victory to Harry Truman over Thomas Dewey (*q.v.*)? Pollsters confessed that there may have been an element of wishful thinking in their claims that the Carter-Reagan race in 1980 was "close" to the very end. When they have been proved grossly wrong, however, why have the pollsters not been discredited? It is possible that the public does not take them seriously enough. Or take its own opinions seriously enough to stand by them, until crisis forces definite decision. Difficulties in continuity (*q.v.*), created by uncrystallized attitudes toward crime, ethnic bodies, distraught families (*q.v.*), and catastrophes abroad might have mixed sincere forgetfulness with impulsive judgments which the respondents did not themselves credit. Late in November 1983 a nationwide telephone poll by *Newsweek*, involving 1,032 people, had three-fourths of them considering Kennedy's Presidency "good to great," and two-thirds of them believing the nation would be much "different" had he lived. Nationwide television focus on the Kennedy at that time, however, almost certainly contributed to that opinion. Other opinions in the same poll suggested that the field of perceived knowledge was wide open. Three out of four people polled, despite all official conclusions, believed that Lee Harvey Oswald had not been alone in the assassination of President Kennedy. As to popularity of Presidents in the poll, after Kennedy came Franklin D. Roosevelt, with 10% of those questioned. Then Harry Truman with 9%, Ronald Reagan with 8%, and Jimmy Carter and Abraham Lincoln tied at 5%. The conservative columnist James J. Kilpatrick was perhaps right to be doubtful of a 1983 study (S. J. Rosenstone, *Forecasting Presidential Elections*), which claimed to have a formula for forecasting the outcome of Presidential elections in advance. But his belief that "a single line" by Reagan in the New Hampshire primaries ("I paid for this microphone, Mr. Green") had "popped the George Bush balloon," and that a second "single line" during Reagan's debate with Carter ("There you go again" [*q.v.*]) had done in Carter, could never be proved or disproved.

**Poor.** By the 1980s the existence of masses of poor people in the U. S., despite great sums regularly contributed by the Federal Government, the states, and the cities, as well as by voluntary (*q.v.*) organizations of every kind, raised questions, the main one being whether any process of rehabilitation was also involved. Although it was generally recognized that social loyalties and responsibilities were in chaos, and in the "inner cities" catastrophic, much of liberal thought divided this condition from the condition of poverty, reluctant to curb the "freedom" of the poor and demanding more welfare without any indication that it would result in greater social stability and improved prospects for the best and worthiest of the poor. Conservatives argued that chaos and catastrophe were related, and that "throwing money" at the problem would do nothing to modify it. Moreover, they pointed to the actual sums expended on the poor. In 1983, Aid to Dependent Children served 3.6 million families receiving $275 a month, food stamps going to some 22 million people, and free medicine under Medicare (*q.v.*) serving some 23 million people. John O'Sullivan, a British conservative in America, then editor of *Policy Review*, noted that with the American "poverty level" officially set at $9,300, "the majority of British workers would be eligible for American food stamps." Liberals, working with statistics on cash benefits, saw the poor as needy and numerous. The non-cash benefits, however, were so substantial as to suggest a desperate need for honesty, if a program leading to improvement was to be found. Conservatives maintained that official caseloads could be cut by over 20%, resulting in billions of dollars of savings and a clarification of human needs if non-cash benefits were also used to determine who was poor. The battle against cheating and corruption with government funds had begun late, and proceeded slowly; only the sheer lack of government funds was forcing attention to the national scandal. Difficulties also attended efforts to force able people to work—"workfare" instead of "welfare"—liberals arguing that this infringed upon their freedom. Yet every gesture toward "workfare" immediately caused substantial numbers of welfare recipients to leave the program. Finally, there was the inevitable detritus of society—bums, vagrants, winos and others—whom liberals included among the poor, but who could not be included with those among the poor who could help make their class a productive, positive element of society. In 1983 the nation also coped with "the new poor": persons who had lived well until deprived of their jobs, and who were then reduced to welfare. Even here, tricks were possible with statistics and "representative" portraits and interviews. Often these portraits and interviews comported with the journalist's or television commentator's point-of-view. Conservatives, in the mid-1980s, were turning over ideas such as Herbert Hoover (*q.v.*) had turned over in 1930: voluntarism (*q.v.*) and an emphasis on business revival which would employ the employable and leave others to their own devices or the assistance of compassionate agencies or individuals. A more responsive family structure would also serve the individual and the neighborhood. But the poor were voters, and to a degree they would help to forge their own destiny.

**Popular Front,** a notorious technique sponsored by the Comintern (*q.v.*) for infiltrating liberal and socialist organizations by proposing united action against presumably common enemies such as fascist organizations. In the late 1930s, it derived from Stalin's slogan of a "united front from below," instructing Communist parties to urge the "workers" of socialist parties to leave their leaders and join in action against the common enemy. Since socialists *were* socialist, the slogan alienated them further and prevented them from creating a united front which could meet the fascist cohorts on their own ground. The "united front from below" was discredited in Germany, and in Republican Spain, where Communists proved more adept at killing other Republicans not of their persuasion than opposing the fascist columns. Communists were then ordered to enlist in "popular fronts," in the United States, in Great Britain, and elsewhere, enlisting socialists, liberals, and unaligned groups which they could then labor to dominate. During World War II the tactic was unnecessary, because of the Grand Alliance which made the Soviet Union seem respectable. By then, the Comintern had been disbanded as unnecessary. However, the "popular front" technique was revived during the "Cold War" (*q.v.*), as Communists in Greece, Turkey, and elsewhere sought to spread their influence according to now-established techniques.

**Population Control,** mainly a liberal concern, dovetailing with such other liberal concerns as abortion, contraception, homosexuality, and Third World problems. The fear of overpopulation of the planet led to the demand that national and international policy be found to prevent the choking up of land with excess population. Marxists (*q.v.*) had scorned Malthus's (*q.v.*) analyses of overpopulation as justifying war and disease as nature's preventatives. They had argued for a better distribution of the world's goods, and, welcoming centralized authority, foresaw measures to control population. Nevertheless, overpopulation was a phenomena in underdeveloped continents which policy could scarcely reach. Conservatives saw vast stretches of world terrain which had been hardly populated at all, and mixed the Biblical command to be "fruitful and multiply" with their sense of social discipline and restraint to resist the arguments favoring abortion. Conservative Catholics argued for "natural" contraception, sexual restraint or the "rhythm" technique of limiting intercourse. Conservatives scorned the argument that homosexuality aided population control. Oddly, the alarmist argument, that much of the world's surface was uninhabitable or unfruitful, persisted despite the fact that transportation facilities made almost any locale reachable with food, and that the capacity of fertile soil had multiplied so as to produce food surpluses in various areas. The program for decreasing population in underdeveloped lands was an entire field of argument between liberals and conservatives. It involved the use of birth-control devices and other elements too often controverted on political rather than human lines.

**Populism,** undoubtedly a liberal trend in the progress of the nation, yet with qualifications meriting note. The distribution of wealth was affected by government policy, but also by changing conditions. In pre-Civil War America, the basis of wealth was land, which state and Federal governments could not avoid administering, and to which entrepreneurs and clients responded with varying degrees of justice. The great events of later decades were the railroads and the development of technology, which centralized power and forced laborers and farmers to organize for their separate purposes. Laborers were less concerned about monopoly than about the development of unions (*qq.v.*), in effect a monopoly of their own. Farmers, separated by distance but linked with the railroads, required protection from destructive storing and carrying charges, discrimination, and the vagaries of export and import charges. Since they saw themselves as the basic national interest—the providers of food, the "original" Americans—it was difficult for them to reconcile themselves to sharing their burden with workers, often "alien" and often crowded in cities. Later conservatives would blame the government for farmers' troubles: a government which had distributed land grants and subsidies rather than opened railroads to private enterprise. Also part of government, however, was the Supreme Court (*q.v.*), which in the late 19th century found for private enterprise of whatever dimension, thus forcing attention to trusts (*qq.v.*) in ways which took legislative decades to bring into relative focus. The famous Populist Platform of 1892 did indeed call for nationalization of the railroads—which actually took place during World War I; populists sought to control gold, demanded a graduated income tax, popular election of senators, the establishment of postal savings banks, and other measures intended to alleviate their anxieties. Overall it was a liberal program, but bearing little relation to the program which grew out of the later New Deal (*q.v.*). Populism had its crackpot fringes, but overall it dealt with real and emergency problems; and it was absorbed by the major parties as conditions changed. Failure to concentrate on these conditions, and the factors affecting them in turn, later produced interpretations of populism by Marxist and "New" historians, with little sense of context, "revealing" matters known before and once seen in perspective—excessive hatred of spirits and joy in life generally, bias toward foreigners and, in the South, toward Negroes—in short, a program leading to reaction. This view of American farming history received spirited rebuttal and wavered from sight as Jimmy Carter (*q.v.*) presented himself as a "New Populist," and the concept was approved in liberal circles. It diminished with Carter's fall, but gave warning that conservatives could profitably review still vibrant history from their standpoints.

**Portable Conservative Reader, The,** edited by Russell Kirk (1982), a collection of prose, fiction, and verse, beginning with an ample selection of Edmund Burke and including selections from conservatives of Revolutionary times—John Adams, Alexander Hamilton, and Fisher Ames; thereafter English and American selections mark the progress of conservatism through constitutional and social crisis. Arguments against leveling, against utilitarian radicalism, and against dangers created by an expanding democracy bring into play a wide variety of authors. Included are American controversialists from John C. Calhoun and James Fenimore Cooper to Paul Elmer More and Irving Babbitt; among the Englishmen included are Thomas Babington Macaulay, John Henry Newman, C. S. Lewis, and Malcolm Muggeridge. A section entitled "Resistance and Hope" features the varied figures of Irving Kristol, Robert Nisbet, and Kirk himself. (*Qq.v.*). See also *Wisdom of Conservatism, The.*

**"Positive" Law**, man-made, as contrasted with Natural Law (*q.v.*), seen as in the nature of humankind, from which durable and just law could be adduced. Murray Rothbard's (*q.v.*) libertarian views emphasized their validity under natural law, as part of his argument that libertarianism (*q.v.*) was not an exotic philosophy, but rooted in the nature of human beings. See also Natural Rights.

**Positivism,** see Comte, Auguste

**Pound, Ezra** (1885-1972) American poet and critic. A key figure in the American poetic "renascence" of the 1920s and 1930s, he sought fresh ways of saying which encouraged such artists as T. S. Eliot (*q.v.*), whose work constituted a criticism of established standards of taste in America. His own taste was shifting and authoritarian; he sneered at the poetry of A. E. Housman but liked the early work of Robert Frost. His own poems were rarely memorable, except for their search for modern expression. His relevance to American life merited closer examination. He entertained worthless theories about American finance, and dangerous views of the worth of fascism and the significance of Jews (*qq.v.*). He spoke on the radio from Rome, in exile, on the values of fascism and the American participation in World War II. He was picked up by American military in 1945 and brought back to the United States to be tried on charges of treason. Many American literary figures came to his defense, however, and he was declared mentally unfit for trial and secured in St. Elizabeth's Hospital. There, later revelations showed, he was accorded the most special consideration. While in the hospital he was awarded the touted Bollingen Prize for poetry.

The question was whether Pound had been responsible for his treasonous activities or had indeed been mentally unfit as claimed. Some argued that the treatment accorded Pound showed that American intellectuals were prepared to be tolerant of treason, especially from one of their own. E. Fuller Torrey, *The Roots of Treason: Ezra Pound and the Secret of St. Elizabeth's* (1984).

**Pragmatism.** As a post-Civil War development, it appeared to have overcome the limitations of an older Utilitarianism (*q.v.*). It depended on more than the pleasure-pain principle. In William James's (*q.v.*) hands, pragmatism became a seeking device to enable him to probe psychological and religious experiences. John Dewey (*q.v.*) originally found in it an experimental means for unfolding human capabilities. Pragmatism as merely practical was closer to commercialism and conformity (*qq.v.*) than to social service and individual enhancement. With the rise of doctrinaire socialism and emotional fascism and, following World War II, philosophies of existentialism, absurdity, and the irrationality (*qq.v.*) of the 1960s youth movements, historical pragmatism seemed securely in history, esteemed neither by conservatives nor liberals.

**Prayer In School**, a controversy especially highlighted following the election of Ronald Reagan to the Presidency in 1980, since he endorsed prayer in school and sought to advance it. Public prayer in the schools was ruled unconstitutional in 1962 (*Engel vs. Vitale*), and this divided conservatives from liberals across the land, though other major social crises, including the youth rebellion, Vietnam, and Watergate (*qq.v.*) drew attention from it. John F. Kennedy, as President, suggested that children pray elsewhere. Others invoked the Constitution, though unclearly as to evidence; they were answered with attacks on "judicial legislation." Prayer in school was the foremost issue among others involving public Christmas observances, "creationism" (*q.v.*), a chaplain for Congress, and other practices. Often overlooked were the opinions of the Founding Fathers (*q.v.*) the long national experience with prayer in school, and the maintenance of religious practices in the armed services. Agitation for an amendment to the Constitution authorizing prayer in school was led by the more religious branches of conservatism. A time in schools for "silent prayer" interested a wide variety of institutions. Meanwhile, it was common knowledge that prayer in schools persisted throughout the land, despite court decisions. Since the pluralistic religious nature of the population had become more evident, thanks to numerous court cases and public manifestations, it was clear that any resolution of the issue, even granted the privilege of public prayer in the schools, would require ecumenical discussion and debates, which did not seem in the offing in the mid-1980s.

**Prejudice,** a persistently difficult subject because of shifting standards of what constitutes permissible and impermissible attitudes. Thus, intellectuals who prided themselves on freedom from prejudice thought nothing of passing on "Polish jokes"—a practice which persisted until Polish resistance against Soviet repression made them obsolete. "Dumb Swede" continued as a mindless impression, even though Swedes were demonstrably the opposite of "dumb." Jews and Negroes carried the burden of prejudice in the first half of the twentieth century, being subject to clouds of forthright discrimination or of rationalizations, such as that blacks would be happiest among their own people or that Jews, being "brilliant," had to be kept to quotas in graduate schools so as to keep the schools "representative." The civil rights drive, implemented with state and federal law, turned the balance the other way, making matters once a question of judgment a question of law and even political power. Although prejudices undoubtedly persisted, including prejudices against WASPS (*q.v.*), they were constrained to take second place to expedience. George Wallace (*q.v.*) of Alabama became the symbol of a renovated, politicalized Southern outlook, winning the support of black voters in his drive to become governor of Alabama. Conservatives faced "affirmative action" (*q.v.*) challenges with an insistence on quality. The anti-prejudice drive uncovered new prejudices long hidden in earlier social fabrics, including prejudices against the aged or aging, against various classes of women, and against homosexuals. The drive for equality made more difficult the search for quality, and, even more, the search for individual preference, especially where business and society intermixed, as in television programming. The courts, finding it difficult to judge between equity and free enterprise, sometimes made decisions involving heavy penalties which inhibited business practices and seemed to many to threaten the foundations of private initiative. As the nation labored to establish working law and habit in an ethnic and politicalized world, there were patent losses. There was little natural humor and daring possible, since any choice of phrases might be interpreted according to partisan prejudices. Spontaneous likings and antipathies had to be carefully laundered in public. Many felt that the nation's heritage of folklore and high culture was in jeopardy, as groups and individuals competed for position and prestige

**Prejudices: A Philosophical Dictionary** (1983), see Nisbet, Robert

**Preparedness,** a major conservative impulse proceeding America's intervention in World War I. It is best recalled in Theodore Roosevelt's exhortation to Americans to *Fear God and Take Your Own Part* (1916), and the efforts of some well-to-do persons to set an example of "preparedness" for wartime emergencies by creating a public consciousness of crisis and patriotic policy. They organized the National Security League, which sought to further citizen "loyalty," and to influence education and immigrant policies; see John C. Edwards, *Patriots in Pinstripe* (1982).

**Preservation,** a grassroots, patriotic impulse intended to emphasize the spiritual as well as material value to the nation of locality of sites, buildings, and artifacts reminiscent of individuals or events useful in understanding the nation's development. Although it often leaned toward antiquarianism, it could be vigorously anti-antiquarian in resisting the ruthless demolition of landmarks in the interests of mere "development" for commercial purposes, and in proving the value of landmarks to local Federal officials. The National Trust for Historic Preservation emerged out of the more limited efforts of earlier preservationists to form an influential body concerned for a wide body of problems and issues. It published *Historic Preservation* and *Preservation News.*

**Press, The,** see Media

**Pressure Groups.** They have always existed in American politics, but became more numerous and influential in the post-World War II era with the multiplication of "minority" (*q.v.*) groups of every kind, made hopeful for new opportunities or advantages by public action, ambitious local political machines, Congressional action, and legal judgments in the courts. Minority groups, activist feminists (*qq.v.*), and others banded together to exert pressure on local authorities. "Single-issue" groups such as "pro-choice" advocates of abortion benefits (*qq.v.*) staged rallies at state houses. San Francisco became famous for its homosexual alliances and demands. Politicians labored to gain votes from special-interest groups, while not losing the votes of the majority. They found it difficult to be adroit, since many groups sought visibility at any cost, and would interpret any gesture or phrase which displeased them as condescending, reactionary, or worse. A *New Yorker* cartoon by Ed Fisher showed an American being glared at by several UN bureaucrats and complaining to a colleague: "Good gracious. You can't say *anything* without insulting them." For national politicians, such responses could seem momentous. Special interests sought to augment their power by finding a common base with other groups. Black leaders projected possible alliances with Hispanics (*q.v.*) in "rainbow coalitions." Women activists, boasting of representing "half" the population, sought to increase their influence on every issue. The National Education Association sought to influence educational policies and finances on all levels of government. In 1983 celebrations of the memory of Martin Luther King, Jr. and the 1963 March on Washington were planned as a "coalition" of reform and liberal causes. They elicited variant accounts of success and failure from liberals and conservatives. Whether radical or liberal politicalization of issues would precipitate counter-politicalization drives, further dividing the country into blocs, or through victories and defeats discredit shallow opportunists among the numerous special interests, was a question for the late 1980s to judge. See also Politicalization.

**Prisons**, see Crime

**Privacy**, universally desired, but emphasized more in principle by conservatives than by others. Law and order seemed to conservatives to limit the rights of the individual in society. Liberals, with a sense of a society in the process of change, were less ready to concede rights to society; for example, the right to arrest individuals on suspicion of committing crimes; see for example Morris L. Ernst's *Privacy: The Right to Be Let Alone*. Struggle over the limits of privacy in post-World War II decades divided into issues involving government and issues involving partisans. Thus radicals, finding liberal sympathy, wanted their private quarters sacrosanct, though they might be stages for what some considered anti-social activity; yet they felt free to use the streets and be seen in neighborhoods—as in San Francisco's notorious Haight-Ashbury section—all the while asserting their right to be free of harassment. Homosexuals fought to "get out of the closet," despite the fact that many considered them immoral. Commercialism and politics which invaded the home with recorded telephone messages complicated the problem of privacy. Although the government began the era with a substantial amount of privacy limited by spy and investigative actions, its prestige was shaken by social unrest, then wounded by such catastrophes as the Bay of Pigs fiasco and the drawn out Pentagon Papers and Watergate episodes. Here journalism mixed together issues of privacy and the right to know. Thus, journalists fought for their right not to reveal sources even though they might involve the most serious consequences to individuals or government. Yet the journalists also emphasized their right to secret information, even though its exposure might serve enemies of the state. The loss of prestige by the F.B.I., the C.I.A., and the presidency brought on the "Freedom of Information Act" of 1974, which exposed to partisan and even frivolous eyes government work done with expectations of security. Although the act was too sweeping to remain unqualified for long, if there was to be government at all to oppose to the rigidly controlled enemies of the nation, it inevitably inhibited government officials and resulted in new methods to control privacy. Although gossip, rumor, and malice never slept, individuals resorted more regularly to the courts in order to curb impudent intruders into their affairs. They were firmer and more careful in their release of private information. They rejected offers of "dialogue." A more relaxed connection between privacy and sociability was not in the offing. John B. Young, ed., *Privacy* (1978); Alan F. Westin, *Privacy and Freedom* (1967); D. H. Flaherty et al., *Privacy and Access to Government Data for Research* (1979); Arthur A. Bushkin, *The Privacy Act* (1976).

**"Privatization,"** a major Conservative goal in Great Britain, where major industries had been nationalized, with enormous effects not only on productivity, quality (*qq.v.*), and other material basics, but on attitudes toward work, individual character, and the scale of values fostered by unions. A famous British film, *I'm All Right, Jack*, satirized the condition. "Peter Simple" (*q.v.*) treated it as one of his themes. The Conservative Party, under Prime Minister Thatcher (*q.v.*), planned to "privatize" once more such industries as coal and railroads. The rollback proved difficult. Large number of workers and families were involved. Workers laid off were eligible for welfare. In addition, they were voters. Private managers had to be ready to run great industries. Although some "privatization" could be achieved by implementing the roles of private firms in industry, large-scale de-nationalization required preparation, publicity, victories at the polls, and the avoidance of further nationalization. In the United States, where no industries had been nationalized, the problem was to cut government intervention which essentially put on government payrolls doctors, educators, job-training and employment personnel, consulting firms, and others. As many as possible, conservatives believed, should be in the marketplace, showing initiative and taking chances with their own money and careers. Here again progress was slow, and for the same reasons. William W. Haynes, *Nationalization in Practice: The British Coal Industry* (1953); Janet Minihan, *The Nationalization of Culture: the Development of State Subsidies in the Arts in Great Britain* (1977); E. Eldon Barry, *Nationalization in British Politics* (1965).

**Pro-Choice**, see Abortion; Euphemisms; "Freedom of Choice"

**Productivity**, a measure of the economic and social health of society. Analysts were concerned for lower productivity, which linked with standards of production, and often with union-management differences. The old American Federation of Labor slogan: time for work, time for rest, time for private life, represented one bottom line of productivity, later superseded by political concerns where the bottom line was a grim falling off of the nation's capacity for competing with international industry, often more dedicated to high and quality productivity than were Americans. A variant on the subject, with serious implications, was government policy of asking or ordering farmers to cut or curb production, in the interests of commodity price control. B. N. Bhattasali, *Productivity and Economic Development* (1972); E. M. Glaser, *Productivity Gains through Worklife Improvement* (1976); C. Prendergast, *Productivity: The Link in Economic and Social Progress* (n.d.).

**Profits**, a basic factor in capitalist economy, identified with incentive to production, economic growth, and the concept of "venture capital": expensive experimentation in hopes of profit. The concept has been clearly a conservative premise, as distinguished from the socialist ideal which emphasized need and preference rather than profit, assuming that there would be sufficient funds or exchange to cover every individual or group need. The welfare state (*q.v.*) was based on this expectation. The growth to monumental proportions of inflation, poor productivity, hideaway capital, and other evils subsequent to the New Deal (*q.v.*) raised new questions of the role of profit in the state's and society's operations. It was observed that "socialist" regimes found it necessary to supply incentives to their industries and that a bedraggled American economy needed to reconsider what constituted an equitable division of funds between financially troubled businesses and wage-hungry unions; see *Profits and the Future of American Society* (1983), by S. Jay Levy and David A. Levy, a volume in praise of profits and the investors who make profits possible by their support of enterprise. It was written by professional economic forecasters and analysts during a period of rising pro-capitalist sentiment.

**Program for Conservatives, A.** (1954), by Russell Kirk (*q.v.*). It was not a political program, but an assertion of principles, in part a polemic confronting such figures as David Riesman, Thorstein Veblen, and John Dewey (*q.v.*) with the ideas of Edmund Burke, Ludwig von Mises, and Wilhelm Röpke, (*qq.v.*) among numerous others. Kirk argued for a whole tradition, including religion, and honoring feeling, community, and loyalty. He found an excessive abstraction, a penchant for dogma, and lack of humanity in liberal thought and action. The full thrust of "proletarianization" struck him as crass, whether it came from commerce (*q.v.*) or socialism. He regretted the use of the atomic bomb over Japan as an expression of the worst side of American assertiveness, as well as being unnecessary. Liberal horror over the House Un-American Activities Committee he saw as hypocritical, its inquiries being normal and appropriate.

**Progress,** not a favorite concept among conservatives, who emphasize religion, tradition as experience, and the eternal verities. Yet conservatives have found uses in the concept which liberals found distasteful. Blaise Pascal (*q.v.*) identified progress with expanded knowledge, yet himself gave up scientific examinations for the higher knowledge of religion. Although Adam Smith (*q.v.*) attacked the established order of mercantilism (*q.v.*), he did it furthering economic freedom, winning the approval of later conservatives. The

American Revolution and French Revolution reveal the differences in liberal and conservative views of progress. J. B. Bury, tracing *The Idea of Progress* (1924), suggested that human beings had goals, of which progress was but one; in time, progress might itself be superseded by other goals. Ellsworth Huntington's long and intensive studies of climate and geography in search of *The Pulse of Progress* (1926) disturbed liberals as suggesting racism (*q.v.*) in listing qualities produced in various peoples by the influence of environment. The gentle liberal Horace M. Kallen studied *Patterns of Progress* (1950), "whose wisdom is science and work civilization." See also F. J. Teggart, ed., *The Idea of Progress: A Collection of Readings* (1949). Simple faith in the ideas of progress can be discerned in commercialism (*q.v.*), which often equates progress with quality. Progressivism (*q.v.*) in politics has had more complex and affirmative implications, but raised questions, as in the course of events from the Progressive Party of 1912 to that of 1948. Philosophically, "progress" appeared differently to optimists and those who questioned whether expanded democracy or technology increased the quality or satisfactions of life or, as with the atomic bomb (*q.v.*), gave less assurance of human continuity.

**Progressive Education,** see Education

**Progressive Historians, The** (1968), by Richard Hofstadter, his major effort to create a liberal historical philosophy. It followed efforts to oppose conservatism through essays which found its proponents to be "pseudo-conservatives," presumably of a lesser breed than those among the Founding Fathers (*q.v.*). His indictment of the new conservatives could be traced in his *Anti-intellectualism in American Life* (1963) and *The Paranoid Style in American Politics* (1965). *The Progressive Historians* apportioned 498 pages in the main to three historians, Frederick Jackson Turner, Charles A. Beard, and Vernon L. Parrington, and dedicated the bulk of analysis to Turner's "frontier thesis," to Beard's economic interpretation of the Constitution, and to Parrington's view of the main currents in American thought. With fulsome references and familiar information, the author found Turner simplistic, Beard often hazy and contradictory, and Parrington already outmoded for lack of esthetic equipment. Hofstadter had already, through his *Social Darwinism in American Thought* (1944), *The American Political Tradition* (1948), and *The Age of Reform* (1955), designated the American tradition as ranging from inadequate to disastrous. What Hofstadter and his admirers did not anticipate was that his own major tenets would affect students with an anti-American bias, and that his scholarship would seem no more consequential than that of his learned predecessors whose love of country and pride in its achievements seemed an offense to discontented people at home and abroad. The youth (*q.v.*) uprisings on campuses in the 1960s attacked not only the established sequence of scholarship in historical studies, but Hofstadter's work as well.

**"Progressive Moderation,"** a phrase used to describe the outlook on society of Nelson A. Rockefeller and Dwight D. Eisenhower (*qq.v.*). They were seen as seeking to serve both New Deal (*q.v.*) and conservative principles. The *National Reivew* saw no positive future in such a viewpoint, and ranged from tepid to antagonistic in its reaction.

**Progressive Tax Rates,** curious in their use of "progressive" as meaning simply regular increase, harking back to earlier Progressives: a fact which gained them regard from neither liberals nor conservatives. They involved essentially a "soak the rich" concept, holding that those who had more should help lift financial burdens from those with less. In the 1930s, the image of "bloated capitalists" in a nation of anxious and needy people was all but impossible to overcome. As the welfare state settled in, however, questions arose as to how much "income transfer," from persons with funds to those without, was reasonable or tolerable. The question most acutely touched the neither rich nor poor, but those subject to "progressive" taxation who might find themselves taking home from labor less pay than others on welfare with housing, medical, child care, and old-age benefits had. In the 1960s and 1970s, questions arose as to whether "progressive" taxation might be driving parts of the public to cheating, the so-called underground economy, and a loss of incentive to manage or produce; and what all this might cost the government in revenues and society in the quality of its people. See *Reaganomics*.

**Progressivism,** see Filler, DASC, a major theme in American life and tradition, under its own name or other rubrics—such as Democratic, Liberal, and Populist (*qq.v.*)—depending on the tone and emphases of the time. It suggested faith in people, concern for their well-being, and the will to do something about it. Though often passionate in temper, it resisted radicalism, and looked for the broadest and most expedient solutions. It was closer to Thomas Jefferson and Andrew Jackson than to John Adams or John Quincy Adams. In its very own time, that of Theodore Roosevelt and Woodrow Wilson, it linked with Pragmatism to shift the national emphasis from the farm to the city, and from the Grange to the trade union, creating a vast body of law to open as much opportunity as a more consolidated nation could permit. It was compromised by having endorsed intervention in World War I. Though its major proponents continued to receive lip-service in the schools, it ceased to be central to the leftward and rightward responses to a new world of high technology, fascist and Communist proliferations, and multiplying elites (*q.v.*). It seemed leftist (*q.v.*) to the new conservatives, concerned for law and order and minimum government, and conservative to the new liberals, who identified it with patriotism, imperialism, and even racism—though Progressives had created the National Association for the Advancement of Colored People. Difficulties with the welfare state, to which liberals had committed themselves, and with a continual crisis in international affairs, awkward for conservatives who had to deal with numerous liberal and radical governments abroad, suggested that both the right and left in America had much to gain from study of Progressive history. It appeared possible that liberals might gain the most because of their traditionally positive view of people professing need, of ethnic minorities at home and abroad, and of using the government for a redistribution of income, as well as because of their sense of being closer to the people. Walter Mondale, 1984 Democratic Presidential candidate, called his branch of the Democratic Party the Progressive branch. (*Qq.v.*, for the above).

**Prohibition**, see Filler, DASC, a patently authoritarian goal, made possible by conjunctive factors during World War I: soldiers abroad or out of politics at home; the need for the grain ("Wheat Will Win the War") which was used in the making of spirits, the women's drive for suffrage (involving powerful female Prohibitionists), anti-German sentiment (Germany being identified with beer production), and the close coordination of Protestant church agitiation. Some of the above involved conservative sentiment, but scarcely all. The element of idealism in American thinking was not to be disputed; many Americans sincerely believed they would take their "last drink" when the Volstead Act became the law of the land. Prohibition undoubtedly contributed to the nationalizing of crime and disrespect for the law. Its overthrow by way of the XXI Amendment with the coming of the New Deal (*q.v.*) in 1933 rid the country of "speakeasies," but could not recreate the warmer taverns of earlier decades. The democratization of hard liquors served commerce (*q.v.*) but not conservatism. In the 1960s, drugs such as marijuana, hallucinogens, and cocaine became popular, rivalling alcohol in their potentially deleterious effects on society. P. E. Isaac, *Prohibition and Politics*...(1965); James H. Timberlake, *Prohibition and the Progressive Movement* (1970); R. S. Bader, *Prohibition in Kansas* (1985).

**Propaganda,** increasingly influential in democratic societies, in which the opinion of ordinary people had to be won and directed in order to move society in preferred directions. Authoritarian states had less trouble with the field since their masses were expected to receive and honor instructions about how to think and feel; hence, they would designate a Minister of Information to administer the process. Although the most democratic societies had their quota of natural followers, the facade of freedom and reason was expected to be upheld and any agenda had to be presented as "fact."

Thus, American publications eager to demean the American effort in Vietnam printed photographs of forlorn South Vietnam children alone on embattled terrain, making no effort to discover comparable conditions in North Vietnam. Nevertheless, the rule of competition (*q.v.*) dictated that persons approving the approach of the American Administration toward Vietnam show their strength by demanding and receiving alternative reports. See also Public Opinion; Filler, DASC.

**Property,** along with the right to private property a classic premise of conservativism. During the youth uprisings of the 1960s and early 1970s, it was a particular target of malcontents who "liberated" (stole) both public and private property, on grounds that they had been victimized by society and were getting back what was their own. During that time, a new theory of property was formulated by a university law professor, Charles Reich, who subsequently wrote *The Greening of America* (1971), and with the proceeds went on to a hippie career in California. Before doing so, however, he had made himself conspicuous among law professors with his ingenious theory of property broadened in meaning to include privileges for the poor. Those on welfare, for example, were not to be seen as receiving aid, charity, or temporary relief. Welfare was an entitlement (*q.v.*) under law, and sufficiently established to be seen as a right, as much so as the most private of property. But property had once been seen as a shield against the state. If welfare was the equivalent of "other" private property, to be administered by the state, there was no ultimate line to distinguish state prerogatives from individual prerogatives. As de Tocqueville and Hayek (*q.v.*) saw, equality threatened property. Reich offered a series of assertions which, if accepted made no distinction between privately owned property and grants as property both of which could be adjudicated by the state. Thus, poverty was not a personal condition but the result of outside forces, which the state should agree to redress. The poor contributed to society as well as (possibly more than) the well-to-do. The state could therefore compel those who had to make up for those who had not. Need was an entitlement, but what was "need"? A heroin addict "needed" heroin; was his claim to heroin a property right? Deservedness was a right, but what constituted "desert"? Those who applauded Reich's reasoning converted property from a defense war against state authority to a means for enabling the state, even in the form of tyranny, to administer property as it chose. One follower of Reich wished to "treat human rights as property rights." Michael B. Levy, 'Illiberal Liberalism: The New Property as Strategy," *Review of Politics*, October 1983.

**Proposition XIII,** see Filler, DASC. It involved an historic tax uprising in California in 1978 against an onerous property assessment which dramatized the connection between burdens placed on property holders and the generous programs for welfare, education, and other entitlements maintained by that state. The successful push for Proposition XIII made its leader, Howard Jarvis, nationally known, and encouraged others elsewhere to work for similar measures. Undoubtedly, the battle over Proposition XIII gave stimulus to the forces which pushed Ronald Reagan for the Presidency. Although liberal apologists continued to emphasize their themes of compassion and the needs of children, the elderly, and others, it became evident that the bottom line was votes, and that those who resisted their appeals and petitions were mobilizing with vigor and results. See *Reaganomics*; Howard Jarvis, *I'm Mad as Hell* (1979).

**Pros and Cons,** a vital element in health-giving debate, less regarded in the United States than in Great Britain, where the elite (*q.v.*) classes, though separated ideologically, might recall associations at the major universities and assimilate the arguments of their opponents, if only for debate purposes. Liberals and conservatives, polarized by the intensity of their differences—on welfare, attitudes toward the Soviet Union, on the Supreme court, abortion, prayer (*qq.v.*)—were more prone to savagery in debate and to one-sided portrayal of their foes. This had been less true when liberals (*q.v.*) had played the part of mediators and "honest brokers" between activists of the Right and activists of the Left (*qq.v.*). But with the middle ground all but filled in and trampled over from the 1960s on, there could only be "clash by night," in Matthew Arnold's immortal phrase in "Dover Beach," with all agreeing on its naked reality, with none to modify it.

**Protectionism,** see Filler, DASC. It was once a clear conservative cause, with Alexander Hamilton's (*q.v.*) advocacy of subsidies to business and tariffs to create difficulties for the goods of foreign merchants. Southern landowners made a Free Trade (*q.v.*) cause of anti-Protection, claiming Protectionism put them at the mercy of New York jobbers, and so made curious union before and after the Civil War with labor sympathizers who asked for cheap woolens to clothe the poor. Nevertheless, Republicans won solid labor votes under the slogan (*q.v.*) of "Home Industries," meaning jobs. Woodrow Wilson (*q.v.*), claiming to speak for the nation, was an advocate of Free Trade, but, with his British allies closing the seas to German shipping, could not deliver. By the 1920s, the issue lost its vestiges of principle, with commerce and labor (*qq.v.*) and international alignments alone giving some rational directions to policy. The government proved more realistic than its political components in striving to determine what ought to be policy toward the post-World War II "West German economic miracle" and the even more formidable Japanese economic revival. The glaring deterioration of American productivity brought on the humiliating slogan (*q.v.*) "Buy American," which many consumers apparently thought it would be foolish to endorse. Conservative regimes in both the United States and Great Britain did their part by attempting to limit the right of workers to strike at will and to lean readily on the state in their quarrels with owners. In the mid-1980s came renewed calls for Protectionist legislation by the U. S. Congress, from farmers, businessmen, and labor leaders.

**Protective Tariff,** a nationalist, conservative program advocated by Alexander Hamilton (*q.v.*), notably in his great report on Manufacturies (1791), in which he recommended high tariffs on foreign goods in order to encourage native enterprise. His program at the time did not require a justification in terms of the laboring classes. Neither did the opposing Free Trade (*q.v.*) doctrine increasingly espoused by Southern planters of cotton who needed to sell their crop in exchange for goods at the lowest price possible and who resented being "enslaved" to New York tradesmen. In post-Civil War decades the Republican Party (*q.v.*) learned to defend its Protective Tariff to the increasing numbers of laborers by denouncing lower-priced foreign products as produced by "slave labor" and, even more doubtfully, of poorer quality, difficult to acquire in wartime, and breeding disloyalty. The expansion of American industry abroad harmed some of these arguments. Worse was the deterioration of American standards of production in the post-World War II decades—despite "quality control" (*q.v.*)—and American preference for foreign cars, clothing, precision instruments, and other products which led to the loss of factories and jobs at home. The call of union leaders to "Buy American" was at least partially to direct attention away from their stewardship, as had once been the case with industrialists advocating a Protective Tariff.

**Protest.** Originally identified with poor and desperate workers and the unemployed, it took the form of marches to city halls and palaces, to cement unity among those who felt oppressed and to appeal for public sympathy and support. Marchers carried banners or such symbolic items as a loaf of bread raised on a pole. A Russian effort to draw compassion before the royal palace in St. Petersburg, on January 22, 1905, resulted in the massacre of protesters by Russian troops, and a legacy of hatred which found expression in the 1917 Revolution (*q.v.*). The 1905 tragedy caused left-wing protesters in America to term police antagonists "Cossacks." Conservatives often found occasions to protest official policies—oppression of minority elements in Europe and the Middle-East, Southern treatment of Negroes at home—but they tended to eschew public protests. With the youth (*q.v.*) eruptions of the 1960s and early 1970s, public protests took exaggerated forms, including the use of "guerrilla theater," designed to win media attention. They included candlelight "vigils," obstructing the streets, chaining individuals in front of the White House and elsewhere, and similar actions. All this depended on the patience and law of Western democracies. There was little protest against atrocities perpetrated by "left-wing" political establishments in Asia, Africa, South America, or Europe. Although such actions subsided with the decline of the 1960s counterculture, they gained some revival with later protests against nuclear energy and with "Anti- Nuke" (*q.v.*) demonstrations intended to force a "freeze" in the proliferation of nuclear weapons.

**Pruriency,** see Victorian Era

**"Pseudo-Conservatives,"** see *Progressive Historians, The*

**Psychiatry,** a long time study of mental disorders dealing also with criminal and irrational behavior. In the twentieth century, due to increased democratization and the widespread distress caused by World War I (*q.v.*) were created numerous schools and clinics. Conservatives generally made less of psychiatry than did liberals, conservatives having more faith in the standards and expectations of society, the importance of will power, and in placing the burden of proof on the individual, rather than society. Neurotic and self-indulgent persons helped create a vast field for psychiatrists who were frequently as self-indulgent as their patients, and not infrequently partisan, as in the case of a pro- Hiss (*q.v.*) psychiatrist who publicly declared that his testimony in the case was directed by partisan considerations. The use of psychiatrists in helping to establish the legal category of "innocent by reason of insanity" disturbed many people, professional and otherwise, and reached a milestone in the innocence verdict regarding Hinckley (*q.v.*), who attempted to murder the President of the United States. Equally reprehensible were "psychiatrists" who used their position to exploit their patients not only financially, but sexually. The youth movement of the 1960s, with its emphasis on experiment, often resulted in anti-social activity which found friends in psychiatry. It welcomed such gurus (see Filler, DASC) as Ronald D. Laing (*q.v.*), who denied that anyone was crazy and who received full hearings from professional associates. It seemed possible that with the proliferation of terrorism, some patently mindless, legal restraints would be found to curb some of their activities. See also Laing, R. D., *Prisons, Capital Punishment.*

**"Psychohistory"** a contemporary development in historical studies. It involved psychological speculation into the motives and personalities of historical figures. Garry Wills's *Nixon Agonistes: The Crisis of the Self-Made Man* (1970) was a prototype of such writings, mixing fact with psychological conjectures. Fawn N. Brodie's (*q.v.*) psychohistory of Thomas Jefferson (*q.v.*) aroused great controversy. The future of psychohistory seemed dependent on the future of history itself.

**Public Interest, The,** influential neo-conservative (*q.v.*) quarterly, edited by Irving Kristol and Nathan Glazer (*qq.v.*). It divided areas of interest with *Commentary* and *Policy Review* (*q.v.*), the former being more responsive to the politics of sensibility, the latter to official or unofficial government programs. Most identifiable conservative figures were likely to appear in all three publications at some time. *The Public Interest* was somewhat more prone to meditate regarding theories by such liberal ideologues as J. K. Galbreath, Lester Thurlow, and Robert B. Reich. Reich's *The Next American Frontier* (1983) was termed by *Public Interest* as advocating a "supply-side economics (*q.v.*) of the Left."

**Public Opinion,** see Gallup Poll, Filler, DASC. Walter Lippmann's *Public Opinion* (1922) recognized that there was not one public, but many publics. Nevertheless, a problem remained, to determine what an *influential* public opinion truly preferred at a given time, since time helped order events and results. Thus, liberals in the contemporary era were seen as gaining control of the *New York Times* and *New York Review of Books,* and giving far less attention and approval to conservatives than conservatives believed they merited. Liberals on these publications even found reason to derogate Alexander Solzhenitsyn (*q.v.*) despite his world-wide fame. Conservative authors received admiration in the conservative press, which also treated works which offended them; but the conservative press wrote from a defensive posture which indicated a sense of weakness. Even the *National Review*, with its wide readership including the White House, admonished readers that it was treating issues and writings of which "you will not learn in the *New York Times*." *Human Life*, publishing Joseph Sobran's *Single Issues* (*q.v.*), declared it would not be reviewed in the liberal press. Although this was true, it did not explain why sufficient word of Sobran's book—if only through the syndicated writings of famous conservatives—would not force the liberals to recognize *Single Issues'* existence, if only to attack it. It thus appeared that the central factor in public opinion was not the press itself, or the polls, or the media, but the public itself, which found or selected whatever it preferred and gave it such weight as it desired. Even William F. Buckley, Jr., though with a national audience in the media and a well-recognized conservative program and line of argument, was constrained to direct his attacks at issues which would keep his readership attentive.

Other conservatives, with less communicative clout, were even more confined to areas in which they had established their status and authority. More limited fields could be more peremptory in their censorship and partiality, when they controlled outlets and editorial chairs. Thus the *American Historical Review*, shifting from its long-established record, was seen by conservatives as committed to a liberal historiography and the advancement of women in the profession, which conservatives disapproved of when based on no more than sex. It was evident that only changes in public, and thus professional, opinion would diminish authoritarian impulses in what were classically nonauthoritarian areas.

**Public Philosophy Reader,** (1978), ed., Richard J. Bishirjiah, concerned for "the nature of public Philosophy," including the philosophies of Gerhart Niemeyer, Michael Novak, and Robert Nisbet (*qq.v.*), and including excerpts from writings by John Courtney Murray, Eric Voegelin, Richard Weaver, and Irving Kristol, (*qq.v.*) among others. It covered such topics as public opinion and the role of classics and of history.

**Public Relations,** an increasingly urgent part of advocacy (*q.v.*) work in a society requiring numerous contacts for impact. Public relations experts were sought to advance politicians, mount campaigns for and against various causes, raise funds, and influence legislators. The general impression that conservatives attracted more money for the affluent causes and could overwhelm the will of others remained unproven. Conservative interests and commercial (*q.v.*) interests did not run tandem. Great expenditures did not necessarily impress voters. Nelson Rockefeller (*q.v.*) spent a substantial sum in his drive for the Presidency and was unsuccessful.

**Public Works,** identified with the relief process launched under the New Deal (*q.v.*), notably the Work Progress Administration (WPA); see Filler, DASC. However, there was a longer tradition, during economic depressions, of municipalities providing work, often needed work on roads, to distribute small sums to unemployed workers. The 1930s Depression appeared so formidable, that given the mandate Franklin D. Roosevelt's (*q.v.*) victory in 1932 seemed to provide, the new President felt free to continue to seek job opportunities as he had during his "little New Deal" in New York, where he had been governor. His Civilian Conservation Corps (CCC) gave jobs to youth under Army supervision—a fact which alarmed both radicals and conservatives—and provided healthy outdoor work, camaraderie, and modest wages. Larger experiments in work projects for unskilled, skilled, and arts workers grew into the famed WPA. Under conservative protest, it built bridges and post offices, renovated schools and public buildings, and provided the art work within, employing many artists later famous. These programs had various careers, but were mostly disbanded or integrated into war work after Pearl Harbor. The costs of the operations were minimal; the results substantial out of all proportion. Although union (*q.v.*) power and opportunities proliferated during World War II, making another WPA and PWA (construction work carried on largely with the unemployed) unnecessary and not possible, after World

War II another CCC might well have been useful. It might have acted to help aimless, unemployed youth in ghettos. However, no work for youth was debated or tried, and antisocial activities proliferated. Later unemployment suggested the idea of a "new WPA," but with too little concern for changes in society. The deterioration of the work ethic, for example, required attention. The existence of welfare, aid to dependent children, old-age assistance, publicly funded medical services, and other public programs raised questions of the relationship of such programs to any projected WPA. Until such questions were debated, the old WPA experience could not be brought to bear on new conditions.

**Puerto Ricans,** see Filler, DASC; and also New and Old Immigration

**Pulitzer, Joseph,** see Dana, Charles A.

**Puppet Governments,** see Surrogates

**Puritanism.** Though it became a synonym for sexual suppression, hypocrisy, and unpleasant history, Puritanism in fact contained elements useful to both liberals and conservatives. Puritans in England had been individuals and had questioned the King's prerogatives as revolutionaries. Some had expressed their radical temperaments by channelling them through the Puritan ethic. American conservatives admired Puritan piety, congregational democracy, and the constructive religious freedom and tolerance associated with Roger Williams and Anne Hutchinson. Puritans had fought Indians (*q.v.*), with right and wrong on both sides and John Eliot, "Apostle to the Indians," on the right. Their small-town morals, and dessicated lives. Puritans lost their place in American thought and feeling, thanks to a consensus of distaste. "Emancipated" modes and opinions, from the Twenties (*q.v.*) on, appeared to make more and more impossible everything that Puritanism had connoted. Arthur Miller's *The Crucible* was an influential statement of public attitudes toward Puritanism. Although there was some doubt that a more accurate version could be communicated to the public soon, it was possible that qualities identified with Puritanism might find their way back to public regard. The very excesses of the youth (*q.v.*) uprisings of the 1960s had produced their own antidote, to a degree. They had divided seekers after euphoria from those who valued security and community. Fundamentalist (*q.v.*) churches manifested a vigor and social energy alarming to such organizations as the American Civil Liberties Union (*q.v.*). The dangers in drugs and alcohol had become a national scandal calling for solution. Sexual promiscuity, touted as the ultimate experience, had proved unfulfilling to many. Although this did not add up to a new Puritanism, or consciousness of the old, it clearly flouted the social attitudes of the 1960s. D. B. Rutman, *American Puritanism* (1970); Perry Miller, *The New England Mind* (1953); Edmund S. Morgan, *Visible Saints: The History of a Puritan Idea* (1963); Francis J. Bremer, *Puritan Experiment: New England Society from Bradford to Edwards* 1976); Sacvan Bercovitch, *Puritan Origins of the American Self* (1977); Michael McGiffert, *Puritanism and the American Experience* (1969). See also Sex and Conservativism; Twain, Mark.

# Q

**Quackery in the Public Schools** (1953), by Albert Lynd. It contributed to the attack on new versions of "progressive" education which took off from John Dewey's (*q.v.*) principles, sometimes without much exposure to them. Lynd demonstrated a turning away from basics and from history as experience. He traced the influence of Dewey, and discussed Professor William Heard Kilpatrick, a prominent proponent of "progressive" education. His book contributed to the streams of criticism which led to the New Conservatism.

**Quality Control,** a phenomenon of post-World War II industry, intended to ensure that mass production was monitored by experts in standards of production, using mathematical and scientific measurements and techniques. Control was particularly necessary because of the theory which went tandem to it of "controlled depreciation"(*q.v.*), which dictated that goods could be scientifically produced which would depreciate according to plan, more rapidly than goods made to last, thus ensuring that demand would guarantee full employment and the money necessary to replenish social and human needs. Such a program required precision production, quality control, and the ability to estimate factors of demand, domestic and foreign competition, availability of materials such as could not be predicted or controlled. Boredom, laxness, greed, and simple lack of information diminished normal incentive and responsibility. "Quality control" emerged as a verbal equivalent for substantive achievement. Notorious became the annual cycle of automobile recalls in the thousands and more, involving brakes, steering wheels, and other crucial elements. Most ironic was the "controlled depreciation" of products which could not be purchased anew because of unemployment or price, while other products did not "move" for lack of sufficient customers. "Controlled depreciation" disappeared from commercial jargon. "Quality control" gave place to the problem of quality production.

**Quality of Life, The,** a topic inconsistently handled, since it involved questions of responsibility, and of financial burdens. Thus it was evident that "inner cities" everywhere were in poor shape, sometimes all but inhabitable. How could they be made livable, and by whom? But even less eroded areas involved problems of expectation and standards. Toronto, Canada's boast, that it was like what American cities used to be was a reminder which raised comparisons, respecting cleanliness, attractiveness, the incidence of crime, the scale and variety of entertainment, of libraries and museums, the sense of courtesy, tolerance of differences, the values shown in work and play. Nor were deficiencies in any areas noticeable solely in cities. Small towns, it was noted, often showed rundown main streets, minimum community, lack of local creativity. The ready culprit seemed always to be television (*q.v.*), prone to violence and "boob tube" fantasies. This did not explain the lassitude which kept hordes of people singlely before them, either for lack of inspiring leaders, or of more interesting duties elsewhere. Liberals tended to be less critical of the quality of life, on television or outside of it. They saw New York (*q.v.*) as "exciting," Chicago as "swinging," San Francisco as "enchanting." They were enraged when Federal funds lagged, and cold to President Reagan's slogan of a " New Federalism," (*q.v.*)

which simply meant holding the cities to their own budgets. Conservatives, concerned for issues, questioned costs and results. Although there were numerous books on "quality control," as for example, R. H. Lester and N. L. Enrick, *Quality Control for Profit* (1977), there were much fewer on the quality of life, and those of doubtful evidence; see B. C. Liu, *Quality of Life Indicators in US. Metropolitan Areas: A Statistical Analysis* (1976).

**Quesnay, Francois** (1694-1774), founder of the Physiocratic (*q.v.*) School of French economists. His articles for the famous *Encyclopédie*, edited by Denis Diderot and others, notably one on farmers (*q.v.*), inspired him to work further with others to elaborate on what came to be seen by him and his colleagues as "laws" governing commercial intercourse. Physiocrats saw land as the sole producer of wealth, and the free movement of agricultural products as the one legitimate means for its distribution. Had they had their way, the state would have fully controlled the movement and exchange of goods. The Physiocrats had a direct influence on Adam Smith's (*q.v.*) views, though they themselves lost credibility because of the rigidity of their formulations. R. L. Meek, *The Economics of Physiocracy* (1962).

**Quids,** the name given to John Randolph's (*q.v.*) faction of Jeffersonian Republicans who protested Jefferson's leading their party away from the states-rights (*q.v.*) position which protected their prerogatives against central government. In 1804 and 1805 Randolph stood out against land frauds perpetrated in Georgia and approved by Congress to the extent of endorsing the claims (known in history as the Yazoo Land Frauds). Though he saw it as a matter of high principle, it cost him his leadership in Congress. He had failed to take into account American desires to expand into the West and the ambitions of the people. His opposition to Jefferson's Embargo (1807) of British and French shipping was essentially intended to prevent America from being drawn into war, but it enraged New England shippers. Randolph's effort to prevent James Madison (*q.v.*), Jefferson's political friend, from attaining the Presidency failed, and he lost his own re-election bid in 1813 to Congress.

**Quincy, Josiah** (1772-1864), son of a distinguished Massachusetts Revolutionary leader. He made his mark as a conservative (*q.v.*) when, as minority leader in Congress from 1805 to 1813, he opposed the admission of Louisiana into the Union, maintained the states-rights argument with the passion of John Randolph (*q.v.*), and opposed Jefferson's Embargo in 1807 and Madison's (*q.v.*) declaration of war against Great Britain in 1812. Quincy continued his career of conservative insurgency in Massachusetts as Speaker of its House of Representatives and as Mayor of Boston. His son Edmund, an abolitionist, wrote his biography (1867).

**Quotas,** originally made notorious by conservatives like U. S. Senator Henry Cabot Lodge, who sought to restrain immigration (*q.v.*) in a burgeoning country. Democrats protested quotas, as the party which welcomed new Americans. Reformers saw quotas as malicious discrimination directed against people modestly endowed with money and education, but of upright character. Quotas were also employed to restrict entrance into college as with Jews, Negroes, and Catholics. A favorite argument was that it was a college's duty to be "representative," and to select students who would enhance their mix of students. The quota systems were shaken by the enormous personnel needs of World War II, the increasing strength of the Catholic (*q.v.*) community, the outlawing of segregation in the armed forces, the bad name given anti-Semitism (*q.v.*) during the era of Nazism, and the increased power of minorities in elections. Quotas received the *coup de grâce* during the civil rights and youth movements from the 1950s through 1980s, with colleges opening doors and administrative posts to numerous groups. The entire subject took on a new character with revelations in the 1970s and early 1980s that illegal immigration from Mexico and elsewhere had gotten out of hand. See also Identity Cards.

# R

**Racism**. Despite the civil rights gains of the 1950s and 1960s, many blacks and members of other minority groups continued to charge that American society was marked by racism. It was philosophically difficult to establish the point that all races and ethnic groups suffered from various forms of discrimination or exploitation, especially with "affirmative action" values fairly well established in practical legal and local operations. A very few successful law suits charging discrimination against "whites" (see Blacks) failed to shake the power of accusations of racism. However, the minority social and political gains of the 1960s and later tended to make such charges less and less credible to many people. Often such charges were made by minority political and community spokesmen to intimidate their opponents and gain or consolidate their own power. By the mid-1980s many blacks and members of other minority groups had come to see that, despite the residual racism they perceived in society, more opportunities than ever were available to those who took individual responsibility for their own lives and careers.

**Rackets**. Organized crime was formalized and made more efficient in the 1920s, a time of consolidation for all businesses aided by swifter communication and transportation facilities. Rackets involving legitimate business, illegal liquor, gambling, and vice were as distasteful when implemented by high-level accountants, lawyers, and friendly politicians as before, but more difficult to reach in an era of "disillusionment" (*q.v.*). The austerity created by the Great Depression (*q.v.*) opened the way for more civic actions, and brought to the fore such public defenders as Thomas E. Dewey (*q.v.*), a conservative in the tradition of "cleaning up" crime. Liberals tended to concentrate on "root causes" (*q.v.*). The youth uprisings of the 1960s revealed the infirm ground on which society was based, especially in the cities. Rackets were required to compete with trade-off arrangements between administrations and labor and business interests. Chicago became famous as "the city that works" by such arrangements. The democratization of drugs (*q.v.*) became an awesome industry attractive to racketeers: a challenge to civilization itself, because of what drugs did to those addicted. Liberals tended to seek meliorative solutions: more money for treatment of addicts, a scale of penalties from no penalties at all to substantial ones. Conservatives sought more drastic approaches. See also Labor Racketeers; *Godfather, The*; Capone, Al.

**Radicals**, once confined to those of the Left (*q.v.*), seen by conservatives indiscriminately as socialists, activist liberals, and even malcontents roused by such causes as poor sanitation, crime tolerated by police, and inequitable taxation. Such historical circumstances as opposition to intervention in World War I and the sluggish response of conservatives to the Great Depression narrowed the word to those who acted directly in opposition to these circumstances. Although the New Deal took some of the edge off the "radical" image, there were diehard conservatives who saw radicalism in all aspects of the New Deal program and its administrators. An oddity was that the most dedicated "radicals," those of Communist allegiance, often adopted conservative modes and tones, in order overtly to deceive New Deal critics. The 1950s brought out a new type of radical, the drop-out, who neither protested nor adapted to a nuclear, assembly-line age. The youth uprisings of the 1960s were less radical than nihilistic. They roused conservatives to new alignments of their own, ranging from Birchite (*q.v.*) formations to the Goldwater (*q.v.*) crusade of 1964. With American fears of Soviet and Red Chinese strength to give conservatives added power, liberals tried to find new criticisms of conservatism. An ingenious approach identified it with "radicalism"; Daniel Bell, a former socialist turned *Fortune* editor, then an influential college professor and social pundit, collected essays first published in 1955 under title *The Radical Right*. He sought to demean conservatives as "pseudo-conservatives," untrue to the genuine and legitimate conservative tradition. The Radical Right, at least as an epithet, was taken up by a wide range of liberal educators and media figures, and appears to have affected public opinion to a degree. Such major conservatives as Goldwater and Ronald Reagan, however, seem to have escaped being readily designated as "radicals," even when it was noted that Reagan was clearly bent on turning the country away from its established welfare-state premises. Elements with a left-wing background or perspective did make an effort to assert their program in *The Radical Papers* (1965), edited by Irving Howe. It included pieces by Daniel Bell, the "action-painting" advocate Harold Rosenberg, the 1930s radical Harvey Swados, permissivist Paul Goodman, and Tom Hayden (then in his anti-liberal phase), among others. However, the shift of attention from group complaints to the high-level difficulties of inflation and unemployment at home and nuclear dangers diminished the impact of "radical" solutions which could not reach the dilemmas involved and took attention from their proponents. Daniel Boorstin (*q.v.*), an old radical in "The New Barbarians: The Decline of Radicalism," (reprinted from *Esquire* [October 1968] in *The Decline of Radicalism* [1969]), made an appeal for radicalism, comparing it to the then-ongoing youth (*q.v.*) uprising, which he saw as a barbaric degeneration of old impulses. His tendency, he admitted, had made mistakes, but, born of the Depression (*q.v.*) era, "had confronted Americans with some facts of life which had been swept under the rug." A more somber aspect of the 1930s radical upsurge was the secretiveness fostered by radical enclaves. Some of it had resulted in contrived academic lectures and instruction by radical instructors which passed as education (see Milton Hindus, "Politics," in Filler, ed., *The Anxious Years* [1963]). Some of it had ended in subversive action which sometimes cost America dearly in distorted lives and damage to national security. The "new barbarians" were gross indeed, though many said they were "the best of their generation." But whether they did as much or as little harm as those who made it unpopular to write critically and accurately of the Soviet Union (*q.v.*) is a matter of comparative history yet to be developed. Vera B. Weisbord, *A Radical Life* (1977); Tom Wolfe, *Radical Chic and Mau Mauing the Flak Catchers* (1970); Donald J. Warren, *The Radical Center: Middle Americans and the Politics of Alienation* (1976); Sally M. Miller, *The Radical Immigrant* (1974); Edward E. Ericson, *Radicals in the University* (1975).

**Radicals (England),** an early nineteenth century development which emerged from philosophical and political dissatisfaction with the earlier Whigs (*q.v.*). The more liberal outlook of the Whigs had opposed the firmer Tory (*q.v.*) stand on Divine Right and Establishment, but their attitude toward industrialism and the increasing misery among poor farmers and factory workers was muddled. The new Radicals looked at the facts of destitute country folk and starving slum-dwellers and sought solutions. Intellectually, they were Utilitarians (*q.v.*), materialists, empiricists. Practically, they asked for a more understanding policy toward Ireland, and the colonies generally. One of the radical answers to the horrors of a growing population and distraught families was to send the excess to the colonies, which they could help develop while themselves living more humanely than was possible in London or Glasgow. All this was in opposition to the Tory emphasis on cruel punishment for criminals at home and exile to penal colonies abroad. Radicals grew with the Reform Bill of 1832, which expanded the suffrage. They made a first principle of freedom of industry; it was the Tories who gave Lord Shaftesbury (*q.v.*) to history, with his pleas for the chimney-cleaning Climbing Boys and for the destitute generally. The Radicals claimed such variant figures as William Cobbett and John Stuart Mill (*qq.v.*), though they had little in background or program between them. They were precursors of what became the Labour Party.

**"Radi-Libs,"** a concept developed by Spiro Agnew (*q.v.*) during his career as an opponent of liberals whose actual sympathies and lifestyles he saw as closer to Communism than to classic liberalism. Agnew's fall and loss of credibility impugned the concept and put it out of general use in the propaganda war between conservatives and liberals. See also Radicals.

**Radio,** see Television

**Radosh, Ronald**, see Isolationism; Rosenberg Case, The

**Rafferty, Max** (1917-1983), educator. Born in the South, he made his reputation as a forceful conservative in California, gaining a national reputation. He taught and administered in schools from 1940 to 1962. In 1963 he bacame Superintendent of California Schools, and from then on found himself in conflict with progressive educators. *Suffer Little Children* (1962) and *What They Are Doing to Your Children* (1964) caused him to be stigmatized as a reactionary, but were praised by proponents of the Basics (see "Back to Basics"). With the advent of Reagan as Governor of California, the struggle among educators intensified. By 1968 Rafferty was famous enough to issue *Max Rafferty on Education* (1968), followed by *Classroom Countdown* (1970). Thereafter, he receded from view, being dean and then distinguished professor of education at the Troy, Alabama teacher's college.

**Rand, Ayn** (1905-1982), American author who played an unusual role in the history of conservatism. She was born in Petrograd, the daughter of a successful businessman. She early exhibited the traits of one who wished to be a writer, and the emotional outlook of one who sought her own preferences. She seized upon Victor Hugo as the greatest writer in the world; later she would describe herself as a "romantic realist." Her absorption of detail as it unfolded about her before and during and following the Bolshevik victory was extraordinary. But it had no outlet in a world which had collapsed about her and her family, as followers of the Revolution on every level deprived them of livelihood, dignity, and hope. Although she lived with others and shared their sorrows to a degree, she had a private self which could forget them with concentration on other things. The dreary and character-destroying life she led gave her a hunger for trivial pleasures which her life as student and museum guide could not satisfy. She therefore eagerly seized the chance to leave the Soviet Union when American relatives offered a chance. But by leaving, she declassed herself more fundamentally than had the bureaucrats who had expropriated her father's business. Her old self died at the frontier as completely as did her alter ego in *We the Living* (*q.v.*), Kira, who died by the rifle of a frontier guardsman as she tried to flee Russia alone and on foot. In the United States, in 1926, she drifted to Hollywood, with funds almost as meager as had sustained her in her old life but with a unique will seeking expression. Her perception was as keen as ever, but she knew little of America apart from Hollywood and her own ideal of indomitable people. In 1929 she married happily to an actor who sustained her during difficult times. Her *We the Living* sold 3,000 copies, and Macmillan broke up the type before it could gain momentum and overcome the distaste of critics. *Anthem* (1937) was a pioneer anti-utopian novel expressing hatred of community as suffocating the individual—with the novel thought of suppressing the word "I"—which community her hero and heroine overcame. But the book lacked a sense of place which gave body to distinguished books in the genre; *Anthem* took place nowhere, not even drawing on the detail which had once been her trademark. Still, her sense of destiny never left her. Bereft as she was of tradition, she was among people who, at least on one level, took little account of the force of tradition, and who gave audience to numerous would-be leaders and panaceas (*q.v.*). Rand had a panacea for them: selfishness, ego, a sense of immediate judgment and satisfaction, unbending and indeed unnatural will and completion—all this in repugnance to and rejection of altruism, cooperation, gentleness, community: these were snares to catch the unwary. She would in her fiction provide role models, male and female, who exemplified the winning qualities. In *The Fountainhead* (1943) she did, and with such publishing success as to make her a legend: an American success story. But Rand did not see it as such. It was a victory of "Objectivism" (*q.v.*), as she termed the new philosophy she presumed to set before the world. She did, with considerable success. Nathaniel Branden joined her to disseminate its truth to the world, and his "institutes" attracted a substantial number of seekers for strength and reassurance. Rand herself was persuaded that she was "challenging the cultural tradition of two and a half thousand years." In her praise of capitalists, her idealization of the doer, the individual, the imperturbable loner and leader, she not only set forth an image for easy approval and dreams but lightened the load of thought and reading for her readers. Why bother with the "cultural tradition" of the past when there were new things to do, new people to know? Well-read conservatives were uncomfortable with some of the implications of Rand's crusade, but libertarians (*q.v.*) saw virtue in it, as did some others. Those with a stronger stake in the religion she flouted, and with a distaste for the violent scenes of sex which she thought illustrated a force for freedom—there has been nothing like them in *We the Living*—were increasingly impatient with Rand. Meanwhile, she underscored her triumph—to her, a triumph of her "philosophy"—with the double-sized *Atlas Shrugged*, which once again became a runaway bestseller. She issued *For the New Intellectual* (1961), expounding her views along with excerpts from her books. *The Virtue of Selfishness* (1961) professed to be "a New Concept of Egoism," *Capitalism* (1966) to reveal an "unknown Ideal." *The Romantic Manifesto* (1970) added nothing to what was known about Romanticism (*q.v.*). Whether her writings did indeed "alter and shape the lives of millions," as one commentator averred, cannot be known and can be doubted. She herself believed she had achieved success "by following strictly and consistently the principles of my philosophy of Objectivism."

**Randolph, John,** (1773-1833), American statesman. Of a distinguished family of Virginia, he was famed for his defense of states rights and fear of augmented central government authority, but most of all for his extraordinary eloquence in pressing his argument at critical instances in the nation's development. He loathed Federalism (*q.v.*), so much so as to welcome the French Revolution. As a young man heading the Jefferson (*q.v.*) Democrats in the U. S. House of Representatives, he seemed to have a great political career ahead. But in 1805, seeing danger in government intervention in the notorious Yazoo Land Frauds and in plans to buy Florida, he broke with Jefferson and thereafter was on his own in Congress: a gadfly who won attention but no victories. He denounced foreign entanglements and the War of 1812, and protested the sanction of the Second Bank of the United States, and the Missouri Compromise of 1820. Although conservatives would remember the man who declared that he loved liberty but hated equality, who loved his native state but was suspicious of a growing power in Washington, and who reminded them of Edmund Burke (*q.v.*) in his passion and felicity of expression, his actual effect declined. At the root of the problem was slavery, which he abhorred but with which he was saddled. A kindly master, he yet defended a doomed-prerogative. Gracious studies of a sick and chivalrous man could do little for his memory. Henry Adams's (*q.v.*) 1882 study of him was interesting as carrying on a family feud, Russell Kirk's 1951 study in several editions provided rich materials for new readers reexamining the past.

**Ransom, John Crowe**, see New Criticism

**Rationalism**, an approach to the world's problems which can be traced back to Scholasticism (*q.v.*), a Medieval system of thought which linked the reasoning process to religion, and continued until it inspired the atheistic Goddess of Reason fancied by French Revolutionary extremists. In less radical form, though not viewed so by fervent religionists, it produced the phenomenon of Deism (*q.v.*), which affected the thinking of such Americans as Thomas Jefferson and John Adams (*qq.v.*) and, in more aggressive form can be traced to a later Humanism (*q.v.*). Rationalism was distasteful—even irrational—to those who found truths in emotional and mystic experiences. T. F. Torrance, *God and Rationality* (1971). Another strain of rationalism proceeded from the long explorations of Jeremy Bentham (1748-1832), widely recalled as believing that that was good which offered the most to the greatest number. On his deathbed he sent out all observers so they should not suffer the sight of his last throes—except for one person, so that he should not suffer them alone. Bentham's most famous intellectual descendant was John Stuart Mill (*q.v.*). See also *Economy of Happiness, The*.

**Rationalism in Politics**, see Oakeshott, Michael

**Reactionary**, one who, technically, refuses to recognize the fact of change, and thus is practically obsolete under existing conditions. However, royalty, despite the "twilight of kings," persisted in major and minor countries; some conservatives, who presumably did recognize change, found themselves secondary in popularity to the "reigning" monarch. Individuals could be perceived as "reactionary" on some issues, though not all, examples including abortion, trade unions, homosexuals, terrorists, and public prayer. Committed Communists, though theoretically in the van of progress, were seen as reactionaries by observers who deplored their authoritarian views expressed in concentration camps, war operations, and a controlled press and controlled cultural standards. Thus, "reactionary" could be an epithet or a description, depending on who was the reactionary in the modern world. The 1950s showed an aggressive conservatism to which the workings of liberals and radicals, which it often associated, were anti-human, demeaning of history and hope. Defenders of the New Deal and its developments in welfare, social security, "affirmative action" (*qq.v.*), and related tenets responded with accusations of being "reactionary." This prompted some exasperated and contemptuous conservatives to assert their willingness to wear the label with pride, if it freed them of complicity in the bureaucracy (*q.v.*), fraud, and chaos which they saw as concomitants of liberalism as it had become. In a world made insecure by weapons of unimaginable power, mass killings in "Marxist" and anti-"Marxist" lands, terrorism and reprisal, it was difficult to determine a stable use of the word "reactionary." "Peter Simple" (*q.v.*) was glad to identify himself as a reactionary, refusing to recognize newly assumed names of African nations, and scorning instruments of speed, efficiency, and government intervention regarding the use of tobacco and seat-belts. Russell Kirk (*q.v.*), though called the "father of modern conservatism," declared his willingness to assume the name of reactionary in his antipathy to "progressive" education (*q.v.*), anti-religious civil rights forces, and other people and issues handled more gingerly by some conservatives. Allan Tate's *Reactionary Essays on Poetry and Ideas* (1936) did no harm to his reputation among libertarians. See also Agrarians.

**Readers's Digest**, founded in 1921 by Dewitt Wallace (1889-1981). It began with a run of 5,000 copies expanded by 1929 to 109,000 copies, and went on to become the largest single publication in America. Using the principle of "digesting" articles printed elsewhere to some one-fourth length, *RD* drew selectively on articles about domestic and world affairs, significant personalities and events, such diverse issues as syphilis and tobacco advertisements, and special features. Basic was its positive view of America, and emphasis on loyalty and family life. Scorned by intellectuals and liberals as the public-affairs equivalent of the *Saturday Evening Post* (*q.v.*), its world-wide circulation in Spanish, Portuguese, Swedish, Arabic, and other editions made it worrisome to those inclined to read reactionary and even "fascist" messages into its articles. The articles changed with the times, broadening positively to tell tales of worthy immigrants and other Americans. It employed Max Eastman, who was once scornful of popular writing, and stayed abreast of abortion, prayer, and other of the newer issues, mainly from the conservative standpoint. Troublesome to some who were not otherwise partisan was the publication's prose, which became highly skilled over the decades, and able to abstract the sense of varied articles and essays, while homogenizing the styles which had made these articles and essays individual and flavorsome. Whatever the *Digest* did or did not do to its readers' outlook, there was some question about what it did to their sense of literary values. In 1982, the *Reader's Digest* published a digest of the Bible (*q.v.*), disclaiming any revisionist goals. Along with other such semi-commercial (*q.v.*) enterprises, it took principled issues out of the hands of intellectuals, and left it for the public to decide whether they considered the book a service.

**Reagan, Ronald** (1911- ), public personality and President of the United States. His earlier years as an actor and exponent of free enterprise constituted a vehicle for conservative ideals, as the public image of such personalities as Frank Sinatra, Helen Gahagen Douglas, and Jane Fonda had typified liberal outlooks, in a time of expanded media (*q.v.*) outlook. Of sound, modestly endowed family, with qualities reminiscent of Gerald Ford (*q.v.*), young Reagan worked, played, and studied; and by way of sports, radio broadcasting, and a winning personality became a successful actor. He took or was given roles which did not strain his natural personality. A Franklin D. Roosevelt (*q.v.*) follower, he early interested himself in the Screen Actors Guild, where the drama of left-wing and conservative politics was to demand his attention for years. The tactics of the Communists in social and political issues turned him to conservatism; and in 1947 he testified freely, along with other actors of his persuasion, before the House Un-American Activities Committee (*q.v.*) with respect to communist penetration of the motion-picture industry. In 1954 he began his long service to General Electric as an intelligent and informed television spokesman and lecturer for free-enterprise ideals. He broadened his scope by addressing numerous social and political gatherings on social and political themes, impressing leaders in California with his personality and with his evident work at grasping issues. When General Electric attempted to make him give up issues on behalf of selling products, Reagan declined to become the salesman they envisioned. His role in the Goldwater (*q.v.*) campaign of 1964 separated him from his past. George Murphy (*q.v.*) that year broke ground by winning election to the U. S. Senate. Although Goldwater was severely defeated for the Presidency, Reagan's speeches on his behalf suggested to Republican politicians his own availability for public office. In 1966 Reagan won the governorship of California on a firm conservative platform of tax cuts, welfare reform, and campus education and tranquillity, beating the liberal Edmond G. Brown, who had defeated Richard M. Nixon (*q.v.*) for the governorship four years earlier. Reagan angered the right-wing branch of California conservatives by making peace with Nelson Rockefeller (*q.v.*) Republicans and avoiding drastic campus and economic measures. But he stopped the high-spending trends, and won the national regard of conservatives, even to the extent of seeming formidable to Nixon strategists in 1968. Reagan served another term as governor, threatened Ford's nomination in 1976, and continued in public as an advocate of limited government and a turning back from what the New Deal had become. His election to the Presidency in 1980 signaled a new era. With the crushing failures of the Carter Administration, the agitation of militant feminists and urban catastrophes, there was an open field for economic argument and controversy over the future of the family, both great concerns of Reagan and the conservative establishment. Once again, Reagan was both fulfilling and disturbing to it. He took severe liberal abuse with an aplomb Nixon had never achieved as President, with wit deflecting charges that he was old, an actor, ignorant, inattentive to issues, and a puppet in his aides' hands. With a Democratic House against him and the thinnest of margins in the Senate, it was expected that his plans for tax cuts, military increases to meet Soviet power, and welfare cuts must fail or be whittled into insignificance. But Reagan displayed amazing ability to win support and keep his popularity. Opponents called him a "great communicator," but they also forecasted continuing inflation, a low Gross National Product, deepening unemployment, and a fall in popularity for him and his program. Militant feminists threatened him for his disapproval of ERA, his anti-abortion stand, and his "sexist" and "racist" policies. They were confounded by his appointment of Sandra Day O'Connor to the Supreme Court, and by other appointments to significant posts which did not hide the fact that he sought women with conservative views. He vigorously counterattacked with evidence that members of minority groups and women were being received in numbers in his Administration. Praising jobs as better than welfare and family as the supreme good, he held on against claims of a "gender gap" and an absence of "compassion." Although he had deplored the deficit, it became a major Democratic concern, as they saw inflation falling, unemployment receding, and an economic recovery—which they would term "weak" and "precarious"—becoming real. Reagan's insistence on full military parity with the Soviet Union made a deficit inevitable, when coupled with a Social Security crisis. It nevertheless appeared that Americans approved of the military buildup. They seemed tolerant of his demand for a Constitutional Amendment mandating a balanced budget. Such conservative organs as *Human Events* and the *National Review* (*qq.v.*) were more uneasy over Reagan's programs: his budget compromises and deferment of farmers' subsidy, Social Security, and other reforms. The New Right (*q.v.*) was plainly angry over his bypassing of New Right personalities for positions in the Administration, and threatened that it might not be able to vote for him in another election. As in California, he held to the middle. His reelection in 1984 was by an overwhelming margin. Since he would be unable to run for re-election in 1988, it remained to be seen how well Reagan would be able to combat the "lame-duck" status of his Second Administration. See his autobiography, *Where's the Rest of Me* (1965), which provides insight into his personality and ways of observation; and Filler, DASC.

**Reaganomics: Supply-Side Economics in Action** (1982 ed.), by Bruce R. Bartlett, a member of Representative Jack Kemp's (*q.v.*) staff. It is a thorough exposition of what tax cuts could be anticipated to accomplish. Retrospectively, it honored Andrew W. Mellon (*q.v.*) for his tax cuts in the 1920s; Calvin Coolidge (*q.v.*), under whom Mellon served; and the John F. Kennedy tax cuts, which Bartlett defended as having done the job so stimulating the economy which Supply-Siders argued such cuts would do again. "The High Cost of Jimmy Carter" criticized his proposal for a steeper progressive income tax (*q.v.*), calculated, Bartlett insisted, not to increase revenue as expected, but to destroy incentive (*q.v.*) and to diminish the revenue so necessary to fighting harmful deficits (*q.v.*).

**Reason**, see Rationalism; Scholasticism

**Recent Conservative Political Thought: American Persepectives** (1979), by Russell G. Fryer, an overview of "conservative" thinkers. It displayed a variety of personalities, emphasizing those who seemed to have a larger public visibility, and including figures who could hardly be considered conservative at all: Reinhold Niebuhr, Daniel Bell, Patrick Moynihan, and George F. Kennan. Murray N. Rothbard (*q.v.*) was included but his "libertarian" views only spasmodically touched the concerns of conservatives or liberals. Ayn Rand (*q.v.*) was a puzzle to many in her individualism and art. Former left-wing figures seemed to create equations between old commitments and new with little regard for conservative traditions as such. Many conservative tenets were associated by Fryer with particular personalities such as Hannah Arendt, Walter Lippmann, and Seymour M. Lipset.

**Reciprocity**, see Tariffs

**Reconstruction Finance Corporation**, see Depressions

**Red**, used to denote a Communist party or its members, or a Communist-controlled country or its cooperative citizens. For many years it was more vaguely applied to persons thought sympathetic to Communists or Communist goals. The diminution of the Communist Party as a center of radical dissent and the need to distinguish various types of radical minded persons increased the use of the term "leftist" (*q.v.*).

**Red Network, The** (1934), by Elizabeth Dilling, a legitimate example of an "extremist" (*q.v.*) work, it being difficut to discern conservative principles in her work of compiling "Red" records of individuals. The journalist Heywood Broun, denounced by Dilling as a "Red," suggested that he was really just a joiner. Although Broun's liberal prestige doubtless aided committed Communists in their work, he merited being distinguished from them. Dilling compiled sometimes interesting information respecting individuals who lived with a degree of furtiveness, but her lack of impact upon more general audiences suggested that they were not so much deceived as troubled by a methodology which would have debarred Albert Einstein from America and gratuitously denounced Sigmund Freud. Dilling's *Roosevelt Red Record and Its Background* (1936) showed no improvement in investigative procedure, and reflected frustration more than it did insight.

**Red Web, The** (1925), by Blair Coán, one of the anti"Red" writings of the era which exploited public fear of Communist influence in the country, rather than illuminating Communist purposes or protagonists. Its actual purpose was to offer a defense of discredited U. S. Attorney-General Harry M. Daugherty, implicated in the Harding (*q.v.*) scandals. Daugherty himself was to make incredible connections between the "worldwide Communist network" and his own trials by government investigators; see his *The Inside Story of the Harding Tragedy* (1932). Closer to corruption than to conservatism, *The Red Web* and comparable works diverted attention from the better heritage of Republicanism.

**Redistribution**, see Income Redistribution

**Reforms and Conservatism**, one of the least understood aspects of the conservative tradition, it being fancied by those with a stake against reform that it was inevitably liberal, when not radical. Yet reforms involved adjustment rather than overthrow, and appealed to those who viewed the social scene with a sense of its needs, for comfort or serious change. Thus, John Eliot (*q.v.*) saw Indians as human beings with souls which required human attention. The American Revolution (*q.v.*) began in efforts at reform, as did the great reform movement of pre-Civil War decades which few of its conservative partisans imagined could bring on the catastrophe of civil war. Henry Bergh's (*q.v.*) efforts in behalf of animals and children constituted an appeal to civility and order during the brutal growth of cities. Dorman B. Eaton's long labors in behalf of a Civil Service Commission and the Pendleton Law (1883), which began the organization of a modern system of government employment, was a necessary check on the excesses of patronage. The great Progressive (*q.v.*) reform era brought "radical" voices to the fore, but municipal reform, conservation, railroad modernization, pure-food measures, and insurance controls among other developments were crucial to societal well-being, and could not have been accomplished without large or small measures of conservative cooperation. The idea of reform as distinguished from revolution, was harmed by the drastic nature of the Great Depression of the 1930s, as well as disappointment with the results of American intervention in World War I (*q.v.*). As a result, the accusations of historians such as Richard Hofstadter that Progressives had "in reality" been conservative appeared credible. Some reformers, such as proponents of the short ballot as making voting more intelligible to the ordinary voter, had meant no more than they declared. Woodrow Wilson (*q.v.*), who esteemed himself of the conservative branch of the Democratic Party, was one such proponent. Others, like Upton Sinclair, meant socialism when they urged reform. It was necessary to distinguish reforms and advocates, in assessing the reform component in a given measure or action. Although the idea of "reform" did not have a good name among latter-day conservatives, they were in effect attempting to apply reform aspects to earlier measures made law by New Dealers (*q.v.*) and their successors. William F. Buckley, Jr. (*q.v.*) proposed *Four Reforms* (1973) as part of his program. The concept of reform remained amorphous, to be used by those who exhibited the greatest energy in its use.

**Regnery, Henry**, see *Memoirs of a Dissident Publisher*

**Regulation**, a major concern of conservatives in post-World War II decades. They noticed the proliferation of agencies with massive budgets which enabled them to become more than mediating offices between varied economic and social elements in the body politics. By publications, subsidies, and ordinances, they were able to make policies which were often in contention. Regulation was related to bureaucracy (*q.v.*), and even to employment, as branch offices of agencies proliferated. Moreover, offices which had had advisory functions became active in directing operations within their sphere, with the power to institute legal actions of wide significance. Thus, Health, Education, and Welfare, which later became separate departments of Education and of Human Services, literally affected activities throughout the land. It was the contention of conservatives that such agencies needed stripping down, absorption by other agencies which they overlapped, and, in some cases, abolition. The Reagan Administration came into office in 1980 with its sights particularly set on the Department of Education and the Department of Energy. It was a sign of the complexities of the Administration, the need of the Executive Office to find friends in Congress and resist foes, and the simple fact of priorities that such steps were never taken. By 1985, the existence of both Departments seemed assured for the foreseeable future. For an overview of regulatory bodies and the problems in law and equity they involve, James Q. Wilson, *The Politics of Regulation* (1983). See also Deregulation, and Susan J. & Martin Tolchin, *Dismantling America: The Rush to Deregulate* (1983).

**Reich, Charles**, see Property

**Reisel, Victor** (1917- ), American newspaper columnist. In his youth he was socialist-minded. He became a follower of labor developments at home and abroad, and was interested in racketeering (*q.v.*), particularly as it besmirched labor unions (*q.v.*). In 1956 he was partially blinded by a gangster who threw acid in his eyes. Adapting to his loss of sight, he followed union developments closely, his syndicated column being especially welcomed in conservative publications. His vendettas against racketeers in unions and malfeasant union officials were more consistent, though less sensational, than what Westbrook Pegler (*q.v.*) had been able to achieve in a shorter space of time.

**"Relevance,"** a term employed by radicals and liberals in the 1960s and early 1970s. Controversies and issues in civil rights, foreign policy, and social duties were not to be judged with reference to history or tradition but only in terms of contemporary "relevance." This allowed such spokesmen of the time as Rap Brown and Abbie Hoffman (*q.v.*) to speak on momentous issues without reference to history or alternative points of view. The passion for "relevance" soon faded along with most of the other passions of the 1960s and early 1970s.

**Relief**, see Entitlements, Welfare State

**Religion**. A key factor in modern conservative thought and activity, religion as viewed by conservatives built on a complex history of veneration and freedom. Earlier conservative religious establishments were firmly founded in tradition, and could survive Deism (*q.v.*), "inner light" deviations from conformity, mob assaults on Catholic (*q.v.*) institutions, and atheistic (*q.v.*), challenges. They could answer or ignore anti-religious implications in Darwinism and the direct scorn of Marxists (*qq.v.*). However, the disillusionment following World War I, the triumphs of an atheistic Soviet Union (*q.v.*), and the psychological upsets caused by extreme affluence and extreme depression (*qq.v.*)—which lost many churches their communicants—raised many questions which new conservatives sought to answer. Fundamentalists sought enlightenment in a literal reading of the Bible (*qq.v.*). Intellectuals looked backward to tradition, authority, and the inspiration of great teachers. The decline of liberalism (*q.v.*) and the failures of the welfare state in the maintenance of families, education and urban centers (*qq.v.*) called for solutions which economics and philosophy seemed unable to provide. Under such conditions, religious tenets seemed more plausible than in past materialistic decades. Moreover, the attack on government-encouraged religious observances by such organizations as the America Civil Liberties Union (*q.v.*) gave religion a new attractiveness to some heretofore passive conservatives. They found their resentment magnified in the sharp writings of conservative journalists, and in such influential public figures as Barry Goldwater and President Reagan (*qq.v.*). Although their goals were opposed to earlier Christian socialists and reformers, who sought in deeds to create a vital church, religious conservatives were in their own way attempting to provide evidence that belief in God was no idle pursuit, but could be the means for finding renewed faith in life and the possibility of improving its chances for good. Wm. G. McLoughlin and R. N. Bellah, eds., *Religion in America* (1968); R. Creel, *Religion and Doubt: Toward a Faith of Your Own* (1976); P. G. Kauper, *Religion and the Constitution* (1964); C. C. Goen, *Broken Churches, Broken Nation* (1986); D. T. Bailey, *Shadow on the Church...1783-1860* (1985). R. L. Moore, *Religious Outsiders and the Making of Americans* (1986).

**Religion and Atheism**. Though on the surface totally opposed, in practice religion and atheism meet at many points. Conservatives made a first point of honoring religion, and religious observance. Deists (*q.v.*), when they were not of the aggressive anti-Bible school of a Thomas Paine, often agreed on the need for a respectful posture toward religion, if only to appease the believing masses. Americans developed a tradition of goodwill toward "the village atheist," often an earnest reader and civic personality who they held was more "truly" religious than mere churchgoers. Modern conservatives saw as foes of society as well as religion militant atheists such as Madalyn Murray O'Hair, whose legal suit against public prayer in the schools (*q.v.*) in 1963 curbed it through a large part of the educational system. See William J. Murray, *My Life Without God* (1982). At least as formidable, however, to conservatives was the atheism preached and practiced by Communists, notably in the Soviet Union. Official persecution of believers, combined with oppression of such minorities as the Jews as well as of lovers of free expression, created religious sentiments among those affected and their sympathizers in the Soviet Union and abroad. Among those famous as having been turned by the workings of atheism to religion was Alexander Solzhenitsyn (*q.v.*), whose extraordinary talent and good fortune enabled him to survive brutal treatment and artistic suppression to become a voice of conscience and religion opposing Soviet practices, to many who were not religious and emphatically opposed to conservatives. W. A. Luijpen and H. Koren, *Religion and Atheism* (1971).

**Religion and the Rise of Capitalism**, see Commercialism

**Rent**, historically a sensitive component in the philosophy of Free Trade (*q.v.*), as giving ownership all but legal rights over the fundamentals of life. David Ricardo (*q.v.*) saw landowners as repressive of human life in Great Britain and even more Ireland, where "absentee landlords" prevailed. The alternative to *rentiers* was harsh hereditary laws, limited ownership, and peasant ownership making for small landholdings. The United States was, in liberal English minds, a model land in this respect, though the process was questioned by such conservatives as James Fenimore Cooper (*q.v.*), even in the face of great land consolidations and hard times which forced small farmers off the land, thus building up days of wrath which more insightful economics might have averted.

**"Reparations,"** see "Affirmative Action"

**Republic**, see Democracy

**Republicans.** Democrats have traditionally called the Republican Party the party of conservatism. Nevertheless Abraham Lincoln headed a party committed to the limitation of, if not its elimination of slavery. (Democratic historians saw Republicans as more concerned for a protective tariff than for the abolition of slavery.) Still, the Free Soil slogan of Republicans spoke better for free enterprise than did the "squatter sovereignty" prospects of the opposition. Post-Civil War Republican Administrations made gestures to the spirit of Lincoln which did the Negro (*q.v.*) community little harm and some good in the form of official respect, some government jobs, and grants in aid—to be sure as part of party policy and organization. Also part of the Republican program was official and unofficial aid to industrial giants, and an unwillingness to fight trusts (*q.v.*). Although Western farmers divided into regular Republicans and Populist elements, the latter in protest against overbearing monopolies, they came together to include Progressives and conservatives, as represented by Theodore Roosevelt and William Howard Taft. The former pressed for laws diminishing the excesses of factory labor, consumer gouging, and trusts; the latter were more interested in social control in law and legislation. The Harding and Coolidge (*qq.v.*) Administrations represented a letdown in civic concerns, resulting from high expectations following World War I and unchecked prosperity and enormous strides in technology. Herbert Hoover (*q.v.*) was expected to provide the executive ability he had manifested during the war, but his program was overwhelmed by the sheer extent of economic woe. The popular acceptance of the New Deal (*q.v.*) program put Republican political power in the hands of New Deal emulators such as Thomas E. Dewey (*q.v.*), who nearly attained the White House. Although Dwight D. Eisenhower did become President, in overwhelming recognition of his wartime prowess, he was too much the soldier, interested in results rather than budgets, to attack the foundations of the New Deal heritage. His Republican successor, Richard M. Nixon, (*q.v.*) was willing to do so. But his Administration blundered and was destroyed by the Watergate scandal. Gerald Ford (*q.v.*), a "caretaker" President, lost the 1976 election despite a strong closing finish. In 1980 the electorate manifested a pronounced turn to conservatism. Ronald Reagan (*q.v.*) ran as a conservative seeking conservative ends. Although he had disappointed his "radical right" followers as governor of California, working with remnants of quasi-New Deal Republicans and striking only moderately at social services, his general purposes had been clearly conservative. All this appeared to be the case again when Reagan was re-elected in 1984.

**Resegregation**, see Segregation

**Restitution**, a problem in the administering of justice in civil and criminal law. Early American practice was to relate as closely as possible law and restitution, not always rational in practice, but creating a terror of law or contract-breaking, and so holding society together. Thus, debt could result in imprisonment, making it difficult for the debtor to pay off his debt unless aided by relatives or friends. Convicted murderers were hanged, shot, or otherwise executed. Imprisoned criminals paid a certain amount of restitution by building the prisons in which they and future criminals were incarcerated. The work of many reformers acted to modify aspects of injustice and social harm created by actual conditions which made prisons into schools of crime (*q.v.*). Prisons were made less dreadful, parole systems gave openings for considering individual cases, and capital punishment was all but eliminated. The great civil rights movement of the post-World War II era created a vast area for reform, with judges, lawyers, and theoreticians, many with stakes in or elected by partisans in high-crime areas, committed to the most generous views of criminals as victims. What was less emphasized or discussed was the potential of restitution, that is, of criminals being required to give as much as they could in compensation for their destruction of property or lives. Earlier systems, notoriously in the South (*q.v.*), which worked convicts on chain gangs or leased their services to outside contractors, had been condemned as barbaric. Some legal impounding of stolen property helped balance society's accounts. But the sheer cost of processing criminals—often for a lifetime of housing, feeding, and clothing—was inadequately examined. The blunt need for housing the burgeoning armies of criminals raised budgets for prisons ever higher. Few solutions were offered, and in many cases crimes were in effect written off like traffic cases. Although restitution could not settle all nuances of crime control, to say nothing of crime diminution, it offered a first step toward tangible action which might give potential criminals second thoughts about the profitability of their vocations. R. Barnett and J. Hagel, *Assessing the Criminal: Restitution, Retribution and The Legal Process* (1977); Stephen Schafer, *Restitution to Victims of Crimes* (1960). P. Brodeur, *Restitution: The Land Claims of the Masphee*...[and other] *Indians of New England* (1986).

**Retirement**. It once depended on individual resources and will as well as, especially among the poor, the ability to continue working. Retirement often meant retiring to the poorhouse. European nations worked earlier than America to stabilize the sequence from early employment to retirement, but the Great Depression of the 1930s brought American government into questions earlier the province of locales, industries, and beneficial societies. See Aged; Social Security. In competitive terms, retirement provided one means for ridding a firm or department of an unwanted member. Lack of preparation for growing old often made for foolish retirements. As early as the 1920s, Ring Lardner, in his "Golden Honeymoon," described the emptiness of many retirement lives. Retirement centers in Florida began to spring up. Actuaries noted the relationship between retirement and early death; Americans needed to keep "busy" to have reasons for staying alive. Post-World War II inflation (*q.v.*) affected retirement; there was less money in real terms for retirees. Journalists and television newscasters found retired individuals subsisting on "dog food." Except for a favored few, such as military men taking "early retirement" often in order to find work elsewhere, prejudice against the old kept them from viable employment, though they were admittedly more conscientious and more adaptable than younger employees. Social Security laws militated against the aged, penalizing them for self-employment and so weakening their stake in society's functions until the penalties were removed in 1984. The social uprisings of the 1960s affected the old as well as the young, and brought forth men and women to state the case for the aged. Laws against discrimination in employment helped. The end of the "baby boom" and the resulting rise in the percentage of older people in society made them a force in politics. Although forced retirement and prejudice continued to work against the aged, they were better positioned as the century moved toward its conclusion. See also Pepper, Claude.

**"Reverse Discrimination**," see "Affirmative Action;" Discrimination

**Revisionists**, a dissident group in historical study, including such disparate figures as Harry Elmer Barnes, the journalist John T. Flynn (*q.v.*), Charles C. Tansill, and to a degree, Charles A. Beard. They held that Franklin D. Roosevelt had played a Machiavellian role in drawing America into World War II, against all reason and necessity. Attention focussed on aid and credits given to the embattled Allies opposing Nazi actions, and on the catastrophe at Pearl Harbor, which revisionists held could have been avoided. Their case supported that of the isolationists (*q.v.*), who were of clear conservative convictions. That the historians should have accepted their status as "revisionists" indicated their sense of representing a minority opinion, and the dominance of liberals in the field.

**Revolt of the Masses**, see Ortega y Gasset, Jose.

**Revolution**, a permanent concept in human and political affairs, there being always a discontented minority or majority of the population to dream of or plot overthrows of governments. In numerous poverty-stricken and repressively administered nations, unrest was permanent, and often resulted in "revolution" which substituted new cliques for old, to little purpose. Thus the word "revolution" caried little weight. It would have carried relatively little weight even in the Soviet Union (*q.v.*), once its credibility as "The Workers' Fatherland" had sufficiently diminished, had it not also acquired the atomic bomb (*q.v.*), in part thanks to treason in the advanced capitalist states. Since the West theoretically was reluctant to foster "revolution" elsewhere, and sought democratic consensus (*q.v.*) in lands "aligned" (*q.v.*) or unaligned with their own, it made little use of the concept of revolution. The Soviet Union, on the other hand, exported it freely wherever it could, except in its own land and in those it dominated. See also Counter-Revolution.

**Reynolds vs. Sims** (1964), see Warren, Earl

**Rhetoric**, see Demagogues.

**Rhodes, James Ford** (1848-1927), American historian. Of a well-established Cleveland, Ohio family, he earned a fortune in the coal and iron business, in company with his brother-in-law Marcus A. Hanna (*q.v.*). Rhodes retired in 1885 to write history. Resettling in Cambridge, Massachusetts, he worked at his *History of the United States from the Compromise of 1850* (1893-1906). In seven volumes and covering no more than the period from 1850 to 1877, it became the cornerstone of his fame. Rhodes was outstanding in his efforts to present clearly and objectively his vast tale, his very first chapter on the origins and growth of slavery in the United States being famous for its evenhandedness. Nevertheless, he was held biased and imperceptive by later liberal historians for pride in his American heritage and insufficient regard for the viewpoints of immigrants and labor activists. Southern historians also criticized him as insufficiently "understanding" of the South; Woodrow Wilson (*q.v.*), in an unsigned review, saw him as merely presenting "facts." Nevertheless, Rhodes was outstanding for his efforts to incorporate opposing viewpoints. His later works included *Historical Essays* (1909) and histories of the Civil War and of Administrations succeeding it. See also Oberholtzer, Ellis Paxson, and R. Cruden, *James Ford Rhodes* (1961).

**Ricardo, David** (1772-1823), British economist, a forerunner in political economic theory whose logic appealed to partisans of free enterprise and made him a pioneer in free-market technical analysis. His emphasis on productivity and his definition of "value" as embodying the labor of individuals made him a foe of Tory landowners, whom he saw as parasites on society. On the other hand, he had little to offer the laborer in his "iron law of wages," which saw them as falling to the lowest point necessary for subsistence. Ricardo's major work, *Principles of Political Economy and Taxation* (1817), set forth "laws" on rent, currency, foreign trade, and other topics which, though heavily qualified by later analyses, organized them for systematic reexamination by others. He accepted Thomas Malthus's (*q.v.*) basic assumptions regarding population. His approval of free trade, sound currency, and the liquidation of the public debt were calculated to provide a heritage for future generations of conservatives. Since Ricardo was Jewish, the approval he won served to encourage those who disapproved of anti-Semitism (*q.v.*) in England and abroad.

**Richberg, Donald R.** (1881-1960), a transitional (*q.v.*) figure between an older liberalism and conservatism. A Tennessean who practiced law in Chicago, he specialized in railroad and labor legislation. His drafting of the bill for a National Recovery Administration (1933) was evidence of the moderate intentions embodied in the Act. When it was declared unconstitutional by the Supreme Court in 1935, Richberg returned to practice, and as the New Deal (*q.v.*) continued, turned to conservative views. See his *Labor Union Monopoly* (1957). See also his *Tents of the Mighty* (1930) and *Government and Business Tomorrow* (1943). Thomas E. Vadney, *The Wayward Liberal, a Political Biography of Donald Richberg* (1970).

**Right**, a term employed mainly by politically minded writers and activists of the Left (*q.v.*), rather than by conservatives proper, except where they felt themselves directly in confrontation with "leftists" and thought it desirable to rally their forces in opposition. "Lefty" was commonly employed by both radicals (*q.v.*) and their opponents; there was no equivalent "righty" in communication, though "a turn to the right" was used to describe industrial and political developments beyond the Depression era and the Cold War which followed the U.S.-U.S.S.R. alliance of World War II. The rise of a new conservatism in the 1950s was widely seen as a right-wing trend, and the Goldwater (*q.v.*) crusade of 1964 as a drive headed by members of the Right. Most confusing to analysts were rightist trends among industrial workers, inspired not by the surly dissatisfactions of neo-fascists (*q.v.*), but by their preference for the promises of conservative candidates for office.

**Right to Life**, see Abortion

**Right to Work**, a cause made difficult to establish in the face of labor's long battle for unions (*q.v.*) and a history of industrial war with heroes (*q.v.*) and villains on both sides. Although industrialists fought a hundred-year battle to maintain their individual prerogatives, in the name of freedom from coercion, the actual war proceeded on many levels, the most reasonable involving the idea of mediation between employers and employees and necessarily endorsing the associated idea of unions. Many employers preferred unions as being the best vehicles for negotiation. Samuel Gompers (*q.v.*) thus stood as a conservative unionist, denouncing martyrdom and heroics and fighting for a representative American Federation of Labor. Workers—often in poverty and needs, and especially in hard or desperate times or when confronted with ruthless employers—won a substantial amount of public sympathy. In reform eras, laws and commissions served to ease their plight, notably the 1914 Clayton Anti-Trust Act, which exempted unions from anti-trust action. Although the Act did not end the tragedy of cruel strikes, boycotts, and other industrial catastrophes, it set a guiding line for humane action. The Great Depression (*q.v.*) with its intolerable burdens, was the turning point in labor-capital relations, resulting in the Labor Mediation Board, intended to end the worst of labor wars. Unions proliferated and thrived, bringing out leaders with power and courage, but now always with bars against the temptation to consolidate power and amass union funds and pensions. The general public had too little access to the interior workings of unions, and even when aroused—by murders or proved theft—scarcely knew how to approach unions which did not touch it directly. Unionists often found themselves under the dictatorship of union chieftains, foremen, and even strong-arm men. They were often better off than their predecessors of a generation past, but subject to burdensome dues, constricted work conditions, and important losses of income during strikes called for reasons of union intrigue rather than legitimate goals. Workers could in effect be blacklisted by unions rather than, as in former years, by employers. They could have their work taken away from them by union bosses. Post-World War II (*q.v.*) affluence undermined many workers' will to resist, but gross scandals and worse in trucking, coal, and other unions stirred the outrage of groups of workers. Some of them protested and were harassed by union officials. Conservative opinon reached them, not for intellectual reasons, but as a result of their own lives. But the magic of labor's long struggle was against them. In the mid-1950s critics denounced an effort to promote "right-to-work" laws arising out of the Taft-Hartley Law (*q.v.*) as furthering industrial strife. Affluent unions were able to persuade the public that a return to the days of prostrate workers and harsh employers was in prospect. In 1968 the National Right to Work Legal Defense Foundation was established to handle the cases of workers who had been prevented from working for refusing to join unions, for protesting involuntary deduction of dues from their pay, and for being unwilling to support unions' political preferences. Although there were cases won, there were also cases lost. The general public found it difficult to concentrate on the idea of the "open shop." Economic depressions, in regions or nationally, complicated questions of labor responsibility to the public weal. See, however, Concessions; Rackets; Unemployment; Unions.

**Rights of Man, The**, see Paine, Thomas

**Ripon Society**. It took its name from the political pioneers who, meeting in Ripon, Wisconsin, made a beginning of founding the Republican Party in 1854. They were protesting the Kansas-Nebraska Act which threatened to open the West to slavery. The young enthusiasts of the Ripon Society, beginning in 1962 and gathering numbers and eloquence in succeeding years, attempted to create what they saw as a new beginning for a Republican Party which had become mired in confusion and defeat. In succeeding years, they were critical of Southern Republicans, of Goldwater and Reagan (*qq.v.*), of the draft, of efforts to curb government expenditures at the expense of the needy, and of curbs on civil liberties, and government support for education. Their foreign policy recommendations comported with these goals and expectations. The problem was to distinguish their opinions from those of many Democrats. They appeared to have a future when Vietnam and Watergate (*qq.v.*) seemed to reduce the ongoing Republican party to chaos. However, it developed that the more conservative elements attaching themselves to the Party proved better at organizing, and had a program which challenged that of the Democrats fundamentally. George F. Gilder (*q.v.*), who had associated with the Ripon Society, emerged as a force in opposition to its expectations. For the despairing response of a Ripon founder to the New Conservatism, see *Ominous Politics*. See also L. W. Huebner and T. E. Perri, *The Ripon Papers 1963-1968* (1968).

**Rise of Radicalism, The** (1973), by Eugene H. Methvin, an ambitious tracing of radical thought and actions arising out of the French Revolution and continuing out of Marx and Marxism to obtain a grip in Russia among its intellectuals and terrorists. A major aspect of the work was to subsume under radicalism both the Bolshevik Revolution and the Nazi Revolution. Since socialists and others had insisted upon the differences between the two successful uprisings, in terms of "class" base and goals, this identification contributed to conservative theory. The full sense of the Stalinist (*q.v.*) tyranny and additional evidence of Soviet barbarism helped support this Nazi-Soviet relationship.

**Road to Reaction**, by Herman Finer (1945). The liberal-socialist response to Friedrich Hayek's *The Road to Serfdom* (1944) (*q.v.*), it presented the case for government planning and social services, arguing, for example, that state health services in Great Britain, Finer's homeland, were a patent success. Moreover, it stated that Hayek, in warning that planning led to dictatorship, passed over or ignored the actual career of "free enterprise," which had brought hardship and worse to toilers and the individual. Since both Hayek and Finer wrote before the full flowering of welfare programs, either in Great Britain or in the United States—or the Soviet Union, toward which Finer was then positive in attitude—it took later unfoldings to create adequate comparisons between the Hayek argument and expectations and those of Finer.

**Road to Serfdom The**, see Hayek, F. A. von

**Robber Barons, The** (1934), by Matthew Josephson. Its title fastened itself on the American consciousness as descriptive of the industrial entrepreneurs of the post-Civil War decades, seen here as the equivalent of the Rhineland buccaneers who made a practice of robbing passersby. Frankly employing anti-capitalist secondary sources and using a vivid prose and illustrative materials, the author, a former Twenties (*q.v.*) litterateur whose career included business activities and pro-Communist attitudes, made a strong impression on readers who made no distinction between financial wreckers of the Jim Fisk-Jay Gould types and such others as Andrew Carnegie and John D. Rockefeller (*qq.v.*). Although the era of Depression (*q.v.*) helped call attention to the "robber barons" concept, it was not totally responsible for its success; readers had had equivalent views presented in popular form which made no distinction between commercialization (*q.v.*) and industrial statesmanship. Scholarly essays and popular successes which treated businessmen with more complex and sympathetic strokes, and the spread of affluence during and after World War II, modified some of the impact of the "robber barons" concept. But it appeared able to revive under other forms; see *Godfather, The*. See also D. E. Shi, *Matthew Josephson: Bourgeois Bohemian* (1981).

**Robertson, Marion Gordon** ("Pat") (1930- ), religious broadcaster who achieved wide popularity, most notably with his syndicated TV program, "The 700 Club." Born and later based in Virginia, he was a graduate of Yale University and the New York Theological Seminary. Work with his Christian Broadcasting Network won him the Religious Heritage of America award of Broadcaster of the

Year in 1976. Robertson's conservative and fundamentalist Christian views led many followers to consider him a potential Republican Presidential candidate in the 1988 election. But repeated calls for a "Christian" United States and his description of himself as a "prophet of God" gave rise to doubts about his ability to attract broad popular support. Some observers regarded him as a dangerous extremist whose effect on the Republican Party could be similar to that of Jesse Jackson on the Democratic Party. He was author of *Shout It from the Housetops* (1972), and *My Prayer for You* (1977).

**Robinson, Edwin Arlington**, see Literature

**Robots**, see Behaviorism

**Roche, George C. III** (1935- ), American educator. He has been president of Hillsdale College (*q.v.*) in Michigan since 1971. A high school and college teacher, he directed seminars for the Foundation of Economic Education (*q.v.*) before assuming his position at Hillsdale. He became conspicuous in his resistance to Federal efforts to apply economic measures in order to force the College to accept Federal educational criteria. He campaigned for untampered education as part of his fund-raising efforts to extend the College's free enterprise program and its influence. His publications include *Power* (1967), *Education in America* (1969), *Legacy of Freedom*(1969), *Frederic Bastiat* (q.v.): *A Man Alone* (1971), *The Bewildered Society* (1972), and *The Balancing Act: Quota Hiring in Higher Edu-*

**Rockefeller, John D.** (1839-1937). Once feared as a threat to American freedom and opportunity as a "Robber Baron" (*q.v.*), he and his activists were the subject of two liberal classics. Henry Demarest Lloyd's *Wealth against Commonwealth* (1894) attacked him with wit and documentation. Ida M. Tarbell's *History of the Standard Oil Company* (1904), serialized in *McClure's Magazine*, took a disinterested tone which roused the public to considering means for regulating companies of such scope and dimensions as Rockefeller's. Rockefeller's own view, that there was no other way but his by which so disorderly a business could have been brought under control, won a measure of acceptance as the "robber baron" view faded out of history, and as Allan Nevins's (*q.v.*) account of Rockefeller's life and work (1940) came before public scrutiny. Moreover, the Rockefeller endowments—notably in the form of the University of Chicago, the Spelman Foundation, Rockefeller University, and the Rockefeller Foundations—were of such palpable public service value as to outlive and even obscure Rockefeller's earlier career. Even such protracted bloody events as those involving the Rockefeller-owned Colorado Fuel and Iron Company—which were directed on the industry side by John D. Rockefeller, Jr. and which resulted in a species of civil war—were dimmed by the passage of time and the bureaucratization of unions (*q.v.*). Grandchildren became prominent in finance, public service, and politics, so as to put the founder's life securely in history. See William Manchester, *A Rockefeller Family Portrait* (1959).

**Rockefeller, Nelson A.** (1908-1979). His rise in public affairs, which all but placed him in sight of the Presidency, was one measure of what had happened to the Rockefeller image since the Progressive era. (See Filler, DASC.) A man of great wealth and with ultimate conservative aims, he and they were not of a quality to attract the sympathy of conservatives who saw as priorities curbing government in the affairs of individuals and commerce and leading resistance to the spread of Communism. Liberal Republicans of Rockefeller's stamp, operating within welfare-state premises, seemed to differ from Democrats only in their promise to bring greater administrative skills to bear on government. It was a program which had all but made Thomas E. Dewey (*q.v.*) President. At the same time as Dewey was at the height of his career, Nelson Rockefeller was making his name as Coordinator of the Office of Inter-American Affairs (1940-1944). He was later Chairman of the International Development Advisory Board (1950-1951) and Chairman of the President's Advisory Committee on Government Organization (1952-1958). Displaying an ability to talk sympathetically to people in the street, he ran for governor of New York in 1958 against another scion of wealth, Averell Harriman, and won. He then instituted a program of expansion of services, urban renewal, and civil-rights legislation, all the while developing the state university system. Considering himself unshakeable in the state, he looked beyond to presidential possibilities. But his divorce and remarriage in 1964 harmed him irreparably; had they occurred later, they would have caused little stir. By 1968 he had to face the fact that the grassroots Republican leaders preferred Richard M. Nixon (*q.v.*) to himself. Nevertheless, liberal Republicans who intensely disliked Nixon pressured Rockefeller to try for the party's Presidential nomination. Rockefeller's swift display of funds and expert publicity campaign proved insufficient. His one great crisis as governor took place when one of the worst prison riots in history began September 9, 1971 at the Attica State Correctional Facility in northern New York State. A portion of the prison was seized by inmates, along with some thirty guards and others, and a variety of demands issued. Protracted negotiations and media coverage roused intense feelings in and out of the prison. On September 13th, Rockefeller placed his authority on the side of law and order by ordering a storming of the prison compound by state troopers and sheriff's deputies. Thirty-two inmates and eleven guards died in the action. Differences in conservative and liberal views of the event were shown when Rockefeller sent telegrams of condolence to the families of the dead prison guards. Tom Wicker of the *New York Times*, covering the crisis, criticized him for not having done the same for the families of the dead prison inmates. Rockefeller resigned the governorship in 1973, and the next year agreed to serve new President Gerald Ford (*q.v.*) as his Vice-President. But, as he said in a phrase which became the title of a book by M. Kramer and S. Roberts (1976), "I never wanted to be Vice-President of anything." He announced that he would step down at the end of Ford's term. Rockefeller's death by heart attack in somewhat compromising circumstances surprised the general public.

**Rockford Institute, The.** Conservative study center whose main effort is directed not at public policy, but at the ethical foundations of a free society. Founded 1976 by John A. Howard, the Institute sponsors conferences, publications, and research, among which are *Chronicles Culture*, The Center on Religion and Society, and Program on the Family in America.

**Roe vs. Wade**, see Abortion

**"Role-Playing,"** see *Behavioral Persuasion in Politics*

**Romanticism**. Not high on the scale of conservative priorities, it has nonetheless been a force to cope with throughout history, involving individualism, love of nature, the attraction of youth to youth, chivalry, and the mysteries of life. Romantic impulses can be perceived throughout literature, but often as fragments in circumstances compelling reverence, duty, and the demands of community. Dante's (*q.v.*) famous line "That night they read no further in the book" appears among many lines with themes more readily associated with his name. Shakespeare gave Romeo the wistful phrase "I meant all for the best," to indicate the power of Fate, elsewhere expressed, over love. Thomas Chatterton's (see Lacy, Ernest) desperate campaign for a freer poetry than Pope's was destined to be that of a forerunner rather than of a victor. Rousseau's (*q.v.*) social conjectures and personal vagaries touched a living chord in society which set off disorder in the name of a new order. Romantics fared less well in America in terms of patrons (*q.v.*) and the capacity to expand. The novelist Charles Brockden Brown was driven to business for a living, William Cullen Bryant (*q.v.*) to journalism. Melville was driven offstage completely; there was no one to indulge his concern for metaphysics or to support Poe's (*q.v.*) peccadilloes. The youth movement (*q.v.*) of the 1910s won some victories for romanticism, but it was directed against its own land, and partially reached its apogee abroad, with expatriates. Although commerce, donors, and foundations stimulated some art, some of it romantic, it took the Federal Arts Projects of the 1930s to turn a fuller attention to American themes and equalize opportunities for members of any class and partisans of any perspective. However, the upheavals of society in post-World War II times were not conducive to art, romantic or otherwise. The New Conservatism was too heavily engaged elsewhere to refine goals and attitudes toward art. Irving Babbitt's (*q.v.*) highly admired *Rousseau and Romanticism* was not calculated to inspire absorption in romantic themes. Nevertheless an interest in their potential could be traced among conservative figures in their religious feelings and imagination. Flannery O'Connor (*q.v.*) hardly appeared a romantic on the surface, but a romantic dream could be discerned beneath her precise prose. Much the same could be said of T. S. Eliot's (*q.v.*) precise verse. C. S. Lewis's science fiction and Russell Kirk's Gothic fantasies (*qq.v.*) looked beyond the cliches dominant in the genres. Romantic development seemed possible in any direction. Mario Praz, *The Romantic Agony* (1933); Owen Barfield, *Romanticism Comes of Age* (1976 ed.); L. R. Furst, *Romanticism* (1976); A. R. Hope-Moncrieff, *The Romance of Chivalry* (1976).

**Roosevelt, Franklin D.** (1882-1945). As President elected to an unprecedented four terms, he initiated the welfare (*q.v.*) system in the United States. As a result he has traditionally been denigrated by Republicans and conservatives. (See Filler, DASC.) Elected governor of New York in 1928, he faced the Great Depression (*q.v.*) which ensued with an outlook contrasting with that of President Hoover (*q.v.*), borrowing from Democratic traditions of public works instituting what came to be seen as a "Little New Deal" (*q.v.*). It offered welfare and temporary jobs from meager budgets. As Presidential candidate in 1932, however, Roosevelt made promises of economy in government operations. He also promised an experimentation which offered a hope Hoover could not bring himself to meet. Roosevelt's first months as President set a revolutionary course. They involved efforts to bring industry together in a semi-voluntary cooperative endeavor to get the economy rolling (National Recovery Administration), to bring farmers together to control production and prevent wholesale bankruptcies, to provide relief for the desperate unemployed through deficit spending, and, later, to institute collective bargaining between labor and industry through Federal mediators (the Wagner Act). The qualifying premise for much New Deal legislation was that it was expected to be temporary, or moderately financed—and with the limited budget available it seemed likely to be. Roosevelt himself appeared to think he was saving capitalism, rather then setting up a novel governmental structure. It was later admitted, even by loyal followers, that his measures did not cure the basic stalemate in the industrial cycle. They did however, offer hope and curb despairing political action. The coming of World War II to America in effect "cured" the depressed economy. But in substituting "Dr. Win the War" for "Dr. New Deal" it failed to eliminate the New Deal's institutions. Government intervention in industry, welfare, and other areas, though secondary to war aims, persisted through the era. Troubling to conservatives, and a heritage to their post-War successors, was the wartime alliance with the Soviet Union (*q.v.*). They insisted Roosevelt should never have permitted Communism to emerge so strong and with dominion over Eastern Europe. Later events seemed to make them prophets in this respect; their liberal opponents argued that the Soviet expansion could not have been halted, during the war itself or after. Although Roosevelt's good opinion of the dictator Stalin (*q.v.*) was embarrassing in retrospect, it did not differ sharply from Eisenhower's (*q.v.*) positive view of his Soviet military allies, and his faith in the ultimate good intentions of the Soviet people. The Roosevelt heritage was cherished by his successor, President Harry S. Truman, and later Democratic politicans sought to keep the spirit of the New Deal and its administrator alive. They learned, however, to concentrate on newer versions of Democratic policy, which sought compassion (*q.v.*) for the needy, a more "equitable" distribution of wealth, and, in foreign policy, an emphasis on peace which saw no harm in "Marxist" (*q.v.*) slogans and modified strictures against the Soviet leadership. Filler, ed.,

*The Ascendant President: McKinley to Lyndon B. Johnson* (1983), John T. Flynn (*q.v.*), *The Roosevelt Myth* (1948).

**Roosevelt, Theodore** (1858-1919). He was considered unforgettable at his death, though recalled bitterly by leading conservatives of the time. The swift "disillusionment" (*q.v.*) of the 1920s culminated in the Henry F. Pringle biography of Roosevelt (1931), which followed his career without respect or sense of achievement, and later in the frank hatred expressed in Richard Hofstadter's *The American Political Tradition* (1948) for Roosevelt's principles and war career. Although conservatives lacked enthusiasm for the Progressive era—which had been the high point of Roosevelt's career, but which they felt had contained the origins of the New Deal (*q.v.*)—they harbored a better opinion of his patriotism and love of country. John M. Blum, in *The Republican Roosevelt* (1954), treated him with scholarly courtesy. A turn in public sentiment was indicated by the interest which attended publication of E. Morris's *The Rise of Theodore Roosevelt* (1979), a bestseller which captured something of the gusto which had attended much of Roosevelt's life and politics. See also Filler, "Theo," in *Appointment at Armageddon* (1976).

**"Root Causes,"** a phrase used mainly by liberals and suggesting that efforts to control social evils such as venereal disease, alcoholism, drug addiction, crime, illiteracy, and child abuse would have to get at the basic reasons for their persistence and growth. The main root cause was usually perceived as poverty, or lack of "green power," as civil rights activists of the 1960s phrased it. George Bernard Shaw once asserted that the only crime *was* poverty. Such thinking resulted in government efforts to place more money in the hands of the poor. The 1960s and 1970s were notorious for such approaches, and also their failure. Conservatives criticized the liberal tendency to "throw money" at problems. Since many social evils were related, as with drug addiction and crime, it seemed better to study their relationships and means for control than to hunt for "root causes" which did not fight present catastrophes. The anti-capitalist bias involved in the "root causes" approach did not explain why the same social phenomena occurred in non-capitalist nations. For a general statement of implicit problems, James Q. Wilson, *Thinking about Crime* (1975) and Wilson, ed., *Crime and Public Policy* (1983).

**Roots of American Order, The** (1974), by Russell Kirk (*q.v.*), see Order

**Röpke, Wilhelm** (1899-1966), economist and humanist, in a tradition which also gave free-enterprise advocates such others as Friedrich Hayek and Ludwig von Mises (*qq.v.*). Röpke's foe was collectivism, which he saw as the opposite of liberalism (understood in the European sense), as "extending the authority and coercive powers of the State" to the detriment of freedom and opportunity. Best known was his *Civitas Humana: A Humane Order of Society* (1948), translated from the German, which looked for alternatives to what had created the late carnage of war. Employing culture, moral values, and fear of overweening intellectual pride and linking them with the workings of economy in totalitarian hands and in "full-employment" ideologies, he pleaded for quiet reason and a free economy that would avoid weighing down nations with intolerable indebtedness, as had happened after World War I. *Civitas Humana* was an essay on order which differed entirely from the "order" imposed by dictators. Other of Röpke's writings included, in translation, *The Solution of the German Problem* (1947) and *The Social Crisis of Our Time* and *Against the Tide* (1969). His colleagues at the University of Marburg in 1968 published a volume in German, *In Memoriam Wilhelm Röpke*.

**Rosenberg Case**. In the early 1950s Julius and Ethel Rosenberg were accused of passing atomic secrets to the Soviet Union. The case became a watershed in conservative-liberal controversy when many liberals of the day proclaimed the Rosenbergs' innocence. They were convicted of treason and executed in 1953, and this began a long effort among Rosenberg sympathizers to prove a miscarriage of justice involving trumped-up charges and fraud by the FBI (*q.v.*). However, research under the Freedom of Information Act led to the same conclusion as in the Hiss (*q.v.*) case. The investigator Ronald Radosh, expected to find proof of innocence. Instead he found evidence of guilt, qualified in his mind by less-than-fair government proceedings. His qualification made no difference to Rosenberg loyalists. They condemned his book *The Rosenberg File: A Search for the Truth* (1983), as a betrayal. As in the Hiss investigation, however, it appeared likely that the incident would at long last be generally considered closed. However, the editor of *The Nation* denounced the sentence of death suffered by the Rosenbergs, and Walter Goodman, in the *New York Times*, accused Radosh of having "succumbed to the facts."

**Rossiter, Clinton** (1917-1970), liberal historian, a tragic victim of the radical uprisings of the 1960s. He made his reputation with works on the Constitution and Constitution-makers which seemed lively and relevant: *Constitutional Dictatorship* (1948), *The Supreme Court and the Commander in Chief* (1951), and particularly *Seedtime of the Republic* (1953), which won the Bancroft Award and other honors. With the rise of conservative thought in the early 1950s, he took his stand with *Conservatism in America* (1955) which placed him with Peter Viereck (*q.v.*) as a critic of its contemporary manifestations. Rossiter chided the new conservatives for not appreciating the liberalism inherent in "true" conservatism. Jefferson (*q.v.*), Rossiter explained, was at the core of the American tradition. Feeling abreast of modern times, he shared the opinions of such authors as Lionel Trilling (*q.v.*), Richard Hofstadter, and Daniel Boorstin (*q.v.*). He found Justice Field and William Graham Sumner (*qq.v.*), whom conservatives admired, to be no more than "upside-down Marxists." Edmund Burke was not John Adams (*qq.v.*). Rossiter continued to win readers and approval with *The American Presidency* (1956), *Parties and Politics in America (1960), Marxism: The View from America* (1960), and *1787: The Grand Convention* (1966). Meanwhile, however, Cornell University, his academic seat, was beleaguered by youthful radicals who found his versions of democracy inadequate. The climax was reached when "students" resorted to carrying rifles to assert their claim to "freedom." Rossiter, as the pride of the campus, denounced this show of force as incompatible with American liberties and education. He was repudiated by his colleagues and committed suicide.

**Rotary**, founded in 1905, a fraternal organization (*q.v.*) dedicated to civic service and voluntarism (*q.v.*), and counting some one million members in the United States and abroad. It attracted mainly businessmen, excluding women from significant involvement, and was especially vigorous on a local level. Although Rotary engaged in benign activities, such as town and city improvement, youth enterprises, and international exchanges, its base was commercial (*q.v.*) rather than ideological. It had little impact on national issues, and none on culture.

**Rothbard, Murray N.** (1926- ), libertarian. His early economic studies (see *The Panic of 1819: Reactions and Policies* [1962]) made him a conservative and a defender of property rights. Impatience with conservative tenets, as in the conservative desire to enforce anti-obscenity laws, caused him to intensify his free-market principles—as in *Man, Economy and State* (1962) and its sequel, *Power and Market* (1970)—and to broaden his studies in the philosophy, logic, ethics, and the history of libertarianism, of which he became the major proponent. A key premise was that libertarianism was a fact in nature; see his *Egalitarianism as a Revolt against Nature and Other Essays* (1974). *For a New Liberty* (1973) was an effort to present his ideas in a more popular vein, and *The Ethics of Liberty* to controvert the "objective," value-free proposals of laissez-faire advocates. In 1975, he undertook to reassess American history in a projected series. It began with two volumes of *Conceived in Liberty* which revealed novelties of interpretation. Other of his writings included *America's Great Depression* (1972), *Toward a Reconstruction of Utility and Welfare Economics* (1977), and *Individualism and the Philosophy of Social Sciences* (1979).

**Rousseau, Jean-Jacques** (1712-1778), French social philosopher. His erratic years of wandering and impulsive living brought him to Paris in 1742, where stimulating intellectual life under the Monarchy excited his thoughts. In 1749 he wrote a prize-winning essay on the question of whether science and the arts had improved or harmed humankind. Rousseau's eloquence in rejecting the hypothesis of improvement made him famous and opened the way for further essays expressing a sense of wrong and inequality. Rousseau's very way of life was in contrast with the formal premises of the age, and, as an incitement to "freedom," was a harbinger of romanticism (*q.v.*). His thought and direction culminated in one of the most potent products of the century, his *Social Contract* (1762), which to men whom he declared to have been "born free," appeared a call to revolution. Rousseau's thought was often intemperate and contradictory, involving rigidities as well as expectations of freedom, as when Rousseau saw society as giving sovereignty the duty to dispense liberty, but according to the "general will." Those who would not comport themselves properly merited death. In the 1930's, such judgments were interpreted as making Rousseau a precursor of fascism (*q.v.*), but in his own time and after he seemed rather a forerunner of emancipation. Harassed by authorities, he accepted an invitation from David Hume (*q.v.*), and at Hume's home began his renowned *Confessions*. He died near Paris. It was symbolic of the course of revolution that in 1794 his remains were interred in Paris, in the Panthéon. In America he was seen negatively by conservatives, as in Irving Babbitt's (*q.v.*) *Rousseau and Romanticism* (1919). As Babbitt stated it, life might indeed be a dream, but it had to be handled carefully, not to turn into a nightmare.

**Royall, Mrs. Anne (Newport)** (1769-1854), a phenomenon in early journalism and "muckraking," whose life and writings were an American heritage. Of obscure and possibly noble birth, she was raised on the Pennsylvania-Virginia frontier. She became the protégé of a wealthy western Virginia farmer, Captain William Royall, who was a friend of George Washington, and he taught her his humanistic philosophy and gave her the run of his library. In 1797 he married her, and, at his death in 1823, left her mistress of his estate. Her travels and gracious living ended that same year, however, when Royall's relatives overturned his will by declaring her an adultress. Her courage in pressing her case for her dead husband's war-service pension, and in gathering materials for the ten books she published about the personages and places of the new country—books which she sold for bread and sustenance, was unexampled in cultural annals. Rudely treated, despised as "unfeminine," and made notorious in 1829 by being convicted as "a common scold," she fought on with *Paul Pry* (1831-1836) and *The Huntress* (1836-1854), publications which exposed Washington machinations and helped create the idea of civic concern. She died a pauper and was buried in the Congressional Cemetery. Although women's rights activists of the 1970s pointed to her as an example of male mistreatment of women, Royall was essentially a conservative whose cause was persons like herself. Her true inheritors were those who persuaded legislatures to permit women to own their own property, to protect women's property from wastrel or cruel husbands, and to permit divorce from obnoxious marriages. See B. R. James, *Anne Royall's U.S.A.* (1972); Filler, "Common Scold," in *Appointment at Armageddon*.

**Rugg, Harold**, see *Imagination*

**"Rule of the Best,"** see Equality

**Rusher, William A.** (1923- ), lawyer and conservative activist. He became publisher of the *National Review* and a lecturer of note in conservative circles. Rusher had been associate counsel for the U. S. Senate Internal Security Subcommittee in 1956 and 1957, and was co-author with Mark Hatfield and Arlie Schardt of *Amnesty?* (1973). His *The Making of the New Majority Party* (*q.v.*) (1975) expressed his revulsion against what he saw as the degradation of the Republican (*q.v.*) Party. See also Rusher's *The Rise of the Right* (1984).

**Russia**, the traditional name of the dominant geographical region of the Soviet Union (*q.v.*). Historically the Russian Czars had extended their rule over various regions and nations having no stake in Russian plans and perspectives. Most notable in this connection was the Ukraine, which prided itself on having a long history of its own, diminished under the Czars and later the Soviets. Other areas controlled by Russia and later the U.S.S.R. found partisans abroad to recall heroes and traditions not honored by Moscow. While the Czars had ruled with the help of an established state church, their Soviet successors enshrined atheism as the official state "religion." But the centralized control from Moscow over a vast "empire" of diverse nations and peoples remained constant, despite the fiction that the U.S.S.R. was really a "voluntary" federation of independent republics. Many exiles from these "republics," such as dispossessed Estonians, Latvians, and Lithuanians, dreamed of some day being able to return home to free and independent nations.

**Russian Revolution**, the most momentous outcome of World War I (*q.v.*). It put into practice what had previously been abstract theory. Proposals for utopias (*q.v.*) could only promise desired results. Communists claimed that the Paris Commune of 1871 could have resulted in a worthy fulfillment, had it not been cut down by the "counter-revolution." The Russian Revolution succeeded, however, and, as the Bolshevik Revolution, put the dictatorship of the proletariat, Marx's panacea for human ills, on trial. It was a product of a decayed Russian military establishment, unable to match the modernization of the Western powers, and a short-sighted German establishment, which permitted Lenin (*q.v.*) to leave Zurich under its protection to contribute to the demoralization of Russians on the Eastern Front. Lenin joined other socialist factions in demanding a constituent assembly, thereby employing what became the Communists' most famous tactic: to demand democratic rights until they could take control in a coup, when they would abandon democracy for naked power. To this general demand, Lenin added a further democratic appeal, for "Land, Bread, and Peace." With power loosely spread between workers' and soldiers' councils (soviets) on the one hand and coalitions of monarchists, republicans, and socialists attempting to form a working government on the other, it was an opportunity for strong, determined forces. Those most determined were the military leaders on one side and the less numerous but highly motivated Bolsheviks on the other. While socialists and republicans struggled to reconcile differences and determine strategies for maintaining a collapsing empire, the Bolsheviks gave full attention to the soviets, which had first been created in the abortive revolution of 1905. Kerensky's attempt to continue the war against Germany only exposed the impotence of his military forces even further. Although a Bolshevik attempt to seize Petrograd was stymied, it revealed the rift between the Soviets and the Kerensky Government. The Bolsheviks had no easy road to power. Hundreds of White Guard and nationalist leaders were spread across the massive Russian terrain working with rifles and bombs not only to seize particular areas, but to extend their power to the seats of Russian government. Poland, the Ukraine, Finland, Siberia, and the Caucasus were all prizes for whoever could establish power. The Bolsheviks, putting their hopes in soviets and guerillas, challenged the warlords to prove their capacity to gain control and hold it. The bloody struggles which ensued following the Bolshevik coup in October 1917 in Petrograd faced them with the need for proving their title to legitimacy. Germany once more partly from necessity because of the terrible pressure on the Western Front, could not resist forcing the Treaty of Brest-Litovsk on the desperate Bolsheviks: a treaty which stripped Russia of Poland and the great "breadbasket" of the Ukraine, among other principalities. Although Allied declarations that Brest-Litovsk exposed German brutality to the world were specious—the Allied naval blockade had caused hunger in Germany—the treaty gave new credence to Bolshevik sincerity among worker and peasant populations, and taught them to distinguish between socialists and reactionaries. It also helps to explain many ardent and brilliant spirits abroad—some later to emerge as conservatives—who, in the course of the long civil war, justified Bolshevik ruthlessness as necessary under counter-revolutionary assault. (For a key account of White Guard campaigns and personalties, Dimitry V. Lehovich, *White against Red: The Life of General Anton Denikin* [1974].) The triumph of the Bolsheviks was a measure of their own power and conviction, and the conviction they inspired at home and among members of the Third International and its sympathizers abroad. They thus shored up a stock of credit which would enable otherwise humanistic people to tolerate evident barbarities and lies later on, with no civil war at hand, with one rationalization or another, until all sympathy eventually dried up. See also Soviet Union. Leon Trotsky, *History of the Russian Revolution* (1932); William H. Chamberlin (*q.v.*), *The Russian Revolution* (1935); Sir Bernard Pares, *The Fall of the Russian Monarchy* (1939); David Footman, *Civil War in Russia* (1962).

# S

**Sacco-Vanzetti Case**, a notorious murder case of the 1920s which became a rallying cry for the left (*q.v.*), inspiring plays, poems, and works of fiction and non-fiction. Sacco and Vanzetti, two Italian immigrants, were convicted of murder in Massachusetts and sent to the electric chair. The American left in general believed them to be innocent, and that the conviction and sentence stemmed from the fact that the two men were aliens and anarchists. See C. L. Joughin and E. M. Morgan, *The Legacy of Sacco and Vanzetti* (1948). See also Filler, DASC. A contrary opinion was put forth in R. H. Montgomery's *Sacco-Vanzetti: The Murder and the Myth* (1960). Other works, reading the evidence, also concluded that certainly Sacco and perhaps Vanzetti had been actually guilty as charged. With continuity in radical history blurred by changing times, and with such Sacco-Vanzetti partisans as John Dos Passos (*q.v.*) repudiating their old commitments, the case lost much of its force in later years. Nevertheless it continued to have meaning for some Italian-Americans. In 1968 the Governor of Massachusetts officially repudiated the original judgement in the case.

**Safire, William** (1929- ), political commentator. His career included journalism, television production, and the presidency of Safire Public Relations from 1960 to 1969. He joined the staff of President Nixon as speechwriter and stayed with him until his resignation. As a writer, he was best known for his *Political Dictionary* (1980) and his interest in language usage; see his *On Language* (1980). His novel, *Full Disclosure* (1977), attempted to make a metaphor of Watergate (*q.v.*), depicting a situation in which a President was struck blind, this being hidden from the public. As columnist for the *New York Times*, Safire presented a conservative viewpoint in a basically liberal newspaper. A curiosity of his column was his impulse to create imaginary speeches for public figures at home and abroad, suggesting that he missed his old role of speech-making.

**"Saints,"** see Scholasticism

**Sakharov, Andrei**, see Dissidents

**Salt**, see Detente

**Samizdat**, underground Soviet publications of the post-Stalin era which carried news and ideas bearing on free speech and human rights. The issuing or possession of *Samizdat* publications brought criminal penalties in the Soviet Union. *Samizdat* (self-publishing) materials drew from among some of the more sensitive and gifted intellectuals, and reported the persecution of dissidents (*q.v.*), the cruel operations of the KGB (*q.v.*), and other transgressions of human rights. Notable publications included the underground news bulletin *Chronicle of Current Events* and *Political Diary*. The latter was made famous by the extraordinary careers of the twin brothers Roy and Zhores Medvedev, sons of a philosopher-soldier father arrested on false charges and exiled to death in a labor camp. Their work as anti-Stalin Soviet loyalists did not save them from less extreme Communist pressure, but it contributed to Western knowledge of Soviet workings and helped open doors to the realities of Soviet suppression and persecution of some of the Soviet Union's finest elements. *Samizdat* materials served Human Rights (*q.v.*) advocates and Amnesty International, but they were also highly prized by conservatives who labored to warn Americans that a nation so rigid in thought control as the Soviet Union could not be turned from its basic purposes. S. F. Chen, ed., *An End to Silence: Uncensored Opinion in the Soviet Union, from Roy Medvedev's Underground Magazine, Political Diary* (1982).

**Sandinistas**, ruling neo-Marxist party in Nicaragua, which American liberals endorsed in 1986, on general ground of approval of the right of nations to such government as they preferred; in opposition to conservatives, who held that the radical leaders constituted a Soviet "foothold" on the American mainland. The Reagan Administration endorsed the opposing "Contras," rebels who hoped to overthrow the regime.

**Santayana, George** (1863-1952), Spanish-American skeptic-philosopher and aesthete, born in Madrid, brought to the United States in 1872. A student of William James (*q.v.*), he developed a style which couched his atheism (*q.v.*) and materialism in agreeable prose. It appealed to the passing generation of the genteel (*q.v.*) and to departments of philosophy and the arts; see his *The Realm of Being* (1927-1940). He attracted the regard of the Soviet apologist Corliss Lamont and the anti-Communist Peter Viereck (*q.v.*). Santayana himself appreciated Catholic (*q.v.*) rituals and material things and had a distaste for Protestant mode. Although he appealed to reason and truth, his judgments were subjective and discriminatory, whether involving Edgar Allan Poe (*q.v.*) or William Faulkner—or indeed the United States, which he left for Europe in 1913. He was sympathetic to the Franco cause in Spain (*q.v.*) and thought Italian fascism created order, though he seemed to judge Mussolini a "bad" man. His view of "The Genteel Tradition at Bay" seemed accurate to its friends and foes. The resounding success of *The Last Puritan* (1935) showed him at his best, weighing his own qualities and those of friends at arm's length and with a sense of everyone's place in the world. See his *Persons and Places* (1944-1953); I. D. Cardiff. ed., *Atoms of Thought* (1950), an anthology; D. Cory, ed., *Letters* (1955).

**Saturday Evening Post**, one of the strongest organs of commercial (*q.v.*) conservative thought in the twentieth century. It aroused much opposition and scorn from liberals and radicals. Under its most powerful editor, George Horace Lorimer (1867-1937), it was positive about America and firmly optimistic. His rigid and selective principles enabled him to use writings of numerous distinguished writers, from Joseph Conrad and Edith Wharton to William Faulkner. F. Scott Fitzgerald, as a young, feisty success, denounced him at lunch, saying he would not have dared to use such vigorous work as that of Frank Norris. He was gently told that several of Norris's most famous works had been serialized in *SEP*. Following Lorimer's death, the magazine sought to fight television competition with "muckraking" (*q.v.*) exposes, and was defeated by diminished reader interest and serious legal mishaps. A revived *SEP* monthly was generally seen as a less vital *Post*. John Tebbel, *George Horace Lorimer and the Saturday Evening Post*. See also *Reader's Digest*.

**Sawyer, Charles**, see Democrats, Conservative

**Sayings of Chairman Malcolm, The** (1978), the title a parody of *The Thoughts of Chairman Mao*, a collection of epigrams and observations by the ruler of Communist China popular among political radicals in America in the 1960s. "Chairman Malcolm" was Malcolm Forbes, the owner and publisher of Forbes magazine, devoted to business and finance. His "sayings" were often more commercial (*q.v.*) than conservative, but contained much food for thought. "Venture nothing and life is less than it should be"; "Ability will never catch up with the demand for it"; "What is inflation? Taxation. Nothing more, nothing less. It's the devastating price of the Free Lunch"; "Socialism will be here the day we share our profits to the degree we share our failure." His commercialism is represented by such thoughts as: "Right? All work and no play makes jack. With enough jack, Jack needn't be a dull boy." And such thoughts as "What's the answer to 99 out of a 100 questions? Money."

**"Say's Law,"** defined by Jean Baptiste Say, (1767-1832), French economist, and prominent in developing Adam Smith's (*q.v.*) ideas on markets and popularizing the concept of "entrepreneur." Only goods, according to Say, ultimately paid for other goods. Thus, productivity was the *sine qua non* of a healthy society. See Thomas Sowell (*q.v.*), *Say's Law: An Historical Analysis* (1972).

**Scapegoats**, see Conspiracy

**Schlafly, Phyllis** (1924- ), one of the most effective of conservative women in the public sector, with an extraordinary career as author, organizer, agitator, and foe of Women's Rights. Though with a large grassroots following, especially among older middle-class women, she appeared "extremist" to many conservative tempers. Her biographer, a journalist, admitted without shame that she had gone to extreme lengths to find derogatory information about Schlafly, but had come up with nothing but malice and lies (Carol Felsenthal, *The Sweetheart of the Silent Majority* [1981]). Schlafly almost certainly helped tip the balance with her three million copies of *A Choice Not an Echo* to make Barry Goldwater (*q.v.*) the Republican candidate for the Presidency in 1964. She organized the "Eagle Forum," a group of conservative women who helped defeat the Equal Rights Amendment. She had been raised in a Depression family which scorned welfare, graduated from Radcliffe and from law school, and during World War II had worked in an ordnance plant. A staunch conservative Catholic, she saw her war against Women's Rights as a religious issue. Her crusade, however, crossed sects. It was her contention that the ERA, if consummated, would hurt men and women both, harming diversity and "neuterizing" society. Her successful uphill struggle against the ERA defeated the combined forces of the National Organization for Women and many prominent politicians including President Carter. Her books raised other questions. Five of them were written with Chester Ward, a law school professor, architect, rear admiral, and Judge Advocate General who had received the Legion of Merit from President Eisenhower. The titles were: *The Gravediggers* (1964), *Strike from Space* (1965), *Safe—Not Sorry* (1967), *The Betrayers* (1968), and *Kissinger on the Couch* (1975). They were all marked by an intense fear and hatred of Communism, and of those in America who appeared tainted with it as sympathizers or collaborators. The number of copies distributed was formidable; two million copies of *The Gravediggers* were distributed in no more than two months. Their impact, however, was debatable. They were doubtless looked at or read, but were they controverted in high places? Many conservatives did not think well of Democratic decision-makers, or even of each other. They backed off, nevertheless, from accusing their opponents of treason or conspiracy. Schlafly did not. Her torrents of facts, for she was a superb student of military hardware, could not substitute for statecraft, which involved conditions at home and abroad. Her impact, therefore, was a function of social logistics, rather than of military. Something more could be said for her *The Power of the Positive Woman* (1977), which spelled out formidable factors in the life of women and downgraded "equality" (*q.v.*) as a chimera harmful to justice and human nature. Schlafly, with her strong grasp of issues and public presence, promised to continue to be a significant factor in the area of women's issues and conservative response.

**Scholasticism** a heritage of the Middle Ages, serving modern conservatism through its Catholic adjuncts, admirers of Aristotle and Plato, and followers of St. Thomas Aquinas and Thomistic reasoning, and of tradition generally (*qq.v.*). It originally drew theologians who worked to relate faith to reason. Once the Divine Will was premised, there were infinite numbers of questions requiring response. St. Augustine (*q.v.*) early saw Plato (*q.v.*) as implementing Christian tenets. Aristotle's (*q.v.*) cosmic views did them no harm. Scholastics quarreled over reason and faith, and the essence of being, and of God (*q.v.*) himself. After the Middle Ages scholasticism began to lose its central place in philosophy. It nevertheless survived effectively in such thinkers as Berkeley and Whatley (*qq.v.*), affecting general impressions, and, in modern times, in the writings of Jacques Maritain. *The New Scholasticism*, published at the University of Notre Dame, gave space to issues and authors engaged in current controversies. Thus, 1983 issues included such writings as M. J. Mathis's "Kindness and Duties in the Abortion Issue," Frederick D. Wilhelmsen's "A Note on the Absolute Consideration of Nature," V. C. Punzo's "Natural Law [*q.v.*] Ethics: Immediate or Mediated Naturalism?" An unusual development was the rise of a species of atheistic scholasticism. Joseph Pieper, *Scholasticism* (1960); J. Weinberg, *A Short History of Mediaeval Philosophy* (1964).

**Schools**, see Education

**Schroeder, Theodore A.** (1864-1953), lawyer and libertarian (*q.v.*). He took pride in having published more controversial matter than any other advocate of unrestricted freedom of speech and press. In temperament he was closer to such a person of principle as John Jay Chapman (*q.v.*) than to the merely licentious or unrestrained. Typical of his writings was *A Challenge to Sex Censors* (1938). It reflected his studies in law and medical history, and also public responses to his arguments for free speech. Unknown to both liberal and conservative commentators, his work came closest to the beliefs of libertarians.

**Schuyler, George S.** (1895-1977), an independent journalist and commentator on Negro and black subjects, a precursor of such writers as Thomas Sowell and Walter Williams (*qq.v.*). Schuyler was born in Providence, Rhode Island, the son of a chef, and educated in Syracuse, New York. He became an editor on the *Pittsburgh Courier*, then expanded his services to Negro-dominated and white publications. As a special correspondent he reported from the Caribbean, South America, and Africa. Although it was soon evident that he did not subscribe to conventional opinions in the black community, it found it hard to repudiate one who had made his own place in the open market. Schuyler's *Black No More* (1931) was a satire on black interests. It told of a cream which could turn Negroes white so that they could disappear into the larger community. He attacked Marcus Garvey's Back-to-Africa movement and as late as the 1950s was unmoved by Martin Luther King's crusade. His articles for the *American Mercury*, the *Reader's Digest*, the *Freeman*, and other publications, including *American Opinion* (*qq.v.*), kept him of interest to white readers and exasperated dominant black leaders. Schuyler's wife Josephine was a painter, and his daughter Philippa (1934-1967) a musical genius who performed in 70 countries and wrote several books, including *Adventures in Black and White* (1960). Following her death, Schuyler established the Philippa Schuyler Memorial Foundation. He was all but unique among his people in insisting on perspective on the slavery (*q.v.*) issue; see his *Slavery Today: A Story of Liberia* (1931). See also his *Black and Conservative: The Autobiography of George S. Schuyler* (1971), published by Arlington House (*q.v.*).

**Science and Ethics**, see Genetic Revolution

**Science Fiction**, although a lucrative and popular genre, hardly a significant factor in disseminating ideas and ideologies. As crime and detection often examined the details of police techniques, so science writers often found ideas in actual science and exploited them in narratives. The key question in both genres was quality, which few writers sought or attained, in tales of good men and bad men, or in appealing to fears for earth's future. Gerald Heard (*q.v.*) mixed genuine science with Christian hope. Ray Bradbury (*q.v.*) was less the scientist than the ponderer on the human condition. C. S. Lewis (*q.v.*) was spectacular in his success as a writer of science fiction, but it was part of a larger success which made him formidable in Christian apologetics; see *Myth, Allegory, and Gospel*. The enormously prolific Isaac Asimov had begun as a professor of biochemistry before discovering his more lucrative profession. How much effect the moralists and religious-minded authors had on readers it is difficult to judge. For a survey of such stories, Asimov, ed., *The Hugo Awards: Twenty-Three Prize-Winning Science Fiction Stories* (1962). See also Gothic Romance.

**Scott, Walter**, see Cooper, James Fenimore

**Screen Actors Guild**, see Reagan, Ronald; Murphy, George; Gavin, John

**Secession**, a painful choice for conservative and Union-raised southerners. They consoled themselves with thoughts that their "revolution" was as similarly justifiable as the first: a

"Second American Revolution" aiming to preserve their "freedoms," including Free Trade (*q.v.*). Woodrow Wilson, in a mediating role, believed that there was honor on both sides of the war, both States Rights and the Union being precious heritages.

**Second Bank of the United States**, see Filler, DASC, a milestone in the liberal-conservative debate over the role of banking (*q.v.*) in a democracy. Did the Bank, charted by Congress, represent a monopolistic threat to commercial freedom, which Andrew Jackson (*q.v.*) properly put down? Or was the Bank doing a proper work and did Jackson, by withdrawing government funds from it and dispensing them among "pet banks," act with authoritarian haste and partiality? What was evident was that no simple extrapolation of 1980s economic principles could be made to fit the categories of the 1830s. Right and wrong would have to be determined with due respect for historical accuracy, and a sense of changing roles of interests in society. Bray Hammond, *Banks and Politics in America* (1957); Robert V. Remini, *Andrew Jackson and the Bank War* (1967); George R. Taylor, ed., *Jackson versus Biddle's Bank* (1972 ed.).

**Sectionalism**, of greater value generally to conservative tradition (*q.v.*) than to liberal, since it brought together those with a stake in roots and local loyalties. The Old South (*q.v.*) was the classic case of a stubborn sectionalism, but sectionalism also had its effects in the Southwest (*q.v.*) and the Old Midwest, where the Tafts (*q.v.*), William McKinley, James A. Garfield, Rutherford B. Hayes, and others were remembered. Sectionalism touched local circumstances, as when Upstate New York disagreed sharply with New York City, and when Southern Californians demanded state separation from Northern Californians. Overall, it was dangerous for politicians not to take the sectional factor seriously. It appeared that Hispanics (*q.v.*) might become a sectional factor in the Southwest, because of their large numbers and their history as a despised underclass. However, they are also family-minded and religious, which would influence their decision as a community. Thomas B. Alexander, *Sectional Stress and Party Strength* (1967); Joseph L. Davis, *Sectionalism and American Politics* (1977); Walter Webb, *Divided We Stand* (1937); Edward W. Chester, *Sectionalism, Politics and American Diplomacy* (1975).

**"Secular Humanists,"** a phrase employed by religious-minded conservatives and Fundamentalists (*q.v.*) to refer to those who believed the Federal Government should not promote the observance of religion, particularly Christianity. The issue affected not only religion per se, but attitudes toward abortion, censorship, deviants, and other matters. See Joseph Sobran, "Secular Humanism" or "The American Way," in *Single Issues* (*q.v.*).

**Sedition Act of 1918**, a wartime measure which severely restricted freedoms guaranteed under the First Amendment. Although wartime exigencies inevitably limited some freedoms, and had done so during the Civil War (*q.v.*), the extreme divisiveness on intervention should ideally have called for restraint in carrying out the law. Instead its enforcement put often brute force in the wrong hands, in terms of peremptory arrest and prosecution, offending libertarian traditions.

**Seeger, Alan** (1888-1916), well-esteemed poet. His most famous work was "I Have a Rendezvous with Death," which he met during service with the French Foreign Legion in World War I. His *Collected Poems* (1916) and letters and diary published the next year seemed to empathetic readers filled with the spirit of youth. As Oliver Wendell Holmes, Jr. phrased it, having himself served in the Civil War, such youth had somehow discovered the secret of life by being able to fling it away as though it were a bagatelle. Had he lived, Seeger would have been the uncle of the radical folksinger Pete Seeger.

**Segregation**, a social process of longstanding and history, in the United States particularly noted with respect to Negroes (*q.v.*), in which persons and families of a kind found themselves in separate areas within a given city or location. Such areas developed their own tone and traditions of language, services, entertainment, and quality. Those wishing to obtrude upon areas not identified with "their kind" were debarred by individual or group resistance, finances, educational facilities for children, or ordinances. Civil Rights Acts intended to protect Negro social prerogatives were superseded by "equal but separate" doctrines, which in turn were struck down by the Supreme Court's *Brown* (*q.v.*) decision. It dealt with the central issue of education, holding that schools segregated by race were inherently unequal. Attendant efforts to "preserve neighborhoods," and the subsequent "White Flight" (*q.v.*), the use of busing across the country to achieve parity of student populations, problems in the erosion of cities and their tax base and the deterioration of educational standards, and especially the "resegregation" of society as a result of social movements and individual preference—all raised questions of whether desegregation would ever work and what the costs might be to society. Strom Thurmond (*q.v.*) took satisfaction in proving by charts and statistics that New York City, despite the sternest laws possible, was more segregated than Atlanta, Georgia. Conservative outlooks were a combination of concern for the individual and states rights (*q.v.*) and the operations of law. The predicaments following from Supreme Court decisions seemed to many conservatives to flout the Constitution (*q.v.*), and thus caused them to consider Constitutional Amendments to curb the Court. In the mid-1980s many conservatives looked for Supreme Court retirements which would allow President Reagan to appoint Justices who would, among other measures (see Supreme Court), reject "affirmative action" as unconstitutional. R. L. Green, *Racial Crisis in American Education* (1969); B. Fancher, *Voices from the South* (1970); Norene Harris, et al., *Integration of American Schools: Problems, Experiences, Solutions* (1975); S. L. Wasby, et al., *Desegregation from Brown to Alexander: An Exploration of Supreme Court Strategies* (1977).

**Self-Help**, an heroic chapter in the efforts of troubled or harassed social groups, notably Negroes and elements of the New Immigration (*qq.v.*), to build morale within their communities, to aid in education, and to sustain life itself in such crises as strikes. Negroes led by forceful ministers set up schools and churches and published newspapers. Poles, Italians, and Jews, among others, worked to overcome language difficulties, problems of women left widowed by industrial accidents, and general problems created by harsh weather, strikes, and often ruthless policies pursued by employers reluctant to give up their individual rights as they defined them. Progressive accident, legal, and union (*q.v.*) gains cut down the need for self-help alternatives, and "good times" created by war and prosperity weakened group loyalty—as did the irregular Americanization and separation into poor and affluent within groups. The advent of the conservative Reagan Administration in 1981 turned new attention on self-help. However, it met opposition from liberals with welfare perspectives and the agencies which administered government social programs. Although crime, violence, battered women, child abuse, and general malaise suggested the need for self-help, bureaucracy (*q.v.*) and uncertain conditions made its uses difficult to define and even suspect. Thus, the Guardian Angels were a voluntary group of young men and women, begun in New York, who watched for muggers and other dangerous persons in subways and other public places. Were they a positive factor in the city's battle against violence? Were they a paramilitary group with no controls, and liable to internal degeneration? New York police—and the police of other cities with Angels chapters—doubted their validity. But whether this was out of jealousy or legitimate professional concern was difficult to say. See also Volunteer Action.

**Senate**, see Congress

**"Senior Citizens,"** a euphemism for the elderly; see Old Age

**Sense of the 60's, The** (1968), edited by E. Quinn and P. J. Dolan. It sought to answer the question "How can you tell your children what it was like to be alive when John Kennedy was a man and not an airport?" It featured such writers as Paul Goodman (*Growing Up Absurd*) and black radical Stokely Carmichael, contributions from other radicals, notes on "camp" dealing with such artifacts as *Flash Gordon* comics, Marshall McLuhan, an essay on black humor, Rachel Carson (with her concern for the environment), and questions about God ("The End of Theism?" and "The Future of Belief"). Of interest to conservatives were Tom Wolfe (*q.v.*), though his examination of "The Pump House Gang" was probably read with empathy rather than irony, and Thomas Merton writing on the death of Pope John. Dwight D. Eisenhower (*q.v.*) wrote on "The Dangers of a Military-Industrial Complex," which liberals found appealing. Norman Podhoretz's (*q.v.*) "My Negro Problem—and Ours" focused on the embittered black attitude toward whites and the need for accepting its intrinsic justice. The book was intended for academic use.

**"Separate But Equal" Doctrine** (1896), Supreme Court doctrine. It was overthrown by its *Brown vs. Board of Education of Topeka* decision of 1954 (*q.v.*), which held that the earlier pronouncement was inherently unequal.

**Sequoyah**, see Indians

**Servants**, a never-ending problem in 19th-century America, since "girls" grew fast, married, followed family or husband West, or, early in the century, left family service for work in factories. It was noticeable that Southern slaveholders, in North-South dialogue, were shy of referring to slaves, preferring to term their "dependents" servants. The post-Civil War era, with its new European immigration, led to a further decline in the availability of servants. The mass production of electrical appliances in the 20th century made servants all but unnecessary for most Americans.

**Service Economy**, once an adjunct of wealth and of its servants at home or abroad, or of more modestly endowed people unusually situated, as during travel or visits to the larger cities. Trains, restaurants, hotels provided services. They were augmented in the 1920s by consolidations of business which diminished the number of shoe and other repair shops, and the prosperity of the time which made it easier to purchase a new commodity than to fix an old one. Salesmen replaced artisans. The rapid growth of the automobile industry created the "service station," employing a high percentage of attendants who "serviced" pumps, rather than the car. With the customer increasingly separated from the product, the quality of the intermediary rose in importance. Whether he knew anything of the product itself, as in a parts department where elements of a car, house implement, or hardware item were handled by number rather than knowledge, his personal qualities of honesty, friendliness, energy, and intelligence could make all the difference to a customer needing a particular service. Troubles could accrue where the service attendant had no reason to see the customer more than once or twice, as during travel on a superhighway. Careless work, insolence, and honest stupidity might have to be endured and even praised and remunerated. Although major companies employed public relations departments to monitor customer dissatisfaction, problems in social morale went too deep to be reached by threats or employee-relations efforts. The quality of service became on indicator of the quality of the society itself. See also Jean S. Wilson, *Tipping* (1965). Since high technology resulted in fewer jobs, it appeared that servicing might become the major conduit for labor and association, and bring liberal and conservative attitudes toward both into confrontation. In 1983 only some 20 percent of the work force had jobs in manufacturing. Only some 14 percent of blue-collar production jobs were available. The rest involved service operations in education (*q.v.*), health, wholesale and retail trade, transportation, communication, and leisure pursuits. Because of the power of traditions, unions (*q.v.*), and inadequate organization of service industries for service, the "production" of services lagged behind human needs. Notorious were service stations which gave little service but charged as though they did. Public fatalism rose in the face of lost contact, broken promises, impersonal misunderstandings, "featherbedding" (*q.v.*), and, in the case of education, non-education. Few people had the visibility and outlets for expressing outrage that William F. Buckley, Jr. (*q.v.*) did, when he was mishandled on airplane flights, overcharged, or subjected to languor and incompetence. To the extent that servicing was a cultural problem, it represented a vast field for theory, action, and exploration as significant as any development in technology.

**"Set-Asides,"** a euphemism for "affirmative action" (*q.v.*), this governmental policy "set aside" portions of official contracts to be allotted to alleged black-owned or -hiring firms. The Reagan Administration, seeking "color blind" contracts, concerned primarily for economy and quality, sought to limit a policy it saw as encouraging false business presentations and questionable standards, especially in small business activities. In 1986, this government effort was protested by liberals and black organizations as reactionary and "racist."

**Settlement Houses**, one of the most notable aspects of the Progressive era. They were created by such distinguished conservatives as Jane Addams (*q.v.*) in Chicago, Lillian D. Wald in New York, and Robert A. Woods in Boston. Helping great numbers of bewildered and exploited immigrants to adjust to American conditions and gain language, organization, and social arts for advancing their control of environment, they gave evidence that conservatism was not the opposite of reform, but an aspect of reform. This fact was blurred in the analyses of such historians as Richard Hofstadter, who taught conservatism was reaction, and that reform was inadequate to need. What settlement houses illustrated, rather, was that some conservatism, interested in family and social order, linked with the liberalism of the time to build connections between established Americans and those who came with foreign heritages. Settlement houses faded as these goals were met; see A. F. Davis, *Spearheads for Reform* (1967).

**1790s**, see Federalists

**Sex and Conservatism**, a long-standing dialogue and debate, involving social attitudes, religious tenets, and the facts of nature. Although Hawthorne's (*q.v.*) *The Scarlet Letter* (1950) was not the reform tract liberals and others imagined it to be, it did probe Puritan principles with unexampled literary power. Herman Melville's *Typee* (1846) contained actual passages which matched primitive morality with that at home in America, which his generation preferred not to notice. Dominant conservative opinion expresed itself variously through emphasis on family, religion, self-control, and status, and conservative principles in such bold ventures as the Oneida Community and Mormonism. Homosexuals (*q.v.*) lived complex lives, most choosing to keep their sexual preferences hidden from public view. Anthony Comstock (*q.v.*) became a target of criticism as reflecting negatively on conservatism; his single-minded crusade, however, included valid as well as invalid elements. How much women suffered from suppression, as compared with men, involves deeper and more objective consideration than partisans are willing to grant. Most women pioneers of the 19th century sought new prerogatives in politics and the world's work, rather than increased sexual opportunities. Conservative groups found some expression in their attitudes toward Henry Ward Beecher, in the notorious. Beecher-Tilton law case of 1872. Conservative Southerners divided in their responses to white-black sexual liaisons. Theodore Dreiser's accounts of drifting women and sex-driven males stirred successful liberal defense despite often doubtful prose. David Graham Phillips' (*q.v.*) *Susan Lenox, Her Fall and Rise*, was actually bowdlerized by Comstock's (*q.v.*) followers, and its plea for female independence ignored. The rising strength of liberalism, thanks to urbanization, the automobile (*qq.v.*), and related factors, presented a challenge to conservative strongholds. By then, "Puritanism" seemed a lost cause, and World War II its *coup de grâce*. The development of the contraceptive pill lessened contraints on sexual behavior, as did the Supreme Court decision which legalized abortion (*q.v.*). Under such conditions, the rebound of conservatism in resistance to the new sexual attitudes was all but startling. Conservative groups fought Federal funding for abortions, and fought it in the states. They fought for what the *New York Times* called the "Squeal Law": the right of parents to know when their young daughters sought to purchase contraceptives without their knowledge. Interestingly, however, they asserted no such parents' rights with regard to young sons. They probed in every detail the fate of fetuses, and of handicapped infants deemed untreatable by medical science. They were critical of sex education outside the home, and of "value-free" standards which, they asserted, denied the difference between babies and animals. Joseph Sobran's *Single Issues* (*q.v.*) even dared to proclaim the values of chastity. Their cause was aided by resurgence of sexual diseases, and the continuance of illegitimate and tragic births. Crusaders for sexual freedom were attacked as immoral and deleterious to society, especially its poor and isolated. Thus conservatives, holding to traditional religious, family, and moral principles, continued their crusades, within the limits of a changing society.

**Sexual Suicide** (1973), by George F. Gilder (*q.v.*), a work which took on the militant feminists of the time and their allegations of male persecution, family enslavement, brainwashed upbringing, and sexual torment. Gilder judged them against personal and universal experience. He saw the feminists as demeaning the womb, seeking the feminization of males, undermining family, and, in their quest for "human beings," working for the ruin of women as women and men as men. Their complaints about lack of power he saw as distorting the meaning of power and fulfillment, a threat to both males and females. They emphasized copulation, he said, while blind to its major purpose: procreation. And they twisted sex to mean no more than copulation, blind to the reality of sex as involving the whole lives of men and women, and determining their differences and associative purposes. Although the book did not match the profeminist best sellers in sales, and received its measure of abuse, it added visibility to Gilder's career and helped open the way to his own best-selling *Wealth and Poverty* (*q.v.*). See also *New Chastity, The.*

**Shaftesbury, Earl of** (1801-1885), British political figure, one of the stars of English conservatism and reform. The key to his career was his Evangelistical Christianity; as with William Wilberforce (*q.v.*) it made him both a symbol of positive change and of social stability. Liberals who wished to move faster and farther, and who were unburdened by religion, tried to ignore him. Shaftesbury's long career constituted a whole movement at humanizing industrial society. He fought child labor, wiping out the institution of "climbing boys" who cleaned chimneys, and the demeaning of women in industry. His Ten Hours Bill (1847) marked a milestone in factory legislation. His enemies sought to mark him down as an agent of farm interests, but Shaftesbury turned on his class to fight the Corn Laws which made bread dear. A towering figure on both sides of the water Shaftesbury lent his support to the "Stafford House Address," which pleaded with American women to act in behalf of the slaves. G. Battiscombe, *Shaftesbury* (1975).

**Shaw, Ann Howard** (1847-1919), suffragist of basically conservative perspectives. She only demanded rights for others which she had won for herself: an individualist rather than a collectivist. Born in England, she was brought to the United States in 1851. She earned her degree in theology in 1878, and received a degree from Boston University in 1885. The Methodist Episcopal Church refused her the right to preach, but she was ordained in 1880. She served several pastorates in Massachusetts before meeting Susan B. Anthony and beginning close association with her and the National American Woman Suffrage Association. She was its president from 1904 to 1915. See her *The Story of a Pioneer* (1915).

**Sheldon, Charles M.** (1857-1946), a Congregationalist minister who in his Topeka, Kansas pastorate became world famous as the author of *In His Steps* (1896). In the United States and around the world it sold more than a million copies. A tale of Christ returned to earth to observe its infirmities and attempt to minister to them, it was an expression of conservative reform expression on a popular level. Sheldon was also editor of the *Christian Herald.*

**Shils, Edward,** see Tradition

**"Siege Psychology,"** a characteristic of Nixon's (*q.v.*) White House which ultimately destroyed his Administration. Nixon won the Presidency in his second, 1968 effort by a narrow-margin. Nevertheless he held to a light rein in the White House while creating accommodations with the welfare system at home and laboring to extricate the country in good order from Vietnam abroad. The constant harassment of the liberal press and Nixon's direct foes, coupled with the anarchy of the youth movement, caused him to tighten his lines further and rely on Executive Privilege—nowhere defined, but leaving loopholes for the least responsible elements in his entourage. Although he had reason to feel exasperation and anger at leaks regarding military and Presidential stratagems, he made no effort to propitiate his more conventional antagonists. His "siege psychology," generally recognized, created an hiatus between his White House and the massive liberal establishments, and encouraged them to treat him as a Constitutional foe. Nixon's overwhelming victory and re-election in 1972 should have given him perspective on the limitations of liberals and radicals, and his consequent opportunities. Inexpertly, he separated himself from his "heartland" (*q.v.*) and middle-of-the-road majority in the interests of petty retainers who impudently imagined he had a duty toward them. This profound miscalculation brought him down with them. The Reagan (*q.v.*) Administration appeared to make conscious efforts to learn from Nixon's errors; see Filler, DASC.

**Sierra Club, The,** see Environment Mentalism

**Silver Issue, The,** see Filler, DASC, undoubtedly a Populist (*q.v.*) issue, but attracting such disparate supporters as Henry Adams (*q.v.*), who had little interest in farmer's troubles but feared what gold (*q.v.*) could do to such incomes as his own if uncontrolled. It was urged that silver be placed on parity to gold by law to curb gold's dominance. Although it failed as a legal measure and lost its place as a panacea (*q.v.*) to class economic troubles, the silver issue earned a place beside such other questions of government responsibility as that involving Free Trade and Protection (*qq.v.*).

**Simon, William E.** (1927- ), American businessman and government official. A prime example of the businessman in government, he served as Administrator of the Federal Energy Office in 1973 and 1974, and as U.S. Secretary of the Treasury from 1974 to 1977. His experience showed him that American production was bound with regulations, and that this spelled disaster for the nation. His book, *A Time for Truth* (1978), was issued with forewords by Milton Friedman and F. A. Hayek (*qq.v.*) and cited the Invisible Hand of Adam Smith and Irving Kristol's (*qq.v.*) charges against a "new class" of government regulators who had no sense of economics but did have a lust for power: it was a model brief in behalf of free enterprise, comparable to *The Incredible Bread Machine* (*q.v.*). Coming from a former Secretary of the Treasury, *A Time for Truth* circulated widely and helped break ground for conservative cases in politics. Simon was an overseer for the Hoover Institute and associated with the Heritage Foundation (*qq.v.*).

**Single Issues,** brought out liberals and conservatives on different sides, sometimes with dedication which all but ruled out interest in any other issue. "Pro-Choice" was a euphemism (*q.v.*) for abortion (*q.v.*), which anti-abortionists denounced in the interests of "Pro-Life." Their major publication was *Human Life Review* (*q.v.*). "Supply-Side Economics" (*q.v.*) was a panacea (*q.v.*) to many conservatives, though not all. Liberals had no direct economic theory to oppose it; they viewed it as wrong-headed and cruel. The ERA (*q.v.*) mobilized vast and influential support, but was countered by Phyllis Schlafly's (*q.v.*) historic drive to derail it. She used no single argument in opposition, but mustered legions of supporters who believed that a woman's place is in the home. Activist homosexuals (*q.v.*) fought for "gay rights," while activist Fundamentalists (*q.v.*) said homosexuals should have no or limited rights. Gun control (*q.v.*) was a basically liberal cause which opposed the "gun lobby" and fought with uncertain success to limit the "right to bear arms" specified in the Constitution. Pro-gun defenders were in the main grassroots and conservative in outlook, and resisted the argument that easy access to guns contributed to the high incidence of crime. Although single-issue liberals had a more impressive record in organizing coalitions and developing rhetoric and media-appeal than conservatives, by the mid-1980s conservatives had come into their own as single-issue proponents.

**Single Issues: Essays on the Crucial Social Questions** (1983), by Joseph Sobran. Although there were numerous single issues, and propagandists and lobbyists for each one, Sobran's book was outstanding in probing into his main issue, abortion, in order to bring out all its implications in terms of feticide, infanticide, euthanasia, homosexuality, the role of fathers, pornography, sex education, public prayer, "secular humanism," and history. To Sobran abortion all but ceased being a "single issue" and became a question of the state of society generally. Sobran used the sharp, economical, precise language of his admired G.K. Chesterton and C.S. Lewis (*qq.v*). He was tenacious in noting the sufferings of fetuses; the connections between infanticide, euthanasia, and killings generally; the paradox of fathers having no say over abortions yet being required to pay child support; and so to other areas which made abortions not a deed but a world. Nevertheless, the book achieved limited circulation and notice, even though there were anti-abortion partisans in every state of the Union, as well as a President who opposed abortion. Evidently, the argument developed best in the give-and-take of state politics and press discussion. Despite the natural constituency of "pro-choice" advocates—those who had or feared they might need abortions—the Sobran book provided source materials certain to stimulate and nourish their opponents.

**Sixties,** see 1960s

**Skepticism,** see Whately, Richard; Berkeley, George; Lewis, C.S.

**Skinner, B.F.,** see Behaviorism

**Slave Labor,** like slavery, an embarrassing fact of life in the world, known best in terms of the Nazi (*q.v.*) experience with its horrendous adjuncts of extermination camps. As well known, and scarcely more humane or subject to melioration has been slave labor in the Soviet Union and in Red China. Slave labor was of enormous use in those lands because it isolated dissidents (*q.v.*) from the general population, because the laborers could be set at onerous work which needed doing, and because the work cost a minimum in terms of worker upkeep. Under Stalin (*q.v.*), slave labor camps operated at maximum harsh efficiency. It appears likely that the "thaw" which followed the dictator's death may have modified the cruelty and death to a degree. It is not certain that Solzhenitsyn's (*q.v.*) epical revelations in *The Gulag Archipelago* (1974) affected Soviet policy; an estimate by Victor Herman, an American who suffered Gulag imprisonment and studied it following his release and return home, noted five million prisoners in slave labor under Yuri Andropov, raised to leadership of the USSR in June 1983. Although slave labor was known to have been employed in Mainland China's massive building projects, no comparable revelations have been publicized. The situation was more complex than appeared on the surface. With representatives of the USSR in the United Nations, along with other states employing slave labor, and with Detente (*q.v.*) identified with peace and the need for finding grounds for cooperation between Communist and non-Communist states, such issues as slave labor have often been put aside. Moreover, there were friends of the communist states in the West, ready to see them in the best light.

**Slavery,** one of the most momentous factors in American development, settled as such by the Thirteenth Amendment to the Constitution (*q.v.*), but carried on as a topic of controversy with respect to the status of blacks in the nation. It went hand in hand with a larger incidence of indentured servitude which was, as John Bach McMaster (*q.v.*) showed and monographs detailed, slavery for white people and their children. It has been difficult to keep this fact in focus, however, because so many citizens have had a stake in forgetting their family past. Although contract labor and "wage slavery" (*q.v.*) perpetuated features of slavery itself, afflicting all ethnic groups, Southern slavery has become the standard example of enslavement in America, furnishing motivation to civil-rights activism in the twentieth century, broader discussion of the subject being avoided. Although slavery continued and even grew around the world in the 19th century, being monitored by the Anti-

Slavery Society of England, it received little attention in the United States, absorbed in its own controversies and tendentious history. (See Filler, ed., *The Rise and Fall of Slavery in America* [1980].) Conservatives tended to make little of the subject, except as roused by those who avoided the facts of modern enslavement in order to denounce America as a land of oppression, past and present. A. Kulikaff, *Tobacco and Slaves* (1986); D. W. Galenson, *Traders, Planters, and Slaves* (1985); J. R. Soderlund, Quakers and Slavery (1985).

**Slogans,** continuously sought to satisfy the needs for succinct statements persuasive in democracy. The general rule was that what survived responded to something real. See "Hoovervilles." See also Epithets.

**Smith, Adam** (1723-1790), Scottish moral philosopher and economist. His famous title, *An Inquiry into the Nature and Causes of the Wealth of Nations* (1776), generally known as *The Wealth of Nations*, marked an era in capitalism. A professor of moral philosophy at the University of Glasgow, he published his *Theory of Moral Sentiments* in 1759. Travelling to France he met "Physiocrats" (*q.v.*) and became acquainted with their doctrines, as explicated by Francois Quesnay and others. They held that land was the basis of all wealth, industrial and commercial interests feeding from its products. Smith was especially drawn to their doctrine of free trade as resulting in full production and economic health. It was scarcely a coincidence that Smith's great book appeared the year of the American Declaration of Independence, since both transgressed mercantilism (*q.v.*), a doctrine which bound trade and its administration to national ministries. With business-adventurers ranging the seas and seeking, within the confines of national wars and intrigues, to make profits wherever possible in buying and selling, Smith's faith in free trade as the "invisible hand" (*q.v.*) which produced the wealth of nations became a justification for, and inspiration to, capitalist enterprise. His prose too was clear and, unlike Physiocrat doctrine, flexible to particular circumstances. See John Rae, *Life of Adam Smith* (1895); Eli Ginzberg, *The House of Adam Smith* (1934).

**Smith, Mortimer B.** (1906- ), a major critic of public education as inadequate and falsely based. He joined the protest against the excesses of "progressive" education in the 1950s, and was a co-founder of the Council for Basic Education (1956). His writings included *And Madly Teach* (1949), *The Diminished Mind* (1954), and, as co-author, *A Consumer's Guide to Educational Innovations* (1972).

**Smith, Reverend Sydney** (1771-1845), British clergyman, famed as a founder of the *Edinburgh Review*, but even more for the wit which gave spirit and relevance to past issues. His *Peter Plymley Letters* (1807-1808), favoring Catholic (*q.v.*) Emancipation, were sensationally received and affected debates until 1829, when Emancipation was achieved in Parliament. His denunciation (1843) of Pennsylvania's cynical repudiation of debts owed British investors, couched in a petition to Congress flashing with brilliant invective, roused patriots, but fair-minded Americans received Smith cordially on his 1844 visit to America. As well-known was his response to an over-intimate Britisher who demanded his attention: "Your face is strange, but your manner is very familiar." Smith's comments on politics, religion, and personalities are readily adapted to later conditions. Hesketh Pearson, *The Smith of Smiths* (1934); N. C. Smith, ed., *Letters* (1956).

**Smoot-Hawley Tariff,** see Depressions

**Smuggling,** a curious element in American individualism which aided or impugned social conservativism. Smuggling was a factor in American determination to advance American trade in defiance of British mercantilist (*q.v.*) laws, and so advanced American nationalism. New Englanders smuggled goods by way of Canada, in defiance of Jefferson's (*q.v.*) embargo and its spirit, though his intention was to avoid being implicated in the war raging between the British and French. Northern shippers and Southern brokers smuggled slaves into the South in defiance of Federal law, and both Northern and Southern adventurers smuggled goods across the battle lines during the Civil War. Individualism manifested itself, more or less, in the traditional production in Border State highlands of "mountain dew": whiskey prepared illegally. Since the offense was made national during the Prohibition era, and resulted in national criminal syndicates, it could be said that the effort to stop drinking was intemperate and in defiance of human nature (*q.v.*). The smuggling of guns to Spain during the 1936-1939 Civil War harmed the operations of the Neutrality Act of 1937, as did the smuggling of guns to Israel in its wars with Arab states.

**"Snivel Service" Reform,** a term of contempt employed by opponents of the Pendleton Act (1883) which established the Civil Service (*q.v.*); evidence of the frustration of political machines to whom government jobs meant patronage and the ability to appoint incompetents whose votes and services kept them in operation. The work of reformers whose efforts improved standards of work in an expanding government and society, the Pendleton Act was a conservative triumph.

**Sobran, Joseph,** see *Single Issues: Essays on the Crucial Social Question*

**Social Contract,** see Rousseau, Jean-Jacques

**"Social Darwinism,"** a concept made famous and notorious by Herbert Spencer (1820-1903). He argued that, as Darwinism (*q.v.*) showed the ascent of man out of the battles among species, so societies were in competition to prove their superiority among others. Conservatives of the time were more sympathetic to this interpretation of the possibilities of man than were liberals and radicals, who argued in response that animals were not in fact in constant competition for survival and that human consciousness and capacity made for a different destiny. Karl Marx's (*q.v.*) vision of society's progress, indeed, was a species of "Social Darwinism" in reverse, seeing an ascent of man as he flung off capitalistic competition in the interest of workers' cooperation. The advent of the atomic bomb made the general argument obsolete, on its own terms.

**Social Dynamics** affected all movements, whether in an "age of romanticism," "a Red decade," "a conservative decade," or any other time. Nevertheless there were centers of concern which highlighted material or intellectual crisis and forced the most unconcerned to be conscious of its slogans and spokesmen. Lenin (*q.v.*) believed that when his revolution came, it would be with arms and funds provided by the enemy. He may have been thinking of Joseph Fels, businessman, who provided the money needed for Lenin's then-socialist comrades to meet in London in 1903, where their famous split between Bolsheviks (the majority) and Mensheviks (the minority) took place. Other proponents of free enterprise became conscious or unconscious laborers in behalf of their foes. Wealthy patrons provided homes and funds for social rebels in the 1910s, finding them personally and even physically interesting and no threat to their personal fortunes, as were pertinacious reformers who feared monopoly, threats to government resources, and anti-union actions (*qq.v.*). The fierce actions of Anti-Red Squads during and after World War I (*q.v.*) created the American Civil Liberties Union and public sympathy for the bruised and maltreated dissidents. Although there were major expositors of free enterprise in the 1920s—Herbert Hoover (*q.v.*), Gerard Swope, E. A. Filene, and, among entrepreneurs proper, Henry Ford (*q.v.*)—they could not touch the minds of their associates sufficiently to inspire a generation of program-builders. They were required to resign their authority to Franklin D. Roosevelt (*q.v.*) and his followers. Roosevelt himself believed that he was saving both capitalism and freedom, and, like Theodore Roosevelt before him, that capitalists were not helping with their stiff-necked resistance to change. The problem of just what constituted legitimate change could not be resolved in philosophic sessions, but they could have helped. There was a conspicuous absence of pro and con debate which suggested that issues of state intervention would be satisfied by force—of majorities, of arms—rather than debate. How, for example, were disaffected Americans able to penetrate sensitive government establishments, with relatively little opposition? There were limits to crying conspiracy (*q.v.*). Conservatives also met and planned programs. They helped carry their constituents through the "temporary" measures of the New Deal and into World War intervention. Roosevelt was indeed the center of events on the American side, but, in assessing his role at Yalta (*q.v.*) and its "giveaways" to the Soviet Union, it is necessary to recall that Winston Churchill (*q.v.*) was also at Yalta and committed to its premises. Whether or not it was a deception which made Alger Hiss (*q.v.*), following hostilities, president of the Carnegie Peace Foundation, its trustees acted on the appointment from conservative presumptions, and were cautious in disassociating themselves from Hiss when all charge and evidence were in the open. Foundations (*q.v.*), run with the pick of successful and approved personnel, were quickly to come under the suspicions of a conscious, conservative *National Review* (*q.v.*), when it opened its campaign in 1955. The mighty Ford Foundation was to be seen making massive grants to clearly radical enterprises, which it presumably found more strategic than others less dubious in goals. So the dynamics of social operations moved on. Whether they would work for Lenin or for heroes (*q.v.*) more indigenous to American ideals depended less on would-be traitors or leaders than on the countrymen to whom they appealed.

**"Social Engineering,"** a liberal concept covering an expectation of rational planning of benefit to all sectors of society. Conservatives found it repugnant: a guise for aggregating power in government intended to serve the official rather than the public. See Lester O'Shea, *Tampering with the Machinery*, which saw liberal "engineering" as having accumulated a sorry record in production for social good. Although Arthur E. Morgan (*q.v.*) conceived of himself as a "social engineer," derived from his actual experience as an engineer, his educational and other projects emphasized "pilot plants": experimental units proving or disproving the validity of projected social programs, rather than foisting them upon communities. However, welfare state (*q.v.*) interventions took the subject out of the areas which persons like Morgan had charted out and gave it the connotation of authoritarian fiats and money-spending endeavors. Although there were, obviously, many things which had to be done by government, employing planners, the concept of "engineering" too much suggested manipulation at the expense of human and individual interests to be useful to a troubled society.

**"Social Fascism,"** see Stalin, Josef; Soviet Union

**Social Sciences.** Once a sensitive field of study under conservative auspices, when it touched upon poverty, labor relations, children, crime, prostitution, slums, and standards of living. It was raised during the Progressive era by empirical studies organized by talented leaders to more substantive areas for research and social action. Thus, University of Chicago urban sociologists helped explain the forms cities took, and the forces which drew ethnic and other groups into patterns replicated in many cities. The Alvin S. Johnson-edited *Encyclopedia of the Social Sciences* (1935) was a storehouse of vibrant studies and analyses summing up decades of experience, in the midst of the Great Depression striking a liberal and reform note. The institutionalizing of poverty and other social sciences areas—by way of welfare departments, mediation boards, psychological counseling, and other official and semi-offical means—separated study from involvement, so that social workers, for example, could pass smoothly from school to work in a welfare department with little significant "field" practice. The remoteness of academics from social conditions created an era of hypothesis, not only in social work but in economics, sociology, and elsewhere. The goal for sharp workers in the area was not to gather data out of living conditions, but to process data in terms of mathematical formulas, in support of, or in qualification of, a given hypothesis. One economist at a professional meeting was quoted as asking, "Must all non-mathematical economists commit suicide?" A mathematical economist declared that if he had the choice of a promising hypothesis and a body of empirical data, he would choose the hypothesis, as having greater promise of long-term usefulness. A new encyclopedia of the social sciences turned away from the long lines of social scientists, their studies, and even their fields which had made the Alvin S. Johnson opus rich and evocative, to concentrate on hypotheses and the special languages created by the newer students in the field for developing their "conceptualizations." The development of computers created a newer breed of social scientists who took pride in being able to project winners in political races, and to determine the preferences of consumers in many areas. Although defenders of the computer—as opposed to humanists who feared its potential for demeaning mankind—protested that it was no more than a tool, and they no more than objective scientists, questions were raised respecting their capacity for error, and even ill. It was a species of good fortune that some specialists exposed their will to manipulate their machines by making gross political and social errors, thus warning non-specialists that they needed to be controlled.

**Social Security,** promising to be one of the formidable challenges to conservatives and liberals in the 1980s. See Filler, DASC. It had not been anticipated that retirees would be so many, and place the burden on the Federal budget that they did. In 1950 one percent of the budget went for Social Security payments. In 1982, 28 percent. By 1985, it was estimated, social security payments would have increased by $150 billion over what they had been in 1980, when Reagan took office. In 1983, retired workers were receiving seven or eight times what they had put in. It had originally not been expected that Social Security would amount to government-bound pensions. Obviously, the money had to come from somewhere. Moreover, there were elections, and mounting millions of aged (*q.v.*), all voters. Hardline conservatives were disturbed to see their President sensitive to the responses of the aged. Modest proposals he had made to stem the drain on government expenditures on Social Security had been stormed down by liberals who brought up visions of starving poor, and, more ominously, by organizations of the aged developing power and publicity skill. Conservatives were made uneasy by Reagan's evident eagerness to persuade the elderly that he was their friend, and to carry the message of increases to them individually and by mail. Reagan was certainly concerned about deficits and the budget; but could he develop a program which would not lose him voters or credibility? Proposals were bruited in Congress: to freeze the cost of living increase for a year; to limit annual increases to match productivity; to levy taxes on social security payments *after life-time payments* (which had been taxed) exactly as on income; to lower the size of payments to citizens who took early retirement; to raise retirement ages by three months every year for at least three years; and to bring civil service workers under the Social Security system. Would such aids to the Social Security dilemmas be acceptable to the electorate? There were large fields for demagogues, who raised the question of the poor even when it was irrelevant to larger subjects. There was also the defense budget, always contrasted invidiously with to the Social Security problem. There were Democrats, and there was Claude Pepper (*q.v.*). Yet some combination of leaders and plans would have to be devised to contain the hemorrhage of Federal funds.

**Social War,** distinguishable from civil war. The American Revolution contained elements of civil war, ranging "rebels" against troops from abroad, including mercenaries, from German Hesse. The war helped to discredit mercenaries, with government fearful of entrusting arms in citizen hands. Although there was genuine disaffection in New England during the War of 1812, with New England Federalists (*q.v.*) wishing "Mr. Madison's War" ill, New Englanders did not take up arms against the government. The crisis had features of social dissent, rather than civil. Although the Mexican War had opposition in New England from pacifists and others who feared a dismembered Mexico would create a tier of slave states in the South and upset the balance of power in Congress, loyal New Englanders helped fill the Army ranks. By 1914 minority people in the North and West had grown so numerous as to create possibilities of social war, though their very numbers militated against war at all. German-Americans were sympathetic to the Fatherland. English-Americans felt for the Old Home, but Irish-Americans were eager for England's defeat. Jews (*q.v.*) with bad memories of Russia longed to see the Czar's throne overthrown. The harsh suppression of isolationists, pro-Germans, and radicals was carried out successfully, but promised trouble in the future. The victory of the Bolsheviks in Russia created a worldwide bank of sympathy and hope from which its Third International gained, to a much greater amount than did the nationalistic Fascism in Italy and Nazism in Germany. Uncommitted Americans were sobered by Soviet excesses at home against their own dissidents, but generally mollified by stories of Soviet "successes" in industrializing; it was held that the Soviets had difficulties in overcoming Russian backwardness inherited from the dark ages of Czars. German barbarism and the Hitler buildup of armaments were easier to grasp. World War II saw Americans substantially united against the Fascist powers. The unearned prosperity of war production, with no sacrifices of comfort—no "victory gardens," not even the saving of tinfoil, since industry produced substitutes—encouraged a greedy affluence which brought the nation a flabby, deficit-spending plenitude. Organization men raised aimless children. They bought off poverty in decaying cities with easy welfare (*q.v.*). Apathy created, in succession, "beats," "hippies," and new social rebels, admiring not Stalin but such as Che Guevara. Although they spoke the language of protest, many had as goal the overthrow of the American establishment. Their arson and explosives brought the nation as close to social war as it had ever been. (See Youth.) Their demonstrations at the 1968 Democratic Convention in Chicago, and their anti-war program, sympathetically reported by the media, led the way to what was accepted by weary citizens as the American "defeat" in Vietnam. Although the social war lost the United States great quantities of prestige in the world, despite continuing disbursements of foreign aid and arms, the rebels themselves disintegrated for lack of program, returning to the establishment itself for lives and influence. Continuing debates on the status of schools, welfare, families, "alternative life-styles," the "military-industrial complex," and rights under civil rights (*qq.v.*) gave evidence that politics had become war carried on by other means. The elections of 1980 and 1984 appeared to erstwhile rebels and their sympathizers an attempt to return the nation to an outmoded past.

**Socialism,** as hateful a word to post-World War II conservative controversialists as Communism (*q.v.*), though sometimes seen in less baleful light when associated with relatively harmless persons such as Eugene V. Debs. As a precursor of Communism it appeared wrong-headed to conservatives, and the instigator of deeds and attitudes harmful to society. Its leading theoreticians were seen as subversive of tradition, family and the individual. Preferred by older conservatives were such counter-philosophies as were offered by William Graham Sumner (*q.v.*) in America and such others abroad as Herbert Spencer (*q.v.*). The Social Democrats who remained loyal to their governments during World War I received honor neither from conservatives, liberals, nor the opponents of the war. The new conservatives of post-World War II picked up the anti-socialist analysis as part of their case for free enterprise, holding that socialist programs were doomed by definition. They followed closely the career of nationalized industries, particularly in great Britain, and felt able to report a record of failure and hardship to the society and the Free World generally. In addition, as they saw liberals (*q.v.*) intensively committed to augmented government power and expenditures, they found an identity between liberals and professed socialists, and held them equally guilty of false analyses, bad faith, and the undermining of freedom. Maurice W. Brainard's *The Modern Conservative and the Liberal Image* (1967) was a summing up of arguments in defense of conservativism, with references ranging from Frederic Bastiat to Friedrich Hayek (*qq.v.*), and including an appendix of conservative organizations and another of books defining "basic social principles" and "government gone wild." A third appendix offered "constructive action programs." See also the Ludwig von Mises (*q.v.*) Lecture Series, *Champions of Freedom* (Hillsdale College [*q.v.*] Press), 1974]. The proliferation of "Marxist" (*q.v.*) and "socialist" governments in underdeveloped countries, with weak governments and confused traditions, made them appear ready prey for Soviet Union machinations. It seemed doubly necessary to conservatives of all stripes that the West harbor no delusions about "socialism," but keep steady eyes on developments which, improperly handled, might decrease the areas open to non-authoritarian governments. A. Fried and R. Sanders, eds., *Socialist Thought: A Documentary History* (1964).

**"Socialism in One Country,"** see Stalin, Josef

**Society.** An evident adjunct of conservativism, emphasizing exclusivity, status, and power, it appeared to be a secondary factor in conservativism's career, thanks to powerful democratizing forces which made it little helpful to an individual's advancement. Aristocracy, society, money, and celebrity mixed in such fashion as to make any of the elements predominant, or none at all. Great Britain seemed to have an advantage over the United States in having an hereditary aristocracy, though it was so infiltrated with knighthoods for money and lordships for services in trade unions, as to make its effectiveness dependent on the individual rather than the title. American politicians were so required to curry favor with the masses as to make their status a matter of judgment, rather than of ascendancy. Franklin D. Roosevelt was judged both an aristocrat—or aristocratic and democratic. Jack and Jackie Kennedy were fancied by admirers as an American "nobility," though with time—despite the "Camelot" fantasy—the idea eroded. Adlai Stevenson's quiet dignity got him no votes, and Nelson Rockefeller's patent efforts to seem what he was not, one of the boys, fared little better. Society, which had once called in celebrities as entertainers, concluded by mixing with them, sometimes to the advantage of one, sometimes of the other. Singer-actor Frank Sinatra, carrying in tow a former Vice-President of the United States, Spiro Agnew, represented a triumph of the city streets over society. Television proved about to make of celebrity and notoriety what it wished, demeaning whom it opposed and dignifying whom it favored, by means of contrived interviews and choice of photographs. In sum, society status had become as much of a burden as a gain, and only exclusivity, once sought mainly by true aristocrats, remained a height to climb, for those who sought it. See Cleveland Amory, *Who Killed Society?* (1960). See also Gentility.

**"Sociobiology,"** see Weyl, Nathaniel

**Sokolsky, George E.** (1893-1962), controversial transitional (*q.v.*) figure in that his turn from left-wing interests and associations to those clearly conservative was impugned by critics as being less ideological than material and self-seeking. A New Yorker and the child of immigrants, he attended Bronx High School of Science and Columbia University, being expelled in 1917 from the latter for undefined "immoral conduct." His subsequent career was so linked with complex associations and experiences as to make his motives and purposes debatable. He left promptly for revolutionary Russia, where he worked on the English-language *Russian Daily News*. The next year, reportedly disillusioned, he left for a long stay in China. Beginning as a reporter on the *North China Star*, he involved himself in the politics of Sun Yat-sen's Kuomintong, then wrote for the *Shanghai Gazette*. His politics were unclear; it would be alleged that he was anxious to become rich, though the means were unclear. He married a Chinese woman and later edited the *Far Eastern Review* (1927-1930). In 1931 he finally returned home, where his foreign experience gave him an entree to writing for the *New York Times* and the *Herald-Tribune*, and also for the *Atlantic Monthly*. Although the settling in of economic depression and the rising clamor of left-wing voices suggested radical uses for his exceptional background, Sokolsky soon made it evident that he had determined on a pro-capitalist use for his talents. His particular analysis of events seemed to make him one who had left the radical fold, as in his revulsion from the New Deal (*q.v.*). Many conservatives saw it as harmful to freedom, but few as moving between communism and fascism, the way Sokolsky did. Sokolsky' s *The Tinder Box of Asia* (1932) took a reporter's stance rather than an ideologue's, as did his *Labor's Fight for Power* (1934), which saw workers as essentially "Kerenskyists"—that is, middle of the road. Sokolsky's outlook attracted business interest and made him an informed spokesman, resented by the Left, for the business point of view, as in his *The American Way of Life* (1939). He debated with Upton Sinclair, who defended socialism, and Earl Browder, who defended Communism. Sokolsky began a column, "These Days," for the *New York Sun*, and when the paper closed, turned to the Hearst press. Though different in character and development from John T. Flynn (*q.v.*), Sokolsky was also a precursor of the later conservative movement, opposing threats to what conservatives saw as American liberties.

**Solidarity,** see Poland

**Solzhenitsyn, Alexander I.** (1918- ), Russian author, a major voice in the conservative campaign to raise the public's consciousness respecting the history and dangers associated with the Soviet Union (*q.v.*). He was a direct product of the Soviet "Thaw," during which Premier Khruschev denounced Stalin (*q.v.*) as a despot and had his corpse removed from Lenin's (*q.v.*) tomb. This permitted the publication of Solzhenitsyn's novel, *One Day in the Life of Ivan Denisovich* (1962), which created a world-wide sensation. It called attention to his life. With degrees in philosophy, literature, mathematics, and physics, he had served as a battery officer in World War II. An intercepted letter by him which contained criticism of Stalin formed the base of an official indictment in 1945 which put Solzhenitsyn in a Siberian slave labor (*q.v.*) camp for eight years, followed by three years in exile. His bold attempts to follow up on the success, in the Soviet Union as well as abroad, of *Ivan Denisovich*—which raised comparisons with Turgenev (*q.v.*), Dostoevsky, Tolstoy, and Maxim Gorky—caused controversy and rebuffs. Eventually Solzhenitsyn was denied Soviet publication for his works. He was denied the Lenin Prize for Literature he plainly merited. Jealous establishment (*q.v.*) critics denounced his "obsession" with labor camps and bureaucracy (*q.v.*), and falsely accused him of cooperating with foreign foes. Remarkable was Solzhenitsyn's literary resourcefulness and art. *The Cancer Ward* (1968) was real, human, yet symbolic, carrying echoes of Russian-Soviet experience with ease and relevance. *August 1914* (1972), a profound novel of the Russian Army's catastrophe at Tannenberg in World War I, added dimensions to his canon of writings. Nothing appeased his foes. His receipt of the Nobel Prize for Literature (1970) aggravated his condition at home. His books, excerpted in *Samizdat* (*q.v.*), flourished outside the Soviet Union, while he groped with questions of survival at home. Eventually exiled from the Soviet Union, he took up residence in the United States. His series of books on *The Gulag Archipelago* (1974-1976)—the "gulag" being on infamous network of prison camps—in which he mixed his personal experiences with study and documentations, gave the world a word in the lexicon of torture and mass murder. Solzhenitsyn's turn to orthodox religion cooled the appreciation of some liberals. His warnings to the West of Soviet evil and unswerving program for world domination struck many liberals as fanatical. Solzhenitsyn's creativity did not flag. His *Lenin in Zurich* (1975) penetrated beneath the clichés to the Soviet founder's essential character. For his account of his long struggle within the Soviet Union, see *The Oak and the Calf* (1980) and G. Grazzini's *Solzhenitsyn* (1973). Italian publishers were active in making his work available to the West. See also the book by a Soviet scientist and dissident who was himself subjected to "psychiatric" (*q.v.*) pressures, before leaving for the West, Zhores A. Medvedev's *Ten Years after Ivan Denisovich* (1973); and Solzhenitsyn et al., *From under the Rubble* (1981).

**Sophistry,** a word traditionally associated with conservatism as unwilling to face the world, its injustice and inequalities, forthrightly and with realism. Children were not born, but came as little gifts from Heaven, people did not die, but passed on, individuals did not age, but entered into their serene years, and the like. That liberals became prone not only to gobbledygook (*q.v.*) but to euphemisms (*q.v.*) became clear only as their long crusades became weathered and susceptible to critical notice.

**South, The,** to be distinguished from the Southwest (*q.v.*), but also from the modern South, required to adjust to new Congressional laws and Supreme Court (*qq.v.*) decisions. The Old South, with its "peculiar institution" of slavery (*q.v.*), its self-identification with Greek and Mediterranean versions of democracy (*q.v.*), its states-rights (*q.v.*) philosophy, its favoring of Free Trade (*q.v.*), its martial record, and its Agrarianism (*q.v.*) was presumably put into history by its Civil War (*q.v.*) defeat. However, it rebounded to an extent by its doctrine of dominance over blacks—celebrated by Ulrich B. Phillips, by Woodrow Wilson's (*q.v.*) attainment of the Presidency, and by Northern agreement on implied Southern premises. The New Deal (*q.v.*) concerned itself little with the Negro problem as such, though many blacks gained by its welfare (*q.v.*) measures. (Interested conservatives argued that they "gained" only trifles by them, and lost family, self-respect, and independence as a result; see Thomas Sowell and Walter Williams [*qq.v.*] as "minority voices" in their ethnic communities, though fully "emancipated" elsewhere.) The overall prosperity of the years after World War II brought to the fore sociological changes which on the surface affected the South, making it much like the North, with white populations moving to suburbs while continuing commercial (*q.v.*) dominance in the major cities, which acquired black mayors and other officials as well as some business expansion. Southern universities and schools, as in the North, acquired black instructors and administrative officers, raising questions about the future of black institutions. Counter-measures in effect led to new policies which labored in the courts and legislatures for clarification. Evidence that the status of blacks, both in the North and the South, lagged far behind court and Congressional intentions, produced no new program. New black leaders could come up with no new programs for the blacks they were supposed to lead. Symbolic programs, such as acquiring a national holiday for Martin Luther King, Jr. rather than Frederick Douglass, did little of themselves for black communities as such. Although white educators intensified Black Studies and created new history (*q.v.*) for the new time, respecters of the old, such as the Agrarians, scholars in pre-Civil War eras, sponsors of the *Southern Partisan*, and especially business people watching their dollars were able to work freely in the South with few restraints so long as they observed the letter of the law. Although, again, this was also the program in the North, its libertarian traditions and language distinguished it from those farther south. See J. I. Copeland, ed., F. M. Gree, *Democracy in the Old South, and Other Essays* (1969) and works by Clement Eaton. See also Filler, "Consensus," in J. Waldmeir, ed., *Essays in Honor of Russel B. Nye* (1978); M.E. Bradford, *Remembering Who We Are* (1985); K.S. Greenberg, *Masters and Statesmen* (1985).

**South Africa, Republic of,** center of controversy once admired in the United States when it resisted British domination (1899-1902) and as an ally in World War I. In 1948, South Africa's policy dictating *Apartheid* (separation of the races) became official. This was in opposition to Western trends toward greater democratic rights for all elements of a country's population. In South Africa, participation in political life was restricted to whites, and the lives of non-whites were governed by many social and legal restrictions. For a time South Africa attempted to create supposedly autonomous "homeland" states for its black population. While some conservatives admired South Africa for its opposition to Communism and pointed to its relatively high standard of living, even among its black citizens, many decried its efforts to restrict political and social rights solely on the basis of race. Its racial policies had caused it to withdraw from the British Commonwealth in 1961 and change its name from the Union of South Africa to the Republic of South Africa. In the mid-1980's leftist agitation for revolutionary change in South Africa reached a peak. Many conservatives, however, were quick to point out that the pressures of a free-market economy in South Africa, especially the growing need for non-whites to fill skilled jobs in industry, were contributing to the gradual erosion of *Apartheid* policies. By 1985 South Africa had granted limited political rights to its so-called coloured population, though blacks remained excluded. *Apartheid* laws of interracial or "mixed" marriages were also eased. The contest was between radical revolutionary turmoil and conservative economic gradualism to produce needed changes in South African society. Meanwhile, many neighboring black states, even Zimbabwe (*q.v.*) turned a blind eye to South Africa's internal racial policies, as a result of political and economic expediency. That the duel within South Africa was in part one uniting western liberals with Soviet policy intended to gain it economic and military strength in Africa generally and in South African ocean waterways was a fact diminished by equalitarian and compassionate demands. See for example A. J. Klinghoffer, *Soviet Perspectives on African Socialism* (1969); Alexander Steward, *The World, The West, and Pretoria* (1980); Rene Lemarchaud, ed., *American Policy in South Africa: The Stakes and the Stance* (1981); Gale S. Hull, *Pawns on a Chessboard: The Resources War in Southern Africa* (1982); K. Osia, *Israel, South Africa and Black Africa: A Study of the Primacy of the Politics of Expediency* (1982). See also Nathaniel Weyl (*q.v.*) *Traitor's End: The Rise an Fall of the Communist Movement in Southern Africa* (1970).

**South America,** see Latin America

**Southern Agrarians,** see Agrarians

**Southern Partisan, The,** begun in 1983, and intended to be the "conservative voice of the unreconstructed...presented with wit and style." "Unreconstructed" suggested an unwillingness to accept, not the results of civil rights legislation, but of Reconstruction. As such, it was in the class of the "Agrarians," (*q.v.*) who in 1983 enjoyed a sense of achievement and acceptance, though hardly of the sort likely to affect developments in the universities. Although *The Southern Partisan* struck the Charleston, South Carolina *News & Courier* as a "breath of fresh air," the journal also saw it as "a voice crying in the wilderness." For a voice driving a pathway through the "wilderness," it appeared that another organ would be necessary. See also South, The.

**Southwest,** first populated by Spanish *conquistadors*—whose explorations took them as far as Kansas—and by Mexicans, it was infiltrated by Americans who, in the Texas war, rooted themselves in the area. They created the Cattle Kingdom (*q.v.*), in which Indians, Mexicans, and blacks had subordinate roles. Southerners ruined by the Civil War augmented its population and gave its language its "Southern" tone, but Northerners also added to its numbers, adjusting themselves to language, interests, and mixed populations. Its politics too were a mixture, ranging from money-grand autocracy to populism (*q.v.*), all overlaid with an individualism which expressed itself in duels and lynchings, and with a firm respect for "good" women, often less admired than the "bad." J. Frank Dobie was the historian of the Southwest's free and easy decades, Walter P. Webb of its passing as railroad, wire fences, and business took the place of free-ranging buffalo and cowboys. Although severely exploited, Mexicans crossed the border in increasing numbers, finding better opportunities than in their birthplaces, which they proved ready to exchange for more humble status, much as the greater numbers of immigrants (*q.v.*) entering the United States in the East. The 1930s Depression (*q.v.*) hit the Southwest as it did the East, sharpening differences between its classes, but finding expression in such New Dealers (*q.v.*) as Lyndon B. Johnson. His odyssey from poor, first-family Southwesterner to multi-millionaire liberal reflected changes in the area's politics and its treatment of the subordinate classes. Mexican illegal immigration increased as commercial (*q.v.*) classes found it difficult to resist the temptation of hiring cheap labor. Immigrants became a social and political force, many of them, by a species of "underground railroad," finding their way as far as Chicago, but substantially more remaining in Southwestern states. Desegregation, voting, and other government acts touching blacks also affected them. Although the Immigration Service sought to join other Federal organizations in policing the Mexican border, it was in disarray due to conflicting signals in government policy and the very increase in numbers of illegal Mexican immigrants. The media (*q.v.*) showed its power by stirring sympathy for the aliens, identifying them with earlier immigrant waves, passing over the fact that these earlier immigrants had been processed by officials before entering into American ways and places. Although the new "citizens" showed traces of "radical" sentiment, responding to the efforts of union (*q.v.*) organizers and emphasizing the word *huelga* (strike) more than they would have dared in Mexico, they also were generally conservative Catholics with a love of family and a desire to get ahead in traditional American ways. As one illegal immigrant—his name and place reported in the *New York Times*, evidently with no fear of being picked up for deportation—put it: admittedly, he was doing much better than he would in Mexico; nevertheless, he wanted still more, for himself and his children. Such was the continuing growth and political influence of Hispanics (*q.v.*) as they were now called, that they were not only able to elect high officials and influence immigration policy, but to push for Spanish as a first language, English as a second. How this would affect national policy—and first of all immigration policy undetermined in the mid-1980s—remained to be seen as voting blocs formed.

**Soviet Union,** the center of world Commmunism, with the power and experience to carry on war with Western nations by all means. It was a measure of the credibility the Soviet regime had attained in the wake of the Russian Revolution (*q.v.*) that it was able to endure massive failures and purges to emerge after World War II (*q.v.*) as one of the world's greatest powers. It suffered its frightful slaughter of kulaks (independent farmers) in the interest of communes and the execution of Old Bolsheviks by Stalin's (*q.v.*) courts and police network. The destruction of the Chinese revolutionary party under Stalin's direction, and the destruction of all parties except Nazi under Stalin's deadly slogan of "Social fascism": that all parties except the German Communist Party were at bottom "fascist." In Spain, the Communists, backed by Soviet cadres, proved more competent at killing anti-Francoists not of the Stalinist persuasion than at killing Francoists. Finally, an isolated Soviet Union first joined the all-but-dead League of Nations, then allied itself with the Nazis, before joining the Allies in an anti-Hitler crusade. The question of how so wholly discredited a regime was not only able to survive, but to rise in power and menace, merited an elaborate and continuing analysis the Soviet Union did not have to endure. It did not suffice to seek scapegoats. The essence of Soviet credibility was hope in socialism and fear of fascism. It enabled partisans to swallow their disappointments with Soviet rule, and to feel chilled by the roll of drums on the Rhine. Although there were many millions of Americans who did not like Communists and distrusted friends of the Soviet Union they could be reached even in the schools with the message that ordinary Russians were just like them: enjoying dances, songs, and family life. The awkward propaganda of conservative groups was not deep enough to touch children and citizens generally with feeling for older American ways. The McCarthy (*q.v.*) cause revealed that there was a strong vein of pro-Americanism in the body politic, but developed more from fear of the Soviet giant than from love of country. By 1950 Soviet leaders no longer needed wooed and subsidized American factions to declare their cause. Their "Iron Curtain" countries they could dominate with local satraps kept to the mark by fear of direct military intervention if necessary, with evidence that there would be no Western intervention to interfere. Truman dismissing MacArthur to avoid "World War III" and Eisenhower refusing to help Hungarian "freedom fighters" for the same reason seemed to conservatives to set a pattern which secured Soviet power at home and abroad. Conservatives protesting Detente (*q.v.*) and arms-limitation negotiations as smokescreens for Soviet aggrandizement sounded like querulous voices among realistic ones welcoming a new time of universal peace and mutual confidence. Still the Soviet Union, much to the amazement of conservatives, did have problems. Chinese "Marxism" proved not to comport with Soviet "Marxism." Poland would not forget the Katyn Forest murders (*q.v.*). The Soviets' African surrogates were not always manageable. Central and South America were as open to American influence as to Soviet. In 1979 Great Britain elected a conservative government, in 1980 the United States did. Most heartening to Westerners not bemused by Soviet power and successes was the flow of information which emanated from the Soviet Union itself in one form or another to stamp out remnants of the old, hopeful sentimentality about the "Workers' Fatherland": the old, false reports by foreign correspondents like Walter Duranty of the *New York Times* and Eugene Lyons (*q.v.*). Alexander Solzhenitsyn (*q.v.*) was a moral and informational force in himself. Informed reports came from authoritative sources. Even dissidents (*q.v.*) could somehow not be kept from reaching Western persons and agencies, though they were kept under rigid surveillance in their homeland. Individual and even nationalistic voices illustrated the indomitable quality of human nature in the Soviet Union even under the threat of the secret police and the Gulag (*q.v.*). Although a disorderly democracy looked and was vulnerable to fools and traitors, it seemed to produce positive results from time to time. For a pioneer exposé of Soviet pretentions, Dagobert D. Runes, *The Soviet Impact on Society* (1953). See also, Levine, Isaac Don; Muggeridge, Malcolm.

**Sowell, Thomas** (1930- ), a senior fellow at the Hoover Institution on War, Revolution, and Peace (*q.v.*), famous along with Walter Williams (*q.v.*) as a black dissenting from the agenda of many better-known black leaders, including affirmative action, increased government power, and increased welfare. Sowell viewed the nation as an area of hope and opportunity, demanding individualism, hard work and an understanding of others, as well as loyalty to the nation's heritage. He denounced the Supreme Court's (*q.v.*) judicial activism, opposed the giving up of the Panama Canal, and opposed Federal subsidies for abortion. Author of *Knowledge and Decision* (1980), *Ethnic America* (1981), and *Pink and Brown People* (1981), he was perhaps a harbinger of an independent sector of the black community, confident of his status in America, intellectual as well as economic, and prepared to defend it.

**Spain,** notable in modern times for the Civil War (1936-1939) which formed a testing ground for the forces supporting the Spanish "Republic," actually controlled by Stalinist Communists, and those standing by the nationalists led by the fascist Francisco Franco. Arms and troops came from the Soviet Union on one side and from Italy and Germany on the other. The United States held to the Neutrality Act of 1937, though guns were smuggled to Spain by Communists and supporters. The fascists, though supposed to disintegrate by historical fiat, emerged victorious over the Stalinists, busy killing or imprisoning dissidents within their ranks. The Franco regime became stabilized, to the chagrin of those sustaining the myth of an anti-Franco assemblage waiting to emerge. As late as 1961, an old Hispanic scholar saw Spain as a "liability" from which the democratic West must disassociate itself. In his *Spain and the Defense of the West*, Arthur Whitaker urged that Spain must be kept out of NATO. We had air bases in Spain, a necessity which such liberal organs as the *New York Times* had "grudgingly" accepted. In 1969, Prince Juan Carlos was designated successor to Franco. Franco's death in 1975 precipitated a democratic revolution, with Franco's institutions discarded and moderates and social democrats emerging as the largest parties. The directions politics were taking in the country were obscurely indicated by the crushing of an attempted coup by Francoists in 1981, and the curious demand of former Republicans, now in old age, for pensions, on the ground that they had been soldiers in a Spanish cause and, with socialists in power, merited their consideration. Hugh Thomas, *The Spanish Civil War* (1961); G. Brennan, *The Spanish Labyrinth* (1962); Max Gallo, *Spain under Franco* (1974).

**Special Interests.** Conservatives and liberals have often accused each other of being supported by or favoring "special interests." To liberals, conservative special interests include the wealthy, the powerful, and the large corporations. To conservatives, liberal special interests include the poor, minorities, and labor unions. In David Graham Phillips's (*q.v.*) *The Treason of the Senate*, "The Interests" were the great corporations which importuned government for special favors.

**Spencer, Herbert** (1820-1903), British philosopher. Extrapolating dubiously from Darwinism (*q.v.*) he created the concept of "Social Darwinism" (*q.v.*) which affected pre-World War I conservativism, mainly as a justification for war and social war (*qq.v.*). His effort to create a "synthetic philosophy" which would literally engross all knowledge, though impressive in its time, was rendered obsolete by the late advances of the several disciplines involved. Even his concept of the "unknowable" did not survive examination; see William F. Lacy, *An Examination of the Philosophy of the Unknowable as Expounded by Herbert Spencer* (1883). Although he at first appeared a libertarian (*q.v.*), in his early *Social Statics* (1850), Henry George was able to trace his progressive decline in later editions of the work in *A Perplexed Philosopher* (1892). Nevertheless, later conservatives cherished his *Man Versus the State* (*q.v.*) (1884), which comported with their principles by emphasizing a minimal role for government.

**Spending,** in politics mainly identified with governmental spending, and thus with taxation (*q.v.*); a significant factor in the lean 1980s, juxtaposing "social" outlays with military or "defense" spending. Liberals argue that, even with inevitable corruption in social welfare programs, it was necessary to help the helpless and needy, and that such spending represented only a fraction of military spending. A curious argument contrasted welfare corruption with corporate corruption, seeing no difference between the family and the corporation. Private spending contrasted with private saving, which could be for hoarding or investment. Eisenhower's (*q.v.*) suggestion in affluent (*q.v.*) times was for spending, but spending judiciously.

**"Spoils System,"** see Bureaucracy

**"Spontaneous Order,"** Friedrich A. Hayek's (*q.v.*) phrase in his *Law, Legislation and Liberty* to explain the regularities in society which were not the result of human planning, but of human action. Essentially, it was Hayek's version of the "Invisible Hand" of Adam Smith (*q.v.*), who saw humanity legislating, and legislating best for itself, by mixing its needs in free enterprise, and coming out with the results which satisfied its needs.

**Sports,** often touching liberal and conservative interests, in the twentieth century, but increasingly less so than entertainment (*q.v.*). Much that appeared "conservative" in sports was mostly commercial (*q.v.*). The prowess of the black fighter Jack Johnson early in the century created the racist call for a "white hope," all of which was recalled during the civil rights drive of later decades. The Negro runner Jesse Owen's refusal to give the Nazi salute at the Berlin Olympics in 1936 contrasted with the refusal of later black Olympic contestants to honor the playing of the "Star-Spangled Banner" during the Olympics in Mexico City. The multiplication of black stars went along with the growth of commerce in sports. It gave ethnic satisfaction to followers of baseball, football, basketball, and other sports, but troubled some libertarians as seeming to indicate that blacks were more adept at physical activities than mental. Nevertheless liberals, probably more than conservatives, expended energy doing justice to blacks in sports. They made much of the black prize fighter Muhammed Ali as a moral figure, a classic fighter, a person of opinions. They told tales of black baseball stars who had not been given entree to the "major leagues" before the advent of Jackie Robinson, and pressed for justice to the Indian Jim Thorpe, deemed cheated of his Olympic honors in 1912 because of an infraction of rules. Much energy was expended in seeking to isolate South Africa (*q.v.*) from international sports, and forcing esteemed competitors to reject invitations to play there. "Peter Simple" (*q.v.*) was persistent in noting how little atrocities perpetrated by the Soviets affected their ability to participate in international events. William F. Buckley, Jr. (*q.v.*) confessed that he had little time to give to sports. Another active conservative, Jeffrey Hart, however, recalled his dedication to tennis with fervor. Michael Novak was even more intense in his faith in sports' significance; see his *The Joy of Sports: and...Consecration of the Human Spirit* (1976). Ronald Reagan's youthful interest in sports and sportscasting was an interesting side-light to his career. In 1980 the summer Olympics took place in Moscow without the presence of American competitors, thanks to President Carter's effort to punish the Soviets for their transgressions in Afghanistan (*q.v.*). In 1984, the Soviets and most of their satellites boycotted the Summer Olympics in Los Angeles.

**"Squeal Rule,"** a *New York Times* description for proposed Federal requirements that subsidized clinics to inform parents when minors received prescription contraceptions. Opponents of the "Squeal Rule" believed that such a requirement would result in greater numbers of teenage pregnancies and abortions under dangerous conditions. Supporters argued that the "Squeal Rule" was intended to protect family prerogatives. The "Squeal Rule" was eventually struck down in Federal court.

**"Stages,"** a term sometimes used to refer to changes in social conditions, often by liberal or radical activists. Radicals claimed to find themselves in early or late stages of capitalist "development," depending on whether the stage was set for further developments or had to "mature." Libertarians (*q.v.*), confronted with the evidence of their minimal impact, were required to look to future stages of economic and social development for justification. Betty Friedan (*q.v.*) and A. Kraditor saw two "stages" in the women's rights movement. Friedan saw feminism's first stage as one of self-assertion and expansion; the second stage would admit the value of old-fashioned female virtues. Kraditor's first stage for male and female was, in effect, equalization of opportunity. The next stage would be conservative. It was unclear how those who had not profited from the earlier stage would fit in.

**Stakhanovism,** see Taylor, Frederick W.

**Stalin, Josef** (1879-1953), Soviet dictator, with Karl Marx and Vladimir Lenin (*qq.v.*) a major target of conservatives as representing socialism's false theory and infamous practice. His life under the Czar as outlaw, terrorist, and bank robber has been viewed unsympathetically as simply that of a thug guided by dogma: the religious seminarian turned inside out. At this point, his defeated opponent Leon Trotsky (*q.v.*), in his study of Stalin published posthumously (1946), was mainly critical of Stalin's mind and spirit rather than his theory; once they had taken power in what had been Russia (*q.v.*), his criticism turned to politics. Stalin opposed Trotsky's projected "permanent revolution" with "socialism in one country," which meant the dominance of the Soviet Union over Communist Parties elsewhere. Stalin's Five-Year Plans forced industrialization upon the nation, attended by extermination of the *kulaks* (landed owners), with debatable industrial results but with clear human failures. Stalin's slaughter of his colleagues made a mockery of law, enduringly etched in Arthur Koestler's *Darkness at Noon* (1940). His followers in Spain lost their country to the Franco forces by carrying on a concerted war against all among them who were not Stalinists. Then, alarmed by his isolation in Europe, Stalin negotiated a non-aggression pact with Hitler, leading to the partition of Poland. These among other policies and actions lost Stalin much support throughout the world. However, when Hitler attacked Soviet Russia, Stalin became an unlikely ally of the West in an anti-Hitler war. Losing a million soldiers in stemming the German advance, many Russians esteemed Stalin as their leader in a close-to-holy war. His policies of slaughter and repression served him to the end, winning him a place beside Lenin in the all-but-sanctified mausoleum in Red Square. Stalin's death coincided with the beginnings of a reaffirmed conservativism in America, dissatisfied with the New Deal heritage at home and alarmed by a Communist dictatorship abroad armed with the atomic bomb. Although the famous "thaw" took Stalin's body out of Red Square and into a more modest grave near the Kremlin Wall, it did not diminish Stalin's program in the hands of his successors. Conservatives made it a major goal to keep this fact before the eyes of all with whom they could make contact. Nikolaus Basseches, *Stalin* (1952); G. R. Urban, ed., *Stalinism: Its Impact on Russia and the World*

(1982); Nikolai Tolstoy, *Stalin's Secret War* (1983).

**Star-Spangled Banner,** national anthem, made an issue when individuals or groups demeaned it in the radical turmoil of the 1960s. Although a non-anti-American argument had been long known respecting the anthem's strain on singers' throats, this was irrelevant to the major contention. Legal efforts to ban desecration, as led by the American Legion and taken up by several congressmen did not advance. The *Star-Spangled-Banner* thus became one indicator of the power of public opinion at any given time.

**State the Enemy, The,** (1953), by Sir Ernest Benn. London publisher and a leading individualist, he wrote many books, including *Confessions of a Capitalist*. He argued against "planners" as having undermined incentives and harmed business initiative with their welfare and nationalizing policies. He concluded his examination of the state as a vehicle of socialism by appending excerpts from Herbert Spencer's (*q.v.*) "The Coming Slavery."

**States Rights,** traditionally more an instrument of conservative principles than of liberal, despite significant exceptions mainly resulting from conservatives having obtained power. With Federalists (*q.v.*) in control of the government in 1798—and that year passing into law their Alien and Sedition acts, inspired by their fear of the French Revolution (*q.v.*)—the more liberal-minded Jefferson and Madison (*qq.v.*) had the legislatures of Virginia and Kentucky pass resolutions declaring that they were not agreed that acts which they deemed unconstitutional deserved to be honored. Similarly, the later abolitionists (*q.v.*) felt free to defy Federal legislation when they deemed it immoral and opposed to religious tenets; for example, they appealed to their fellow-citizens in their states to join them in disavowing fugitive slave laws. Nevertheless, for the most part, "states rights" was a slogan of conservatives, before the Civil War in defense of slavery, after the War in defense of doctrines intended to keep the Negro freedmen in subordinate status. States-rights principles were invoked to slow down the post-World War II drive to increase black voting; Strom Thurmond (*q.v.*) in 1948 ran as Presidential candidate for the States Rights Party. He won over a million votes, and the electoral votes of Alabama, Mississippi, Louisiana, and South Carolina. (See also Wallace, George.) Aroused conservatives of the 1960s and later periods, while seeking national power, also denounced the Federal bureaucracy and liberalism which was interfering with state action regarding education, busing, (*q.v.*) and other issues. At the same time, conservatives labored to turn public and Congressional opinion to their side, and looked for opportunities which would create a more conservative Supreme Court (*q.v.*). See also Tenth Amendment.

**Statism,** like "Collectivism" (*q.v.*) seen without positive qualities by conservatives; a program or viewpoint interpreted as looking to the state for solution, rather than to individual effort.

**Steinbeck, John** (1902-1968), major American author whose misconstrued goal was not for justice but for faith. This should have been evident in such titles as *To a God Unknown*, *The Grapes of Wrath*, and *East of Eden*. Even *In Dubious Battle* drew its attempted theme from John Milton's *Paradise Lost*: "Innumerable force of Spirits armed,... In dubious battle on the plains of Heaven." Liberals who complained that Steinbeck had written "only" *The Grapes of Wrath* were confessing their lack of understanding, their impression that the book was a novel of haves against have-nots. It was, in fact, a vast parable of a religious quest, from an oppressive Egypt to a hoped-for land of milk and honey. It featured, among others, a Jim Casy, an erstwhile evangelist, who denied that he loved Jesus, only people, and whose last words to his vigilante killers were: "You fellows don't know what you're doin." The trek of the Joads in search of of a decent life ends in a chaos of storm and flood, with a man found who is dying of hunger, too far gone to absorb bread. He must have milk. Rose of Sharon, her baby lost, is put to feeding him from her full breasts. Steinbeck was not afraid of sentimentality, and some of it made him a best-seller. But there was not a sentimental phrase in *The Grapes of Wrath*. His search for meaning in life kept him in touch with both life and death: in nature, which he explored with a scientist and reflected upon in *Sea of Cortez* (1941); and in primitive life, as in *The Pearl* (1947). Communists did not like it because it seemed to tell peasants to be happy with simple things. Conservatives had no interest. There were other masterpieces among the tales in *The Pastures of Heaven* (1932) and *The Long Valley* (1938), notably "The Red Pony," which honored youth and also old age. The Left took *In Dubious Battle* (1936) as belonging to them, but Steinbeck's heart was not in class struggle. So formidable was literary contempt for his work that Steinbeck was himself abashed when he received the Nobel Prize for Literature, in 1962.

**Stephen, James Fitzjames** (1829-1894), distinguished British jurist, brother of Sir Leslie Stephen, essayist and editor of the *Dictionary of National Biography*, who wrote his brother's biography (1895). James Stephen became the foremost British authority on criminal law, beginning with his *General View of the Criminal Law* (1863) and maturing his views in *A History of the Criminal Law of England* (1883). He also published essays which showed his increasing skepticism about democratic trends. The reluctance of Parliament to put into law the criminal code he saw necessary underscored for him the harm being done by such libertarians as John Stuart Mill (*q.v.*). He wrote his conclusions into a major conservative volume of the era, *Liberty, Equality, Fraternity* (1873).

**Stereotypes,** a major factor in public opinion (*q.v.*), often requiring not only intellectual revisions but a willingness of public opinion to accept or reject them. Although the use of stereotypes was often identified with conservative malice and epithets (*q.v.*), liberals had their own stereotypes. Thus, WASP (*q.v.*) suggested a cohesiveness of community which often did not exist. Heroes (*q.v.*) were often accorded stereotypes and counter-stereotypes, as in the case of George Washington and Abraham Lincoln (*qq.v.*). Stereotypes of both liberals and conservatives clearly merited more conscious attention than they received.

**Stewardship,** see Commercialism; Tappan, Lewis; Carnegie, Andrew

**Stockman, David A.** (1946- ), Republican government official, whose short, brilliant career in the Reagan Administration seemed all but wrecked in adversary politics, providing lessons in techniques employed in the competition between advocates of the welfare state and those favoring limited government. Stockman attended Divinity School at Harvard (1968-1970), became an assistant to Republican Congressman John Anderson, then director of the Republican Conference of the House of Representatives. A member of the 95th Congress himself, Stockman was then made chairman of the Republican Economic Policy Task Force, and as such helped prepare Ronald Reagan for his debate with President Jimmy Carter. He so impressed Reagan with the keenness of his economic grasp that, on winning the Presidency, Reagan appointed Stockman director of the Office of Management and Budget. Stockman came under close scrutiny for his opposition to entitlements, and for his faith in supply-side economics (*qq.v.*). He was criticized for having attended Divinity School, perhaps in order to avoid military service. His own budget projections evidently worried him, as well as his ill-wishers. He confided some of his doubts to William Greider, whose article in the *Atlantic*, "The Education of David Stockman" (December, 1981), produced a sensation. It appeared to say that Stockman and the Administration did not truly know what they were about, and that the economic tenets they were following were flimsy. *Forbes Magazine* saw him as "Benedict Stockman." *America* interpreted the interview as a "confession," the *New Republic* as evidence that the Reagan team was "Marching to Dunkirk"; that is, its program was collapsing. There was wide expectation that Stockman would be jettisoned. But he was "taken to the woodshed" for a briefing by the President, then returned to office. The public was given to understand that budget figures were tentative, and dependent for validity on results, involving not only the Administration but social and economic elements proper. Stockman maintained his program for holding down government spending by such means as could be justified. He finally resigned his Administration post in 1985. Although Stockman's *The Triumph of Politics* (1986) was critical of his former colleagues, including the President, Owen Ulmand's *Stockman: The Man, the Myth, the Future* (1986) did not spare the former director in its account of his qualities.

**Story, Joseph** (1779-1845), American jurist, a favorite of conservatives because of his firm defenses of property and determination that Christian doctrine was part of the common law, and also because of the fine logic and learning which informed his decisions and treatises. Beginning his career as a Jeffersonian (*q.v.*), his emergence as a believer in property rights scarcely marked him as transitional (*q.v.*) from Democratic-Republicanism to Whiggery (*q.v.*). Story's emphasis was not on party politics. Although he voted for repeal of Jefferson's peace-intended Embargo, he had moved with refinements from a pro-Embargo position. President Madison's (*q.v.*) appointment of him as the youngest member of the Supreme Court (1811) was a tribute to his reputation as a keen interpreter of the law. Story joined Marshall (*q.v.*) in his nationalistic version of the Constitution. In the *Dartmouth College* case (1819), he held to the sanctity of contracts irrespective of the changes wrought by time. He held to this view in the *Charles River Bridge Case* (1837), but was outvoted by a Jacksonian (*q.v.*) majority with less regard for the indestructible nature of contracts. Story's views of slaves as property were less respectful of owner's rights. In the *Amistad Case* (1839), involving slaves in revolt, he interpreted them as "property rescued from pirates," and in *Prigg v. Pa.* (1842), he refused to invoke the Fugitive Slave Act of 1793 in behalf of slave catchers. (See Supreme Court.) Although Story's decision did little for abolition, it involved an equity for which he was internationally famous, which aided anti-slavery developments in a difficult era. Story's *Commentaries on the Constitution*, his studies in the common law and other contributions were marked by their durability, as well as their firm sense of continuity in American law.

**Straight, Michael,** son of Willard and Dorothy Whitney Straight, founders of the *New Republic* who were once influential in the Woodrow Wilson (*q.v.*) Administration and after in liberal opinion. Straight was representative of what liberalism became under the impact of leftist views generated by the Thirties Depression (*q.v.*) and the fascist-communist duel throughout the world. Straight took on Communist views at Cambridge University where he was friendly with the traitors Anthony Blunt, Guy Burgess, and others. Although he knew them to be Soviet agents, he used the excuse—also adopted by Secretary of State Dean Acheson with respect to Alger Hiss (*q.v.*)—that the duties of friendship overrode duties to the nation. Straight therefore kept his knowledge to himself until 1963, when President John F. Kennedy offered to appoint him Deputy Director of the National Endowment for the Arts. Persuaded that an official investigation would reveal his connection with the traitors, he informed the FBI (*q.v.*) of his association—a fact which, passed on for British investigation, was nevertheless kept secret. It was the subsequent exposure of Blunt which finally led to Straight's exposure. In the meantime he had become connected with the *New Republic*, where he distinguished himself in his hatred and scorn of "McCarthyism": a fact which was not lost on those conservatives who had written in its defense. See Straight, *After Long Silence* (1983).

**Strauss, Leo** (1899-1973), German scholar whose philosophy of natural law (*q.v.*) helped conservatives clarify the source of virtue and the dangers in pragmatic solutions to the world's problems. Strauss's work took him into research which was rudely interrupted by the advent of Nazism. Of Jewish birth, he fled their persecution. Strauss was especially interested in the work of Hobbes (*q.v.*). He analyzed him in *The Political Philosophy of Hobbes* (1936), and saw him as repudiating the natural law (*q.v.*) tradition—one of instinctive virtue and fraternity—for a "natural rights" conception which placed individual appetites above society's needs. This produced Leviathan, and, according to Strauss, Nazism. Strauss much admired the ancient Greek view of society. His "classical paganism" disturbed Frank Meyer (*q.v.*), who held that Christianity better estimated the worth of the individual. He held suspect too Strauss's willingness to have the state serve the public in benign ways. Nevertheless, Strauss was found evocative by rising conservative factions, at the New School for Social Research and, after 1949, as professor of political philosophy at the University of Chicago. His works included *Natural Right and History* (1953), *Thoughts of Machiavelli* (1958), for whom he felt distaste, and *What Is Political Philosophy? and Other Studies* (1959). See also Voegelin, Eric.

**Strausz-Hupé, Robert** (1903- ), Vienna-born foreign-policy analyst. His services to American conservativism were somewhat comparable to those of Bertrand de Jouvenel and Eric Kuehnelt-Leddihn (*qq.v.*) in adding a European dimension to American concerns. Strausz-Hupé came to the United States in 1928, and did not take up scholarship for many years. He became associated with the University of Pennsylvania, where he developed the Foreign Policy Research Institute, which published several of his books. They included *Geopolitics* (*q.v.*), *The Struggle for Space and Power* (1942), *The Balance of Tomorrow* (1945), *The Zone of Indifference* (1952), and *A Forward Strategy for America* (1961). He believed that China did not have to be lost to the Communists, and that Stalin's (*q.v.*) purposes could have been earlier perceived and resisted. He served as U. S. Ambassador to Ceylon, Belgium, Sweden, and Turkey. For his autobiography, *In My Time* (1965).

**Street Corner Conservative** (1975), by William F. Gavin, an employee of then U. S. Senator James F. Buckley. It was intended to explain persons like himself, from Jersey City, N. J., who were Irish-Catholic, of modest working-class background, and wanted nothing from government but to be left alone. They were not envious of others, or with grievances to display. But they were mightily disturbed, Gavin said, by those who wished to explain them to themselves and, in effect, tell them what to feel and how to act.

**Students,** a factor in national life and politics from the time of Plato's Academy to the more recent Students for Democratic Action, and their conservative opponents. The academic milieu as a place for books and issues, as well as job preparation, attracted evangelical types and also opportunists, and contributed leaders for changing times. James Wechsler, later editor of the *New York Post*, and Joseph Lash, later prize-winning biographer of Eleanor Roosevelt, were left-wing student agitators in the 1930s. They constituted a debatable highpoint over such later voices as Bob Dylan, and agitator Jerry Rubin of the same era. Although students had long played serious roles in such European crises as the revolutionary upsurge in Europe in 1848, there had been no comparable tradition in America. The experiences of the 1960s and early 1970s indicated that events were bringing domestic America closer to foreign modes of thought. Indeed, the American youth uprisings were accompanied by similar upheavals in Europe, though different traditions and ways of thought gave different results. A notable development of the late 1970s and early 1980s—the latter certainly influenced by the rise of Ronald Reagan—was the flowering of a vigorous conservative campus student establishment. Significantly, it disturbed academic administrators of the time. The president of Dartmouth College, for example, made efforts to impede the work of its conservative activists. This allowed conservative spokesmen to argue that such administrators were betraying the liberal tenets they claimed to cherish. With students increasingly more interested in a material, rather than idealistic or ideological, future, it remained to be seen whether liberal and radical adventurers on campuses were playing out their New Deal heritage, or would find means for renewing it. See also Youth.

**"Subliminal Advertising,"** see Advertising

**Suburbia,** seen benignly during the expansion eras of urban (*q.v.*) development as offering "breathing space" for the growing cities and home in the country for the well-to-do. The movement to the suburbs before and during World War II (*q.v.*) did not have the character of "White Flight" (*q.v.*) but of dissatisfaction with city pressures. After the war Federal support of housing and highway construction led to an enormous expansion of the suburbs as the expense of the urban areas. In the 1950s evidence of mounting crime and a lowered quality of life in the cities raised questions about their future, and the pressures resulting from desegregation laws following Supreme Court orders implementing the *Brown* (*q.v.*) decision in 1954 led to "White Flight" to maintain separation in housing and schooling. Suburbs received a bad press as housing faceless Organization Men (*q.v.*), and as evading social responsibilities toward the poor and dissatisfied. By the mid-1980s many suburbs had become afflicted with problems somewhat similar to those endemic to the central cities. Although suburbs were generally weak in creativity and bold social experimentation, their future was undetermined. Harlan P. Douglas, *Suburban Trend* (1925); John E. Ullmann, ed., *Suburban Economic Network* (1977); Scott Donaldson, *The Suburban Myth* (1969); L. H. Masotti and Jeffrey K. Hadden, eds., *Suburbia in Transition* (1974).

**Subversives,** a key word with shifting connotations. It was weighted in terms of pro-Communist treason (*q.v.*) by conservatives, of dissent opinion in a free society by liberals—who also invoked Constitutional guarantees and the sanctity of privacy. In 1984 the determination of Great Britain's Conservative government to debar union (*q.v.*) members from work at Cheltenham Communications Centre, and offering £1,000 separation fee to Centre workers who left the union and its perquisites, was interpreted by union officials as strike-breaking and unnecessary. They held that workers were loyal, more so than such known traitors as Anthony Blunt and Kim Philby, who had come from the upper classes and elite schools. "Peter Simple" (*q.v.*) retorted in his *Way of the World* that workers had been more loyal for lack of access to government secrets, but that, subject to union discipline and consensus, they would welcome Soviet forces invading Great Britain. A majority of workers intended for GCHQ opted for the £1,000 and non-union status. The unions threatening a general strike were declared by Government partisans to be giving proof of what they were capable of doing in critical national situations.

**Suicide,** rejected by many conservatives as an impugning of life and of religion (*q.v.*). According to these conservatives, life is a test and trial before entrances into another life. Suicide was often tolerated or approved by liberal opinion as involving individual choice, as being a tolerable alternative to pain and psychological agony, and as being an appropriate adjunct to inevitable death. Technically, suicide is a legal crime. But the *New York Times* reported on a planned suicide the facts of which had been shared by a wide variety of people. As a result of the uncertain social ethic of the time, absurdities in the field abounded. Thus, "professionals" in the field were annoyed by non-professionals interposing their aid and concern by helping a potential suicide; they should have telephoned for a professional. The suicides of Arthur Koestler and his wife in 1983 attracted attention. A quadraplegic's request that she be allowed to starve to death was turned down in a California Superior Court, on grounds that "our society values life. The plaintiff is not terminal." A. Alvarez, *The Savage God: A Study of Suicide* (1972); H. Hendin, *Suicide in America* (1982).

**Sumner, William Graham** (1840-1910), American author and educator. Although trained for the ministry, he was caught up in the social concerns of the post-Civil War era and became a principled proponent of Social Darwinism and Free Trade (*qq.v.*). Appointed at Yale, first professor of political and social science in 1872, the next year he published *What Social Classes Owe to Each Other*, in which he concluded that they owed nothing. An opponent of labor union's he saw life as a necessary struggle in order to produce the finest human elements: essentially the doctrine of Herbert Spencer (*q.v.*). Nevertheless he was held suspect by Yale trustees to whom Free Trade (*q.v.*) was a "radical" policy and who favored Protection. Sumner made much of hard work and proof of superiority, and set an example of diligence with the publication of works which helped create the discipline of sociology. His most enduring concept was that of "Folkways," which attempted to trace the habits and rituals of primitive and other civilizations. In *The Forgotten Man and Other Essays* (1919), he saw the "forgotten" man as one who simply wished to be let alone. In Franklin D. Roosevelt's (*q.v.*) later lexicon the "forgotten man" was one who was in need and required help. Sumner's work was carried on at Yale by A. G. Keller, who appears to have influenced John Chamberlain (*q.v.*) in his transitional (*q.v.*) career from neo-Marxist to admirer of American entrepreneurs and businessmen.

**Supply-Side Economics,** see Reaganomics; Laffer, Arthur

**Supreme Court.** In tendency it was generally a conservative body, but, subject to Presidential nomination and Congressional approval, it could be and was affected by circumstances which gave it intermittently a liberal image offensive to several classes of conservatives. The Marshall Court (*q.v.*) was notable for establishing the Supreme Court as interpreter of the Constitution. The Marshall decisions were strongly nationalistic, Marshall finding in *McCullough vs. Maryland* (1819) "implied powers" in the Constitution which expanded the government's ability to act. However, the government itself under Jackson (*q.v.*) refused to act when Marshall (*Cherokee Nation vs. Georgia* [1830]) ruled that the government had jurisdiction over Cherokee Indian (*q.v.*) lands and that Georgia law abrogating this jurisdiction was invalid. With Marshall deceased in 1835, the Court turned Jacksonian under Chief Justice Roger B. Taney (*q.v.*) and mixed liberal decisions with others which struggled with slavery dilemmas. *Prigg vs. Pennsylvania* (1842) had found that a fugitive slave law of 1793 did not require the states to enforce it, thus giving rise to a host of Northern "personal liberty" laws which impeded the return of runaways. But Taney's 1857 dictum in *Dred Scott vs. Sandford* that the temporary presence of a slave in a free state did not make him free on his return to a slave state, among other findings, divided North from South. The fact that decision had been withheld until after the election of President Buchanan roused charges of conspiracy. Free Soilers (*q.v.*) believed that had it been known before election that Taney was in effect rubbing out the borders between free states and slave, the Republican candidate Frémont would have won the 1856 election. During the Civil War, the Supreme Court was quiescent, once it was clear that Lincoln would not obey rulings which interfered with his power (in *Ex Parte Merryman* [1861]) to suspend issuance of writs of *habeas corpus* as a war measure. In post-Civil War decades, the Court became increasingly loathe to interfere with business expansion. Although the Granger Cases (1877) increased the power of states to limit the authority of big business over those requring its services, the increase in "due process" (*q.v.*) proceedings, enabling railroad and other interests to carry their pleas against containment to the Supreme Court itself, made it the final arbiter even on the subject of fair rates to customers, among other issues. The Sherman Anti-Trust Law of 1890 was kept ineffective by inaction and narrow interpretation. In 1896 the Court's notorious *Plessy vs. Ferguson* decision approved segregation for Negroes so long as "equal" accommodations were provided. During the Progressive era (*q.v.*) rifts appeared in the Court's long conservative record. A law controlling working hours for women (*Muller vs. Oregon* [1908]) was held valid and no "impairment" of the liberty of contract. In 1911, the Standard Oil Company of New Jersey and the American Tobacco Company were dissolved as trusts, though the effect of the decisions remained doubtful. Child labor laws, however, were lost. Secondary labor boycotts were held to be conspiracies and subject to penalty (*Lowe vs. Lawler* [1908]). An espionage act enacted during World War I was upheld. Although such decisions made famous the names of Holmes and Brandeis (*qq.v.*) in dissent, their views were not the law of the land. Court decisions on crucial New Deal (*q.v.*) measures infuriated the Franklin D. Roosevelt Administration and impelled it to seek legislation "packing" the Court, but events intervened. Though the Supreme Court struck down the National Industrial Recovery Act in 1935 and the Agricultural Adjustment Act on grounds of excessive government authority, business had inadequately worked to mend its establishment and a 1935 National Labor Relations Act promised more interaction between labor and industry. A second AAA was drawn up to meet the Court's objections. Moreover, Justices retired or died, and were replaced with individuals closer to Roosevelt's outlook. The ascent of Earl Warren, former Republican governor of California, to the Chief Justiceship in 1953 coincided with the stirring of conservative unrest over lost traditions and a purposeless materialism (see Warren, Earl). Warren's retirement in 1969 gave conservatism a new chance to install a Chief Justice closer to its principles. President Nixon's choice of Warren Earl Burger to fill the office, though he was all but unknown as a justice in the U. S. Appeals Court in Washington, seemed sound. Burger favored a stern approach to crime and criminals. He had expressed disagreement with the *Miranda* decision (1966) which required what conservatives saw as undue care to protect the right of criminals against self-incrimination, police and, inevitably, justice. He had criticized the high Court for making law, even while expressing respect for its having set down "landmarks on basic rights." He had had in mind, presumably, the great case of *Brown vs. Board of Education of Topeka* (1945), which overthrew the "separate but equal" doctrine. Burger had worried too about Supreme Court decisions which depended on case-to-case judgment rather than the "mechanisms" provided by Congress. In sum, he had apparently feared judicial legislation. Burger was, however, surrounded by acknowledged civil libertarian justices, and decisions under his leadership took unexpected turns. He favored "equality" (*q.v.*), a controversial word in the conservative lexicon. In his case, it meant approval of busing (*q.v.*), though the tortuous ways in which the issue led forced modifications of judgment. The Burger Court concluded (1972) that capital punishment (*q.v.*) as administered by the states was unconstitutional (*Furman vs. Georgia*). It concluded that questions of school prayer, abortion, pornography and busing (*q.v.*) could not be left to the states. They required national—Supreme Court—adjudication. Such was the authority of constitutionalists that Raoul Berger (*q.v.*), a maverick law scholar at Harvard University, created a sensation by concluding that the Court had ceased being a interpreter of the Constitution and became an "activist" Court. The problem, however, was only partly with the Supreme Court. Congress was lax in its willingness to create laws which would give national direction to national findings. As a result, the Court found itself able to take on a docket of cases which finally all but overwhelmed it. James J. Kilpatrick (*q.v.*), an influential conservative journalist and commentator, observed that the Court had so broadened "the rights of an accused" that it had invited "frivolous petitions from jailhouse lawyers." While Robert Nisbet's *Prejudices* (*q.v.*) perceived "no end to the process of creating victims who overflowed the Court's dockets," state courts were being petitioned, and were responding variously, to do something for victims of crime, inequity, and abuse. Capital punishment was reinstituted in various states, and roused growing debate in others. Public prayers in schools was in continuous debate, and given limited opportunity in some states, despite monitoring by the American Civil Liberties Union and other interested groups. The question of when fetuses became human beings continued to be controversial, and opponents of abortion brought it constantly to the nation's attention. Overshadowing the Court was the fact that by the mid-1980s five of the nine Justices, including the Chief Justice, were over 75 years old. Burger himself seemed to Court-watchers an "elusive" figure, less peremptory in his personal judgment of what the Constitution implied or ought to imply, but by no means a firmly "conservative" justice. He did appear to be a firm Republican, and, though he was in evidently sound health, this raised questions whether he might not choose to resign before the Reagan Administration had run its course, in order to give the President a chance to appoint another younger, certainly conservative Chief Justice to head a drive for change in the Court's direction. L. Friedman and F. Israel, *The Justices of the United States Supreme Court* (1969); F. G. Lee, ed., *Neither Conservative nor Liberal: The Burger Court on Civil Rights and Civil Liberties* (1983). See also Legal Services Corporation.

**"Surplus Value,"** a Marxist concept which held that capitalists deprived workers of a large part of what they produced and deserved to receive in order to purchase equivalents through funds. Capitalists, weighed down with unearned profits and unable to sell their goods to their underpaid employees, had to look elsewhere for customers, and so were driven to imperialist and war (*q.v.*) measures, creating at home an army of defrauded workers with nothing to lose but their chains. The Marxist (*q.v.*) analysis failed to take into account the value of enterprise, the achievements of reformers, the marvels of technology, and the force of competition, cooperation, and "welfare capitalism" (*q.v.*)—all serving to render simplistic the "surplus value" formula. Problems with unions, productivity, (*qq.v.*) and other aspects of labor also worked against the "surplus value" hypothesis.

**Surrogates**, or "clients," an increasingly employed concept as governments and groups disported themselves in behalf of causes, and with arms and other assistance provided by more affluent or influential powers or people. Thus, conservative governments of Guatemala fighting left-wing forces could be seen as surrogates for United States interests in the Caribbean, with a 10,000-member U. S. Southern Command based in Panama which permitted aid to be shifted in the area as needed. Surrogates assumed an Administration which could not survive without support. The pro-American Marcos Philippine government, however, rested on the assumption that its basic principles assured support—that the Americans required Marcos as much as he required them. "Third World" governments favoring "Marxist" principles were more patently pawns—surrogates—for Soviet interests as in Angola, where Cuban soldiers sustained black revolutionaries seeking to demoralize and undermine the Republic of South Africa (*q.v.*). Many Soviet-dominated areas such as Afghanistan (*q.v.*), Czechoslovakia, and Latvia had what were called "puppet" governments by their foes, but which accomplished surrogate ends for the Soviets—and could be distinguished from Yugoslavia, Albania, and Poland (*q.v.*), where leaders either directly defied Soviet causes, or felt it necessary to appear to do so.

**Symbolic Acts**, highly developed during the 1960s, and, as furthered by the rise in television viewing by millions of people, made into an art form by partisans able to generate publicity for their causes. Symbolic acts built on the experiences of "guerrilla theater," which had utilized actors and mimes who claimed to represent the poor, "oppressed" women, and the like. For example, in the 1960s radical protesters against American involvement in Vietnam burned their draft cards as symbolic acts of protest. The effort was to find succinct actions which vividly embodied causes or statements. It was closely studied by Black leaders who found television exposure for scenes of Negroes in shabby surroundings, children in rags, persons who claimed to have suffered outrage at the hands of gangs or to have been deprived of their vote. The drama of "Reaganvilles," thought to be the modern equivalent of "Hoovervilles" (*q.v.*), appeared not to have been effective. Overall, it seemed that the value of symbolic acts to partisans of several kinds would have to be thought through with a better grasp of the content of changing times.

# T

**Tabletalk of the Late Samuel Taylor Coleridge** (1835), edited by Henry Nelson Coleridge, Coleridge's nephew and son-in-law. He made assiduous notes of Coleridge's famous conversations in the last twelve years of his life following his long and eccentric slavery to opium. Although he was incapable of a systematic life and writing, following the poetic era which made him famous, Coleridge traveled, read, and met innumerable persons in all ways of life. His views, founded in mysticism, poetic fancies, and often detailed reading in religion, biography, and aesthetics made for an inexhaustible fountain of views and judgments, mainly serving the most conservative sense of duty and ideals, though certainly in large part an apology for the helpless and irresponsible life he had lived. Coleridge believed that the "result of [his] system will be to show that, so far from the world being a goddess in petticoats, it is rather the devil in a strait waistcoat." He opposed the abolition of the French hereditary peerage. He talked of the ideal Tory and the ideal Whig, and would have wanted to "trace the rise, the occasion, the progress, and the necessary degeneration of the Whig spirit of compromise, even down to the profound ineptitudes of their party in these days." The fate of the national church occupied his mind with great intensity. He met a "loose, slack, not well-dressed youth" in a lane near Highgate, who was introduced to him as John Keats. They parted, but Keats soon returned to say: "Let me carry away the memory, Coleridge, of having pressed your hand." Coleridge later observed to his campanion, "There is death in that hand"; the consumption had showed itself distinctly. A single day's conversation, on May 15, 1833, brought out observations on Wycliffe, Luther, "Reverence for Ideal Truths," Johnson the Whig (not Dr. Johnson [*q.v.*]), Asgill, and James I.

**Taft, Robert A.** (1889-1953), American politician, "Mr. Republican," who represented a firm Republicanism in a New Deal era demoralizing to its aims and program. He attacked Franklin D. Roosevelt's (*q.v.*) readiness to spend, opposed intervention in World War II (*q.v.*)—but welcomed the United Nations (*q.v.*). Most famous of his legislative coups was the Taft-Hartley Act of 1947, intended as a curb on unwarranted labor power as represented by the National Labor Relations Act (1935) and the Federal Anti-Injunction Act (1932). Taft opposed Truman's entrance into the Korean (*q.v.*) conflict, protested Truman's confrontation with the steel industry (1952), and, though he approved aid to anti-Communist Turkey and Greece, was disappointed in the "Point Four" program of economic aid to underdeveloped countries. He disapproved of the Nuremberg Trials of captured Nazi leaders on criminal charges, which he feared might raise strange legal fruit. "Taft-Hartley," as it was universally known, slowed down and impeded union action, qualified unions' power to force workers to join them, and forced democratic procedures on unions. Although they fought back by all manner of tactics, the Act set up a standard of free choice which sustained conservatives during times difficult for free-enterprise ideals. Taft hoped to be the Republican nominee for President in 1952, but could not resist the party elements which thought Eisenhower (*q.v.*) a better choice. Taft was admired by principled conservatives. See *The Political Principles of Robert A. Taft*, by

Russell Kirk (*q.v.*) and James McClellan (1967); see also James T. Patterson, *"Mr. Republican"* (1972).

**Taft, William Howard** (1857-1930), American President, Chief Justice of the Supreme Court. He had been an "injunction judge" in his native Ohio, more ready than others to issue writs impeding strikes. As Governor General of the Philippines, he prided himself on his patronage toward what he saw as an inferior people. His road to the Presidency was paved with friendship for Theodore Roosevelt (*q.v.*), whose vigor and adroitness in behalf of his conservative following Taft did not inherit. Although, like Roosevelt, he was judicious in assessing the buccaneers of Wall Street and approved anti-trust legislation, he had no insight into even conservative labor aspirations. His son Robert Taft (*q.v.*), with his firm free-enterprise principles, better expressed the feelings of the most legitimate of social conservative forces. As Chief Justice of the Supreme Court (1921-1930) William Howard Taft expressed reasonably his old 1894 conviction that the Constitution made ours "a conservative government,...strongly buttressed by written law, against the attacks of anarchy, socialism, and communism." Praised as Chief Justice for his reorganization of the Judiciary, giving it greater power and flexibility, he worked within a framework of personal principles, as when he opposed President Harding's (*q.v.*) selection of Chief Justice of the New York Supreme Court Benjamin N. Cardozo to the U. S. Supreme Court because he might "herd with Holmes and Brandeis" (*qq.v.*)—"herd" being representative of Taft's class-minded vocabulary. As Chief Justice Taft maintained his defense of private property by endorsing injunction relief (*Truax v. Corrigan*, 257 U. S. 312 [1921]), calling forth a Brandeis dissent. Taft's other views, often mixing his own preferences with national need, embodied little more than an attempt to stop the growth of a nation become larger and more complex. Although Taft revered John Marshall (*q.v.*), he left little legacy in law to a nation which urgently required a working law.

**Taft-Hartley Act** (1947). A major conservative victory of the post-World War II era, it sought to put a curb on union (*q.v.*) expansion and consolidation during the war and to keep labor fluid and independent. It permitted the hiring of non-union people, stipulated a cooling-off period before strikes, stopped automatic deductions of employees' salaries for union use, demanded union official declarations of non-Communist affiliation, and set down other criteria ensuring freedom for workers and employers. Gallup polls traced the course of Taft-Hartley in public estimate, and found centrist opinion dominant: the public approved, but also approved a variety of changes. Although official labor fought the law without pause, its only result was the Landrum-Griffin Act of 1959, which excised the non-Communist affidavits and gave unions somewhat more leeway in prosecuting their strikes. Much that Taft-Hartley intended was frustrated in practice: union dues could be collected against an employee's will; he could find himself forced into the union; labor racketeers (*q.v.*) found ways to persuade workers to see union operations their way. Conservatives watched such matters closely and praised right-to-work (*q.v.*) advocates and freedom of choice in union affairs, yet saw a long road ahead to the free society.

**Taiwan**, see China

**Tammany Hall**, see Jacksonian Era

**Taney, Roger B.** (1777-1864), Chief Justice of the Supreme Court of the United States, appointed in 1835 following the death of John Marshall (*q.v.*). He is a notable example of a transitional (*q.v.*) figure, complicated by a Southern heritage which qualified both his liberalism and conservatism. Having rejected Federalism (*q.v.*), Taney became Attorney General in Andrew Jackson's Cabinet, as such approving Jackson's belief that he was not bound by the Supreme Court's interpretations of the Constitution. His removal of government deposits from the embattled Second Bank of the United States (*q.v.*) was as distinct an act of liberalism as the time produced, as was his 1837 decision in *Charles River Bridge v. Warren Bridge* which modified Marshall's more conservative *Dartmouth College* finding in 1819 protecting monopolies. The slavery controversy, however, brought out Taney's sectional and racial bias, and resulted in his momentous decision in the Dred Scott case (*q.v.*). *Ex Parte Merryman* (1861) was liberal on its face, defending as it did the rights of civilians during wartime, but, if followed, would have hobbled President Lincoln in his efforts to hold down and resist the secessionist operations. See C. W. Smith, Jr., *Roger B. Taney, Jacksonian Jurist* (1936), and Walker Lewis, *Without Fear or Favor: A Biography of Chief Justice Roger Brooke Taney* (1965).

**Tappan, Lewis** (1788-1873), American reformer, representative of business in its heroic age. He placed piety on the level with reform, and denied that the good man had a right to die rich. His conservative achievements were many, including development of the one-price system, the founding of the *Journal of Commerce*, and of the first credit-rating agency, as well as of churches, colleges, and missionary societies. His achievements as a reformer were even more formidable, involving abolitionist societies and journals, the subsidizing of a wide range of abolitionists and of abolitionist institutions: one of a line of distinguished conservatives not well remembered by advocates of conservatism in later decades. See also Filler, DASC.

**Tariffs**, a major issue in the nineteenth century, ranging Free Traders (*q.v.*) against Protectionists, in 1826 producing the grandly named "Tariff of Abominations," which John Randolph (*q.v.*) held had no purpose serving manufactures but to help manufacture a President. The South here held, with its Free Trade program, that it was defending freedom, and that Northern industrialists had no goal as Protectionists but to keep out of the country cheaper basic goods. In the post-Civil War years, the South, still favoring Free Trade, was joined by Democratic reformers who claimed to speak for working men and their families who needed cheaper woolens and food. William McKinley's high 1890 Tariff proudly presented itself as aiding home industries, from which presumably the worker gained in jobs and better wages; but a sense of injustice persisted into the Woodrow Wilson (*q.v.*) Administration, when tariff schedules were sharply diminished. However, World War I and German submarines rendered them meaningless. The fact that war-time prosperity and increased technology brought "good times" helped underscore that tariffs were but one unit in a nation's economic well-being. Republican tariffs in the 1920s were nationalistic and protectionist. How much they contributed to growing imbalances which would result in the stock market crash of 1929 and subsequent Depression (*q.v.*) were matters of controversy, which new problems of unemployment, radicalism, and war diminished, and which a new prosperity and a matured welfareism (*q.v.*) diminished further. The precipitous urban decline, social "activism," and other problems of the 1960s added to radical changes in foreign affairs should have made tariffs an historical and specialized interest. The rise of Japanese and West German industries, and humiliations dealt the once-imperial American automobile (*q.v.*), created parochial suspicions inimical to Free Trade. Unions demanded Protection. A Republican Administration, however, which had to concern itself for American investments abroad, military friends, and other facts of international life, could not assume attitudes feasible in the 1890s or even in the 1920s. It appeared that, at the very least, reciprocal agreements would have to suffice to satisfy American unions (*q.v.*). American workers would have to produce more, and better, in competition with others for the patronage of consumers at home and abroad. Tom E. Terrill, *Tariff, Politics, and American Foreign Policy, 1874-1901* (1973); F. W. Taussig, *Tariff History of the United States* (1931); L. E. Lloyd, *Tariffs: The Case for Protection* (n.d.); William J. Ashley, *The Tariff Problem* (1920 ed.).

**Tarkington, Booth** (1869-1946), Indiana novelist, whose *Penrod* (1914) came to be identified as a watered-down *Tom Sawyer*. However, Tarkington's *The Magnificent Ambersons* (1918) served as the basis of an Orson Welles film, and *Alice Adams* (1921) was not only an extraordinary film vehicle for Katherine Hepburn, but focussed attention as a true life. John Chamberlain (*q.v.*), on his road back to conservatism, praised Tarkington as distinguished, but without providing substantive analysis of his work. Central to Tarkington's achievement was his *Growth* trilogy: *The Turmoil* (1915), *The Magnificent Ambersons* (1918), and *The Midlander* (1923). See James Woodress, *Booth Tarkington, Gentleman from Indiana* (1955).

**Tate, Allen**, see New Criticism

**Tawney, Richard H.**, see Commercialism; Equality

**Taxation**, see Filler, DASC. A key tenet of New Conservatives held that inordinate taxation no more than augmented the welfare state and socialism (*qq.v.*). Libertarians (*q.v.*) rejected the idea of an income tax. Oil interests argued that excessive taxation diminished their power for oil exploration and incentive, that it no more than augmented the government treasury without cutting prices or producing more oil. Although welfare perquisites took some of the air out of "bloated capitalists" stereotypes (*q.v.*), liberals fought a constant battle for Federal allotments for welfare, the arts, urban renewal, and employment. Depleted economies and tax revolts forced them, during the Reagan Administration, to focus on the military as over-endowed with funds, fighting tax cuts which diminished the state's capacity for spending. Conservative economists seemed to liberal ideologues (*q.v.*) committed to programs at the expense of people. Since their own strategies involved spending which was no longer feasible, they sought new formulas denouncing economies of "greed" and arguing for a new relationship among government, industry, and labor which would somehow satisfy all three. The implication was that conservative government was operating against the interests of labor. Conservatives believed that tax cuts would bring back an energetic economy. Martin A. Larson, *Tax Rebellion, U. S. A.* (1973); R. Brandon, *Tax Politics* (1976); A. C. Harberger, *Taxation and Welfare* (1978); D. D. Kaufman, *The Tax Dilemma* (1978). See also Proposition XIII; Income Tax.

**Taylor, Frederick W.** (1856-1915), "father of scientific management." As an industrial engineer he introduced efficiency techniques in factory operations which Henry Ford (*q.v.*) made famous with his assembly line (*q.v.*). It was welcomed by those seeking efficiency and production, denounced by unionists (*q.v.*) who feared the "speed-up" system. See Taylor's *Principles of Scientific Management* (1911). Praised under Stalin (*q.v.*) and by Communists everywhere was "Stakhonovism" in the 1930s, named for a worker who presumably extracted extraordinary quantities of coal in Soviet mines, inspired by Soviet dreams of production quotas, but no more than the "speed-up" itself under watchful foremen's eyes.

**Telegraph, The** (London), with the decline of *The Times*, the leading conservative paper in England, influential among American conservative journalists and theoreticians. A supporter of the Thatcher (*q.v.*) Government, it found little to resist or repudiate, in her policies of denationalizing industry ("privatization"), curbing trade-union perquisites, bolstering defense, cooperating with the European Economic Community (EEC) without relinquishing British advantages, and maintaining obligations in Northern Ireland despite Irish Republican Army (IRA) terror. The American conservative program being somewhat similar, the *Telegraph* was generally cordial toward the Reagan Administration, though free to criticize when it felt necessary. It took pride in "Peter Simple" (*q.v.*) and in Garland's editorial cartoons, as well as in a host of journalists and conservative Members of Parliament whose columns covered religious, political, and military subjects, and also manners and the lore of the countryside. The *Telegraph* featured significant atrocities as news, but maintained old traditions in limiting news about simple crime and events. In debate with the liberal *Guardian* and *Observer* and the socialist *New Statesman* it employed cold, exact language, and mixed in irony as occasion suggested. There was no comparable journal in the United States. See, however, *Washington Times*.

**Television**, see Filler, DASC, momentous in conservative affairs as well as liberal. It was felt by many conservatives that television had become more an instrument for liberal causes and attitudes than for conservative.

Liberals had learned to use images against conservatives and their causes by photographic techniques and by choice of materials, personalities, and skills of presentation (Edith Efron, *The News Twisters* [1973]; Efron and C. Chambers, *How CBS Tried to Kill a Book* [1973]). The role of television as a soporific, a hypnotic force, a mind-numbing, manipulative instrument struck many observers as alarming (R. Stavins, *Television Today: The End of Communication and the Death of the Country* [1971]). The feelings of TV commentators, their roles in elections, their attitudes toward Republicans and Democrats furnished materials for comment which took form slowly. Their attitudes toward the Watergate crisis and Vietnam (*qq.v.*) affected the nation. Republicans from Nixon onward often utilized radio to reach their constituents, as being cheaper, better directed, and less subject to liberal bias. (Giraud Chester et al., *Television and Radio* [1978 ed.].) William F. Buckley, Jr. (*q.v.*) was a major triumph for conservatives in television as in other fields, but there were relatively few such triumphs. By 1980, with Reagan victorious and able to assert himself on television as earlier conservatives had not, light shone harder on the medium and its directors than ever before. Liberals were called upon to explain themselves by conservatives. Key programs were examined for format and presentation by conservatives. The weighty responsibility of television to let the people judge became more evident. So basic a point as announcing "projection" of winners before the polls had closed, thus discouraging masses of people from voting, was seen as unfair by both liberals and conservatives. The indignation of press and TV for having been kept out of Grenada (*q.v.*), when troops made a surprise landing on its shores, called up memories of Vietnam (*q.v.*) and what conservatives regarded as bias in media coverage there. By the mid-1980s the national television networks were even beginning to evaluate their own news-gathering operations, with as yet uncertain results. H. J. Skornia, *Television and Society* (1965); D. Cater and R. Adler, *Television as a Social Force* (1975); Robert S. Alley, *Television: Ethics for Hire?* (1977); Jay G. Blumler and Denis McQuail, *Television in Politics* (1969); Joseph Keeley, *The Left-Leaning Antenna: Political Bias in Television* (1971), the last a publication of Arlington House (*q.v.*).

**Temperance**, a development in American conservative reform which gave evidence that blanket approval or disapproval of historical developments could only result in poisonous conclusions, useful to narrow partisans. Temperance originally asked only moderation in drinking habits, and could be readily contrasted with the results of intemperance, especially when the latter affected not only the individual but his family. The ready appearance, however, of degraded people, soaked in gin and spirits, suggested to austere social leaders the need for more than temperance. Welch Grape Juice was created as a substitute for wine, though wine was well-regarded in many middle-class homes. Abolitionists were almost always teetotalers, though to scorn their cause because of their fear of alcohol is to debase American history. Prohibitionists entered into politics with notorious results. As notorious, however, became the results of triumphant anti-Prohibitionists. With drinking encouraged in the nation and drunk-drinking a deadly menace on the nation's highways, moderation in drinking seemed a plausible goal for drinkers and non-drinkers. The recognition of the potentially addictive nature of alcohol created a renewed awareness of the dangers of intemperance. Drinkers contended that alcoholism was a "disease," rather than a failure of will or degradation of society. See also Prohibition. Sean D. Cashman, *Prohibition: The Lie of the Land* (1981); M. E. Lender and J. K. Martin, *Drinking in America: A History* (1982).

**Tenth Amendment**, one of the hopes of conservatives wishing to buttress States Rights (*q.v.*) and slow down or limit Supreme Court (*q.v.*) decisions which prevented individual states from responding differently to national questions. Amendment X stipulated that "the powers not delegated to the United States by the Constitution, nor prohibited by it to the States, are reserved to the States respectively, or to the people." Since many of the vital

issues had been judged by the Supreme Court in ways troubling to conservatives, they sought decisions which encouraged state independence. They seemed to find one in a 1974 decision (*National League of Cities v. Usery*) which held unconstitutional a 1974 amendment to the Fair Labor Standards Act extending Federal minimum wage and hour regulations to state and local government employees. Although further challenges to Congressional legislation were turned back by the Court, they were interpreted in so narrow a way as not to shake the apparent strengthening of state independence. In 1983, however, the Court reviewed a Wyoming decision depending on its *National League of Cities* decision and holding that the Federal Age Discrimination in Employment Act did not require Wyoming to keep employees deemed too old for their jobs. The *Cities* decision had passed on a 5 to 4 vote. The Wyoming decision reversed the count, 5 to 4 against Wyoming. This practically negated the usefulness of the *Cities* decision. The close vote suggested that any further developments involving the Amendment would depend on whether new appointees to the Supreme Court would be favorable to its use. See also Bill of Rights.
Rights.

**Teresa, Mother** (1910- ), Roman Catholic nun world famous for her works of charity. Born Agnes Gomxha Bozaxhim in what became Yugoslavia, she joined the Sisters of Loretto in 1928, beginning a career of charity and compassion which made her a world figure. Her missions took her to Ireland and India. She opened homes for the destitute and for lepers, and received the Nobel Peace Prize in 1979. During the awards ceremonies and subsequent tours, full media coverage was given her opinions: her sweeping repudiation of abortion, her lack of interest in women's rights activism. In view of the reverence she was accorded, resentment appeared, particularly among some American nuns who disagreed with her conservative views. But her reputation continued unassailable through the mid-1980s.

**Terrorism**, see Filler, DASC. Once identified with the deeds of revolutionaries claiming to act in the name of oppressed people, and risking martyrdom to fell high officials or industrialists. The Soviet Union and Red China, with records of and rationales for terror, and the rise of Third World countries, whose emergence has been preceded by terror campaigns, created new conditions for terror and new terrorist types, often with surrogate (*q.v.*) resources and rewards. In the six British northern counties of Ireland, there were 43,000 violent incidents and 2,300 deaths between 1969 and 1983, involving Protestant Loyalists and the Catholic minority's Irish Republican Army. Notable were the atrocities which spared no one and which raised murderers almost from the cradle. To speak of terrorists as soldiers or as patriots was to make a mockery of language. On the Continent, in the democracies, new terrorist gangs, mainly left-wing, usually of good family and education, engaged in bombings and other acts which took a heavy toll of innocents, in order to bring their countries' governments into disrepute. In the main, they had no program for righting society's alleged wrongs. Their plan, such as it was, was to raze social bonds and considerations and to take over from there. Their foes were men like Sandro Pertini, president of Italy, who had served time in prison for his opposition to Fascism. The Palestine Liberation Organization was a key organization, dedicated to the destruction of Israel, and practicing unrestrained atrocities to call its cause to the world's attention. Behind such organizations was often the Soviet Union, and such governments as that of Libya, itself directly engaged in terrorism against dissenting Libyans abroad. Peter Duignang, a fellow of the Hoover Institution (*q.v.*), described terrorism as a growth industry, with such notable practitioners as the international terrorist "Carlos," and enterprises everywhere. From 1968 to 1980, political kidnapings in the West rose from 1 to 401, bombings from 79 to 21,371, hijacking from 3 to 173, letter-bombings from 8 to 470, and armed attacks from 12 to 278. Such matters were confined to the West because operators sensed the irresolution of Western authorities, the legal processes which worked in their favor, and the availability of friends and collaborators. They knew that, in the Soviet Union, they and theirs would be fought with unlimited counter-terror. Liberals were more prone to find reasons for terrorists than conservatives. The PLO received international credibility from the United Nations and from numerous nations; its leader, Yasir Arafat, was even received by the Pope. An exasperated Father Greeley (*q.v.*) asked if he would be recognizing, similarly, the IRA. Liberals and conservatives tended to be selective in their sympathies, with liberals favoring opponents of conservative regimes and conservatives favoring the opponents of Marxist regimes throughout the world. The shooting of the Pope in St. Peter's Square (1981) aroused universal consternation and the revelation that it might well have been planned within the Kremlin. There was speculation that, for reasons of policy, the U. S. Government was curbing discussion of the somber act. The democracies worked to impede the plots of terrorists, and succeeded in slowing down or stopping some of their operations. Paradoxically, doing so required that they infringe to a degree on privacy and individual judgment. But these had long been eroded by frayed family ties, diluted patriotism, and other social impulses attacking cohesion and civilized expectations. They would have to be renewed, if terrorists were to be made outlaws in human society, and differences between war and terror relearned. James W. Clarke, *American Assassins* (1982); William Eggers, *Terrorism: The Slaughter of Innocents* (1975); Walter Laqueur, *Terrorism Reader: A Historical Anthology* (1975); C. Dobson and R. Payne, *The Terrorists: Their Weapons, Leaders, and Tactics* (1979); Claire Sterling, *The Time of the Assassins* (1983).

**Thatcher, Margaret** (1925- ), Prime Minister of Great Britain since 1979. As Conservative Party leader she came to power with a mandate to turn back the program which labor had built and directed. She denied that she wished to disassemble the Welfare State, only its dire aspects. As the London *Economist* summarized, she believed "that the best help was self-help, that work deserved reward, not taxation, that the cake must be baked before it was distributed, that there was no free welfare lunch; that Whitehall or tripartite consensus-makers cannot know best, that small business is better than state corporations, that government cannot regulate the economy but only control key factors like the money supply, with effects that others would ignore at their peril; that prices matter more than jobs, that getting real jobs meant cutting phony ones; that the economy needed surgery not aspirins, and that Keynes (*q.v.*) was no cure but part of the disease." But this was only the economic aspect of her challenge. She was a woman, with a husband named Dennis, for whom she prepared breakfast, and a son whom she deeply cared for. She spoke well and under pressure in a Parliament where speaking effectively was a vital part of the job. She was subjected to scorn, suspicion, innuendo, satirical cartoons, and vulgar attacks by Labor and union foes; there were even attempts to derogate her as a woman, which gained little public favor. She was the Iron Lady, to be sure, but personable and clear in her program and presentations. Although she tacked and swerved in pursuit of her goals, her message was clear. It became evident following the American elections in 1980 that it was not far from that which the new President Reagan displayed for his countrymen. Great Britain intended curbs on nationalization and Marxist goals, and America intended its equivalent. Mrs. Thatcher sponsored "Victorian values" and, despite parody and attack, it appeared that she had not lost stature by the avowal. As leader during the Falkland Islands crisis in 1982, involving war with Argentina thousands of miles from home, she was upbraided as a bloody adventuress who placed Great Britain at risk, unwilling to accept the "mediation" of the United Nations. With British victory, she was accused of having "tried, quite deliberately, to cover up her administration's nakedness by wrapping herself in the Falklands' bunting" (according to David Steel, Liberal Party leader). Despite efforts by labor and the new Social Democratic Party, the nation returned Mrs. Thatcher to power in a general election. Whatever the future, she had made her mark, nor only for conservatism, but for the intrinsic merits of feminine goals her tenure had inevitably involved.

**"Thaw"** (Soviet), see Solzhenitsyn, A. I.

**Theory of Education in the United States**, see Nock, A. J.

**"There You Go Again**," Ronald Reagan's memorable response in his 1980 pre-election debate with Jimmy Carter. The phrase was repeated around the country, and even in private conversation, reminding hearers of the vagueness and repetitiveness of the Carter presentation. It was an example of accidental or deliberate phrasing which caught the sensibilities of the American public.

**They'd Rather Be Right: Youth and Conservatism** (1963), by Edward Cain, a serious effort to consider the prospects for conservatives to become social and political factors in America. Written before the great eruption of anti-American radicalism in the 1960s, it operated from liberal premises and expectations. It identified much of conservatism with Fundamentalism (*q.v.*) and treated Robert Welch, Ayn Rand, and Senator Goldwater (*q.v.*) as almost similar in belief. It was limited by not being able to foresee the proliferation of civil libertarian causes and organizations, the radical turmoil on the campuses, or the deep involvement in Vietnam (*q.v.*) and its consequences. It thought conservatives overemphasized their anti-Communism; there was little Communism in America, and the fixation on the Soviet Union confused perspective. Liberals were smug about their principles, according to Cain, but theirs was the accepted and acceptable tradition. William F. Buckley, Jr. (*q.v.*) was witty and interesting, but not only had he committed himself to the cause of McCarthy (*q.v.*), he had quarreled in divisive ways with officials and publications of his own Catholic Church. The future of conservatism, such as it was, was not with him but with Peter Viereck and Clinton Rossiter (*qq.v.*). Cain conducted useful inquiries into campus attitudes and "Young Men and Business and Politics," highlighting many individuals whose names have faded from the local and national spotlight.

**Thinking about Crime** (1975), by James Q. Wilson, a conservative who, however, noted even-handedly fallacies projected by conservatives as well as liberals. These included too great faith in criminals, as well as over-expectations from "law and order." Interest groups—police, prisoners, unions—blurred the scene. No solutions would erase crime, but, for example, a 20 percent fall in crime would mean thousands of fewer assaults. Some analysts equated predatory crime with corruption (*q.v.*): but predatory crime undermined society at its base. Those emphasizing "root causes" (*q.v.*) could not face facts, such as that many unemployed and poor did not want to work, and that most poor people were not criminals. A key element in crime was repeaters; were they handled properly, crime statistics would fall dramatically. Uniform sentencing—sentencing taken away from local magistrates—would help keep repeaters off the streets. On the death penalty (*q.v.*), Wilson counseled not deterrence, which was problematic, but justice.

**Third Parties** (see Filler, DASC), most often radical in some aspect of their purpose or program, and as often set upon some highly particular purpose, as with the nativist (*q.v.*) groups which feared immigrants and sought to persuade voters that they should be protected from them. The American Party in the early 1850s provided troubled Democrats and Whigs with a halfway house in which they could struggle as Southerners and Northerners, while they sensed what the direction of politics respecting slavery might be. The later Prohibition (*q.v.*) Party seemed a threat to the major parties in a close election. Embittered conservatives in 1975, despairing of the Republican Party, sought to explore possibilities for a new Conservative Party; see Rusher, William A. See also Wallace, George; Thurmond, Strom.

**Third World, The**, see Equality

**Thirties, The**, catastrophically in contrast with the "affluent" (*q.v.*) Twenties (*q.v.*), despite the serious pockets of social trouble and dissatisfaction in such areas as textiles, coal production, and union (*q.v.*) differences with industrialists during the Twenties. Herbert Hoover's (*q.v.*) bold expectations of a great American era following his election in 1928 were rudely shaken by a market crash of unmistakable proportions, and a continuing stalemate which defied his bravest efforts to hold the line for normal values. John Kenneth Galbraith's studiously urbane account of *The Great Crash, 1929* (1954) had fairly legitimate fun with the labored efforts of politicians, businessmen, and economists to speak and act in the crisis. Although Franklin D. Roosevelt (*q.v.*) had little more knowledge of economics than Hoover, he did indicate a greater willingness to experiment. Although it has been theorized that Hoover would ultimately have done what Roosevelt did, his abrupt action against the "Bonus Marchers" in 1932 not only lost him an opportunity to show special regard for the veterans, but also gave alarming suggestions of intransigence in a tense time. Radicals were perceiving American capitalism in trauma and filling the air with promises. But Roosevelt's "New Deal" experiments took the edge off such lure as they could dangle before anxious citizens. Meanwhile, Twenties (*q.v.*) literature had been deflated. Although the general public sought glamorous escape in musicals and fantasies, the stage was filled with radicalism as well as romance, Clifford Odets's *Waiting for Lefty* as well as light comedies. Although conservative solutions to trouble overlapped into the dark era, amid ominous words at home and abroad from Fascists and Communists, conservatism as a working philosophy was in short supply. A worker for Roosevelt's Works Progress Administration (WPA) might indeed do an honest day's work, but he was working by leave of the government. A farmer caught in a drought of the time or ruined by the Mississippi River flood might feed on emergency funds, but there was no proud, independent farmer here such as American dreams cherished. Yet young Ronald Reagan (*q.v.*) at the time—and others like him—though approving of humanitarian and economic needs, began to notice how soon bureaucratic (*q.v.*) elements entered into the operation of Federal regulations. The economic crisis continued, and was complicated by ominous possibilities abroad: fascism (*q.v.*) in Germany, Italian aggression in Ethiopia, unnatural bloodletting in the Soviet Union. Although the 1930s produced the best of John Steinbeck, Archibald MacLeish, Meyer Levin, William Saroyan, Sidney Hook, and Pare Lorenze, it was not a happy time, and few people drew inspiration from it. And yet it was significant that Hoover's reputation revived with time, and that many who were in despair when Roosevelt died, picked up life again and recognized, to a degree, that there was a difference between welfare (*q.v.*) in despair and welfare as offered by Roosevelt's successors during affluent times. The heritage of the 1930s promised to be different for liberals and conservatives. Filler, ed., *The Anxious Years* (1964). See also 1933.

**Thirties, 1930-1940 in Great Britain, The**, (1940), by Malcolm Muggeridge (*q.v.*), helpful in tracing his development to devout conservatism. Surveying the Thirties, he saw a Church which abided by conventions and anti-conventions, rather than by religious tenets, and a political establishment which veered between nationalistic appeals and slogans which followed dire economic news, unable to move beyond the "illusions of Liberalism." Yet he saw Stalin (*q.v.*) as a tyrant, and scorned British Communists who raged at the Nazi trial of Communists, but accepted as real the staged Soviet trials of disgraced Communists. Muggeridge already had the large view of life in which portentous figures passed from headlines into obscurity. He observed with sad irony England's movement from pacifism to rearmament, from interest and even admiration of Hitler to a sense of fate, as the dictator absorbed Austria, Czechoslovakia, and divided Poland with his erstwhile foe, Stalin. England, which had swallowed Mussolini's war on Ethiopia and rationalized Japan's movements in Mongolia, had in effect stood by while the League of Nations had expired. In 1940 it was preparing to fight for its life.

**Thomism**, basic in conservative Catholic (*q.v.*) doctrine and philosophical outlook, but also well-respected in conservative thought generally, as representing dependence on God's will and certainly that it could be perceived through the exercise of reason. St. Thomas Aquinas (1225-1274) himself was a force bridging the distance between the pagan Aristotle (*q.v.*)

and Christianity, and held faith and reason to be equally gifts of Deity. His *Summa Theologica* was interwoven with religious debates, but also with understandings of societal rights and duties, affecting theorists from David Hume to Leo Strauss (*q.v.*). Thomism was often at the base, when not on the surface, of conservative outlooks and projections, as in the work of Harry V. Jaffa (*q.v.*). Jacques Maritain (*q.v.*) sought to apply Thomism to contemporary problems: see also his *St. Thomas Aquinas* (1958). G. K. Chesterton (*q.v.*) solved one of his Father Brown plots by exposing a false priest through noticing that he had denied reason. See also Etienne Gilson, *The Christian Philosophy of St. Thomas Aquinas* (1956).

**Thurmond, Strom** (1903- ), American political figure, States Rights (*q.v.*) proponent who held that his cause was the Constitution, rather than opposition to civil rights (*q.v.*). By force of personality, he made an impact on his state and national issues. A strong, virile man with a good war record, he won the governorship of South Carolina in 1946. In 1948, denouncing President Truman's move toward civil-rights legislation, he ran for President on the States Rights (*q.v.*) ticket, making the best third-party showing till that time. In 1954 he made national news by winning a United States senatorship on a write-in vote. In Washington he helped form a Southern bloc which issued a "Declaration of Constitutional Principles," and in 1957 set a record for filibustering in an attempt to stop the passage of the Civil Rights Bill of that year. Thurmond resisted with some success efforts to curb armed forces educational efforts to inform the public of the threat of Communism, and carefully followed the crisis over Soviet attempts to introduce weapons dangerous to American security in Cuba. He criticized American foreign policy as a "no-win" policy which influenced conservative approaches. In 1964 he joined the Republican party and fought on Barry Goldwater's (*q.v.*) side, winning South Carolina for his candidacy. An early opponent of force except as it comported with law, he created a persuasive public image of sincerity, as when he argued that there was more segregation in New York than in his own state, using charts which spelled out the population distribution. A. Lachicotte, *Rebel Senator Strom Thurmond* (1967).

**Time**, see Luce, Henry R.

**Times, The** (London), once one of the great conservative papers of the world, distinguished by its precision of language—critics said, affectionately, that it read as though translated from the Latin—its distinguished letter columns, and its unequivocal loyalty to traditional England and Empire. The modification of the one and dissolution of the other, and the turmoil at home caused by welfare burdens, shaken loyalties, troubled industries, immigration from former British colonies such as Pakistan and India, and Labor policies intensifying the effects of all the preceding, caused the *Times* to lose much of its individuality and purpose. Economic difficulties with labor and staff acted to undercut further its base of operations. The *Times* was eventually purchased by the Australian newspaper magnate Rupert Murdoch. See also *Telegraph, The* (London).

**Tipping**, a post-Civil War phenomenon which persisted as a middle-class problem in values. It transgressed "waste not, want not" principles. It suggested "conspicuous consumption," such as had earned Thorstein Veblen's contempt. The impersonal city raised problems in civility and ostentation which could not be as readily institutionalized as it was abroad, where the *pour boire* (for drinking) was established, and even added to dining charges. William Dean Howells (*q.v.*) provoked arguments by questioning tipping as demeaning of honest workmanship; and quarrels were precipitated as service industries built in tipping perquisites as part and even major part of salaries. Americans abroad and soldiers in countries with economies ruined by war or with no economies to ruin found problems in tipping created by traditions or expectations, or simple greed. Jean S. Wilson, *Tipping* (1965).

**Tocqueville, Alexis De** (1805-1859), author of the classic *Democracy in America* (in French, 1835), which has drawn generation after generation because of the vividness of his contacts and observations and his social and philosophical generalizations respecting the American character. Tocqueville was a liberal who believed democracy was inevitable, not only in the United States but in Europe, and himself was associated with the French revolution of 1848. Nevertheless, conservatives have claimed him as one of their own, because of his unvarnished reports on American conditions and his evident hope that the pressures of equality would not degrade civilization. His famous chapter on Presidents as being inevitably mediocre can be compared with Henry Adams's treatment of the theme in his *Democracy*. See also Bryce, James; Grund, F.D.

**Toledano, Ralph De** (1916- ), American journalist. From a background of socialism and interest in music, he brought a variety of talents to bear on conservative concerns. He co-edited *Jazz Information* (1938-1939), and served as associate editor of the socialist *New Leader* (1941-1943). He was managing editor of *Plain Talk* (1946-1947), and publicity director for the International Ladies Garment Workers Union (1947-1948). Toledano served *Newsweek* in various posts from 1948 to 1960. He then became a syndicated columnist for King Features. Meanwhile, he had also become a contributing editor for the *National Review* (*q.v.*). With Victor Lasky (*q.v.*) he wrote *Seeds of Treason* (1950), covering the Alger Hiss-Whittaker Chambers (*q.v.*) confrontation. He contributed to *The Goldwater Story* (1964), and to *Nixon* (1956) and *One Man Alone: Richard M. Nixon* (1969). Toledano co-edited *The Conservative Papers* (1964), wrote *J. Edgar Hoover: The Man in His Time* (1973) and *Hit and Run: The Ralph Nader Story* (1975). Although his verses and continuing interest in music did not win significant attention, they helped to define his style and approach.

**Tolkien, J. R. R.** (1892-1973), British philologist, Oxford professor, friend of C. S. Lewis and Charles Williams (*qq.v.*). He studied myths and language formations in Northern lands and resolved to write a saga of his own, locating it in Middle Earth. His creation *The Hobbit* (1937) opened the way for the extraordinary success of his trilogy, *The Lord of the Rings* (1954-1955), which secular critics hardly knew how to handle, but which were welcomed by religious intellectuals, and read by students who were not concerned for the theology their mentors traced in them. It was the story-line which disturbed esthetic critics, who were unmoved by Tolkien's own fascination with names and new words, and wondered about the validity and depth of his evil and good people, their goals and substance. If the musings of elves, dwarfs, hobbits, and men were uneventful, and the songs Tolkien made up dull, if the battles with the miserable orcs did not have the sharpness and persuasiveness of real battles, why did the young in many countries read of them? One response, for those who were not taken with the saga of Middle Earth, was that Tolkien represented escape from an ominous and perhaps doomed industrial civilization; and that, with all its intricate linguistic artifacts, *The Lord of the Rings* did not present such a challenge of imagination as did Sir Thomas Malory's *La Morte D'Arthur*. However, considering the Christian ideals which Tolkien's admirers found in his work, which moved them and which may well have moved a portion of his readers, it appeared that there might be more interior movement in his protagonists than skeptics discerned, and that this might carry Tolkien's writings beyond his era. See references in *Myth, Allegory, and Gospel*; see also H. Carpenter, ed., *The Letters of J. R. R. Tolkien* (1981).

**Tories**, in America forebears of later conservatives who emerged under commercial auspices, as from John Jacob Astor to John D. Rockefeller (*q.v.*) or as from such conservative idealists as Ralph Adams Cram (*q.v.*). The irony surrounding Tories was that they had to be repudiated by many of their descendants who saw themselves as patriots (*q.v.*), committed to the revolution of 1776. Over the years they have received some justice and softening of lineaments, as well as attention in the historical fiction of Kenneth Roberts; see his *Oliver Wiswell* (1940). See also Hutchinson, Thomas.

**Tories and Aristocracy**, see *Aristocracy, the*

*Transition from 1832 to 1867* by O. F. Christie

**Tory Party (England)**, popular name for the Conservative Party (*q.v.*), with its roots in loyalty to the Crown and identification with the Church of England. It prized country gentlemen, made Bolingbroke (*q.v.*) great, but fell with him. It opposed freedom for the American colonies, and was excited by the French Revolution (*q.v.*) to a firm Establishmentarianism. The rising democracy of the early nineteenth century, capped by the Reform Bill of 1832, caused turbulence and change in its membership which reached fulfillment under Disraeli (*q.v.*). It struggled for form and philosophy before it emerged as the Conservative Party. W. H. Speck, *Tory and Whig* (1970); William J. Wilkinson, *Tory Democracy* (1971); John Biggs Davison, *Tory Lives* (1952).

**Tory Socialism**, see Disraeli, Benjamin; Tory Party

**"Totalitarian States,"** see "Authoritarian States"

**Tradition**, a major conservative concern, yet requiring close handling by conservatives who chose to work at current effectiveness. Thus, although there were long traditions of capital punishment, school prayer, opposition to abortion, a sense of Christian priority in law and expectation, and regard for Anglo-Saxon roots, new conditions required conservative competitors to bend their arguments to show awareness of minority elements whose stake in such traditions might be less than their own, and indeed might transgress their very own traditions. The diminished historical factor in public controversy forced an emphasis on what the Founding Fathers (*q.v.*) were alleged to have thought, on what "human rights" (*q.v.*) were supposed to involve, and on sheer numbers and influence. The evidently changing nature of human relations and international necessities paradoxically worked positively for tradition, because of the necessity to find reason for giving relatively uprooted groups programs which helped their case in dealing with other groups. Since traditions were mainly cultural, an effective use of traditions would have called for more knowledgable use of distinguished artifacts in literature, folklore, memoirs, and other accreted materials. Thanks to the manipulative use of historical materials as in the work of E. L. Doctorow, politically motivated claims for interest groups, the creation of "fakelore," and other pseudo-cultural materials, the reconstruction of legitimate cultural social supports was slow in maturing. *Tradition*, by Edward Shils (1981) was an effort at defining its qualities. It noted that tradition was by no means confined to conservatives. There was a social tradition, a tradition of modernity, a "tradition" of the new. In addition, it could be noted that there was a powerful liberal tradition which intermingled with conservatism; an obvious example was that which had both separated and joined Thomas Jefferson and John Adams (*qq.v.*), but which neither party was able to handle with the sense of tradition required; see Filler, "Crimes and Blunders, but Merely Intellectual, after All," *University Bookman*, Winter, 1973.

**Tragic Sense of Life in Men and Nations, The**, see Unamuno, Miguel de

**Transcendentalism**, one of the greatest intellectual movements in America, inspiring to such figures as Ralph Waldo Emerson (*q.v.*), Henry D. Thoreau, Margaret Fuller, Bronson Alcott, Orestes Brownson (*q.v.*), and others among a small but highly influential group of writers and religious seekers. In its own, pre-Civil War time, it was seen as radical in its unwillingness to conform to traditional church doctrine and observances. It sought truth in nature, in German idealistic speculations, in inner light, in Eastern spiritual disciplines. All this disturbed conservatives but had the respect of the open-minded. In post-Civil War decades, the situation was reversed. Emerson's emphasis on self, on self-reliance, pleased conservatives faced by incoming hordes in cities and factories, who demanded attention as people in groups. Newer intellectuals grappling with the implications of Darwinism, and persuaded that "nature [was] red in tooth and claw," were more skeptical of Emerson's boundless optimism and joy in life. Henry James's *The Bostonians* (1886) was satiric regarding reform and reformers. He portrayed Bronson Alcott as a bumbling egotist. Harold Frederic protrayed abolitionists as mean-minded, small-town tyrants. E. W. Howe's *The Story of a Country Town* (1883) saw nothing but darkness at noon. As Emerson and his cohorts lost influence, they appeared as untrustworthy adventurers to new conservatives seeking a tradition of free enterprise and social stability. Aside from a few vagaries, such as youthful rebels of the 1960s imagining that Thoreau was their predecessor, the Transcendentalists appeared to require rediscovery for a new era. Perry G. Miller, ed., *Transcendentalists: An Anthology* (1950); M. Simon and T. H. Parsons, eds., *Transcendentalism and Its Legacy* (1966).

**Transition From Aristocracy, 1832-1867, The**, by O. F. Christie, an account of the first Reform Bill of 1832 , which "transferred the centre of gravity in the [British] Constitution from the Upper to the Lower House," held to be the decisive act which changed morals, customs, and expectations of all classes in Great Britain. It roused Radicals to demand more of the commercial-minded Whigs, and caused Tories to consider what could be done for the depressed classes. Between John Bright and Disraeli (*q.v.*), there were non-negotiable differences, but both—one for the towns, the other for the landed squires—changed England at the expense of the aristocrats. Christie, rich with anecdotes and regretful of change, saw in the rising suffrage a threat to standards and unity which would make for a second-rate nation. Yet his very account revealed vitality in all classes, constantly under each other's eyes, and with a Queen for whom there was no American parallel. American conservatives learned from Burke and Disraeli (*q.v.*), but there were no equivalent texts for Britishers to ponder and digest. The American Progressive (*q.v.*) Era was roughly equivalent to the British Liberal era, there being no American Liberal Party to stand between Labour and Conservatism; and in the 1930s the New Deal learned from John Maynard Keynes (*qq.v.*). American "aristocratic" families, such as the Roosevelts (*q.v.*), sought a democratic image, which a Winston Churchill (*q.v.*) did not require. Although appeal to tradition carried some weight in the United States in earlier Republican decades, it faded more steadily than in England in the twentieth century. "Sir Robert Peel was the first recognisably modern [conservative] leader.... He accepted the 1832 Reform Act and...a policy of cautious reform.... [His] party bears a clear resemblance to the party as we know it today; that of Lord Liverpool does not" (from F. F. Lindsay and Michael Harrington, *The Conservative Party 1918-1970* [1974]). See also Nigel Birch, *The Conservative Party* (1949); Keith Feiling, *Toryism* (1913); R. J. White, *The Conservative Tradition* (1950).

**Transitional Figures**. They cut across the social and political barriers, sometimes growing out of or enriching old attitudes, but not infrequently changing their characters abruptly, in effect creating new and contradictory careers with which social analysts were required to cope. Often the individual's changes were of such a nature that he existed in two versions. Thus, the Fulton Oursler who wrote *Behold This Dreamer!* (1924), in which H. L. Mencken (*q.v.*) appeared as without virtue, became the Fulton Oursler of *The Greatest Story Ever Told* (1949), a popular version of Jesus' life. John T. Flynn (*q.v.*), a highly respected liberal journalist and critic of capitalism, became the almost notorious author of *The Roosevelt Myth* (1948). The condition operates in reverse. C. Wright Mills put into motion an impressive sociological career involving research, judicious assessment, and the like in such books as *The New Men of Power* (1948)—analyzing "left" and "right" tendencies in labor—and even *White Collar* (1951), which saw middle-class America with something less than awe. He soon emerged as a fully based radical who earned the editorial plaudits of the Communist Herbert Aptheker. Such developments, illuminating as they were of the causes embraced or abandoned, had to be distinguished from social groundswells which took moderately opinioned people and turned them into abolitionists or abolitionist-sympathizers, or 1930s radicals who, once they had jobs in the war economy, gave up their "Marxism," threw their radical publications away, and took to worrying over government taxation policies. Although they were in transitional times they were hardly transitional figures. See also Neo-Conservative.

**Transportation,** a key factor bearing on changing social circumstances in post-Civil War America. Railroads not only contributed to the rapid growth of cities; they robbed farmers (*q.v.*) of their sense of being central to the economy by pitting them against the railroads which carried their food to market, and the world's goods to them. Railroads drew farmers's youth (*q.v.*) to the cities, taking from them labor and voting constituents. The automobile (*q.v.*) later played a similar role in permitting dissatisfied family members to find mobility and privacy in cars, and to leave the countryside for the city as opportunity and will permitted. Democratized air travel later affected all aspects of American prospects and points of view. D.V. Harper, *Transportation in America: Users, Carriers, Government* (1978).

**Treason**, see Filler, DASC. The subject was one of continuous adjustment, as definitions moved from the "higher law" of pre-Civil War years—duty to God being greater than duty to the Constitution (*q.v.*)—to a species of higher law which made it legitimate, and not only in the minds of direct traitors, to pass on secrets of American policy to Soviet agents; there was less regard in America for fascist agents. The new treason, which conservatives identified with liberalism, filled out its program with long views of history, other services to humanity, (such as Anthony Blunt's expertise in art), general hatred of McCarthyism, the alleged cunning and contrivances amounting to persecution by the FBI (*q.v.*), and the fact that the Soviets had been America's wartime ally. *The Nation*, in a lengthy effort to diminish R. Radosh's *The Rosenberg* (*q.v.*) *File*, complained of his overconcern for the facts, meaning to conservatives that the mere facts of treason did not take into account such other "facts" as the above. See also Hiss Case, The.

**Treason of the Intellectuals** (1927), by Julien Benda (1867-1956), French critic and novelist. He was repelled by what he saw as a movement among writers and philosophers who might have been expected to be in search of truth, but who had engaged their minds in political questions and shown themselves willing to abandon old prerogatives in behalf of party lines. With the increasing emergence of right-wing and left-wing apologists for fascism and Communism, the aptness of Benda's formulation became more and more evident. It established itself as a constant in intellectual life. Malcolm Muggeridge's (*q.v.*) autobiographical volumes were filled with accounts of journalists and litterateurs who passed off fantasies and falsehoods as real to readers worldwide.

**Treason of the Senate, The** (1906), see Phillips, David Graham; Congress

**Trilling, Lionel** (1905-1975), Columbia University professor whose "liberalism" was taken to be a model for a mature sense of its values in the modern world by elements in academic criticism who issued his collected works in twelve volumes (1978-1980). In fact, only his first book, *Matthew Arnold* (1939), showed a broad sweep of study and critical issues which could serve intellectuals. Later writings were blurred by his ambivalent political tendencies, as shown in his novel, *The Middle of the Journey* (1947) (*q.v.*) and critical essays in *The Liberal Imagination* (1950). Curiously trivial to many were his views of George Orwell's (*q.v.*) *Homage to Barcelona* as not being a work of genius, though it involved truth or falsehood in the bloody Spanish Civil War, and Henry James' *Princess Casamassima* as being the product of genius, without asking whether James understood late nineteenth-century European anarchism. Trilling was thus seen by conservatives as a sign of the difficulty of lifting the cultural debate between liberals and conservatives. See also *When the Going Was Good! American Life in the Fifties*, by J. Hart, and *Liberal Imagination, The*.

**"Trimmer, The,"** a nickname associated with Viscount Halifax (1633-1695), known for his skill at balancing factions in the British government when he was in position to do so. Working between pro-Catholic factions and their opponents, he subscribed to neither group, but helped mediate the succession to the throne of James II (1685), from which he gained politically. He labored to temper the change from James to William of Orange during the Glorious Revolution (1688). In 1684 he wrote in defense of the trimmer, as one who sought the middle way and kept public life on an even keel. *The Character of the Trimmer* (1688) was thus his apologia, but he could not prevent posterity from choosing to make of "the trimmer" a two-faced and small-spirited opportunist. See H. C. Foxcroft, *A Character of the Trimmer* (1946), a biography of Halifax.

**Trotsky, Leon** (1879-1940), a legend of the Bolshevik Revolution, organizer of its Red Army, a companion of Lenin (*q.v.*). He was victimized by the rise of nationalism in the Soviet Union and driven from it in the late 1920s by Stalin, who at the time did not dare to have him assassinated. Though harassed by governments reluctant to grant the revolutionary asylum, Trotsky marshalled groups in many countries and sought to reconcile his demand for party democracy with his belief in a "dictatorship of the proletariat." Before his murder by an agent of Stalin, he had declared the Third (Communist) International a dead letter, and sought to launch a Fourth. Though he was admittedly a brilliant writer, especially when compared with Stalin, Trotsky's deterministic outlook, energized by Marxist predictions, had nothing to offer conservatives. It did, however, give him a postmortem intellectual triumph over Stalin, inspiring would-be revolutionaries in the capitalist countries—though surprisingly few, on any evidence, in the Soviet Union itself. In the early 1980s, "Trotskyites" made the British news as being active and successful among radicals of the Labor Party and in unions. Exposed by conservative journalists as "moles," they protested that they no more than sought what they could gain by democratic dialogue. Critics in and out of Labor saw them as conspirators, rather than legitimate activists or trade-union sympathizers.

**"Truly Poor,"** a concept of the Reagan (*q.v.*) Administration, which sought to separate mere parasites on the state from those—dependent young and old, women with children, the handicapped—who merited the state's attention. Though satirized by liberal journalists and cartoonists (*q.v.*), the phrase offered some guidance through a jungle of entitlements (*q.v.*) which burdened society and made difficult the problem of recapturing a viable social ethic (*q.v.*)

**Trust**, a potent word in nineteenth-century and early twentieth-century business and social politics. It appeared to offer legal means for individuals to buy into sufficient control of an industry to dominate its power structure and policies. Spread sufficiently throughout American business, it would place the economic control of the country in a few hands. Several decades of seething unrest in such key industries as the railroads, oil, steel, lumber, and shipping created a national antipathy to trusts which seemed met by the passage of the Sherman Anti-Trust Act in 1890. However, the reluctance of the Attorney-General of the United States to act in trust prosecutions and the Supreme Court's unwillingness to recognize their existence created a mood of discouragement which contributed to the rapid build-up of the Progressive (*q.v.*) movement early in the twentieth century. The breakup of the Standard Oil Trust by action of the Supreme Court in 1911, and subsequent evidence that great corporations could not be forced into drastic competition, raised further questions about controls of industry. Passage of the Clayton Act in 1914, with its enduring observation that labor was not a commodity and so subject to anti-trust regulation, though it did not prevent further labor-industry confrontations, did encourage the building up of labor unions (*q.v.*) as a bulwark against great industries. Although anti-trust actions became part of the legal scene in the following decades, the emphasis shifted from fear of trusts as such to the monitoring of labor, industry, and government relations, with Congress becoming a major repository of law governing all.

**Turgenev, Ivan**, (1818-1883), one of the greatest of Russian writers, whose works continue to be read in Russia: a link between Old Russia and the Soviets. Turgenev's dedication to art saved him from much, not all, suppression under the old regime, though the extraordinary clarity of his prose and delineation of Russian types affected social attitudes. His *A Sportsman's Sketches* (1852), with their descriptions of the workings of serfdom, contributed to the spirit which brought on the emancipation of the serfs in 1861. Turgenev's *Fathers and Sons* (1861) gave the world "nihilism," a desperate youth alienation which expressed itself in apathy, then radical terrorism. Turgenev was a conservative in subordinating other causes to his art. He urged Leo Tolstoy to give up his evangelical crusades and return to writing fiction. Tolstoy, however, feared death as making pursuits other than immortality futile, and sought meaning in social justice and religious texts. Most of Turgenev's writings had social implications.

**Turncoats**, a term of opprobrium often applied to transitional (*q.v.*) figures by their late associates, as well as to such obvious turncoats as Benedict Arnold—who indeed are often defended with eloquence and point as having had good cause for their actions. Samuel Adams and Patrick Henry (*qq.v.*) were too well imbedded in Revolutionary lore to suffer severe criticism for their conservative actions. Abolitionists made Daniel Webster (*qq.v.*) appear a traitor for his "Seventh of March" speech pleading for acceptance of the compromise of 1850, even though Webster had never claimed abolitionist perspectives. Robert E. Lee's chivalrous dedication to duty saved him from the scorn attending his refusal to accept command of the Union forces in order to lead Confederates during the Civil War. The rise of a new conservative produced, in post-World War II decades, numerous persons who turned mainly from liberal or radical premises to those of conservatism. Among many others, John T. Flynn, John Dos Passos, James Burnham, John Chamberlain, Frank S. Meyer, John P. Roche, and Norman Podhoretz (*qq.v.*) had turned from left or liberal to conservative stances. Morrie Ryskind of the satirical *Of Thee I Sing* and *Strike Up the Band*, musical-comedies of the 1930s, tired of his left-wing associates and contributed wit to the *National Review*. Max Eastman, who had already astounded watchers of the New York scene by turning on his non-conformist past to become a roving editor of *Reader's Digest* (*q.v.*), tried to become part of the *National Review* group, but found their principles too hard to assimilate. Peter Viereck (*q.v.*) asserted his conservatism, then turned from the New Conservatism as reaction, but maintained his anti-Soviet stance. Garry Wills (*q.v.*) turned from the conservatism which had given him his start to what seemed to many an essentially contemporary liberalism.

**Twain, Mark** (1835-1910), noted American author, born Samuel Langhorne Clemens. His life of writing and commenting on American ways, his travels and associations, his movement from rural and Western areas to more decorous Connecticut make him an inexhaustible fund of references and examples to all. However, Van Wyck Brooks's *The Ordeal of Mark Twain* (1920) portrayed him as a victim of Puritanic (*q.v.*) repression and American—that is, conservative—lack of respect for art. Central to the indictment was the influence of Twain's mother, who fostered fears of hell and brimstone in the child, and Twain's wife, who called him "Youth" and suppressed his natural bardic expression. The indictment included an America which encouraged fixations on money, and caused Twain, though amply paid for publications and lectures, to seek out millionaires for companionship and to try himself to become a millionaire. To Brooks, *Huckleberry Finn* was the best "boy's" book ever written, and Twain's other writings unworthy of what he might have done if less bound by native conventionalities. The indictment failed on many counts, being answered directly in Bernard De Voto's *Mark Twain's America* (1932). Twain's work was subsequently read and analyzed by a host of critics, who particularly exalted *Huckleberry Finn* as a masterpiece. Nevertheless Brooks's persisted as part of the indictment of Puritan and conformist America. See also Censorship.

**Twenties, The**. The 1920s are largely identified with youth seeking emancipation from older taboos and a literary renascence highlighted by bold experiments. In fact, there was a conservative aspect to the era, even in business. In the Twenties business formulated the underestimated installment plan, which enabled people of modest income to spend beyond their actual assets, shoring up trouble for the future as they set aside old ideals of frugality, debtlessness, and moderation. Thus, the era had its "conservative" side, but without built-in controls. Similarly, the democratization of the automobile (*q.v.*) cut space and time, but inadvertently contributed to the diminution of the home and family (*q.v.*), unexpectedly creating freedoms for youth (*q.v.*) even in conventional circumstances. To such developments, disillusionment (*q.v.*) with the "Great Crusade" of World War I contributed its share. Affluence, transportation (*q.v.*), and the importance of youth made the matrix for the greatest rush forward of creative talent since the pre-Civil War era in fiction, drama, and poetry. For the first and only decade poets produced bestsellers of distinction, with such authors as Edwin Arlington Robinson (*q.v.*), Edna St. Vincent Millay, and Carl Sandburg being read as though reading poetry was a natural American proclivity. The era was shocked and titillated by critics and experimenters, and knew of them: James Joyce, James Branch Cabell, H. L. Mencken, Sinclair Lewis (*qq.v.*). It would have surprised many readers, however, to know that of these writers only Joyce was not essentially conservative. So many brilliant talents, scornful of tradition, religion, and homely virtues, disported themselves in America or abroad—F. Scott Fitzgerald. Ernest Hemingway, Gertrude Stein, Eugene O'Neill, Hart Crane, John Dos Passos (*q.v.*), e. e. cummings—that it is possible to forget the numerous artists who contributed to the conservative vision of life. Willa Cather, Stephen Vincent Benét, Robert Frost, the Agrarians (*q.v.*), and the Regionalists—avant-garde Southerners whose verse was metaphorical beyond ordinary readers but whose sustenance was in the past. The "boldest" of all experimenters was the most conservative of all, T. S. Eliot (*q.v.*), whom the avant-garde saw as one of its own and a satirist of despised America, but whose dedication to classicism, Anglicanism, and royalty came to his erstwhile friends as a revelation. Yet the trend of society was with the avant-garde, rather than the conservatives, intrinsic or otherwise. Even in their time, such conscious conservatives as Paul Elmer More and Irving Babbitt (*qq.v.*) and the Neo-Humanism they sought to further were subject to the raucous satire of Mencken and Sinclair Lewis and the lumbering sarcasm of Theodore Dreiser. Readers gave lip-service to distinguished figures of conservatism, but soon accorded "classic" status to the expatriates of the 1920s, notably Hemingway and Gertrude Stein, who were able to persuade the government in the case of Ezra Pound (*q.v.*) that he had been an aberrant, rather than a wartime traitor. For two decades, Henry Miller, whose writings seemed to many little more than pornography, was treated as a classic author and master of prose. Thus, despite the latent power of conservatism as a tradition and font of creativity, it took dissatisfaction with the results of World War II (*qq.v.*) and the development of the New Deal (*q.v.*) to stir a renewed interest in the substance of conservatism, as displayed by Russell Kirk (*q.v.*), and to make the *National Review* (*q.v.*) an organizer of conservative thought and opinion. Nevertheless, the Twenties continued to be identified with inventive rebels and legitimate emancipation. F. J. Hoffman, *The Twenties* (1949), J. K. Hutchens, ed., *The American Twenties* (1952).

**"Two Nations, The,"** famous phrase by Disraeli (*q.v.*) in his *Sybil* (1845) to describe the condition of England, as divided into the rich and the poor.

**Tyrrell, Emmett, Jr.** (1943- ), American author and columnist. He was editor of the conservative student magazine *The Alternative*, published at Indiana University, which attracted well-known conservative figures and varied contributions, by 1975 claiming a national circulation of 25,000. In 1977 it assumed the name which had been its first inspiration, *The American Spectator*—first associated with George Jean Nathan, the critic and associate of H. L. Mencken (*q.v.*). Although firmly conservative, it sought wit, irreverence, and a sense of superiority to common foibles. The advent of the Reagan Administration gave it a new authority and augmented circulation. Though it dealt with many ephemeral figures, such as E. L. Doctorow, it also probed important national issues such as the Vietnam war and the cancer problem. Its reviews, though few, were among the more responsible and varied in conservative journals. Tyrrell's works includes *The Future That Doesn't Work: Social Democracy's Failures in Britain* (1977), and *Public Nuisances* (1979), a series of portraits written with rough strokes.

# U

**Ulyanov, Vladimir Ilyich**, see Lenin
**UN**, see United Nations
**Unamuno, Miguel De** (1864-1936), Spanish philosopher and academic, an individualist whose *The Tragic Sense of Life in Men and Nations* (1913) won him wide regard for his sense of the human condition. A man of the faith, and a romantic, he at first approved of the Republican regime in Madrid, but before the civil war got under way was repelled by the directions it was taking. His works included a study of Don Quixote and Sancho (1905), *The Agony of Christianity* (1925), and *Three Exemplary Novels and a Prologue* (1930). Mario J. Valdes, *Death in the Literature of Unamuno* (1966).
**Underachievers,** see Overachievers
**Underdeveloped Nations**, see Foreign Aid; Equality
**Underground Grammarian, The**, see *Graves of Academe, The*
**Unemployment**, a social problem not easily fitted into the conservative program because of its possible affect on elections, yet subject to some of its philosophy. Although the 1930s were notorious for unemployment, it was evident that it was made more acute by the relatively meager benefits available to the deprived. Since then, unions (*q.v.*) have built unemployment benefits into their contracts which have done much to ease the tension and needs associated with temporary or full loss of a job. Welfare payments, food stamps, government-supported medical services, and allowances for children and the aged (*qq.v.*) have created buffers against poverty which raw unemployment statistics overlook, intentionally or not. Multiple-income families and an "underground economy" are also necessary to seeing the contemporary picture whole. Nevertheless, the high rate of 10.1 percent unemployment in the second year of the Reagan (*q.v.*) Administration required a response which a Reagan defender, William F. Buckley, Jr. (*q.v.*), only partially provided. Citing a jobless university graduate in physics, he suggested that the young man needed to look around, possibly for a job not in physics. The suggestion was reminiscent of 1930s reasoning: that any job was better than none. Although there was some truth in Buckley's comment, there was still the question of what might happen to the young man's skill if it was not kept active. All workers did not have equal stamina, or the talent of a George Bernard Shaw, who put it that, had he been a "good" person jobless in London in the late 1870s and early 1880s, he would have found a job. Instead, he had lived on his mother's income and made a man of himself. In the 1970s and 1980s, job markets were changing. Whatever errors had been made by labor and industry, however opportunities had been mishandled, as with wages (*q.v.*), a program dealing with unemployment needed to be prepared. President Truman had sought a Full Employment Act in 1946. In undergoing "considerable changes," however, as Truman noted, it essentially ended as rhetoric rather than fact. Later job-training and retraining efforts spent money but did little more than discredit the methods or directions taken. Notorious was the Comprehensive Employment and Training Act (CETA). Over seven years ending in 1982 it spent some $53 billion, with little to show in personal or material results. The problem was complicated by the eagerness of Democrats to show themselves responsive to

popular need in the spirit of the New Deal (*q.v.*), but limited by deficit and inflation (*qq.v.*) warnings. Reagan's program for creating jobs by inspiring industry to expand seemed calculated to harm him severely with voters who, in basically one-industry states such as Michigan were suffering 17.6 percent unemployment. Reagan's game plan, however, and his successes with inflation and other measures, though they did not appease his foes, appeared to hold the respect of the more general public. Even his willingness to impose an income tax on unemployment benefits lost him little popularity. It appeared that a section of the population at least agreed with him that employment had not always demanded the best from the employed, and that some modification of job expectations was in order.

**UNESCO**, see United Nations Educational, Scientific, and Cultural Organization

**Unheavenly City, The**, see Banfield, Edward C.

**Unilateral Disarmament**, see Nuclear War

**Unions**, once the first demand of embattled workers who sought them in order to gain strength through union, and who were resisted as infringing upon the prerogatives of employers. The fight for unions produced many martyrs and forgotten men who found themselves blacklisted, hounded from jobs, discredited. The American Federation of Labor (see Gompers, Samuel) was built on the premise of business unionism: of unionism not intent on heroics but on the ability to survive and grow in good times and bad. Nevertheless, it was required to help or endorse less secure or unskilled workers, dependent on jobs and needing to bend employers and public opinion to a recognition of their need. The Progressive Era (*q.v.*) helped with publicity and such laws as the Clayton Act (1914), which exempted labor from anti-trust regulations. This did little to remove laborers from threats of prosecution and violence by police, company agents, and vigilantes. Radicals of various kinds, including Communists, worked for positions in labor unions, and were helped by opportunities for organization opened by the stalemates of the Great Depression (*q.v.*). The National Labor Relations Board (1935) created a mediating agency which labor was able to influence in its behalf. World War II, with its need for manpower, was a critical period enabling labor leaders to strengthen their hold over union workers. They augmented their hold in the affluent times which followed, despite the Taft-Hartley Act (*q.v.*). The unprecedented prosperity made it easier for business and industry to work "with" unions, corrupt or otherwise, than to be concerned for the rights of workers who were manipulated by union leaders unresponsive to their desires. Union contracts which mandated the automatic collection of dues from individual workers, union-ordered strikes, and union input into work rules contributed as much to deterioration of production standards as did employer incompetence and greed. Although union thugs and corrupt officials were exposed in crime investigations, and by police and federal crime-fighting units, official labor found it more expedient to close ranks against them than to join in pursuit of the same objectives. Although right-to-work (*q.v.*) laws were passed in a number of states they were difficult to enforce. Labor presented itself as a large army which could make or break politicians and Presidential aspirants: a "special interest" (*q.v.*) which could swing elections, especially for Democrats supportive of their New Deal (*qq.v.*) tradition. Thus, labor had come far from its own history; it was now Big Labor, as business had once been and continued to be. Depressed economic circumstances in the late 1970s and during the Reagan Administration, with workers being laid off in every industry, forced labor to reconsider its course and whether it could deliver its own workers at the polls. The effort of controllers to strike against the Federal Government for better working conditions, despite Federal law, caused their wholesale firing and the downfall of their union. The attempt of union leaders to mass a protest march in Washington against Reagan Government policies brought little success. Although they created a rhetoric of action, compassion, and appeals for social justice, it was evident that their workers wanted to work, and that they would be forced to give "concessions" (*q.v.*) to harassed industrialists. It was evident that the future of unions would be the future of other constituencies seeking to marshall influence at the polls. Lane Kirkland, leader of the AFL-CIO, complained that people who criticized "special interests" wanted to exclude "working people, young people, environmentalists, and the poor" from politics, leaving "a handful of prosperous, middle-aged white males to run the country." The Chicago *Tribune* columnist Stephen Chapman commented: "Why Kirkland resists being governed by replicas of himself is a matter for his psychiatrist." A curious development was a division among unionists with respect to illegal immigration (*q.v.*), which put aliens into the work force at lower than going wage rates. Established unions generally viewed those from south of the U. S. border as scabs, "wetbacks," interlopers, and threats to native workers. Independent union organizers, however, took steps to organize them. Their problems, it appeared, "rooted in the structure of the Mexican economy," could be better handled by unions than by Congress and the Bureau of Immigration. Arizona Farm Workers Union spokesmen tried to portray the illegal immigration as normal between neighboring countries and in the best American tradition. They held that there was no labor law to prevent the immigrants from receiving all benefits due all workers, and claimed there were employers who recognized these facts and cooperated in meeting wage and other standards. Moreover, the immigrants were engaging in "self-help immigration reform," putting their savings to work on both sides of the border. Although information on this was meager, and Immigration authorities offered no comments, Congress appeared determined to legislate in the area.

**United Fruit Company**, made symbolic of American imperialism in Central America, maker and breaker of "banana republics"; see Scott Nearing and Joseph Freeman, *Dollar Diplomacy: A Study in American Imperalism* (1926). It was seen differently in Frederick Upham Adams's *Conquest of the Tropics: The Story of the Creative Enterprises Conducted by the United Fruit Company* (1914). Much of the issue of imperialism (*q.v.*) versus commerce and philanthropy (*qq.v.*) was bound up in the career of Sam Zemurray (1878-1961). He was a poor immigrant from Russia who interested himself in the growth and sale of bananas, grew important in the industry from meager beginnings, and through force of personality and bold use of resources won control of United Fruit and warring factions in Honduras and Nicaragua. He was said once to have outfitted an exiled Honduran president and two soldiers of fortune with rifles, ammunition, and a yacht. They overthrew the current regime, in turn protecting Zemurray's interests. He spent lavishly to support sanitary conditions for workers, providing health clinics, schools, housing, and even archeological research funds. It was doubtful whether any group of native politicians could have done as much for the populace involved. Although the tone and language of social operations changed in the post-World War II political configurations, the question of proper relations between small countries and business from abroad continued to match realism against demagoguery. Stuart and Eleanor Bruckey, eds. *United Fruit Company in Latin America* (1958).

**United Nations**. It has been haunted by memory of the impotence displayed by its predecessor, the League of Nations, but presents a different configuration, thanks to the rise of the Soviet Union, the creation of African states, and the inclusion of numerous "Third World" states—often with small budgets, unstable governments, and minimal democracy: surrogate (*q.v.*) lands which demanded parity with the largest states to which they were indebted for existence. The United Nations Educational, Scientific, and Cultural Organization (UNESCO) (*q.v.*), which had embodied much hope for civilizing the world to peace and cooperation, was little more than an agency for publishing essays by literate spokesmen for self-interested governments. The United Nations Human Rights Commission proved political in its judgments and information. Conservatives were impatient with its government's patience with UN slurs, slights, and demands. The Reagan Administration, however, come to power in

1980, judged that if the UN was a forum for opportunists and foes, it was also a forum from which American representatives could utter hard truths which went around the world and heartened its friends. Also, that words were better than blows, and the UN therefore worth sustaining as an instrument which could deceive only those who intended to be deceived, but one which could provide a platform for negotiations. See also Human Rights.

**United Nations Educational, Scientific, and Cultural Organization (UNESCO)**, intended to be a humanistic arm of the world-wide United Nations. With majorities of anti-American, pro-Marxist, and Third World representatives, it turned into an organization disseminating propaganda in deprecation of the United States and all its works. Since the nation subsidized UNESCO's operations to a high degree, it seemed self-destructive to continue association with the organization. Conservatives had been in the forefront demanding separation from it, and often received criticism as being isolationist, racist, and anti-democratic. In 1984 the Reagan Administration gave the necessary one-year notice that it intended to leave UNESCO. Remarkably, many liberals agreed, reflecting how UNESCO had fallen in the eyes of what were once its staunchest supporters. However, they seemed to hope that UNESCO officials would "shape up," moderating their criticism of the United States, and so permitting a revival of relationships.

**University Bookman, The**, a quarterly founded and edited by Russell Kirk (*q.v.*). It sought to maintain something of the tradition of the essay, involving free, unhackneyed prose with respect for institutional aspects and the variety of books a university should notice and weigh.

**Unraveling of America, The** (1984), by Allen J. Matusow, a liberal effort subtitled "A History of Liberalism in the 1960s." It was possibly a forerunner of more such efforts, as the Democratic establishments sought fresh formulas for the end of the century. It contrasted drastically with the 1960s (*q.v.*) as perceived for example in the *National Review* (*q.v.*), unnoticed in this volume. The *National Review* saw civil rights (*q.v.*) as a matter of law and social stability. It fought on behalf of public morality, asking how federal funds could be used for education with students tearing up campuses. It viewed the Supreme Court (*q.v.*) with alarm, and Communism as a massive threat abroad. It feared Americans for Democratic Action (ADA), with its anti-anti-Communist (*q.v.*) approach, its welcome of world government, and infiltration of Democratic Administrations. The Matusow book intended to appear realistic and historically valid. Its basic infirmity to conservative critics of modern society lay in its placing the "unraveling" in the Sixties. There was no consensus (*q.v.*) prior to that time, according to conservatives. Unraveling began during World War II (*q.v.*) when the nation divided between those at war and those at home enjoying—many for the first time in a decade—good wages. Unraveling continued painlessly in the 1950s, with urbanites departing for the suburbs (*qq.v.*), leaving their former homes to those conservatives regarded as untried minorities. Matusow took up the Democratic cause, and measured it by civil rights, asking not what those demanding rights were prepared to give their country, but what could be demanded or forced from it. The nation's "best and brightest" on swollen campuses had led the drive which Matusow approved. He called the goal of "redistribution of income" (*q.v.*) by the name of "liberal reform," cutting both liberalism and reform (*qq.v.*) away from their roots in moral and pragmatic movements from Andrew Jackson to the Progressives, and even from the early New Deal (*qq.v.*). He held it against the Democratic Establishment that it could not achieve the "redistribution" of income sought through welfare, housing, equal opportunity, Medicare, unemployment compensations, retraining, affirmative action, anti-discrimination efforts, and child, maternal, and family aid—"Community Aid" generally (*qq.v.*). This thesis was to him sufficient for a study of the 1960s. In his 440 pages of text, involving national elections, technical discussions of Keynesian theory, and the "imprudent" Vietnam War, there were fourteen chapters, nine of which treated with circumstantial detail civil-rights protests, the "War on Poverty," and the rise and fall of the New Left and the "Counterculture." "Black rage" was seen as a legitimate weapon of social change. (See Anger.) Tom Hayden, a youth activist (*q.v.*) of the Sixties, emerged as a major American figure, in Matusow's view, presumably meriting study on the plane of figures from Tom Paine to Robert M. LaFollette. Hayden's *Port Huron Statement* of Left student goals was "one of the most successful radical documents in American history" (p.313). Yet, if there was anything conservatives found profoundly missing in the book it was American history. Even more startling was the number of contemporary topics, heavy with controversy, which found no place in its pages. The Supreme Court—more basic to the civil rights movement than marches and riots—Communism, religion, Hispanics, the deference of many educators to their students, public and private corruption, the Cold War (*qq.v.*)—none of these was noticed as affecting the course of civil rights and the "War on Poverty," from John F. Kennedy to the 1968 election victory of Richard M. Nixon. Matusow appeared realistic to conservatives in depicting John F. Kennedy—and others about him with "glittering images"—as shallow and ambitious; but he concluded that Kennedy was learning and could have done better had he lived longer. Conservatives saw Kennedy and Democrats generally as capable of little. Lyndon B. Johnson's "War on Poverty" was paved with good intentions, and might have done better too had the Vietnam War not interposed, drawing away money from rehabilitation of the black ghettoes. A strange thought in the book had the liberal reformers *by their victories* in economic "redistribution" driving the blacks toward "black nationalism": from civil rights to "liberation." The Democrats had done too little, too late. The public had given up on "redistribution." By contrast, the conservatives had been grotesque, in the Goldwater (*q.v.*) Presidential fiasco of 1964. Nixon's call in 1968 for "law and order" (*q.v.*) showed him "at his demagogic worst" (p. 401). The author perceived a "long-term trend" toward a conservatism he had not so much as previously noticed except in an aside on "white backlash." He saw Reagan winning easily in 1980 by "running on a platform to repeal the cultural as well as the political legacy of the sixties" (p. 439). The "cultural" achievements included the "modern classics" Ken Kesey's *One Flew over the Cuckoo's Nest* and Norman Mailer's "brilliant" *Armies of the Night*, Mailer's account of his presence at a student assault on the Pentagon. Whether liberals, following Matusow in discontinuity from American history, would similarly cling to their "legacy" of civil rights, counterculture, and militant students and minorities, in refreshing their public image for the last part of the century, the author, "reared in the liberal tradition," would not or could not say.

**Up From Communism**, by John P. Diggins (1975), a study of "conservative odysseys in America," in essence accounts of the development of leftist (*q.v.*) intellectuals Max Eastman, John Dos Passos, Will Herberg, and James Burnham (*q.v.*). Although a variety of disillusioned "fellow travelers" (*q.v.*) and communists became involved with William F. Buckley, Jr. and his *National Review*, not all were of equal weight. Eastman carried an aura from his Greenwich Village years but contributed little to the *National Review*. John Dos Passos was more cultural than political. Will Herberg left a bankrupt Communist faction ("Lovestoneites") to involve himself in mystic concerns involving Christian and Jewish philosophy. James Burnham became a durable figure in *National Review* (*q.v.*) annals.

**"Upward Mobility,"** a sociological concept descriptive of the democratic process which interfered with pressures making for stability in the social order and authoritarianism among classes. Both liberalism and conservatism accepted this modern concept, liberals with greater conviction. "Mobility" was highly material in its components. However, the same factors which created equalitarian slogans and demagogic movements also created new levels of individual with status and prerogatives to conserve, many of whom turned on older concepts and associates. See Neo-conservatives.

**Urban Problem**, (see Filler DASC), a development out of older conditions which saw cities in a process of growth, adding new neighborhoods and ethnic components, with transportation and other services subject to political chicanery, but also to reform movements with competent leadership and appreciative citizenry which could call them to account. The reform movement of pre-World War I years produced classics of analysis and leaders who entered into folklore. Poverty, "skid rows," and ghettoes produced tragedies, but also picturesque enclaves all of which were spelled out in such works as *Sister Carrie* by Theodore Dreiser, but also in classic vaudeville which reflected zest in living. Cities were ringed by suburban towns which increasingly gave some classes of city workers a choice of small-town or country living and the interests and amusements of the "big city." As the city burgeoned and grew more complex, choices became more pressing. The easy money of World War II, after the austerities of the 1930s, was too much for its recipients to take in ways approved of by conservatives. "White flight" (*q.v.*) to the convenient suburbs left their former city neighborhoods open to minority groups. Their rapid proliferation in politics led to their leaders being called demagogues (*q.v.*) who would appeal to their prejudices rather than to their need for order and improvement. In such an atmosphere of what conservatives called political shuffling and deals, there was no room for reformers. The lengthy prosperity of the Post-World War II decades meant political payoffs in all sectors, according to conservatives, who saw schools and families eroded on all levels. Despite a generation of "city planners" and social workers, no major figures emerged, as in the past, to lead in movements against crime, broken families, empty-handed youth, and the "low-income housing" which often baffled the mind with its desolation and expense. The sums spent futilely and impotently in all these areas were astronomic. City defenders found no alternative to asking for more. When President Reagan, discussing unemployment, observed that over $60 billion had been spent on "job skills and retraining" and no jobs created, he appeared to make little impression. Reagan's own two answers to the situation were at first a "New Federalism" (*q.v.*) and "Enterprise Zones." In effect, he would have taken city rehabilitation out of the hands of Washington bureaucrats and made grants to cities for their own rehabilitation and responsibility. This meant less money and more accountability, neither of which stipulation sat well with urban officials. Secondly, he would have encouraged "zones" of the needy where energetic and resourceful businessmen could receive benefits to encourage them to rebuild neighborhoods, working with their inhabitants to mutual benefit. Reagan's proposals involved infringing on many union (*q.v.*) gains, notably the minimum hourly wage, in order to put money into poor hands. The alternative to such proposals according to Reagan and his defenders was more city erosion, with more guarded buildings to provide for corporation headquarters and the few favored city dwellers. Much of urban "literature" is a study in futility to conservatives. Several works give a sense of conservative approaches available. S. E. Clarke and J. L. Obler, eds., *Urban Ethnic Conflict* (1976); Diana Klebanow et al., *Urban Legacy: The Story of America's Cities* (1977); E. C. Banfield and J. Q. Wilson, *City Politics* (1963); Ray C. Rist, *The Urban School: A Factory for Failure* (1977); Mark V. Melosi, *Garbage in the Cities...1880-1980* (1981); M. L. Stackhouse, *Ethics and the Urban Ethos: An Essay in Social Theory and Theological Reconstruction* (1972).

**Utilitarianism**, see Rationalism; Mill, John Stuart

**Utopia**, unpopular with conservatives, despite such inspiration as it provided for Plato (*q.v.*) in his study of the ideal Republic, and Sir Thomas More, who invented the word, meaning "nowhere." It appeared to modern conservatives to excite futile and harmful dreaming and experimentation. It was often identified with socialism (*q.v.*) though one of the fathers of socialism, Friedrich Engels, also denounced it in his *Socialism, Utopian and Scientific.*

Edward Bellamy's *Looking Backward* (1888) was a novel which was picked up by readers who not only took his account of a peaceful and cooperative world as feasible, but created a movement which influenced the growth and development of Progressivism (*q.v.*) and was found in the fabric of the early New Deal (*q.v.*). Arthur E. Morgan, the biographer of Bellamy, even sought to prove that the "utopia" was in fact real, and that More's *Utopia* was not fiction at all, but an account of post-Columbian explorations; see Morgan's *Nowhere Was Somewhere* (1946). Although the idea of utopias had continued to attract attention and experiments, it has been matched by anti-utopian sentiments reflecting a fear of what people are capable of doing to themselves, as in Aldous Huxley's (*q.v.*) *Brave New World* (1932) and George Orwell's (*q.v.*) *1984* (1949). Pro-utopians and anti-utopians continue to build their cases; see Thomas Molnar (*q.v.*), *Utopia: The Perennial Heresy* (1967) and R. Buckminister Fuller, *Utopia or Oblivion: The Prospects for Mankind* (1969).

# V

**"Value-Free Society,"** see Morality

**Van Buren, Martin**, see Free Soilers; Panaceas

**Vatican Council II** (1962-1965), held in limited esteem by conservatives as having encouraged "progressive" tendencies in Catholic (*q.v.*) centers of opinion, and so encouraged less responsible elements in the durable structure of the Church. Its key tendency, to encourage lay understanding of church services and participation in its workings, disturbed conservatives, who foresaw increased pressure from Catholic "progressives." When it came with participation in the youth uprisings of the 1960s and later with anti-nuke demonstrations, conservatives traced it to Vatican II. H. Daniel-Rops, *The Second Vatican Council* (1962); G. A. Lindbeck, *The Future of Roman Catholic Theology* (1970); A. Flannery, ed., *Vatican Council II* (1976).

**Vers De Société**, "society verses," in a nineteenth century cultural tradition, intended to amuse, exhibit wit or light satire, or graceful expression. As phrased in French, it tended to indicate the sophistication and well-being of those who were well-traveled. Its best exponent, Charles Stuart Calverley (1831-1884), published *Fly Leaves* in 1872, which helped destroy *vers de société* as a tradition with his satire of its more shallow examples. Increased democratization, and the determination of university men to reach the widening audience and deeper issues, robbed readers of poetry of charming verses. In the United States it was a sign of increased democracy that society verse tended to be more "serious," as in William Allen Butler's criticism of frivolous women who claimed to have *Nothing to Wear* (1857), and reached a nonsense level in Gelett Burgess's later verse on the "Purple Cow," which entered into folklore, to Burgess's chagrin. As he wrote still later: "Yes, I wrote the Purple Cow,/ I'm sorry now I wrote it./ But I can tell you anyhow,/ I'll kill you if you quote it." See Dreele, W. H. von.

**"Victimless Crime,"** a liberal concept intended to control the amount of surveillance society would set over individuals to limit freedom and make punishable that which harmed no one. High among "victimless crimes" were alleged to be drug use and distribution, especially that of marijuana, for which harmless properties were claimed; a favorite argument was to compare its use with hard liquors, the latter as more dangerous to impressionable persons. Evidence suggested to many that such claims were specious, and the "victimless crime" phrase a euphemism (*q.v.*). Youth did suffer from drug addiction. Marijuana was an open door to exploitative activities, which drew and created victims. Drug distributors had a stake in creating drug addicts. Those who advocated decriminalizing drugs argued that laws against drugs created more social harm than good.

**Victorian Era**, made notorious by post-World War I liberals, disillusioned participants in the Wilsonian Crusade, and radicals (*qq.v.*) looking forward to a better world. Accusations against the age of Queen Victoria included racist egotism, imperialist exploitation of other lands, hypocritical religion, heartless repression of the poor and toiling, and pruriency (*qq.v.*)—the latter linked with evasion of the facts of life. Notorious was the alleged penchant of the middle classes to term legs "limbs," and to hide even the legs of pianos. Identified with Victorianism too was its crusade against liquor: "The lips that touch liquor will never touch mine." Above all, Victorianism stood charged with conformity and the suppression of individuality. "Victorianism" was seen by its foes as considerably present in the United States as well. The fact that the bill of particulars was not qualified with obvious, representative individuals who deviated in various ways from the stereotype was evidence to those who defended the Victorian Era that the charges constituted a war against society, caused by revulsion to the futility of World War I, by hopes of a new, socialist world, and by tearings in the fabric of established society. The stereotype failed to give attention to forces which limited its impact. The American West honored motherhood and social graces, but took in stormy characters of every kind. "Bourbon" liquor was nurtured in the South. Imperialism and expansion (*qq.v.*) there were, but also *anti*-imperialism, sponsored by straight-laced and more flexible Easterners. Mark Twain (*q.v.*) was one among many scribes who commented heartily and with more or less kindly malice on American peccadilloes (*q.v.*), and with effect. There were poor, and there was harsh treatment of minority people, but there was never a time which did not inspire such ladies as Jane Addams (*q.v.*) to dedicate themselves to their problems. There were good-morals societies and efforts to quell prostitution, but there was also the *Police Gazette* to be scanned by men of every class who visited barber shops. Tribute was paid to the norms of society, but, once paid, could be and was honored in the breach. Anthony Comstock (*q.v.*) was a fact of life in the American Victorian saga, but there were few who could match him in dedication. The charge of conformity required special attention. Its implication was that the accusers were persons of generous character, always ready to recognize the vagaries of others so long as they did not interfere with their own. In fact, the "proper attitude" toward drink, sex, Communists, privacy, and the rest was insisted upon by the anti-"Victorian" partisans, and often went deeply into the feelings and preferences of deviationists from the anti-"Victorian" line. It finally reached its apogee in the 1960s quip: "I am a non-conformist just like all the rest of you." The worst of the Victorian stereotype was that it cut connections between contemporaries and the past, preventing them from learning its lessons.

**Viereck, Peter** (1916- ), American poet and conservative-liberal polemicist. He was the son of George Sylvester Viereck, a poetaster whose more serious role as a German agent made him notorious in two wars. (See Niel M. Johnson, *George Sylvester Viereck, German-American Propagandist* [1972].) Viereck himself was a soldier in World War II, following a brilliant career in history and poetry at Harvard. His first book, *Metapolitics: From the Romantics to Hitler* (1941), offered the original thesis that the "liberal" movement of the early nineteenth century in Germany was actually a precursor of fascism, including its racist component, and that Metternich's "international conservatism" gave more to the poor than did the "freedom" slogans of such nationalists as Richard Wagner. Following wide appearances in publications as a poet, Viereck published *Terror and Decorum: Poems 1940-1948*, which won the Pultizer Prize. The next year saw issue of his *Conservatism Revisited*, heralding the coming New Conservatism. While not rationalizing Metternich's reactionary policies (better, Viereck thought, called Emperor Francis's policies), he praised aristocratic democracy as opposed to mass democracy, the nurturer of fascism and Stalinism. The former was gracious, humanistic, and, from Edmund Burke (*q.v.*) through others, carrying the human heritage of several thousand years. Viereck contrasted this with Manchester Liberalism (*q.v.*), reflected, he thought, in the tasteless labors of Herbert Hoover and Robert A. Taft (*qq.v.*). See also his *Conservatism: From John Adams to Churchill* (1956), essays and documents. By 1962, a second section had been added to the original of *Conservatism Revisited*, entitled: "What Went Wrong?" The key quarrel with the new Buckley-Kirk-*National Review* (*qq.v.*) enterprises was over "McCarthyism," which Buckley defended and Kirk would not repudiate. In addition Viereck scorned free enterprise as sterile and as welfare in the "Tory socialism" tradition (*qq.v.*). Viereck joined the New Liberal Richard Hofstadter in seeing conservatives as "pseudo-conservatives." However, he shared with conservatives hatred of the totalitarian Soviets and their American apologists, whom he satirized and dissected in *Shame and Glory of the Intellectuals* (1953) and *The Unadjusted Man* (1962). Increasingly, his concern was for poetry, which he saw as strict form, as in "Would Jacob Wrestle with a Flabby Angel?" (*Critical Inquiry*, Winter 1978.) His major poetic effort involved *The Tree Witch* (1961). See his "Conservatism," *Encyclopaedia Brittanica* (1974); see also C. G. Ryn, "Peter Viereck: Unadjusted Man of Ideas," *Political Science Reviewer*, Fall, 1977; M. Renault, *Peter Viereck, Historian and Poet* (1969).

**Vietnam**, see Filler, DASC, an unfinished saga of war in recent American annals, though apparently established in retrospect as a thorough and well-deserved defeat: the result of blind aggression, unwillingness to read the record of French ignominy in the area, support of corrupt South Vietnam leaders, and the "Domino Theory"—holding that, if South Vietnam fell to the Communists, so would the other nations of Southeast Asia. That there was a breakdown in Johnson Administration's military perspective, even when compared with that of the earlier Korean (*q.v.*) involvement, there can be no doubt. But as important was the unforeseen cooperation which developed between American correspondents and the news media and the anti-Vietnam cause which the massive youth uprising embraced, linking anti-war, pro-North Vietnam feelings and ideas which, as deaths mounted and victory receded before ordinary people watching television, persuaded the public that the nation was in a no-win situation and its sons were being victimized as soldiers. In such circumstances, dialogue at home was impossible, and the succeeding Nixon Administration sought to disengage the nation from Vietnam with honor. Although it brought back a majority of the soldiers, and attempted to curb war-related atrocities, the pressure at home on the public and on Congress was such as to limit what an Administration could do. Nixon resigned from office as a result of Watergate (*q.v.*) and his successor, Gerald Ford, pleaded with Congress to permit an orderly departure, to no avail. The disarray in which American troops fled became evidence of American defeat. The ruthless Communist takeover which followed disillusioned many American supporters of the North Vietnam war effort. Although "another Vietnam" became a general warning used especially by liberals who feared foreign entanglements, conservatives too weighed choices respecting involvement in the Middle East, and such military actions as in Grenada (*q.v.*). Vietnam war veterans were distinctly up-graded in public estimation, as the debates over the Vietnam War Memorial in Washington showed, probing esthetic and moral as well as substantive values. What were needed were retrospective examinations of the nature of media-reporting on wartime developments in Vietnam, and on responses at home. In addition to Filler, DASC, bibliographical suggestions; Bernard Fall, *The Two Vietnams* (1967); D. S. Zagoria, *Vietnam Triangle: Moscow, Peking, Hanoi* (1967); Al Santoli, *Everything We Had: An Oral History...As Told by 33 American Soldiers* (1981). See also Cambodia.

**Viewpoints: The Conservative Alternative** (1973), ed., David Brudnoy, a spectrum of conservative essays, some critical of liberals and their causes, others intent on defining aspects of conservatism, and revealing a striking coherence of views on contemporary problems.

**Viguerie, Richard A.** (1933- ), vigorous "right wing" proponent. He became known for his highly efficient direct-mail techniques which proved effective in mobilizing conservatives in political and other causes. A former secretary of Young Americans for Freedom, he founded the Viguerie Company to carry on his operations. Publisher of the *Conservative Digest* from 1975 on, and of the *New Right Report*, Viguerie viewed proper conservative action in such terms that by the middle of 1982 he was accusing President Reagan of "deserting conservatives." He was author of *The New Right: We're Ready to Lead* (1980), which included autobiographical chapters as well as surveys of New Right (*q.v.*) actions and personalities. Viguerie's was one of the major operations which stirred liberal alarm as expressed in *Ominous Politics* (*q.v.*).

**Violence**, always a problem in society, but, with the "confrontation" drives of the 1960s and after, and the swift deterioration of the "inner cities," rendered more difficult to control. It received justifications as well as expressions of frustration and alarm. The sociologist Daniel Bell, a former socialist, argued that there had always been violence, and pointed to that recorded in New York in the 1830s. He passed over the fact that the violence described had taken place in the notorious "Five Points" district of downtown New York, a seedbed of degradation which dedicated reformers sought bravely to penetrate. The violence of Bell's time permeated all New York, creating a species of democracy, but also of despair accelerating the flight of many residents to the suburbs. The situation was made more complex by the "exclusionary rule." In 1961 the Supreme Court extended this long-time feature of American law to rule out in criminal cases evidence acquired by the police in violation of the Fourth Amendment to the Constitution. This Amendment prohibited "unreasonable" and improperly warranted searches and seizures. As applied, it permitted many apparently guilty defendants to walk out of courts to perpetrate further violence. Organizations such as the American Civil Liberties Union, however, feared police violence and malice more than that of criminals. Along with tired or partisan judges, law and order in large cities seemed to many mainly a matter of chance, leaving only questions concerning the scope of capital punishment and the housing of criminals. In general liberals seemed to look out for the rights of defendants more than they did for victims. Although conservatives in general emphasized law and order, they divided in respect to the death penalty, and in solutions to violence. Society itself seemed unsure of how to approach the matter. The 1963 murder of a President should have sobered it to the issue and forced action. Instead, its inaction led to further assassinations and attempted assassinations. A strange development in the 1960s was the appearance of "black anger" as an explanation of violence, not an anti-social feeling which merited suppression but a quasi-legitimate expression of justified rage. Studies of more violence in general centered on television violence, and other alleged encouragements to irresponsible actions. The insanity plea (*q.v.*) aroused great controversy with its use and abuse. But the basic question still lay with the general public. Did it fear criminal violence less than it did the police? Did it quietly prefer to make individual decisions, moving from high-violence areas to low-violence areas? Why was it uninterested in the uses of restitution (*q.v.*)? Was it looking for leadership, from liberals or conservatives? Fredric Wertham, *A Sign from Cain: An Exploration of Human Violence* (1966); J. D. Carthy, F. J. Ebling, eds., *The Natural History of Aggression* (1964); J. Feiffer, *The Great Comic Book Heroes* (1965); see also Crime, and Richard Harris, *The Fear of Crime* (1968), a liberal view underscoring the need for controls over police, with an introduction by former Attorney General Nicholas D.B. Katzenbach, expressing the opinion that "there is no real connection between the rise in street crime and other forms of civil disorder."

**VISTA** (Volunteers in Service to America), see Volunteer Action

**Vivas, Eliseo** (1901- ), American aesthetician who began his intellectual career as a follower of John Dewey (*q.v.*) and naturalism, mainly as a professor and reviewer of books. Persuaded that neither brought him close to the meaning of art and to "metaphysical reality," he probed further to values beyond things and politics. The latter, one of his interpreters thought, could only result in vulgar progressivism and reform. Vivas also preferred Henry James's fictional penetration to his brother William's (*qq.v.*) "utilitarianism." He concluded that art without religious insight was not whole. His books included *The Moral Life and the Ethical Life* (1950), *Creation and Discovery* (1955), *D. H. Lawrence: The Failure and the Triumph of Art* (1960), and *The Artistic Transaction* (1963). Some of his work was supported by the publisher Henry Regnery (*q.v.*). Conservatives united to honor his seventy-fifth birthday with essays published in ¡Viva Vivas! (1976), edited by Peter J. Stanlis. It included essays by Regnery, by Stanlis on "The Aesthetic Theory of Eliseo Vivas," by Stephen J. Tonsor on "Eliseo Vivas: Philosopher in Spite of Himself," and others. Russell Kirk's (*q.v.*) "Vivas, Lawrence, Eliot (*q.v.*), and the Demon" brought together a number of related issues from personal knowledge and analysis.

**Vocational Education**, once a natural development out of older apprenticeship systems which directed youths unsuited to more intensive academic disciplines into useful craft and technical pursuits. Vocational education was given more modern direction and support under the George-Dean Act of 1936, a time of Depression. The needs of World War II created a wide variety of schools intended rapidly to prepare people for use in the war industries. Postwar affluence, however, made it possible to suggest the ideal of offering everything to everyone, an aim which muddled perspectives between academics and potential industrial workers and technicians. Community colleges were intended to provide ample opportunities for the vocational-minded who might or might not prefer to go beyond two years of training, but so politicalized did many of them become as to fall into the hands of incompetents. Campus turmoil in the 1960s affected all education, and could not fail to waste community time and funds as well as student potential. The Vocational Education Act (1963), aimed at "disadvantaged youth," lacked the power to define its terms or objectives and was no more than one more step in a social process requiring confrontation and educational decisions. Although it was argued that society had reached a point requiring high skills from students, it was evident that that same society needed hands and hearts for clearing rubble and creating good fellowship: goals not achieved by computers or electrical equipment. It was possible that some system not unlike apprenticeship might be useful as a supplement to other curricula for rebuilding community. F. J. Keller, *The Double-Purpose High School* (1953); Rupert N. Evans, *Foundations of Vocational Education* (1971); G. C. Somers and J. K. Little, *Vocational Education: Today and Tomorrow* (1971).

**Voegelin, Eric** (1901-1985), religious historian whose overview of human social developments was inspiring to conservative intellectuals, especially those who found intolerable as guides to life the pessimistic interpretations of a Spengler. Voegelin was trained at the University of Vienna, where he made a reputation with books on race and religion. He was forced to flee the Nazis in 1938. In America, he joined the faculty of Louisiana State University. His *The New Science of Politics* (1952) denounced "Gnosticism," a movement of ideas which he saw as first, under Christianity, "de-divining" temporal power and personalities, but then, under "Gnostic" leaders, increasingly reestablishing divinity as on earth. "Gnosticism" he discerned in England's Puritan Revolution, in Hobbes's (*q.v.*) materialistic philosophy, distinctly in the unfolding of the French Revolution (*q.v.*), and increasingly in the exalted tenets of Communism and fascism. Voegelin made no mystery in successive volumes of *Order and History* (1956-1974). He wrote of *Israel and Revelation*, which he saw as "reduced" by Toynbee and Spengler—who thought man believed because "he needs" to believe, not because Revelation is true. *The World of the Polis, Plato and Aristotle*, and *The Ecumenic Age* maintained his argument. *From Enlightenment to Revolution* was edited by John H. Hallowell (1975). See also Eugene Webb, *Eric Voegelin: Philosopher of History* (1981).

**Volunteer Action**, with many variations important to the modern conservative as resisting the advances of welfarism (*q.v.*) and creating steps for cutting it back. Its roots were in charity, which became less and less reputable as democratic aspirations grew in post-Civil War decades, even though the New York State Board of Charities gained from the distinguished work of Josephine Shaw Lowell (*q.v.*). Voluntarism differed from self-help (*q.v.*), which saw hard-pressed labor elements and Negro communities raising money and means among themselves for health and sustenance purposes. Volunteers of America stemmed from Salvation Army religious and social purposes, after 1896. Numerous other agencies, from coast to coast, local and of larger scope, developed or emerged from particular crises to minister to want, homelessness, and meager or helpless conditions, especially in the great cities. Volunteers were organized by hospitals and prisons to console, encourage, or "enhance the quality of lives." Old newsboys in Detroit who recalled their poverty-shadowed youth organized in 1914 to raise money for the city's waifs; in 1982 they raised $375,000 to add glow to Christmas for some 36,500 of Detroit's children. Federalism entered into the field in 1971 with the creation of ACTION, intended to mobilize volunteers through VISTA (Volunteers in Service to America), seeking to reach needy elements through state offices. Conservative critics argued that such agencies in practice served mainly their administrative staffs. Fear of crime and desperation in the great cities created neighborhood watch groups to patrol the embattled streets. These groups for a while were given funds from the Federal Law Enforcement Assistance Administration (LEAA), though the heart of the grassroots program was citizen concern. The Reagan Administration came in with high enthusiasm for volunteer services and self-help ideas, but also with a will to curb bureaucracy, particularly as it spread out from Washington. It closed down LEAA. It expressed admiration for local efforts of all kinds, centered in hospitals, in community service agencies, involving the "new poor" hit by economic depression, and highlighting determined individuals with the power to attract support. Reagan worked under liberal criticism, to diminish the long list of Federal agencies created under Lyndon B. Johnson (*q.v.*) and his "War on Poverty." Reagan's call for the observance of "National Volunteer Week" mentioned not only the needy and harassed, but the larger society which required individual cooperation. He urged the "private sector" to help cut down the escalating costs of health care. He praised the "volunteer" spirit which inspired several Indiana banks to cut interest rates on loans for automobile purchases, to help local business. Volunteer services were an old, established function of society. Whether they had been hurt or impeded by new traditions of welfare was unclear. Whether they could be rebuilt and augmented to substitute for government welfare services and affect positively society's workings, while satisfying its needs, was undetermined. Carolyn Chiechi, *Private Foundations* (1974); Richard Ellis, *Corporative Giving in a Free Society* (1956); Burton Weisbrock, *The Voluntary Nonprofit Sector* (1977).

**Voting Rights Act** (1965), momentous law passed by a bi-partisan majority, intended to overcome state stipulations which denied or tended to deny the vote of sections of the population, notably blacks, but affecting elements in every state. States-rights (*q.v.*) partisans fought the bill as transgressing local traditions and the general will, and as filling the voting booths with unready people. The bill becoming law, the next issue was as to its effectiveness. Black partisans protested that insufficient numbers of Federal examiners were provided for overseeing state and local compliance with the law. Tradition affected not only whites but blacks, many of whom were used to not voting, or joined other Americans in their indifference to the vote. Black organizers, and increasingly organizers in other ethnic groups, labored to create blocs of voters representing their interests and favoring preferred candidates, using the time-honored means of slogans, neighborhood agitators, and transportation to the polls for the old, infirm, or languid and united them behind preferred candidates. Black mayors were elected in such major cities as Los Angeles, Chicago, and Philadelphia. Candidates increasingly emphasized, however, that they represented all population sectors. George Wallace (*q.v.*), though once famous as a segregation politician, reversed himself, persuading Alabama blacks that he was their friend determined to benefit them economically. As a result, he was re-elected as Governor with substantial black support. With others newly conscious of the power of bloc voting, it remained to be seen what might occur in the large constituency of white voters.

**Vulgarity**, compared by some to "puritanical," life-hating, hypocritical standards of deportment, speech and attitudes. Persons and situations assessed as puritanical, and identified with "gentility" (*q.v.*), received growing disregard or ridicule following World War I. Vulgarity was equated with earthiness by protesters of the 1960s and after, who publicly flaunted "loose" styles and language. Although vulgarity as a cause gave way to the exigencies of jobs and practical relations, it continued to merit the social criticism it had received from such authors as Mark Twain, George Ade, Ogden Nash, and S. J. Perelman.

# W

**Wage and Price Controls,** a major liberal panacea for inflation (*q.v.*) shortages, imbalances in production, banking (*q.v.*) defects, and other economic evils. Conservatives fought such controls in every way possible. They held that, far from curing inflation, controls augmented it. It created another bureaucracy (*q.v.*) to undermine the free market and discourage industry, serving no one but the bureaucrats. It undermined public morality by creating a black market. Yet the impulse toward regulation was always about, putting pressure on executives, tempting the public to experiment with it. Although President Nixon (*q.v.*) denounced controls, his Administration instituted them. A confusing halfway house to wage and price controls was "guidelines," which, pressuring business to hold the line on wages, were seen by their opponents as inevitably affecting prices and sowing discontent and demoralization among workers and entrepreneurs. The conservative Administration which took over in Washington in 1980 set itself rigidly against controls, and sought to avoid "guidelines." R. L. Schuttinger and E. F. Butler, *Forty Centuries of Wage and Price Controls: How Not to Fight Inflation* (1979).

**Wage Fund Theory.** It held that there was a fixed amount of capital to pay for goods, manufacture, and distribution, leaving whatever remained for wages. Increase in population thus forced wages to diminish, increasing suffering and death among laborers and their families, for which nothing remained but social efforts to accept the results, or, in liberal theory, to encourage colonization for draining off an "excess" population. This theory left a heritage of fatalism among the favored classes which their compassionate reformers could not stir to new solutions. The cooperative or socialist solution was for a redistribution of income, or later, Keynesian (*q.v.*) manipulation of currency, involving inflation which struck most harshly at the laborers and their families, and required social services and black-market enterprise for survival.

**"Wage Slavery,"** a formulation of post-Civil War eras when industry, freed of war duties, and with a "New Immigration" (*q.v.*) pool of workers to utilize, was denounced by labor leaders and liberals for onerous treatment of its employees. In fact, treatment differed in different industries and sections of the country. Disappointed miners, formerly drawn to gold, silver, and copper mines seeking riches, found themselves rudely employed by men who were like themselves and used to bitter, competitive struggle. More reprehensible to reformers seemed the operators of "sweatshops," who gathered helpless and ignorant girls into inhumane places of labor and made them desperate with crushing wages and hours of work. Such hapless workers needed unions. Workers who worked separately in their own homes, with air filled with lint or tobacco, its space with materials for processing, needed laws to control or change the business. Conservatives appealed to individualism (*q.v.*) in their defense of mining and lumbering. They appealed to free enterprise (*q.v.*) in their defense of sweatshops. However, among the reformers who protested the sad conditions which accompanied the varied forms of labor were distinguished conservatives of the stamp of Josephine Shaw Lowell and Jane Addams (*qq.v.*), who added brilliant chapters to the history of American industries and institutions. Samuel Gompers (*q.v.*) saw himself not as a conservative or radical, but as one directing American labor into ways of opportunity and strength. Louis D. Brandeis (*q.v.*), as "people's advocate" and Supreme Court Justice, saw himself as bringing law to bear upon actual conditions, rather than economic or social theory, as did a host of figures in the Progressive era (*q.v.*). Paradoxically, though assessed by later conservatives as having begun the process which culminated in the New Deal (*q.v.*), they were perceived by more radical-minded liberals such as Richard Hofstadter to have done too little.

**Wages,** a long-time issue in strikes and other labor-capital episodes. Traditionally part of the tragic history of labor, particularly during hectic eras of the Industrial Revolution, wages spurred the battle for unions (*q.v.*) and collective bargaining. Conservative theoreticians of the 19th century tended to see the question of due wages according to the framework of their economics. Made notorious by compassionate observers and socialists was the Wage Fund theory (*q.v.*), which held that there was only so much money left from which wages could be paid after the capitalists had attended to rent, interest, and other necessities. (See *Cyclopedia of Political Science.*) Although there were obvious differences in the wages of skilled and unskilled employees, it took generations of conflict and negotiations to set up going rates of wages in the various trades. Conservatives argued for a free market which would set levels satisfactory to both workman and employer, but minimum wage laws, the full employment of the World War II period, and the succeeding prosperity put the history of wages into the past. Big labor (*q.v.*) could challenge big business on equal, or better than equal, terms. Unions (*q.v.*) could sway legislators. "Skill" on automated machines became a matter of definition. The notorious "featherbedding" (*q.v.*), employing unnecessary workers in unnecessary jobs, lowered the meaning of productivity (*q.v.*) and quality. Such services as fire-fighting and garbage collection were dangerously politicalized in some cities. "Cost of living" increases led to greater expectations from workers. A protracted series of catastrophes interposed. Inflation (*q.v.*), increased costs of production, a spectacular rise in the price of oil (*q.v.*), loss of markets to better-perceived foreign products, war and defense expenditures, and what many saw as arrogant strikes combined to force industry to curb expenses by closing plants, cutting the work force, and denying "cost of living" increases whenever possible. There were often demands that wages be cut back. Although pro-labor statisticians sought to discredit capitalists in traditional ways—by publicizing their large salaries, perquisites, and general affluence, it was evident that labor had lost much of its ancient prestige. To many the free market seemed as reasonable a means for determining due returns to labor and capital as any other measure of justice. See also Concessions. At issue also in these fluid conditions was the minimum-wage law. Conservatives argued that the minimum wage should be lowered for youth employment. Liberals argued that this would result in the loss of jobs by higher-paid adult workers. An interesting phenomenon of mid-1980s was the quiet proliferation of companies remaining free from unionization by granting their workers higher pay and benefits than under prevailing union contracts in exchange for greater company control over work rules and productivity.

**Waite, Morrison R.** (1816-1888), Chief Justice of the Supreme Court (appointed 1874). His decisions in the *Granger Cases* (1877) were intended to implement state authority, much weakened by the exigencies of the Civil War and by the swift growth of industries at the expense of farmers and others who required their services. In effect, the Waite Court held that "business affected with a public interest" was subject to law and could be controlled by state legislatures even when their laws affected operations in other states. Although such a decision seemed Populist (*q.v.*) and disruptive of commerce to such partisans of business as E. L. Godkin and William Graham Sumner (*qq.v.*), Waite's Court was generally conservative. But it sought to strike a balance which did not leave small farmers and small business people at the mercy of giant combines and railroads. Waite himself helped to modify state power by implementing "due process" (*q.v.*) which gave business confined by state laws options for carrying their cases beyond state adjudication to circuit courts, and to the Supreme Court itself. See Filler, "Morrison R. Waite," in Friedman, Israel, eds., *The Justices of the Supreme Court* (1969).

**Wallace, George C.** (1919- ), Democratic Alabama governor and Presidential candidate. He exemplified the turnings Southern (*q.v.*) states made in order to accommodate themselves to Supreme Court rulings and Congressional laws mandating desegregation and an end to racial discrimination (*qq.v.*). Closer to demagogue than to conservative (*qq.v.*), Wallace, as governor of Alabama, first took a defiant stance toward national law, vowing that segregation would endure in the South then and forever. In February 1968 he announced his determination to run as a third-party candidate for the Presidency, and made national tours, where he was well received despite liberal and radical agitation. In the elections proper, he far outdid comparable parties, winning the electoral votes of five Southern states and a total of almost ten million votes nationally. Believing that he had laid a foundation for national power, Wallace continued to assert states rights, scorn of radicals, and opposition to forced desegregation—which was as equally undesired in the North as in the South. In the 1972 Presidential race, when he seemed to be gaining ground as a third-party candidate he was shot and partly paralyzed by a disturbed would-be assassin, and his national hopes were curtailed. However, he continued strong in Alabama, working from his wheelchair, overcoming marital upsets, and finally announcing a full change of heart. His old resistance to desegregation was gone. He was a friend of the blacks, and went among them expressing his good will and desire to help them in their troubles. His program was to help the poor and jobless, without distinction of race. Although some black spokesmen urged their communities to beware of Wallace as a deceiver, he was well received among them and, reelected as governor. In 1982, twenty years after his first inaugural speech, he pledged his aid to the needy of all races in Alabama. "A nation that forgets its poor will lose its soul," he told his black and white auditors. At that moment, he appeared to speak for a new conservatism in Alabama.

**Wanniski, Jude** (1936- ), supply-side economist. At first a writer for the editorial page of the *Wall Street Journal*, he later became president of a business-consultant firm, Polyconomics. Well regarded by conservative theoreticians was his popularly written *The Way the World Works: How Economies Fail—and Succeed* (1978), published by Basic Books.

**War,** see Filler, DASC. Made momentous in the 1980s by fear of nuclear (*q.v.*) war, as distinguished from the numerous conventional wars, almost all with atrocious aspects, being waged from Lebanon to Cambodia. Missing was a sense of the philosophy of war, which had once made it a legitimate occupation for those with the proper temperament and abilities. Total war, since World War I (*q.v.*), had broadened the meaning of professional soldier to take in almost anybody so that, given particular conditions, it could embrace millions of people, male and female, willing and unwilling. Franklin D. Roosevelt (*q.v.*) was the last President who, as Commander in Chief, was able to conduct war and peace almost unrestrained. (See Revisionists.) Truman and Eisenhower, facing Cold War (*q.v.*), moved diplomatically rather than through military power. Kennedy, in connection with Cuba, faltered at the Bay of Pigs but stiffened during the Cuban Missile Crisis. Johnson's Presidency was brought down by the Vietnam War (*q.v.*). The same war, though it was being wound down, helped cost Nixon his Presidency. Ford, despite adverse criticism, put up a creditable display for his troubled country. The "hostages" nightmare of Carter's Administration lost America much prestige. Reagan's struggles over the military budget were moved by the need to resist Communists abroad and pacifists at home and among friendly nations. Events in the Middle East and in the Caribbean and domestic and European resistance to Reagan military policies made it evident that the Commander-in-Chief could not avoid mixing politics with the movement of troops and arms. The German theoretician of war, Karl von Clausewitz, had said that war was politics carried on by other means, and this was never more relevant. It was as important to Soviet planners of expansion to encourage pacifists in the West as to prepare to encounter Western troops anywhere in the world. Being unhampered by democratic processes, their strategy differed fundamentally from that which Western democracies were required to develop. See also Detente. Richard Nixon, *The Real War* (1980); M. S. Stohl, *War and Domestic Violence* (1976); T. A. Taracousia, *War and Peace in Soviet Diplomacy* (1975); Michael Howard, *War and the Liberal Conscience* (1978); James T. Johnson, *Just War Traditions and the Restraint of War* (1981). See also Social War.

**"War on Poverty,"** see Volunteer Action

**Ward, Chester,** see Schlafly, Phyllis

**Warren, Earl** (1891-1974), Chief Justice of the Supreme Court (1953-1969). He provided a record of court decisions which dismayed conservatives, who accused him of subverting the Constitution. Although all conservatives would not go the length of the John Birch Society (*q.v.*), which purchased billboard space to declare to the public that Earl Warren ought to be impeached, there were doubtless more than just members of the Society who agreed with this demand. Yet he had been appointed by President Eisenhower, who had had no expectation of such decisions as gave Warren his place in history. Although Warren could not have gained them without a majority of the Court being composed of civil libertarians—William O. Douglas, Hugo Black, William J. Brennan, Arthur J. Goldberg (who, retiring from the Court, made place for Abe Fortas)—Warren himself put his stamp upon the Court. Eisenhower, who in time regretted the appointment, knew that Warren favored expansion of citizen rights, but he knew too that Warren as governor of California had among other views accepted the necessity for internment of Japanese-Americans during World War II. He was given no inkling of Warren's belief that justice, as he viewed it, took precedence to precise or associated readings of the Constitution itself. His Court's most momentous decision, with himself writing the majority ruling, was *Brown vs. Board of Education of Topeka* (1954) (*q.v.*), which opened wide the field of desegregation. But the great reapportionment case, *Reynolds vs. Sims* (1964), which struck down traditional districts in all the states and ruled that only population could be the basis for appointment was a blow to a rural primacy of long establishment. Anthony Lewis, a Warren admirer, wrote, Warren "did not ask whether the Constitution applied to the whole issue of appointment, or if so what theories of representation ought to be considered. He began with the premise that the democratic norm was equal treatment of individual voters and then asked what departures from absolute population equality the Constitution would countenance." (See Lewis, "Earl Warren," in Friedman, Israel [eds.], *The Justices of the Supreme Court of the United States.*) Such was the process of examination into feasible solutions. Justice Harlan, dissenting, maintained: "This view, in a nutshell, is that every major social ill in this country can find its cure in some constitutional 'principle,' and that this Court should 'take the lead' in promoting reform when other branches of government fail to act." The Warren Court's war against "unreasonable" searches and seizures, against "self-incrimination," and guaranteeing the right of counsel; its work in cutting the lines between state law and Federal law in behalf of what it interpreted as constitutional rights—in effect depriving states of authority—reached one plateau in the famous case of *Miranda vs. Arizona* (1966), which sought to insure that police procedures would not jeopardize the constitutional rights of those arrested. What effect such decisions would have on the society proper conservatives presumed to spell out, in their search for constitutional order. With the Court firmly in the hands of acknowledged civil-rights partisans, conservatives followed their proceedings with care, and also looked into congressional possibilities for redress, and even constitutional change.

**Warsaw Pact,** including the Soviet Union, East Germany, Rumania, Bulgaria, Hungary,

Czechoslovakia, and Poland. Begun in 1955 under Soviet control, it was intended to give notice to NATO that interference with its concerns would bring Soviet retaliation. Although most members were obviously captive (*q.v.*) nations, as the Hungarian uprising the following year gave evidence, the Pact gave dramatic indication of how times had changed since there had been a Comintern (Communist International), which had marshalled worldwide strength for the defense of the "Worker's Fatherland," the Soviet Union. The progress of the various Warsaw Pact nations was varied enough to give hope to some observers that there were limits to Soviet tyranny beyond its borders. Conservative analysts tended toward a hard line which saw the "softening" of Soviet objectives only subject to displays of power it could not resist.

**Washington, Booker T.** (1856-1915), American Negro educator, recognized as the successor to Frederick Douglass, though less militant in his public demands than Douglass—whose circumstances as a runaway, an outlaw, and an advocate of all rights identified with the Revolution's goals place him necessarily within a liberal-radical spectrum. Washington, though born in slavery, having risen to the headship of Tuskegee (Alabama) Normal and Industrial Institute for Negroes, found himself working for leadership in the South, and among Negro communities spread through the South and North, and challenged by more aggressive and demanding elements. He had therefore to engage in intergroup politics which angered some of his co-workers. Of the South and for the nation he offered a program of gradualism which in effect accepted "equal but separate" stipulations, though indicating hope for better things. H. Hawkins, ed., *Booker T. Washington and His Critics* (1962); S. R. Spencer, Jr., *Booker T. Washington and the Negro's Place in American Life* (1955); A. Meier, *Negro Thought in America* (1963); and Washington's own classic *Up from Slavery* (1910).

**Washington, George** (1732-1799), for decades following the American Revolution the enshrined figure in national annals, as first in war and first in peace: the one who had held a wavering alliance of planters, merchants, laborers, and even slaves together for republican principles, and carried it through treachery and ill-faith against a powerful force of arms supported by Americans loyal to the Crown. Washington's readiness to endure beside his men, his patience with adversaries, and steadiness under all but catastrophic conditions were central to the long campaign, and gave the new nation credibility abroad as well as at home. His rejection of overtures of his conservative associates who would have made him a king, and his modest but firm building of Presidential prerogatives established the Executive office on constitutional grounds. Although popular adulation following his death tended to deprive him of the human traits which would have made him more interesting to school children and newer immigrants, enough remained in memory of his brilliant stroke at Trenton, his endurance at Valley Forge, and the general strategy by which he kept together a difficult people to make his principles credible to all but those of disloyal sentiment. Abraham Lincoln's (*q.v.*) rise as a savior of the Union, his humble beginnings and democratic sentiments, tended to diminish Washington's stature in perspective. But enough of it remained to remind the least history-minded student that the circumstances under which Lincoln had fought the Civil War differed widely from those under which Washington had been born and matured. Not until the 1920s, when "disillusionment" with the results of World War I created an interest in "debunking" American heroes, were questions raised respecting Washington's character in sophisticated circles. Rupert Hughes' *George Washington* (1926-1930) provided some sense of shock in indicating that Washington had been less than elegant in some of his actions and expressions. If anything, it served to counteract the still prissy and dehumanizing treatments accorded to Washington in the lower schools. Later, less friendly attempts to prove that Washington had sought to defraud the Congress in his accounts of funds due him for services in the field, which seemed to many to be based on misconceptions about the value of money in colonial times, probably did as much for modernizing attention to the hero as for anything else. The work of editing his writings and analyzing his character and life never flagged, in modern times reaching a highpoint in Douglas S. Freeman's magisterial *George Washington* (1948-1957), in seven volumes. Subsequent social turmoil called attention to Washington as a slaveholder. It remained to be seen how modern statements and surveys might accommodate themselves to such American heroes (*q.v.*) as Washington.

**Washington Times,** a newspaper founded in 1982 by the Unification Church leader Sun Myung Moon in order to present the Capitol with a conservative viewpoint. It was intended to oppose the *Washington Post*'s established liberal program on national politics and the world. The *Times* had to overcome public skepticism regarding Reverend Moon's interest in influencing the paper's editorial policy. Although the *Times* attracted outstanding conservative writers and developed an attractive format, it at first grew slowly. Several editorial changes later, however, and with the accession of Arnaud de Borchgrave as editor-in-chief, the *Times* picked up momentum and advertising. By August 1985 it was able to announce publicly that it had achieved a circulation of almost 84,000 in less than three years, putting it among the top 20 percent of daily newspapers. By 1986, its circulation had risen to 150,000, and it had added a magazine, *Insight*, to its offerings. In 1986 they launched a 700-page monthly publication, *The World and I*, discussing modern thought, natural science, intellectually significant books.

**WASPs (White Anglo-Saxon Protestants),** held to be the original dominant force in the nation's direction, and under heavy challenge in the twentieth century. Notorious were the claims of demagogues and even such distinguished representatives as Samuel F. B. Morse, inventor and artist of the nineteenth century, that this was a white man's country, that Catholics (*q.v.*) were suspect, and Jews (*q.v.*) grasping in money affairs. Although political exigencies reduced blatant race hatred, blunt discrimination against Negroes (*q.v.*), malicious rumors against Catholics, and crude quotas against Jews—who were alleged to be "too smart" to move freely into medical schools—continued until the shocks of social demoralization following World War II (*q.v.*) made such policies untenable. Negroes and Jews were found to head famous institutions. Catholics were leaders in society, produced best sellers, and were forced to face internal crises similar to those of other groups. The New Conservatives attracted persons of all status and condition, including so-called WASPs. Prejudice as such had no place in New Conservative policies and organization. Remarkably, the strong emphasis in those policies on constitutionality, tradition, local and state preferences, the Tenth Amendment (*q.v.*), and opposition to the Federal bureaucracy and Federal expenditures and domination caused many liberals to charge New Conservatives with racial, religious, ethnic, and social bias. But WASPs were not alone in protesting urban deterioration, busing, "affirmative action" procedures, crime, and abortion. Many Catholics, Jews, and others favored some sort of public encouragement for religious observances, even though such encouragement had traditionally been Protestant-oriented. Many women found the extremes of pro-abortion policies distasteful. Thus, the original WASPs, in their newfound social image, were less the foes of ethnic minorities than they had been some decades before, and might prove to be part of a new majority. For derogatory academic portrayals of the WASP tradition, John G. Sproat, "*The Best Men*" (1965); S. Persons, *The Decline of American Gentility* (1973); J. Tomisch, *A Genteel Endeavor* (1971).

**Watch and Ward Society,** see Censorship

**Watergate**, see Filler, DASC. The Watergate Affair was a problem for conservatives, since many of them were ambivalent about the break-in on Democratic Party headquarters, and considered Daniel Ellsberg's publication of the so-called Pentagon Papers in the *New York Times* reprehensible at a time when American troops were engaged in battle. Yet conservatives were aware that even many conservative-minded citizens were dubious over the ethics of undercover operations emanating from the White House and involving President Nixon. It helped a little that such activities were not unique, as Victor Lasky showed in *It Didn't Start with Watergate* (1977). Nevertheless the Administration had been disgraced; it had associated with dubious personalities and had given ammunition to its foes. It had forced painful adjustments, harmful to espionage and security operations, and had made a deadly foe of the *New York Times* (*q.v.*), a major organ of the nation as well as of liberalism. Nevertheless, new conservatives could come into power with clean hands and a chance to appeal to citizens under more sophisticated terms. Although many liberals continued to point to Watergate in subsequent elections, its impact declined. Nixon made the bestseller lists, and he was soon in demand as an analyst at home and abroad. Other Watergate participants grew rich from best selling books and other dealings. *Time* polls soon indicated that the public had "softened" toward the entire matter and had concluded that Watergate had been "politics as usual." Thus, the "legacy of Watergate" appeared in danger of fading into insignificance.

**Watson, J.B.,** see Behaviorism

**Watt, James G.** (1938- ), as Secretary of the Interior a controverisal figure in President Reagan's (*q.v.*) first Administration. Watt became one symbol of the struggle waged between conservatives and liberals in the early 1980s. The son of Wyoming homesteaders, and himself raised among western rangers, Watt was steeped in the lore of soil, water, and air. From 1966, when he served the U. S. Chamber of Commerce as secretary to its natural resources committee, through the 1970s he held posts involving outdoor recreation, federal power authority, and conservation legalities. He was notorious to such liberal watchdog agencies as the Sierra Club. They followed Watt's career as president of the Mountain States Legal Foundation (1977-1980), during which he fought restrictions on gas and oil explorations in wildlife sanctuaries, air pollution, and strip-mining. His program of less law and more private enterprise was approved by Reagan, who appointed him Secretary of the Interior. The Sierra Club worked to oppose Watt's five-year plan, which, by mid-1982, called for releasing some 35 million acres of Federal land for gas and oil exploration. Watt pointed out that this involved only some five percent of Federal holdings. He urged that in a crisis the nation needed a backlog of energy resources, and an established group of specialists and business people who could provide them as required. Watt enjoyed great popularity in the Western states. His tenure as Secretary was halted by a public outcry when he joked that his commission on coal pricing included "a black, a woman, two Jews, and a cripple." The subsequent clamor emphasizing his insensitivity did more to discredit him and embarrass President Reagan than had his land policies. Administration efforts to quell public indignation failing, Watt was asked to resign. R. Brownstein and N. Easton, *Reagan's Ruling Class* (1982); see also Environment.

**Waugh, Evelyn** (1903-1966), British author, like Graham Greene a gift from Great Britain to Catholic conservatives. But his satirical novels lacked the adventure and dramatic excitement which drew to Greene's work many readers of varied social and political persuasions. Waugh's *Brideshead Revisited* (1944) made timeless and unpolitical the feelings and preferences of an upper class removed from the aspirations of other classes for which Waugh had little feeling. He found particularly obnoxious the "pushing" elements of society whose egotism deprived them of the sympathy of all classes. In a subsequent television serialization, *Brideshead Revisited* was an outstanding popular success, in America and Great Britain. Whether it had any notable influence on public views, however, may be doubted. See also Catholicism; Society; Cozzens, James Gould; Chesterton, Gilbert Keith.

**Wave of the Future, The,** see Lindbergh, Charles A.

**"Waving the Bloody Shirt,"** see Patriotism

**W.C.T.U.,** see Willard, Frances E. Union

**We The Living** (1936), by Ayn Rand (*q.v.*), her powerful novel of the Petrograd she knew before and after the Russian Revolution (1917): soaked in drabness and hypocrisy. The city affected not only her declassed and demeaned bourgeois family and associates. It twisted and turned its friends and enemies. It closed and opened doors, took bread and gave champagne underneath the slogans of the New Society. Rand's memory of the streets, sounds, houses, the appurtenances of life, the nuances of meeting and response in her new language of English was phenomenal; the memory of a born writer who had seen and felt intensely, and from a firm center of individuality. The slogans and symbols of Communism, her Argounovs, Dunaevs, Kovalenskys, Comrade Pavol Syerov, Comrade Sonya, the speculator Mazarov, Comrade Andrea Tagonov of the GPU, the adventuress Antonina Pavlova, Stepan Timoshenko, the peasant Lavrov—who had given their all to the Revolution—were people with pasts, in Czarist times and after. The University was a place of forms and features and professors, as were the unions and clubs which could mean sustenance or harassment, a place to live or a place to die. All this Rand recounted with the cold balance and bitter memories of art. The book took her four years to write, two to get published—publishers were reluctant to print an anti-Soviet novel. The book was a failure until the success of *The Fountainhead* (*q.v.*) put it back into print. But print did nothing for one of the fine novels of the twentieth century. Being "bourgeois," it gave her no status with dissenters (*q.v.*), or with conservatives who read it as a tract. Rand herself imagined that she was not writing of Russia but of dictatorship, as to an extent she was. But it was vastly more the story of her own life, and of the humanity of others. While Soviet apologists said that "Russians" were just like Americans, interested in singing, dancing, and the simple things of life, *We the Living* said that they were indeed just like others: subject to forces which they rarely had the capacity to resist, and which could lead to defeat in the midst of "victory." It would appear that Rand wrote herself out. Her subsequent work had no more to do with *We the Living* than she had to do with the family which had given her birth or brought her to the United States. For some details, in the midst of dogma, Nathaniel Branden, *Who Is Ayn Rand*? (1964).

**Wealth and Poverty** (1981), by George Gilder (*q.v.*), his best seller of that year. It gained by the incoming Reagan (*q.v.*) Administration, and the known fact that the new President believed in supply-side (*q.v.*) economics and would work for a tax cut, a war on inflation (*q.v.*), and related measures opposed by many liberals. But it won attention as a matured example of Gilder's old-fashioned moral concern for family, free enterprise, and "faith"—not explicitly identified as to religion, but implying a sense of social destiny. "The Mandate for Capitalism" noted the strange lack of regard for capitalism by conservatives—Daniel Boorstin (*q.v.*), for example, finding it "morally vacant." Although Gilder saw "real poverty" as a state of mind and capitalism strongest in the area of psychology, he buttressed his moral argument with numerous statistics to attack the liberal claims for "income distribution" and "welfare," which he saw as at the root of urban decay, family demoralization, and the undermining of the human nature of men and women. The base of a living society was work. Hard, fulfilling work and upward mobility (*q.v.*) had been the lot of all the nation's poor and minorities. Liberal laws intended to make them secure and equal had degraded them and made more hopeless their inequality. Gilder was especially caustic about the long record of dependency the government had fostered among the poor: "The attempt of the welfare state to deny, suppress, and plan away the dangers and uncertainties of our lives—to domesticate the inevitable unknown—violate not only the spirit of capitalism but also the nature of man." Although he gave substantial space to the theories of Laffer (*q.v.*) and related economists, it was his probings into the actions and responses of the poor themselves, including blacks (*q.v.*), buttressed with statistics, which gave bite to his judgments and beliefs, adding up to an "Economy of Faith." Compare with Richard H. Fink, ed., *Supply Side Economics: A Critical Appraisal* (1983).

**Weaver, Richard M.** (1910-1963), American author and educator. His life was a development of Southern feeling and conservatism which proved stimulating and evocative to others formulating new conservative views. Born in North Carolina, he studied at the University of Kentucky, explored socialism, and was taken by the writings of the Agrarians (*q.v.*). In 1940, dissatisfied with his own state of mind and social trends, he undertook a re-examination of both. Ortega's (*q.v.*) *Revolt of the Masses* provided him with one clue to social order, the Southern tradition and the results of Civil War another. The ideals of chivalry and religion seemed to him as necessary as ever. He joined the English Department of the University of Chicago in 1945. His first book made him famous. *Ideas Have Consequences* (1948) was a precursor of a coming literature of conservatism. Willmoore Kendall (*q.v.*) saw it as an indictment of "modern man": an egotist with no sense of moral responsibility. Based on the Platonic-Christian tradition, the book resisted what it saw as a crass empiricism endemic in society. Kendall's one criticism was that Weaver did not directly identify the liberal as the enemy. Weaver's *The Ethics of Rhetoric* (1953) built on the idea of words as deeds. Standing between Old South traditions and the new conservatism, Weaver's essays and reviews contributed to developments in both sectors. Following his death, his essays were collected in *Visions of Order* (1964), with an introduction by Russell Kirk (*q.v.*), and *Life without Prejudice* (1965).

**Webster, Daniel** (1782-1852), American statesman. Once admired as a rock of the Union and of constitutional stability, he daunted even abolitionists by his national passion and the power of his analyses of law. His foes could only conclude that it was the Union itself which was expendible. Beginning his public career as a loyal New Englander, he denounced Jefferson's (*q.v.*) peace-seeking "Embargo" against commercial intercourse, essentially with warring nations, as an attack on New England shipping. He also denounced the 1816 Tariff the Protective features of which would do the same. By the next decade, he had become a thorough nationalist who praised Protection as good for native industry and who sought internal improvements to bind the states, defended the sanctity of contracts, and approved Army and other Federal expenditures. His great orations reached their peak in his debate with the southern senator Robert Y. Hayne over the validity of nullification (see Calhoun, John C.). In them Webster declared for the North: "Liberty *and* Union, now and forever, one and inseparable." Deprived of the Presidency, he served as Secretary of State and Senator. In 1850 he delivered his appeal for compromise on the slavery issue, speaking "not as a Massachusetts man, nor as a Northern man, but as an American....Hear me for my cause." Although Free Soilers (*q.v.*) professed to be shocked by Webster's "treason," he was saying no more than he had ever said, and was honored in following decades as one of the great men of the nation. John Bach McMaster (*q.v.*), *Daniel Webster* (1902); C. M. Fuess, *Daniel Webster* (1930).

**Welch, Robert** (1899-1985), founder and director of the John Birch Society (*q.v.*), made notorious by liberals and handled with care by many active conservatives in public life. Welch, a brilliant youth and successful candy manufacturer, fought for Robert A. Taft's Presidential aspirations in 1952. He was persuaded by the defeat of Nationalist China and the expansion of Soviet Russia in Eastern Europe and elsewhere that this could not have happened without the American government's program and actions, which he saw as amounting to a conspiracy (*q.v.*) with the Communists against American interests. He expressed his views in a speech published by Regnery (*q.v.*) in 1952, *May God Forgive Us*, which sold 200,000 copies. He seized on the murder by Chinese Communists of a Baptist minister, John Birch, to make him a symbol of American failure and misdemeanor in opposing Communist plans. Welch founded the John Birch Society in 1958, an organization he ran totally. His broad denunciations, which took in President Dwight D. Eisenhower (*q.v.*) stirred excitement and concern among politicians. Liberals held him to be an "extremist," typical of conservatives who used him and his society as arguments in their literary and political campaigns. Welch, however, had tapped a segment of society dissatisfied with the language and view of liberals. His book *The Politician*, as published in 1963, though ignored by regular reviewers and book distributors sold some 250,000 copies. His Society at its peak had some 80,000 members, most of them older, upper-class whites, a force with which conservatives had to reckon in some areas of the nation. Ronald Reagan, running for governor in California, put it that he could not stop anybody who wanted to vote for him. The Birch insistence on a "conspiracy" favoring Communism—and including such persons as Secretary of State John Foster Dulles (*q.v.*) and his brother Allen, director of the CIA (*q.v.*)—shocked many conservative-minded people, as did the Society's lurid campaign to impeach Chief Justice Warren (*q.v.*) which many believed harmed the conservative cause rather than helped it. Welch's magazine *American Opinion* (*q.v.*), with its open scorn of democracy, which it insisted the Founding Fathers had never intended, and with its drastic program for achieving peace at home and abroad, could be clearly distinguished from the more pertinent operations of conservatives involved in day-to-day dialogue. A Senate Internal Security Subcommittee eventually concluded that the Society was protected by free-speech rights and was patriotic in its intention. Welch retired in 1983 from rule over a clearly declining operation. See G. E. Griffin, *The Life and Words of Robert Welch* (1975), and Welch's own *The Life of John Birch* (1954).

**Welfare,** one of the formidable issues dividing liberals and conservatives. It involved assessments of the proper role of government in social problems. Once the province of voluntary (*q.v.*) organizations in the United States, welfare assistance instituted as relief during the difficult Thirties (*q.v.*), maintained during World War II despite full employment, and institutionalized in the affluent Fifties (*q.v.*), when the deterioration of cities and family life among the poor became notorious. Eisenhower's Welfare and Pension Fund Disclosure Act of 1958 made efforts to obtain some control over private fund manipulations, mainly those of labor. Difficulties were increased in the public sector since public welfare was often concentrated in minority areas which could claim racism (*q.v.*) and harassment. The youth and civil rights (*q.v.*) urprisings of the Sixties (*q.v.*) revealed a reckless disregard of civil authority and demoralized many administrators more fearful of their clients than of higher authority. Although President Carter (*q.v.*) in 1978 planned abolition of the welfare system, to be succeeded by job incentives and other measures, he could not reach his Democratic Congress for action. The one factor working for change was the economic depression and rising unemployment, along with a government deficit which demanded cuts in government expenditures. Although Reagan Administration cuts in social services were denounced as cruel, new attention was forced on the welfare problem, including its scale of benefits from direct relief to housing subsidies, with much attention given to voluntary (*q.v.*) agencies as aids to diminished budgets. Whether they would grow at the expense of welfare programs was a question for future elections. R. H. Haveman, ed., *A Decade of Federal Antipoverty Programs* (1977), M. Anderson, *Welfare: The Political Economy of Welfare Reform* (1978). See also "Workfare."

**"Welfare Capitalism,"** a concept deriving from Progressive era efforts to diminish class warfare and make firmer the bonds uniting the interests of workers and capitalists. Most notable of the entrepreneurs pressing for cordiality and cooperation were Owen D. Young and Gerard Swope of General Electric. Swope especially sought good conditions of work, profit-sharing plans, voluntary (*q.v.*) aid to the needy, rehabilitation schemes for those wounded in war, and other necessities and amenities. The Great Depression (*q.v.*) "wiped out the ideological base" of the program, as the New Deal itself undertook welfare responsibilities of a more basic kind. Josephine Young Case and Everett Needham Case, *Owen D. Young and American Enterprise* (1982); E. Berkowitz and Kim McQuaid, *Creating the Welfare State* (1980).

**Welfare State,** see Capitalism and Welfare

**Welfare State in U.S. and Great Britain.** The term had a different connotation in Great Britain—with its long tradition of patronage and royalty, where "poor house" had a humble but dignified meaning, and in America—with its traditions of independence and contempt for improvidence and lack of means. The Keynesian (*q.v.*)-based logic of manipulated currency in the interests of social use, however, operated similarly in both countries, as directed by the Democrats in the United States and Labour in the United Kingdom. The attack on the welfare state was directed in America by the Republican Party, though with little success in the Eisenhower (*q.v.*) Administration, he having the military man's indifference to cost. There was no more success under Nixon (*q.v.*), sympathetic though he was to traditional values, his goal being party and power rather than their underpinnings. The moral fervor of a Goldwater (*q.v.*) responded to the demands of traditionalists who deplored permanent welfare roles, decayed work and ethics standards, and other byproducts of the welfare state, but not sufficiently so as to win those who approved his program but not its specifics: farmers accustomed to subsidies, businessmen accustomed to ready contracts, and minority elements of every kind who recalled the New Deal (*q.v.*) with respect, though they did not approve many of its results. Reagan (*q.v.*), as a man of modest birth and small-town and college background, and with governmental programs in California which resisted the easy deficit spending of his predecessor Pat Brown cutting welfare loans and tightening school policies toward students better appealed to attitudes of traditionalists. These specifics plus others gave Reagan his chance at solving the national problem. A somewhat similar background of the Tory Margaret Thatcher (*qq.v.*) in Great Britain enabled her to launch her attack on subsidized and nationalized industry, on random and destructive education, and on welfare clients. Nevertheless Thatcher insisted that she was not attacking the welfare state, only its harmful byproducts. Not only was she given her second chance at governing Great Britain, but with a massive majority. Since other factors entered into the national decision, it remained to be seen how much of it related to the government's welfare policies.

**Weyl, Nathaniel** (1910- ), American social scientist and author, representative of a small but challenging element of the conservative spectrum. His credentials were impeccable in his antagonism to Communism and treason in its behalf, as in *Treason: The Story of Disloyalty and Betrayal in American History* (1950), *Red Star over Cuba: The Russian Assault on the Western Hemisphere* (1960), *Traitor's End, the Rise and Fall of the Communist Movement in Southern Africa* (1970). More controversial were his studies in elitism (*q.v.*), creativity, and ethnicity (*q.v.*) and races (*q.v.*)—which raised emotional memories of the Nazi Holocausts though their intention and content were the exact opposite. The premise of *The Creative Elite in America* (1966) and *The Geography of Intellect* (1963), (written with Stefan T. Possony) was to give evidence that creativity and I.Q. endowments could be traced and explained by social conditions and heredity. These books summed up years of findings by Weyl and others in science and social studies, and recognized self-interest and prejudice as in such manifest racist doctrines as could be found in Houston Chamberlain and Count de Gobineau. On the other the books employed such factors as time sequence and climate in explanation of the rise and fall of civilizations. Statistics seemed incontrovertible in terms of Jewish excellence, and the concept of a "despised elite" helpful in explaining *The Jew in American Politics* (1968). Weyl had occasion to recall John Nevin, an abolitionist in his family background, in *The Negro in American Civilization* (1960), to show that he sought the well-being of blacks in detailing their qualities and relations. With R. Travis Osborne and Clyde E. Noble, he prepared the volume *Human Variation: The Biopsychology of Age, Race, and Sex* (1978). It was dedicated to Sir Francis Galton, the founder of behavioral genetics and eugenics: a cooperative work involving scientists and experiments fulsomely reported and covering theory and statistics respecting genes and intellectual differences. A lengthy chapter covered "Fallacies in Arguments on Human Differences." A significant fact about the potential impact of such investigations was that they did not rank high on the larger conservative agenda, which involved winning over majorities in a democracy. Although conservatives could denounce "the treason of intellectuals" (*q.v.*) and voice contempt for those who opposed the "racist" opinions of Nobel-prize-winner William T. Shockley, they had problems enough with national and international issues without indulging themselves in scientific disputes. In theory, the Weyl theses were addressed to government elites with a stake in excellence. In practice these elites had not only to maintain a hold on their constituents, but to resist the propaganda of such foes as the Soviet Union, which denounced "racism" whatever its own actual practice. There were even difficulties within the field of human behavior. Thus, the implications of "biopsychology" were that genes and group history set limits to a group's potential. But Paul Johnson (*q.v.*), reporting the work of the Harvard scientist Edward Wilson in his *Sociobiology: The New Synthesis* (1975), noted the radical (*q.v.*) assault which forced the Harvard Medical School to give up its long-term research project in genetic abnormality and social patterns. Yet Wilson's target had been Darwinism (*q.v.*) not ethnic groups. He believed that human societies were different because of learning and social conditioning, not heredity. Whether such emphases involved contradictions or could be reconciled was uncertain, but they could not be made primary subjects for general dialogue. At issue were the parameters of civil rights, freedom of speech, the quality of education, and of research.

**Wharton, Michael** (1913- ), see "Peter Simple"

**What is Conservativism?** (1964), edited by Frank S. Meyer (*q.v.*), symposium displaying aspects of New Conservative thought. It ranged from Meyer's repugnance to "collectivist liberalism" to Friedrich Hayek's "Why I Am Not a Conservative" (originally published in 1960 in his *The Constitution of Liberty*). Among others, Russell Kirk spoke for "ordered freedom," Willmoore Kendall for his understanding of the Bill of Rights, Wilhelm Röpke for "economic liberty," and John Chamberlain for the morality of free enterprise. William F. Buckley, Jr.'s "Notes toward an Empirical Definition of Conservativism" used his own experiences to reach a larger public (*qq.v.*).

**Whately, Richard** (1787-1863), witty English prelate, whose famous *Historic Doubts Relative to Napoleon Buonaparte* (1819 and in numerous reprints thereafter) was a forceful effort to combat skepticism by demonstrating that the very existence of the French conqueror could be doubted on the evidence available. Essentially Whately set out to prove that faith was as substantial a guide as were alleged "facts": a conservative argument which gave heart to numerous persons assailed by doubts raised by David Hume (*q.v.*) and the Utilitarians (*q.v.*), and later to others plagued by the implications of the Darwinism (*q.v.*) hypothesis. Whately later added *Historic Certainties Respecting the Early History of America*.

**When the Going was Good! American Life in the Fifties**, by Jeffrey Hart (1982), a controversial view of the Eisenhower (*q.v.*) era, using individual memories, vignettes, and other devices to present a picture of the times. Hart had enjoyed his youth in New York City, which emphasized baseball, tennis, musical comedy, and other activities. He felt enriched by Columbia University's English Department, and especially by Lionel Trilling (*q.v.*). Having become a conservative, Hart assimilated the program of the *National Review*, which he set forth in his *The American Dissent* (1966) (*qq.v.*). Although his journalistic writings were clear on the conservative position, his cultural interpretations were controversial to conservatives who had no affinity for 20th-century literature. Hart praised Faulkner and Hemingway and F. Scott Fitzgerald's *The Great Gatsby*. He called the poet Allen Ginsberg "the Jewish Whitman," and noted the influences of Herbert Marcuse, Norman O. Brown, and Paul Goodman in the 1950s without judging the weight of their work. Although he honored Eisenhower and had a clear distaste for Communism-inspired treason, he found more that was liberal or merely commercial to approve of in the 1950s than conservatives with a distaste for modern life would admit: avant-garde art, modernist architecture, suburban developments such as Levittown, computer technology, the "roots" of the Sixties sexual and civil rights revolutions, the growth of air travel and national highways, and the development of advertising. He quoted a Hitler refugee as urging that "history must be told," and attempted to carry out this intention in his work. Hart had been a speech writer for Ronald Reagan and Richard M. Nixon (*qq.v.*) in 1968, but his sympathy for modern society jolted those conservatives who longed for the past as meriting parity with the present.

**Whigs.** In the conservative succession from Federalists (*q.v.*), they harked back to British Whiggery, with its roots in commerce and suspicion of unbridled monarchy. In the 1830s they emerged out of a variety of political elements opposed to the peremptory democracy headed by Andrew Jackson (*q.v.*). They offered statesmen of distinction, notably John Quincy Adams and Henry Clay (*qq.v.*), and attracted abolitionists repelled by the pro-slavery attitudes of the popular Democratic Party. But it was only by matching Democrats in demogogy and expedience that they were able to win elections, with General Harrison (1840) and General Taylor (1848). Rising Free Soil (*q.v.*) sentiment in the North divided Whig strength. Its disintegration by 1852 gave rise to Republican alliances, interpreted in the South as sectional. By then, however, antislavery possibilities below the Mason-Dixon Line had been stamped out. A. C. Cole, *The Whig Party in the South* (1913); G. R. Poage, *Henry Clay and the Whig Party* (1936).

**White, Edward Douglass** (1845-1921), Chief Justice of the Supreme Court. He studied at Jesuit College, New Orleans, and at Georgetown College, which later became Georgetown University (*q.v.*). At age sixteen, he enlisted in the Army of the Confederacy, was taken prisoner following the Federal siege of Port Hudson, Louisiana, and with others permitted to return home. Following the war, he was one of the Redeemers who struggled against Carpetbagger rule and joined the Ku Klux Klan in the effort. Popular at home and of well-to-do family, he served in Louisiana as lawyer, judge, and politician before joining the U. S. Senate in 1891. In 1894, as part of a political struggle, he found himself appointed to the Supreme Court as an Associate Justice. He became Chief Justice in 1910. Overall, he proved a conservative in his legal judgments, his decisions being modified by his States Rights (*q.v.*) leanings, which sometimes gave them a liberal cast. Notable was his dissent in the case of *Lochner vs. New York* (1905), in which a Court majority struck down a law setting maximum hours of work. Legal observers, however, noted inconsistencies in White's reasoning, for he also dissented from the majority in *Bunting vs. Oregon* (1917), which upheld the state's ten-hour work law. Those emphasizing "liberal" interpretations of law approved his endorsement of the Adamson Act (*Wilson vs. New* [1917]), which gave railroad workers an eight-hour day. White's greatest fame was related to the "rule of reason" which he laid down in his opinion dissolving the Standard Oil Company and the American Tobacco Company in 1911: a clearly conservative decision, in effect distinguishing between "good" and "bad" trusts. His colleague John M. Harlan protested that the Sherman Anti-Trust Law made no such distinctions; it outlawed trusts. White's florid style in legal writing disturbed commentators who did not appreciate his Southern background or political training. Sr. Marie Carolyn Klinkhamer, *Edward Douglas White* (1943).

**"White Flight,"** a momentous feature of the movement in the 1950s and afterward, from cities to suburbs. The flight of whites to suburbs after World War II, encouraged by Federal highway and housing policies, was accelerated when many saw their neighborhoods threatened by the infiltration of "undesirable" elements, notably blacks. The movement was further accelerated by unscrupulous realtors who spread rumors of such infiltration, bought up abandoned property at cheap rates, and sold it at inflated prices thus bringing down the area. "Blockbusting" became the netherside of what had begun as an effort to rise socially or to seek the peace and quiet of less-inhabited locales. White and black conservatives tended to opt for individual rights, liberals for ideals of equality and government interposition; which had more responsibility for "urban blight" was difficult to determine, for lack of open debate. See also Busing.

**White Guilt.** Although actively pressed by liberals over the ancient system of slavery, it touched conservatives to the extent that they accepted the liberal version of slavery's history in America, or accepted without qualification black rhetoric on the subject or the legal sanctions of "affirmative action" (*q.v.*). Fewer conservatives were moved by demands for "reparations" (*q.v.*) to make up for ancient wrongs. The general appeal for ethnic parity toward blacks—soon joined by similar demands touching other ethnic groups—was fed by comparable demands for the freedom of black African nations. Conservatives tended to push such agitation aside as irrelevant to practical issues of productivity, individuality, humane rule, privacy, and crime control. Conservatives also rebuffed agitation against "racism" which took no account of cost and experience. As with other social traumas, many such issues ended up in the courts—or, abroad, in an appeal to arms.

**"White Hope,"** see Sports.

**Widener, Alice,** (died 1985) conservative journalist. In 1951 as a free-lance political writer she was engaged by the official Voice of America, but in five months was let go as "too hard-hitting, too anti-Communist, not in line with our policy." In 1952 she wrote a series for *The Freeman* (*q.v.*) which became part of her book *Behind The U.N. Front* (1955), published by The Bookmailer (*q.v.*). It spelled out the anti-American front within the organization, and named American U.N. employees engaged in anti-American cooperation with it. (For differences in climate and approach, see Kirkpatrick, Jeane J.) In 1954, Mrs. Widener began her own magazine, *USA—An American Bulletin of Fact and Opinion*. A close student of the Left (*q.v.*), of which she wrote in various conservative publications, in 1970 she published *Teachers of Destruction: Their Plan for a Socialist Revolution*, vastly more authoritative than the earlier work by Elizabeth Dilling (*q.v.*) as being literally what she called it, "An Eyewitness Account." Her almost verbatim reports on meetings by revolutionary-minded professors circulated in conservative enclaves, and persuaded them that the professors constituted a conspiracy against American laws and municipal and university bylaws—though relatively few of them suffered or were inconvenienced as a result of their violent actions or encouragement of violence. What Mrs. Widener seemed unable to explain, in her glaring accounts of anti-American hatred and subversion, was what gave the participants the strength to do their work, and even to grow with it. Her researches, which touched such obvious figures as Jerry Rubin and Herbert Aptheker, as well as Eugene Genovese, might profitably have extended to her "Heartland" (*q.v.*) readers. Some of them rose to administrative posts and as authorities gave acceptability to erstwhile activists, in effect endorsing the validity of the activists' old-time causes and those which they went on to modernize for "civil rights" (*q.v.*) and other purposes. The confusion in the minds of otherwise patriotic citizens came from the conflict between horror of radical excesses and interest in their social experimentation: both involving components of entertainment and envy (*qq.v.*) of the freedom the adventurers enjoyed, and some dampening the impact of Mrs. Widener's revelations. The actress Jane Fonda, on a higher level of affluence and interest to Heartlanders, exemplified the process. Mrs. Widener also published *Gustave Le Bon, the Man and His Works* (Liberty Press, 1979).

**Wilberforce, William** (1759-1833), a British antislavery partisan of such magnitude, thanks to his Evangelical Christianity, that he was famous even in the American South. Its pro-slavery spokesmen had none of the usual arguments for refuting him, and were daunted by his patent piety and disinterestedness. Wilberforce was wakened to the antislavery cause by Thomas Clarkson about 1787, and entered Parliament, where he worked with William Pitt the Younger to further the cause. The major goal was to end the slave *trade*, slavery in England having been abolished in law. American critics, however, held that child and factory labor was a more atrocious form of slavery (see John C. Cobden, *The White Slaves of England* [1853]). Others fought the battle against shipping, trading, and colonial interests. Wilberforce contributed a presence and oratory which kept his cause live and formidable; not all the "economic interpretations" could touch the man deemed sacrosanct. He had his reward in 1807, when the slave trade was abolished and the battle for enforcements began, extending into the crusade to abolish slavery in the British colonies. John Pollack, *Wilberforce* (1978):

**Will, George E.** (1941- ), social commentator. He called himself a conservative, but kept himself aloof from conservative enclaves and party lines, and dissented from their emphasis on economics as it encroached on commercialism (*q.v.*). A successful columnist and television personality, he denounced professional pro-abortionists and lock-step female activists, and honored religious observances. He was noted for the felicity of his quotations from classic authors and the range of his interests. His prose attracted notice as differing from the flat phrasing of most commentators. His faith in compassion caused his conservative critics to hold him closer to New Deal (*q.v.*) than to conservative tenets. His books include *The Pursuit of Happiness and Other Sobering Thoughts* (1978), *The Pursuit of Virtue and Other Tory Notions* (1982), and *Statecraft as Soulcraft* (1983).

**Willard, Frances E.** (1839-1898), American activist caught, for modern purposes, between two reputations, one of which made her admired in her time as urging and aiding education for women, the other of which, added to the first, made her adored as a person of inimitable qualities for her support of temperance (*q.v.*). She served the cause of temperance with eloquence and effect. As president of Evanston (Illinois) College for Ladies, she pioneered the expansion of educational vistas for professionals. As president of the National Women's Christian Temperance Union (W.C.T.U.), her reputation followed the sagging fortunes of the Prohibition crusade, and diminished her public personality, which was notable. See her *Glimpses of Fifty Years* (1889); and M. Earhart, *Frances Willard* (1944).

**Williams, Charles,** see *Myth, Allegory and Gospel*

**Williams, Walter E.,** (1936- ) conservative economist, professor at George Mason University in Virginia. He was made all but notorious along with Thomas Sowell (*q.v.*) for opposing liberal programs for black people which he held harmed them in their circumstances and in their potential. Himself black and raised in North Philadelphia slums, he observed the crime, vice, and demoralization fostered by welfare and related policies. Strictly committed to free enterprise, he resented "drug raids" by police as no more than raising the cost of drugs, and thereby the incidence of crime. He opposed the draft as an imposition on freedom, creating an army of incompetents. His solution was higher pay for soldiers. His views outraged black partisans and startled his white readers and auditors. A syndicated columnist, he chose a sardonic title for his first book of essays, *America: A Minority Viewpoint* (1982), and a turn of language for his second, *The State against Blacks* (1983). As a "minority" voice, Williams was an indicator of both black and white attitudes toward intellectual desegregation. He resented being considered a "token" black, noting that anyone was free to be a Republican and to subscribe to principles of free enterprise.

**Wills, Garry** (1934- ), American author and columnist, a curious figure in modern conservativism and a transition (*q.v.*) figure to what liberalism had become. As a student in Catholic colleges, his language and ready flow of words attracted the attention of William F. Buckley, Jr. (*q.v.*), who permitted Wills to express himself freely on all subjects in the early pages of the *National Review*—in effect conducting his social education in public while acquiring his Ph.D. at Yale University. The key to his style in earlier works was a sense of authority through interpretations of language and increasingly bold judgments, often abusive, as he separated from one or another of his colleagues. His *Chesterton: Man and Mask* (1961) appealed to his Catholic base. By 1970, his *Nixon Agonistes* employed a psychohistory (*q.v.*) framework which satisfied liberals. His introduction to Lillian Hellman's *Scoundrel*

*Time* (1976) showed further linkage with liberalism balancing critical attitudes toward America with selective realism toward pro-Communist impulses. His *Confessions of a Conservative* (1979) explained that "confession" referred to a profession of faith, but in fact separated him from his earlier conservatism. Wills' *Inventing America* (1978) was a publishing success, applying psychohistory to history, and, in a bad time, seeming witty and fresh; journalists took to "inventing" women, extended families, and whatever else their columns required. He became Henry R. Luce Professor of American Culture and Public Policy at Northwestern University and a syndicated columnist. To many conservatives he was predictably liberal, as in *The Kennedy Imprisonment* (1982).

**Wilson, James Q.**, see *Thinking about Crime*

**Wilson, Woodrow** (1856-1924), a transitional (*q.v.*) figure between hardline pre-Progressive (*q.v.*) conservatism and a newer conservatism bent on responding to public demands for great control over unforeseen urban and technological forces. Wilson, as a Southerner who had tasted the bitter fruit of Congressional Reconstruction seized on the idea of a stronger President and Cabinet to offset Congress. He followed a career as popular professor and lecturer with a presidential decade at Princeton University during which he mixed conventional deportment and morality with a demand for more democratic processes involving rich and poor students and their mentors. Democrats saw him as a promising opponent of Theodore Roosevelt (*q.v.*). He preceded his challenge to Republicans with a challenge to the New Jersey political machine; but was made President by the historic split between Old Guard and Progressive Republicans. Wilson fought the Southern fight for Free Trade (*q.v.*), which never materialized because of the advent of World War I and the patrolling of the seas by British and German ships. His Progressive reforms mainly consolidated the gains carved out during high points of the era. Wilson's institution of segregation (*q.v.*) in government departments, though little noted at the time, would be angrily recalled by civil-rights partisans on campuses in the 1960s. However, his crusade for democracy, which brought American soldiers to European battlefields, was offset, to peace-minded factionalists, by his subsequent crusade for a League of Nations. Wilson was little honored by hard-bitten conservative critics of his own time or noticed by new conservatives of post-World War II years. Liberals, however, found materials amid his considerable eloquence which suited their anti-business and pro-union views and longings for peace abroad. See Filler, DASC and *The Ascendant President* (1983); J. M. Blum, *Woodrow Wilson and the Politics of Morality* (1956); Herbert Hoover et al., *The Ordeal of Woodrow Wilson* (1958). Most important are Arthur Link *et al*, eds. The Papers of Woodrow Wilson, now in over fifty volumes. They give, sometimes in dramatic detail, a history of the era seen from the standpoint of an essentially conservative society and its involvement with the larger American public.

**Wisdom of Conservatism, The,** edited by Peter Witonski, in four volumes, a compendious assortment of selections, as significant for what it failed to include as for what it included. Peter Viereck (*q.v.*) disillusioned with the conservative movement he helped give visibility, in his lengthy *New York Times Book Review* article found much to criticize. He found the inclusion of Ronald Reagan and the non-inclusions of Adlai Stevenson a fault and also the failure to include materials directly critical of the workings of the John Birch Society and Joseph McCarthy. The publishing of Dante, Plato, Aristotle, Lincoln and Aquinas did not compensate, in his view, for the display of "modern rightists" views. He approved of the "organic continuity" of Coleridge and the "Tory anti- Nazism" of Churchill, but believed that contemporary young people needed more "relevant" selections for modern ideological dilemmas. He also saw "rightist thought-control vs. a free [Edmund] Burke-[John] Adams conservativism" an issue not addressed. Compare Russell Kirk, ed., *The Portable Conservative Reader* (1982); (*qq.v.*) for the above.

**"Witchhunt,"** identified with official interrogations, especially under Martin Dies and

Joseph McCarthy (*q.v.*), by liberals and radicals. The credibility which the slogan attained was one measure of the strength pro-Communist forces were able to exercise on public thinking, in effect by suggesting that there were no more Communists than there had been witches in colonial New England. A second measure of the strength of such attitudes was the success of Arthur Miller's *The Crucible* (1953), which drew an analogy between the trials of witches in colonial New England and the investigations of McCarthy.

**Wolfe, Tom** (1931- ), American author, a pioneer of the "new journalism," which sought to enter into the spirit of disturbed social elements and report them in terms which mimicked their own minds and those who took their cases seriously. Wolfe's *The Kandy-Kolored Tangerine-Flake Streamlined Baby* (1965) vividly reflected the mindless urgency of youth and black and female "revolt" which all could see but lacked the will to answer. His devastating analysis of "radical chic" gave a memorable phrase to the language. The veteran liberal columnist James Wechsler, aware of his group's odyssey from simplistic radicals to affluent welfare-state (*q.v.*) partisans admitted to the "radical chic" label, but held that the cause was just. Wolfe's investigations made him conservative in outlook, but successful enough to be unavoidable. In a curious way D. Keith Mano, of the *National Review* (*q.v.*), engaged in comparable work, describing sex bazaars, Russian apologists in William Sloane Coffin's Riverside Church, a pretentious playwrights' conference, and a more crudely pretentious gathering of van owners in a similar "new journalism" style.

**Woman's Record** (1853), a compendious work by the writer and journalist Sara Josepha Hale (1788-1879), editor of *Godey's Lady's Book* for forty years. Her chief claim to fame, the formidable *Woman's Record*, scoured history to give conscientious accounts of the lives of distinguished women, including a substantial number of Americans who had made names as wives of principals in history and as participants in social developments, historic events, literature and the arts, and public pursuits.

**Women,** see Filler, DASC. Women as conservatives—that is, as living and acting according to the tenets of their age—have achieved distinction in all ages. In America, their opportunities for advancement were augmented by the open nature of its environment and by the Revolution (*q.v.*), which drew in conservatives as well as the democratically-inclined. Although the turmoil of the 1960s and 1970s affected conservative women as well as liberals or radicals, the highest visibility went to those with demands, for the most part radical, who attacked the history of women in America with little opposition from conservatives. Strongly symbolic was the volume *Notable American Women*. First published at Harvard in 1971, it sought experts in history regardless of sex. But a subsequent volume was wholly in the hands of women "activists." The momentous fact about the era was that, for the first time in history, half the labor force in America was composed of women. Adjustments in respect to families, social relations, proper work conditions, political leaders, law, and other areas became necessary. Although some demands of women seemed not so much liberal or conservative as self-advertising, such as women who demanded the right to play on all-male sports teams, some demands were deemed more serious and seriously considered. A General Motors woman employee was fired when she asked to be called "Ms.," and won $119,985 in damages. Indeed, the deep wounds to the family produced not only by work but the unsettled nature of women's identity made law the major arbiter between conflicting viewpoints. Thus, the idea that women were not like men had long slowed down the drive for women's "equality." In the 1960s and 1970s the law was required to make decisions involving gender. A judge who ruled that women's provocative clothing mitigated the violence of rape was recalled by an enraged community. But efforts to establish rights of "palimony"—resulting from unmarried couples living together—moved slowly beyond older common-law arrangements. "Pre-menstrual tension" as a mitigating factor in crime was ruled-out in a British case which was closely watched on both sides of the water. Most pitiful was the need for law to strive to curb "wife battering" and "child abuse"—repulsive byproducts found at all levels of society. The 1970s produced the fight for an Equal Rights Amendment (ERA) to the Constitution. Buttressed by contributions and White House, political, and media (*q.v.*) support, and using commercial threats against opponents, ERA activists seemed ready to sweep the field. However, they met a formidable foe in Phyllis Schlafly (*q.v.*), whose marshalling of conservative women slowed their drive and, despite the frantic appeals of the National Organization of Women (NOW), overcame it. Nevertheless, Schlafly's was a negative program to the extent that it aimed to *stop* ERA, rather than to minister to the wants and needs of women. Ronald Reagan, coming to Washington as a foe of ERA, was not perceived as a foe of women, but was watched by women as well as his liberal opponents to see what his program for them was. Although he was not eager to fill posts with women merely because they were women, as was happening in some areas, it did appear that the very nature of society required a greater attention to qualified women than he seemed willing to give. In July 1981, he achieved a publicity coup by appointing Sandra Day O'Connor, an Arizona appeals court judge, to the Supreme Court. Although her qualifications for the post were mercilessly analyzed, especially on such key issues as abortion (*q.v.*), there was almost no mention of her sex as a factor in the appointment. Partisanship lost ground in the event. Other Presidential appointments—Elizabeth Dole as Secretary of Transportation, Margaret Heckler as Secretary of Health and Human Services—felt for a balance between political expedience and due recognition of women's modern role. As the 1984 election approached, a "gender gap" was perceived, especially by liberal analysts who noted disenchantment among "moderate" Republican women with Reagan's policies on women, as well as a clear disparity in polls between male and female support for Reagan. Was it because of his slow movement on activist causes? Many women were expressing themselves—in the press, in publications—as wanting to be women, rather than political pawns. Was it because of economic problems which Democrats were promising to deal with? Many women wanted day-care centers, jobs, or better jobs. Was it because of abortion, which many women seemed to tolerate and for which some women wanted Federal support? In any event, the 1984 election, and Reagan's re-election gave little evidence of the existence of such a "gender gap."

**Women's Christian Temperance Union,** see Willard, Frances E.

**"Workfare,"** a conservative answer to welfare (*q.v.*). Workfare was difficult to institute because of bureaucratic processes and liberal appeals to "compassion" (*q.v.*) and fear of forced labor. Unions also dreaded workfare as possibly infringing on the minimum wage (*q.v.*). It was publicized by Governor Ronald Reagan in California and praised as giving work to those who wanted it, while driving from the relief rolls those unwilling but able to work. Reagan brought the idea with him to Washington as President. He and his sympathizers maintained that they had no intention of depriving worthy recipients of needed aid, especially as it affected dependent children and the incapacitated. At the end of 1982, a *Washington Post* survey estimated that from twenty to twenty-five states had installed "workfare" programs. See also Outdoor Work.

**"Working Class,"** a concept often identified with radical and revolutionary concepts and alignments. It was repudiated by conservative ideologues as a fantasy in America, the land of opportunity, but encouraged in early Soviet (*q.v.*) years in their appeals for world leadership of "workers and farmers" (*q.v.*). It received further endorsements during the decade of the Depression (*q.v.*), which added the unemployed to those laboring under duress and with little hope. The subsequent war prosperity changed perspectives for workers, giving them middle-class (*q.v.*) dreams and ambitions which postwar prosperity proceeded to fulfill in terms of housing, union gains, entertainment, and life-styles. Although there was dire poverty and absence of hope among large areas of blacks, migrant workers, and others in cities and on farms, the developed welfare (*q.v.*) system took the edge off their conditions and mitigated appeals to class, particularly among such groups as migrant workers. The effort by President Johnson to surpass the New Deal with his Great Society created a welter of economics, rather than a marshalling of classes. Tiny pockets of "revolutionaries" remembering Marx, Lenin, the Cuban revolutionaries, and heroes of Marxist groups elsewhere did little to rouse "class consciousness" among Americans. Such radicalism as there was found mainly among left-leaning intellectuals seeking a stake in national alignments.

**Works Progress Administration (WPA),** see Filler, DASC, and Public Works

**World and I, The**: A Chronicle of our Changing Era, an ambitious offshoot of *Washington Times* (*q.v.*) publications, launched in 1986 somewhat on the order of its other organ of commentary, *Insight*, but vastly larger and covering topics from "special reports," to the arts, individually examined. It sought to direct a conservative prospectus on the world, significant personalities, books, and even such diversions and interests as food, gardens, and fashion.

**World Council of Churches,** an ecumenical body important in East-West dialogue, especially as entering into national quarrels between surrogate (*q.v.*) nations. It was held in some suspicion by conservatives who feared it was too willing to find hope in Soviet peace gestures and paid too little attention to the Soviet Union's long-term goals. The Council's slogan during the 1970s and after was: "The world sets the agenda for the church."

**World Research,** see *Incredible Bread Machine, The*

**World War I,** a momentous event of the twentieth century, overturning the expectations of leading civilizations, and still subject to historic revaluation. Despite the ominous tramp of armies, it seemed incredible that cultured, dominant classes could unleash such weapons as they had developed. Sarajevo, famed as the "beginning" of the war, involved minor ambitions which should have been properly adjusted between Russia and the Austro-Hungarian Empire, with others acting as intermediaries. Their failure to rise to the crisis constituted a major charge against their ruling classes which their mutual recriminations did not lessen. See *Myth of a Guilty Nation, The*. As serious were the alliances between conservatives and liberals for the prosecution of war, which left radicals free of responsibility for its workings, while raising popular armies for future work not anticipated by the promoters and administrators of war. Their narrow aims were symbolized by the decision of the German statesmen to permit Lenin (*q.v.*) to return to Russia in a sealed train, in order to disaffect elements of the Russian state and demoralize still further its capacity for operation. The will of British statesmen to draw the United States into the holocaust was short-sighted. All too successful was Allied propaganda, at home and in America. It exploited idealistic sentiments, but also gave space to malicious and small-minded "patriots" (*q.v.*) who could harm by their actions the cause they were supposed to defend. The young humanist Randolph Bourns, made a radical by events, pleaded that by intervention America would lose its moral force and influence; see Filler, "Trial by Fire," in *Randolph Bourne*. The Woodrow Wilson (*q.v.*) Administration turned from such prospects to the will-o'-the-wisp of a League of Nations, which produced its own disillusionments (*q.v.*). The war was a turning point for the conservative tradition in America, for, though "popular" at the time and productive of a wide array of heroes (*q.v.*), from "Black Jack" Pershing to Sergeant Alvin York, it was made popular by a vast network of journalists at the expense of crushed "foreign-born" or second-generation citizens, and of radical and reform personalities and leaders such as Charles A. Lindbergh, Sr., and Robert M. La Follette. The war's cause was impugned by President Wilson's marked bias against Germany, by the practical abrogation of civil rights (*q.v.*) in America, and by capitalism's apparent financial stake in Great Britain's victory. The munitions industry's stake in war as such gave an ugly aspect to American war aims. "Disillusionment" (*q.v.*) with both capitalism and reform served radical ideology. Though stifled in the 1920s, this ideology was able to expand with idyllic pictures of the Soviet Union's "progress," in the Depression era, and prophecies of capitalism's collapse. The war produced numerous conservatives of distinction, but it was the experimenters and innovators who were more active in interpreting the world created by war. Although alienated youth was conspicuous for radical outlooks, as ominous was the Babbitt (*q.v.*) psychology which made clichés of tradition. The rise of fascism (*q.v.*) gave new validity to left-wing postures. It was significant that persons traveling to Spain to support its "Republic" in 1936 termed themselves the Abraham Lincoln (*q.v.*) Brigade, seeking to clothe themselves in his reputation. The Nazi-Soviet Pact of 1938 disillusioned many with radical perspectives, passive or active, but the Grand Alliance against Hitler undermined those who had hoped, following the outbreak of Soviet-German war, that the two lands would overthrow their leaders. America First (*q.v.*), mordantly criticized, had no alternative but to close shop. Publishers' efforts to capitalize on the pictorial aspects of World War I were only partially successful; apparently, German, Jewish, Irish, and other Americans were sufficiently disaffected by the treatment they had been accorded as to have no interest in the war even as spectacle, and "loyal" Americans found no nourishment in its saga. This gave patriotism (*q.v.*), therefore, largely over to such organizations as the American Legion (*q.v.*). Americans were properly perplexed, even when unconfused by dual loyalties, by the manifestations of "total war"—that is, war which did not have a particular foe or goal, as in earlier wars. The Soviet Union (*q.v.*) represented an idea, rather than merely specific land or resources; see Raymond Aron, *The Century of Total War* (1954). John Keegan's *The Face of Battle* (1976) sought to isolate the war itself, independent of the cause which was given to or assumed by the soldiery. Cyril Falls's *The Great War, 1914-1918* (1959) sought in conservative fashion to penetrate the slaughter and find in it the red badge of courage and nobility it had not destroyed. As he said: "Despite many reckless and brutal deeds done in high places, this terrible war of material was for the most part directed by statesmen and conducted by commanders who, for all their faults and errors and despite the trammels of nationalist and racialist bigotry, did not altogether lose their sense of the meaning and value of civilization...." Something of that sense is captured, on the British side, in John Terraine's *To Win a War: 1918, the Year of Victory* (1981). See also Pacifism.

**World War II,** different from the first World War in being regarded as a just war, requiring the demolition of the evil power of Nazi Germany, militaristic Japan, and their associates. It did, however, also involve relations with the Soviet Union, which conservatives saw equal in evil to Nazi Germany. Although there was an indeterminate number of business or ideological conservatives with fascist sympathies, left-wing propagandists made them more numerous than evidence warranted. Some America First (*q.v.*) partisans were sincere isolationists. Others hoped that the Nazi-Soviet war would decimate both sides, to the benefit of the free world. The American decision to intervene was of great benefit to the image of Soviet leaders in America. It was responsible for the collapse of Martin Dies's (*q.v.*) Congressional war against Communist influence in and out of government. The war itself, as it progressed, troubled conservatives mainly as it seemed to endorse Soviet actions and programs, which included the notorious "Katyn Forest" slaughter of Polish officers: a genocidal action. Although the full extent of Stalinist crimes, at home and abroad, was not fully known, or credited, the nation had been exposed to such revelations as were included in Benjamin Gitlow's *I Confess* (1940), and Isaac Don Levine's (*q.v.*) books. On the other hand, the full power of the Hitlerite assault could not be known until the end, and contained justifications for the credit accorded, or reluctantly given, Stalin (*q.v.*). Some of the conservative discontent was later to be turned on Eisenhower (*q.v.*), as having insufficiently limited Soviet war gains during combat: too readily gulled by their professed peaceful and democratic intentions. See Revisionists (*q.v.*); L. B. Namier, *Europe in Decay* (1950); Herbert Feis, *Churchill, Roosevelt, Stalin* (1957); Arnold Toynbee, ed., *Survey of International Affairs, 1939-1946* (1955); D. D. Eisenhower, *Crusade in Europe* (1948); John R. Deane, *The Strange Alliance: The Story of Our Efforts at Wartime Cooperation with Russia* (1947); Stanislaw Mikolajczk, *The Rape of Poland* (1948).

**WPA,** see Public Works; New Deal; Youth

# X

# Y

**Yale Literary Magazine,** "America's Oldest Review," an elegant quarterly which engaged the university's ire recently by turning conservative, and drawing contributions from such writers as William F. Buckley, Jr., Ralph de Toledano, John Chamberlain, Thomas Molnar, and George Gilder (*q.v.*). Such partisanship dismayed Yale's president, and he sought court action forcing the word "Yale" off of the cover, unsuccessfully.

**Yalta Conference,** notorious to conservatives, held in the Crimea by Churchill, Franklin D. Roosevelt, and Stalin (*qq.v.*) from February 4 to 11, 1945. The agreements arrived at pledged Stalin to join the Allies in the Far Eastern theater of World War II. In exchange, the Soviet Union was given extensive promises in respect to the war's anticipated aftermath: promises which would make it a dominant force not only in the Far East, but in Eastern Europe. The Soviets proved not to be a significant factor in Japan's capitulation, and the war ended sooner than expected, with Stalin breaking promises—as in Poland, promised a democratic regime—without redress. Conservatives later noted Alger Hiss's (*q.v.*) role in these negotiations. Liberals denied conspiracy and pro-Stalin sympathies, and argued that Stalin could not have been stopped from doing what he in fact did, that no one could know how long the war would take.

**Year that Changed the World, The,** by Brian Gardner (1964), though possibly offering more than it could deliver, nevertheless added up events of 1945 to include military actions in Europe and the Pacific, the Potsdam and Yalta (*q.v.*) Treaties, Winston Churchill's political defeat in Great Britain—leaving reconstruction to the Labour Party—and the death of Franklin D. Roosevelt (*q.v.*). Above all, it was the year of the first purposeful explosion of the atom bomb.

**Young Americans for Freedom,** an offshoot of the Young Republicans organization. The organizers of the YAF had campaigned for Richard M. Nixon in 1960 and, disappointed, came together to form a youth organization with wider ramifications. Fired by the challenge offered in Barry Goldwater's (*q.v.*) 1960 bestseller, *The Conscience of a Conservative*, of which YAF distributed 100,000 copies, they continued to build campus organizations which, contrary to general assumptions, attracted not scions of wealth and family, but middle-class and poor youths. With time, the YAF produced a substantial number of notable figures, from journalists to Congressmen, and rooted itself in colleges and political work; for details, James C. Roberts, *The Conservative Decade* (1980) (*q.v.*).

**Youth,** momentous in all movements, but identified with radicalism and radical movements; see Filler, DASC. It appeared to move independently, as was so seen by its "leaders" and by adults. Lacking funds, status, experience, followers, and often talent or purpose youth movements generally subsisted and grew with the support or tolerance of adults. In the Twenties (*q.v.*) and earlier, it was first of all the adults, many inhabiting major cities, who were restless, purchased cars—mobile rooms,—and defied Prohibition (*q.v.*). Small wonder that their children developed from the "Turkey Trot," which shocked the elders in Booth Tarkington's fiction, to raccoon coats, hip flasks, and joy rides in the 1920s. "He who has the youth has the future," proclaimed V. I. Lenin (*q.v.*), and his adult followers worked hard to marshall youth for Communism in the Depression era, with "freedom" demeaned as a "bourgeois" term meaning frivolous goals, Babbittry (*q.v.*), and immaturity. Although most young people at the time were no doubt conservative, they had no consequential organization or visibility. Youth meant radical youth, standing up for "free speech" in the schools, scorning athletics (see sports); it meant sympathy for the plight of workers and farmers at home, approval of "workers and peasants" movements abroad. It meant "literature" on tables at mass rallies in protest and endorsement. The collapse of Depression politics and society, making way for wartime affluence and disturbance of the family (*q.v.*), produced a new youth, well fed, comfortably housed, and easily accommodated. With adults busy with new enterprises, often away from home and with inchoate dreams of expanded opportunities, youth grew in disaffection. The Beats of the 1950s were overwhelmed by a sense of the power of government. In the 1960s many youths turned to protest against the war in Vietnam and over the problems of miners, blacks, and others at home. In the vanguard all too often were those intent on levelling society in the interests of a truly free world, admirers of the new Cuba, the new China and other "liberated" areas. With the full revolt of these and related elements, led by demagogues on and off the campuses, radical youths and disaffected "hippies" congregated in New York, San Francisco, and Berkeley, with points in between. They were now sufficiently powerful to be able to influence styles of clothing and "life styles" in the population in general. Their tastes dominated popular music and éntertainment, and, linked with the "civil rights" (*q.v.*) movement, they were strong enough to be a major factor in education, commerce, journalism, and other areas of society. Thus, adults and youths met on almost equal terms. Although many young people were conservative throughout this turbulence, sometimes even achieving a measure of visibility for their opposition to it, and in such places as Hillsdale College (*q.v.*) being actively courted, they had greatest coherence as attached to conservative Republican or religious organizations. See the *National Review* for the 1950s and on; see Conservative Party of New York for later youth involvement. A phenomenon of the 1970s and 1980s was the rise of informed and influential groups of conservative youth on campuses. Since their interests were opposed to and collided with those of the civil rights, women's rights, and other activist movements—often sponsored or encouraged by the administrations themselves—there were sometimes unseemly actions taken to still their voices by administrative and faculty members. The *National Review* and other such organs kept close watch on such developments. See *Yale Literary Magazine*. See Filler, *Vanguards and Followers: Youth in the American Tradition*.

# Z

**"Zero Funding,"** see Communication
**Zimbabwe,** see Africa
**Zinsser, Hans** (1878-1940), American humanist and scientist whose gracious concern for the quality of life merited the regard of all shades of native opinion, but whose distinction did not survive his life work. His studies of typhus and anti-typhus immunizations made him a hero of World War I and later efforts to control epidemics. His essays in genteel (*q.v.*) publications, while expressing traditional values, were understanding of the vagaries of postwar social unrest and radicalism. Zinsser's best-selling *Rats, Lice, and History* (1935) was an antidote to fashionable cynicism. His *As I Remember Him: The Biography of R. S.* (1940) was obviously autobiographical, but written as though about someone else. It was revealed that Zinsser knew he was dying of cancer, and conjectured that "R. S." stood for "romantic self."

# Index

Elisabeth Döpp, Christian Willrich, and Jörn Rebbe

# GRAINS

PHOTOGRAPHY

Heinz-Josef Beckers

Translated from the German by Elizabeth D. Crawford

## TABLE OF CONTENTS

# Small Grains—Big Trend

### Small Grains—Big Trend

Now you can enjoy to your heart's content: the days when cooking with grains was equated with asceticism are past. These days, more and more kinds of grains are becoming available, a sign that these tiny, round things are very much on the road to success.
On this book's back gatefold flap you will find all the unfamiliar grains listed, with brief notes and pictures. You will find detailed descriptions in the introductions to the individual chapters. Soaking and cooking times for the various grains are listed in the table on the front gatefold flaps.

### Inviting Dishes

Delicacies like couscous and bulgur from North African cooking, amaranth and quinoa from Latin America, and basmati and jasmine rice from Asia were hardly available in the West until recently. Wheat, corn, and barley now have exotic competition.

### Sophisticated and Fast

Want to cook something special in a hurry? Wonderful grain products with short cooking times let you do it. After about half an hour you can treat your family or friends to a nutritious, inexpensive dish: Oriental couscous salad, herb tabouleh, kasha with mushrooms, or buckwheat risotto. Using couscous, bulgur, or buckwheat, you can conjure up a side dish at a moment's notice.

### Fine Eating

Brown rice for a fine meal? Today, depending on the variety, unhulled natural rice is no longer humble. Basmati and other aromatic rices go fantastically well with curries and subtly flavored vegetable dishes.
• Cooking tip: It takes about 40 minutes for brown rice to cook—a handicap when you're in a hurry. So just cook a double portion. Cooked rice will keep in the refrigerator for a few days; and in the freezer—packed flat for fast thawing—for several months.

### Healthy Food for Satisfying Eating

You want to eat to your heart's content and still do something good for yourself? Put your money on grains! They are nourishing for body and soul.

Here's why a grain-based diet is now endorsed by so many nutritionists:

• Whole grains are important sources of carbohydrates and protein.Their fat content is low, between 2% and 4%; only oats have 7%. And the fat contains lineoleic acid, an essential nutrient.

• Grains provide B vitamins and folic acid, essential nutrients that tend to be undersupplied in the American diet.

• Grains are rich in minerals. The most important are magnesium, iron, and potassium—found particularly in the outer layer and the germ, as are the vitamins.

**Tips for a Vital Cuisine**

Know how to use them, taking best advantage of what grains have to offer.

• Eat some of your grain raw, either soaked ahead of time, as sprouts in salad, or as muesli. When grains are uncooked, their heat-sensitive nutrients are retained: folic acid, saponine in oats, phytoserine in wheat and corn, and tocotrieneole in barley, oats, and wheat, all of which work to lower cholesterol.

• Eat some of your grain cooked, as bread or in grain dishes. The fiber is broken down during heating and its associated minerals can then best be utilized.

• Less is more: Grains stimulate the digestive tract. Important for beginners: Start your "fitness training" with small portions.

**Grains for Weight Control**

The carbohydrates in grains are broken down slowly by the body, making them ideal for the weight conscious. They are comfortably filling, and they satisfy for a long time. So they are particularly suitable for breakfast and between meals—in muesli, generous slices of bread, grain tabouleh, or grain salads.

***Energy Drink—a refreshing pick-me-up for breakfast***

*This drink is simple to prepare and also makes a terrific between-meal refresher.*

*For 2 people, bring 2 tablespoons rolled oats to boil in 7 Tbs (3½ oz/100 ml) low-fat or nonfat milk. Set aside. In a blender container mix 7 Tbs (3½ oz/100 g) yogurt, a grated apple, and 1 finely diced apricot or ¼ mango, peeled. Add 1 tablespoon each honey, lemon juice, and flax oil, and a dash of vanilla extract. Add the oat milk and puree. If desired, chill the drink for 30 minutes before serving.*

Vital
FOOD

# Salads and Side Dishes

In the United States as well as in Europe, easy couscous, bulgur, and sprout salads are appearing in sophisticated restaurants everywhere. Here are some important tips, tricks, and pointers for last-minute cooking.

### Bulgur

Bulgur, or cracked wheat, can be used to prepare fast salads, soups, pilafs, and casseroles.

• Buying tip

Bulgur may be labeled as burghul or bulgar in Middle Eastern grocery stores. It is available in several sizes, from coarse to very fine. Bulgur is also sold in natural food and health food stores.

• Tips for basic preparation

For salads, simply pour hot water over the bulgur and let soak, covered, for 30 minutes to 1 hour. If the recipe calls for cooking, bulgur should be simmered over low heat, stirring—it burns very easily.

### Couscous

Durum wheat semolina is used to make couscous, which is actually tiny balls of pasta. It is used for fine fast salads, vegetable dishes, and desserts.

• Tips for basic preparation

*Boiling:* Stir into the same quantity of boiling salted water; cook covered over low heat for 5 minutes; remove from the burner and let stand for about 15 minutes. Toss with a fork and mix with melted butter.

*Steaming:* Let soak in warm water for about 10 minutes; then steam in a steamer insert, covered, over boiling water for about 15 minutes.

• Steamed couscous in the traditional Arabic way

Let soak as described above, then loosen with the fingers to separate grains. Place in a steamer insert over the dish with which the couscous is to be served and steam uncovered for about 30 minutes. Toss with a fork and transfer to a bowl. Sprinkle with salt water and mix in some clarified butter. Return to the steamer insert and steam for another 30 minutes. Toss again and serve.

### Green Spelt

This grain is unfamiliar to most Americans but is very popular in

Southern Germany and the Alps. It is ideal for boiling but is less suitable for baking and not at all suitable for sprouting.

• Buying tip

Green spelt has a greenish shimmer if the grain is harvested at the right time. Green spelt groats are wonderful for fast cooking, and are also available prepared.

• Tips for basic preparation

Substitute green spelt groats in dishes that call for bulgur or couscous.

*Boiling:* Bring groats to boil with 2 times their volume of water, stirring to keep them from sticking. Remove from heat, and let stand for 15–20 minutes.

### Sprouts—Pure Vitality Food

Most grains are suitable for sprouting, with the exception of rice, millet, and green spelt.

Don't underestimate grain sprouts. As the seed sprouts, vitamins and fiber content increase, minerals become easier to assimilate, and the nutrient value of the protein (page 63) increases.

At the same time, the proportion of calories and fat decreases.

### Grains for Sprouting

Quantities given make about 3½ oz (100 g) of sprouts.

| Grain/ Seed | Hrs. of Soaking | Days to Harvest |
|---|---|---|
| Pearl barley (1½ oz [40 g]) | 6–12 | 2–3 |
| Wheat (1½ oz [40 g]) | 12 | 2–3 |
| Spelt (1½ oz [40 g]) | 12 | 2–3 |
| Rye (1½ oz [40 g]) | 12 | 2–3 |
| Hulled Oats (1½ oz [40 g]) | 4 | 2–3 |
| Buckwheat (1½ oz [40 g]) | 1–2 | 3–4 |
| Sunflower seeds (1¾ oz [50 g]) | 4 | 1–3 |
| Pumpkin seeds (1¾ oz [50 g]) | 4 | 1–3 |
| Lentils (scant 1 oz [25 g]) | 6–12 | 3–4 |
| Chickpeas (1¾ oz [50 g]) | 6–12 | 3–4 |
| Mung beans (1 oz [30 g]) (green soybeans) | 6–12 | 3–5 |
| Fenugreek (1 oz [30 g]) | 5 | 3 |
| Radish (1¾ oz [50 g])* | 4 | 4 |
| Cress (20 g) | 4 | 5–6 |
| Alfalfa (20 g) | | 4–5 |

### *Tips for Sprouting*

- *Buy untreated, unprocessed grains and seeds capable of sprouting.*
- *You can get sprouting jars and equipment in health food or natural food stores or in the housewares section of many department stores.*
- *Soak grains in three times as much water as you have seeds.*
- *Pour out seeds, rinse, and place in sprouting jar.*
- *Rinse the sprouts thoroughly two or three times a day to discourage the growth of bacteria or mold. Drain thoroughly.*
- *Mixing in some radish seed helps prevent mold. Don't confuse white roots with mold!*
- *Wash the sprouts thoroughly once more before using. The later you harvest them, the lower the nitrate content. The bigger and greener the sprouts, the less sweet they taste. Oats, fenugreek, and pumpkin seed can even taste bitter.*
- *Sprouts from legumes—lentils, chickpeas, and mung beans—should be blanched for 2–5 minutes before using.*

**Pumpkin Salad with Barley Sprouts**
*1 Tbs white wine vinegar*
*1 Tbs soy sauce*
*salt and pepper*
*2 Tbs sunflower oil*
*3½ oz (100 g) raw pumpkin*
*2 scallions*
*3½ oz (100 g) barley sprouts*
*1½ oz (40 g) pumpkin seed sprouts*
*1 Tbs pumpkin seed or olive oil*
*1 ripe tomato*
*1 bunch watercress*
*1 bunch chives*

*Preparation time: about 20 minutes*

**Buckwheat Sprout Salad**
*2 shallots*
*2 Tbs cider (or balsamic) vinegar*
*2 Tbs walnut oil*
*3½ oz (100 g) cabbage*
*salt and pepper*
*pinch of caraway seeds*
*3½ oz (100 g) celery root*
*1 small tart apple*
*3 Tbs (1 oz/30 g) raisins*
*3½ oz (100 g) lentil sprouts*
*1¾ oz (50 g) buckwheat sprouts*
*8 each radicchio and savoy cabbage leaves*
*1 oz (30 g) alfalfa sprouts*
*¼ cup (1 oz/30 g) walnuts*

*Preparation time: about 20 minutes*

# Pumpkin Salad with Barley Sprouts

**Fast • Pictured**

• Mix vinegar, soy sauce, salt, and pepper and whisk in the oil. Peel the pumpkin, and cut into ½-inch (1 cm) diamond-shaped pieces. Toss with the vinaigrette and let stand 5 minutes.

• Trim the scallions, wash, and chop fine, including the green part. Wash the barley sprouts and pumpkin seed sprouts and let drain. Mix the scallions and sprouts with the pumpkin and season with additional salt, pepper, and oil.

• Wash the tomato and cut into small pieces, removing the base of the stem. Wash the watercress and drain. Wash the chives and chop fine. Divide watercress among 4 plates, and top with the sprout-pumpkin salad. Garnish with tomato and chives.

Makes 4 servings.

| PER SERVING: | 176 CALORIES |
|---|---|
| NUTRITIONAL INFORMATION | |
| Fat (47% calories from fat) | 10 g |
| Protein | 7 g |
| Carbohydrates | 18 g |
| Cholesterol | 0 mg |
| Sodium | 270 mg |

# Buckwheat Sprout Salad

**Easy to make • Sophisticated**

• Peel the shallots, dice, and mix with vinegar and oil. Wash the cabbage, trim, and cut into ¾-inch (2 cm) diamond-shaped pieces. Season in a bowl with salt, pepper, and caraway seeds. Mix with the vinaigrette.

• Peel the celery root and grate fine. Core and dice the apple; peel if desired. Add both to the cabbage with the raisins.

• Bring 2 cups (500 ml) water to boil. Wash the lentil sprouts and blanch for about 2 minutes. Wash the buckwheat sprouts in hot water. Let all drain well and mix into the salad. Wash the greens and alfalfa sprouts and shake dry. Coarsely chop the walnuts. Arrange the sprout salad with the greens, alfalfa, and nuts.

**Tip**

Substitute other sprouts as you wish.

Makes 4 servings.

| PER SERVING: | 160 CALORIES |
|---|---|
| NUTRITIONAL INFORMATION | |
| Fat (37% calories from fat) | 7 g |
| Protein | 5 g |
| Carbohydrates | 23 g |
| Cholesterol | 0 mg |
| Sodium | 35 mg |

# Colorful Salad with Spelt Sprouts

**Different • Fast**

• Bring 1 quart (1 liter) water to boil. Blanch the sprouts in it about 2 minutes, rinse in ice water, and drain. Place in a bowl.

• Peel the shallots and chop fine. Stir the vinegar, salt, pepper, oil, broth, and shallots together. Mix into the sprouts. Wash the vegetables. Peel the carrots and dice into about ⅛-inch (5 mm) squares, cut the celery into ¼-inch (1 cm) diamonds, and cut the cheese into small squares. Mix all with the sprouts. Remove stems from the sorrel, wash, and cut into strips. Mix with the salad and season to taste.

• Wash the currants and garnish the salad with them.

### Menu

For the main course, Borscht (with diced potato instead of barley, page 39); for dessert, Sweet Polenta (page 82).

Makes 4 servings.

| PER SERVING: | 300 CALORIES | |
|---|---|---|
| NUTRITIONAL INFORMATION | | |
| Fat (49% calories from fat) | 17 | g |
| Protein | 15 | g |
| Carbohydrates | 24 | g |
| Cholesterol | 15 | mg |
| Sodium | 94 | mg |

# North African Couscous Salad

**Fast • Pictured**

• Season the broth with salt and bring to boil. Stir in the couscous and cook, covered, over low heat for 5 minutes. Remove from heat and let stand about 15 minutes.

• Meanwhile, soak the currants in hot water to cover. Dissolve a little salt in the vinegar and mix with the pepper and oil. Wash the coriander, shake dry, chop fine, and stir into the vinaigrette with the cumin.

• To prepare the vegetables, cut the celery into small diamonds and the zucchini into small cubes. Mix both into the dressing. Pit the dates and cut into sixths. Drain the currants. Quarter the nuts. Peel and halve the oranges; cut each half into pieces. Add all to the salad. Fluff up the couscous so the grains are well separated and mix in. Garnish with mint.

Makes 4 servings.

| PER SERVING: | 287 CALORIES | |
|---|---|---|
| NUTRITIONAL INFORMATION | | |
| Fat (11% calories from fat) | 4 | g |
| Protein | 14 | g |
| Carbohydrates | 53 | g |
| Cholesterol | 0 | mg |
| Sodium | 181 | mg |

**Colorful Salad**

*3½ oz (100 g) spelt sprouts*
*2 shallots*
*¼ cup (2 oz/60 ml) cider (or balsamic) vinegar*
*salt and pepper*
*¼ cup (2 oz/60 ml) sunflower or other light vegetable oil*
*3 Tbs vegetable broth*
*8 oz (250 g) carrots*
*7 oz (200 g) celery*
*5 oz (150 g) sheep's milk cheese*
*2 oz (60 g) sorrel*
*½ cup (2 oz/60 g) red currants (optional)*

*Preparation time: about 25 minutes*

**Couscous Salad**

*7 Tbs vegetable broth*
*salt*
*7 Tbs couscous*
*¼ cup (1 oz/30 g) dried currants*
*¼ cup (2 oz/60 ml) cider (or balsamic) vinegar*
*pepper*
*2 Tbs cold-pressed walnut oil*
*1 bunch fresh coriander (cilantro)*
*½ tsp ground cumin*
*3 ½ oz (100 g) celery*
*3 ½ oz (100 g) zucchini*
*4 dates*
*¾ cup (3½ oz/100 g) pecans*
*2 oranges*
*mint leaves*

*Preparation time: about 25 minutes*

¾ cup (3½ oz/100 g) soft dried apricots
5 oz (150 g) carrots
5 oz (150 g) parsnips or celery root
5 oz (150 g) red onions
5 oz (150 g) snow peas
½ cup (2 oz/60 g) pine nuts
3 Tbs cold-pressed olive oil
7 Tbs bulgur
¾ cup (6 oz/200 ml) vegetable broth
salt and pepper
¾ cup (3½ oz/100 g) hazelnuts
2 limes or 1 lemon
1 bunch chives
lemon balm leaves, optional
2 oz (50 g) arugula

*Preparation time: about 40 minutes*

# Bulgur Nut Salad with Apricots

**Unusual • For company**

• Cut the apricots into raisin-size cubes. Wash the vegetables. Peel the carrots and parsnips. Cut the carrots into ½-inch (1 cm) cubes and the parsnips into ¼-inch (.5 cm) cubes. Peel the onions and chop fine. Trim the pea pods and halve them on the diagonal.

• Heat an ungreased frying pan over medium heat and toast the pine nuts in it until golden brown and aromatic.

• In a large frying pan or wok, heat 2 tablespoons olive oil over low heat. Add the bulgur and brown about 5 minutes. Add the vegetable broth and bring to boil. Stir in the apricots. Season to taste with salt and pepper. Cook the mixture for about 5 minutes, then transfer to a salad bowl.

• Wipe out the frying pan. Heat 1 tablespoon olive oil over medium heat and fry the carrots, parsnips, onions, and peas about 5 minutes or until the onions are transparent.

• Mix the vegetables with the bulgur. Coarsely chop the hazelnuts and mix in. Squeeze the limes and stir in the juice. Wash the chives and cut into small rings. Mix into the salad, along with the lemon balm leaves.

• Just before serving, pick over the arugula leaves, wash, and shake dry. Cut them into the salad. Divide the salad among the 4 plates and sprinkle with the pine nuts.

**Variations:**

**Green Spelt Nut Salad**

• Instead of bulgur use green spelt. Soak the spelt in ¾ cup (6 oz/200 ml) water 12 hours and cook about 40 minutes. Brown in a frying pan in 1 tablespoon clarified butter over high heat for about 2 minutes, then add to the salad.

• Instead of chives use ½ cup (2 oz/60 g) grated Parmesan cheese.

Makes 4 servings.

| PER SERVING: | 415 CALORIES |
|---|---|
| NUTRITIONAL INFORMATION | |
| Fat (39% calories from fat) | 20 g |
| Protein | 11 g |
| Carbohydrates | 59 g |
| Cholesterol | 1 mg |
| Sodium | 503 mg |

# Vegetable Salad with Sweet Rice

**Easy to prepare • Pictured**

• Combine 1 cup (8 oz/250 ml) salted water with rice and bring to boil. Cook, covered, over low heat about 20 minutes. Drain and set aside.

• Meanwhile, bring 3 cups (24 oz/ 750 ml) water to boil. Add fava beans and cook, covered, over low heat about 10 minutes. Drain the beans, plunge into ice water and drain again. Place in a bowl. Heat an ungreased frying pan and fry the nuts until golden brown and aromatic.

• Season the vinegar with salt and pepper; whisk in the oil. Wash basil and arugula and shake dry. Peel the shallots. Chop all fine and mix well. Mix into the beans along with rice. Wash vegetables and peel any that need it. Cut the kohlrabi and carrots into thin sticks and mix into the salad. Dice the tomato, leaving out the base of the stem, and scatter on top with the nuts.

Makes 4 servings.

| PER SERVING: | 337 CALORIES | |
|---|---|---|
| NUTRITIONAL INFORMATION | | |
| Fat (47% calories from fat) | 18 | g |
| Protein | 9 | g |
| Carbohydrates | 38 | g |
| Cholesterol | 0 | mg |
| Sodium | 57 | mg |

# Tabouleh with Herbs

**Popular . Middle Eastern specialty**

• Bring the broth to boil. Add the bulgur and boil about 2 minutes, stirring. Remove from heat and let stand, covered, about 30 minutes.

• Heat an ungreased frying pan and toast the pine nuts until golden yellow. Whisk the lemon juice with salt, pepper, and oil. Peel and mince the garlic and mix in.

• Wash and trim the vegetables. Cut the celery into pieces about ¼-inch (1 cm) long. Cut the fennel into small dice. Dice the peppers. Quarter the tomatoes. Halve the cucumber lengthwise and slice. Wash the herbs, shake dry, chop fine, and add to the salad. Stir in the bulgur and taste for seasoning. Sprinkle with pine nuts.

Makes 4 servings.

| PER SERVING: | 421 CALORIES | |
|---|---|---|
| NUTRITIONAL INFORMATION | | |
| Fat (24% calories from fat) | 12 | g |
| Protein | 16 | g |
| Carbohydrates | 68 | g |
| Cholesterol | 1 | mg |
| Sodium | 510 | mg |

***Vegetable Salad with Sweet Rice***

*salt*
*¾ cup (3½ oz/100 g) sweet rice (Mochi rice, page 47)*
*¾ cup (3½ oz/100 g) shelled fava beans*
*¾ cup (3½ oz/100 g) cashews*
*¼ cup (2 oz/60 ml) mild cider vinegar*
*pepper*
*3 Tbs cold-pressed olive oil*
*1 bunch basil*
*2 oz (60 g) arugula*
*2 shallots*
*3 oz (100 g) kohlrabi*
*3 oz (100 g) carrots*
*1 tomato*

*Preparation time: about 30 minutes*

***Tabouleh with Herbs***

*Scant 2 cups (15¼ oz/450 ml) vegetable broth*
*1½ cups (10½ oz/300 g) bulgur*
*3 Tbs pine nuts*
*6 Tbs lemon juice*
*salt and pepper*
*3 Tbs cold-pressed olive oil*
*1 clove garlic*
*3½ oz (100 g) celery*
*2 oz (60 g) fennel*
*3½ oz (100 g) red bell peppers*
*3½ oz (100 g) cherry tomatoes*
*3½ oz (100 g) cucumber*
*mixed fresh herbs (plenty of parsley, plus basil, dill and other herbs to taste)*

*Preparation time: about 40 minutes*

*Makes 4 servings*

**Pacific Rim Salad**

*¼ cup (1½ oz/40 g) pearl barley*
*3 Tbs cider vinegar*
*1 Tbs lime juice*
*salt and pepper*
*2 Tbs cold-pressed walnut oil*
*1 tsp small mint leaves*
*1 Tbs chopped fresh chives*
*2 pink grapefruit*
*3½ oz (100 g) spinach leaves*
*1 head iceberg lettuce*
*2 avocados*
*3½ oz (100 g) fresh shiitake mushrooms*
*1 Tbs sunflower or vegetable oil*

*Preparation time: about 30 minutes (+6–15 hours soaking time)*

**Millet Salad**

*1 oz (30 g) dried chickpeas*
*¼ cup (2 oz/60 ml) cider vinegar*
*salt and pepper*
*¼ cup (2 oz/60 ml) peanut oil*
*3½ oz (100 g) cabbage*
*⅓ cup (2 oz/60 g) red rice*
*3 Tbs millet*
*2 scallions*
*2 firm-ripe tomatoes*
*1 red bell pepper*
*1 bunch Italian parsley*

*Preparation time: about 1¼ hours (+1 hour soaking time)*



# Pacific Rim Salad with Barley

**Unusual . Easy to make**

• Soak barley in 1 cup (8 oz/250 ml) cold water for 6–15 hours.

• Mix vinegar, lime juice, salt, pepper, walnut oil, mint, and chives in a bowl.

• Peel grapefruit, removing all the white pith and membrane. Halve crosswise, cut into sections, and add to the vinaigrette. Remove stems from spinach and tear into pieces. Tear the lettuce. Wash both and shake dry. Peel and pit avocados; dice the flesh. Mix with the lettuce and spinach in the dressing.

• Wipe mushrooms with a damp cloth, remove stems, and cut caps into sixths. Wash and drain barley. Heat sunflower oil in a frying pan. Brown the barley in it over medium heat about 2 minutes, stirring constantly. Add mushrooms and fry about 2 minutes or until brown. Remove from heat. Divide salad among 4 plates and garnish with mushrooms and barley.

| PER SERVING: | 238 CALORIES |
|---|---|
| NUTRITIONAL INFORMATION | |
| Fat (53% calories from fat) | 15 g |
| Protein | 5 g |
| Carbohydrates | 25 g |
| Cholesterol | 0 mg |
| Sodium | 25 mg |

# Millet Salad with Red Rice

**Economical • Pictured**

• Boil chickpeas in 3 cups (24 oz/750 ml) water for 2 minutes. Remove from heat and let stand 1 hour.

• Mix vinegar, salt, pepper, and oil. Wash cabbage and cut the leaves into ¼-inch (1 cm) pieces. Mix with the marinade and let stand.

• Meanwhile, return chickpeas to the boil and add salt. Stir in rice and cook together, covered, over low heat 10 minutes. Rinse millet in hot water, add to the chickpeas, continue cooking 30 minutes or until the chickpeas are tender. Let cool.

• Wash the vegetables and parsley. Trim the scallions and chop fine, including the green parts. Cut tomatoes into eighths, leaving out the stem bases. Halve the pepper, clean, and dice. Mince the parsley. Drain the grain mixture and mix into cabbage along with the pepper, parsley, and scallions. Garnish with tomatoes.

| PER SERVING: | 206 CALORIES |
|---|---|
| NUTRITIONAL INFORMATION | |
| Fat (40% calories from fat) | 9 g |
| Protein | 5 g |
| Carbohydrates | 27 g |
| Cholesterol | 0 mg |
| Sodium | 10 mg |

# Buckwheat Noodle Salad

**Savory • Easy to make**

*salt*
*3 Tbs sunflower or other light vegetable oil*
*5 oz (150 g) buckwheat noodles (see Tip)*
*1 Tbs rice or sherry vinegar*
*2 Tbs sherry vinegar or red wine vinegar*
*1 Tbs soy sauce*
*pepper*
*1 Tbs Asian sesame oil*
*1 Tbs freshly grated ginger*
*1 tsp chopped fresh coriander (cilantro) or Italian parsley*
*5 oz (150 g) carrots*
*5 oz (150 g) zucchini*
*2 oz (60 g) leek*
*2 scallions*
*1 clove garlic*
*⅓ cup (2 oz/60 g) buckwheat*
*2 Tbs sesame seeds*

*Preparation time: about 30 minutes*

• Bring 2 quarts (2 liters) salted water to boil with 1 tablespoon sunflower oil. Drop in the noodles and boil 3–4 minutes. Drain, rinse with cold water, and drain again.

• Mix the vinegars, soy sauce, salt to taste, and pepper in a salad bowl. Whisk in sesame oil and 1 tablespoon sunflower oil. Season with ginger and coriander.

• Wash and trim the vegetables. Peel the carrots and cut them and the zucchini into matchsticks. Slice open the leek lengthwise, wash well, and cut into thin strips. Slice the scallions into thin rings. Peel and mince the garlic. Mix all into the dressing, and add the noodles.

• Wash the buckwheat in hot water and drain. Heat the remaining sunflower oil in a frying pan over moderate heat until hot but not smoking. Brown the sesame seeds in it about 1 minute. Roast the buckwheat about 2 minutes, stirring. Sprinkle both over the salad.

**Tip**

Buckwheat noodles are available in Japanese groceries or specialty stores. But you can also make them yourself: For 14 ounces (400 g) noodles, grind 1 scant cup each (150 g) buckwheat and spelt to the fineness of flour. Knead to an elastic dough with 2 eggs, 1 teaspoon salt, a pinch of nutmeg, and 2 teaspoons olive oil. Let rest, covered, about 30 minutes. Then roll out thin and cut into ribbon noodles.

**Menu**

For a festive meal, start with the salad, offer Rice Soup (page 32) as the second course, and stir-fried Chinese vegetables as the third. Finish with a salad of lichis and oranges. A semi-dry Riesling or green tea is a good beverage.

Makes 4 servings

| PER SERVING: | 261 CALORIES | |
|---|---|---|
| NUTRITIONAL INFORMATION | | |
| Fat (25% calories from fat) | 7 | g |
| Protein | 8 | g |
| Carbohydrates | 43 | g |
| Cholesterol | 0 | mg |
| Sodium | 260 | mg |

# Buckwheat Pancakes with Eggplant

**Pictured • Can be prepared ahead of time**

• Preheat the oven to 350°F (170°C). Score the eggplant several times and bake for about 20 minutes.

• Meanwhile, blend flour, kasha, milk, and eggs together. Wash and trim vegetables. Grate the carrots. Cut the leek into strips and the celery root into thin sticks. Peel and chop shallots. Wash parsley, shake dry, and chop fine. Mix all into the batter, along with the thyme, nutmeg, salt, and pepper.

• Wash the basil and cut the leaves into strips. Peel the eggplant and dice fine. Mix with salt, pepper, half the basil and half the oil.

• In a large frying pan over moderate heat, heat 1 tablespoon oil and fry pancakes in batches until golden, 3–4 minutes. Divide among plates along with remaining basil and eggplant.

| PER SERVING: | 485 CALORIES | |
|---|---|---|
| NUTRITIONAL INFORMATION | | |
| Fat (30% calories from fat) | 15 | g |
| Protein | 20 | g |
| Carbohydrates | 59 | g |
| Cholesterol | 455 | mg |
| Sodium | 2 | mg |

# Spelt Patties with Almonds

**Inexpensive • For company**

• Crush ⅓ cup (2½ oz/70 g) spelt and the green spelt fine and grind the rest of the spelt to flour. Bring the broth to boil, add both types of spelt and cook over low heat, stirring, for 5 minutes. Remove from heat and let stand, covered, for about 20 minutes.

• Meanwhile, peel onion. Wash parsley and basil and chop the leaves fine. Wash mushrooms, trim, and dice fine.

• Heat an ungreased frying pan and toast the almonds until golden; set aside. Heat 1 tablespoon olive oil in the pan. Fry the onion over moderate heat until transparent, about 2 minutes. Stir in the mushrooms and sauté 3 minutes. Let cool. Mix the almonds, parsley, basil, salt, pepper, and cheese into the batter. Form into 16 patties. Wipe out the frying pan, heat 1 tablespoon oil in it and cook the patties in batches for 2–3 minutes per side, adding more oil as needed. Serve hot.

| PER SERVING: | 479 CALORIES | |
|---|---|---|
| NUTRITIONAL INFORMATION | | |
| Fat (41% calories from fat) | 25 | g |
| Protein | 23 | g |
| Carbohydrates | 58 | g |
| Cholesterol | 14 | mg |
| Sodium | 1594 | mg |

**Makes 4 servings**

**Buckwheat Pancakes**

*2 eggplants (about 8 oz/220 g each)*
*1 scant cup (3½ oz/100 g) whole-wheat flour*
*2¾ cups (18 oz/500 g) fine buckwheat kasha*
*⅔ cup (5 oz/150 ml) whole milk*
*3 eggs*
*2 oz (60 g) each carrots, leek, and celery root*
*2 shallots*
*1 bunch Italian parsley*
*½ tsp fresh thyme*
*pinch of freshly grated nutmeg*
*salt and pepper*
*1 bunch basil*
*4 Tbs cold-pressed olive oil*

*Preparation time: about 50 minutes*

**Spelt Patties**

*½ cup (3½ oz/100 g) spelt*
*7 Tbs green spelt*
*3 cups (24 oz/750 ml) vegetable broth*
*1 red onion*
*1 bunch Italian parsley*
*1 bunch basil*
*3½ oz (100 g) button mushrooms*
*⅓ cup (2¾ oz/75 g) chopped almonds*
*3 Tbs cold-pressed olive oil*
*salt and pepper*
*½ cup (2 oz/60 g) freshly grated Parmesan cheese*

*Preparation time: about 45 minutes*

# Green Spelt Medallions with Herbed Crème Fraîche

**Elegant • For company**

*For the medallions:*
*¾ cup (5 oz/500 g) green spelt*
*1 garlic clove*
*2 shallots*
*2 cups (16 oz/450 ml) vegetable broth*
*2 pinches curry powder*
*¼ tsp fresh thyme*
*salt and pepper*
*freshly grated nutmeg*
*1 bunch parsley*
*1 egg*
*1 Tbs freshly grated Parmesan cheese*
*2 Tbs cold-pressed olive oil*

*For the herb cream:*
*1 bunch chives*
*1 sprig basil*
*1 sprig chervil*
*1 lime*
*2 Tbs plain yogurt*
*3 Tbs crème fraîche or sour cream*
*salt and pepper*

*For the vegetable confetti:*
*3 Tbs vegetable broth*
*1 tsp mild prepared mustard*
*2 Tbs white wine vinegar*
*2 Tbs sunflower or other light vegetable oil*
*salt and pepper*
*1 carrot*
*3½ oz (100 g) celery root*
*1 small zucchini*
*½ red bell pepper*

*Preparation time: about 45 minutes*

• For the medallions, finely grind the green spelt. Peel the garlic and shallots and chop fine. Bring the vegetable broth to boil. Stir in the garlic, shallots, and spelt and season with curry, thyme, salt, pepper, and nutmeg. Cook all together, stirring, for about 5 minutes. Remove from heat and let stand, covered, about 15 minutes.

• Meanwhile, wash the herbs for the herbed cream, shake dry, and chop fine. Wash the lime under hot water, dry, and grate the peel. Stir together the herbs, lime zest, yogurt, and crème fraîche; season with salt and pepper. Chill.

• For the vegetable confetti, blend the vegetable broth, mustard, vinegar, oil, salt, and pepper in a salad bowl. Wash and trim the vegetables. Cut the carrots, celery root, and zucchini into small dice. Cut the pepper into small squares. Let all marinate in the dressing.

• For the medallions, wash the parsley and finely chop the leaves. Mix the cooled green spelt mixture with egg, Parmesan, and parsley. Form 16 small, round medallions.

• Heat 1 tablespoon oil in a large, heavy frying pan and fry half the medallions in it about 3 minutes per side, first over medium heat, then over low. Fry the remaining medallions. Serve with the vegetable confetti and herbed crème fraîche.

**Variation:**
**Bulgur Medallions with Mustard Yogurt**
Instead of using herbed crème fraîche, mix ½ cup (4 oz/125 g) plain yogurt and 2 tablespoons coarse-grained mustard. For medallions, use bulgur instead of green spelt and 2 ounces (60 g) arugula instead of parsley.

Makes 4 servings.

| PER SERVING: | 343 CALORIES | |
|---|---|---|
| NUTRITIONAL INFORMATION | | |
| Fat (33% calories from fat) | 13 | g |
| Protein | 14 | g |
| Carbohydrates | 45 | g |
| Cholesterol | 161 | mg |
| Sodium | 529 | mg |

*Makes 4 servings*

***Oat Pancakes***

*½ cup (3½ oz/100 g) wheat berries*
*3 eggs*
*1 cup (3½ oz/100 g) rolled oats*
*1¼ cups (10 oz/300 ml) whole milk*
*3½ oz (100 g) assorted sprouts*
*freshly grated nutmeg*
*salt and pepper*
*2 scallions*
*2 tomatoes*
*14 oz (400 g) button mushrooms*
*3 Tbs cold-pressed olive oil*
*2 Tbs chopped Italian parsley*

*Preparation time: about 45 minutes*

***Quinoa Cakes***

*1 cup (6½ oz/180 g) quinoa*
*¼ cup (1¾ oz/50 g) spelt*
*¼ tsp active dry yeast*
*7 Tbs lukewarm milk*
*1 tsp honey*
*4 Tbs olive oil*
*3 eggs, beaten*
*1 oz (30 g) sprouts*
*salt and pepper*
*pinch of mace or freshly grated nutmeg*
*1 red onion*
*5 tomatoes*
*1 small sprig rosemary*
*1 yellow bell pepper*
*1 small eggplant*
*1 cup (4½ oz/125 g) black olives, chopped*

*Preparation time: about 45 minutes*



# Oat Pancakes with Sprouts

**Inexpensive • Satisfying**

• Grind the wheat to flour fineness. Separate eggs. Stir wheat, egg yolks, rolled oats, and milk together and let stand about 20 minutes. Wash the sprouts, dry, and mix into batter. Season with nutmeg, salt, and pepper. Beat the egg whites stiff and fold into batter.

• Wash the scallions, trim, and cut into rings, including the green part. Wash the tomatoes and dice, omitting stem base. Wash mushrooms, trim, and quarter.

• Heat 1 tablespoon oil in a heavy frying pan over moderate heat. With a tablespoon drop in six cakes and cook 2–3 minutes per side. Repeat with remaining batter, adding more oil as needed. Meanwhile, in another frying pan, heat 1 tablespoon oil over medium heat and braise mushrooms for about 3 minutes. Add onions and continue braising 2 more minutes. Stir in tomatoes, parsley, salt, and pepper. Serve the pancakes with the mushroom mixture.

| PER SERVING: | 378 CALORIES | |
|---|---|---|
| NUTRITIONAL INFORMATION | | |
| Fat (30% calories from fat) | 13 | g |
| Protein | 19 | g |
| Carbohydrates | 51 | g |
| Cholesterol | 148 | mg |
| Sodium | 317 | mg |

# Quinoa Cakes with Vegetable Salsa

**Pictured • For company**

• Bring 1 scant cup (7½ oz/220 ml) water to boil. Add ½ cup (2¾ oz/80 g) quinoa and cook over low heat 15 minutes. Remove from heat and let stand 10 minutes.

• Meanwhile, grind the rest of the quinoa to consistency of coarse cornmeal. Grind the spelt to flour. Mix the yeast with the ground quinoa, flour, milk, and honey. Let stand 10 minutes, then stir in 1 tablespoon oil, eggs, sprouts, salt, pepper, and mace.

• Peel the onion and dice. Wash tomatoes and dice, leaving out stem base. Heat 1 Tbs oil in a sauce pan. Add onion, tomatoes, rosemary, salt, and pepper, and cook over low heat about 10 minutes. Wash pepper and eggplant, trim, and dice fine. Add to the tomato mixture with olives and simmer 5 minutes. Set the salsa aside.

• Mix cooked quinoa into batter. Heat 1 Tbs oil in each of two frying pans over medium heat. Fry eight cakes in each pan for 3–4 minutes per side. Serve with salsa.

| PER SERVING: | 436 CALORIES | |
|---|---|---|
| NUTRITIONAL INFORMATION | | |
| Fat (36% calories from fat) | 19 | g |
| Protein | 16 | g |
| Carbohydrates | 59 | g |
| Cholesterol | 141 | mg |
| Sodium | 354 | mg |

With
Pizazz!

# For the Small Appetite

Grains add more to a meal: They give soups and small dishes nutritional weight. All the dishes in this chapter can be served as part of a meal or with a raw vegetable for lunch or supper.

### Oats

The number-one power pack among the various grains: Oats provide higher-quality protein than wheat; they are higher in many unsaturated fatty acids; and they have a positive effect on cholesterol levels. The grain is rich in minerals, 2 ounces (60 g) providing 22% of the daily requirements for magnesium and vitamin $B_1$. Only gluten protein is missing.

• Preparation tip

Oat grains are particularly soft; soaking them is unnecessary.

• Recipe variations

Try using oats instead of barley, rice, or rye in the following recipes in this chapter: Pumpkin Soup, Winter Soup, Buckwheat-Ricotta Dumplings, Kasha, and Barley Balls.

### Millet

Millet brings beauty from within; with its high iron content (2 oz [60 g] of the grain provides 30% of our daily requirement) as well as fluoride and silicic acid, millet is good for healthy teeth, skin, and hair. Because millet is gluten-free (important for those who are allergic!), it is not suitable for baking when used alone.

• Preparation tips

Wash millet in hot water before using. It is sold hulled, so that the germ is often bruised; oil oozes out and may become rancid and bitter. But it can easily be washed away. Millet does not need to be softened and goes well with other grains, such as barley, oats, rice, rye, or green spelt.

• Recipe variations

Try the following recipes in this chapter with millet instead of rice or buckwheat: Pumpkin Soup, Buckwheat Dumplings. Also tasty and popular in African countries is steamed millet instead of couscous. To make it, cover raw millet with water and let soak about 1 hour. Then drain and steam like couscous.

### Barley

A handful of toasted barley tossed into the soup is exactly the right thing after

a stressful day, as barley quiets the stomach. Why was one of the oldest grains replaced by wheat? Barley lacks the gluten protein that is important for baking and is thus a grain for boiling. It tastes particularly good pan-toasted and steamed.

• Recipe variations

Try barley in the following recipes instead of oats, rice, and rye: Leek Soup, Pumpkin Soup, Winter Soup, and Buckwheat Dumplings.

### Corn

A body builder, completely in tune with the times—in recent years polenta has been transformed from a rustic standby to an elegant dish. Polenta meal is made from ground corn; popcorn comes from special popping corn; and sweet corn serves as the vegetable. Corn is rich in carotene, which supports the immune system and from which our bodies build vitamin A (7 oz [200 g] sweet corn provides 24% of the daily requirement). Corn is gluten-free.

### Rye

With more total protein but less gluten than wheat, rye gives dishes a hearty touch. Bread made with rye takes longer to rise, and may require more leavening.

• Recipe variations

Try rye in the following recipes in this chapter instead of rice, buckwheat, and barley: Pumpkin Soup, Winter Soup, Buckwheat Dumplings, and Barley Balls.

### *Tips for Cooking with Whole Grains and Groats*

- *You will find precise details about cooking times on the front endpapers.*
- *Do not soak groats; they will retain their nutrients and fragrance better.*
- *The short cookers—millet, buckwheat, and quinoa—are also not soaked. Wash buckwheat and millet in hot water before cooking.*
- *Amaranth, oats, green spelt, and rice (with moderate cooking times) need not be soaked, but soaking does shorten the cooking time.*
- *The long cookers—wheat berries, spelt, kamut, rye, and barley—must be soaked because of their hard hulls. The soaking water is used for cooking.*
- *Toasting produces a hearty aroma. Toast groats, meal, or soaked grains in a dry pan or toast in a little oil for 5–10 minutes over moderate heat, stirring constantly.*
- *Salt the grains with medium and longer cooking times toward the end of cooking, which shortens the cooking time slightly.*

***Makes 4 servings***

***Leek Soup***

*1 cup (3½ oz/100 g) rolled oats*
*2 Tbs spelt*
*1 egg*
*1 egg yolk*
*¾ cup (6 oz/175 ml) whole milk*
*salt and pepper*
*1 tsp fresh thyme leaves*
*3 shallots*
*10 oz (300 g) leeks*
*1 apple (about 5 oz/150 g)*
*1 medium potato (about 3½ oz/100 g)*
*3 Tbs cold-pressed olive oil*
*1 Tbs curry powder*
*1¼ cups (10 oz/300 ml) vegetable broth*
*1 tsp freshly grated ginger*
*7 Tbs cream*

*Preparation time: about 30 minutes*

***Rice Soup***

*2 red onions*
*5½ oz (160 g) snow peas*
*2 Tbs sunflower or other light vegetable oil*
*½ cup (3½ oz/100 g) whole-grain fragrant rice*
*3¼ cups (26 oz/800 ml) vegetable broth*
*salt and pepper*
*1 tsp Asian sesame oil*
*1 Tbs freshly grated ginger*
*¼ cup (2 oz/60 ml) soy sauce*
*½ leaf nori seaweed (see Tips)*

*Preparation time: about 30 minutes*

# Leek Soup with Oat Cakes

**Inexpensive • From India**

• Grind the oats and spelt to fine flour and stir together with egg, egg yolk, milk, salt, pepper, and thyme.

• Peel shallots and mince. Wash vegetables and fruit. Slice leeks crosswise. Peel apple and potatoes and dice.

• In a saucepan heat 2 tablespoons oil over medium heat. Add the shallots, apple, and curry and braise about 3 minutes, stirring constantly. Add the potato and leek and continue braising about 5 minutes. Add vegetable broth and bring to boil. Season with ginger, salt, and pepper and simmer over low heat, covered, about 25 minutes. Puree in blender or processor and return to the saucepan. Stir in the cream and bring to boil, then remove from heat.

• Meanwhile, heat 1 tablespoon olive oil in a heavy frying pan over moderate heat. Fry eight batter cakes over low heat, 3–4 minutes per side. Serve with the soup.

| PER SERVING: | 350 CALORIES | |
|---|---|---|
| NUTRITIONAL INFORMATION | | |
| Fat (30% calories from fat) | 12 | g |
| Protein | 13 | g |
| Carbohydrates | 51 | g |
| Cholesterol | 127 | mg |
| Sodium | 805 | mg |

# Rice Soup with Snow Peas

**Pictured • From Japan**

• Peel the onions and dice. Wash the snow peas, trim, and halve on the diagonal.

• Heat sunflower oil in a saucepan over moderate heat but do not let it smoke. Fry the rice and onions together gently for about 2 minutes.

• Pour in the vegetable broth; add the snow peas and salt. Bring the soup to boil and simmer, covered, over low heat about 20 minutes. Season with pepper, sesame oil, salt, ginger, and soy sauce, and garnish with nori cut into strips.

## Tips

You can change the taste of the soup by slicing ½ stalk lemongrass into rings and adding with the snow peas, or by seasoning the soup with lime juice.

Nori and lemongrass are available in Asian grocery stores.

| PER SERVING: | 328 CALORIES | |
|---|---|---|
| NUTRITIONAL INFORMATION | | |
| Fat (23% calories from fat) | 8 | g |
| Protein | 12 | g |
| Carbohydrates | 53 | g |
| Cholesterol | 2 | mg |
| Sodium | 2525 | mg |

# Pumpkin Soup with Rice Dumplings

**Hearty • Pictured**

• Bring 1 cup (8 oz/250 ml) salted water to boil. Cook the rice in it about 40 minutes, drain, and let cool.

• Puree the tofu and knead with the egg, egg yolk, bread crumbs, parsley, salt, pepper, and rice. Chill.

• Peel and mince shallots. Wash the pumpkin, peel, and chop into small pieces. In a saucepan, heat oil over moderate heat and braise the shallots and pumpkin in it for about 3 minutes. Add broth, bring to boil, and cook about 10 minutes. Puree in processor or blender and return to the saucepan. Wash the spinach, dry, cut into strips, and add. Season soup with salt and pepper and remove from heat.

• While the soup is cooking, bring 2 cups (16 oz/500 ml) salted water to boil. With two tablespoons, form dumplings from the rice dough and poach about 10 minutes, then add to the soup. Garnish with chervil.

| PER SERVING: | 279 CALORIES | |
|---|---|---|
| NUTRITIONAL INFORMATION | | |
| Fat (34% calories from fat) | 11 | g |
| Protein | 13 | g |
| Carbohydrates | 35 | g |
| Cholesterol | 100 | mg |
| Sodium | 929 | mg |

# Winter Soup with Rye

**Inexpensive • Easy to make**

• Soak the rye in ⅔ cup (5 oz/150 ml) water in the refrigerator for 10 hours.

• Drain the rye. Bring 2 cups (16 oz/500 ml) salted water to boil. Wash vegetables. Peel rutabaga, dice, blanch about 2 minutes in the salted water, and drain. Cut the savoy cabbage into thin strips; slice the leek into strips. Peel celery root, carrot, and potato and grate. Cut the chard into strips.

• Heat a frying pan over moderate heat and toast the rye in it for about 3 minutes, shaking constantly to prevent burning.

• Heat butter in a saucepan and braise the vegetables in it with the rye about 5 minutes. Add the broth and bring to boil. Season with salt and pepper. Add the bay leaves and cloves and simmer about 15 minutes. Wash the mushrooms, trim, and cut into fine strips. Garnish the soup with the mushrooms.

| PER SERVING: | 295 CALORIES | |
|---|---|---|
| NUTRITIONAL INFORMATION | | |
| Fat (24% calories from fat) | 8 | g |
| Protein | 10 | g |
| Carbohydrates | 48 | g |
| Cholesterol | 11 | mg |
| Sodium | 1811 | mg |

***Makes 4 servings***

***Pumpkin Soup***

*salt and pepper*
*¼ cup (1¾ oz/50 g) red rice*
*7 oz (200 g) tofu*
*1 egg*
*1 egg yolk*
*2 Tbs bread crumbs*
*1 Tbs chopped Italian parsley*
*3 shallots*
*14 oz (400 g) fresh pumpkin*
*2 Tbs sunflower or other light vegetable oil*
*2 cups (16 oz/500 ml) vegetable broth*
*1 oz (30 g) spinach or fresh basil*
*1 Tbs chopped fresh chervil*

*Preparation time: about 1¼ hours*

***Winter Soup with Rye***

*¼ cup (1¾ oz/50 g) rye*
*salt and pepper*
*1 rutabaga (about 3½ oz/100 g)*
*3½ oz (100 g) savoy cabbage*
*1 thin leek*
*3½ oz (100 g) celery root*
*1 carrot*
*1 large potato*
*1 oz (30 g) chard, beet greens or spinach*
*1 Tbs clarified butter*
*1 qt (1 liter) vegetable broth*
*2 bay leaves*
*2 whole cloves*
*2 button mushrooms*

*Preparation time: about 45 minutes (+10 hours soaking time)*

*For the dumplings:*
*1 generous cup (7 oz/200 g) buckwheat kasha*
*1 cup (8 oz/250 ml) vegetable broth*
*salt*
*⅔ cup (5 oz/150 g) ricotta*
*2 eggs*
*1 egg yolk*
*3 Tbs whole-wheat flour*
*pepper*

*For the green sauce:*
*1 medium potato (about 3½ oz/100 g)*
*5 oz (150 g) leeks*
*2 shallots*
*1 scant cup (7 oz/100 ml) vegetable broth*
*⅔ cup (5 oz/150 g) cream*
*3½ oz (100 g) mixed fresh herbs (see Note)*
*2 tsp lemon juice*

*For the vegetables:*
*1 red onion*
*1¼ lb (20 oz/600 g) celery*
*1 apple*
*1 Tbs sunflower or other light vegetable oil*
*salt and pepper*
*freshly grated nutmeg*

*Preparation time: about 45 minutes*

# Buckwheat-Ricotta Dumplings with Green Sauce

**Piquant • Inexpensive**

• For the dumplings, wash the kasha in hot water and drain well. Toast in a dry frying pan over medium heat, stirring constantly, about 3 minutes. Bring 1 cup (8 oz/250 ml) broth to boil. Add the buckwheat and keep hot, covered, over low heat for about 10 minutes. Remove from heat and let cool.

• For the sauce, wash the potato, peel, and grate it. Wash the leeks, trim, and cut into rings. Peel the shallots and dice. Combine all in a saucepan with the remaining broth and bring to simmer; cook 10 minutes. Stir in the cream and simmer for another 5 minutes. Wash the herbs, shake dry, chop coarsely, and stir into the sauce. Puree in processor or blender and season to taste with lemon juice.

• Bring a saucepan of salted water to simmer. Mix the ricotta, eggs, yolk, flour, salt, and pepper. Using two tablespoons, form dumplings and poach in the water about 10 minutes; do not boil. Remove and drain.

• For the vegetables, peel the onion and chop fine. Wash the celery, trim, and cut into diamonds about ¼ inch (1 cm) in size. Wash the apple, peel if necessary, and cut into matchsticks, leaving out the core.

• Heat the oil in a frying pan over moderate heat. Add the onion and sear slightly. Add the celery and braise 5 minutes. Season to taste with salt, pepper, and nutmeg. Divide the dumplings, vegetables, and sauce among 4 plates and garnish with apple.

### Note

Use a combination of several or all of the following: sorrel, chervil, parsley, dill, chives, tarragon, and lovage or celery leaves.

Makes 4 servings.

| PER SERVING: | 649 CALORIES |
| --- | --- |
| NUTRITIONAL INFORMATION | |
| Fat (32% calories from fat) | 25 g |
| Protein | 26 g |
| Carbohydrates | 91 g |
| Cholesterol | 198 mg |
| Sodium | 1101 mg |

# Couscous with Pumpkin

**Middle Eastern delicacy • Easy to make**

• Soak couscous in 7 tablespoons broth for about 30 minutes.

• Meanwhile, peel and chop the onion. Peel and dice the pumpkin. Wash the basil and mince the leaves. Halve the hot pepper lengthwise, seed, and chop. Wash the snow peas, trim, and halve on the diagonal.

• Heat the oil in a saucepan and braise the onion, pumpkin, and hot pepper over moderate heat about 3 minutes. Add the remaining broth and simmer for about 10 minutes.

• Line a metal steamer insert with a clean towel and add the couscous. Place over the vegetables and cook over low heat, covered, about 25 minutes. Wash the tomatoes and heat with the basil and peppers about 5 minutes. Season to taste with salt, pepper, and Parmesan, and serve with vegetables.

Makes 4 servings.

| PER SERVING: | 392 CALORIES | |
|---|---|---|
| NUTRITIONAL INFORMATION | | |
| Fat (15% calories from fat) | 7 | g |
| Protein | 14 | g |
| Carbohydrates | 71 | g |
| Cholesterol | 2 | mg |
| Sodium | 622 | mg |

# Borscht with Sprouts

**Inexpensive • Pictured**

• Bring 1 quart (1 liter) salted water to boil. Core the cabbage and cut into small diamonds. Blanch in the salted water about 2 minutes; drain. Peel the onions and parsley root and cut into small dice. Wash the remaining vegetables and peel. Grate potato and carrot; dice the pepper and beets. Remove the stem base from the tomatoes and cut into sixths.

• Heat clarified butter in a saucepan and braise the onions, parsley root, potato, carrot, and pepper about 4 minutes. Add broth and bring to boil, stirring in salt, pepper, beets, caraway, and barley sprouts. Simmer, covered, over low heat about 15 minutes. Stir in the parsley and tomatoes. Ladle into 4 bowls and garnish with sour cream.

Makes 4 servings.

| PER SERVING: | 462 CALORIES | |
|---|---|---|
| NUTRITIONAL INFORMATION | | |
| Fat (28% calories from fat) | 15 | g |
| Protein | 20 | g |
| Carbohydrates | 70 | g |
| Cholesterol | 23 | mg |
| Sodium | 1495 | mg |

***Couscous with Pumpkin***

*1 generous cup (8¾ oz/250 g) couscous*
*1¼ cups (10 oz/300 ml) vegetable broth*
*1 red onion*
*14 oz (400 g) fresh pumpkin*
*1 bunch basil*
*1 small hot pepper*
*3½ oz (100 g) snow peas*
*1 Tbs cold-pressed olive oil*
*7 oz (200 g) cherry tomatoes*
*salt and pepper*
*1 Tbs freshly grated Parmesan cheese*

*Preparation time: about 1 hour*

***Borscht with Sprouts***

*salt and pepper*
*7 oz (200 g) cabbage*
*2 onions*
*3½ oz (100 g) parsley root (optional)*
*1 large potato*
*1 carrot*
*½ red bell pepper*
*2 small beets*
*2 tomatoes*
*2 Tbs clarified butter*
*3 cups (24 oz/750 ml) vegetable broth*
*1 Tbs caraway seeds*
*3½ oz (100 g) barley sprouts*
*1 Tbs chopped fresh parsley*
*2 Tbs sour cream or crème fraîche.*

*Preparation time: about 50 minutes*

**Makes 4 servings**

**Kasha**

*2 onions*
*2 scallions*
*7 oz (200 g) parsnips or carrots*
*14 oz (400 g) button mushrooms*
*1½ bunches Italian parsley*
*2½ cups (600 ml) vegetable broth*
*salt*
*3 Tbs clarified butter*
*1 cup (7 oz/200 g) buckwheat kasha*
*pepper*
*¼ cup (4 oz/100 g) sour cream*

*Preparation time: about 30 minutes*

**Chili Succotash**

*⅔ cup (4½ oz/125 g) dried lima or other beans*
*salt*
*4 ears fresh corn (or 1 cup/ 7 oz/200 g canned corn)*
*3 shallots*
*10 oz (300 g) green beans*
*2 red bell peppers*
*⅓ hot pepper*
*3 Tbs clarified butter*
*½ cup (4 oz/125 ml) vegetable broth*
*pepper*
*1 avocado*
*1 Tbs chopped chives*

*Preparation time: about 35 minutes (+ 1 hour soaking time)*



# Kasha with Mushrooms

**From Russia • Fast**

• Peel onions and dice. Wash vegetables. Trim the scallions and chop, including the green parts. Peel parsnips and dice. Wash the mushrooms and quarter. Wash parsley and chop fine.

• In a pot, salt the broth and bring to boil. In a frying pan heat 1 tablespoon clarified butter over moderate heat. Gently sear the onions and kasha in it for about 3 minutes, then add the broth and simmer about 10 minutes.

• Meanwhile, heat 1 tablespoon clarified butter in another pan over moderate heat. Sear the parsnips and scallions in it for about 1 minute. Stir in parsley and season with salt and pepper. Add contents of pan to kasha mixture. In the saucepan, heat the remaining tablespoon of butter over moderate heat. Add mushrooms and braise about 5 minutes. Season with salt and pepper.

• Stir sour cream into kasha mixture over moderate heat until heated through. Correct the seasonings and serve with mushrooms.

| PER SERVING: | 453 CALORIES |
|---|---|
| NUTRITIONAL INFORMATION | |
| Fat (35% calories from fat) | 19 g |
| Protein | 15 g |
| Carbohydrates | 65 g |
| Cholesterol | 37 mg |
| Sodium | 143 mg |

# Chili Succotash

**Colorful • Pictured**

• Boil the lima beans in 2 cups (16 oz/ 500 ml) water for about 3 minutes, then cover and let stand 1 hour. Place over low heat and cook 20 more minutes, covered, adding salt after 15 minutes.

• Meanwhile, wash the vegetables. Cut the corn kernels from the cob. Peel the shallots and mince. Trim the green beans and cut them into thirds. Clean the peppers and cut them into ¼-inch (1 cm) diamonds. Seed the hot pepper and chop it fine.

• Heat clarified butter in a deep frying pan and sear the shallots, corn, and hot pepper about 3 minutes. Add the green beans, lima beans, and pepper and cook 5 minutes. Pour in the broth and bring to boil. Season to taste with salt and pepper.

• Peel the avocado, halve, and remove the pit. Dice the avocado and distribute among the 4 plates. Spoon the succotash on top. Sprinkle with chives.

| PER SERVING: | 363 CALORIES |
|---|---|
| NUTRITIONAL INFORMATION | |
| Fat (37% calories from fat) | 16 g |
| Protein | 12 g |
| Carbohydrates | 48 g |
| Cholesterol | 23 mg |
| Sodium | 355 mg |

# Barley Balls with Tofu and Bean Cassoulet

**Easy to make • Hearty**

*For the barley balls:*
*⅔ cup (4 oz/120 g) pearl barley*
*1 Tbs wheat berries*
*8 oz (250 g) tofu*
*3 Tbs ricotta or cottage cheese*
*2 Tbs soy sauce*
*salt and pepper*
*dash Tabasco*
*2 tsp Asian sesame oil*
*1 piece fresh ginger (about ¾ in/2 cm)*
*1 bunch Italian parsley*
*7 Tbs whole-wheat bread crumbs*
*2 Tbs olive oil*

*For the cassoulet:*
*7 oz (200 g) red onions*
*1 clove garlic*
*1¼ lb (20 oz/600 g) green beans*
*14 oz (400 g) cherry tomatoes*
*2 Tbs cold-pressed olive oil*
*1¾ cups (14 oz/400 ml) vegetable broth*
*grated peel of ¼ lemon*
*2 Tbs balsamic vinegar*
*1 Tbs chopped fresh savory*
*1 tsp chopped fresh mint*
*salt and pepper*
*1 bunch chives*

*Preparation time: about 1¼ hours (+6–12 hours soaking time)*

• For the barley balls, soak 3 tablespoons barley in 7 tablespoons water 6–12 hours.

• Crush the remaining barley. Grind the wheat to flour. Puree the tofu and mix with crushed barley, ground wheat, cheese, soy sauce, salt, pepper, Tabasco, and sesame oil. Peel the ginger and grate. Wash parsley, shake dry, and chop the leaves. Thoroughly wash the soaked barley and drain well. Mix the ginger, parsley, and soaked barley into the dough and let rest about 30 minutes.

• Meanwhile, for the cassoulet, peel the onions and garlic and chop fine. Wash the green beans, trim, and cut in thirds. Wash tomatoes and halve. In a pot heat 2 tablespoons olive oil and over low to medium heat fry onions and garlic till onions are transparent. Add the beans and cook about 4 minutes. Add the broth, bring to boil and cook, covered, over low heat about 10 minutes. Add the tomatoes. Season with lemon peel, vinegar, savory, mint, salt, and pepper; remove from heat.

• Preheat oven to 160°F (70°C). Form 20 little "meatballs" from the barley mixture and roll in the crumbs. Heat 1 tablespoon oil in a large, heavy frying pan and fry the barley balls in batches over low to medium heat, about 4 minutes per side. Keep warm in the oven.

• Wash the chives, shake dry, and cut into rings. Divide the barley balls and cassoulet among 4 plates and sprinkle with chopped chives.

**Menu**

Serve endive salad with walnuts as a first course, and follow with Muesli Parfait (page 85).

Makes 4 servings.

| PER SERVING: | 423 CALORIES | |
|---|---|---|
| NUTRITIONAL INFORMATION | | |
| Fat (26% calories from fat) | 13 | g |
| Protein | 20 | g |
| Carbohydrates | 59 | g |
| Cholesterol | 2 | mg |
| Sodium | 1273 | mg |

GORGEOUS
grain

# From Pot and Pan

Ordinarily just side dishes, grains are the very center in this chapter. Here you will find such dishes as bulgur, pasties, and jambalaya, as well as delicious rice dishes like risotto and pilaf.

**Brown Rice for All Occasions**

As the cuisines of Asia have become more familiar, the variety of rices available has simply exploded. Because of its easy availability, brown rice is especially suitable for newcomers to natural cooking. Brown rice (which still retains the silvery hull and germ) is more filling and more nourishing than polished white rice. Two ounces (60 g) of brown rice provide 22% of our daily requirement of vitamin $B_6$ and 27% of the daily magnesium requirement. Rice is gluten-free.

• Buying tips

Brown rice does not keep indefinitely because of the germ. Pay attention to the expiration date!

Wash rice from Asia before using.

But don't wash enriched rice, or you will be rinsing off the added nutrients, which are in the form of a surface coating.

**Long-grain Brown Rice** is firm-cooking, chewy, and ideal as a side dish. It is neutral in taste and very versatile in hearty cooking.

**Short-grain Brown Rice** easily becomes sticky and soft and therefore is perfect for risotto and rice pudding. It is fine for fillings and casseroles, too, but it is also—especially for the beginner—a lovely side dish.

• Cooking tip

If rice pudding doesn't get creamy enough, grind some rice to flour and use it for thickening.

**Medium-grain Brown Rice** is a newly available variety that has somewhat plumper grains than long-grain rice. It is very well suited for stews and other hearty everyday dishes.

**Parboiled Natural (Converted) Rice** is treated with a steam-pressure process that forces about 80% of the nutrients in the hull to the inside of the grain. Its cooking time is as short as that of white rice, but the price for this is a loss of nutrients and fiber.

Arborio rice, a specialty of Italy, is a parboiled rice from which the hull has been removed; it is a soft medium-grain rice for risotto and rice pudding.

**Sweet Rice (Brown Rice), also Mochi Rice** is the fastest-cooking of the brown rices, with a cooking time of only about 20 minutes. It is a delicacy with fine flavor. Originally it came from Japan, but it is also grown in the United States today. It is smaller-grained than short-grain rice. Mochi rice needs less liquid than other types (1 cup/7 ounces/200 g rice to 1¼ cups/10 ounces/300 g fluid). It is marvelous for risottos and desserts, for fillings, and as a side dish.

**Fragrant Rice (Brown Rice, also Basmati)** is ideal for Asian dishes—such as curries. Particularly good is brown jasmine rice from Thailand, a narrow long-grain rice that gives off a delicate jasmine fragrance while cooking. Excellent fragrant rices of the Basmati type are grown in the United States.

**Brown Basmati Rice** is a classic Indian specialty with a nutty aroma. It is perfectly suited for Asian cooking in particular. It comes from India, Pakistan, and the United States.

• Cooking tip

Wash brown basmati rice before cooking, let soak for 30 minutes, and cook in fresh water for about 20 minutes. Let stand off heat for about 10 minutes before serving.

**Red Rice** is a piquant, nutty-tasting specialty with a natural red color. Fine for salads, stuffings, soups, dumplings, and risotto, it gives dishes a subtle note.

**Grain-Rice Mixtures**

*Served with a nutty mixture of grains, a simple vegetable dish suddenly turns into something special. Such mixtures can be bought already prepared, but you can also assemble them yourself:*

- *2-grain mixture: long-grain brown rice with a small portion of wild rice*
- *3-grain mixture: basmati-type fragrant rice, with a small portion of red rice and wild rice*
- *7-grain mixture: brown short-grain rice, wild rice, red rice, green spelt, oats, soaked barley, soaked spelt (see table on front endpapers). To make 7 oz (200 g) of a seven-grain mixture, use 1 oz (30 g) of each except for wild rice; use ¾ oz (20 g) wild rice.*

**Makes 4 servings**

**Bulgur with Caponata**

*12 black olives*
*3 shallots*
*1 garlic clove*
*5 small plum tomatoes*
*1 eggplant*
*4 Tbs cold-pressed olive oil*
*2½ cups (20 oz/600 ml) vegetable broth*
*2 tsp chopped fresh thyme*
*salt and pepper*
*3 Tbs small capers*
*3 Tbs honey*
*3 Tbs balsamic vinegar*
*1 small zucchini*
*1 cup (7 oz/200 g) bulgur*
*1 Tbs freshly grated Parmesan cheese*
*3 basil leaves*

*Preparation time: about 30 minutes*

**Red Rice Risotto**

*1 qt (1 liter) vegetable broth*
*3 shallots*
*3 Tbs olive oil*
*1½ cups (10 oz/300 g) red rice*
*1¼ lb (20 oz/600 g) oyster mushrooms*
*4 Tbs freshly grated Parmesan cheese*
*2 Tbs cream*
*1 tsp chopped fresh tarragon*
*freshly grated nutmeg*
*salt and pepper*

*Preparation time: about 45 minutes*



# Bulgur with Caponata

**Pictured • Inexpensive**

• Remove pits from olives and halve. Peel shallots and garlic and chop fine. Wash tomatoes and eggplant and dice.

• Heat 2 tablespoons oil in a frying pan over medium heat. Brown the eggplant in it for about 3 minutes; remove. Add another 1 tablespoon oil, two thirds of the shallots and the garlic and fry until shallots are transparent. Add ½ cup (4 oz/100 ml) broth, tomatoes, thyme, salt, and pepper and simmer 10 minutes. Add olives, capers, eggplant, honey, and vinegar, and keep warm.

• Meanwhile, wash the zucchini and dice. Heat the remaining oil in a saucepan over medium heat. Fry the remaining shallots and bulgur until shallots are transparent, then add the remaining broth and bring to boil. Cook over low heat, covered, for about 10 minutes. Add zucchini and Parmesan and cook 2 more minutes. Serve with caponata and basil.

| PER SERVING: | 422 CALORIES | |
|---|---|---|
| NUTRITIONAL INFORMATION | | |
| Fat (20% calories from fat) | 10 | g |
| Protein | 14 | g |
| Carbohydrates | 77 | g |
| Cholesterol | 3 | mg |
| Sodium | 1243 | mg |

# Red Rice Risotto with Mushrooms

**Elegant • For company**

• Heat the broth. Peel the shallots and chop.

• In a large frying pan heat 2 tablespoons oil and fry the shallots and rice over low heat about 5 minutes until shallots are transparent. Cover with some of the broth and boil briskly, uncovered, 35–40 minutes, stirring. As the broth cooks down, keep adding more. The risotto should be creamy and moist but still firm to the bite.

• Meanwhile, clean the mushrooms and cut into strips. Just before the rice is done, heat the remaining oil in a frying pan over moderate heat. Fry the mushrooms in it about 3 minutes; set aside.

• Mix the rice with the Parmesan, cream, tarragon, mushrooms, salt, and pepper. Serve hot.

| PER SERVING: | 588 CALORIES | |
|---|---|---|
| NUTRITIONAL INFORMATION | | |
| Fat (18% calories from fat) | 12 | g |
| Protein | 29 | g |
| Carbohydrates | 95 | g |
| Cholesterol | 19 | mg |
| Sodium | 2037 | mg |

*For the pastry:*
*1 generous cup (7 oz/200 g) spelt*
*2 eggs*
*2 egg yolks*
*salt and pepper*
*2 Tbs sunflower or other light vegetable oil*
*freshly grated nutmeg*

*For the filling:*
*4 Tbs quinoa*
*¾ cup (7 oz/200 ml) vegetable broth*
*salt and pepper*
*2 oz (50 g) each leek, celery root, and carrot*
*1 clove garlic*
*1 bunch arugula*
*5 sun-dried tomatoes*
*4 Tbs freshly grated pecorino cheese*
*2 Tbs fresh goat cheese*

*For the sauce:*
*2 shallots*
*½ cup (4 oz/100 ml) vegetable broth*
*5 Tbs white wine (or 1 Tbs lemon juice)*
*2 sage leaves*
*½ cup (2 oz/50 g) pine nuts*
*2 Tbs crème fraîche or sour cream*
*scant ½ tsp carob powder*
*salt and pepper*
*flour*

*Preparation time: about 1¼ hours*



# Quinoa Dumplings with Pine Nut Sauce

**Savory • Unusual**

• To make the pastry, grind the spelt to flour. Separate 1 egg, reserving the white. Knead the spelt with the second egg, all the yolks, 1 tablespoon water, salt, oil, and nutmeg to form a firm dough. Shape into two balls and let rest 20 minutes, covered.

• Meanwhile, combine broth and quinoa and bring to boil. Add salt and cook, covered, over low heat about 20 minutes. Drain.

• In the meantime, wash the vegetables. Trim the leek, celery root, carrot; peel the garlic. Chop all very fine. Place in bowl. Shake the arugula dry, chop, and add to the vegetables, reserving 2 tablespoons. Chop the tomatoes fine. Stir into the vegetables along with the cooked quinoa, pecorino, goat cheese, salt, and pepper.

• For the sauce, peel the shallots and chop. In a saucepan bring the broth, shallots, wine, sage, and pine nuts to boil and cook over medium heat 5 minutes. Puree in processor or blender. Stir in the crème fraîche. Stir the carob powder into 4 tablespoons water and stir into the puree. Bring to boil, stirring, and season to taste with salt and pepper. Set aside.

• Bring 2 quarts (2 liters) salted water to boil. Beat the remaining egg white.

• Roll out the pastry on a floured work surface and with a round cutter make 12 circles 2½–3 inches/6–8 cm in diameter. Brush edges with beaten egg white. Place filling on half the circle, fold pastry over, and press the edges together with a fork. Cook dumplings in simmering water 5 minutes.

• Meanwhile, reheat the sauce. Lift out the dumplings with a slotted spoon, drain on paper towels, and divide among 4 plates. Top with the sauce and garnish with the remaining arugula.

Makes 4 servings.

| PER SERVING: | 639 CALORIES | |
|---|---|---|
| NUTRITIONAL INFORMATION | | |
| Fat (31% calories from fat) | 26 | g |
| Protein | 33 | g |
| Carbohydrates | 96 | g |
| Cholesterol | 215 | mg |
| Sodium | 2254 | mg |

# Pumpkin Mixed Vegetables with Kamut

**Pictured • Inexpensive**

• Grind the kamut very coarsely. Peel the onions and chop. Heat the oil in a large, deep saucepan and fry the onions and kamut over low heat, stirring, for about 3 minutes. Add the broth and simmer 20 minutes.

• Meanwhile, wash the vegetables and trim. Cut the peeled pumpkin into small cubes; cut the celery into diamond-shaped pieces about ¼ inch (1 cm) in size. Cut the fennel into sixths. Quarter the mushrooms. Stir all, including the peas, into the kamut. Season with turmeric, nutmeg, salt, and pepper. Cook, covered, about 8 minutes. Wash the parsley; chop the leaves and stir in.

• Halve the tomatoes. Divide the vegetable mixture among 4 plates and garnish with tomatoes and cress.

Makes 4 servings.

| PER SERVING: | | 378 CALORIES |
|---|---|---|
| NUTRITIONAL INFORMATION | | |
| Fat (19% calories from fat) | 8 | g |
| Protein | 21 | g |
| Carbohydrates | 61 | g |
| Cholesterol | 2 | mg |
| Sodium | 1056 | mg |

# Quinoa Pilaf with Asparagus

**Fast • Sophisticated**

• Peel the onions and chop fine. Wash the asparagus, peel, and cut into thin slices. Heat the oil in a deep frying pan over low heat. Fry the onion and asparagus about 3 minutes until the onion is transparent, then remove. Add the quinoa to the pan with the broth and bring to boil. Add salt and bay leaves. Cook the quinoa, covered, 15 minutes. Remove the bay leaves.

• Wash the kohlrabi, cut into small diamonds, and stir into the quinoa along with the cream. Cook 5 minutes. Wash the parsley, chop the leaves, and stir into the asparagus and onions. Season with salt and pepper.

• Wash the tomatoes. Divide the quinoa and asparagus among 4 plates. Garnish with teardrop tomatoes.

Makes 4 servings.

| PER SERVING: | | 298 CALORIES |
|---|---|---|
| NUTRITIONAL INFORMATION | | |
| Fat (37% calories from fat) | 13 | g |
| Protein | 8 | g |
| Carbohydrates | 40 | g |
| Cholesterol | 25 | mg |
| Sodium | 401 | mg |

***Pumpkin Vegetables***

*1 cup (7 oz/200 g) kamut*
*2 red onions*
*2 Tbs sunflower oil*
*3½ cups (28 oz/850 ml) vegetable broth*
*14 oz (400 g) fresh pumpkin*
*7 oz (200 g) celery*
*1 small fennel bulb*
*7 oz (200 g) button mushrooms*
*¾ cup (3½ oz/100 g) fresh or frozen peas*
*1 tsp turmeric*
*freshly grated nutmeg*
*salt and pepper*
*1 bunch Italian parsley*
*3½ oz (100 g) cherry tomatoes*
*2 Tbs watercress or garden cress*

*Preparation time: about 30 minutes (+6–12 hours soaking time)*

***Quinoa Pilaf***

*1 onion*
*12 stalks green asparagus*
*1 Tbs sunflower or other light vegetable oil*
*1 cup (5 oz/150 g) quinoa*
*¾ cup (6 oz/200 ml) vegetable broth*
*salt and pepper*
*2 bay leaves*
*3½ oz (100 g) kohlrabi*
*5 Tbs cream*
*1 bunch Italian parsley*
*3½ oz (100 g) yellow teardrop tomatoes*

*Preparation time: about 45 minutes*

# Fragrant Rice with Baby Corn

**Unusual • For company**

*3 oz (80 g) dried chickpeas*
*1½ cups (10 oz/300 g) whole-grain fragrant rice*
*salt*
*2 red onions*
*1 clove garlic*
*2 Tbs sunflower or other light vegetable oil*
*1⅔ cups (13 oz/400 ml) vegetable broth*
*7 oz (200 g) baby corn*
*7 oz (200 g) okra*
*5 Tbs cream*
*2 Tbs tandoori seasoning (Indian or Asian groceries)*
*pepper*
*1 cup (8 oz/250 g) plain yogurt*
*1 tsp chopped fresh mint*
*1 Tbs chopped fresh coriander (cilantro)*
*2 oz (50 g) cashews*
*1 scallion*
*2 limes or lemons*

*Soaking time: overnight*
*Preparation time: about 1 hour*

• Soak chickpeas overnight in 1 cup (8 ounces/250 ml) water.

• Wash the rice; drain. Soak in water to cover about 20 minutes.

• Bring salted water to boil in saucepan and blanch the chickpeas about 3 minutes. Drain and rinse with cold water. Drain again.

• Peel the onions and garlic and mince. Heat oil in a frying pan and fry the onions, garlic, and uncooked rice over low heat about 5 minutes, stirring. Add the broth and bring to boil. Cook, covered, about 15 minutes.

• Wash the vegetables. Trim the corn and halve diagonally. Leave the okra whole, but remove the base of the stem without injuring the pod (otherwise the milky fluid will ooze out). Mix both vegetables and the chickpeas into the rice. Stir in the cream and tandoori seasoning. Bring the mixture to boil and cook, covered, 10 minutes. Season to taste with salt and pepper and remove from heat.

• Mix the yogurt, mint, and coriander in a bowl. Season to taste with salt and pepper.

• Toast the cashews to a golden brown in a frying pan over moderate heat. Chop coarsely. Wash the scallion and trim. Cut the white part into small dice and the green into thin rings. Halve the limes. Divide the rice mixture among 4 plates and sprinkle with the cashews and scallion pieces. Offer the yogurt sauce and lime halves separately.

**Variation:**

**Fragrant Rice with Green Beans**

Instead of okra use 7 oz (200 g) green beans, cut into small pieces, and instead of corn use 7 oz (200 g) red bell pepper, cut into small dice. Add both to the rice with the chickpeas. Instead of tandoori seasoning use 1 tablespoon ginger.

Makes 4 servings.

| PER SERVING: | 672 CALORIES |
|---|---|
| NUTRITIONAL INFORMATION | |
| Fat (26% calories from fat) | 20 g |
| Protein | 25 g |
| Carbohydrates | 104 g |
| Cholesterol | 25 mg |
| Sodium | 757 mg |

# Risotto with Radicchio

**From Italy • Subtle**

• Boil the beans in 2 cups (16 ounces/500 ml) water about 2 minutes. Remove from heat and let stand 1 hour. Then cook until tender, 20–30 minutes. Wash the rice and soak in 2 cups (16 ounces/500 ml) water about 20 minutes. Drain the beans and rice.

• Meanwhile, peel the onions and chop coarsely. Wash the vegetables and basil. Cut the cabbage into fine strips, omitting the stem. Dice the tomatoes, removing the stem base. Quarter the radicchio and cut into fine strips. Cut the basil leaves into strips.

• Heat the oil in a deep frying pan over low heat and fry the onions and rice about 5 minutes. Add the broth and bring to boil; cook, covered, 20–30 minutes. Add the beans, cabbage, radicchio, and tomatoes and cook 5 minutes. Season with salt and pepper. Mix in the basil. Divide the risotto among 4 plates and sprinkle with Parmesan.

| PER SERVING: | 577 CALORIES | |
|---|---|---|
| NUTRITIONAL INFORMATION | | |
| Fat (17% calories from fat) | 11 | g |
| Protein | 20 | g |
| Carbohydrates | 99 | g |
| Cholesterol | 12 | mg |
| Sodium | 1579 | mg |

# Buckwheat with Savoy Cabbage

**Easy to make • Pictured**

• Bring 1 quart (1 liter) salted water to boil. Wash the savoy cabbage, quarter, cut into strips (omitting the stalk), and blanch in the water for about 2 minutes. Wash the buckwheat in hot water. Drain the cabbage and buckwheat. Peel the onion and dice.

• Heat the oil in a deep frying pan over low heat. Fry the onion until transparent. Add the broth and bring to boil. Stir in the buckwheat, bay leaf, cloves, caraway, thyme, allspice, and cabbage. Cook, covered, over low heat about 10 minutes.

• Wash the carrot, peel, and grate. Wash the parsley root, peel, and dice. Cook both with the buckwheat 5 minutes. Add cream, salt, and pepper and bring just to boil. Remove from heat. Wash the beet, peel, and cut into thin strips. Garnish the buckwheat with beet.

| PER SERVING: | 410 CALORIES | |
|---|---|---|
| NUTRITIONAL INFORMATION | | |
| Fat (27% calories from fat) | 13 | g |
| Protein | 13 | g |
| Carbohydrates | 66 | g |
| Cholesterol | 18 | mg |
| Sodium | 961 | mg |

**Makes 4 servings**

**Risotto with Radicchio**

*2 oz (50 g) white beans (cannellini)*
*1½ cups (10½ oz/300 g) short-grain brown rice*
*2 red onions*
*10 oz (300 g) Chinese cabbage*
*7 oz (200 g) tomatoes*
*3 oz (80 g) radicchio*
*1 bunch basil*
*2 Tbs cold-pressed olive oil*
*3 cups (750 ml) vegetable broth*
*salt and pepper*
*4 Tbs freshly grated Parmesan cheese*

*Preparation time: about 1 hour (+1 hour soaking time)*

**Buckwheat with Savoy Cabbage**

*salt and pepper*
*1 generous pound (18 oz/500 g) savoy cabbage*
*1 generous cup (7 oz/200 g) buckwheat*
*1 medium onion*
*2 Tbs sunflower or other light vegetable oil*
*2 cups (500 ml) vegetable broth*
*1 bay leaf*
*2 whole cloves*
*¼ tsp caraway seeds*
*½ tsp chopped fresh thyme*
*1 pinch ground allspice*
*1 medium carrot*
*3½ oz (100 g) parsley root*
*5 Tbs cream*
*1 small red beet*

*Preparation time: about 30 minutes*

# Multigrain Jambalaya

**Creole specialty • Zesty**

*About 1½ cups (10 oz/300 g) mixed grains (spelt, barley, wheat, rye)*
*2 red onions*
*3 Tbs clarified butter*
*1 tsp sweet paprika*
*1 tsp cayenne pepper*
*3 cups (24 oz/750 ml) vegetable broth*
*12 oz (350 g) celery*
*4 ripe, fleshy tomatoes*
*7 oz (200 g) pineapple*
*1 mango*
*2 green bell peppers*
*1 bunch Italian parsley*
*½–1 green hot pepper*
*4 oz (125 g) shallots*
*salt and pepper*

*Soaking time: overnight*
*Preparation time: about 45 minutes*

• Soak the mixed grains overnight in 1 quart (1 liter) water.

• Peel the onions and chop fine. In a deep frying pan heat the clarified butter and toast the grains in it over moderate heat for about 2 minutes, stirring. Stir in the onions, paprika, and cayenne pepper and cook 3 minutes. Add the broth, bring to boil and cook over moderate heat 20 minutes.

• Wash the vegetables, fruit, and parsley and trim. Cut 7 ounces (200 g) celery into pieces about ¾ inch (2 cm) long, cut the rest into thin strips, and set aside. Cut the tomatoes into small dice, leaving out the stem base. Cut the pineapple into ½-inch (1 cm) dice. Peel the mango, remove the pit, and dice. Cut the pepper into ¼-inch (1 cm) diamonds. Chop the parsley leaves fine. Seed the hot pepper and cut the pod into fine rings. Peel the shallots and chop. Mix the peppers, celery, pineapple, mango, and tomatoes into the grain mixture. Let all come to the boil and cook 5 minutes. Season with salt and pepper. Divide among 4 plates and garnish with parsley, celery strips, hot pepper, and shallots.

**Variation:**

**Jambalaya with Rice**

Instead of grains, use short-grain brown rice. Don't soak the rice, but after frying in butter, cook in 2¼ cups (18 oz/550 ml) broth, covered, 40 minutes. Instead of mango use 7 ounces (200 g) diced tofu. Offer a Creole sauce on the side. To make it, mix 2¼ cups (10 oz/300 g) chopped tomatoes, 1 tablespoon lime juice, 1 teaspoon each chopped fresh thyme, oregano, and sage, 2 tablespoons olive oil, ¼ cup (2 ounces/60 ml) balsamic vinegar, 1 pressed garlic clove, and ½ chopped hot pepper, and season to taste with salt and pepper.

**Menu**

Serve vegetable sticks with avocado dip first, and finish with fruit salad with mango.

Makes 4 servings.

| PER SERVING: | 677 CALORIES |
|---|---|
| NUTRITIONAL INFORMATION | |
| Fat (23% calories from fat) | 18 g |
| Protein | 23 g |
| Carbohydrates | 116 g |
| Cholesterol | 33 mg |
| Sodium | 1631 mg |

# Fire up the Oven!

# Hearty Dishes from the Oven

Grains are perfectly suited for soufflés and stuffed vegetables done in the oven. Here the stars are the wheat-like grains; they add a festive note and are good for special occasions.

**Grain or Not Grain?**
**Grain-like Plants**

Grains consist of the seeds or fruits of various food plants. Grain-like plants, on the other hand, mostly grow where climate and soil are unsuitable for grains. They can be used like grains in cooking because of their nutrients and the ways they are prepared.

**Amaranth**

These tiny seeds of a spinach-like plant that grows in the Andes are higher in protein, calcium, magnesium, and iron than wheat. Amaranth has recently been rediscovered after having been forgotten for a long time. It is gluten-free.

• Recipe variations

Try the following recipes in this chapter using amaranth instead of polenta meal, red rice, or green spelt: Stuffed Zucchini, Stuffed Kohlrabi, and Stuffed Peppers.

**Buckwheat**

Great for fast cooking, this is ready to use as a side dish (like rice) in 15–20 minutes. It already has a secure place in Breton and Russian cooking, and gives vegetarian dishes a rustic stamp. Buckwheat is a wheat-like plant rich in minerals and vitamins—2 ounces (60 g) provides 25% of the recommended daily allowance of vitamin $B_1$.

• Recipe variations

Try the following dishes in this chapter with buckwheat instead of red rice or green spelt: Stuffed Kohlrabi, Stuffed Peppers.

**Quinoa**

Fast and delicate: These are the advantages of quinoa (like amaranth, a vegetable plant from Latin America). Its small grains are similar in appearance and nutrient content to millet, and its protein content is higher than that of wheat. Quinoa is gluten-free.

• Recipe variations

Try the following recipes in this chapter with quinoa instead of amaranth, polenta meal, or rice: Eggplant-Amaranth Casserole, Stuffed Zucchini

and Kohlrabi, Stuffed Peppers, Amaranth Soufflé.

**Wild Rice**

This delicacy is not rice but the seed of a wild North American grass. It obtains its dark brown color and its nutty taste when, like spelt, it is kiln-dried after harvest.

• Buying tip

Wild rice is expensive, but it can be easily mixed with long-grain rice. Various combinations are available already mixed. Very intriguing is a gourmet rice mixture of long-grain brown rice, red rice, whole-grain fragrant rice, and wild rice.

• Serving tip

Because of its characteristic flavor, you should serve pure wild rice as a fine, festive side dish, perhaps together with mushrooms and a mixed plate of Mediterranean vegetables.

**Happily Meatless**

Grain is not only a good source of carbohydrates but also an important source of protein. Though its protein is of lesser quality than animal protein, this is easily remedied by combining grain with other protein-containing foods. You can find suggestions in the right-hand column on this page.

• Info

The quality of a food's protein depends on how many essential amino acids it contains. We use the protein in our food to replenish our own body protein.

***Vital Foods—Knowledgeable Mixing (Protein Combinations)***

*For a good vegetarian daily diet, which should be nourishing, satisfying, and at the same time tasty and interesting, it pays to combine foods to maximize their protein value.*

*Use whole-wheat and whole-grain products, because much of the higher-value protein in grains is located in the hulls. Good combinations are:*

- *Grains and eggs (noodles, pancakes, soufflés, baked goods, puddings)*
- *Grains and milk or milk products (dumplings, risotto, cheese dishes, puddings)*
- *Grains and legumes (salads, stews, rice dishes, stuffed vegetables)*
- *Grains and yeast (breads)*
- *Grains, milk, and eggs (pancakes, dumplings, soufflés, casseroles)*
- *A grain-based main dish and a dairy-based dessert.*

*Makes 4 servings*

***Eggplant-Amaranth Casserole***

*1 red onion*
*¾ cup (5 oz/150 g) amaranth*
*1¼ cups (10 oz/300 ml) vegetable broth*
*salt and pepper*
*2 ears corn*
*3 eggplants*
*3 Tbs cold-pressed olive oil*
*3½ oz (100 g) leeks*
*5 tomatoes*
*3½ oz (100 g) sheep's milk cheese*
*1 tsp chopped fresh marjoram*

*Preparation time: about 1 hour*

***Polenta Gratinée***

*4½ cups (36 oz/1.2 l) vegetable broth*
*1 scant cup (7 oz/200 g) polenta*
*juice and grated peel of 1 lemon*
*freshly grated nutmeg*
*salt and pepper*
*3½ oz (100 g) fresh basil*
*3 cloves garlic*
*¾ cup (3 oz/90 g) freshly grated Parmesan cheese*
*¼ cup (1 oz/30 g) pine nuts*
*7 Tbs cold-pressed olive oil*
*4 red onions*
*10 oz (300 g) mozzarella cheese*

*Preparation time: about 50 minutes*

# Eggplant-Amaranth Casserole

**Easy to make • Pictured**

• Peel and chop the onion. Cook the amaranth in broth with salt and onion over low heat 20–30 minutes.

• Meanwhile, bring 1 quart (1 liter) water to boil. Husk the corn. Trim the eggplant and wash. Cut off the corn kernels and blanch in boiling water 2 minutes. Cut the eggplant in lengthwise slices. Brush with oil.

• Preheat the oven to 350°F (170°C). In a large, heavy frying pan heat the remaining oil over medium heat. Brown the eggplant in it, 2–3 minutes per side. Wash the leeks and tomatoes, trim the leeks, and slice them all. Crumble the cheese.

• Line a baking dish with eggplant. Seasoning as you go with salt and pepper, make alternating layers of amaranth, leek, tomato, eggplant, and cheese. Bake until cheese is melted, about 25 minutes.

| PER SERVING: | 465 CALORIES | |
|---|---|---|
| NUTRITIONAL INFORMATION | | |
| Fat (30% calories from fat) | 17 | g |
| Protein | 17 | g |
| Carbohydrates | 69 | g |
| Cholesterol | 23 | mg |
| Sodium | 841 | mg |

# Polenta Gratinée

**Economical • For company**

• Bring 1 quart (1 liter) broth to boil and cook the polenta with the lemon peel and nutmeg, stirring, for about 5 minutes over moderate heat. Add salt and pepper. Spread in a greased rectangular mold and let cool.

• For the pesto, wash the basil and pull the leaves apart. Peel the garlic and chop coarsely. Puree both in food processor with Parmesan, pine nuts, lemon juice, and 6 tablespoons oil.

• Preheat oven to 400°F (200°C). Grease a baking sheet. Peel onions and dice. Heat remaining oil in a frying pan and fry onions in it over moderate heat for about 3 minutes. Season with salt and pepper. Cut mozzarella and polenta into 12 slices each. Lay 3 slices of polenta next to each other on the sheet in a fan shape, paint with pesto, and cover with mozzarella. Repeat with remaining polenta. Bake 15–20 minutes until cheese is melted and crusty.

| PER SERVING: | 941 CALORIES | |
|---|---|---|
| NUTRITIONAL INFORMATION | | |
| Fat (44% calories from fat) | 47 | g |
| Protein | 40 | g |
| Carbohydrates | 94 | g |
| Cholesterol | 86 | mg |
| Sodium | 2789 | mg |

*½ cup (2 oz/60 g) cashews*
*2 cups (16 oz/500 ml) vegetable broth*
*¼ cup (1 oz/50 g) polenta*
*freshly grated nutmeg*
*1 tsp chopped fresh mint*
*¼ tsp Asian sesame oil*
*⅔ cup (2¾ oz/80 g) freshly grated Parmesan cheese*
*salt and pepper*
*4 small zucchini*
*2 meaty tomatoes*
*3 shallots*
*5 oz (150 g) fresh spinach*
*1 Tbs cold-pressed olive oil*
*4 oz (120 g) red lentils*
*1 tsp fresh thyme or lemon thyme*
*5 Tbs cream*
*12 nasturtium flowers for garnish*

*Preparation time: about 1 hour*

# Zucchini with Polenta-Nut Filling Over Lentils

**Flavorful • For company**

• Heat a frying pan over moderate heat until hot and toast the nuts in it for about 1 minute, or until golden brown. Chop coarsely.

• Bring 1¼ cups (10 oz/300 ml) broth to boil in a saucepan. Stir in the polenta, nutmeg, mint, cashews, and sesame oil and cook for about 5 minutes, covered, over low heat. Remove from heat. Stir in part of the cheese and season to taste with salt and pepper. Let the polenta stand, covered, about 20 minutes.

• Wash the zucchini and tomatoes. Trim the zucchini, halve lengthwise, scoop out the insides with a spoon and dice the removed flesh very fine. Season with salt and pepper. Slice the tomatoes after removing the stem bases. Salt and pepper the halved zucchini and the tomatoes.

• Preheat the oven to 400°F (200°C). Grease a baking dish. Fill the zucchini with the scooped-out flesh, cover with tomatoes, and spread polenta over each. Sprinkle with the remaining cheese and arrange in the baking dish. Bake until golden, about 20 minutes.

• Peel the shallots and chop. Pick over the spinach, wash, chop coarsely, and drain. Heat the olive oil in a saucepan and briefly fry the shallots and lentils in it over medium heat. Add the remaining broth, bring to boil, and cook about 4 minutes, covered, over low heat. Stir in the spinach, thyme, and cream. Cook the lentil mixture 3 minutes longer and season with salt and pepper.

• Wash and dry the nasturtium blossoms. Distribute zucchini on plates and serve with lentils. Garnish with the flowers.

Makes 4 servings.

| PER SERVING: | 567 CALORIES | |
|---|---|---|
| NUTRITIONAL INFORMATION | | |
| Fat (36% calories from fat) | 23 | g |
| Protein | 29 | g |
| Carbohydrates | 66 | g |
| Cholesterol | 34 | mg |
| Sodium | 1814 | mg |

# Kohlrabi with Rice Filling

**Inexpensive • Pictured**

• Bring rice to boil with 2 cups (16 oz/ 500 ml) broth, add salt, and cook 45 minutes, covered, over low heat.

• Meanwhile, bring 1 quart (1 liter) salted water to boil. Wash the kohlrabi and peel it. Cut off the tops and set aside. Hollow out the kohlrabi and blanch for 10 minutes.

• Preheat the oven to 325°F (160°C). Wash and trim the vegetables and peel the onions. Dice all the vegetables, onions, and kohlrabi trimmings. Drain the rice and mix with vegetables, currants, pine nuts, cheese, salt, and pepper. Fill the kohlrabi with the mixture and replace the tops. Arrange in a baking dish and pour in ½ cup (4 oz/ 125 ml) water. Bake about 20 minutes.

• Peel the shallots and chop fine. Peel the potato and grate. Cook both in ¾ cup (6 oz/200 ml) broth over moderate heat for about 10 minutes. Stir in crème fraîche and puree until smooth. Season to taste with lime juice, salt, and pepper. Serve the sauce with the kohlrabi.

| PER SERVING: | 315 CALORIES |
|---|---|
| NUTRITIONAL INFORMATION | |
| Fat (41% calories from fat) | 14 g |
| Protein | 7 g |
| Carbohydrates | 40 g |
| Cholesterol | 34 mg |
| Sodium | 2398 mg |

# Peppers with Green Spelt Filling

**Piquant • Can be prepared ahead of time**

• Peel the onions and chop. Bring 1¼ cups (10 oz/300 ml) broth to boil. Add the green spelt, onions, nutmeg, paprika, thyme, cheese, and salt, and simmer, stirring, about 5 minutes. Remove from heat and let stand 20 minutes.

• Preheat the oven to 350°F (180°C). Wash the peppers, cut off the tops, and clean out the insides. Sprinkle with salt and pepper and fill with the green spelt mixture. Replace the tops and arrange the peppers in a baking dish. Pour in the remaining broth and bake 30–35 minutes.

• Meanwhile, peel the shallots. Wash the parsley. Chop both fine. Clean the mushrooms and cut into strips. Heat the butter in a frying pan. Braise the mushrooms and shallots in it over moderate heat about 5 minutes. Season with salt and pepper. Stir in parsley and crème fraîche. Serve with the peppers.

| PER SERVING: | 339 CALORIES |
|---|---|
| NUTRITIONAL INFORMATION | |
| Fat (26% calories from fat) | 11 g |
| Protein | 18 g |
| Carbohydrates | 56 g |
| Cholesterol | 19 mg |
| Sodium | 1027 mg |

***Makes 4 servings***

***Kohlrabi with Rice Filling***

*5 Tbs natural red rice*
*2¾ cups (28 oz/700 ml) vegetable broth*
*salt and pepper*
*4 kohlrabi (about 10 oz/300 g)*
*1 each small carrot, green bell pepper, leek*
*1 red onion*
*2 Tbs dried currants*
*2 Tbs pine nuts*
*1 tsp grated Parmesan cheese*
*3 shallots*
*1 small potato*
*½ cup (4 oz/100 g) crème fraîche or sour cream*
*fresh lime juice*

***Peppers with Green Spelt Filling***

*2 red onions*
*2¼ cups (18 oz/550 ml) vegetable broth*
*¾ cup (5 oz/150 g) fine green spelt grits (or groats)*
*freshly grated nutmeg*
*¼ tsp paprika*
*1 tsp fresh thyme*
*1 oz (30 g) Gruyère cheese, grated (¼ cup)*
*salt and pepper*
*4 red bell peppers*
*2 shallots*
*1 bunch Italian parsley*
*10 oz (300 g) oyster mushrooms*
*1 tsp butter*
*1 Tbs crème fraîche or sour cream*

*Preparation time (both recipes): about 1 hour*

# Savoy Cabbage with Wild Rice Stuffing and Thyme Sauce

**Complex • Can be prepared ahead of time**

*3 cups (24 oz/750 ml) vegetable broth*
*1 red onion*
*2 Tbs clarified butter*
*⅓ cup (2 oz/60 g) wild rice*
*⅓ cup (2 oz/60 g) short-grain brown rice*
*salt and pepper*
*1 small head savoy cabbage (about 28 oz/800 g)*
*5 oz (150 g) parsley root*
*2 Tbs pumpkin seeds*
*1 tsp fresh marjoram*
*freshly grated nutmeg*
*1 shallot*
*2 Tbs white wine (optional)*
*7 Tbs cream*
*1 Tbs fresh lemon thyme (or 1 tsp fresh thyme and ¼ tsp grated lemon peel)*
*2 Tbs lemon juice*

*Preparation time: about 1½ hours*

• Heat 1¾ cups (14 oz/400 ml) of broth. Peel the onion and chop fine. Heat 1 tablespoon clarified butter in a saucepan. Fry the onion in it over moderate heat until transparent, then fry the rice with it about 3 minutes. Add the heated broth and bring to boil. Season with salt and cook about 40 minutes, covered, over low heat.

• Meanwhile, remove about 12 leaves of savoy cabbage and cut the rest into fine strips, omitting the stalk. Rinse the cabbage and drain. Scrub the parsley root and cut 3½ ounces (100 g) into small dice. In a saucepan heat 1 tablespoon clarified butter over medium heat. Braise the chopped vegetables in it about 5 minutes. Season with salt and pepper.

• Bring 1 quart (1 liter) water to boil. Blanch the cabbage leaves in it about 2 minutes. Rinse with cold water and let drain. Cut out the stalk.

• If necessary, drain the rice; let cool slightly. Chop the pumpkin seeds and mix with the cabbage strips, diced parsley root, rice, marjoram, salt, pepper, and nutmeg.

• Preheat the oven to 325°F (160°C). Lay one cabbage leaf at a time in a soup plate with the underside up, overlapping the sections where the stalk was cut out. Place a spoonful of filling on the leaf and fold the leaf around it to enclose the filling. Arrange the stuffed cabbage leaves in a greased baking dish, seam side down. Pour in ½ cup (4 oz/125 ml) broth. Bake 10–15 minutes.

• Grate the remaining parsley root; peel and mince the shallots. Combine both in a saucepan with the remaining broth and the wine and bring to simmer; simmer over moderate heat for about 10 minutes. Stir in the cream and cook 3 minutes. Puree until smooth. Season with thyme, lemon juice, salt, and pepper. Serve the sauce with the stuffed cabbage.

Makes 4 servings.

| PER SERVING: | 447 CALORIES | |
|---|---|---|
| NUTRITIONAL INFORMATION | | |
| Fat (34% calories from fat) | 18 | g |
| Protein | 13 | g |
| Carbohydrates | 63 | g |
| Cholesterol | 41 | mg |
| Sodium | 1357 | mg |

# Amaranth Soufflé with Eggplant

**Pictured • For company**

• Grind the amaranth fine. Bring the milk to boil with the saffron. Stir in the amaranth and the whole-wheat meal and cook, covered, over low heat about 15 minutes.

• Preheat oven to 350°F (175°C). Grease the baking cups. Separate eggs. Stir egg yolks into amaranth mixture and let cool about 5 minutes. Beat the egg whites stiff and fold in. Divide among 4 ovenproof coffee cups or ramekins. Bake 25 minutes.

• Meanwhile, peel the onions and garlic and chop. Wash the vegetables. Coarsely chop the tomatoes after removing the stem bases. Heat the oil in a deep frying pan. Fry the onion and garlic until the onion is transparent. Add the tomatoes and thyme and cook, covered, over low heat 10 minutes. Trim and dice the eggplant. Add to the frying pan and cook 10 minutes, uncovered. Season with salt, pepper, and vinegar. Dice the mozzarella and serve with the eggplant mixture and the soufflés.

| PER SERVING: | 495 CALORIES | |
|---|---|---|
| NUTRITIONAL INFORMATION | | |
| Fat (39% calories from fat) | 22 | g |
| Protein | 23 | g |
| Carbohydrates | 55 | g |
| Cholesterol | 184 | mg |
| Sodium | 272 | mg |

# Spelt-Ricotta Soufflé

**Mediterranean • Easy to make**

• In a frying pan, toast the almonds over medium heat until golden brown. Chop the tomatoes into small pieces. Stem the basil and arugula, wash, and chop fine. Wash the spelt sprouts thoroughly and drain. Peel the garlic and mince.

• Preheat the oven to 350°F (175°C). Grease a soufflé dish and sprinkle with crumbs. Separate the eggs. Beat the whites stiff with a pinch of salt and refrigerate. Stir the ricotta and cream together. Mix in the whole-wheat meal, yolks, spelt sprouts, basil, arugula, tomatoes, almonds, garlic, salt, and pepper. Fold in the egg whites. Transfer the soufflé mixture to the baking dish and bake 1 hour. Serve immediately.

### Menu

For a first course serve a plate of raw vegetables with dip. Accompany the soufflé with an eggplant compote, such as the one on this page.

| PER SERVING: | 434 CALORIES | |
|---|---|---|
| NUTRITIONAL INFORMATION | | |
| Fat (54% calories from fat) | 27 | g |
| Protein | 24 | g |
| Carbohydrates | 28 | g |
| Cholesterol | 256 | mg |
| Sodium | 734 | mg |

***Makes 4 servings***

***Amaranth Soufflé***

*generous ½ cup (3½ oz/100 g) amaranth*
*1¼ cups (10 oz/300 ml) milk*
*2 pinches saffron*
*⅓ cup (1¾ oz/50 g) whole-wheat meal*
*3 eggs*
*2 red onions*
*2 cloves garlic*
*2 lb (1 kg) tomatoes*
*7 oz (200 g) eggplant*
*2 Tbs olive oil*
*1 sprig thyme*
*salt and pepper*
*2 Tbs balsamic vinegar*
*5 oz (150 g) mozzarella cheese*

*Preparation time: about 1 hour*

***Spelt-Ricotta Soufflé***

*2 Tbs slivered almonds*
*2 dried tomatoes*
*1½ bunches basil*
*3½ oz (100 g) arugula*
*3½ oz (100 g) spelt sprouts*
*1 clove garlic*
*fine whole-wheat bread crumbs*
*4 eggs*
*salt and pepper*
*14 oz (400 g) ricotta*
*7 Tbs cream*
*3 Tbs whole-wheat meal*

*Preparation time: about 1½ hours, of which 1 hour is baking time*

# Rutabaga-Green Spelt Casserole with Peppers

**Hearty • Can be prepared ahead of time**

*For the casserole:*
*1 generous cup (7 oz/200 g) green spelt*
*salt*
*2 small rutabagas (about 10 oz/300 g each)*
*1 medium carrot*
*1 medium leek*
*1¼ cups (10 oz/300 ml) vegetable broth*
*1 Tbs chopped Italian parsley*
*1 pinch freshly grated nutmeg*
*pepper*
*2 eggs*
*4 oz (125 g) Emmentaler cheese, grated (1 cup)*

*For the sauce:*
*2 scallions*
*7 Tbs vegetable broth*
*1 Tbs crème fraîche or sour cream*
*Scant ½ tsp carob powder*

*For the vegetables:*
*salt*
*1 small red bell pepper*
*1 medium parsnip (or carrots)*
*3½ oz (100 g) snow peas*
*2 shallots*
*1 Tbs olive oil*
*pepper*

*Preparation time: about 1¼ hours*

• For the casserole, bring half the green spelt to boil in ¾ cup (6 oz/200 ml) water and cook, covered, over low heat about 40 minutes. Drain. Coarsely grind the remaining green spelt.

• Bring 1 quart (1 liter) salted water to boil. Peel the rutabagas and cut into slices about ⅛ inch (5 mm) thick. Blanch 2 minutes. Rinse with cold water and drain. Peel and grate the carrot. Clean the leek and cut into strips.

• Preheat the oven to 350°F (180°C) Grease baking dish. Bring the broth to boil over moderate heat. Add the ground green spelt and bring just to boil, stirring constantly. Stir in the carrot, leek, parsley, and nutmeg. Remove from heat and add salt and pepper. Blend in the cooked whole green spelt with the eggs and half the cheese.

• Cover the bottom of the baking dish with rutabaga slices; top with some of the green spelt-vegetable mixture. Continue layering rutabaga and filling, ending with rutabaga. Sprinkle with the remaining cheese and bake 25 minutes.

• Meanwhile, for the sauce, wash the scallions, trim, and chop. Bring broth to boil in a saucepan. Stir in the crème fraîche and let scallions simmer about 5 minutes, then puree. Mix the carob powder with 3 tablespoons water and stir in. Remove from heat.

• Wash and trim the vegetables. Bring 1 quart (1 liter) salted water to boil. Cut the pepper into small diamonds, the parsnip into sticks. Cut the peas in thirds. Blanch them all for about 2 minutes. Peel the shallots and dice. Heat oil in a frying pan and briefly fry the shallots. Swish the vegetables around in the flavored oil and add salt and pepper. Serve the vegetables and sauce with the casserole.

Makes 4 servings.

| PER SERVING: | 540 CALORIES |
|---|---|
| NUTRITIONAL INFORMATION | |
| Fat (34% calories from fat) | 21 g |
| Protein | 28 g |
| Carbohydrates | 61 g |
| Cholesterol | 326 mg |
| Sodium | 759 mg |

# Spelt-Amaranth Bread

**Substantial • Pictured at left**

• Bring ⅔ cup (5 oz/150 m) salted water to boil. Cook ¼ cup (1¾ oz/50 g) amaranth in it, covered, over low heat 30 minutes. Set aside.

• Meanwhile, grind the spelt and the remaining amaranth to a fine flour. Dissolve the yeast in 2 tablespoons lukewarm water. Combine the yeast mixture, about 1¼ cups (10 oz/300 ml) water, 2 teaspoons salt, the flour, and the oil and knead to form an elastic dough. Let rise, covered, at room temperature 1 hour.

• Grease a baking sheet. Chop the olives. Knead the olives and cooked amaranth into the dough. Form the dough into six balls and roll out on a floured surface into flat cakes about ⅛ inch (5 mm) thick. Place on the baking sheet and cover with a moist cloth. Let rise 30 minutes. Preheat the oven to 425°F (220°C). Place a small pan of water in the oven. Spray the loaves with water and bake 20–25 minutes.

| PER SERVING: | 352 CALORIES | |
|---|---|---|
| NUTRITIONAL INFORMATION | | |
| Fat (19% calories from fat) | 7 | g |
| Protein | 13 | g |
| Carbohydrates | 58 | g |
| Cholesterol | 1 | mg |
| Sodium | 73 | mg |

# Millet Bread

**Easy to make • Pictured at right**

• Bring 1¼ cups (10 oz/300 ml) salted water to boil. Add half the millet and cook, covered, over low heat 10 minutes. Set aside.

• Grind the remaining millet, spelt, and wheat to fine flour. Dissolve the yeast in 2 tablespoons lukewarm water. Combine 1¼ cups (10 oz/300 ml) water, flour, yeast mixture, caraway, coriander, and fennel and knead to form an elastic dough. Cover and let rise at room temperature 30 minutes.

• Grease a loaf pan. Add 2 teaspoons salt and the cooked millet to the dough and knead to blend well. Place in the pan and let rise, covered, 30 minutes. Meanwhile, preheat the oven to 450°F (230°C). Place a pan of water in the oven. Prick the dough several times with a fork, brush with water, and bake 20 minutes. Reduce the heat to 375°F (190°C) and finish baking about 40 minutes, or until the loaf sounds hollow when tapped.

Makes 28 slices, about 70 calories per slice

| PER SERVING: | 72 CALORIES | |
|---|---|---|
| NUTRITIONAL INFORMATION | | |
| Fat (8% calories from fat) | 1 | g |
| Protein | 3 | g |
| Carbohydrates | 14 | g |
| Cholesterol | 0 | mg |
| Sodium | 0 | mg |

***Spelt-Amaranth Bread***
***(Makes six flat loaves)***

*salt*
*1 scant cup (5¼ oz/150 g) amaranth*
*2¾ cups (14 oz/400 g) spelt*
*3¼ tsp active dry yeast*
*1½ Tbs sunflower or other light vegetable oil*
*½ cup (2 oz/50 g) pitted black olives*

*Preparation time:*
*about 50–60 minutes*
*(+50 minutes–1½ hours rising time)*

***Millet Bread***
***(Makes 10-inch [25 cm] loaf)***

*salt*
*1 cup (7 oz/200 g) millet*
*1⅔ cups (10 oz/300 g) spelt*
*½ cup (3½ oz/100 g) wheat berries*
*3¼ tsp active dry yeast*
*2 tsp caraway seeds*
*1 tsp coriander seeds*
*½ tsp fennel seeds*

*Preparation time:*
*about 1 hour and 20 minutes*
*(of which 1 hour is baking time)*
*+40–60 minutes rising time*

So sweet...

# Sweets with Grains

Sweet polenta, muesli parfait, millet soufflé—there are more delicious desserts to be made with grains than you might think. Warm grain-based sweets are also great for breakfast or for a light, nourishing but self-indulgent supper.

### Wheat and the Like

If you consider the history of wheat in cooking, it is striking that traditionally the grain has only been used for baking. Wheat and spelt deserve to be put to more versatile uses: as breakfast cereal, as sprouts for salads, as ingredients for marvelous main courses.

**Wheat:** This king of grains contains the gluten that gives bread and other baked goods their structure. It is rich in vitamins and minerals: 2 ounces (60 g) of wheat provides 21% of the recommended daily requirement of vitamin $B_1$, 31% of phosphorus, 25% of magnesium, and 58% of manganese. In addition to the unprocessed wheat grains, there are other products made from wheat, such as bulgur and couscous (both on page 6).

**Spelt:** The original form of wheat. Its fine aroma, good baking qualities, and light-colored flour are earning it growing numbers of fans. Green spelt (page 6) is produced from spelt.

**Durum wheat:** Homemade noodles of whole durum flour are a delicacy. Durum wheat is often available in natural food stores, sometimes by special order. Try our noodle recipe (page 20) without egg, but with 1 scant cup (3½ oz/100 g) buckwheat flour, 1½ cups (8¾ oz/250 g) whole durum flour, 7 tablespoons water, and 2 tablespoons oil.

**Kamut:** A novelty in the market. This rediscovered ancient grain has outstanding baking qualities. Wheat and spelt recipes also work extremely well with kamut. If your natural foods dealer does not have kamut in stock, he can order it for you.

### Muesli Snacks with a Flip of the Wrist

Muesli, granola, and muesli bars make a quick snack for breakfast or between meals. Accompanied by milk or yogurt, they provide a balanced light meal.

**Muesli**

For a week's batch, mix and store in a tightly closed container:
½ cup (2 oz/60 g) each rolled oats and wheat flakes, 3 tablespoons (1½ oz/40 g) each soft dried apricots and dates, diced to raisin size, 3 tablespoons (¾ oz/20 g) raisins, 1½ tablespoons (¾ oz/20 g) sesame seeds, ¼ cup (1¾ oz/50 g) coarsely chopped walnuts, 2 tablespoons (1 oz/30 g) sunflower seeds. Use 4 tablespoons per serving with milk or yogurt.

**Granola**

Preheat the oven to 350°F (180°C). In a bowl mix 1 cup (3½ oz/100 g) rolled oats, ½ cup (1¾ oz/50 g) wheat flakes, 1½ tablespoons (¾ oz/20 g) sunflower seeds, ¼ cup (1¾ oz/50g) shelled almonds, 2 teaspoons sesame seeds, 1 tablespoon light vegetable oil, and a pinch of salt. Spread out on a baking sheet and roast for about 20 minutes, turning occasionally. Transfer to a bowl and mix in 6 tablespoons raisins, 3 tablespoons (1½ oz/40 g) chopped soft dried apricots, a pinch of cinnamon, and 1½ tablespoons honey. After cooling, store in tightly covered jars.

**Fresh Grain Muesli**

(1 portion)

Grind 2–3 tablespoons oats fine or crush to flakes and mix with ½ cup (4 oz/100 g) yogurt, ½ grated apple, ½ mashed banana, 1 tablespoon chopped nuts, and a dash of vanilla. Garnish with 2 tablespoons of fruit or berries.

All other grains must be softened in cold water or yogurt in the refrigerator, fine-ground ones for about 30 minutes and coarse-ground ones for 10 hours. Best suited are the soft grains wheat and spelt; do not use barley or rye. Wash buckwheat in hot water before softening.

• Tips

Soften dried fruit separately from the grains. Do not use milk or milk products for softening; always add it directly to the muesli when serving.

***Muesli Bars***

*(Makes 25)*

*In a food processor, puree ½ cup (4½ oz/125 g) chopped soft dried apricots; add, pureeing after each addition, 7 tablespoons raisins, ½ cup (3½ oz/100 g) chopped hazelnuts, 7 tablespoons acacia honey, and 7 tablespoons melted butter. Work in 7 tablespoons mineral water, 3½ tablespoons apple juice, 1¾–2½ cups (7–10½ oz/200–300 g) spelt flour, ¼ tsp each ground cloves and cinnamon, and ½ teaspoon vanilla. Let the mixture rest 6 hours. Mix in 1 cup (3½ oz/100 g) rolled oats and 2 tablespoons (1 oz/30 g) sunflower seeds. Let stand 30 minutes. Preheat the oven to 400°F (200°C). Mix 1½ teaspoons grated lemon peel into the dough. Form into a roll, slice, and shape into 2¾ × 1½ in (7 × 4 cm) bars. Decorate with dried currants and slivered almonds. Bake 20–30 minutes.*

***Sweet Polenta***

*2 lemons*
*⅔ cup (5 oz/150 ml) whole milk*
*¼ tsp vanilla*
*3 Tbs polenta*
*2 Tbs honey*
*2 egg yolks*
*1½ cups (6 oz/180 g) mixed dried fruit*
*½ tsp cinnamon*
*½ tsp ground ginger*
*pinch of powdered anise*
*2 pinches cardamom*
*2 Tbs butter*
*4 sprigs lemon balm (optional)*

*Preparation time:*
*about 35 minutes*
*(+30 minutes cooling time)*

***Sweet Risotto***

*½ cup (4 oz/125 ml) apple juice*
*¼ tsp vanilla*
*2 star anise*
*2 Tbs honey*
*salt*
*⅔ cup (4½ oz/125 g) short-grain brown rice*
*⅔ cups (13½ oz/400 ml) whole milk*
*4 Tbs raisins*
*1 lemon*
*3 Tbs pine nuts*
*5 oz (150 g) red currants*
*2 nectarines*
*1 apple*
*3½ oz (100 g) blackberries*
*3 mint leaves*

*Preparation time:*
*about 45 minutes*
*(+30 minutes soaking time)*

# Sweet Polenta with Compote

**Pictured • Economical**

• Wash the lemon in hot water and dry it. Using a zester, cut off strips of lemon peel. Bring the milk to boil with the vanilla. Stir in the polenta, honey, and lemon peel and cook over low heat, stirring until thickened, about 10 minutes.

• Let cool to lukewarm, then stir in the egg yolks. Grease a small baking dish. Pour in the polenta and smooth the top. Cover with plastic wrap and chill.

• Place dried fruit in a bowl and barely cover with boiling water. Stir in cinnamon, ginger, anise, and cardamom.

• Cut the polenta into squares. Heat the butter in a frying pan over moderate heat—don't let it smoke. Brown the polenta slices about 3 minutes per side. Serve with the compote and garnish with lemon balm.

Makes 4 servings.

| PER SERVING: | 285 CALORIES | |
|---|---|---|
| NUTRITIONAL INFORMATION | | |
| Fat (29% calories from fat) | 10 | g |
| Protein | 5 | g |
| Carbohydrates | 50 | g |
| Cholesterol | 127 | mg |
| Sodium | 90 | mg |

# Sweet Risotto with Fruits

**Exclusive • For company**

• Bring the apple juice to boil with the vanilla, star anise, honey, and salt. Sprinkle in the rice and gradually stir in the milk. Simmer over medium heat 10 minutes, stirring constantly.

• Meanwhile, soak the raisins in warm water. Wash the lemon in hot water and remove the zest with a zester. Squeeze the lemon. Heat a dry frying pan and roast the pine nuts in it over medium heat. Add the pine nuts, zest, and raisins to the rice and remove from heat. Let stand about 30 minutes.

• Wash the fruit. Stem the currants. Pit the nectarines and core the apple; slice both. Cut the mint into strips. Mix the fruits with lemon juice and mint. Serve with the lukewarm risotto.

Makes 4 servings.

| PER SERVING: | 351 CALORIES | |
|---|---|---|
| NUTRITIONAL INFORMATION | | |
| Fat (15% calories from fat) | 6 | g |
| Protein | 8 | g |
| Carbohydrates | 71 | g |
| Cholesterol | 14 | mg |
| Sodium | 62 | mg |

# Muesli Parfait with Papaya

**Subtle • Pictured**

- In a heated frying pan toast first the rolled oats, then the nuts. Rub the skins off the nuts and chop the nuts. Finely dice the dried fruits. Wash the orange in hot water and dry it. Remove the peel of half the orange in strips and mince them. Squeeze the orange juice. Beat the cream stiff and chill it.
- In a bowl beat the egg yolks, 3 tablespoons of honey, vanilla, and 2 tablespoons lukewarm water until creamy. Mix in the cream, dried fruit, oats, hazelnuts, and orange zest. Mix in half the juice, reserving the remainder. Divide the mixture among 4 1-cup molds and freeze 2–3 hours.
- Peel the papayas, halve them, and remove the pits. Cut one half into 16 thin slices; coarsely chop the remaining papaya and puree with the remaining orange juice and honey. Serve the parfaits with papaya and sauce.

| PER SERVING: | 499 CALORIES | |
|---|---|---|
| NUTRITIONAL INFORMATION | | |
| Fat (40% calories from fat) | 24 | g |
| Protein | 7 | g |
| Carbohydrates | 73 | g |
| Cholesterol | 214 | mg |
| Sodium | 69 | mg |

# Buckwheat Mini-Loaves

**Unusual • Easy to make**

- Grind the wheat berries to flour. Coarsely grind the poppyseeds. Mix both with the kasha, cream, milk, sugar, and salt and let the dough stand about 30 minutes.
- Meanwhile, wash the cranberries and drain. Heat 1 tablespoon butter and the honey in a frying pan over medium heat until browned and caramelized, about 3 minutes. Stir in the cranberries and orange juice and cook 2 minutes. Let the sauce cool.
- Form the buckwheat dough into small loaves. Heat 1 tablespoon butter in a frying pan over moderate heat. Cook half the buckwheat loaves until golden on both sides, about 4 minutes per side. Repeat with the remaining butter and loaves.
- Spread the sauce on dessert plates. Arrange the buckwheat loaves in it. Garnish with pistachios.

| PER SERVING: | 133 CALORIES | |
|---|---|---|
| NUTRITIONAL INFORMATION | | |
| Fat (28% calories from fat) | 4 | g |
| Protein | 3 | g |
| Carbohydrates | 22 | g |
| Cholesterol | 6 | mg |
| Sodium | 6 | mg |

***Muesli Parfait***
***Makes 4 servings***

*4 Tbs rolled oats*
*1/4 cup (1 3/4 oz/50 g) hazelnuts*
*1 3/4 cups (7 oz/200 g) dried fruit (apricots, pears, apple, figs)*
*2 oranges*
*1 cup (8 oz/250 g) whipping cream*
*3 egg yolks*
*4 Tbs honey*
*1 tsp vanilla*
*2 papayas*

*Preparation time: about 45 minutes (+2–3 hours freezing time)*

***Buckwheat Mini-Loaves***
***(Makes 20)***

*1/2 cup (3 1/2 oz/100 g) wheat berries*
*1/2 cup (3 1/2 oz/100 g) poppyseeds*
*1 scant cup (5 oz/150 g) kasha*
*5 Tbs cream*
*7 Tbs milk*
*2/3 cup (5 1/4 oz/150 g) sugar*
*pinch of salt*
*7 oz (200 g) cranberries*
*3 Tbs butter*
*5 Tbs honey*
*5 Tbs orange juice*
*1 Tbs chopped pistachios*

*Preparation time: about 45 minutes (+30 minutes soaking time)*

# Green Spelt Pudding with Almonds and Elderberries

**Can be prepared ahead of time • For company**

*1 quart (1 liter) whole milk*
*½ tsp vanilla*
*salt*
*1 cup (7 oz/200 g) green spelt grits or groats*
*½ cup (2¾ oz/80 g) slivered almonds*
*¼ cup (1 oz/30 g) sliced almonds*
*2 lemons*
*4 eggs*
*¾ cup (8½ oz/250 g) honey*
*7 oz (200 g) elderberries or blackberries*
*¾ cup (6 oz/200 ml) blackberry liqueur or juice*
*½ teaspoon cinnamon*
*¾ tsp carob powder*
*8 mint leaves*

*Preparation time: about 45 minutes (+1 hour baking time)*

• Bring the milk to boil with the vanilla and salt. Sprinkle in the green spelt and cook over low heat, covered, 10 minutes. Remove from heat and let stand about 15 minutes.

• Heat a frying pan and separately toast the almond slivers and slices about 1 minute each until golden yellow. Wash the lemons in hot water and dry. Grate the peel. Squeeze one of the lemons. Separate the eggs.

• Preheat the oven to 350°F (180°C). Beat the egg yolks and 7 tablespoons honey with an electric mixer until creamy. Stir in the lemon zest. Using clean beaters, beat the whites until stiff. Fold the egg whites, the green spelt mixture, and the slivered almonds into the yolks. Place the pudding mixture in a soufflé dish and bake 1 hour.

• Pick over and wash the berries. Place in a saucepan with the liqueur, the remaining honey, and the cinnamon and bring to boil. Simmer over low heat about 5 minutes. Stir in the lemon juice and mix in the carob powder to thicken. Cook about 2 minutes, stirring constantly.

• Serve the pudding with the sauce and sliced almonds. Garnish with mint.

**Variation:**

**Kamut Pudding with Blueberries**

Instead of green spelt, grind ¾ cup (5½ oz/150 g) kamut and stir into the cold milk along with ⅓ cup (1½ oz/40 g) whole-wheat meal, salt, and vanilla. Bring to boil over low heat, stirring constantly, then remove from heat and let cool. Before folding in the beaten egg whites, stir in ½ teaspoon of baking powder.

Makes 4 servings.

| PER SERVING: | 764 CALORIES |
|---|---|
| NUTRITIONAL INFORMATION | |
| Fat (31% calories from fat) | 30 g |
| Protein | 28 g |
| Carbohydrates | 122 g |
| Cholesterol | 220 mg |
| Sodium | 199 mg |

**Quinoa Soufflé**
*1 scant cup (5 oz/150 g) quinoa*
*1¼ cups (10 oz/300 ml) milk*
*4 eggs*
*3½ oz (100 g) black currants*
*4 fresh figs*
*¼ cup (2 oz/60 g) sugar*
*7 Tbs (100 ml) black currant juice*
*⅔ cup (5 oz/150 g) cottage cheese*
*5 Tbs (100 g) honey*

*Preparation time: about 1 hour*

**Couscous Savarin**
*¾ cup (6 oz/200 ml) orange juice*
*2 Tbs honey*
*pinch of saffron*
*½ tsp cinnamon*
*½ cup (3½ oz/100 g) medium-fine couscous*
*2 Tbs dried currants*
*¼ cup (1 oz/30 g) slivered almonds*
*1 orange*
*¼ cup (1 oz/30 g) pistachios*
*1 Tbs chopped fresh mint*
*1 grapefruit*
*1 kiwi*
*2 bananas*
*1 pomegranate*
*10 dates*
*2 Tbs maple syrup*

*Preparation time: about 45 minutes*

# Quinoa Soufflé with Figs

**Refined • For company**

• Grind the quinoa. Bring the milk to boil in a saucepan and stir in the quinoa. Simmer over low heat, stirring, about 10 minutes. Remove from heat and let cool.

• Meanwhile, separate the eggs. Pick over and wash the currants. Peel the figs and cut into sixths.

• Stir the egg yolks into the quinoa mixture one at a time. Preheat the oven to 400°F (200°C). Butter baking dish and sprinkle with sugar.

• Bring the juice, berries, and sugar to boil in a saucepan and simmer about 5 minutes. Puree coarsely. Add the figs and let cool.

• Stir the cottage cheese and honey into the quinoa mixture. Beat the egg whites until stiff and fold in. Place the mixture in the prepared baking dish and bake 25 minutes. Serve the soufflé immediately with the sauce.

Makes 4 servings.

| PER SERVING: | 664 CALORIES |
|---|---|
| NUTRITIONAL INFORMATION | |
| Fat (24% calories from fat) | 16 g |
| Protein | 25 g |
| Carbohydrates | 87 g |
| Cholesterol | 610 mg |
| Sodium | 2 mg |

# Couscous Savarin with Fruit

**Can be prepared ahead of time • Pictured**

• Bring the orange juice, honey, saffron, and cinnamon to boil. Pour over the couscous and currants and let stand, covered, about 10 minutes.

• Heat a frying pan and briefly toast the slivered almonds in it. Wash the orange in hot water and grate the peel. Mix into the couscous with the pistachios and mint. Grease 4 small savarin molds and divide the couscous mixture among them.

• Peel the orange and grapefruit, removing white pith. Halve crosswise and cut into sections, omitting the membranes. Peel the kiwi and quarter it lengthwise. Peel the bananas. Slice both fruits. Quarter the pomegranate and remove the seeds. Pit the dates and cut into sixths. Mix all with the maple syrup.

• Unmold the savarins onto plates and garnish with the fruit.

Makes 4 servings.

| PER SERVING: | 660 CALORIES |
|---|---|
| NUTRITIONAL INFORMATION | |
| Fat (9% calories from fat) | 7 g |
| Protein | 11 g |
| Carbohydrates | 146 g |
| Cholesterol | 0 mg |
| Sodium | 49 mg |

*1 cup (8 oz/250 ml) milk*
*salt*
*½ tsp vanilla*
*7 Tbs sugar*
*1 scant cup (5¼ oz/150 g) whole-grain semolina*
*1 Tbs butter*
*2 eggs*
*1 lemon*
*7 Tbs mango juice or nectar*
*1 tsp chopped fresh rosemary*
*1 Tbs honey*
*14 oz (400 g) small yellow plums*
*7 oz (200 g) apricots*
*2 Tbs slivered almonds*

*Preparation time: about 35 minutes*

# Whole-Grain Semolina Dumplings with Plums

**Easy to make • Inexpensive**

• In a saucepan bring milk, a pinch of salt, vanilla, and sugar to boil. Sprinkle in the semolina and stir over low heat about 1 minute until the mixture forms a firm mass. Remove from heat and let the mixture cool about 5 minutes. Mix in the butter and the eggs, one at a time. Let stand, covered, about 10 minutes.

• Meanwhile, wash the lemon in hot water and dry it. Grate the peel. Squeeze the juice. Mix the mango juice, lemon juice, lemon zest, rosemary, and honey in a bowl. Wash and pit the plums and apricots. Halve the plums and slice the apricots. Mix the fruits with the mango juice mixture and let marinate.

• Bring 1½ quarts (1.5 liters) salted water to boil. Also have a small pot of hot water ready. Using two teaspoons, make about 20 little dumplings of the semolina mixture and drop them into the boiling water. To keep the semolina mixture from sticking, keep dipping the spoons into the hot water. Poach the dumplings about 10 minutes.

• Heat a dry frying pan over medium heat and toast the slivered almonds until golden.

• Divide the fruits among 4 plates and add the dumplings. Pour marinade over them and sprinkle with the slivered almonds.

**Variation:**

**Kamut Dumplings**

Grind ⅓ cup (3 oz/80 g) kamut and mix with ½ cup (4 oz/125 ml) milk. Bring the remaining milk to boil with the flavorings as described in the recipe, then stir in ⅓ cup (1¾ oz/50 g) whole-grain semolina and the mixed kamut. Proceed with the recipe.

Makes 4 servings.

| PER SERVING: | 469 CALORIES |
|---|---|
| NUTRITIONAL INFORMATION | |
| Fat (20% calories from fat) | 11 g |
| Protein | 11 g |
| Carbohydrates | 86 g |
| Cholesterol | 108 mg |
| Sodium | 92 mg |

# Millet Pudding with Yogurt Sauce

**Can be prepared ahead of time • Pictured**

• Finely grind the millet and wheat. Mince the dried fruit. Coarsely chop the raisins. Wash the apple and grate coarsely. Coarsely chop the walnuts. Wash the lemon in hot water, dry, and grate the peel.

• Preheat the oven to 350°F (180°C). Grease baking dish. Separate the eggs. Beat the yolks with 3 tablespoons honey until creamy. Mix in the millet, wheat, cottage cheese, dried fruit, raisins, apple, walnuts, lemon zest, and cinnamon.

• Beat the egg whites stiff and fold into the dough. Place the mixture in the baking dish and bake 1 hour.

• Meanwhile, squeeze 1 tablespoon lemon juice. Whip the cream stiff and mix with the yogurt, remaining honey, lemon juice, and lemon balm. Serve the pudding on plates with the yogurt-lemon sauce.

Makes 4 servings.

| PER SERVING: | 886 CALORIES | |
|---|---|---|
| NUTRITIONAL INFORMATION | | |
| Fat (27% calories from fat) | 21 | g |
| Protein | 22 | g |
| Carbohydrates | 107 | g |
| Cholesterol | 215 | mg |
| Sodium | 121 | mg |

**Millet Pudding**

*¾ cup (5¼ oz/150 g) millet*
*⅓ cup (2¾ oz/80 g) wheat berries*
*1 cup (5 oz/150 g) mixed dried fruit*
*4 Tbs raisins*
*1 apple*
*¾ cup (3 oz/90 g) walnuts*
*1 lemon*
*4 eggs*
*5 Tbs honey*
*½ cup (4 oz/120 g) cottage cheese*
*1 tsp cinnamon*
*½ cup (4 oz/125 g) whipping cream*
*1 cup (8 oz/250 g) yogurt*
*1 tsp chopped fesh lemon balm*

*Preparation time: about 30 minutes (+1 hour baking time)*

# Amaranth Cake with Apricots

**Rich • Easy to make**

• Grind the amaranth and wheat to fine flour. Cut the apricots into raisin-sized pieces. Soak the raisins in the cognac and 2 tablespoons of water. Separate the eggs. Melt the butter.

• Preheat the oven to 350°F (180°C). Grease the springform and dust with flour. Beat the egg whites until stiff with the salt, then beat in 1 tablespoon honey. Chill the meringue. Beat the egg yolks with the remaining honey until creamy. Mix in the amaranth, wheat, baking powder, cinnamon, and cardamom. Stir in the melted butter, apricots, and raisins. Then fold in the meringue. Spread the batter in the springform. Bake 50 minutes.

| PER SERVING: | 701 CALORIES | |
|---|---|---|
| NUTRITIONAL INFORMATION | | |
| Fat (36% calories from fat) | 28 | g |
| Protein | 24 | g |
| Carbohydrates | 88 | g |
| Cholesterol | 787 | mg |
| Sodium | 6 | mg |

**Amaranth Cake**
**(1 10-inch [26 cm] springform)**

*⅔ cup (3½ oz/100 g) amaranth*
*⅓ cup (2¾ oz/80 g) wheat berries*
*1 cup (5 oz/150 g) dried apricots*
*2 Tbs raisins*
*2 Tbs cognac or orange juice*
*5 eggs*
*¼ cup (2 oz/60 g) butter*
*¼ tsp salt*
*7 Tbs honey*
*½ tsp baking powder*
*½ tsp cinnamon*
*pinch of cardamom*

*Preparation time: about 30 minutes (+50 minutes baking time)*

# INDEX

Published originally under the title *Korn & Co.*



German edition by Elisabeth Döpp, Christian Willrich, and Jörn Rebbe

Photography by Heinz-Josef Beckers

English translation by Elizabeth D. Crawford



*All inquires should be addressed to:*
Barron's Educational Series, Inc.
250 Wireless Boulevard
Hauppauge, NY 11788
**http://www.barronseduc.com**

Library of Congress Catalog Card No. 98-51590

International Standard Book No. 0-7641-0930-8

**Library of Congress Cataloging-in-Publication Data**
Döpp, Elisabeth.
[Korn & Co. English]
Grains, etc. / Elisabeth Döpp, Christian Willrich, Jörn Rebbe; photography by Heinz-Josef Beckers; [English translation by Elizabeth D. Crawford].
p. cm.
Includes index.
ISBN 0-7641-0930-8
1. Cookery (Cereals) 2. Grain. I. Willrich, Christian. II. Rebbe, Jörn. III. Title.
TX808.D6713 1999
641.6'31—dc21 98-51590
CIP

Printed in Hong Kong

9 8 7 6 5 4 3 2 1

**Elisabeth Döpp** worked for a long time as an editor for a large publishing house. Since 1985 she has been a cookbook author and a nutrition and cooking instructor.

**Christian Willrich** began working as a chef in premier French restaurants in 1980. Since 1990 he has been active as a cookbook author and culinary consultant.

**Jörn Rebbe** was trained as a cook in a Japanese hotel. As a head chef, he specializes in Japanese and Chinese cooking. He has authored cookbooks since 1995, and in 1997 he completed his training as a dietician.

**Heinz-Josef Beckers** specializes in communications design, food, still-life, and experimental photography. He also does conceptual and graphics work for corporations, publishers, and advertising agencies.

# Grains at a Glance

**Amaranth** (page 62)
These fine seeds are an exotic addition to cakes, soufflés, and vegetable dishes. Amaranth is not a grain but a vegetable from the Andes, whose seeds are exported as grain. The seeds can be ground into flour for bread or used as cereal. They are very rich in vitamins and minerals.

**Bulgur** (page 8)
One of the oldest foodstuffs in the world, bulgur is durum wheat that has been coarsely ground, steamed, and then dried. Bulgur, also called *burghul,* has a tender, chewy texture and is available in coarse, medium, and fine grinds. Good flavor and short cooking time make this Middle Eastern staple a favorite.

**Buckwheat** (page 62)
Buckwheat's distinctive aroma makes everyday dishes into delicacies; Russian blini are famous, as is the galette from Brittany. Buckwheat is not a grain but a plant of the *Polygomum* family (like rhubarb). It is not a product of intensive hybridization but thrives well in poor soils.

**Couscous** (page 8)
In North Africa, couscous, or granular semolina, is steamed over braised dishes and eaten as a side dish. It is wonderfully versatile,

appearing in hearty main dishes and delicate desserts. For example, cooked, it may be served with milk as porridge, with a dressing as a salad, or sweetened and mixed with fruits for dessert.

WINES
CHARDONNAY
4.75
VINTAGES

# A Recipe of Memories

Chef
Joe Brancatella

Photos
Carlos Avalos

Authors
Carmen Amato
Stefano Colacitti

15 years and still Yonge.

Visit the GRAZIE website at: www.GRAZIE.ca

First published in Canada in 2005

ISBN: 0-9739000-0-8



Produced by
Redbean Design Group Ltd.
185 Claireport Cres.
Toronto ON M9W 6P5

Art Director: Stefano Colacitti
Project Manager: Carmen Amato
Photographer: Carlos Avalos
Photographer Assistant: Besar Xhelili
Food Stylist: Joe Brancatella
Editor: Domini Clark

Designed By
Leap Creative Design
Graphic Design: Leonardo Tamburri & Ben Panton
Layout: Luciano Sebastian De Monte

Printed in Canada by Friesens Printing Ltd.

Grazie would like to dedicate this book to our guests who have supported us through our past 15 years.

In Memory of Mohammed "Babuji"
For teaching us that friends are only a memory away.

DEWALT

GRAZIE
RISTORANTE
www.grazie.ca
TORONTO LIFE

# Table of Contents

# Foreword:

It's 9:00pm in the middle of the summer, the Yonge St. festival is in full swing; Saturday night, the patio makes a special guest appearance under the *GRAZIE* sign in front of the restaurant. The atmosphere is electric, as the alcohol stirs the appetites of waiting customers who watch with anticipation, as plates of food make their way around the restaurant at a hectic pace. The music is loud with the guests even louder as the buzz can be felt from the back of the restaurant to the front, where the street festival is turning Toronto into a hub of live activity, if you didn't know any better you would swear you were somewhere on the streets of Italy. There is something special in the air tonight, and whatever it is you just hope that the boys at *GRAZIE* continue to serve it.

Fifteen years after their initial doors opened – three doors south of the current location – and *GRAZIE* still feels as alive and raw as it did when it took the Yonge and Eglington area by surprise. Now, instead of being the new guy on the block having to prove itself to the cynic demanding the highest of standards for an area known for its prestigious restaurants, it has become a measure for quality and consistency amongst restaurant enthusiasts. Though the landscape of the Yonge and Eglinton area has changed since the arrival of *GRAZIE*, some would even say for the better, Joe Brancatella believes that it is the Yonge and Eglinton area that has allowed *GRAZIE* to be so successful for so long. For this he and his partners would like to thank the community and its people for all their support over the years.

Since their humble opening the boys at *GRAZIE* would never have believed that their dream would have turned out this way. Three brothers and some friends coming together almost by happenstance to create one of the most successful restaurants the area has seen in the last 15 years. In the beginning there was no master plan, the only idea running through Joe Brancatella's head and former partner Louie Granicolo was survival. All they were concerned with was, were people going to walk through the front door, and when they did, were they going to be happy with what they found. Now sitting here writing a foreword to a cookbook that has long been in the imagination of Joe, I feel honoured to have been included in the creation of this project.

*GRAZIE*, from the beginning has been more than just a place where you could come to for a plate of food. It has transcended all boundaries of what a restaurant should be and has risen to prominence because of intangibles that simply cannot be replaced by any one formula; timing, chance, luck, whatever it is that people have called it, it would seem that the boys at *GRAZIE* have managed to harness it for their own biding. Though when I think about it, having been a part of the *GRAZIE* family for 15

years myself, and ironically being part of the real family that extends beyond the walls of the restaurant, I can honestly say that there is and was no magic, it was just three brothers, some friends and a lot of hard work and determination.

Never let anybody tell you anything different, the restaurant business is anything but easy and without work, but when it is done right there is a seamlessness to it that looks almost effortless. It's that hard work and dedication to quality and consistency that has had GRAZIE running at such a high level for so many years. But in the end maybe there is one thing underlying everything else that in retrospect may be responsible for the magic everyone speaks about; love! If you truly do not love the restaurant business there is no substitute or formula that will ensure that all the work that needs to be done will ever get done properly. Anyone can paint by numbers, but the great ones will tell you that without love you will never be inspired to do what it takes to see what happens when you paint outside the normal boundaries of your contemporaries.

No one can ever really tell you the amount of work it is going to take to get your dream off the ground; all they can ever tell you is that if you want it, you have to believe in it first and foremost, followed by a lot of work and sacrifice to get it. Considering GRAZIE Ristorante's rise to prominence over the last fifteen years, I think Chef Joe Brancatella and his partners will tell you that they are glad that they made the sacrifices and will never regret the day to day work that was involved in making it grow to the success that GRAZIE has become

To that end I leave you with what we believe to be a collection of memories through recipes that we have all shared in throughout the years. Moments of fun, laughter and sometimes tears. Stories of customers that have come and gone who have continued to define what GRAZIE is and can be. Memories of Staff that have given more than any one establishment can ask of, of its employees. Memories of an extended family that has grown with us; from inspired marriage proposals to pizza landing in the lap of an unsuspecting guest, from the good to the bad we are defined. GRAZIE is not perfect, but it does represent a place that we can all go to and find a sense of home. We hope that this book brings the magic of GRAZIE to your home and that you continue to share with us in creating new memories for our untold future ahead.

GRAZIE per tutti,
Stefano Colacitti

# In The Beginning...

GRAZIE began 15 years ago, quietly opening its doors to the public. It hasn't been quiet since. But the restaurant known for its boisterous atmosphere lined with customers waiting to be seated almost never happened. In the beginning, Chef Joe Brancatella and Louie Granicolo had the idea to go into business together, but it wasn't a restaurant that they had in mind.

Their initial idea was to start a catering company with Louie's wife, Mary, as the three had been friends for years. Joe, aware that Mary had grown up in a restaurant family and consequently had a great deal of cooking experience, thought it would be the perfect fit. Louie, though excited about the prospect, felt that they could be more successful opening their own restaurant. Although it had always been a dream of Joe's, he questioned the idea at first citing their limited experience, but after a week of deliberation, Joe decided that he was up for the challenge.

Despite the fact that they were young and ambitious, they had the presence of mind to recognize they had never done anything like this before, and would need some help if they were going to be successful. At the time, Mary was raising her first child and as much as she wanted to be part of the business, felt the timing wasn't right. So in stepped Mary's mother, Rosa. Having already cultivated one successful restaurant, she felt that she could lend her support and experience to these two young men. And so the journey of GRAZIE began.

From there, the pieces of the puzzle started to fall into place — or so they thought. Joe and Louie began looking for a location but for one reason or another every prospect began to slide away. As doors closed, deals went sour and opportunities were squandered. Their initial drive and passion started to wane.

Joe, 24 and impulsive, had quit his job to focus all his efforts on starting up the restaurant. He was getting nervous and restless as the bills were beginning to pile up. He began to wonder whether their dream would have to be put on hold. He was still young, and felt there would be plenty of time for their dream to happen. At that moment, he just needed a job. As fortune would have it, an associate of Joe's called out of the blue and asked whether the chef would be interested in running his kitchen. Not thinking too much about it, but recognizing the offer as a great opportunity — and a chance to get some work — Joe pulled himself out of his doldrums and went down to the restaurant for a meeting.

Turns out his friend Michael had a lot on his mind. He was not only looking for a new chef, but also hoping to get out of day-to-day operations of the business. As he listened, something triggered inside him. Joe knew he had to seize the opportunity. He asked his friend whether he would be interested in selling the restaurant. Needless to say, a phone call was made and Louie was soon on his way down to look at the location. Within the hour an agreement had been made and the boys were in business.

Yonge and Eglinton had always been on top of Joe and Louie's wish list, but their earlier attempts to find something in the area had been fruitless. This was the perfect spot, in size and location: a 60-seat room in an area surrounded by some of the top restaurants in the city. For what more could aspiring entrepreneurs ask?

Six months into the business after the boys had found their footing and the restaurant showed signs of sticking around, Rosa felt that it would be okay to step aside and let the boys run their own show. In stepped Joe's older brother Vito to pick up where Rosa left off.

From the first day, Vito was part of the restaurant, helping with the renovations and day-to-day tasks. He saw what his brother and friend had started and wanted nothing more than to be part of the fun. And so the initial team was complete. The remaining family members were drawn in, almost as if compelled by a familial bond that intrinsically defies the laws of business.

As the years passed, changes were inevitable. After six years, Louie felt that his time with the restaurant had reached its pinnacle: He was ready for a new challenge. Joe and Vito were suddenly faced with the task of what to do with Louie's share. Vito and Joe made a bold move to offer shares in the restaurant to long-standing members of the *GRAZIE* family — Bruno, their youngest brother; Rob Prete, their cousin; Marco Puntillo, manager and one of their first staff members; and Angelo Moretti, a former restaurant owner himself — with the hope of cultivating a strong and unified team.

What began as nothing more than a dream has turned into a home away from home where people flock to for great food, great friendships and lasting memories. For Joe, the dream of opening up a successful restaurant is now an everyday reality. Where Joe and his partners decide to take their dreams from here, we can only wait and see.

Thanks to all who have supported *GRAZIE* throughout the years!

*GRAZIE*, circa 1990

# Dressing Your Kitchen

Cooking can be made more enjoyable by havine the right utensils on hand for the job. Here are a few items that I suggest so that you can get your kitchen started off on the right foot. "Always remember to keep your knives sharp and your senses sharper."

1 - Chef's Knife or French Knife
2 - Cleaver
3 - Serrated Knives
4 - Filleting Knife
5 - Paring Knife
6 - Turning Knife
7 - Oyster Shucker
8 - Peeler
9 - Channel Knife
10 - Zester
11 - Melon Baller
12 - Pizza Cutter
13 - Cooking Shears
14 - Grater
15 - Measuring Cups
16 - Offset Spatula
17 - Ladle
18 - Wooden Spoon
19 - Tongs
20 - Slotted Spoon
21 - China Cap
22 - Colander
23 - Rubber Spatula
24 - Spider

ISTORANTE
HAIR
485-2575

GRAZIE

# Antipasti

Bruschetta
Crostini Di'Bosco
Carpaccio with Fennel and Arugula
Four Onion Tart with Blue Cheese
Grilled Calamari
Stuffed Sardines
Fresh Mussels in a Tomato Sauce
Fresh Mussels with Beer
Mixed Olives
Gorgonzonla Stuffed Pears

# Bruschetta

## Ingredients

*Serves: 4*
*Prep time: 10 minutes*
*Cook time: 0 minutes*
*Total time: 10 minutes*

**6 plum tomatoes, diced**

**1 garlic clove, minced**

**5 sprigs of parsley, chopped**

**5 basil leaves, chopped**

**1/2 tsp dry oregano**

**1 loaf Italian bread**

**salt to taste**

**pepper to taste**

## Directions

In a mixing bowl, combine tomatoes, garlic, parsley, oregano, basil, salt and pepper. Set aside for 10 minutes, allowing the flavours to come together. In the meantime, slice and toast the bread (for added flavor, lightly rub the toasted bread with a clove of garlic). Top each slice of bread with the tomato mixture and enjoy

# Crostini D'Bosco

## Ingredients

*Serves: 4*
*Prep time: 15 minutes*
*Cook time: 10 minutes*
*Total time: 25 minutes*

**1 medium onion, finely diced**

**2 1/2 cups mushroom (suggested: button, oyster and portobello)**

**3 oz dry white wine**

**1/2 cup 35% cream**

**1/2 cup milk**

**1 tbsp flour**

**1/2 tsp rosemary, finely chopped**

**2 tbsp butter**

**pinch of nutmeg**

**1 baguette**

**1/4 tsp salt**

**1/4 tsp white pepper**

## Directions

Sauté onions with butter in a medium saucepan over medium heat until onion are translucent. Turn heat to high, add mushrooms and sauté for 4-5 minutes. Add seasonings and flour. Stir and cook for about 1 minute. Add white wine and cook for 2 minutes. Slowly add cream and milk, reduce heat to medium and cook for 4-5 minutes. Remove from heat and let cool.

When ready to serve, slice baguette on a bias into 1/2-inch thick slices. Place one heaping tablespoon of the mushroom mixture on each slice. Place bread on a cookie sheet and bake at 450 F until edges are golden brown.

# Carpaccio
## with Fennel and Arugula Salad

Serves: 4
Prep time: 15 minutes
Cook time: 3-5 minutes
Total time: 20 minutes

### Ingredients

**3/4 lbs beef tenderloin or sirloin**

**2 tbsp extra-virgin olive oil**

**1 tbsp rosemary, finely chopped**

**1 tbsp thyme, finely chopped**

**3 oz Parmesan cheese, thinly sliced**

**1 lemon, cut into wedges**

**1 tbsp dried porcini mushroom, ground**

**2 sprigs parsley, leaves only**

**2 tbsp capers**

**salt to taste**

**pepper to taste**

### Directions: Carpaccio

Coat the meat with olive oil and place in a hot cast-iron skillet over high heat. Sear the meat on all sides and set aside. Place a flat sheet of plastic wrap on the counter, then cover it with thyme, rosemary, salt, pepper and porcini mushrooms. Place meat on top of mixture. Roll the plastic wrap up tightly and refrigerate for 8-12 hours.

### Ingredients

**1 bulb fennel, sliced**

**1/4 cup lemon, juiced**

**1/4 cup parsley, coarsely chopped**

**2 bunches arugula**

**3 tbsp virgin olive oil**

**1 large button mushroom**

**salt to taste**

**pepper to taste**

### Directions: Arugula and Fennel Salad

Place your fennel, parsley and arugula into a bowl. Add oil, lemon juice and seasonings. Toss everything together and grate raw button mushroom over the salad.

### Directions: Plating

For each portion, cut 6 or 7 very, very, very thin slices of beef by hand or with an electric slicer. Arrange on a chilled plate. Drizzle the meat with a few drops of olive oil, then top with Parmesan shavings, parsley and capers. Place arugula and fennel salad in the middle of the plate, on top of the carpaccio. Add two lemon wedges to the side of the plate and serve.

# Four Onion Tart
## with Crumbled Blue Cheese

### Ingredients: Filling

**1 1/2 cups 35% cream**

**5 eggs**

**1 tbsp butter**

**1 tbsp vegetable oil**

**1 large Spanish onion, chopped**

**1 leek, chopped, green and white pieces separated**

**5 green onions, finely chopped**

**1 medium red onion, chopped**

**1/3 cup Parmesan cheese, grated**

**pinch of nutmeg**

**4 tbsp of blue cheese, crumbled**

**salt to taste**

**pepper to taste**

### Directions:

Over medium heat, sauté oil, butter, Spanish onion and green pieces of leek in a large pan for 10 minutes. Add red onion, white pieces of leek, green onion and salt. Cook for 10-15 minute or until the onions are soft. Remove from heat and set mixture aside to cool.

In a medium bowl, mix eggs, cream, Parmesan cheese, nutmeg, salt and pepper.

Roll out the dough and place it in a pie pan. Add the onion mixture followed by the cream mixture. Crumble blue cheese on top and place into 350 F oven for 30-40 minutes.

### Ingredients: Pastry Tart

**1/2 tsp vegetable oil**

**1/2 cup cold butter, cut into 1/2-inch cubes**

**1 cup all-purpose flour**

**1 egg**

**1 tbsp ice water**

**pinch of salt**

### Directions:

Add flour and salt to a food processor and pulse for a couple of seconds. Add butter and pulse for 3-5 second intervals until mixture has a sandy texture. Add egg, water and oil and pulse for 5-10 seconds. Place ball of dough in plastic wrap and refrigerate for 1-2 hours.

*Serves: 4*
*Prep time: 20 minutes*
*Cook time: 40 minutes*
*Total time: 60 minutes*

# Grilled Calamari
## with Tomato and Olives

## Ingredients

*Serves: 4*
*Prep time: 10 minutes*
*Cook time: 8 minutes*
*Total time: 18 minutes*

**4 large calamari tubes, cleaned**

**2 tbsp capers**

**1/2 red onion, diced**

**1/2 cup niçoise olives, pitted and chopped**

**1 lemon, zested and juiced**

**8 parsley sprigs, torn and chopped, stems removed**

**2 tomatoes, coarsely chopped**

**2 garlic cloves, chopped**

**6 tbsp extra-virgin olive oil**

**2 anchovies fillets, finely chopped**

**salt to taste**

**pepper to taste**

## Directions: Calamari

To cut the calamari, slice 3⁄4 of the way into the tube, making 1⁄2-inch incisions along the length. Be careful to keep the calamari intact. Drizzle calamari with 2 tablespoons of olive oil and place on a grill over medium-high heat. Cook for 3-4 minutes on each side. Remove from heat. In a medium-size mixing bowl, toss calamari with 2 tablespoons olive oil, garlic clove, salt and pepper.

## Directions: Tomato and Olives

In a mixing bowl, combine red onion, capers, olives, tomatoes, parsley, remaining garlic, lemon juice, anchovies, remaining olive oil, salt and pepper. Marinate for 15-20 minutes. Serve at room temperature with grilled calamari.

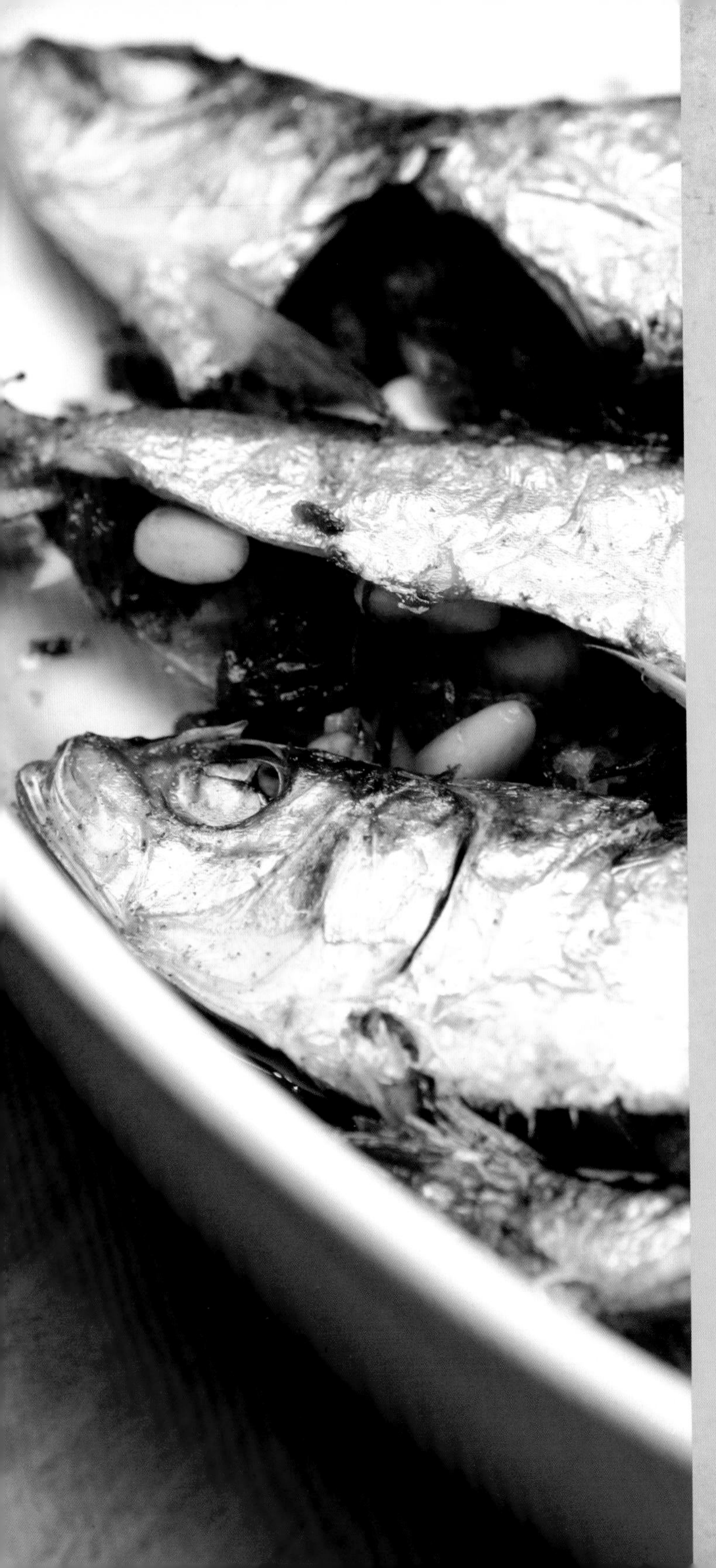

# Stuffed Sardines

## Ingredients

*Serves: 6*
*Prep time: 15 minutes*
*Cook time: 10 minutes*
*Total time: 25 minutes*

**12 sardines**

**1/4 cup bread, cubed into 1⁄4-inch pieces (for best results use day-old Italian bread with the crust removed)**

**2 tbsp butter**

**4 tbsp extra-virgin olive oil**

**4 tbsp raisins**

**2 tbsp lukewarm red wine vinegar**

**2 tbsp parsley, chopped**

**2 oz white vermouth**

**2 anchovies fillets, finely chopped**

**2 garlic cloves, minced**

**1 shallot, diced**

**salt to taste**

**pepper to taste**

## Directions: Deboning Sardines

Remove backbone from sardines and rinse fish under cold water. Pat the sardines dry and store in the fridge.

## Directions: Stuffing

In a sauté pan over medium-high heat, combine 1 tablespoon butter, 2 tablespoons olive oil and the cubed bread. Allow bread to toast to a golden colour, then add all other ingredients except sardines and remaining olive oil and butter. Cook for 2 minutes and place mixture in a bowl and cover with plastic wrap for 10-15 minutes. Remove from bowl and fill sardines with stuffing. In a large sauté pan over medium heat, combine 2 tablespoons olive oil and 1 tablespoon butter. Season stuffed sardines with salt and pepper and place in the pan. Cook on one side for 1 minute, flip, then place in a 450 F oven for 10 minutes. Remove and serve hot.

# Fresh Mussels
## with Tomato and Olives

### Ingredients

*Serves: 4-6*
*Prep time: 10 minutes*
*Cook time: 10 minutes*
*Total time: 20 minutes*

**3 lbs mussels, with shell**

**2 tomatoes, chopped**

**1 can of tomatoes, chopped (28 oz can)**

**1 cup white wine, dry**

**2 tbsp olive oil**

**2 garlic cloves, smashed**

**1/3 cup parsley, chopped**

**pinch hot chili flakes**

**salt to taste**

**pepper to taste**

### Directions

Rinse and scrub mussels under cold running water, discarding any that have opened. Add oil and garlic to a large sauté pan and cook over medium-high heat for 1 minute. Add mussels and cook for 1-2 minutes. Add canned tomatoes, parsley, chili flakes, salt and pepper. Increase heat to high, add white wine and fresh tomatoes. Bring to a boil, cover with a lid and cook for 4-5 minutes or until mussels have opened. Enjoy with crusty Italian bread.

# Fresh Mussels
## with Beer

### Ingredients

*Serves: 4-6*
*Prep time: 10 minutes*
*Cook time: 10 minutes*
*Total time: 20 minutes*

**3 lbs mussels, with shells**

**2 tbsp extra-virgin olive oil**

**2 garlic cloves, smashed**

**24 341-ml bottles pilsner beer (one for the mussels and the remainder for your guests, chilled!)**

**4 tomatoes, chopped**

**1/3 cup parsley, chopped**

**pinch chili flakes**

**salt to taste**

**pepper to taste**

### Directions

Rinse and scrub mussels under cold running water, discarding any that have opened. Add oil and garlic to a large sauté pan and cook over medium-high heat for 1 minute. Add mussels and cook for 1-2 minutes. Add tomatoes, parsley, chili flakes, salt and pepper. Increase heat to high and add 1 bottle of beer. Bring to a boil and cover with lid. Cook for 4-5 minutes or until mussels open. Enjoy these mussels on their own or over pasta with crusty Italian bread to sop up all the fantastic flavours.

# Mixed Olives

Serves: 6-8
Prep time: 10 minutes
Cook time: 10 minutes
Total time: 20 minutes

## Ingredients

2 cups of mixed olives (suggested: Gaeta, kalamata, colosso)

1/3 cup extra-virgin olive oil

1/2 red pepper, chopped

1/2 small onion, cut into wedges

3 garlic cloves, whole

1 bunch rosemary

2 sprigs thyme

1/4 cup flat-leaf parsley, leaves only

Preheat a sauté pan over medium heat. Add oil, onion, red pepper and garlic. Sauté for 5-6 minutes or until garlic and onion are lightly browned and pepper is soft. Add rosemary and thyme and allow flavours to mellow. After about 1 minute, add olives and sauté for a couple of minutes more. Remove from heat and add parsley. Let the olives rest for 1-2 hours at room temperature in the pan and serve. The olives should be good for up to a week refrigerated in a sealed container.

# Gorgonzola
## Stuffed Pears

Serves: 6
Prep time: 10 minutes
Cook time: 0 minutes
Total time: 10 minutes

## Ingredients

**3 firm ripe pears**

**1 lemon, juiced**

**4 oz Gorgonzola cheese**

**4 tbsp white sugar**

## Directions

Using a melon baller, core the pears. Drizzle lemon juice into each cavity to prevent pear from browning. Pack Gorgonzola tightly into cavity, making sure there are no air pockets. Wipe excess cheese from bottom of the pear for a clean presentation. Refrigerate for 25 minutes to allow cheese to set. When ready to serve, line a baking sheet with foil and fill a shallow bowl with white sugar. Cut pears in half, lightly coat the cut side of the pear with the sugar, lay them on the baking sheet cut side up. Using a kitchen torch, caramelize the coated side of the pear running the torch along the outer sides of the pear. This process should only take between five and ten seconds.
(excersise caution when using kitchen torch.)

# Salads

Goat Cheese and Eggplant Salad
Prosciutto with Melon and Fig
Tomato Salad
Watercress and Fennel Salad
Caprese Branca Salad
Sila Salad
Two-Can Tuscan Tuna Salad
Caesar Salad

# Goat Cheese
## and Eggplant Salad

### Ingredients: Salad

*Serves: 4*
*Prep time: 20 minutes*
*Cook time: 15 minutes*
*Total time: 35 minutes*

**2 bunches arugula**
**1 shallot, finely chopped**
**3 sprigs parsley, chopped**
**3 tbsp extra-virgin olive oil**
**1 oz sherry vinegar**
**salt to taste**
**pepper to taste**
**12 oz goat cheese, sliced or piped**
**2 red bell peppers, cut into wedges**
**1/4 head frisée**

### Breading the eggplant

**SEE LEFT COLUMN**

**1 large eggplant, peeled and sliced**
**2 eggs**
**1 tbsp milk**
**1 cup bread crumbs**
**1/2 cup flour**

### Directions: Grilled Peppers

Drizzle olive oil over peppers. Grill peppers over medium-high heat until grill marks appear. Do not burn.

### Directions: Arugula Salad

In a large bowl, mix together arugula, olive oil, parsley and shallots. Add sherry vinegar and season with salt and pepper.

To assemble salad refer to picture.

### Breading

There are three stages of breading:

1. The flour: helps the breading stick to the food.
2. The egg wash: a mixture of eggs and milk, necessary to bind the breadcrumb to the food.
3. Bread crumbs: fine, dry bread crumbs provide the best results.

Have your flour in a shallow bowl, your egg wash in another shallow bowl and your bread crumbs spread out over a flat plate. Dredge the eggplant with flour and then dip it into the egg wash, being sure to coat the entire eggplant.
Pat the eggplant into the bread crumbs, covering both sides. (This is the fundamental breading process for all food types.)

# Prosciutto with Melon and Fig

## Ingredients

*Serves: 4*
*Prep Time: 5 minutes*
*Cook Time: 0 minutes*
*Total Time: 5 minutes*

**1/2 cantaloupe**

**1/2 honeydew melon**

**8 thin slices prosciutto**

**4 figs, halved**

## Directions: Grill Peppers

Remove skin and seeds from cantaloupe and honeydew. Slice melons into four, then wrap each piece with a slice of prosciutto. Slice figs in half. To serve, place one slice of each melon on a plate, along with a halved fig.

*The Three Musketeers!*
*Ricardo, Frank and Giovanni*

# Tomato Salad

## Ingredients

Serves: 4
Prep time: 5 minutes
Cook time: 0 minutes
Total time: 5 minutes

**8-10 tomatoes, sliced**
**1/2 red onion, thinly sliced**
**3 tbsp parsley, chopped**
**1/2 tsp dried oregano**
**1/3 cup extra-virgin olive oil**
**4 basil leaves**
**1/2 tsp salt**
**1/2 tsp pepper**

### Directions:

Combine all ingredients in a medium-size mixing bowl. Toss and serve. Yes, it is that easy!

# Watercress and Fennel Salad

## Ingredients

Serves: 4
Prep time: 10 minutes
Cook time: 0 minutes
Total time: 10 minutes

**1/2 english cucumber, cut into thin strips**
**1/2 fennel bulb, thinly sliced**
**2 tbsp parsley, chopped**
**1 shallot, finely diced**
**2 radishes, julienned**
**1 granny smith apple, julienned**
**1 bunch watercress, torn**
**4 tbsp white wine vinegar**
**1 lime, juiced**
**4 tbsp extra-virgin olive oil**
**2 tbsp honey**
**1/2 tsp sea salt**
**pepper to taste**

### Directions:

Place ingredients in a large mixing bowl. Toss and enjoy.

# Caprese Branca Salad

Serves: 4
Prep time: 20 minutes
Cook time: 30 seconds
Total time: 20 minutes

**Black Olive Dressing**

**4 tomatoes, sliced**
**1 red onion, thinly sliced**
**24 small bocconcini**
**1/3 cup Gaeta olives**
**1 bunch frisée**
**2 bunches watercress**
**2 bunches arugula**

**Black Olive Dressing**

**1/2 shallot, finely diced**
**1/4 cup of niçoise olives, chopped**
**1 tbsp parsley, finely chopped**
**4 tbsp extra-virgin olive oil**
**2 tbsp red wine vinegar**
**salt to taste**
**pepper to taste**

**Basil Dressing**

**1 cup parsley, fresh**
**1 cup basil, fresh**
**3/4 cup olive oil**
**1/4 tsp salt**
**pinch of ground pepper**

## Directions: Salad

Toss watercress, frisee, arugula and red onion with black olive dressing. Place tossed salad in the middle of a plate. Arrange tomatoes, olives and bocconcini on the plate, drizzle with basil dressing and serve.

## Directions: Black Olive Dressing

Mix all ingredients well in a bowl. Allow flavours to come together for 10-15 minutes and use as needed.

## Directions: Basil Dressing

Blanch basil and parsley in boiled salted water for 30 seconds. (Blanching refers to cooking an item partially and very briefly). Immediately chill in ice bath or cold running water (to keep vibrate colour). Place basil and parsley in a blender, squeezing out any excess water. Drizzle in olive oil and add salt and pepper. Blend until mixture is a loose liquid (if necessary add more olive oil). Set aside, refrigerate and use when needed.

# Sila Salad

## Ingredients

*Serves: 6*
*Prep time: 15 minutes*
*Cook time: 5 minutes*
*Total time: 20 minutes*

**Poaching Liquid for Shrimp and Calamari**

**5 litres water**

**3/4 lbs shrimp, peeled**

**3/4 lbs calamari rings**

**3 celery ribs, halved**

**3 cloves garlic, whole**

**1/2 medium onion, whole**

**2 bay leaves**

**1/2 cup white wine vinegar**

**1/2 lemon**

**1/4 cup peppercorns**

**3/4 cup salt**

**2 cups of ice**

**2 tbsp extra-virgin olive oil**

**Salad**

**1 medium red onion, finely julienned**

**3 celery ribs, peeled and julienned**

**1/2 red bell pepper, julienned**

**1/2 green bell pepper, julienned**

**pinch dried oregano**

**1/2 cup white wine vinegar**

**3 tbsp extra-virgin olive oil**

**5 sprigs parsley, chopped**

**2 tsp salt**

**1/2 tsp pepper**

## Directions: Poaching Liquid for the Shrimp and Calamari

Add onions, garlic and 2 tablespoons extra-virgin olive oil to a large pot. Cook over medium-high heat for 3-4 minutes. Add bay leaves, lemon, vinegar, celery, peppercorns, 4 litres water and 1/2 cup salt. Bring to a boil. Place shrimp in the boiling water. Bring water back to a boil and cook shrimp for 1 minute. Remove shrimp from pot and place in a bowl filled with 1 litre water, 1/4 cup salt and 2 cups ice. Repeat these steps with calamari, leaving calamari in the boiling water for 2 minutes after it has returned to a boil. The shrimp and calamari must be drained very well. Set them in a colander, place a bowl under the colander to catch excess water, cover with paper towel and refrigerate for 10-20 minutes.

## Directions: Salad

Place all ingredients in a large mixing bowl along with poached and drained shrimp and calamari.
Marinate for 1 hour in the fridge and serve.

# Two-Can Tuscan Tuna Salad

## Ingredients

*Serves: 4*
*Prep time: 10 minutes*
*Cook time: 0 minutes*
*Total time: 10 minutes*

**2 cans tuna in oil, drained**

**1 can white kidney beans, rinsed under cold water**

**1/2 medium red onion, finely diced**

**2 celery ribs, chopped**

**5 sprigs fresh parsley, chopped**

**2 tbsp fresh basil, chopped**

**2 tbsp red wine vinegar**

**3 tbsp extra-virgin olive oil**

**1/2 cup black olives, pitted**

**salt to taste**

**pepper to taste**

## Directions

Mix all ingredients together in a medium-size mixing bowl. Refrigerate for 15 minutes, then serve.

## The Anchovy

To anchovy or not to anchovy: That is the question — at least when it comes to Caesar salad. Joe has found through the course of his career that many people are unaware that the anchovy is a fundamental ingredient in Caesar salad dressing. It provides a salty yet subtle fish flavour that creates the unique taste of the dressing. Without it, the dressing would lack the necessary bite for which it is famous.

# Caesar Salad

## Ingredients

*Serves: 6*
*Prep time: 15 minutes*
*Cook time: 5 minutes*
*Total time: 20 minutes*

**2 heads of romaine lettuce**
**1/2 loaf Italian bread**
**1 garlic clove**
**4 anchovy fillets**
**2 egg yolks**
**1 lemon, juiced**
**6 oz extra-virgin olive oil**
**3 oz Parmesan cheese, grated**
**2 tbsp Dijon mustard**
**1 tbsp capers**
**2 oz red wine vinegar**
**salt to taste**
**pepper to taste**

## Directions: Salad

Wash, clean and dry lettuce. Tear into bite-size pieces. Place leaves in a large bowl and set aside.

## Directions: Dressing

Place garlic, anchovy, capers, mustard, egg yolk, vinegar, lemon juice, salt and pepper in a blender and mix until they form a paste. Drizzle in olive oil to get a smooth and creamy texture. (For an extra layer of flavour, add 1 oz Parmesan cheese.)Use immediately or refrigerate in a sealed container for up to 4 days. If you don't like the idea of raw eggs in your dressing, substitute whole hard-boiled eggs. The creaminess of the dressing will not be the same, but the flavour will be just as good. Spoon dressing over lettuce and toss until fully coated. Sprinkle remaining Parmesan cheese over salad.

## Directions: Croutons

Slice bread on a bias into 1⁄4-inch slices and toast until brown. Rub a raw piece of garlic on the bread and drizzle with olive oil. Cut the slices of bread in half, place on the salad and enjoy.

# Soups / Zuppa

Minestra
Minestrone
Chicken Stock
Beef Stock
Shrimp Stock
Roasted Red Pepper Puree
Pasta Fagioli
Roasted Butternut Squash Soup
Potato Puree with Smoked Salmon
Stracciatella Soup

# Minestra

## Ingredients

Serves: 6

Prep time: 15 minutes

Cook time: 70 minutes

Total time: 85 minutes

**3 oz pancetta, finely diced**

**3 tbsp olive oil**

**1 can white kidney beans, rinsed under cold water**

**1 lb collard greens, coarsely chopped**

**1 head escarole, coarsely chopped**

**1 bunch rapini, coarsely chopped**

**1 cup broccoli, stems peeled**

**1 cup green onion, finely diced**

**4 sprigs parsley, chopped**

**1 sprig thyme, chopped**

**1 1/2 litres chicken stock, heated**

**2 garlic cloves, whole**

**2 potatoes, diced**

**3 Italian sausages, whole**

## Directions

Heat the oil in a large saucepot over medium-high heat.
Add sausages. Once the sausage has started to brown, add pancetta and garlic and sauté for two minutes.
Add collard greens, escarole, rapini, broccoli and the heated chicken stock. Simmer for 45 minutes.
Add the kidney beans and potato. Simmer for 20 minutes.
Add parsley, thyme and green onion. Simmer for 5 minutes and serve.

# Minestrone

## Ingredients

*Serves: 4*
*Prep time: 10 minutes*
*Cook time: 45 minutes*
*Total time: 55 minutes*

**1 garlic clove, whole**

**2 tbsp extra-virgin olive oil**

**1 large onion, diced**

**5 ribs of celery, diced**

**1 cup cabbage, coarsely chopped**

**2 zucchini, quartered and seeded (keep seeds)**

**4 carrots, diced**

**3⁄4 cup tomato, diced**

**2 potatoes, diced**

**1 litre chicken stock, heated**

**1 cup fresh green beans, cut into 2-inch pieces**

**5 oz piece hot pancetta (keep whole)**

## Directions

Heat oil in a large saucepot over medium heat.
Add pancetta, garlic and onions. Cook for 3 minutes.
Add celery, carrot and cabbage and cook for 2 minutes.
Add chopped tomato and zucchini seeds and cook for another 2 minutes. Add stock, bring to boil, skim and simmer for 15 minutes.
Add zucchini, green beans and potato. Bring to a boil and simmer for another 20-25 minutes and serve.

P.S. This tastes even tastes better the next day!

# Chicken Stock

**Yields 3 liters**

## Ingredients:

**3 lbs chicken bones, cut into 3-4 inch pieces**
**4 litres water**
**3 carrots, chopped**
**2 medium onions, quartered**
**3 ribs celery, chopped (include leaves)**
**2 bay leaves, whole**
**10 black peppercorns, whole**
**2 tbsp vegetable oil**

## Directions:

Cut bones into 3-4 inch pieces and rinse under cold water (this removes some of the impurities that make stock cloudy). Add oil, carrots, onion and celery to a large saucepot over medium-high heat and sauté for 1-2 minutes. Add water and bring to a boil. Add chicken bones, peppercorns and bay leaves. Cook at a gentle simmer for 3-4 hours, skimming the scum that comes to the surface.

When the stock is ready, remove from heat and allow it to cool. Strain through a china cap (fine meshed strainer) lined with cheesecloth into a container. Cover the container and refrigerate for up to 3 days. If you decide to freeze the stock, it is good for up to 6 months.

The same steps are used for vegetable stock: Simply eliminate chicken bones.

# Beef Stock

**Yields 3 liters**

## Ingredients:

**3 lbs beef and veal bones**
**4 litres cold water**
**2 tbsp vegetable oil**
**3 carrots, chopped**
**2 medium onions, quartered**
**3 celery ribs, chopped**
**2 bay leaves, whole**
**4 garlic cloves, whole**
**10 black peppercorns, whole**
**4 thyme sprigs**
**1 cup red wine**

## Directions:

Cut bones into 3-4-inch long pieces (do not wash) and place in a roasting pan, making sure not to stack them. Lightly drizzle vegetable oil over bones. Place roasting pan in the oven at 450 F for approximately 15-20 minutes. Remove from oven and add carrots, celery, garlic and onion. Roast for another 10-15 minutes. Remove pan from oven and deglaze with red wine on the stove over medium-high heat. Once the wine has evaporated, transfer all the roasted ingredients into a large saucepot over medium-high heat. Cover with water, bring to a boil, then add bay leaves, thyme and peppercorns and reduce to a simmer. Simmer for 3-4 hours, skimming off excess fat and scum as necessary.

Remove stock from heat and allow it to cool. Strain through a china cap (fine meshed strainer) lined with cheesecloth into a container. Cover and refrigerate for up to 3 days. If you decide to freeze the stock, it is good for up to 6 months.

# Shrimp Stock

**Yields 3 liters**

## Ingredients:

**1 tbsp butter**
**4 litres water**
**3 medium carrots, chopped**
**3 celery ribs, chopped**
**2 medium onions, quartered**
**1/2 medium onion, diced**
**2 bay leaves**
**1 1-inch cinnamon stick, whole**
**10 anise seeds**
**10 black peppercorns, whole**
**1 tbsp tomato paste**
**5 oz tomato juice**
**1 lemon, halved**
**10 fennel seeds**
**50 shrimp shells**
**1 cup dry white wine**
**1 tbsp vegetable oil**

## Directions:

Add butter and onion to a large sauce pot over medium heat and sauté for 1-2 minutes. Add shrimp shells and cook for 2 minutes. Remove the shrimp shells and quartered onion from pot and set aside in a bowl. Add all remaining ingredients except water, tomato paste, tomato juice and white wine to original pot. Sauté for 1 minute, then add tomato paste and stir, cooking for 1-2 minutes. Add white wine and cook for 2-3 minutes. Finally, add tomato juice, water and cooked shells and onion. Increase the heat to medium-high, skim as needed and simmer for 2 hours. Never allow the stock to boil or it will become cloudy.

When the stock is ready, remove from the heat and allow it to cool. Strain through a china cap (fine meshed strainer) lined with cheesecloth into a container. Cover the container and refrigerate for up to 3 days. If you decide to freeze the stock, it is good for up to 6 months.

# Roasted Red Pepper Puree

## Ingredients

- 1 tbsp extra-virgin olive oil
- 1 tbsp butter
- 5 roasted red peppers, coarsely chopped
- 4 oz carrot, finely diced
- 2 oz celery, finely diced
- 2 oz onion, finely diced
- 1 garlic clove, whole
- 1 16-oz can tomatoes
- 1 1/2 litres chicken stock, heated
- 3 parsley stems, coarsely chopped
- 1 bay leaf
- 3 sprigs thyme
- 1/2 cup long-grain rice, uncooked
- salt to taste
- pepper taste

## Directions

Heat the butter and oil in a large saucepot over medium heat.

Add the carrots, celery, onion, garlic and bay leaf. Cook the vegetables for 2 minutes until they are about half cooked. Do not let them brown.

Add the can of tomatoes and cook for 3-4 minutes.

Add the uncooked rice and stir for 1-2 minutes. Then add the roasted red peppers.

Add heated chicken stock and bring to a boil. Skim the soup and add thyme and parsley.

Cook for about 15 minutes or until the rice is tender.

Remove bay leaf, place the soup in a food processor and blend until smooth.Place through a strainer, adjust seasonings and serve hot.

# Pasta Fagioli

## Ingredients

*Serves: 4*
*Prep time: 10 minutes*
*Cook time: 70 minutes*
*Total time: 80 minutes*

**1 19-oz can cannellini beans**

**1 litre chicken stock, heated**

**2 tbsp extra-virgin olive oil**

**1 onion, finely chopped**

**2 ribs of celery, finely diced**

**3 garlic cloves, minced**

**1 carrot, finely diced or grated**

**1 green pepper, chopped**

**4 oz pancetta, diced**

**2 fresh plum tomatoes, diced**

**1 cup small macaroni, cooked to al dente**

**4 basil leaves, torn**

**1 bay leaf**

**1 garlic clove, rubbed on Italian bread**

**salt to taste**

**pepper to taste**

## Directions

In a medium saucepot, heat olive oil over medium to medium-high heat. Add pancetta and onion and cook until onion becomes translucent (do not brown). Add garlic, celery, carrot, green pepper and bay leaf and continue to sauté for 2 minutes.

Pass canned tomatoes through a food mill or pulse in a processor, then pass through a strainer to extract the seeds. Add tomatoes to pan and simmer for 5-7 minutes. Add the beans, chicken stock and salt and pepper to taste. Raise the heat, bring to a boil and allow to simmer for 30-40 minutes, stirring occasionally.

Add the precooked pasta (al dente), the basil leaves and allow the macaroni and sauce to marry for about 10-12 minutes. Serve with toasted garlic-rubbed Italian bread.

## A View from the Kitchen

It's Saturday night,
Music is pumping
Sauces slowly bubbling.
Feet on the run,
Flip the pan,
Plate the pasta,
Ladle the demi to finish the chicken,
Get it to the table on time!
Not done yet, still another hundred to go!
Give me this,
Get me that,
Move to the right,
Watch it doesn't get burned,
We can do it.
In the groove,
The groove is where you need to be.
Plate that steak,
Pump out those salads,
Finish that sauce,
More pleased patrons,
Bring it on,
We can handle it.
Best pizza maker in the city,
Fling the dough,
Add the sauce gently,
Then come the toppings,
Bake it, take it out slice it up,
No time to relax, there's more to come.
Drinks pouring, people laughing,
This is *GRAZIE* to me ...
Sublime.

Jonathan Pyke. Legend
(Chef De Parti, *GRAZIE*)

# Roasted Butternut Squash Soup

## Ingredients

*Serves: 4*
*Prep time: 10 minutes*
*Cook time: 75 minutes*
*Total time: 85 minutes*

**1 large butternut squash, halved and seeded**
**1 medium onion, diced**
**2 ribs of celery, diced**
**1 carrot, diced**
**1 tsp brown sugar**
**pinch nutmeg**
**1 2-inch piece of cinnamon stick**
**2 bay leaves**
**2 sprigs thyme**
**2 garlic cloves, whole**
**2 litres chicken stock**
**2 tbsp butter**
**3 tbsp extra-virgin olive oil**
**salt to taste**
**pepper to tatse**

## Directions: Roasting Butternut Squash

Cut squash in half, spoon out seeds and score the flesh.
Fill the fleshy center of each half with butter, bay leaves, thyme, garlic, cinnamon, nutmeg and brown sugar.
Drizzle flesh with olive oil and season with salt and pepper.
Cover with foil and place in 450 F oven for 20-25 minutes.
Remove cinnamon and bay leaves, scoop flesh from skin and set aside.

## Directions: Soup

Heat 2 tablespoons of olive oil in a large saucepot over medium heat.
Add onion, carrot and celery and cook for 4-5 minutes.
Add chicken stock, bring to a simmer and cook for 20 minutes.
Add roasted squash to stock. Allow squash to warm through, then place mixture in a food processor and blend until smooth.
Strain through fine sieve and adjust seasoning.
Bring strained soup to a boil and serve.
Option: Garnish with caramelized squash.

# Potato Puree Garnished with Smoked Salmon

## Ingredients

**6 large russet potatoes, cut into 1/4-inch thick slices**

**3 celery ribs, chopped**

**1 medium carrot, chopped**

**1 medium Spanish white onion, chopped**

**2 litres chicken stock, heated**

**3 tbsp butter**

**spice bag (1 sprig rosemary, 2 bay leaves and 1 tbsp whole black pepper-corns wrapped and tied in cheesecloth)**

**Smoked Salmon**

**salt to taste**

**pepper to taste**

## Directions

*Serves: 4*
*Prep time: 10 minutes*
*Cook time: 25 minutes*
*Total time: 35 minutes*

Heat the butter in a large saucepot over medium heat.
Add the carrots, celery and onions.
Cook for 2 minutes and then add the potatoes, spice bag and sauté for another 2 minutes.
Add the chicken stock, bring to a boil and reduce to a simmer and cook for 15-20 minutes until the potatoes are tender. Add salt and pepper to taste.
Place in a food processor, remove the spice bag and blend until smooth.
Place through strainer, adjust for seasonings and serve hot.

*Garnish with boiled potato and smoked salmon*

# From Rags to Riches

GRAZIE became the local hot spot for the cast and crew of the hit musical Ragtime during its run at the Ford Center for the Performing Arts. Almost every night you could find at least one member of the cast at GRAZIE, either before or after a show. It wasn't out of the ordinary for cast members to call up after a late show and ask whether the restaurant could stay open just a bit longer because they were on their way down.

Here is a shot of the Ragtime cast having their Thanksgiving dinner with us. Though they may have been forced to spend time away from their real families, they will always be remembered as part of the GRAZIE extended family. Our doors are always open.

"Thanks for the fun, thanks for the laughs; for the friendships we had, as leaving is sad; from the sharing of drinks, to being our shrinks, we stand with applause, with roses for this cause. We bid you adieu, but never goodbye. Till next we meet, the memories will keep."

# Stracciatella Soup with Spinach

## Ingredients

Serves: 4
Prep time: 5 minutes
Cook time: 15 minutes
Total time: 20 minutes

**2 eggs**

**3 tbsp Parmesan cheese, grated**

**1 tbsp fresh parsley, chopped**

**1 litre chicken stock**

**1 1/2 cups fresh spinach**

**salt to taste**

**pepper to taste**

## Directions

Beat eggs in a small bowl. Mix in cheese, parsley, salt and pepper. In a medium saucepot, bring chicken stock to a simmer.

Pour egg mixture slowly into the simmering stock and cook gently, increase the heat slightly while breaking the egg with a knife or fork.

Once the soup has returned to a boil remove from heat and add spinach immediately, letting it wilt in the hot soup.

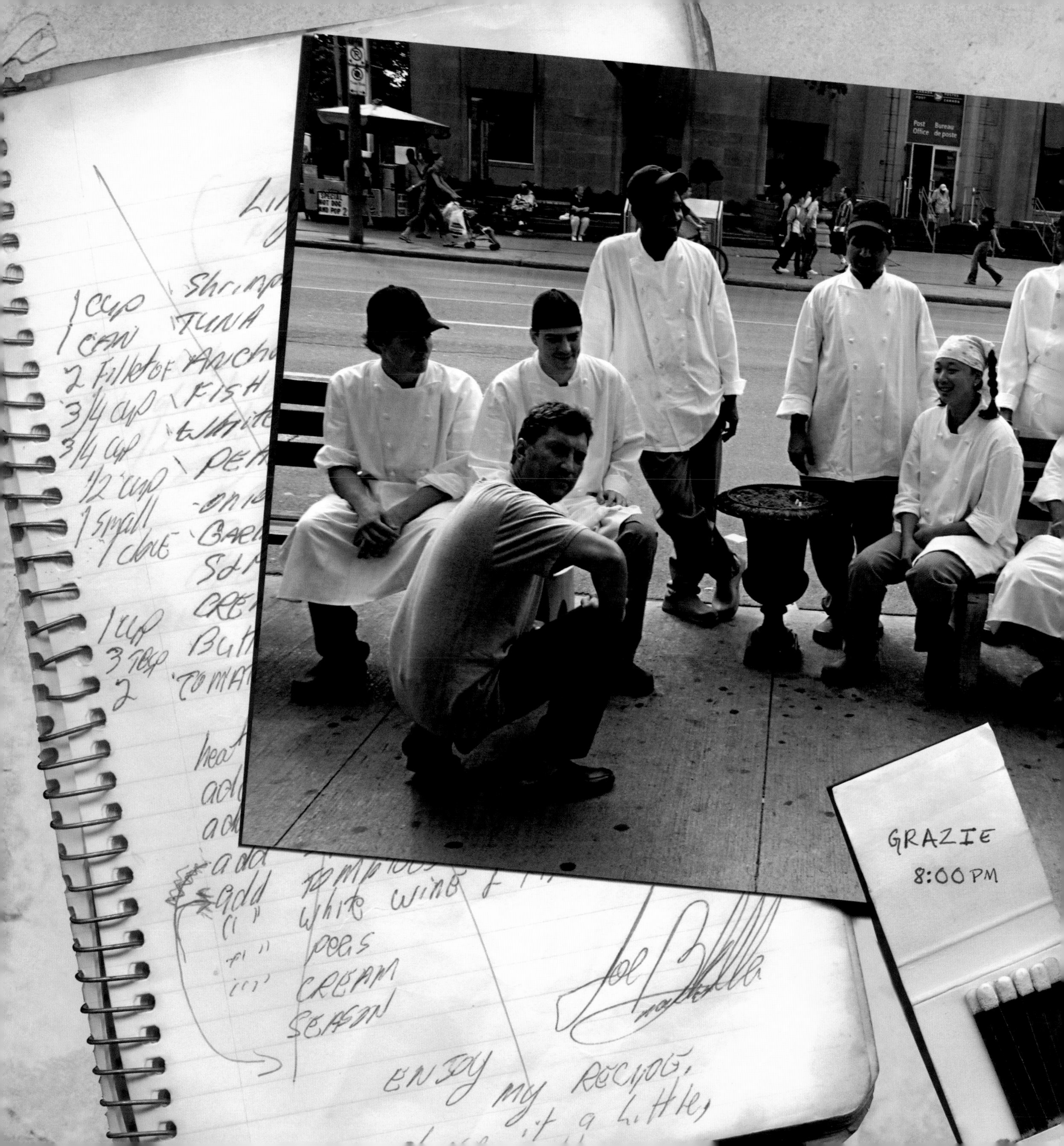

Post Office
Bureau de poste
1 cup
1 can TUNA
2 Fillet of
3/4 cup FISH
3/4 cup
1/2 cup
1 small
1 clove
1 cup
3 Tbsp
2
white wine
peas
CREAM
SEASON
ENJOY my RECIPE,
GRAZIE
8:00 PM

GRAZIE
RISTORANTE

# Pizza

# Pizza Dough Recipe

## Ingredients

*Yields 4 doughs, approximately 10 inches in diameter.*

**4 cups all-purpose flour**

**1 oz whole-wheat flour**

**1/2 teaspoon salt**

**1 1/2 cups lukewarm water**

**1 package yeast**

**1 tbsp sugar**

**1/4 cup olive oil**

## Directions:

In a small bowl, mix together lukewarm water, sugar, oil and yeast. Set mixture aside, allowing contents to come to room temperature.

Using a food mixer with a dough hook, combine all-purpose flour, whole-wheat flour, rosemary and salt. When everything is combined evenly, add yeast/water mixture. The dough should be sticky enough that it begins to grab the hook of the mixer. (You may need to adjust the amount of water or flour.)

Remove dough from the mixer and place it on the countertop. Knead dough by hand briefly and then cover with a damp cloth for 20-30 minutes. Cut dough into 8-9-oz portions. Knead each portion into a ball, forcing out any remaining air. Oil a baking sheet or tray. Brush dough balls with olive oil, cover with plastic wrap and place on the baking sheet. Refrigerate immediately. (If you are using the dough the same day, allow the dough to remain at room temperature for another hour before refrigerating. This will give the dough a chance to rise). The dough is good for 3 days if refrigerated.

## Just stopped to smell the Roses

GRAZIE has been a special place for many staff members who have come and gone. It's given some the opportunity to get their feet wet, while trying to balance their lives and career aspirations. Others have found GRAZIE the perfect place to lay the groundwork for future endeavors. None have exemplified this more than John Gramarossa.

After beginning his tenure with GRAZIE as an inexperienced waiter, Gramarossa left with a new skill set and a passion for food. John credits Joe's passion for food and quality for inspiring him to follow his dream.

*"John and I were the same age, and I remember him always questioning things and sampling foods that he had never tried before. He was genuinely enamored by the cooking process and enjoyed watching what we created on a nightly basis. You could see that he wanted to learn as much as he could. I guess he just felt the buzz and wanted to see where it would take him."*

*continued on next page*

# Margherita Pizza

## Ingredients

**1 pizza dough**

**4 oz tomato sauce (refer to p107)**

**3⁄4 cup mozzarella cheese, grated**

**6 basil leaves, torn**

**1 tbsp extra-virgin olive oil**

**pinch oregano**

**salt and pepper to taste**

*Serves: 1-2*
*Prep time: 5 minutes*
*Cook time: 7 minutes*
*Total time: 12 minutes*

*For best results a pizza stone is recommended*

## Directions

Preheat pizza stone in a 450-475 F oven for at least 45 minutes. Roll out dough and ladle tomato sauce into the middle, spreading evenly over the surface. Sprinkle salt, pepper and oregano over sauce, followed by mozzarella. Bake pizza on stone until bottom is golden brown, approximately 6-8 minutes. Remove from oven, drizzle with olive oil and place fresh basil evenly over pizza.

*continued from previous page*

The experience left John wanting to learn more. Pairing his new love with his primary passion — travel — John trained and worked in Italy, England and the Caribbean until he finally found a home in the Provence region of France, where he joined the Alain Ducasse group. Now an accomplished chef, he officiates as a trainer chef at the ADF.

What began as a simple quest for a part time job lead John on a journey that altered the course of his life! Inspiration is found in the smallest of seedlings. Sometimes all it needs is a bit of light.

John Gramarossa
Former GRAZIE employee

# San Vito

## Ingredients

**1 pizza dough**

**4 oz tomato sauce (refer to p107)**

**1/2 cup mozzarella cheese, grated**

**1/4 cup roasted red peppers**

**8 thin slices sopresata**

**1/4 cup green olives, not pitted**

**pinch oregano**

**salt and pepper to taste**

*Serves: 1-2*
*Prep time: 5 minutes*
*Cook time: 7 minutes*
*Total time: 12 minutes*

*For best results a pizza stone is recommended*

## Directions

Preheat pizza stone in a 450-475 F oven for at least 45 minutes. Roll out dough and ladle tomato sauce into the middle, spreading evenly over the surface. Place mozzarella, salt, pepper and oregano evenly over sauce, followed by sopresata, roasted red peppers and green olives. Bake pizza on stone until bottom is golden brown, approximately 6-8 minutes.

# Pescara

## Ingredients

Serves: 1-2
Prep time: 5 minutes
Cook time: 7 minutes
Total time: 12 minutes

For best results a pizza stone is recommended

**1 pizza dough**

**2 tbsp pesto (recipe on p 59)**

**1/2 tomato, diced**

**1/4 cup mozzarella cheese, grated**

**8 mussels, whole and uncooked**

**6 shrimp, peeled**

**1 calamari tube, cut into rings**

**pinch oregano**

**salt and pepper to taste**

## Directions

Preheat pizza stone in a 450-475 F oven for at least 45 minutes. Roll out dough and spread pesto evenly over the surface. Sprinkle salt, pepper, oregano and mozzarella over pesto, followed by diced tomato. Add mussels, shrimp and calamari. Bake pizza on stone until bottom is golden brown, approximately 6-8 minutes.

## AN UNASSUMING GENTLEMAN

12:30 p.m., Monday. The sun makes its way through the windows as the regular lunchtime crowd shuffles in, greeted at the door by a smile. It's business as usual since the doors opened four years earlier.

An elderly gentleman in a straw hat walks through the doors with an unassuming manner. He takes his seat at the corner of the bar, a seat he has sat in everyday for the last five years. No one has noticed him yet: They are all rushing around attending to their duties. He takes off his long grey trench coat and hangs it on the back of the bar stool. He is quiet and reserved on this day, different from his usual jovial self, a sign of the disease starting to control him.

A moment later the bartender recognizes the usual face at the corner of his bar and shouts a big hello from the opposite end: "Good afternoon Mr. Stephens." With a nod and a slight smile, the guest takes his seat. Promptly and without having to be asked, the bartender moves across the bar, lays a napkin down in front of him and places a beer on top of it. "There you go Mr. Stephens."

*GRAZIE* has become a home away from home for Mr. Stephens — a place where he could come to for a quick bite, some conversation, the occasional beer and a good smoke. After his doctor informed him that he had Lupus which forced him into early retirement, he found himself with more time on his hands and fewer friends around to help him fill it with. When *GRAZIE* opened its doors it seemed the two were destined to find each other. Mr. Stephens became an instant regular to the quaint Italian restaurant. With his charming personality it didn't take him long to endear himself to the staff and owners. If you didn't know better, you would have sworn he had stock in the place how often he

*continued on next page*

*continued from previous page*

was there, but he was never a nuisance, in fact, quite the opposite. Today however, will be one of the last times Mr. Stephens sets foot through the doors of GRAZIE. The family has made a decision to move to Winnipeg to support the success of Mrs. Stephens, new position with the University of Winnipeg. They will be leaving by train in a few weeks. Sadly he will miss the restaurant and all the friends that he has made over the years, but looks forward to his new adventure and welcomes the starry nights of Winnipeg. Mr. Stephens leaves behind a lasting piece of his heart and charm here at GRAZIE, and will always be missed. He was given a farewell party at GRAZIE, were everyone drank and toasted to their celebrated friend.

Over the years, Mr. Stephens has become a symbol for all that GRAZIE stands for. His memory makes us believe in the magic that people can share between each other, and how limited that time can be. He shows us how we should live everyday amongst friends, never taking them for granted. There is magic at GRAZIE, but the magic is in the people and what they bring with them.

Mr. Stephens died soon after having arrived in Winnipeg, quietly in his sleep. The Lupus had become too much for his body to handle.

At GRAZIE, Mr. Stephen still sits at the same spot he did 10 years ago. And if you listen quietly on a Monday afternoon, when the sun begins to come through the windows of the front doors, you might just hear the laughter of one the first guests GRAZIE ever had the pleasure of serving.

*"To our resident guardian angel, with one hand holding a beer and the other holding a smoke, we raise a glass and say: GRAZIE!"*

# Romana

## Ingredients

*Serves: 1-2*
*Prep time: 5 minutes*
*Cook time: 7 minutes*
*Total time: 12 minutes*

*For best results a pizza stone is recommended*

**1 pizza dough**

**1/2 potato, sliced extremely thin**

**1/4 cup pancetta, finely diced**

**1 tomato, diced**

**1/2 cup mozzarella cheese, grated**

**2 tbsp Parmesan cheese, grated**

**1 tsp rosemary, finely chopped**

**salt and pepper to taste**

## Directions

Preheat pizza stone in a 450-475 F oven for at least 45 minutes. Roll out dough and sprinkle evenly with rosemary, salt and pepper. Place the thinly sliced potato over the dough, being careful not to overlap slices, followed by mozzarella, pancetta, 1/2 of diced tomato and Parmesan cheese. Bake pizza on stone until bottom is golden brown, approximately 6-8 minutes. Remove pizza from oven and evenly distribute remaining diced tomato.

# Pastore

## Ingredients

*Serves: 1-2*
*Prep time: 5 minutes*
*Cook time: 7 minutes*
*Total time: 12 minutes*

*For best results a pizza stone is recommended*

**1 pizza dough**

**4 oz tomato sauce (refer to p107)**

**3⁄4 cup mozzarella cheese, grated**

**1/4 cup roasted red peppers**

**2 artichoke hearts, quartered**

**4 oz goat cheese, thinly sliced or piped**

**1/4 cup sun-dried tomatoes, julienned**

**pinch oregano**

**salt and pepper to taste**

## Directions

Preheat the pizza stone in a 450-475 F oven, for at least 45 minutes. Roll out the dough and ladle tomato sauce into the middle, spreading evenly over the surface. Distribute salt, pepper, oregano, mozzarella cheese, roasted red peppers, artichoke hearts and goat cheese evenly over dough. Bake pizza on stone until bottom is golden brown, approximately 8-12 minutes.
Add the sun-dried tomatoes a couple of minutes before the pizza is finished (this allows them to warm through but not overcook).

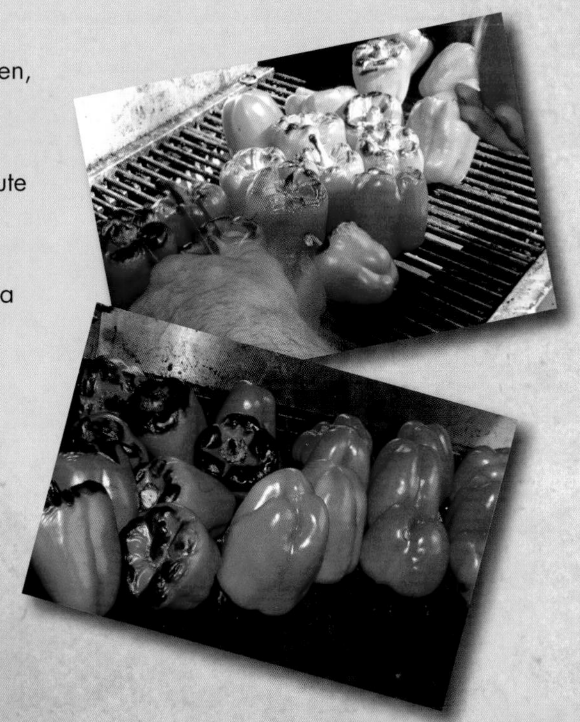

## Roasting and peeling peppers

There are two different methods for roasting peppers, the oven or the BBQ; both are effective. If you are using your oven, preheat it to 250 F; for the BBQ, set the grill to medium-high heat. In the oven, placing the peppers whole on a baking tray and bake until they are soft and blistered. The BBQ is the same process only you can place them directly on top of the grill. Once they have blistered, remove them and place into a bowl. Cover with plastic wrap for 15 to 20 minutes.
Once they have cooled, remove the skin from the peppers along with the seeds. It is important that after peeling the peppers you do not to wash them.

# Firenza

## Ingredients

*Serves: 1-2*
*Prep time: 5 minutes*
*Cook time: 7 minutes*
*Total time: 12 minutes*

*For best results a pizza stone is recommended.*

**1 pizza dough**

**1⁄2 cup grilled chicken, sliced**

**3⁄4 potato, sliced extremely thin**

**1⁄4 cup grilled eggplant, cut into 1⁄4-inch slices**

**2 tbsp pesto (view right column)**

**1 tomato, diced**

**pinch oregano**

**salt and pepper to taste**

## Directions

Preheat pizza stone in a 450-475 F oven for at least 45 minutes. Roll out dough and spread pesto evenly over the surface. Place sliced potato over pesto, being careful not to overlap slices. Add salt, pepper, oregano, chicken, eggplant and tomato. Bake pizza on stone until bottom is golden brown, approximately 6-8 minutes.

*Grazie is not just a restaurant, but an emotion. One that we hope reaches out to everyone who walks through the door. – Angelo Moretti*

# Pesto

*Yields 1 cup*
*Prep time: 10 minutes*
*Cook time: 0*

## Ingredients:

**1 1⁄2 cups fresh basil leaves**

**4 tbsp pine nuts, toasted**

**1 garlic clove**

**1⁄2 tsp salt**

**1⁄2 cup olive oil**

**1/3 cup Parmesan cheese**

## Directions:

Rinse, dry and coarsely chop basil. Place in a blender along with pine nuts, garlic and salt. While ingredients are blending, slowly drizzle in olive oil until mixture is a thick creamy paste. Add cheese and adjust seasonings if necessary.

Heineke

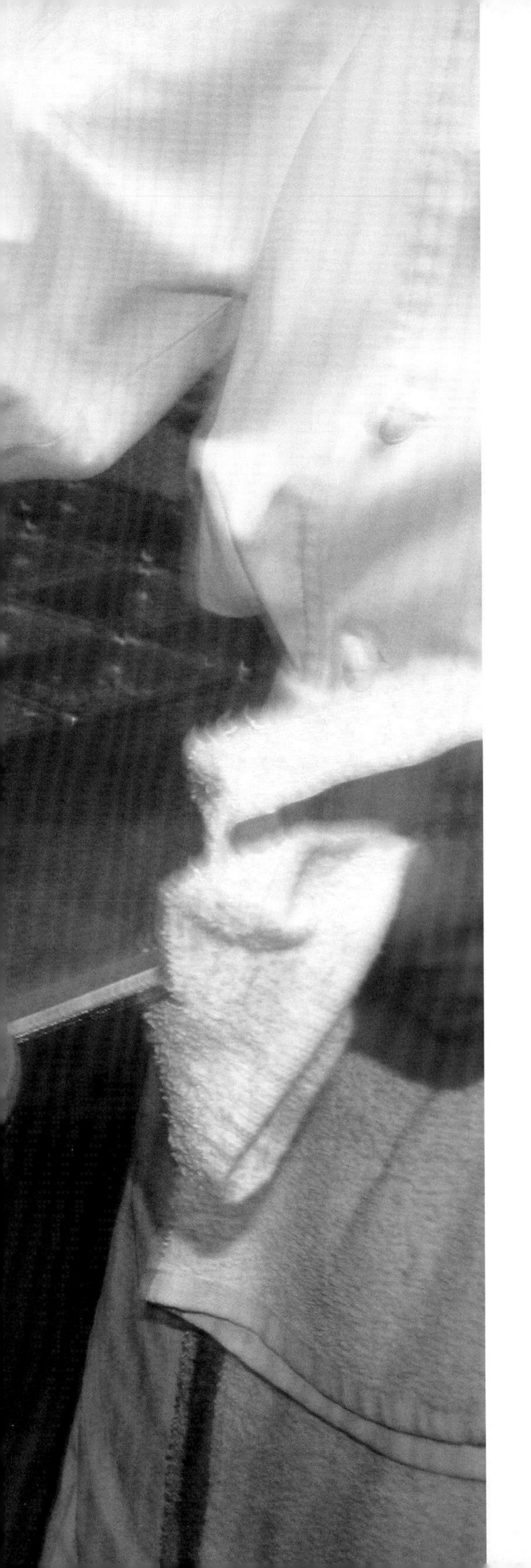

# Pasta

Termini
Nonna Franca
Penza
Torino
Catrina
Capri
Bianca
Milano

# Termini

## Ingredients

*Serves: 4*
*Prep time: 10 minutes*
*Cook time: 10 minutes*
*Total time: 20 minutes*

**3 cloves garlic,**

**8 parsley sprigs, chopped**

**4 tbsp extra-virgin olive oil**

**12 oz chicken stock**

**16 oz tomato sauce (refer to page107)**

**salt to taste**

**pepper to taste**

**500 g spaghetti**

## Directions

Begin by cooking spaghetti in boiling salted (1 tbsp) water to al dente.

To make the sauce, heat 3 tablespoons of olive oil in a large sauté pan over medium-high heat. Add garlic cloves and sauté until golden brown; do not allow the garlic to burn. Add parsley (be careful, it may splatter), then immediately add chicken stock and tomato sauce. Bring to a boil, reduce heat and let simmer. Season with salt and pepper and cook for 4-5 minutes. Add spaghetti, drizzle in 1 tablespoon of olive oil and cook for another 30 seconds, allowing the pasta to marry with the sauce.

## The Origin of the Tomato

Tomatoes are native to western South America. A yellow variety was taken to Spain by the conquistadors in the 16th century, making that country the first in the Old World to use them in cooking, stewing them with oil and seasoning. Italy soon followed suit, but elsewhere they were treated with suspicion.

The first red tomatoes arrived in Europe in the 18th century, brought to Italy by two Jesuit priests. But it wasn't until the 19th century that they were accepted in Northern Europe.

Today, along with onions, tomatoes are arguably the most important fresh ingredients used in Mediterranean cooking. They are an essential ingredient, along with garlic and olives, creating the basis of so many Italian, Spanish and Provençal recipes that it is hard to find any such dish that does not feature them.

There are more than 7,000 different varieties of tomatoes, with new hybrids becoming available all the time. The leaves of tomatoes are actually toxic, and if eaten can result in very bad stomach aches.

Source: Cooking Ingredients; by Christine Ingram

## Nonna Franca

This recipe, which originated in Palermo, Sicily, many geerations ago, was brought to *GRAZIE* by Mary Granicolo's grandmother. Joe took an instant liking to the powerful flavors that embodied this traditional Sicilian pasta. The hint of anchovy begs the recipe to remember the influence the sea has had on Sicilian cooking. It is balanced by the richness of raisins.

Thank you, Nonna Franca, for offering a recipe that has been in the family for generations and now has become a staple of the *GRAZIE* menu. Nonna Franca passed away in the summer of 2005 and will always be remembered as part of the *GRAZIE* tradition.

"Buon Appetito!"

# Nonna Franca

## Ingredients

*Serves: 4*
*Prep time: 10 minutes*
*Cook time: 10 minutes*
*Total time: 20 minutes*

**4 tbsp extra-virgin olive oil**

**3 garlic cloves, minced**

**4 anchovy fillets, chopped**

**1/2 tsp chili pepper flakes**

**1/2 cup parsley, chopped**

**1/2 cup toasted pine nuts**

**1/2 cup raisins**

**1/2 head broccoli, trimmed (flowers only)**

**1 cup chicken stock**

**20 oz tomato sauce (refer to p107)**

**1/4 cup toasted sesame seeds**

**1/4 cup toasted breadcrumbs**

**salt to taste**

**pepper to taste**

**500 g spaghetti**

## Directions

Using a large saucepan over medium heat, add olive oil and sauté garlic, anchovy fillets and chili flakes for a few minutes. Add parsley, pine nuts, raisins, salt and pepper and sauté for about a minute. Add broccoli and sauté for another minute. Add chicken stock and bring to a simmer, add tomato sauce and simmer for another five minutes. Add pasta and cook for another 30 seconds, allowing the pasta to marry with the sauce. Garnish with sesame seeds and breadcrumbs.immediately add vegetable stock and tomato sauce. Bring to a boil, then reduce heat and let simmer. Add seasonings and cook for 4-5 minutes. Add the spaghetti, drizzle in 1 tablespoon of olive oil and cook for another 30 seconds to 1 minute, allowing the paste to marry with the sauce.

# Penza

## Ingredients

*Serves: 4*
*Prep time: 10 minutes*
*Cook time: 10 minutes*
*Total time: 20 minutes*

**2 tbsp butter**

**1 medium onion, finely diced**

**5 oz pancetta, thinly sliced**

**3 oz vodka**

**8 oz 35% cream**

**16 oz tomato sauce (refer to p107)**

**pinch nutmeg**

**4 oz chicken stock**

**2 green onions chopped**

**salt to taste**

**pepper to taste**

**500 g rigatoni cooked aldente**

## Directions:

To make the sauce, add butter, onion and pancetta to a large saucepan over medium-high heat. Sauté until onions are translucent and pancetta begins to brown and crisp up.. Add chicken stock, tomato sauce and cream. Add vodka (being very cautious, the alcohol may create a flame). Bring sauce to a boil, simmer and add seasonings. Cook for 5-6 minutes and add green onions. Add pasta and cook for another minute or so, allowing the pasta to marry with the sauce.

*Penza is a city located 650 miles southeast of Moscow. It's a fitting name for a rigatoni a la vodka that has the overtones of strong man — and a feisty personality to match. The spicy combination of chili pepper and pancetta yields explosive results.*

*Prepare to enjoy one of the restaurant's signature dishes in the comfort of your own home.*

*A young chef in training.*

# Torino

## Ingredients

Serves: 4
Prep time: 5 minutes
Cook time: 10 minutes
Total time: 15 minutes

**2 tbsp butter**

**1 medium onion, finely diced**

**16 oz tomato sauce (refer to p107)**

**8 oz 35% cream**

**4 oz chicken stock**

**salt to taste**

**pepper to taste**

**pinch nutmeg**

**40 agnolotti**

## Directions:

Begin by cooking agnolotti in boiling salted (1 tbsp) water to al dente.

To make the sauce, add butter and onion to a large saucepan over medium heat and sauté until onions are translucent. Add chicken stock and tomato sauce and cook for 1 minute. Add cream. Bring to a simmer, add seasonings and cook for 4-5 minutes. Add agnolotti to sauce and cook for another 30 seconds, allowing the flavours to marry.

*Grazie has given me a lot over the years, but nothing more important than my beautiful wife and three wonderful children. Happy Anniversary Grazie!*

*Vito Brancatella*

## The Story of Karma

Before I started at GRAZIE, I used to manage restaurants for corporate companies, but I was never satisfied with what I was doing. Young and restless and needing a break from the 80-hour work week, I set about to find a summer job and a new direction. In 1996 I had a job interview just down the street from where GRAZIE is; not being a person to miss an opportunity, I dropped my resume off at the bar on the way to my car.

A month later, I received a call from Angelo at GRAZIE asking whether I would be able to come in for an interview. The thing was, I had dyed blue streaks into my hair a few days earlier. Knowing full well that I couldn't show up to an interview with blue hair, I went out and purchased some black spray paint normally used for Halloween. Just before my interview, I sprayed my hair black to appear a little less rebellious — but, of course, that didn't stop me from wearing six rings, three earrings and two gold chains as I headed for GRAZIE.

Angelo greeted me at the bar with a smile, and then we proceeded to a corner table near the window. I had a pretty impressive resume and felt very confident, but confidence is a funny thing. As we talked, the sun started beating down on me and I started to sweat, and the black colour I

# Catrina

## Ingredients

*Serves: 4*
*Prep time: 10 minutes*
*Cook time: 10 minutes*
*Total time: 20 minutes*

**3 cloves garlic, smashed**

**1 medium onion, diced**

**5 oz pancetta, thinly sliced**

**2 grilled chicken breasts, sliced**

**8 oz chicken stock**

**3 oz extra-virgin olive oil**

**1 tsp crushed black peppercorns**

**salt to taste**

**pinch chili flakes**

**8 sprigs parsley, chopped**

**500 g spinach linguini**

## Directions:

Begin by cooking linguini in boiling salted (1 tbsp) water to al dente.

To make the sauce, add olive oil and garlic to a large sauté pan over medium heat. Allow garlic to flavour oil for about 30 seconds, then add onion and pancetta. Once pancetta begins to crisp, add parsley and grilled chicken; allow chicken to warm through. Add chicken stock and seasonings and reduce heat to medium-low. Add linguini to sauce, cook for 30 seconds and finish with a drizzle of olive oil in the pan.

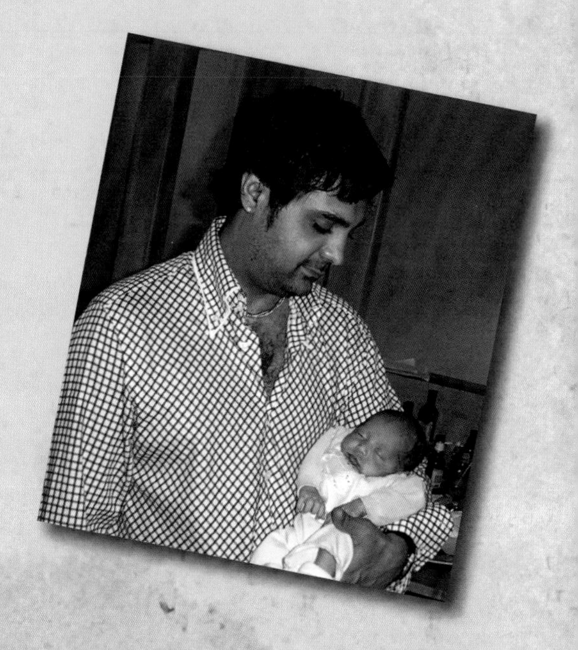

# Capri

## Ingredients

Serves: 4
Prep time: 10 minutes
Cook time: 10 minutes
Total time: 20 minutes

**4 cloves garlic, smashed**
**1 cup clams**
**12 shrimp, peeled**
**1/2 tsp chili flakes**
**5 oz shrimp stock**
**3 oz dry white wine**
**4 sprigs parsley, chopped**
**1 medium tomato, diced**
**5 tbsp extra-virgin olive oil**
**salt to taste**
**pepper to taste**
**500 g linguini**

## Directions

Begin by cooking spaghetti in boiling salted (1 tbsp) water to al dente.

To make the sauce, add olive oil and smashed garlic to a large pan over medium-high heat and sauté until garlic is golden brown. Add parsley, shrimp and clams and cook for 1-2 minutes. Add fennel seeds and seasonings. Once shrimp have changed colour to a light pink, add white wine and shrimp stock. Reduce liquid slightly. Add diced tomato, then spaghetti just seconds later. Cook pasta with sauce for 30 seconds and finish with a drizzle of olive oil in the pan.

had put in my hair started to drip down my forehead. As I sat there, I suddenly remembered the label on the bottle: "Do not spray on wet hair." Just when you think you've got it all figured out, you forget to follow the directions.
I'm sure Angelo saw the dye and was just being polite by not mentioning it. When I left GRAZIE that day I was positive I hadn't gotten the job, but obviously that wasn't the case. I started in May of 1996.

My summer job ended up lasting eight years. More importantly, I made a great deal of new friends and a new family. I travelled to Barbados, Trinidad and Africa with Robbie, threw countless parties with the guys and even opened and closed a business. Best of all, I met my wife at GRAZIE.
We now have two-year-old twins; Angelo and and his wife are the godparents of my son. I wear only one ring, no earrings and no gold chains. I manage the food and beverage department at a golf and country club and own my own home. The only parties I throw are for my children's birthdays.
When I look back on my time at GRAZIE, it's as though I went into the restaurant a boy and came out a man.

I just want to wish GRAZIE a Happy 15th Anniversary!

Amir Karmali

# Bianca

## Ingredients

Serves: 4
Prep time: 10 minutes
Cook time: 10 minutes
Total time: 20 minutes

**3 tbsp butter**

**3 tbsp onion, finely diced**

**10 oz chicken stock**

**12 oz 35% cream**

**3 tbsp Parmesan cheese, grated**

**500 g fettuccine cooked aldente**

**salt to taste**

**pepper to taste**

## Directions

Begin by cooking fettuccini in boiling salted (1 tbsp) water to al dente.

To make the sauce, add butter and onion to a large sauté pan over medium heat and cook for 1-2 minutes. Add chicken stock, cream and seasonings. Allow sauce to reduce slightly. Add Parmesan cheese and cook for another minute or so. Add fettuccine to sauce and cook for another 30 seconds, allowing all the flavours to come together.

# Milano

## Ingredients

*Serves: 4*
*Prep time: 10 minutes*
*Cook time: 10 minutes*
*Total time: 20 minutes*

**3 tbsp butter**
**1 medium onion, diced**
**2 grilled chicken breasts, sliced**
**5 oz sun-dried tomatoes, coarsely chopped**
**10 oz 35% cream**
**10 oz chicken stock**
**1 cup snow peas, julienned**
**salt to taste**
**pepper to taste**
**500 g linguini**

## Directions

Begin by cooking linguini in boiling salted (1 tbsp) water to al dente.

To make the sauce, add butter and onion to a large sauté pan over medium-high heat and cook for 1-2 minutes. Add grilled chicken and sun-dried tomatoes and sauté for 1-2 minutes. Add chicken stock, cream, salt and pepper, reducing sauce slightly. Add snow peas, then linguini just seconds later. Allow linguini to cook with sauce for 30 seconds and enjoy.

*Get ready to enjoy one of the restaurant's signature dishes in the comfort of your own home.*

WARNING

# Entrees

Linguini di Mare

Ossobucco with Mushroom Risotto

Veal Chop Milanese

Toasted Sesame Tuna

Baccala with Tomato and Olives

Braised Halibut

Grilled Swordfish

Monkfish

Grilled Tenderloin

Roasted Rack of Lamb

Duck Leg Confit

Rabbit Cacciatore

# Linguini di Mare

## Ingredients

*Serves: 4*
*Prep time: 10 minutes*
*Cook time: 15 minutes*
*Total time: 25 minutes*

**31/2 lbs fresh mussels**
**2 grouper fillets, cut into small pieces**
**1lb calamari, fresh**
**3/4 lbs shrimp, peeled**
**3 cloves garlic, smashed**
**1 Spanish onion, diced**
**1/2 cup dry white wine**
**2 large cans plum tomatoes, chopped**
**4 tbsp extra-virgin olive oil**
**4 sprigs parsley, coarsely chopped**
**chili flakes to taste**
**salt to taste**
**pepper to taste**
**500 g linguini**

## Directions:

Place 2 tablespoons of olive oil and onion in a large sauté pan and cook over medium-high heat until onions begin to sweat. Add garlic, salt, pepper and chili flakes and stir for about 1 minute. (It is important to make sure none of the ingredients start to burn.) Add calamari and sauté for about 1 minute, then add white wine. Add chopped tomatoes, bring mixture to a boil and decrease heat to medium. Simmer for 2-3 minutes. Add mussels, cover with a lid and cook until they open, approximately 3 minutes. Place shrimp and grouper in pan, partially cover with lid and continue to simmer for 3-4 minutes.

Bring a large pot of salted (1 tbsp) water to boil. Add pasta. The average cooking time for dried linguini is 8-10 minutes; fresh linguini takes about 5-6 minutes. When the pasta is ready remove from heat and strain.

Before linguini is cooked, ladle a few cups of sauce into a large sauté pan, without any fish. Bring to a boil (it may be watery, so you want to reduce the sauce to a thicker consistency). Once the sauce is ready, add strained pasta to the pan along with coarsely chopped parsley and 2 tablespoons olive oil. Stir the pasta and sauce together. Plate and serve.

When plating the dish you have a couple of options. The simplest is to serve the pasta separate from the fish. Putting the seafood into a large serving bowl and placing the bowl in the middle of the table allows the meal to be an interactive experience — and it offers your guest the ability to take as much or as little as they want. The alternative is to combine the pasta with the fish and plate them together.

# Ossobucco
## with Mushroom Risotto

### Ingredients

6 cuts veal shanks, (approx. 2 inches thick)

1/2 cup flour

2 tbsp extra-virgin olive oil

1/2 cup onion, diced

1/4 cup carrot, diced

1/4 cup celery, diced

1 garlic clove, finely chopped

2 tbsp tomato paste

2 oz dry white wine

1 litre beef stock

6 sprigs parsley

5 sprigs thyme

5 garlic cloves, whole

6 sprigs rosemary

salt to taste

pepper to taste

### Ingredients
### For Risotto

2 tbsp butter

1 tbsp extra-virgin olive oil

1 medium onion, finely chopped

2 cups Arborio rice

2 garlic cloves, finely chopped

1 litre chicken stock

2 tbsp Parmesan cheese

1/2 cup variety of mushrooms, including porcini

salt to taste

pepper to taste

*Serves: 6*

*Prep time: 10 minutes*

*Cook time: 2 hours*

*Total time: 2 hours 10 minutes*

*Serves: 6*

*Prep time: 5 minutes*

*Cook time: 25 minutes*

*Total time: 35 minutes*

## Directions: Ossobucco

Season veal shanks with salt and pepper, then lightly coat meat in flour. In a large saucepot, heat oil over medium-high heat, then sear veal to a deep brown color. Remove shanks from the saucepot, place them on a plate and set aside. To the same saucepot add onions and cook to a golden brown. Add carrots, celery and garlic, cook for a few minutes, then add tomato paste, cook for 1 minute. Then add white wine and deglaze (dissolving with white wine the small amounts of flavour-rich brown food particles attached from the bottom of the pan). Return veal shanks to pot, along with juices left on plate. Pour heated beef stock into the pot (enough to cover about 2/3 of the veal shanks). Reduce heat to medium-low, a gentle simmer, and add parsley, rosemary, thyme and garlic. Cover pot and place it in the oven at 350 F for approximately 1 1/2 hours.

You will know the shanks are ready when the meat is tender and almost falling off the bone. Remove veal from oven and transfer to a large roasting pan along with the sauce. Reduce the oven to 200 F and bake for another 10 minutes, allowing the sauce to reduce.

Remove from oven and serve with mushroom risotto.

## Directions: Risotto

Add 1 tablespoon butter and olive oil to a large saucepot over medium heat. Add onion, garlic, a pinch of salt and pepper and sauté until onion is translucent. Add arborio rice and sauté until rice is well coated with butter and oil.

Using a 6-oz ladle, pour 1 scoop of stock into the pot and stir until risotto absorbs the liquid. Continue this process, 1 ladle at a time, until you have added the litre of stock. The rice will become creamy as it absorbs the liquid. When you notice that you only have about a 1/4 litre of stock left, add the mushrooms. Remember, a risotto must be stirred continuously throughout the process; otherwise the rice will stick together and burn. Once the risotto is cooked, remove from heat and stir in remaining butter and grated Parmesan cheese.

# Veal Chop Milanese

*Serves: 4*
*Prep time: 12 minutes*
*Cook time: 8 minutes*
*Total time: 20 minutess*

## Ingredients

**4 10-oz veal chops**

**3 eggs**

**1 tbsp 2% milk**

**1 cup bread crumbs**

**1 cup all-purpose flour**

**1/2 tsp dried basil**

**1/2 tsp dried thyme**

**1/2 tsp dried oregano**

**1 1/2 cups vegetable oil**

**1/4 cup parmesan cheese**

**1 lemon, cut into wedges**

**salt to taste**

**pepper taste**

## Directions:

For the veal chops, pound them out with a mallet until they are 1/2 inch thick.

For breading the veal pounded veal chops, in a shallow dish, beat eggs, milk, parmesan cheese and season with salt and pepper. Pour flour into another shallow dish. Mix together the bread crumbs, basil, oregano and thyme in a third shallow dish. Refer to page 18 for the breading technique.

In a large skillet with high sides, heat the oil to 375 F. Carefully place 2 pieces of breaded veal in the hot oil at a time and fry until golden brown on both sides, about 6 to 8 minutes total. Serve with lemon wedges.

# Toasted Sesame Tuna

## Ingredients

### Tuna

**4 8-oz tuna steaks**

**8 green onions, whole**

**3 tbsp toasted sesame seeds**

**1 garlic clove, chopped**

**3 tbsp soy sauce**

**1 tbsp olive oil**

**pepper to taste**

### Sushi Rice

**2 cups Japanese short-grain rice**

**3 tbsp rice wine vinegar**

**1 tsp white sugar**

**Pinch salt**

### Sauce

**1/4 cup soy sauce**

**1 1/4 cup water**

**1/4 cup white sugar**

**1 tsp ginger**

**1 garlic clove**

**4 green onion tops**

**1/2 tbsp cornstarch**

**1/4 cup rice wine vinegar**

**1 dry red chili, finely chopped**

*Serves: 4*

*Prep time: 10 minutes*

*Cook time: 20 minutes*

*Total time: 30 minutes*

## Directions: Tuna

In a mixing bowl combine olive oil, 2 tablespoons soy sauce, garlic and pepper. Allow to sit in the fridge for 15 minutes. Rub tuna steaks in soy/garlic mixture and marinate for 5 minutes at room temperature. In a large sauté pan over high heat, sear tuna for 1 1/2 -2 minutes on either side, tuna is best cooked rare.
Have toasted sesame seeds ready in a small plate (to toast seeds, place them in a small sauté pan and cook over a low heat until they reach a light golden colour). Once tuna is cooked, place one side in the toasted seeds and slice on a bias or leave whole.

For the Green Onions, place whole green onions in a large piece of foil along with 2 tablespoons water and 1 tablespoon soy sauce. Wrap foil tightly and broil for 4-5 minutes.

## Directions: For the Green Onions

Place whole green onions in a large piece of foil along with 2 tablespoons of water and 1 tablespoon of soy. Wrap foil tightly and broil for 4-5 minutes..

## Directions: Sushi Rice

Wash the rice in several changes of cold water. When cooking the rice, cover the rice with water (have 1 inch of water above the rice) and bring to a boil cook until all the water has been absorbed. Place the rice into a wooden bowl (if you do not have a wooden bowl any serving bowl will do) then add sugar, vinegar and salt. Once mixed, it is ready to be served.

## Directions: Sauce

Combine soy sauce, 1 cup water, sugar, ginger, garlic, onion, rice wine vinegar and chili in a saucepot and bring to a boil. Immediately bring down the temperature to a gentle simmer for 10-15 minutes. In a small bowl mix together cornstarch and a 1/4 cup water. When the sauce is cooked, add the cornstarch mixture and bring to a boil. Remove from heat, strain and set aside until ready to use.

When plating, place tuna steaks on plate alongside sushi rice and broiled green onions. Pour sauce over tuna.

# Baccala
## with Tomato and Olives

### Ingredients

*Serves: 4*
*Prep time: 10 minutes*
*Cook time: 30 minutes*
*Total time: 40 minutes*

**1 1/2 lbs of 6-oz cod fillets**

**1/2 large onion, chopped**

**3 cloves garlic, smashed**

**6 tbsp extra-virgin olive oil**

**2 tbsp capers**

**1/2 cup Gaeta olives**

**1 fennel bulb, quartered, cored and sliced**

**1 19-oz can plum tomatoes**

**1 cup dry white wine**

**1/2 cup shrimp stock, heated**

**1/3 cup flour**

**pinch dry oregano and thyme**

**salt to taste**

**pepper to taste**

### Directions:

Lightly coat the baccala (cod) with flour. In a cast-iron or heavy-gauge skillet over medium-high heat add 4 tablespoons of olive oil and brown the baccala on both sides. Remove fish from the heat. In another saucepan, sauté garlic, onion and remaining olive oil for 2 minutes. Add capers, olives and fennel, cook for couple of minutes more and add tomatoes, white wine, stock and seasonings. Cook for 8 minutes, then place cooked fish on top of vegetable mixture and place skillet in 400 F oven. Bake for 15 minutes and enjoy.

*A picture of calm and consistency and a driving force behind Grazie's longevity, managing the highwire between success and failure with his affable smile. - Marco Puntillo*

# Braised Halibut
## in a Grappa Miso Sauce

*Serves: 4*

*Prep time: 15 minutes*

*Cook time: 20 minutes*

*Total time: 35 minutes*

### Ingredients

**4 7-oz halibut fillets, skin on**

**12 oz taro root, diced into 1/2-inch cubes**

**1 tbsp extra-virgin olive oil**

**1 cup onion, diced**

**1 tbsp ginger, minced**

**2 tbsp Dijon mustard**

**1/2 cup miso**

**1/4 cup rice wine vinegar**

**3 1/2 cups water**

**2 oz grappa**

**1/4 cup white sugar**

**24 fresh mussels, with shell**

**12 pieces baby bok choy**

**1 cup carrot, julienned**

**5 tbsp green onions, sliced**

### Directions:

Whisk together Dijon mustard, miso, rice wine vinegar and water in a medium-size mixing bowl. Add grappa and sugar and mix until smooth. Heat 1 tablespoon olive oil in a large saucepan over high heat. Add taro root, ginger and diced onion and cook for 2 minutes. Pour Dijon and miso mixture into saucepan. Bring to a boil and immediately reduce heat to medium-low, allowing the sauce to simmer for 3-4 minutes. Place halibut skin-side down in saucepan and cover with lid. After 5 minutes lift the lid and add mussels, baby bok choy, and carrots. Place lid back on and braise for another 3-4 minutes. Remove from heat add the green onions, just allowing them to warm through and serve.

# Grilled Swordfish
## with Mango Salsa

*Serves: 4*

*Prep time: 10 minutes*

*Cook time: 30 minutes*

*Total time: 40 minutes*

### Ingredients

**4 swordfish steaks, 8 oz each**

**2 tbsp extra-virgin olive oil**

**2 garlic cloves, minced**

**1 tsp salt**

**1 tsp pepper**

### Mango Pepper Salsa

**1 red pepper, diced**

**1 mango, diced**

**2 shallots, finely chopped**

**1/2 small red onion, diced**

**1 jalapeno pepper, seeded and diced**

**2 limes, juiced**

**1/4 cup coriander, chopped**

**2 tbsp extra-virgin olive oil**

**3 sprigs parsley, coarsely chopped**

**salt to taste**

**pepper to taste**

### Directions: Swordfish

Wash and clean swordfish. Combine garlic and olive oil together in a small bowl, then rub it over the fish and allow to sit at room temperature for 5-10 minutes. Season with salt and pepper, don't be shy with seasoning and then immediately place fish on a hot grill (medium-high heat). Cook for 2 minutes, turn steaks 90 degrees, to create diamond marks, cook for another 2 minutes then turn over for2 minutes more (if needed turn 90 degrees for another 2 minutes). The steaks should be cooked to medium any more and the fish will become dry.

### Directions: Salsa

Combine red pepper, mango and shallots in a mixing bowl. Add red onion and jalapeno, and squeeze in the lime juice. Stirring ingredients together, add coriander, parsley, salt and pepper. Drizzle olive oil over the salsa and mix everything together. Set in the refrigerator and allow too sit for at least 30 minutes.

*Option: substitute swordfish with Marlin, Tuna or Mahi-Mahi*

# Monkfish

## Wrapped in Prosciutto and Potato with Warm Lentil Salad

*Serves: 4*

*Prep time: 10 minutes*

*Cook time: 25 minutes*

*Total time: 35 minutes*

### Ingredients

**Monk Fish**

**4 8-oz monkfish fillets**

**8 slices prosciutto, thinly sliced**

**2 tbsp extra-virgin olive oil**

**2 sprigs rosemary**

**5 oz water**

**1 lemon, zested**

**3 oz honey**

**1 Yukon Gold potato, sliced extremely thin**

**Lentil Salad**

**3 cups dried lentils**

**1 medium onion, coarsely chopped**

**2 cloves garlic (1 whole, 1 minced)**

**1 bay leaf**

**1 sprig thyme**

**1 shallot, diced**

**2 sprigs rosemary**

**2 tbsp butter**

**salt and pepper to taste**

**1 1/4 cups strong shrimp stock**

**3 cups water**

### Directions: Monk Fish

Bring water and honey to a simmer in a small saucepot over low heat. You want to thin the consistency of the honey just a bit, so that you will be able to coat the monkfish evenly. Add lemon zest and rosemary sprigs, stirring for 30 seconds. Remove glaze from the heat and allow to cool. Brush glaze on monkfish, which has rested at room temperature for 10-15 minutes. Wrap prosciutto slices around fish, making sure to go all the way around. Finally, wrap potato slices around prosciutto (the moisture in the potato will make it stick).

Brush potato slices with olive oil and sear wrapped fish in a saucepan over medium-high heat until potato is brown. Remove pan from stove and place in a preheated oven at 375 F for 6-8 minutes, depending on the thickness of the fish. Remove from oven and let sit for a few minutes before serving.

### Directions: Lentil Salad

Place lentils in a saucepot with water, onion, 1 whole garlic clove, bay leaf and thyme. Bring to a boil and cook until lentils are tender, approximately 10-15 minutes. Remove from heat and strain.

In a sauté pan combine butter, shallots and 1 garlic clove minced. Cook for 2 minutes, then add rosemary, salt, pepper and shrimp stock. Reduce liquid by half. Add cooked lentils and let them absorb the flavours. Serve once liquid has dissipated.

# Grilled Tenderloin
## in a Caramelized Shallot and Thyme Sauce

*Serves: 4*
*Prep time: 10 minutes*
*Cook time: 20 minutes*
*Total time: 30 minutes*

## Ingredients
### Tenderloin

**4 beef tenderloins, 8-10 oz each**
**2 tsp coarse sea salt**
**1 tbsp fresh black pepper corns, cracked**
**3 tbsp olive oil**
**2 garlic cloves, minced**
**3 sprigs thyme, chopped**

### Mashed Potatoes

**6 Yukon Gold potatoes, peeled**
**1/2 cup Parmesan cheese, grated**
**3 tbsp butter**
**1/3 cup 35% cream**
**1/3 cup chicken stock, heated**
**hint of nutmeg**
**salt and pepper to taste**

### Caramelized Shallots

**8 shallots, whole**
**1/3 cup sugar**
**1/3 cup red wine vinegar**
**1/2 tsp salt**

### Thyme Sauce

**8 caramelized shallots**
**3 tbsp butter**
**2 oz dried porcini mushrooms, soaked and drained**
**1 cup dry red wine**
**3/4 cup strong beef stock, heated**
**2 shallots, diced**
**1 garlic clove, minced**
**6 sprigs thyme, stalk and leaves, chopped**
**5 sprigs thyme, leaves only, chopped**
**salt to taste**
**pepper to taste**

## Directions: Grilling

Marinate meat for 1 hour in oil, garlic and thyme. Bring tenderloin to room temperature and preheat grill to 400 F. Five minutes before grilling season meat with salt and pepper. Place meat on grill, cook about 3 minutes, then turn 90 degrees (to get cross-hatching) and cook for another 3 minutes. When you notice blood rising to the surface it's time to flip. Repeat turning process. The average steak, depending on size, takes about 8-10 minutes to cook. The meat should be cooked to medium rare.

## Directions: Potatoes

Boil peeled potatoes in salted water until fork-tender. Drain and begin to mash while adding heated stock and cream (do not add all the liquid at once; judge the consistency to your liking). Add salt, pepper, nutmeg and butter. Check the consistency and add more or all of the liquid. Add the Parmesan cheese and combine well.

## Directions: Caramelized Shallots

Put sugar in a heavy-based saucepan and cook over low heat. It is important that you do not stir the sugar. Watch carefully: When it begins to smoke, a thin foam shows on the surface, followed by a thicker one. At this point add the vinegar and allow sugar and liquid to combine. Add shallots and salt and continue to cook at low heat. Simmer for 15-20 minutes or until shallots are soft and sauce is syrupy. For added flavour, combine caramelized sauce with thyme sauce.

## Directions: Sauce

In a large saucepan over medium heat add 1 tablespoon butter, diced shallots, mushroom, garlic, salt and pepper and sauté for 2-3 minutes. Add red wine and reduce by two-thirds. Add 6 thyme sprigs (stalks and leaves) and beef stock. Reduce by half and strain through a fine meshed strainer lined with cheesecloth. Place sauce in a saucepot and check consistency. If the sauce is thin continue to reduce until it is a light syrup. Add caramelized shallots and warm through. Stir in thyme leaves and 2 tablespoons butter. Serve immediately; do not allow sauce to boil.

# Roasted Rack of Lamb
## with Minted Eggplant

### Ingredients

**2 racks of lamb, 4 bones per person**

**1 lb new potatoes, whole**

**5 tbsp parsley, finely chopped**

**1 tbsp chives, finely chopped**

**1 large eggplant, grilled and sliced**

**2 tbsp fresh mint, chopped**

**1/2 tsp dry oregano**

**1/2 shallot, chopped**

**1 tbsp butter**

**1 garlic clove, minced**

**6 tbsp extra-virgin olive oil**

**salt and pepper to taste**

### Directions:

*Serves: 4*
*Prep time: 15 minutes*
*Cook time: 30 minutes*
*Total time: 45 minutes*

Preheat your oven to 450 F. Season lamb with salt and freshly ground pepper. Sear seasoned rack in a large sauté pan, fat-side down, for 2-3 minutes over medium-high heat. Flip lamb over and finish in oven for 15-18 minutes (it should be cooked to medium-rare). Remove from oven and let rest for 3-4 minutes.

While the lamb is in the oven, place potatoes in a pot of cold salted (1 tbsp) water and bring to a boil. Reduce to a simmer and cook until potatoes are fork tender. Drain the water and let potatoes cool. Slice potatoes in half and place them in a mixing bowl. Drizzle 2 tablespoons olive oil over potatoes and add salt and pepper to taste. Mix gently with hands, then place potatoes cut-side down on a baking sheet lined with parchment paper. Bake in oven 10 minutes or until light golden brown.

Remove from pan and toss in a large mixing bowl with garlic, 3 tablespoons of parsley, chives, butter and 1 tablespoon of olive oil. Plate and serve alongside the lamb.

### Directions: Minted Eggplant

Place sliced and grilled eggplant in a mixing bowl with mint, oregano, shallots, 2 tablespoons of parsley and 3 tablespoons extra-virgin olive oil. Serve along side the lamb.

# Duck Leg Confit
## with Ginger Blueberry Sauce

### Ingredients

**Duck**

**4 duck legs**

**3/4 cup salt**

**1/2 cup black pepper**

**1/2 cup white sugar**

**4 potato discs, 1/2-inch thick, steamed**

**3 cups duck fat (purchase from local butcher or specialty store)**

**Ginger and Blueberry Sauce**

**2 tbsp butter**

**1 tbsp extra-virgin olive oil**

**3 shallots, chopped**

**1/4 cup leek tops, chopped**

**3 garlic cloves, sliced**

**1 2-inch piece ginger, sliced**

**2 tbsp honey**

**1/4 cup red wine vinegar**

**3 cups duck stock or chicken and veal stock combined**

**1 cup fresh blueberries**

### Directions: Duck

Coat duck evenly and generously with sugar, salt and pepper. Place on a perforated pan, cover with plastic wrap and refrigerate for 36 hours. After the duck has been cured remove from fridge, rinse off and pat dry.

In a roasting pan submerge duck in duck fat, then place it in a 180 F oven for 21/2-3 hours. It is important that the fat never boils. Once the duck is cooked allow too cool at room temperature in fat. (At this point, if you chose to double the recipe, transfer the extra duck to a clean container with the duck fat and freeze).
To crisp the duck, place steamed potato discs and 4 tablespoons duck fat at the bottom of a cast-iron skillet. Put each leg on a potato disc, not allowing the duck to touch the pan, and cook for 10 minutes at 450 F.

### Directions: Blueberry Sauce

Combine 1 tablespoon butter, olive oil, shallots, leek tops, ginger and garlic in a medium-sized saucepot over medium heat and cook for 4-5 minutes. Once shallots and leeks are soft, add honey and red wine vinegar. Cook for 2-3 minutes, then add stock and bring to a simmer. Add 1/3 cup blueberries. Reduce sauce to approximately 1 cup, then strain through a fine meshed strainer lined with cheesecloth. Place sauce in a saucepan over medium-high heat and whisk in 1 tablespoon butter. When butter has melted add remaining blueberries and cook for 10-15 seconds. Use jus immediately.

*Serves: 4*

*Prep time: 25 minutes*

*Cook time: 21/2 -3 hours*

*Total time: 3-31/2 hours (there are many steps involved, this recipe requires a couple of days)*

*This recipe requires an ample amount of time.*
*You can double the recipe, freeze the extra and use it at a later date*

# Rabbit Cacciatore

*Serves: 4*

*Prep time: 25 minutes*

*Cook time: 1 hr 15 min*

*Total time: 1 hr 40 min*

## Ingredients

### Rabbit

**2 rabbits, cut into pieces and trimmed**

**3 tbsp extra-virgin olive oil**

**1 large onion, diced**

**1 garlic clove, minced**

**1/2 cup tomato concasse (peeled, seeded and diced tomatoes)**

**1 cup button mushrooms, sliced**

**1/4 cup dried porcini mushrooms, soaked and drained**

**3 oz dry white wine**

**2 oz all-purpose flour**

**1 tbsp lemon zest, grated**

**2 cups chicken stock, heated**

**1 tbsp tarragon, chopped**

**1 tbsp parsley, chopped**

**1 tbsp thyme, chopped**

**salt and pepper to taste**

### Polenta

**6 1/2 cups water**

**1 tbsp salt**

**2 1/2 cups cornmeal**

## Directions: Rabbit

Blot rabbit pieces dry and season with salt and pepper.

Heat oil in a large casserole dish. Place rabbit carefully in oil and sear to a light brown on all sides. Remove to a separate pan. Add onions to original casserole dish and cook for 3-4 minutes or until golden brown. Add garlic and cook for 1 minute. Add tomatoes and mushrooms and sauté for a couple minutes more.

Add wine, stirring to release all the drippings, and reduce by nearly half. Add flour and stir well to make a roux. Cook roux, stirring frequently, for 3-4 minutes. Whisk in stock to make a smooth sauce. Return rabbit and any juices that may have been released.

Bring to a gentle simmer over medium-low heat. Cover pot and continue to braise in a 350 C oven. Braise for 45 minutes or until rabbit is fork tender. Remove rabbit and keep warm while finishing sauce.

Return braising liquid to a simmer on stovetop and reduce until the sauce has a good flavour and consistency. Skim thoroughly to degrease. Add lemon zest and herbs and adjust the seasoning with salt and pepper.

Serve rabbit on heated plates with the sauce.

## Directions: Polenta

Bring the water to the boil in a large heavy saucepan and add the salt. Reduce the heat to a simmer and begin to add the cornmeal slowly. Stir constantly with a whisk until the polenta has all been incorporated.

Switch to a long-handled wooden spoon and continue to stir the polenta over low to moderate heat until it is a thick mass and pulls away from the sides of the pan. This may take 20-45 minutes, depending on the cornmeal used. For best results, never stop stirring the polenta until you remove it from the heat.

Here's a photo of GRAZIE'S two biggest supporters over the last 15 years.
Mille GRAZIE, your son Joseph Brancatella

# La Signora

Tomato Sauce
Polpetini and Meatballs
Stuffed Roasted Peppers
Breaded Involtini

1
2
4
5
6
7

# Tomato Sauce
## a.k.a. "Sunday Sauce"

This method of slow cooking will allow all the flavours in your pan to come alive, giving you that authentic feeling of being in Mama's kitchen.

*Serves 4*
*Prep time: 5 minutes*
*Cook time: 50 minutes*
*Total Time: 55 minutes*

## Ingredients:

**3 tbsp extra-virgin olive oil**

**1/2 large onion, diced**

**2 garlic cloves, diced**

**1 large can whole, peeled plum tomatoes, crushed by hand**

**1 tbsp basil, chopped**

**5 sprigs fresh parsley, chopped**

**1 Bay leaf**

**salt to taste**

**pepper to taste**

## Directions:

Add oil, chopped onions and garlic to a large saucepot over medium-high heat and sauté until golden brown. Add tomatoes and juice from the can. Add a few pinches of salt and pepper to taste, then freshly chopped basil and parsley. Simmer for 45 minutes, taste and adjust for seasoning.

La Signora's

# Polpetini and Meatballs

## Ingredients

**1 lb mincemeat (1/2 pound minced pork and 1/2 pound minced veal)**

**1 large garlic clove, finely chopped**

**1 tsp salt**

**2 eggs**

**1 tbsp parsley, finely diced**

**1 cup Parmesan cheese, grated**

**1 cup fine bread crumbs**

**1 tsp basil, finely diced**

**2 cups tomato sauce**

**1 cup vegetable oil**

*Serves 4*

*Prep time: 15-20 minutes*

*Cook time: 15-20 minutes*

*Total Time: 40 minutes*

## Directions: Polpetini

Place minced meat in a large mixing bowl. Add garlic and salt. Add eggs, parsley, basil and Parmesan cheese, then the bread crumbs. Finally, add cooled Sunday Sauce to the mix. Mix until the consistency is even. (Don't be afraid to get your hands dirty.)

Roll meat mixture into tiny balls (keep one hand flat and move the other counter-clockwise). They should be about the size of large marbles. Continue process until you have desired amount of polpetini.

Heat vegetable oil in a deep frying pan over high heat (enough to cover the polpetini). Never use olive oil when deep frying; the oil will burn long before you ever get it to the heat you require. Test oil by placing 1 polpetini in the pan. Once it beings to sizzle, the oil is ready. Place polpetini in pan and cook until they are golden brown, about 5 minutes. Use a slotted spoon to remove balls. Pat excess oil off with a paper towel and place polpetini in a bowl. Once all of them are fried, place them in simmering tomato sauce and cook for another 10 minutes.

***What's the difference between polpetini and meatballs?***

The answer is simple, size. Polpetini are smaller versions of their cousin the meatball. They get to have a lot more fun on a plate of spaghetti, swimming around in the tomato sauce. The meatball usually gets taken out of the sauce before the spaghetti even gets near it, placed on a separate plate to be eaten after the pasta has been finished.

## Directions: Meatballs

Roll about 2 tablespoons of meat mixture into a ball (about the size of a golf ball). Meatballs do not need to be fried. Put them in with the Sunday Sauce as it is being prepared; they will cook with the sauce, in about 45 minutes.

# Stuffed Roasted Peppers

## Ingredients:

*Serves 4*

*Prep time: 15 minutes*

*Cook time: 45 minutes*

*Total Time: 1 hour*

**2 whole red peppers**

**1/2 clove garlic, minced**

**1 egg**

**1 1/2 cups arborio rice, cooked**

**1/4 cup Parmesan cheese**

**1 cup minced veal and pork**

**2 tbsp tomato sauce**

**2 tbsp extra-virgin olive oil**

## Directions:

Cut peppers in half and remove seeds. In a large bowl mix together garlic, egg, rice, Parmesan cheese, minced veal and pork and tomato sauce. Stuff halved peppers with the mixture. Heat 2 tablespoons oil in a large sauté pan over medium-high heat. Sear the peppers, stuffed-side down, in the oil for about 30 seconds to 1 minute. Turn peppers over, cook for another 1-2 minutes, then cover pan with foil and place it in a 350 F oven. Bake for 40-45 minutes.

# Breaded Involtini

## Ingredients:

*Serves 6-8*

*Prep time: 20 minutes*

*Cook time: 10 minutes*

*Total Time: 30 minutes*

**2 lbs veal cutlets, thinly sliced**

**1 clove garlic, thinly sliced**

**4 tbsp Parmesan cheese**

**1/2 lbs spinach, sautéed**

**3 oz mozzarella cheese, sliced**

**1/4 cup parsley, chopped**

**1/4 cup basil, chopped**

**4 tbsp vegetable oil**

**salt to taste**

## Directions:

Place meat between two layers of plastic wrap and pound to an even thickness. Spread garlic slices evenly among the cutlets, keeping them close to the middle of the veal. Place 1 slice of mozzarella on top of the garlic, then put 1 tablespoon of Parmesan cheese on top of the mozzarella. Roll up the meat, trying to keep all ingredients in one spot. Grab one side and fold it over, tucking one side under and leaving room for stuffing. Fill pocket with spinach, parsley, basil and a pinch of salt. Do not overfill. Fold in open end to create a seal.

Once the meat has been folded, it is time for the breading.

To cook, heat oil in a large sauté pan over medium-high heat. Cook involtini on all sides until golden brown. Remove with slotted spoon, straining excess oil, and pat dry with a paper towel.

# Dolci / Desserts

Tiramisu with a Twist
Panna Cotta
Lemon Tart
Grilled Peaches
Biscotti *GRAZIE*

# Tiramisu with a Twist

Tiramisu like you've never tasted.

*Serves 6-8*

*Prep time: 3-4 hours*

*Cook time: 0 minutes*

## Ingredients

**2 cups mascarpone cheese**

**2 cups 35% whipping cream**

**4 egg yolks**

**5 tbsp white sugar**

**3 oz amaretto liqueur**

**3 oz Kahlua liqueur**

**6 oz espresso coffee**

**24-32 savoyardi (lady finger biscuits)**

## Directions:

In a large bowl, mix egg yolks with sugar. Add mascarpone cheese. In a separate bowl whip 35% cream until soft peaks form. Fold whipped cream into cheese and egg mixture. Spoon mixture into martini glasses and allow to set in the refrigerator for 3-4 hours.

In a medium bowl combine espresso and liqueurs, then spoon them into 2-oz shot glasses and refrigerate.

Remove martini and shot glasses from the fridge and place four savoyardi cookies inside each martini glass. When presenting the tiramisu, present a martini glass and a shot glass to each guest and tell them to dunk and scoop; dunk the cookie into the coffee/liqueur and then scoop the creamy cheese mixture from the martini glass.

# Panna Cotta

## Ingredients
### Cream

**16 oz 35% whipping cream**

**7 oz sugar**

**4 gelatin sheets**

**16 oz buttermilk**

**zest of 2 oranges**

*Severs 4*

*Prep time: 15-20 minutes*

*Cook time: 0 minutes*

*Here's to a new beginning!*

## Ingredients
### Fruit Topping

**1/2 cup fresh raspberries**

**1/2 cup fresh strawberries**

**1 cup water**

**3 oz sugar**

**4 gelatin sheets**

## Directions: Cream Mixture

Blanch orange zests in boiling water for 10-15 seconds. In a small bowl, dip gelatin sheets in cold water and let bloom.

Place cream, buttermilk, sugar and orange zests in a medium-sized saucepot and bring to a boil over high heat. Reduce heat to low and add bloomed gelatin (strained of excess water). Stir, allowing gelatin to dissolve. Place liquid into desired serving glass/bowl and refrigerate for 4 hours.

## Directions: Fruit Topping

In a small bowl, dip gelatin sheets into cold water and let bloom.
Place 4-oz water, fruit and sugar in a medium-sized saucepan and cook over medium heat until fruit becomes soft. Add gelatin and stir until gelatin has dissolved. Pass mixture through a fine strainer to remove seeds. Cool, then spoon over set custard mixture and refrigerate for another 2 hours.

# Lemon Tart

*Servers 4-6*

*Prep time: 15 minutes*

*Cook time: 15 minutes*

## Ingredients
### Pie Tart

**1 cup flour**

**2 tbsp almonds, ground**

**3⁄4 cup butter, cold and cubed**

**31⁄2 tbsp water, cold**

**1 egg**

**pinch salt**

## Ingredients
### Tart

**6 lemons, juiced**

**6 eggs**

**1⁄4 cup butter, soft**

**zest of 4 lemons, chopped**

**2 cups white sugar**

**1⁄2 cup blueberries**

## Directions: Pie Crust

Add flour, ground almonds and salt to a food processor and pulse for 5 seconds to distribute ingredients evenly. Add butter and pulse for 5 seconds at a time. Do this roughly 3-4 times, until the dough has a sandy consistency. Add water and egg, pulsing for another 10 seconds. Remove dough from processor and place on clean countertop. Form into a ball, wrap with plastic and refrigerate for a least 1 hour. Remove dough from the refrigerator and let stand for 5 minutes. On a floured countertop, roll dough to 1/8-inch thickness and place in tart shell or cast-iron pan (the shell makes a more formal crust; the pan, a more rustic one). Preheat oven to 325 F and bake until the shell is golden brown. Let pie crust stand in a cool, dry place until ready for use.

## Directions: Tart

Combine all ingredients, except for butter, in a stainless-steel mixing bowl. In a double boiler, whisk ingredients together over a simmering heat. Stir for 10 to 15 minutes, turning the bowl for even heating. When the mixture begins to thicken, turn off heat and whisk in butter, a little at a time. The mixture will begin to thicken as it cools. Pour the warm mixture into the tart shell and refrigerate for 3-4, allowing it to set. When ready to serve, remove from the refrigerator, slice and garnish with blueberries.

# Grilled Peaches
## with a Red Wine and Rosemary Reduction

*Serves 4*
*Prep time: 3-4 hours*
*Cook time: 4 minutes*

## Ingredients

### Grillled Peaches
**4 fresh peaches**
**8 basil leaves**

### Yogurt Cheese
**1 litre whole-fat yogurt**
**1/2 cup powdered sugar**
**1/2 cup honey**
**2 tbsp vanilla extract**
**2 oz amaretto liqueur**

### Red Wine Sauce
**3/4 cup red wine**
**1/3 cup honey**
**1 sprig rosemary**
**pinch salt**

### Almond Crisp
**1 1/2 cups sugar**
**1/4 tsp salt**
**3 cups whole almonds, ground**
**1/3 cup butter, soft**

## Directions: Grilled Peaches

Cut peaches in half, remove pits and place on a grill flesh-side down over medium-high heat. Cook for 3-4 minutes (no need to flip).

## Directions: Yogurt Cheese

Combine all ingredients in a bowl except amaretto liqueur. Place in a strainer lined with cheesecloth sitting over a bowl. Allow liquid to drain through. Cover bowl with plastic wrap and refrigerate for 3-4 hours. Remove cheesecloth, add amaretto and set aside until needed.

## Directions: Red Wine Sauce

In a small sauté pan, combine red wine, rosemary, salt and honey. Bring to a boil, simmer and reduce to a syrup consistency.

## Directions: Almond Crisp

Put dry sugar in a heavy-based pan and cook over low heat. Do not stir! Watch carefully, when it begins to smoke, a thin foam will show on the surface, followed by a thicker one. At this point, add butter and stir gently, then remove from the pan and place on a lightly buttered piece of parchment paper. Let cool until solid. Remove from parchment and place in a food processor, pulsing until it becomes a powder.
Combine almonds, powdered sugar mixture and salt in a medium non-stick pan over medium heat. Stir and cook until almonds have toasted and sugar is sticky. Remove and place almonds on parchment paper. Fold paper over the mixture and flatten with a rolling pin until thin. While still warm, cut into desired shapes.

To serve, place a dollop of cheese in the centre of each plate. Perch the grilled peach alongside the cheese. Drizzle red wine reduction over half of peach and place almond crisp in the cheese, creating height. The basil leaves are used as a garnish; you will be pleasantly surprised how well basil and peaches complement each other.

# Biscotti GRAZIE

## Ingredients

*Yields 34 cookies*

*Prep time: 10-15 minutes*

*Cook time: 40 minutes*

**1 tbsp shortening**

**1 1/2 cups slivered almonds, finely chopped**

**1 tsp vanilla extract**

**2 tsp baking powder**

**2 eggs**

**1 egg yolk**

**2/3 cup sugar**

**2 cups all-purpose flour**

**1/3 cup butter, at room temperature**

**3 tbsp milk**

## Directions: Cream Mixture

In a large bowl mix butter, 1 cup flour, sugar, 2 eggs, shortening, baking power and vanilla until combined. Once mixture is at a dough-like texture, add remaining flour and almonds.

Divide dough in half. Form each portion into an 8-9 inch log, flattening to approximately 1 inch high. Place logs on a lightly greased cookie sheet. For a shiny glaze, mix together milk and 1 egg yolk and brush on top of the logs.

Bake in a 375 F oven for 20-25 minutes. Let cool for 1 hour. Using a serrated knife, cut the log diagonally into 1/2-inch thick slices.

Place the cut biscotti slices on a cookie sheet and bake in a 325 F oven for 16 minutes, turning cookies over after 8 minutes.

# Drinks

Italian Surfer
Azzuri
Espresso Martini
Liscio
Classico

1
2
3
4

# Martini List

1. **Italian surfer:** 1 oz Vodka, 1/2 oz Coconut Rum, 1/2 oz Amaretto, 1 oz of pineapple juice and 1 oz of cranberry juice.

2. **Azzuri:** 1oz White Rum, 1/2 oz Raspberry Rum, 1/2 Blue Curacao, 1/2 lime juice, 1 oz cranberry juice, (add ice, shake well), strain into martini glass and add 3/4 oz 7 up or sprite, garnish with purple grapes.

3. **Espresso Martini:** 1 oz Vodka, 1/2 oz Kahlua, 1/2 oz Talea (an amaretto cream). 2 oz of espresso (add ice, shake well), strain into martini glass. Before straining, rim the martini glass with a mixture of coffee grinds and sugar.

   *Riming the glass: the glass must be moistened first. Put your mixed coffee grinds and sugar onto a flat plate. Put the moistened martini glass on top of the mix with the rim side down and turn in a clockwise direction. Flip glass over, rim should be coated with the mix.*

4. **Liscio:** 1 oz Vodka, 1/2 oz Banana liqueur, 1/2 oz Lycee liqueur, 1 oz pineapple juice, (shake well with ice), strain and serve, garnish with pineapple, or banana.

What are you drinking at?

# Classico

**2 oz Vodka,**

**splash of 1⁄4 oz Scotch,**

**stir, garish with green olive**

Garnishing options:(onion, gherkins, or green tomato)

Option: Vodka can be substituted with GIn, depending on your preference.

*Two guys who have been setting the tone from the beginning, with their exciting drinks and outlandish personalities.*

*- Rob Prete and Bruno Brancatella*

# The Jacob's Ladder
## Foundation

*GRAZIE* is proud to donate a portion of the proceeds received from, *GRAZIE*: a recipe of memories, to the Jacob's Ladder. Jacob's Ladder is a Canadian Foundation, which began in 1998 as a local effort to help prevent and diagnose degenerative neurological disorders. Jacob Schwartz, the inspiration behind the movement, has turned eight this year and continues to inspire and encourage work towards finding new ways to treat, diagnose, and prevent neurological disease. Jacob suffers from a rare neurological disorder, which occurs mainly in young children called Canavan disease.

Canavan disease is an inherited, progressive neurodegenerative disease that strikes in early infancy causing progressive mental and physical disabilities. Although Canavan disease is rare, it is one form belonging to a group of disorders called leukodystrophies.

Leukodystrophies are a group of progressive disorders that affect the brain, spinal cord, and nerves. They result from inherited defects in various enzymes in lipid (fat) metabolism, which affect the production of myelin.

Funds raised through Jacob's Ladder, continue to be directed towards groundbreaking work in the areas of education, prevention and treatment. The efforts of all of our supporters are resulting in substantial gains, not only in our understanding of Canavan's disease, but in the whole area of neurodegenerative disease.

For more information on Jacob's Ladder please visit
Our website at: www.jacobsladder.ca

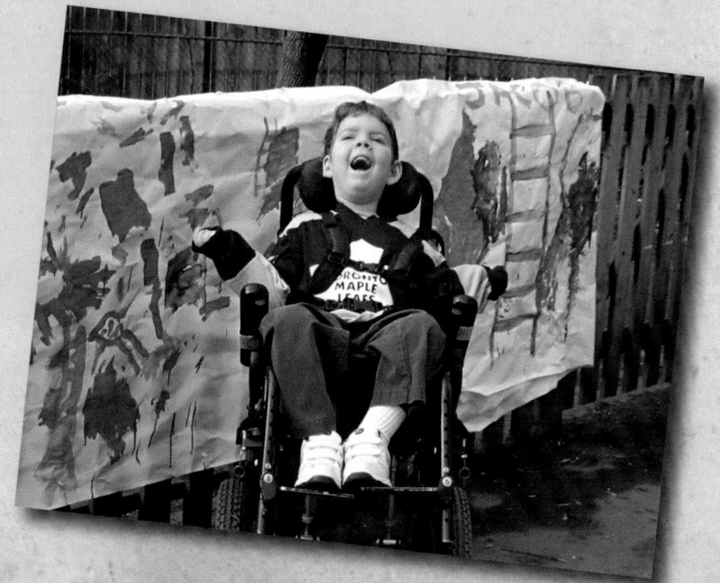

# Acknowledgements

Joe Brancatella, Carmen Amato and Stefano Colacitti, would like to take a moment to thank a few people who without their constant support this book would not have been possible: Steellite for donating all the plates; Nella Cutlery for donating all cutlery (kitchen utensils) used in the photo shoot. To Antonietta Brancatella and Kahlil Nekzai, for coming in on those early mornings to help prep for the shoot, their tireless efforts have not gone unnoticed. Mike Prete and Johnathen Pyke, for being there when no one else could be. Thasan Thirunavukkarasu, Raj Ratnasabapthy, Baskaran Apputhurai, for being part of the GRAZIE family since the beginning. Sandro Bustamante, for helping the process moving along. Mark Klepec, for his diligent work. Owen Steinberg and wife Laura Doyle, because Jov was just another way of expressing Love! Didier Leroy, for your constant words of encouragement and understanding of possibility. Amir Karmali, for taking the time to remember, Nick Brancatella for always having a smile. Larry Fridman, for being himself. Greg Colacitti, don't say we forgot you! Demetria Georgopulos, for her kind words, advice and guidance along the way. Carlos Avalos, an applause is only the beginning soon they will be standing. Besar, you were right about the Catrina. Leo Tamburri, Ben Panton, Luciano Sebastian De Monte, for all your work and countless nights of lost sleep for the sake of this project. We want to thank Jack Zoulalian for contributing photos that he has taken over the years. Mary Bartucci, for playing everyone's shrink. Vito Brancatella, Marco Puntillo, Rob Prete, Bruno Brancatella, Angelo Moretti, and all the staff at GRAZIE, because we forget sometimes to say thank you for all that you have done, big and small; and finally to Louie Granicolo and family, we couldn't of done any of this with out you.

Thanks for the new memories.

Salut to the next fifteen years!

*Ciao! A prossimo.*

# Index